RELIGION of the SEMITES

RELIGION of the SEMITES

William Robertson Smith

With a new introduction by
Robert A. Segal

Transaction Publishers
New Brunswick (U.S.A.) and London (U.K.)

Second printing, 2012

This book is printed on acid-free paper that meets the American National Standard for Permanence of Paper for Printed Library Materials.

Library of Congress Catalog Number: 2001058132
ISBN: 978-0-7658-0936-0
Printed in the United States of America

Library of Congress Cataloging-in-Publication Data

Smith, W. Robertson (William Robertson), 1846-1894.
[Lectures on the religion of the Semites]
Religion of the Semites / William Robertson Smith ; with a new introduction by Robert A. Segal.
p. cm.
Originally published: Lectures on the religion of the Semites. New ed. A. & C. Black, 1894. With new introd.
Includes bibliographical references and indexes.
ISBN 0-7658-0936-2 (pbk.: alk. paper)
1. Semites—Religion. I. Title.

BL1600 .S6 2002
299'.2—dc21 2001058132

CONTENTS

LECTURE IX

LECTURE X

LECTURE XI

TRANSACTION INTRODUCTION

*Religion of the Semites** comprises lectures delivered at the University of Aberdeen in three series from October 1888 to December 1891. At the outset William Robertson Smith (1846-1894) declares his subject to be "the religion of the Semitic peoples" (2nd ed. [1894], p. 1). The Semites include "the Arabs, the Hebrews and Phoenicians, the Aramaens, the Babylonians and Assyrians, which in ancient times occupied the great Arabian Peninsula, with the more fertile lands of Syria, Mesopotamia, and Irac, from the Mediterranean coast to the base of the mountains of Iran and Armenia." From the Semites emerged "three of the great faiths of the world": Judaism, Christianity, and Islam. On the one hand these three religions, which Smith labels "positive religions," broke away from ancient "heathenism." Where ancient heathen religions grew up "under the action of unconscious forces operating silently from age to age," the positive religions arose from "the teaching of great religious innovators," who "spoke as the organs of a divine revelation" and "deliberately departed from the traditions of the past" (p. 1). On the other hand the positive religions arose out of ancient heathenism:

---

* Originally published under the title *Lectures on the Religion of the Semites.*

> The positive Semitic religions had to establish themselves on ground already occupied by these older beliefs and usages; they had to displace what they could not assimilate, and whether they rejected or absorbed the elements of the older religion, they had at every point to reckon with them and take up a definite attitude towards them. No positive religion that has moved men has been able to start with a *tabula rasa*, and express itself as if religion were beginning for the first time; in form, if not in substance, the new system must be in contact all along the line with the older ideas and practices which it finds in possession. (p. 2)

Smith proceeds to show at once how "primitive" ancient Semitic religion originally was and how far Christianity, above all, advanced beyond its primitive origins.

Semites as Primitive

Just as in *The Elementary Forms of the Religious Life* (1912) Emile Durkheim, in seeking the nature of religion per se, turns to Australian aborigines as the earliest extant and therefore presumably clearest case, so in *Religion of the Semites* Smith, in seeking the nature of Semitic religion, turns to "heathen Arabia" as the earliest and therefore presumably clearest case: "In many respects the religion of heathen Arabia, though we have little information concerning it that is not of post-Christian date, displays an extremely primitive type, corresponding to the primitive and unchanging character of nomadic life" (p. 14). Smith here evinces the fundamental assumption of his book: that the Semites were initially at a *primitive* stage of culture, so that the key to understanding them is to see them as akin to primitives worldwide. Smith thus uses the terms "primitive" and "ancient" (or "antique") almost interchangeably. Unlike Edward Tylor and James Frazer, who are concerned with only the similarities among primitives the world over, Smith is concerned with the differences as well as the similarities between early Semites and other primitives, just as he is concerned with the differences as well as the similarities between early and later Semites. But it is his focus on the similarities that is revolutionary and controversial. As he says of his initial lecture,

> But though my facts and illustrations will be drawn from the Semitic sphere, a great part of what I shall have to say in the present lecture might be applied, with very trifling modifications, to the early religion of any other part of mankind. The differences between Semitic and Aryan religion, for example, are not so primitive or fundamental as is often imagined.... [T]he two races, Aryans and Semites, began on lines which are so much alike as to be almost indistinguishable, and the divergence between their paths, which becomes more and more apparent in the course of ages, was not altogether an affair of race and innate tendency, but depended in a great measure on the operation of special local and historical causes. (p. 32)

Primitive and Ancient Religion as Ritualistic

The basic religious divide for Smith is not, then, between Semites and Aryans. It is between primitives and moderns. Where the heart of modern religion is its beliefs, the heart of primitive religion is its rituals. That difference, we are told, has often been missed by modern scholars, ingrained as they are as moderns "to look at religion from the side of belief rather than of practice." Thus "we naturally assume that" in primitive no less than in modern religion "our first business is to search for a creed, and find in it the key to ritual and practice" (p. 16). In actuality, primitive religion "had for the most part no creed" and consisted entirely of institutions and practices. While acknowledging that "men will not habitually follow certain practices without attaching a meaning to them," in ancient religion we ordinarily find that "while the practice was rigorously fixed, the meaning attached to it was extremely vague, and the same rite was explained by different people in different ways, without any question of orthodoxy or heterodoxy arising in consequence" (p. 16). "It was imperative that certain things should be done, but every man was free to put his own meaning on what was done" (p. 399). Smith goes as far as to declare that "mythology was no essential part of ancient religion" (p. 17) and that "ritual and practical usage were, strictly speaking, the sum-total of ancient religions" (p. 20).

Smith's focus on practice rather than belief as the core of primitive and ancient religion is revolutionary. For example, Tylor devotes only a small section of *Primitive Culture* (1871) to ritual, and sees ritual as the mere application of belief (see Tylor 1958:II, ch. 18). By contrast, Smith devotes six of the eleven lectures in the First Series of Burnett Lectures to rituals—specifically, to the ritual of sacrifice—and devotes most of the other lectures not to beliefs but to such topics as holy places. Smith might as well have been directing himself against Tylor in stating that "religion in primitive times was not a system of belief with practical applications" but instead "a body of fixed traditional practices" (p. 20).

Yet on ritual, as on other aspects of religion, Smith's revolution stops short, and abruptly so. He does not propose that modern religion as well be looked at from the side of ritual foremost. He draws a rigid hiatus between primitive and modern religion. He approaches modern religion no differently than do others. It is creedal first and ritualistic second—no doubt a reflection of Smith's anti-ritualistic, Protestant viewpoint. Where twentieth-century theorists of religion, if one dare generalize, tend to stress the similarities between primitive and modern religion, Smith stresses the differences.

Primitive and Ancient Religion as Mythic

In place of creed in ancient and primitive religion there was myth. Where in modern religion creed prescribes ritual, in ancient religion myth explained ritual. Myth explained how a ritual came to be. While the myth would attribute the ritual to a god and to that degree bolster the ritual, the myth would be taken lightly, and there could be competing myths. Unlike ritual, myth was not obligatory:

> [I]t [myth] had no sacred sanction and no binding force on the worshippers. The myths connected with individual sanctuaries and ceremonies were merely part of the apparatus of the worship; they served to excite the fancy and sustain the interest of the worshipper; but he was often offered a choice of several accounts of the same thing, and, provided that he fulfilled the ritual with accuracy, no one cared what he believed about its origin. (p. 17)

In connecting myth to ritual, Smith is again revolutionary. Where Tylor views myth as an explanation of the world, Smith proposes myth as an explanation of ritual. Where for Tylor myth explains physical events, for Smith myth explains social events. But here, too, Smith stops short. While he indisputably pioneers the myth and ritual theory, myth for him plays a minor role. Not only is it optional rather than mandatory for adherents, but—so Smith hypothesizes—ritual at first existed alone. Only when the purpose of the ritual was somehow forgotten was myth concocted to give ritual a purpose:

> Now by far the largest part of the myths of antique religions are connected with the ritual of particular shrines, or with the religious observances of particular tribes and districts. In all such cases it is probable, in most cases it is certain, that the myth is merely the explanation of a religious usage; and ordinarily it is such an explanation as could not have arisen till the original sense of the usage had more or less fallen into oblivion. (p. 18)

Even the explanation provided by myth was less a justification for the ritual than an account of its origin, for ancient religion "was so ruled by precedent" that worshippers required no "adequate moral explanation even of the most exorbitant demands of traditional ritual," including human sacrifice. Worshippers "were content to explain" those demands "by some legend that told how the ritual first came to be set up" (p. 409). Where for Bronislaw Malinowski, for example, myth accompanies ritual from the outset and traces ritual back to primordial times exactly to enhance its aura and thereby justify the practice of it, for Smith myth is almost incidental even when it arises. Myth-ritualists after Smith give myth more significance. For Frazer, myth is indispensable to ritual, and indispensable from the start, providing the script for the magical ritual. Going beyond Frazer, classicist Jane Harrison and biblicist S. H. Hooke ascribe magical potency to myth itself.

But Smith is still revolutionary. If he substitutes myth for creed in primitive and ancient religion, he also downplays the importance of myth there. His subordination of myth to ritual means that "mythology ought not to take the prominent place that is too often assigned to it in the scientific study of ancient faiths" (p. 18). For Smith, the importance wrongly accorded mythology is part of the importance wrongly accorded belief. While he allows for the subsequent development of myths independent of rituals, he takes these kinds of myths to be "products of early philosophy, reflecting on the nature of the universe"—for example, creation myths; or "political in scope, being designed to supply a thread of union between the various worships of groups, originally distinct, which have been united into one social or political organism"; or else the results of "the free play of epic imagination." But then, as he writes, "philosophy politics and poetry are something more, or something less, than religion pure and simple" (p. 19). For Tylor, religion pure and simple *is* philosophy (see, e.g., Tylor 1958:I, 285). For Smith, it is anything but.

Smith allows for the increasing importance of mythology in the "struggle" of ancient heathenism against skepticism on the one hand and Christianity on the other. Traditional myths were interpreted allegorically to defend heathenism against its nemeses. Myth now became part of creed. But "the [allegorical] theories thus developed are the falsest of false guides as to the original meaning of the old religions" (p. 19). For myth taken philosophically was late myth, not, as for Tylor, pristine myth.

After presenting the ritualist theory in the first lecture of *Religion of the Semites*, Smith tends no more to myth save in passing (see especially pp. 173, 191, 409-13). He concentrates almost wholly on rituals, which he sees not merely as activities but as institutions. Not until the last lecture of the third series of lectures, the notes for which have only recently been discovered and published, does he return to myth. There he considers myth on its own, apart from ritual, and discusses the ideas of God in pagan and biblical creation myths (see Smith 1995:96-112). In effect, he approaches myth as if it was philosophical all along.

Primitive and Ancient Religion as Collective

To drive home the point that in primitive and ancient religion ritual precedes belief, Smith compares religion with politics, noting that "political institutions are older than political theories" and that "in like manner religious institutions are older than religious theories" (p. 20). But Smith then asserts that in ancient times religion and politics were more than analogous. They were "parts of one whole of social custom." Religion was "a part of the organised social life into which a man was born, and to which he conformed through life in the same unconscious way in which men fall into any habitual practice of the society in which they live." Religious duty was civic duty, so that "religious nonconformity was an offence against the state." Nonconformity meant nonconformity in practice, not belief, so that "so long as the prescribed forms were duly observed, a man was recognised as truly pious, and no one asked how his religion was rooted in his heart or affected his reason." Just like political duty, of which Smith now declares religion a part, religious duty "was entirely comprehended in the observance of certain fixed rules of outward conduct" (p. 21).

Once again, Smith is revolutionary—here in seeing ancient and primitive religion as collective rather than individual. Because "to us moderns religion is above all a matter of individual conviction and reasoned belief" (p. 21), we assume the same of ancient religion. But ancient religion was in fact the opposite of modern. Because Smith takes for granted that modern religion really is a matter of the individual, his revolutionary approach once again stops abruptly. Where, notably, Durkheim argues that religion per se is collective rather than individualistic, Smith distinguishes rigidly between the collective nature of ancient religion and the individualistic nature of modern.[1] His "sociologizing," as original as it is, is confined to ancient and primitive religion. For him, modern religion transcends the group. At the same time not only the organization but also the function of ancient and primitive religion was social: "Religion did not exist for the saving of souls"—the individualistic function of modern religion—"but for the preservation and welfare of society" (p. 29).

Primitive and Ancient Religion as Materialist

Another, equally fundamental difference for Smith is that where modern religion is spiritual, primitive and ancient religion is materialist. God is conceived of as physically related to worshippers:

> The relation between the gods of antiquity and their worshippers was expressed in the language of human relationship, and this language was not taken in a figurative sense but with strict literality. If a god was spoken of as father and his worshippers as his offspring, the meaning was that the worshippers were literally of his stock, that he and they made up one natural family with reciprocal family duties to one another. (pp. 29-30)

God as father has moral as well as physical consequences. Physically, "the father is the being to whom the child owes his life, and through whom he traces kinship with the other members of his family or clan." The key physical linkage is "participation in one blood, which passes from parent to child and circulates in the veins of every member of the family" (p. 40).[2] Morally, god as father dictates social obligations, with "the parent protecting and nourishing the child, while the child owes obedience and service to his parent" (p. 41).[3]

In the positive religions, going all the way back to the Hebrews, "the idea of divine fatherhood is entirely dissociated from the physical basis of natural fatherhood." According to Genesis 1, humans were created *by* God and *in the image of* God but not *from* God. "God-sonship is not a thing of nature but a thing of grace." By contrast, "in heathen religions the fatherhood of the gods is physical fatherhood" (p. 41). Smith rejects the conventional view that where the original conception of god among Aryans was concrete and human-like, that of the Semites was "abstract and transcendental"—as if Semitic religion "sought to remove the gods as far as possible from man, and even contained within itself from the first the seeds of an abstract deism" (p. 48; see also pp. 194-95). According to this conventional view, anthropomorphic depictions of Semitic gods were meant merely allegorically, not literally. The purported evidence for this divergence between Semites and Aryans is that Aryan kinds of myths, "in which gods act like men, mingle with men, and in fact live a common life with mankind, have little or no place in Semitic religion" (p. 49). While granting the paucity of Semitic mythology, Smith points to "traces" of anthropomorphic mythology—for example, the mating of the "sons of God" with the "daughters of men" in Genesis 6.

Smith also notes the tradition among Semitic nations of "habitually feign[ing] themselves to be of one kin" (p. 51), when in fact nations are usually distinguished from kinship groups like clans. It is not clear how for Smith nationhood based on kinship bears on kinship between god and worshippers. Perhaps because a nation represents the union of tribes and because its head is also a god, a god is considered as biologically tied to his subjects as he is to individual clans. But for Smith a god eventually "comes to be thought of as king *rather than* as father" (p. 61 [italics added]). In any event kingship, like fatherhood, is meant not metaphorically, as conventionally assumed, but literally:

> [T]he two leading conceptions of the relation of the god to the his people are those of fatherhood and of kingship. We have learned to look on Semitic society as built up on two bases—on kinship, which is the foundation of the system of clans or gentes, and on the union of kins, living intermingled or side by side, and bound together by common interests, which is the foundation of the state. (p. 40)[4]

Just as god as father "belongs to the family or clan," so god as king "belongs to the state" (p. 40). But even if the god is literally the king and his worshippers his subjects, how, again, is that relationship one of kinship? Whatever Smith's logic, his point is that in any stage of primitive and ancient religion "the indissoluble bond that unites men to their god is the same bond of blood-fellowship which in early society is the one binding link between man and man" (p. 53).

Primitive and Ancient Religion as Moral

Tylor places morality outside of primitive religion. It is not that primitives are amoral but that their morality is independent of their religion, which itself is amoral (see Tylor 1958:II, 11). Antithetically to Tylor, Smith, in seeing moral obligation as a consequence of physical kinship, places morality at the center of primitive religion:

> And thus we see that even in its rudest forms religion was a moral force; the powers that man reveres were on the side of social order and tribal law; and the fear of the gods was a motive to enforce the laws of society, which were also the laws of morality. (p. 53)[5]

The moral link between god and worshippers is wholly beneficent. The god of a clan or nation is friendly, solicitous, and above all loving. Unfriendly, malevolent forces fall under magic or sorcery rather than religion:

> From the earliest times, religion, as distinct from magic or sorcery, addresses itself to kindred and friendly beings, who may indeed be angry with their people for a time, but are always placable except to the enemies of their worshippers or to renegade members of the community. It is not with a vague fear of unknown powers, but with a loving reverence for known gods who are knit to their worshippers by strong bonds of kinship, that religion in the only true sense of the word begins. (pp. 54-55)

Because the forces in magic are unfriendly, they can only be controlled, not obeyed. Thus no morality arises from dealings with them. Smith even associates magic with the individual rather than, like religion, with the group—a distinction later adopted by, especially, Durkheim (see Durkheim 1965:57-63, 472-74): "In better times the religion of the tribe or state has nothing in common with the private and foreign superstitions or magical rites that savage terror may dictate to the individual" (p. 55). Magic is not merely private but anti-social and therefore immoral: "private and magical superstitions were habitually regarded as offences against morals and the state" (p. 55). Modern religion may be individualistic, but it is not thereby anti-social.

Primitive and Ancient Conceptions of God

For Smith, the materialist conception of primitive and ancient religion has further consequences. Because a god is material, he is limited physically. He is neither omnipotent nor omnipresent but is instead tied to a specific place, where alone he has power. In earliest religion a god is assumed to reside in, say, a tree or a stone rather than simply to visit it (see pp. 194, 209-10). If one wants to find a god, one seeks him in his home, which may be in the sky or in the water as well as on earth. Later, the home becomes a temple. Smith maintains that "it was not agriculture that created the conception that certain places were the special haunts of superhuman powers" (pp. 113-14). Rather, agriculture assumed this view and deemed those haunts "a garden of God, cultivated and fertilised by the hand of deity" (p. 113). The view derives from the materialist conception of god: "That the gods are not ubiquitous but subject to limitations of time and space, and that they can act only when they or their messengers are present, is the universal idea of antiquity and needs no explanation." The idea of "existences raised above space and time" comes only later (p. 114). By the time of Isaiah "the residence of Jehovah in Zion is almost wholly dematerialised" (p. 117)—but not fully so since Isaiah still conceives of God's activity as King of Israel as "going forth from the capital of the nation." Isaiah "has not risen to the full height of the New Testament conception that God, who is spirit and is to be worshipped spiritually, makes no distinction of spot with regard to His worship, and is equally near to receive men's prayers in every place" (p. 117).

A yet further consequence of the materialist conception of god in primitive and ancient religion is that god need not be human-like. He can, alternatively, be an animal or even a plant. Smith thus roots what for him is the earliest form of religion—totemism—in this materialist or, better, biological conception. And just as an anthropomorphically conceived god is taken to be the father of his worshippers, so an animal is taken to be their brother:

> In the totem stage of society each kinship or stock of savages believes itself to be physically akin to some natural kind of animate or inanimate things, most generally to some kind of animal. Every animal of this kind is looked upon as a brother, is treated with the same respect as a human clansman, and is believed to aid his human relations by a variety of friendly services. (p. 124)

Strictly, totems for Smith are not gods—precisely because they are not human-like—but they are the basis for gods. Like gods, who are originally local, totems "are invested with gifts such as we should call supernatural, and of the very same kind which heathenism [later] ascribes to the gods—for example with the power of giving omens and oracles, of healing diseases and the like." In "races which we know only in a state of society higher than savagery," it is dubious to argue that the conception of god developed independently of totemism. In "savage races" the conception of local superhuman powers with whom worshippers have a biological "affinity" "is invariably put in the totem form" (p. 125). Yet totemism is not the earliest stage of belief. The belief in demons comes earlier and is pre-religious. Smith's chronology is: first demons, then totems, then local gods, then national gods, and finally universal gods. The issue of the origin of totemism he calls a "problem" but to it offers no solution (p. 125).

The Comparative Method

Smith insists that the Arabian *jinn* are exactly the Semitic version of totems: "This conception of the communities of the *jinn* is precisely identical with the savage conception of the animal creation" (p. 127; see pp. 126-39). Smith's argument for taking the *jinn* as totems is twofold: he appeals both to internal evidence and to cross-cultural cases. Like totems, the *jinn* appear as animals, have no individuality, inhabit a particular locale, are united by bonds of kinship, and wreak collective vengeance for any injury done to a member. But Smith appeals as well to the cases of other "savage" peoples:

> [I]f my analysis of the nature of the *jinn* is correct, the conclusion that the Semites did pass through the totem stage can be avoided only by supposing them to be an exception to the universal rule, that even the most primitive savages have not only enemies [i.e., demons] but permanent allies (which at so early a stage in society necessarily means kinsfolk) among the non-human or superhuman animate kinds by which the universe is peopled. And this supposition is so extravagant that no one is likely to adopt it. (p. 137)[6]

Overall, Smith's procedure is to begin with the Semitic evidence, make sense of it internally, and then turn to cases elsewhere to confirm the analysis. As he writes of sacrifice,

> To construct a theory of sacrifice exclusively on the Semitic evidence would be unscientific and misleading, but for the present purpose it is right to put the facts attested for the Semitic peoples in the foreground, and to call in the sacrifices of other nations to confirm or modify the conclusions to which we are led. (pp. 214-15)

Smith's approach is almost the opposite of that of his fellow comparativist Frazer, who, in the work closest to Smith's *Religion of the Semites*, *Folk-lore in the Old Testament* (1918), begins with some Israelite custom that makes scant sense internally and turns to cases elsewhere to explicate, not merely confirm, the case at hand.[7]

Primitive and Ancient Religion as Amoral

Still another consequence of the materialist nature of primitive and ancient religion is that the sacredness, or "holiness," of a god, person, or place stems from other than character. To moderns, holiness is "an ethical idea" and is based on character: "God, the perfect being, is the type of holiness; men are holy in proportion as their lives and character are godlike; places and things can be called holy only by a figure, on account of their association with spiritual things" (p. 140). By contrast, to ancients, "holy persons were such, not in virtue of their character but in virtue of their race, function, or mere material consecration" (p. 141). Persons practicing the worst immoralities could be labeled "holy." The same Smith who credits primitive and ancient religion with the instillment of morality simultaneously disparages that stage of religion as amoral. How he reconciles these positions it is not easy to see.

In ancient and primitive religion the attribute "holy" was applied less to persons than to gods, seasons, things, and, most of all, places. While persons, things, and times were, as in modern religion, holy because of their association with gods, their holiness was tied to the places—the physical spots—where the gods were present: "Holy persons things and times, as they are conceived in antiquity, all presuppose the existence of holy places at which the persons minister, the things are preserved, and the times are celebrated." In fact, the holiness of the gods themselves "is an expression to which it is hardly possible to attach a definite sense apart from the holiness of their physical surroundings" (p 141).

Holiness and Uncleanness in Primitive and Ancient Religion

One more consequence or likely consequence of the materialist nature of primitive and ancient religion is the conflation of holiness with uncleanness. True, holiness stems from association with gods and uncleanness from association with demons. Holiness is thus tied to religion and uncleanness tied to magic. But both involve contact. One becomes holy by contact with something holy, just as one becomes unclean by contact with something unclean: "Holiness...is conceived as infectious, propagating itself by physical contact." This notion "was never eliminated from the Semitic conception of holiness, and figures even in the ritual parts of the Old Testament" (p. 161). Contact with either the holy or the unclean is tabooed, and to make contact with either is to become tabooed oneself:

> Thus alongside of taboos that exactly correspond to rules of holiness, protecting the inviolability of idols and sanctuaries, priests and chiefs, and generally of all persons and things pertaining to the gods and their worship, we find another kind of taboo which in the Semitic field has its parallel in rules of uncleanness. Women after child-birth, men who have touched a dead body and so forth, are temporarily taboo and separated from human society .... In these cases the person under taboo is not regarded as holy, for he is separated from approach to the sanctuary as well as from contact with men; but his act or condition is somehow associated with supernatural dangers, arising, according to the common savage explanation, from the presence of formidable spirits which are shunned like an infectious disease. In most savage societies no sharp line seems to be drawn between the two kinds of taboo just indicated, and even in more advanced nations the notions of holiness and uncleanness often touch. (pp. 152-53)[8]

For Smith, the differentiation between the holy and the unclean marks "a real advance above savagery" (p. 154), and Smith credits the Semites, or some of them, with making the distinction. But there is more to the advance than the differentiation between a physical property—uncleanness—and a spiritual one—holiness. The differentiation is also that between magic and more advanced religion, and that differentiation has social, not merely theological, ramifications:

> All taboos are inspired by awe of the supernatural, but there is a great moral difference between precautions against the invasion of mysterious hostile powers and precautions founded on respect for the prereogative of a friendly god. The former belong to magical superstition—the barrenest of all aberrations of the savage imagination—which, being founded only on fear, acts merely as a bar to progress and an impediment to the free use of nature by human energy and industry. But the restrictions on individual license which are due to respect for a known and friendly power allied to man, however trivial and absurd they may appear to us in their details, contain within them germinant principles of social progress and moral order. (p. 154)

By appealing to fear, magic secures only "slavish" submission to a stronger power. By appealing to respect, religion inculcates self-discipline and good character. Because the power to which one submits in religion is the god of the community, the restrictions imposed by that god are assumed to be done for the sake of the community: "the development of law and morals is made possible...by the belief that the restrictions on human license which are necessary to social well-being are conditions imposed by the god for the maintenance of a good understanding between himself and his worshippers" (pp. 154-55).

Primitive and ancient religion thus regains its moral stature and, with it, its social function. But if the morality of religion derives from the friendliness of gods, it is hardly clear how more advanced religion, even with its differentiation of the holy from the unclean, improves upon the moral fiber of earlier religion. For to quote

Smith anew, "From the earliest times, religion, as distinct from magic or sorcery, addresses itself to kindred and friendly beings" (p. 54).

Smith celebrates as progressive economically as well as socially the steady displacement of demons by gods. Where demons rule, the land lies fallow. Where gods rule, they can be called upon to make the land arable:

> The triumph of the gods over the demons, like the triumph of man over wild beasts, must have been effected very gradually, and may be regarded as finally sealed and secured only in the agricultural stage, when the god of the community became also the supreme lord of the land and the author of all the good things therein. (p. 122)

Sacrifice in Primitive and Ancient Religion

For Smith, the key relationship between god and his worshippers in any religion is that of communication. Therefore the key function of the key ritual, sacrifice, is as a "means of converse between God and man" (p. 216). In sacrifice the worshipper not merely "comes into the presence of his god with gestures of homage and words of prayer" but also "lays before the deity some material oblation" (p. 213). It was as yet a further consequence of the materialist conception of ancient and primitive religion that sacrifices "were taken by the ancients as being literally the food of the gods" (p. 224). In the earliest Semitic religion the "difficulty of conceiving that the gods actually partake of food is partly got over by a predominant use of liquid oblations," for liquid substances, "which sink in and disappear, are more easily believed to be consumed by the deity than obstinate masses of solid matter" (p. 229; see also p. 235). The gods, it is supposed, drink rather than eat and so "must be thought of as having a less solid material nature than men" (p. 235). In the "higher forms of heathenism" the "crass materialism" of the sacrifice of even solids is "modified," at least in the case of burned offerings, "by the doctrine that man's food must be etherealised or sublimated into fragrant smoke before the gods partake of it" (p. 224).

Smith is obsessed with arguing that the act of sacrifice constitutes not "a gift made over to the god" but "an act of communion, in which the god and his worshippers unite by partaking together of the flesh and blood of a sacred victim" (pp. 226-27). Sacrifice as gift, which is Tylor's view (see Tylor 1958:II, 461-96), must come only later. For a gift is intended to alleviate guilt and to secure forgiveness, and originally there is no guilt to be alleviated or forgiveness to be secured, for worshippers have in no way fallen short. Because the god is considered a father or a king, whatever demands he makes are pitched at a human level and so are capable of being met: "Civil and religious morality have one and the same measure, and the conduct which suffices to secure the esteem of men suffices also to make a man perfectly easy as to his standing with the gods." Therefore "there is no room for an abiding sense of sin and unworthiness, or for acts of worship that express the struggle after an unattained righteousness, the longing for uncertain forgiveness." Worshippers "are satisfied with their gods" and "feel that the gods are satisfied with them" (p. 256). Worshippers have "confidence in their god, untroubled by any habitual sense of human guilt." Worshippers enjoy "the firm conviction that they and the deity they adore are good friends, who understand each other perfectly and are united by bonds not easily broken" (p. 255). Smith's emphasis on a personal relationship with god as the heart of religion doubtless reflects his Protestant upbringing.[9]

Where Freud in *Totem and Taboo* (1913) sees the father-like character of a god as the source of guilt, the more innocent Smith sees that same father-like quality as protection against guilt. For Freud, a god represents the projection onto the world of the human father. The deification of the father only exacerbates the hostility and in turn guilt felt toward him. For Smith, the earliest god may be deemed the worshipper's actual father, but he thereby stirs the unblemished love felt toward any human father. Smith's depiction of "god" may reflect his idealized image of his own father.

For Smith, "a sacrifice ordinarily involves a feast," and "a feast cannot be provided without a sacrifice" (p. 255). Because the relationship between god and worshippers is so happy, so is the annual feast at which both gather to partake of the sacrifice:

> Then the crowds streamed into the sanctuary from all sides, dressed in their gayest attire, marching joyfully to the sound of music, and bearing with them not only the victims appointed for sacrifice, but store of bread and wine to set forth the feast. The law of the feast was open-handed hospitality; no sacrifice was complete without guests, and portions were freely distributed to rich and poor within the circle of a man's acquaintance. Universal hilarity prevailed, men ate drank and were merry together, rejoicing before their God. (p. 254)

While the life of no worshipper can be "perfectly happy and satisfactory," primitive and ancient religion nevertheless "assumes that through the help of the gods it is so happy and satisfactory that ordinary acts of worship are all brightness and hilarity, expressing no other idea than that the worshippers are well content with themselves and with their divine sovereign" (p. 257). Where David Hume or, for Smith, Ernest Renan roots religion in fear, Smith roots it in blissful joy. As already quoted, "It is not with a vague fear of unknown powers, but with a loving reverence for known gods who are knit to their worshippers by strong bonds of kinship, that religion in the only true sense of the word begins" (pp. 54-55).

Smith acknowledges that catastrophes like famine, pestilence, or loss in war may be attributed to a god's anger but maintains that the happy relationship between god and worshippers is unaffected, for the catastrophe is blamed on "some one for whom the community is responsible," and the damaged relationship is "put right" by a suitable "reparation." When the rain resumes falling, the pestilence ceases, or the next battle ends in victory, worshippers "at once recover their old easy confidence, and go on eating and drinking and rejoicing before their god with the assurance that he and they are on the best of jovial good terms" (p. 257).

Yet eventually, as nations emerged from "childhood" and grew up, they could no longer be so "insouciant." Either they "became less concerned to associate all their happiness with the worship of the gods," in which case they simply became less religious, or they "were unable to think of the divine powers as habitually well pleased and favourable," in which case they saw the anger of the gods as more than episodic. "The old joyous confidence" in the gods gave way to "a painful and scrupulous anxiety in all approach to the gods" (pp. 257-58). Consequently, sacrifice ceased to be an expression of sheer communion and became as well a quest for penance. In the case of Israel sin as penance arose in reaction to the conquest of the Northern and Southern Kingdoms by Assyria and Babylonia—a conquest that seemed to spell God's abandonment of his people: "the nations of Palestine in the seventh century B.C. afford an excellent illustration of the development of a gloomier type of worship under the pressure of accumulated political disasters" (p. 258). "The distressful times that preceded the end of Hebrew independence drove men to seek exceptional religious means to conciliate the favour of a deity who seemed to have turned his back on his people" (p. 238).

One reason that the idyllic view lasted as long as it did was that gods were assumed to concern themselves with the nation as a whole and not with individual members. Thus the benefits expected from the gods "were of a public character, affecting the whole community, especially fruitful seasons, increase of flocks and herds, and success in war." Individual misery "reflected no discredit on divine providence, but was rather taken to prove that the sufferer was an evil-doer, justly hateful to the gods" (p. 259). Individuals turned to magic to serve private needs, especially when those needs stood not merely outside but "against the interests of the community." Once again, magic is anti-social. It is "illicit" (p. 264). Magic is black magic.

Ordinarily, Smith does not pit the individual against society. Usually, their interests coincide. In fact, the happiness of the individual is fulfilled in the happiness of the community, and religion serves

> to maintain the civil virtues of loyalty and devotion to a man's fellows at a pitch of confident enthusiasm, to teach him to set his highest good in the prosperity of the society of which he is a member, not doubting that in so doing he has the divine power on his side and has given his life to a cause that cannot fail. This devotion to the common weal was, as every one knows, the mainspring of ancient morality and the source of all the heroic virtues of which ancient history presents so many illustrious examples. (p. 267)

Durkheim's impassioned description of the euphoria felt by individuals during religious gatherings echoes Smith (see Durkheim 1965:245-51).

Smith contrasts the social function of religion not merely to the individual function of magic but also to the universal function of "ethical universalism." Once religion and nationality diverge, the gods become guardians of a universal morality. Whatever the virtues of that universalism, there is lost the "intensity and strength of religious feeling" found in communal religion (p. 268). Again, Durkheim, for whom religion and society rightly go hand in hand, echoes Smith.

Sacrificial Meal in Primitive and Ancient Religion

In ancient and primitive religion the sacrificial meal had an especially socializing effect. Not only did god and worshippers jointly partake of the food, but "the very act of eating and drinking with a man was a symbol and a confirmation of fellowship and mutual social obligations." Those who ate together were "united for all social effects." Those who did not were "aliens to one another" (p. 269).

It was not enough for the food to be shared. It had to be slaughtered: "there is no sacrificial feast according to Semitic usage except where a victim is slaughtered" (p. 280). In totemism the animal killed was ordinarily sacrosanct because it was kin: "Thus the conjecture that sacrificial animals were originally treated as kinsmen, is simply equivalent to the conjecture that sacrifices were drawn from animals of a holy kind, whose lives were ordinarily protected by religious scruples and sanctions" (p. 289). On annual feast days, however, killing what was otherwise prohibited was not merely allowed but required—for Freud, in contrast to Smith, a cover-up for unconscious parricide (see Freud 1965:141-42). Precisely because the killed animal was kin, the common eating of it by god and worshippers strengthened the kinship between them:

> Nevertheless the slaughter of such a victim is permitted or required on solemn occasions, and all the tribesmen partake of its flesh, that they may thereby cement and seal their mystic unity with one another and with their god. In later times we find the conception current that any food which two men partake of together, so that the same substance enters into their flesh and blood, is enough to establish some sacred unity of life between them; but in ancient times this signifi-

> cance seems to be always attached to participation in the flesh of a sacrosanct victim, and the solemn mystery of its death is justified by the consideration that only in this way can the sacred cement be procured which creates or keeps alive a living bond of union between the worshippers and their god. (p. 313)

Smith speculates that while in "the later days of heathenism" a distinction was drawn between the "ordinary" sacrifices of animals habitually eaten and the "extraordinary" sacrifices of animals otherwise forbidden to be eaten, originally all sacrifices were of forbidden animals. Smith uses this point to argue yet again that the earliest form of Semitic religion was totemism, for an animal prohibited from being killed was at once a sacred animal and an unclean one. Furthermore, the sacrifice of a sacred, unclean animal was "generally limited to certain solemn occasions, usually annual" and so constituted a "public celebration" (p. 294). In all these respects earliest Semitic practice "is exactly what we find among totem peoples" (p. 295).

Smith argues that worldwide, and therefore among Semites as well, the earliest sacrifices were of wild animals, for animals had not yet been domesticated: "observation of savage life in all parts of the world shows that the belief in sacred animals, akin to families of men, attains its highest development in tribes which have not yet learned to breed cattle and live on their milk." Totemism is the worship of wild animals and "seems always to lose ground after the introduction of pastoral life." As totem clans began to breed cattle and to live on the milk, they "transferred to their herds"—to oxen, sheep, goats, and camels—"the notions of sanctity and kinship which formerly belonged to species of wild animals" and so to totems (p. 355). Yet "the very fact" that wild animals were no longer regularly sacrificed preserved their aura, and "long after the sacrificial flesh of beeves and sheep had sunk almost to the rank of ordinary food" (p. 356).

From Sacrifice as Communion to Sacrifice as Atonement

In the pastoral stage of early religion domesticated animals were originally considered kinsmen of the tribe and therefore worthy candidates for sacrifice. Smith rejects the view that sacrifices were at first of humans and only subsequently of animals. For "in the oldest times there could be no reason for thinking a man's life better than that of a camel or a sheep as a vehicle of sacramental communion" (p. 361). But gradually animals did come to be seen as less sacred than humans, who were therefore sacrificed in times of extreme peril or even periodically "at solemn annual rites" (p. 366). Still, "even savages commonly refuse to eat their own kinsfolk," and to more civilized societies "the idea that the gods had ordained meals of human flesh...was too repulsive to be long retained" (p. 367). Insofar as human sacrifices were not eaten, the function could not be communion and, at least when offered at times of peril, instead became atonement.

Smith offers another explanation for the development of sacrifices of atonement: the emergence of the concept of private property. Without explaining how that concept emerged, he attributes to it the shift from the view of sacrificial animals as inherently sacred to the view of them as mere "chattel," to be used as the worshipper pleased. Because the animal belonged to the worshipper, the presentation of it at the altar constituted the surrender of ownership to the god as a gift. And why offer a gift except as penance?

Now it was the selection of the animal for sacrifice that conferred sacredness on it (see pp. 390-91). But then the "most characteristic" aspect of sacrifice, "the application of the blood to the altar, and the burning of the fat on the sacred hearth" (p. 392), turned the gift into food and made the god beholden to his worshippers for "daily nourishment," even while the worshipper was supposedly beholden to the god for every bounty. The gift of food to a god who controlled the food supply seemed superfluous. If in times of prosperity this inconsistency could be glossed over, in times of adversity it could not be, for how could a god who controlled the food supply be persuaded by the offer of food to relent in his punishment? The result was the diminution of the place of sacrifice altogether. Instead, there emerged the notion, forged by the Hebrew Prophets, that "what the true God requires of His worshippers is not a material oblation, but 'to do justice, and love mercy, and walk humbly with thy God'" (pp. 393-94).

Smith attributes to the emergence of the notion of private property at once a step forward and a step forward in the development of religion. The notion that an animal, having been given as a gift to the god, became sacred only as the property of the god was "undoubtedly beneficial, for the vague dread of the unknown supernatural" presupposed by the notion of the inherent sacredness of the animal "paralyses progress of every kind, and turns man aside from his legitimate task of subduing nature to his use" (p. 395). Smith generalizes from the idea that sacred things were now forbidden to humans by virtue of "the wrath of a personal god, who will not suffer his property to be tampered with" (p. 395), to the idea that "all supernatural processes are referred to the will and powers of known deities, whose converse with man is guided by fixed laws" (pp. 395-96). But he laments that the fixed laws were linked to property, for "the notion of property materialises everything that it touches," so that "its introduction into religion made it impossible to rise to spiritual conceptions of the deity and his relations to man" (p. 396). For Smith, property means tangible property. The notion of "intellectual property" would be meaningless.

Smith acknowledges that even the conception of sacrifice as communion rather than as gift was likewise originally understood materially—as a physical bond between a god and his worshippers. Hence the ritual of the common ingesting of the sacrificed animal. But he contends that sacrifice taken as communion "contained an element of permanent truth wrapped up in a very crude embodiment." That element of truth was the spiritualized conception of the bond between a god and his worshippers, and the embodiment was exactly the material manifestation of the conception. Smith seems to be maintaining that the spiritualized conception was also to be found in the conception of sacrifice as gift, at least in times of crisis, when it was recognized that the anger of a god could be alleviated only by acts beyond "the payment of gifts and tribute" (p. 396). Atonement required the restoration of the right relationship with the god.

In fact, Smith contends that sacrifice as atonement developed out of sacrifice as communion, "whose atoning efficacy rested on the persuasion that those in whose veins the same life-blood circulates cannot be other than friends, bound to serve each other in all the offices of brotherhood" (p. 398). As Smith asks, "[H]ow can the impurity of sin be better expelled than by a draught of sacred life? and how can man be brought nearer to his god than by physically absorbing a particle of the divine nature?" (p. 356). Atonement, which itself means "at one," presupposes a relationship of friendship that the act of sacrifice is intended to restore. The initial kind of sacrifice as atonement was called "piacular," and its communal aspect testifies to its origin:

> The characteristic features in piacular sacrifice are not the invention of a later age, in which the sense of sin and divine wrath was strong, but are features carried over from a very primitive type of religion, in which the sense of sin, in any proper sense of the word, did not exist at all, and the whole object of ritual was to maintain the bond of physical holiness that kept the religious community together. (p. 401)

Sacrifice as atonement was initially offered as more or even other than a gift and thus, far from arising "when the gift-theory of sacrifice began to break down," antedated sacrifice as gift exclusively (p. 397).

If sacrifice as communion gave way to sacrifice as atonement because travails came to be seen as chronic punishment by a god, sacrifice as communion also gave way to sacrifice as atonement because the animals sacrificed came to be seen as ever more sacred. So sacred did they become that the consumption of them by worshippers came to be considered sacrilegious. The blood, the fat, and eventually even the flesh dared only be poured out or burned or else given to the priests:

> In the later forms of Syrian heathenism the sacrificial meal practically disappears, and almost the whole altar service consists of piacular holocausts, and among the Jews the highest sin-offerings, whose blood was brought into the inner sanctuary, were wholly consumed, but not upon the altar, while the flesh of other sin-offerings was at least withdrawn from the offerer and eaten by the priests. (p. 348)

These "holocaust" sacrifices dissolved the communal element in atonement.[10]

From Material to Spiritual Conception of Religion

For Smith, uncleanness was originally assumed to arise from physical contact and was remedied by a physical act:

> Among the Semites the impurities which were thought of as cleaving to a man, and making him unfit to mingle freely in the social and religious life of his community, were of very

> various kinds, and often of a nature that we should regard as merely physical, *e.g.* uncleanness from contact with the dead, from leprosy, from eating forbidden food, and so forth.... They were dealt with, where the uncleanness was of a mild form, mainly by ablutions; or where the uncleanness was more intense, by more elaborate ceremonies involving the use of sacrificial blood, of sacrificial ashes, or the like. (p. 428)

Where, however, uncleanness stemmed from the murder of a fellow tribesman, the washing away of the blood did not suffice. Semitic religions "provide no atonement for the murderer himself," who therefore cannot be restored "to his original place in his tribe." Thus Hebrew law "does not admit piacula for mortal sins." Only the community can be cleansed, and only by "disavow[ing] the act of its impious member." Atonement "is bound up with the notion of the solidarity of the body of worshippers—the same notion which makes the pious Hebrews confess and lament not only their own sins, but the sins of their fathers" (p. 429).

The combination of collective responsibility for "the maintenance of holiness" with "the thought that holiness is specially compromised by crime" led to the conception of the community as "a kingdom of righteousness," which is to say, a kingdom based on ethics. Where ethics rules, "there is no atonement for mortal sin" on the part of individuals (p. 429). Smith seems to conflate the rejection of the possibility of atonement with the rejection of a physical means of atonement. He certainly conflates the rejection of a physical means of atonement with the rejection of the sin as physical. While bloodshed was obviously still involved, the real sin was now taken to be ethical.

Smith credits the Prophets with this spiritualized conception of sin, a conception that "raised the religion of Israel altogether out of the region of physical ideas with which primitive conceptions of holiness are bound up" (p.

430). Just as communion was initially understood physically and only subsequently spiritualized, so atonement was initially understood physically and only subsequently spiritualized (see p. 435).

On the one hand Smith maintains that even the post-exilic Israelite notion of sacrifice as atonement rested on the primitive notion of sacrifice as communion: "all atoning rites are ultimately to be regarded as owing their efficacy to a communication of divine life to the worshippers, and to the establishment or confirmation of a living bond between them and their god." On the other hand Smith maintains that even primitive and pre-exilic Israelite notions of sacrifice harbored the supposedly exclusively higher concepts of atonement: "Redemption, substitution, purification, atoning blood, the garment of righteousness, are all terms which in some sense go back to antique ritual" (p. 439). Within primitive religion itself misfortunes like plague and famine were originally attributed to the weakening of the bond between god and community, and sacrifice served to restore the bond. Eventually, the weakening came to be attributed to sin, and sacrifice came to be taken as atonement. Nevertheless, the ultimate aim of atonement was the restoration of the bond between god and community.

In its fullest, Christian form, God sacrifices himself to atone for the sins of the worldwide community, though Jesus' death still serves primarily to restore the fellowship between God and humanity. Indeed, Smith comes increasingly to downplay the atoning aspect of Jesus' death, and in the second edition of *Religion of the Semites*, the edition reprinted here, he deletes the following comparison of the Crucifixion as an atoning death with the deaths of other gods:

> That the God-man dies for His people, and that His death is their life, is an idea which was in some degree foreshadowed

> by the oldest mystical sacrifices. It was foreshadowed, indeed, in a very crude and materialistic form, and without any of those ethical ideas which the Christian doctrine of the atonement derives from a profounder sense of sin and divine justice. And yet the voluntary death of the divine victim, which we have seen to be a conception not foreign to ancient sacrificial ritual, contained the germ of the deepest thought in the Christian doctrine: the thought that the Redeemer gives Himself for His people, that "for their sakes He consecrates Himself, that they also might be consecrated in truth." (Smith 1889:393)

Smith never finds a satisfactory place for atonement in his irenic characterization of Christianity.[11] The ineluctable link between atonement and fear, in contrast to that between communion and love, cannot but push religion based on fear in the direction of, by Smith's own criteria, magic *rather than* religion. Frazer noted Smith's reluctance to acknowledge the place of fear in religion and attributed that reluctance to Smith's own belief in a god of love rather than of fear:

> I may add that it had long seemed to me that Smith, influenced probably by his deeply religious nature, under-estimated the influence of fear, and over-estimated the influence of the benevolent emotions (love, confidence, and gratitude), in moulding early religion. Hence his view of sacrifice as mainly a form of communion with the deity instead of a mode of propitiating him and averting his anger. The latter is the ordinary view of sacrifice, and I believe it on the whole to be substantially correct. Not, of course, that I would deny sacrifice sometimes to involve a form of communion with the deity, but I believe it to be far oftener purely propitiatory, that is, intended to soothe and please a dreaded being by giving him something that he likes. (quoted Black and Chrystal 1912:518-19)[12]

Despite Smith's insistence on the presence of both communion and atonement in primitive and higher religion alike, the gulf between these stages of religion remains wide because primitive religion still conceives of both materially, where higher religion conceives of both spiritually. In primitive religion spiritual ideas like atonement, while present, "are very vaguely defined; they indicate impressions produced on the mind of the worshipper by features of the ritual, rather than formulated ethico-dogmatical ideas." In "primitive ritual" communion "is grasped in a merely physical and mechanical shape, as indeed, in primitive life, all spiritual and ethical ideas are still wrapped up in the husk of a material embodiment" (p. 439). In primitive religion the goal is physical contact with a god—a goal achieved through the shared eating of a sacrifice, which in its earliest form is the eating of the totemic god itself. At first, little attention is paid to the cause of the separation from a god or to the justification for it.

"To free the spiritual truth from the husk was the great task that lay before the ancient religions, if they were to maintain the right to continue to rule the minds of men." Smith grants that "some progress in this direction was made, especially in Israel" (p. 439). It was the Prophets who severed communion from material sacrifice—Smith taking the Prophets as entirely anti-ritualistic. Once communion with a god came to be conceived of spiritually, separation from the god came to be conceived of ethically, as a matter of the justification for the separation and of the amends needed for overcoming it. But the subsequent, post-exilic restoration of material sacrifice conflated anew the spiritual with the material. Only with Christianity was the spiritual fully disentangled from the material.

Smith's account of the evolution of sacrifice is theological in a straightforward sense: he appeals to God as a cause of the evolution. He contends that "on the whole it is manifest that none of the ritual systems of antiquity was able *by mere natural development* to shake itself free from the congenital defect inherent in every attempt to embody spiritual truths in material forms. A ritual system must always remain materialistic" (pp. 439-40 [italics added]). In other words, Israelites and Christians on their own could never have made the leap from a material conception of sacrifice to a spiritual one. Only God's intercession, undertaken indirectly through inspiration, can account for the jump.[13]

Smith is rightly viewed as a pioneering, as perhaps even *the* pioneering, sociologist of religion. He shifts the focus of the study of primitive and ancient religion from beliefs to institutions and from the individual to the group. For Smith, the function of primitive and ancient religion is the preservation of the group, even if he does not, like the more relentlessly sociological Durkheim, make group experience the origin of religion or make the group itself the object of worship.

Whether Smith can reconcile his sociological account of religion with his theological one is a philosophical issue. Certainly God for him operates behind the scenes, by inspiring religious innovators. The direct causes of religious evolution are for him natural. They are a mix of external factors—political, economic, environmental, and cultural (contact with other cultures)—and internal ones. For example, the beginning of the religion of the individual stems internally from individual Israelites' being left to themselves once sacrifice was centralized.

Smith was the last great theological theorist of religion. With conspicuous contemporary exceptions like John Hick, theorists after him have shied away from appealing to God to account for religion and have restricted God to the object of religion. Disputes since Smith's day have been over the natural causes of religion. God is never invoked. Smith straddled the move from a theological to a secular account of religion. His sociological approach to primitive and ancient religion opened the door to the sociology of religion. But his theological approach to higher religion sought to keep the door closed to a wholly secular account of religion.

ROBERT A. SEGAL

Notes

1. See Beidelman 1974:30-31. Still, it would be going much too far to deny for Smith the centrality of the group for individual Christians: see Nelson 1969, pp. 179-80.

2. Smith also links kinship with the collective rather than individualistic nature of ancient religion: "With the ancients the conception of life, whether divine or human, was not so much individualised as it is with us; thus, for example, all the members of one kin were conceived as having a common life embodied in the common blood which flowed through their veins" (p. 190).

3. For all Smith's focus on the ancient god as father, he is prepared to grant that the earliest god was female: see pp. 51-52, 55-58. See also Jones 1984:40.

4. Smith argues that polytheism arose when aristocrats toppled the king: see pp. 73-74.

5. Yet Smith simultaneously states that in ancient religion the physical kinship between god and worshippers *lessened* the ethics: "heathenism shows its fundamental weakness, in its inability to separate the ethical motives of religion from their source in a merely naturalistic conception of the godhead and its relation to man" (p. 58).

6. Smith contends not merely that Semites passed through a totemic stage but also that subsequent stages emerged out of it, so that "some of the Semitic gods are of totem origin" (p. 138).

7. On the difference between Frazer and Smith on the comparative method see Segal 2001:359-72.

8. On holiness and uncleanness see also Additional Note B (pp. 446-54).

9. On this point, made by many commentators, see, for example, Nelson 1969:176-78.

10. See Black and Chrystal 1912:516-17.

11. On Smith's conspicuous neglect of the issue of Jesus' death as atonement see Bediako 1997:355-72; Riesen 1985:174-86.

12. Smith replies to an earlier statement by Frazer of this view, a statement not directed at Smith himself: "I think Mr. Frazer goes too far in supposing that mere fear of ghosts rules

in all these observances. Not seldom we find also a desire for continued fellowship with the dead, under such conditions as make the fellowship free from danger" (p. 370 note 1). See also p. 336 note 2.

13. As Rogerson writes of Smith on Israel, "Smith believed that if the Old Testament were compared with the religion of other ancient Semitic peoples, the superiority of Israelite religion would be clear for all to see, and that it would be possible to draw the conclusion that this superiority could not have been a human achievement, but was made possible only by the self-revealing activity of God" (Rogerson 1995, pp. 146-47). On this issue Smith and the Dutch biblical scholar Abraham Kuenen parted company (see Bailey 1970:ch. 5), though Bailey argues that Smith eventually moved in the naturalistic direction of Kuenen: see Bailey 1970:291-93. In reply, see Rogerson 1995:147-49; Bediako 1997:117-18.

References

Bailey, Warner McReynolds, 1970, *Theology and Criticism in William Robertson Smith.* Ph.D. Dissertation, Yale University.

Bediako, Gillian M., 1997, *Primal Religion and the Bible.* Sheffield: Sheffield Academic Press.

Beidelman, T. O., 1974, *W. Robertson Smith and the Sociological Study of Religion.* Chicago: University of Chicago Press.

Black, John Sutherland, and George Chrystal, 1912, *The Life of William Robertson Smith.* London: Black.

Brown, Jesse H., 1964, *The Contribution of William Robertson Smith to Old Testament Scholarship, With Special Emphasis on Higher Criticism.* Ph.D. Dissertation, Duke University.

Durkheim, Emile, 1965, *The Elementary Forms of the Religious Life* [1912]. Tr. Joseph Ward Swain. New York: Free Press. (Original pub. of translation 1915.)

Frazer, James George, 1918, *Folk-lore in the Old Testament.* 3 vols. London: Macmillan.

Freud, Sigmund, 1965, *Totem and Taboo* [1913]. Tr. James Strachey. New York: Norton. (Original pub. of translation 1950.)

Johnstone, William, ed., 1995, *William Robertson Smith.* Sheffield: Sheffield Academic Press.

Jones, Robert Alun, 1981, "Robertson Smith, Durkheim, and Sacrifice: An Historical Context for *The Elementary Forms of the Religious Life.*" *Journal of the History of the Behavioral Sciences* 17:184-205.

_____, 1984, "Robertson Smith and James Frazer on Religion: Two Traditions in British Social Anthropology." In *Functionalism Historicized*, ed. George W. Stocking, Jr., 31-58. Madison: University of Wisconsin Press.

_____, 1986, "Durkheim, Frazer, and Smith: The Role of Analogies and Exemplars in the Development of Durkheim's Sociology of Religion." *American Journal of Sociology* 92:596-627.

Nelson, Ronald Roy, 1969, *The Life and Thought of William Robertson Smith, 1846-1894*. Ph.D. Dissertation, University of Michigan.

Riesen, Richard Allan, 1985, *Criticism and Faith in Late Victorian Scotland*. Lanham, MD: University Press of America.

Rogerson, J. W., 1995, *The Bible and Criticism in Victorian Britain*. Sheffield: Sheffield Academic Press.

Segal, Robert A., 2001, "In Defense of the Comparative Method." *Numen* 48:339-73.

Smith, William Robertson, 1889, *Lectures on the Religion of the Semites*. First Series. 1st ed. Edinburgh: Black.

_____, 1894, *Lectures on the Religion of the Semites*. First Series. 2nd ed. Edinburgh: Black.

_____, 1995, *Lectures on the Religion of the Semites*. Second and Third Series, ed. John Day. Sheffield: Sheffield Academic Press.

Tylor, Edward Burnett, 1958, *Primitive Culture*. 2 vols. 5th ed. New York: Harper Torchbooks. (Original pub. of 5th ed. 1913.) 1st ed. 1871.

PREFACE TO THE FIRST EDITION

In April 1887 I was invited by the trustees of the Burnett Fund to deliver three courses of lectures at Aberdeen, in the three years from October 1888 to October 1891, on "The primitive religions of the Semitic peoples, viewed in relation to other ancient religions, and to the spiritual religion of the Old Testament and of Christianity." I gladly accepted this invitation; for the subject proposed had interested me for many years, and it seemed to me possible to treat it in a way that would not be uninteresting to the members of my old University, in whose hall the Burnett Lectures are delivered, and to the wider public to whom the gates of Marischal College are opened on the occasion.

In years gone by, when I was called upon to defend before the courts of my Church the rights of historical research, as applied to the Old Testament, I had reason to acknowledge with gratitude the fairness and independence of judgment which my fellow-townsmen of Aberdeen brought to the discussion of questions which in most countries are held to be reserved for the learned, and to be merely disturbing to the piety of the ordinary layman; and I was glad to have the opportunity of commending to the notice of a public so impartial and so intelligent the study of a branch of comparative religion which, as I venture to think, is indispensable to the future progress of Biblical research.

In Scotland, at least, no words need be wasted to prove that a right understanding of the religion of the Old Testament is the only way to a right understanding of the Christian faith; but it is not so fully recognised, except in the circle of professed scholars, that the doctrines and ordinances of the Old Testament cannot be thoroughly comprehended until they are put into comparison with the religions of the nations akin to the Israelites. The value of comparative studies for the study of the religion of the Bible was brought out very clearly, two hundred years ago, by one of the greatest of English theologians, Dr. John Spencer, Master of Corpus Christi College in Cambridge, whose Latin work on the ritual laws of the Hebrews may justly be said to have laid the foundations of the science of Comparative Religion, and in its special subject, in spite of certain defects that could hardly have been avoided at the time when it was composed, still remains by far the most important book on the religious antiquities of the Hebrews. But Spencer was so much before his time that his work was not followed up; it is often ignored by professed students of the Old Testament, and has hardly exercised any influence on the current ideas which are the common property of educated men interested in the Bible.

In modern times Comparative Religion has become in some degree a popular subject, and in our own country has been treated from various points of view by men of eminence who have the ear of the public; but nothing considerable has been done since Spencer's time, either in England or on the Continent, whether in learned or in popular form, towards a systematic comparison of the religion of the Hebrews, as a whole, with the beliefs and ritual practices of the other Semitic peoples. In matters of detail valuable work has been done; but this work has been too special, and for the most part too technical, to help the circle to whom the Burnett Lectures are addressed; which I take to be a circle of cultivated and thinking men and women who have no special acquaintance with Semitic lore, but are interested in everything that throws light on their own religion, and are prepared to follow a sustained or even a severe argument, if the speaker on his part will remember that historical research can always be made intelligible to thinking people, when it is set forth with orderly method and in plain language.

There is a particular reason why some attempt in this direction should be made now. The first conditions of an effective comparison of Hebrew religion, as a whole, with the religion of the other Semites, were lacking so long as the historical order of the Old Testament documents, and especially of the documents of which the Pentateuch is made up, was unascertained or wrongly apprehended; but, thanks to the labours of a series of scholars (of whom it is sufficient to name Kuenen and Wellhausen, as the men whose acumen and research have carried this inquiry to a point where nothing of vital importance for the historical study of the Old Testament religion still remains uncertain), the growth of the Old Testament religion can now be followed from stage to stage, in a way that is hardly possible with any other religion of antiquity. And so it is now not only possible, but most necessary for further progress, to make a fair comparison between Hebrew religion in its various stages and the religions of the races with which the Hebrews were cognate by natural descent, and with which also they were historically in constant touch.

The plan which I have framed for my guidance in carrying out the desires of the Burnett trustees is explained in the first lecture. I begin with the institutions of religion, and in the present series I discuss those institutions which may be called fundamental, particularly that of sacrifice, to which fully one half of the volume is devoted. It will readily be understood that, in the course of the argument, I have found it convenient to take up a good many things that are not fundamental, at the place where they could most naturally be explained; and, on the other hand, I daresay that students of the subject may sometimes be disposed to regard as fundamental certain matters which I have been compelled to defer. But on the whole I trust that the present volume will be found to justify its title, and to contain a fairly adequate analysis of the first principles of Semitic worship. It would indeed have been in some respects more satisfactory to myself to defer the publication of the first series of lectures till I could complete the whole subject of institutions, derivative as well as primary. But it seemed due to the hearers who may desire to attend the second series of lectures, to let them have before them in print the arguments and conclusions from which that series must start; and also, in a matter of this sort, when one has put forth a considerable number of new ideas, the value of which must be tested by criticism, one is anxious to have the judgment of scholars on the first part of one's work before going on to further developments.

I may explain that the lectures, as now printed, are considerably expanded from the form in which they were delivered; and that only nine lectures of the eleven were read in Aberdeen, the last two having been added to complete the discussion of sacrificial ritual.

In dealing with the multiplicity of scattered evidences on which the argument rests, I have derived great assistance from the researches of a number of scholars, to whom acknowledgment is made in the proper places. For Arabia

I have been able to refer throughout to my friend Wellhausen's excellent volume, *Reste arabischen Heidenthumes* (Berl. 1887), in which the extant material for this branch of Semitic heathenism is fully brought together, and criticised with the author's well-known acumen. For the other parts of Semitic heathenism there is no standard exposition of a systematic kind that can be referred to in the same way. In this country Movers's book on Phœnician religion is often regarded as a standard authority for the heathenism of the Northern Semites; but, with all its learning, it is a very unsafe guide, and does not supersede even so old a book as Selden, *De diis Syris*.

In analysing the origin of ritual institutions, I have often had occasion to consult analogies in the usages of early peoples beyond the Semitic field. In this part of the work I have had invaluable assistance from my friend, Mr. J. G. Frazer, who has given me free access to his unpublished collections on the superstitions and religious observances of primitive nations in all parts of the globe. I have sometimes referred to him by name, in the course of the book, but these references convey but an imperfect idea of my obligations to his learning and intimate familiarity with primitive habits of thought. In this connection I would also desire to make special acknowledgment of the value, to students of Semitic ritual and usage, of the comparative studies of Dr. Wilken of Leyden; which I mention in this place, because Dutch work is too apt to be overlooked in England.

In transcribing Oriental words, I have distinguished the emphatic consonants, so far as seemed necessary to preclude ambiguities, by the usual device of putting dots under the English letters that come nearest to them in sound. But instead of *ḳ* (ק) I write *c*, following a precedent set by eminent French Orientalists. In Eastern words both *c* and *g* are always to be pronounced hard. But where there is a conventional English form for a word I retain it; thus I write "Caaba," not "Kaʿba;" "Caliph," not "Khalīfa"; "Jehovah," not "Yahveh" or "Iahwé." As regards the references in the notes, it may be useful to mention that *CIS.* means the Paris *Corpus Inscriptionem Semiticarum*, and *ZDMG.* the *Zeitschrift* of the German Oriental Society; that when Wellhausen is cited, without reference to the title of a book, his work on Arabian Heathenism is meant; and that *Kinship* means my book on *Kinship and Marriage in Early Arabia* (Cambridge, University Press, 1885).

Finally, I have to express my thanks to my friend, Mr. J. S. Black, who has kindly read the whole book in proof, and made many valuable suggestions.

W. Robertson Smith.

Christ's College, Cambridge,
1st *October* 1889.

NOTE TO THE SECOND EDITION

The failure of Professor Smith's health from 1890 onwards made it impossible for him to prepare for publication the Second and Third Series of Burnett Lectures, delivered in March 1890 and December 1891; but the subject never ceased to interest him, and the comparatively manageable task of embodying in a new edition of the First Series the results of further reading and reflection, as well as of criticisms from other workers in the same field, was one of his latest occupations. On March 17th, only a fortnight before his lamented death, he handed over to my care the annotated print, and also the manuscript volume of new materials, with the remark that, apart from some adjustments in detail, which he hoped he might yet find strength to make as the work passed through the press, he believed the revision was practically complete. In making the adjustments referred to, it has been my endeavour to carry out with absolute fidelity the author's wishes so far as I knew or could divine them; and in the majority of instances the task has not been difficult. My best thanks are due to Mr. J. G. Frazer, and also to Professor Bevan (both of Cambridge), for much valuable help in correcting the proofs.

J. S. B.

Edinburgh, *3rd October* 1894.

LECTURE I

INTRODUCTION: THE SUBJECT AND THE METHOD OF ENQUIRY

THE subject before us is the religion of the Semitic peoples, that is, of the group of kindred nations, including the Arabs, the Hebrews and Phœnicians, the Aramæans, the Babylonians and Assyrians, which in ancient times occupied the great Arabian Peninsula, with the more fertile lands of Syria Mesopotamia and Irac, from the Mediterranean coast to the base of the mountains of Iran and Armenia. Among these peoples three of the great faiths of the world had their origin, so that the Semites must always have a peculiar interest for the student of the history of religion. Our subject, however, is not the history of the several religions that have a Semitic origin, but Semitic religion as a whole in its common features and general type. Judaism, Christianity and Islam are *positive* religions, that is, they did not grow up like the systems of ancient heathenism, under the action of unconscious forces operating silently from age to age, but trace their origin to the teaching of great religious innovators, who spoke as the organs of a divine revelation, and deliberately departed from the traditions of the past. Behind these positive religions lies the old unconscious religious tradition, the body of religious usage and belief which cannot be traced to the influence of individual minds, and was not propagated on individual authority, but formed part of that inheritance from the past into which successive generations of the Semitic race grew up as it were instinctively, taking it as a matter of course that they should believe and act as their fathers had done before them. The positive Semitic religions had to establish themselves on ground already occupied by these older beliefs and usages; they had to displace what they could not assimilate, and whether they rejected or absorbed the elements of the older religion, they had at every point to reckon with them and take up a definite attitude towards them. No positive religion that has moved men has been able to start with a *tabula rasa*, and express itself as if religion were beginning for the first time; in form, if not in substance, the new system must be in contact all along the line with the older ideas and practices which it finds in possession. A new scheme of faith can find a hearing only by appealing to religious instincts and susceptibilities that already exist in its audience, and it cannot reach these without taking account of the traditional forms in which all religious feeling is embodied, and without speaking a language which men accustomed to these old forms can understand. Thus to comprehend a system of positive religion thoroughly, to understand it in its historical origin and form as well as in its abstract principles, we must know the traditional religion that preceded it. It is from this point of view that I invite you to take an interest in the ancient religion of the Semitic peoples; the matter is not one of mere antiquarian curiosity, but has a direct and important bearing on the great problem of the origins of the spiritual religion of the Bible. Let me illustrate this by an example. You know how large a part of the teaching of the New

Testament and of all Christian theology turns on the ideas of sacrifice and priesthood. In what they have to say on these heads the New Testament writers presuppose, as the basis of their argument, the notion of sacrifice and priesthood current among the Jews and embodied in the ordinances of the Temple. But, again, the ritual of the Temple was not in its origin an entirely novel thing; the precepts of the Pentateuch did not create a priesthood and a sacrificial service on an altogether independent basis, but only reshaped and remodelled, in accordance with a more spiritual doctrine, institutions of an older type, which in many particulars were common to the Hebrews with their heathen neighbours. Every one who reads the Old Testament with attention is struck with the fact that the origin and *rationale* of sacrifice are nowhere fully explained; that sacrifice is an essential part of religion is taken for granted, as something which is not a doctrine peculiar to Israel but is universally admitted and acted on without as well as within the limits of the chosen people. Thus, when we wish thoroughly to study the New Testament doctrine of sacrifice, we are carried back step by step till we reach a point where we have to ask what sacrifice meant, not to the old Hebrews alone, but to the whole circle of nations of which they formed a part. By considerations of this sort we are led to the conclusion that no one of the religions of Semitic origin which still exercise so great an influence on the lives of men can be completely understood without enquiry into the older traditional religion of the Semitic race.

You observe that in this argument I take it for granted that, when we go back to the most ancient religious conceptions and usages of the Hebrews, we shall find them to be the common property of a group of kindred peoples, and not the exclusive possession of the tribes of Israel. The proof that this is so will appear more clearly in the sequel; but, indeed, the thing will hardly be denied by any one who has read the Bible with care. In the history of old Israel before the captivity, nothing comes out more clearly than that the mass of the people found the greatest difficulty in keeping their national religion distinct from that of the surrounding nations. Those who had no grasp of spiritual principles, and knew the religion of Jehovah only as an affair of inherited usage, were not conscious of any great difference between themselves and their heathen neighbours, and fell into Canaanite and other foreign practices with the greatest facility. The significance of this fact is manifest if we consider how deeply the most untutored religious sensibilities are shocked by any kind of innovation. Nothing appeals so strongly as religion to the conservative instincts; and conservatism is the habitual attitude of Orientals. The whole history of Israel is unintelligible if we suppose that the heathenism against which the prophets contended was a thing altogether alien to the religious traditions of the Hebrews. In principle there was all the difference in the world between the faith of Isaiah and that of an idolater. But the difference in principle, which seems so clear to us, was not clear to the average Judæan, and the reason of this was that it was obscured by the great similarity in many important points of religious tradition and ritual practice. The conservatism which refuses to look at principles, and has an eye only for tradition and usage, was against the prophets, and had no sympathy with their efforts to draw a sharp line between the religion of Jehovah and that of the foreign gods. This is a proof that what I may call the natural basis of Israel's worship was very closely akin to that of the neighbouring cults.

The conclusion on this point which is suggested by the facts of Old Testament history, may be accepted the more readily because it is confirmed by presumptive arguments of another kind. Traditional religion is handed down from father to child, and therefore is in great measure an affair of race. Nations sprung from a common stock will have a common inheritance of traditional belief and usage in things sacred as well as profane, and thus the evidence that the Hebrews and their neighbours had a large common stock of religious tradition falls in with the evidence which we have from other sources, that in point of race the people of Israel were nearly akin to the heathen nations of Syria and Arabia. The populations of this whole region constitute a well-marked ethnic unity, a fact which is usually expressed by giving to them the common name of Semites. The choice of this term was originally suggested by the tenth chapter of Genesis, in which most of the nations of the group with which we are concerned are represented as descended from Shem the son of Noah. But though modern historians and ethnographers have borrowed a name from the book of Genesis, it must be understood that they do not define the Semitic group as coextensive with the list of nations that are there reckoned to the children of Shem. Most recent interpreters are disposed to regard the classification of the families of mankind given in Genesis x. as founded on principles geographical or political rather than ethnographical; the Phœnicians and other Canaanites, for example, are made to be children of Ham and near cousins of the Egyptians. This arrangement corresponds to historical facts, for, at a period anterior to the Hebrew conquest, Canaan was for centuries an Egyptian dependency, and Phœnician religion and civilisation are permeated by Egyptian influence. But ethnographically the Canaanites were akin to the

Arabs and Syrians, and they spoke a language which is hardly different from Hebrew. On the other hand, Elam and Lud, that is Susiana and Lydia, are called children of Shem, though there is no reason to think that in either country the mass of the population belonged to the same stock as the Syrians and Arabs. Accordingly it must be remembered that when modern scholars use the term Semitic, they do not speak as interpreters of Scripture, but include all peoples whose distinctive ethnical characters assign them to the same group with the Hebrews, Syrians and Arabs.

The scientific definition of an ethnographical group depends on a variety of considerations; for direct historical evidence of an unimpeachable kind as to the original seats and kindred of ancient peoples is not generally to be had. The defects of historical tradition must therefore be supplied by observation, partly of inherited physical characteristics, and partly of mental characteristics, habits and attainments such as are usually transmitted from parent to child. Among the indirect criteria of kinship between nations, the most obvious, and the one which has hitherto been most carefully studied, is the criterion of language; for it is observed that the languages of mankind form a series of natural groups, and that within each group it is possible to arrange the several languages which it contains in what may be called a genealogical order, according to degrees of kinship. Now it may not always be true that people of the same or kindred speech are as closely related by actual descent as they seem to be from the language they speak; a Gaelic tribe, for example, may forget their ancient speech, and learn to speak a Teutonic dialect, without ceasing to be true Gaels by blood. But, in general, large groups of men do not readily change their language, but go on from generation to generation speaking the ancestral dialect, with such gradual modification as the lapse of time brings about. As a rule, therefore, the classification of mankind by language, at least when applied to large masses, will approach pretty closely to a natural classification; and in a large proportion of cases the language of a mixed race will prove on examination to be that of the stock whose blood is predominant. Where this is not the case, where a minority has imposed its speech on a majority, we may safely conclude that it has done so in virtue of a natural pre-eminence, a power of shaping lower races in its own mould, which is not confined to the sphere of language, but extends to all parts of life. Where we find unity of language, we can at least say with certainty that we are dealing with a group of men who are subject to common influences of the most subtle and far-reaching kind; and where unity of speech has prevailed for many generations, we may be sure that the continued action of these influences has produced great uniformity of physical and mental type. When we come to deal with groups which have long had separate histories, and whose languages are therefore not identical but only cognate, the case is not so strong; but, on the whole, it remains true that the stock which is strong enough, whether by numbers or by genius, to impress its language on a nation, must also exercise a predominant influence on the national type in other respects; and to this extent the classification of races by language must be called natural and not artificial. Especially is this true for ancient times, when the absence of literature, and particularly of religious books, made it much more difficult than it has been in recent ages for a new language to establish itself in a race to which it was originally foreign. All Egypt now speaks Arabic—a Semitic tongue—and yet the population is very far from having assimilated itself to the Arabic type. But this could not have happened without the Coran and the religion of the Coran.

The Semitic nations are classed together on the ground of similarity of language; but we have every reason to recognise their linguistic kinship as only one manifestation of a very marked general unity of type. The unity is not perfect; it would not, for example, be safe to make generalisations about the Semitic character from the Arabian nomads, and to apply them to the ancient Babylonians. And for this there are probably two reasons. On the one hand, the Semite of the Arabian desert and the Semite of the Babylonian alluvium lived under altogether different physical and moral conditions; the difference of environment is as complete as possible. And, on the other hand, it is pretty certain that the Arabs of the desert have been from time immemorial a race practically unmixed, while the Babylonians, and other members of the same family settled on the fringes of the Semitic land, were in all probability largely mingled with the blood of other races, and underwent a corresponding modification of type.

But when every allowance is made for demonstrable or possible variations of type within the Semitic field, it still remains true that the Semites form a singularly well marked and relatively speaking a very homogeneous group. So far as language goes the evidence to this effect is particularly strong. The Semitic tongues are so much alike that their affinity is recognised even by the untrained observer; and modern science has little difficulty in tracing them back to a single primitive speech, and determining in a general way what the features of that speech were. On the other hand, the differences between these languages and those spoken by other adjacent races are so fundamental and so wide, that little or nothing can be affirmed with certainty as to the relation of the Semitic tongues to other linguistic stocks. Their nearest kinship seems to be with the languages of North Africa, but even here the common features are balanced by profound differences. The evidence of language therefore tends to show that the period during which the original and common Semitic speech existed apart, and developed its peculiar characters at a distance from languages of other stocks, must have been very long in comparison with the subsequent period during which the separate branches of the Semitic stock, such as Hebrew Aramaic and Arabic, were isolated from one another and developed into separate dialects. Or, to draw the historical inference from this, it would appear that before the Hebrews, the Aramæans, and the Arabs spread themselves over widely distant seats, and began their course of separate national development, there must have been long ages in which the ancestors of all these nations lived together and spoke with one tongue. And as this was in the infancy of mankind, the period of human history in which individuality went for nothing, and all common influences had a force which we moderns can with difficulty conceive, the various swarms which ultimately hived off from the common stock and formed the Semitic nations known to history, must have carried with them a strongly marked race character, and many common possessions of custom and idea, besides their common language.

And further, let us observe that the dispersion of the Semitic nations was never carried so far as the dispersion of the Aryans. If we leave out of account settlements made over the seas,—the South Arabian colonies in East Africa, and the Phœnician colonies on the coasts and isles of the Mediterranean,—we find that the region of Semitic occupation is continuous and compact. Its great immovable centre is the vast Arabian peninsula, a region naturally isolated, and in virtue of its physical characters almost exempt from immigration or change of inhabitants. From this central stronghold, which the predominant opinion of modern scholars designates as the probable starting-point of the whole Semitic dispersion, the region of Semitic speech spreads out round the margin of the Syrian desert till it strikes against great natural boundaries, the Mediterranean, Mount Taurus, and the mountains of Armenia and Iran. From the earliest dawn of history all that lies within these limits was fully occupied by Semitic tribes speaking Semitic dialects, and the compactness of this settlement must necessarily have tended to maintain uniformity of type. The several Semitic nations, when they were not in direct contact with one another, were divided not by alien populations, but only by the natural barriers of mountain and desert. These natural barriers, indeed, were numerous, and served to break up the race into a number of small tribes or nations; but, like the mountains of Greece, they were not so formidable as to prevent the separate states from maintaining a great deal of intercourse, which, whether peaceful or warlike, tended to perpetuate the original community of type. Nor was the operation of these causes disturbed in ancient times by any great foreign immigration. The early Egyptian invasions of Syria were not followed by colonisation; and while the so-called Hittite monuments, which have given rise to so much speculation, may afford evidence that a non-Semitic people from Asia Minor at one time pushed its way into Northern Syria, it is pretty clear that the Hittites of the Bible, *i.e.* the non-Aramaic communities of Cœle-Syria, were a branch of the Canaanite stock, though they may for a time have been dominated by a non-Semitic aristocracy. At one time it was not uncommon to represent the Philistines as a non-Semitic people, but it is now generally recognised that the arguments for this view are inadequate, and that, though they came into Palestine from across the sea, from Caphtor, *i.e.* probably from Crete, they were either mainly of Semitic blood, or at least were already thoroughly Semitised at the time of their immigration, alike in speech and in religion.

Coming down to later times, we find that the Assyrian Babylonian and Persian conquests made no considerable change in the general type of the population of the Semitic lands. National and tribal landmarks were removed, and there were considerable shiftings of population within the Semitic area, but no great incursion of new populations of alien stock. In the Greek and Roman periods, on the contrary, a large foreign element was introduced into the towns of Syria; but as the immigration was practically confined to the cities, hardly touching the rural districts, its effects in modifying racial type were, it would seem, of a very transitory character. For in Eastern cities the death-rate habitually exceeds the birth-rate, and the urban population is maintained only by constant recruital from the country, so that it is the blood of the peasantry which ultimately determines the type of the population. Thus it is to be explained that, after the Arab conquest of Syria, the Greek element in the population rapidly disappeared. Indeed, one of the most palpable proofs that the populations of all the old Semitic lands possessed a remarkable homogeneity of character, is the fact that in them, and in them alone, the Arabs and Arab influence took permanent root. The Moslem conquests extended far beyond these limits; but, except in the old Semitic countries, Islam speedily took new shapes, and the Arab dominations soon gave way before the reaction of the mass of its foreign subjects.

Thus the whole course of history, from the earliest date to which authentic knowledge extends down to the time of the decay of the Caliphate, records no great permanent disturbance of population to affect the constancy of the Semitic type within its original seats, apart from the temporary Hellenisation of the great cities already spoken of. Such disturbances as did take place consisted partly of mere local displacements among the settled Semites, partly, and in a much greater degree, of the arrival and establishment in the cultivated lands of successive hordes of Semitic nomads from the Arabian wilderness, which on their settlement found themselves surrounded by populations so nearly of their own type that the complete fusion of the old and new inhabitants was effected without difficulty, and without modification of the general character of the race. If at any point in its settlements, except along the frontiers, the Semitic blood was largely modified by foreign admixture, this must have taken place in prehistoric times, or by fusion with other races which may have occupied the country before the arrival of the Semites. How far anything of this sort actually happened can only be matter of conjecture, for the special hypotheses which have sometimes been put forth—as, for example, that there was a considerable strain of pre-Semitic blood in the Phœnicians and Canaanites—rest on presumptions of no conclusive sort. What is certain is that the Semitic settlements in Asia were practically complete at the first dawn of history, and that the Semitic blood was constantly reinforced, from very early times, by fresh immigrations from the desert. There is hardly another part of the world where we have such good historical reasons for presuming that linguistic affinity will prove a safe indication of affinity in race, and in general physical and mental type. And this presumption is not belied by the results of nearer enquiry. Those who have busied themselves with the history and literature of the Semitic peoples, bear uniform testimony to the close family likeness that runs through them all.

It is only natural that this homogeneity of type appears to be modified on the frontiers of the Semitic field. To the West, if we leave the transmarine colonies out of view, natural conditions drew a sharp line of local demarcation between the Semites and their alien neighbours. The Red Sea and the desert north of it formed a geographical barrier, which was often crossed by the expansive force of the Semitic race, but which appears to have effectually checked the advance into Asia of African populations. But on the East, the fertile basin of the Euphrates and Tigris seems in ancient as in modern times to have been a meeting-place of races. The preponderating opinion of Assyriologists is to the effect that the civilisation of Assyria and Babylonia was not purely Semitic, and that the ancient population of these parts contained a large pre-Semitic element, whose influence is especially to be recognised in religion and in the sacred literature of the cuneiform records.

If this be so, it is plain that the cuneiform material must be used with caution in our enquiry into the type of traditional religion characteristic of the ancient Semites. That Babylonia is the best starting-point for a comparative study of the sacred beliefs and practices of the Semitic peoples, is an idea which has lately had some vogue, and which at first sight appears plausible on account of the great antiquity of the monumental evidence. But, in matters of this sort, ancient and primitive are not synonymous terms; and we must not look for the most primitive form of Semitic faith in a region where society was not primitive. In Babylonia, it would seem, society and religion alike were based on a fusion of two races, and so were not primitive but complex. Moreover, the official system of Babylonian and Assyrian religion, as it is known to us from priestly texts and public inscriptions, bears clear marks of being something more than a popular traditional faith; it has been artificially moulded by priestcraft and statecraft in much the same way as the official religion of Egypt; that is to say, it is in great measure an artificial combination, for imperial purposes, of elements drawn from a number of local worships. In all probability the actual religion of the masses was always much simpler than the official system; and in later times it would seem that, both in religion and in race, Assyria was little different from the adjacent Aramæan countries. These remarks are not meant to throw doubt on the great importance of cuneiform studies for the history of Semitic religion; the monumental data are valuable for comparison with what we know of the faith and worship of other Semitic peoples, and peculiarly valuable because, in religion as in other matters, the civilisation of the Euphrates-Tigris valley exercised a great historical influence on a large part of the Semitic field. But the right point of departure for a general study of Semitic religion must be sought in regions where, though our knowledge begins at a later date, it refers to a simpler state of society, and where accordingly the religious phenomena revealed to us are of an origin less doubtful and a character less complicated. In many respects the religion of heathen Arabia, though we have little information concerning it that is not of post-Christian date, displays an extremely primitive type, corresponding to the primitive and unchanging character of nomadic life. With what may be gathered from this source we must compare, above all, the invaluable notices, preserved in the Old Testament, of the religion of the small Palestinian states before their conquest by the great empires of the East. For this period, apart from the Assyrian monuments and a few precious fragments of other evidence from inscriptions, we have no contemporary documents outside the Bible. At a later date the evidence from monuments is multiplied, and Greek literature begins to give important aid; but by this time also we have reached the period of religious syncretism—the period, that is, when different faiths and worships began to react on one another, and produce new and complex forms of religion. Here, therefore, we have to use the same precautions that are called for in dealing with the older syncretistic religion of Babylonia and Assyria; it is only by careful sifting and comparison that we can separate between ancient use and modern innovation, between the old religious inheritance of the Semites and things that came in from without.

Let it be understood from the outset that we have not the materials for anything like a complete comparative history of Semitic religions, and that nothing of the sort will be attempted in these Lectures. But a careful study and comparison of the various sources is sufficient to furnish a tolerably accurate view of a series of general features, which recur with striking uniformity in all parts of the Semitic field, and govern the evolution of faith and worship down to a late date. These widespread and permanent features form the real interest of Semitic religion to the philosophical student; it was in them, and not in the things that vary from place to place and from time to time, that the strength of Semitic religion lay, and it is to them therefore that we must look for help in the most important practical application of our studies, for light on the great question of the relation of the positive Semitic religions to the earlier faith of the race.

Before entering upon the particulars of our enquiry, I must still detain you with a few words about the method and order of investigation that seem to be prescribed by the nature of the subject. To get a true and well-defined picture of the type of Semitic religion, we must not only study the parts separately, but must have clear views of the place and proportion of each part in its relation to the whole. And here we shall go very far wrong if we take it for granted that what is the most important and prominent side of religion to us was equally important in the ancient society with which we are to deal. In connection with every religion, whether ancient or modern, we find on the one hand certain beliefs, and on the other certain institutions ritual practices and rules of conduct. Our modern habit is to look at religion from the side of belief rather than of practice; for, down to comparatively recent times, almost the only forms of religion seriously studied in Europe have been those of the various Christian Churches, and all parts of Christendom are agreed that ritual is important only in connection with its interpretation. Thus the study of religion has meant mainly the study of Christian beliefs, and instruction in religion has habitually begun with the creed, religious duties being presented to the learner as flowing from the dogmatic truths he is taught to accept. All this seems to us so much a matter of course that, when we approach some strange or antique religion, we naturally assume that here also our first business is to search for a creed, and find in it the key to ritual and practice. But the antique religions had for the most part no creed; they consisted entirely of institutions and practices. No doubt men will not habitually follow certain practices without attaching a meaning to them; but as a rule we find that while the practice was rigorously fixed, the meaning attached to it was extremely vague, and the same rite was explained by different people in different ways, without any question of orthodoxy or heterodoxy arising in consequence. In ancient Greece, for example, certain things were done at a temple, and people were agreed that it would be impious not to do them. But if you had asked why they were done, you would probably have had several mutually contradictory explanations from different persons, and no one would have thought it a matter of the least religious importance which of these you chose to adopt. Indeed, the explanations offered would not have been of a kind to stir any strong feeling; for in most cases they would have been merely different stories as to the circumstances under which the rite first came to be established, by the command or by the direct example of the god. The rite, in short, was connected not with a dogma but with a myth.

In all the antique religions, mythology takes the place of dogma; that is, the sacred lore of priests and people, so far as it does not consist of mere rules for the performance of religious acts, assumes the form of stories about the gods; and these stories afford the only explanation that is offered of the precepts of religion and the prescribed rules of ritual. But, strictly speaking, this mythology was no essential part of ancient religion, for it had no sacred sanction and no binding force on the worshippers. The myths connected with individual sanctuaries and ceremonies were merely part of the apparatus of the worship; they served to excite the fancy and sustain the interest of the worshipper; but he was often offered a choice of several accounts of the same thing, and, provided that he fulfilled the ritual with accuracy, no one cared what he believed about its origin. Belief in a certain series of myths was neither obligatory as a part of true religion, nor was it supposed that, by believing, a man acquired religious merit and conciliated the favour of the gods. What was obligatory or meritorious was the exact performance of certain sacred acts prescribed by religious tradition. This being so, it follows that mythology ought not to take the prominent place that is too often assigned to it in the scientific study of ancient faiths. So far as myths consist of explanations of ritual, their value is altogether secondary, and it may be affirmed with confidence that in almost every case the myth was derived from the ritual, and not the ritual from the myth; for the ritual was fixed and the myth was variable, the ritual was obligatory and faith in the myth was at the discretion of the worshipper. Now by far the largest part of the myths of antique religions are connected with the ritual of particular shrines, or with the religious observances of particular tribes and districts. In all such cases it is probable, in most cases it is certain, that the myth is merely the explanation of a religious usage; and ordinarily it is such an explanation as could not have arisen till the original sense of the usage had more or less fallen into oblivion. As a rule the myth is no explanation of the origin of the ritual to any one who does not believe it to be a narrative of real occurrences, and the boldest mythologist will not believe that. But if it be not true, the myth itself requires to be explained, and every principle of philosophy and common sense demands that the explanation be sought, not in arbitrary allegorical theories, but in the actual facts of ritual or religious custom to which the myth attaches. The conclusion is, that in the study of ancient religions we must begin, not with myth, but with ritual and traditional usage.

Nor can it be fairly set against this conclusion, that there are certain myths which are not mere explanations of traditional practices, but exhibit the beginnings of larger religious speculation, or of an attempt to systematise and reduce to order the motley variety of local worships and beliefs. For in this case the secondary character of the myths is still more clearly marked. They are either products of early philosophy, reflecting on the nature of the universe; or they are political in scope, being designed to supply a thread of union between the various worships of groups, originally distinct, which have been united into one social or political organism; or, finally, they are due to the free play of epic imagination. But philosophy politics and poetry are something more, or something less, than religion pure and simple.

There can be no doubt that, in the later stages of ancient religions, mythology acquired an increased importance. In the struggle of heathenism with scepticism on the one hand and Christianity on the other, the supporters of the old traditional religion were driven to search for ideas of a modern cast, which they could represent as the true inner meaning of the traditional rites. To this end they laid hold of the old myths, and applied to them an allegorical system of interpretation. Myth interpreted by the aid of allegory became the favourite means of infusing a new significance into ancient forms. But the theories thus developed are the falsest of false guides as to the original meaning of the old religions.

On the other hand, the ancient myths taken in their natural sense, without allegorical gloss, are plainly of great importance as testimonies to the views of the nature of the gods that were prevalent when they were formed. For though the mythical details had no dogmatic value and no binding authority over faith, it is to be supposed that nothing was put into a myth which people at that time were not prepared to believe without offence. But so far as the way of thinking expressed in the myth was not already expressed in the ritual itself, it had no properly religious sanction; the myth apart from the ritual affords only a doubtful and slippery kind of evidence. Before we can handle myths with any confidence, we must have some definite hold of the ideas expressed in the ritual tradition, which embodied the only fixed and statutory elements of the religion.

All this, I hope, will become clearer to us as we proceed with our enquiry, and learn by practical example the use to be made of the different lines of evidence open to us. But it is of the first importance to realise clearly from the outset that ritual and practical usage were, strictly speaking, the sum-total of ancient religions. Religion in primitive times was not a system of belief with practical applications; it was a body of fixed traditional practices, to which every member of society conformed as a matter of course. Men would not be men if they agreed to do certain things without having a reason for their action; but in ancient religion the reason was not first formulated as a doctrine and then expressed in practice, but conversely, practice preceded doctrinal theory. Men form general rules of conduct before they begin to express general principles in words; political institutions are older than political theories, and in like manner religious institutions are older than religious theories. This analogy is not arbitrarily chosen, for in fact the parallelism in ancient society between religious and political institutions is complete. In each sphere great importance was attached to form and precedent, but the explanation why the precedent was followed consisted merely of a legend as to its first establishment. That the precedent, once established, was authoritative did not appear to require any proof. The rules of society were based on precedent, and the continued existence of the society was sufficient reason why a precedent once set should continue to be followed.

Strictly speaking, indeed, I understate the case when

I say that the oldest religious and political institutions present a close analogy. It would be more correct to say that they were parts of one whole of social custom. Religion was a part of the organised social life into which a man was born, and to which he conformed through life in the same unconscious way in which men fall into any habitual practice of the society in which they live. Men took the gods and their worship for granted, just as they took the other usages of the state for granted, and if they reasoned or speculated about them, they did so on the presupposition that the traditional usages were fixed things, behind which their reasonings must not go, and which no reasoning could be allowed to overturn. To us moderns religion is above all a matter of individual conviction and reasoned belief, but to the ancients it was a part of the citizen's public life, reduced to fixed forms, which he was not bound to understand and was not at liberty to criticise or to neglect. Religious nonconformity was an offence against the state; for if sacred tradition was tampered with the bases of society were undermined, and the favour of the gods was forfeited. But so long as the prescribed forms were duly observed, a man was recognised as truly pious, and no one asked how his religion was rooted in his heart or affected his reason. Like political duty, of which indeed it was a part, religion was entirely comprehended in the observance of certain fixed rules of outward conduct.

The conclusion from all this as to the method of our investigation is obvious. When we study the political structure of an early society, we do not begin by asking what is recorded of the first legislators, or what theory men advanced as to the reason of their institutions; we try to understand what the institutions were, and how they shaped men's lives. In like manner, in the study of Semitic religion, we must not begin by asking what was told about the gods, but what the working religious institutions were, and how they shaped the lives of the worshippers. Our enquiry, therefore, will be directed to the religious institutions which governed the lives of men of Semitic race.

In following out this plan, however, we shall do well not to throw ourselves at once upon the multitudinous details of rite and ceremony, but to devote our attention to certain broad features of the sacred institutions which are sufficiently well marked to be realised at once. If we were called upon to examine the political institutions of antiquity, we should find it convenient to carry with us some general notion of the several types of government under which the multifarious institutions of ancient states arrange themselves. And in like manner it will be useful for us, when we examine the religious institutions of the Semites, to have first some general knowledge of the types of divine governance, the various ruling conceptions of the relations of the gods to man, which underlie the rites and ordinances of religion in different places and at different times. Such knowledge we can obtain in a provisional form, before entering on a mass of ritual details, mainly by considering the titles of honour by which men addressed their gods, and the language in which they expressed their dependence on them. From these we can see at once, in a broad, general way, what place the gods held in the social system of antiquity, and under what general categories their relations to their worshippers fell. The broad results thus reached must then be developed, and at the same time controlled and rendered more precise, by an examination in detail of the working institutions of religion.

The question of the metaphysical nature of the gods, as distinct from their social office and function, must be left in the background till this whole investigation is completed. It is vain to ask what the gods are in themselves till we have studied them in what I may call their public life, that is, in the stated intercourse between them and their worshippers which was kept up by means of the prescribed forms of cultus. From the antique point of view, indeed, the question what the gods are in themselves is not a religious but a speculative one; what is requisite to religion is a practical acquaintance with the rules on which the deity acts and on which he expects his worshippers to frame their conduct—what in 2 Kings xvii. 26 is called the "manner" or rather the "customary law" (*mishpat*) of the god of the land. This is true even of the religion of Israel. When the prophets speak of the knowledge of God, they always mean a practical knowledge of the laws and principles of His government in Israel,[1] and a summary expression for religion as a whole is "the knowledge and fear of Jehovah,"[2] *i.e.* the knowledge of what Jehovah prescribes, combined with a reverent obedience. An extreme scepticism towards all religious speculation is recommended in the Book of Ecclesiastes as the proper attitude of piety, for no amount of discussion can carry a man beyond the plain rule to "fear God and keep His commandments."[3] This counsel the author puts into the mouth of Solomon, and so represents it, not unjustly, as summing up the old view of religion, which in more modern days had unfortunately begun to be undermined.

The propriety of keeping back all metaphysical questions as to the nature of the gods till we have studied the practices of religion in detail, becomes very apparent if we consider for a moment what befel the later philosophers and theosophists of heathenism in their attempts to con-

[1] See especially Hosea, chap. iv. [2] Isa. xi. 2. [3] Eccles. xii. 13.

struct a theory of the traditional religion. None of these thinkers succeeded in giving an account of the nature of the gods from which all the received practices of worship could be rationally deduced, and those who had any pretensions to orthodoxy had recourse to violent allegorical interpretations in order to bring the established ritual into accordance with their theories.[1] The reason for this is obvious. The traditional usages of religion had grown up gradually in the course of many centuries, and reflected habits of thought characteristic of very diverse stages of man's intellectual and moral development. No one conception of the nature of the gods could possibly afford the clue to all parts of that motley complex of rites and ceremonies which the later paganism had received by inheritance, from a series of ancestors in every state of culture from pure savagery upwards. The record of the religious thought of mankind, as it is embodied in religious institutions, resembles the geological record of the history of the earth's crust; the new and the old are preserved side by side, or rather layer upon layer. The classification of ritual formations in their proper sequence is the first step towards their explanation, and that explanation itself must take the form, not of a speculative theory, but of a rational life-history.

I have already explained that, in attempting such a life-history of religious institutions, we must begin by forming some preliminary ideas of the practical relation in which the gods of antiquity stood to their worshippers. I have now to add, that we shall also find it necessary to have before us from the outset some elementary notions of the relations which early races of mankind conceived to subsist between gods and men on the one hand, and the material universe on the other. All acts of ancient

[1] See, for example, Plutarch's *Greek* and *Roman Questions*.

worship have a material embodiment, the form of which is determined by the consideration that gods and men alike stand in certain fixed relations to particular parts or aspects of physical nature. Certain places, certain things, even certain animal kinds are conceived as holy, *i.e.* as standing in a near relation to the gods, and claiming special reverence from men, and this conception plays a very large part in the development of religious institutions. Here again we have a problem that cannot be solved by *à priori* methods; it is only as we move onward from step to step in the analysis of the details of ritual observance that we can hope to gain full insight into the relations of the gods to physical nature. But there are certain broad features in the ancient conception of the universe, and of the relations of its parts to one another, which can be grasped at once, upon a merely preliminary survey, and we shall find it profitable to give attention to these at an early stage of our discussion.

I propose, therefore, to devote my second lecture to the nature of the antique religious community and the relations of the gods to their worshippers. After this we will proceed to consider the relations of the gods to physical nature, not in a complete or exhaustive way, but in a manner entirely preliminary and provisional, and only so far as is necessary to enable us to understand the material basis of ancient ritual. After these preliminary enquiries have furnished us with certain necessary points of view, we shall be in a position to take up the institutions of worship in an orderly manner, and make an attempt to work out their life-history. We shall find that the history of religious institutions is the history of ancient religion itself, as a practical force in the development of the human race, and that the articulate efforts of the antique intellect to comprehend the meaning of religion, the nature of the gods, and the principles on which they deal with men, take their point of departure from the unspoken ideas embodied in the traditional forms of ritual praxis. Whether the conscious efforts of ancient religious thinkers took the shape of mythological invention or of speculative construction, the raw material of thought upon which they operated was derived from the common traditional stock of religious conceptions that was handed on from generation to generation, not in express words, but in the form of religious custom.

In accordance with the rules of the Burnett Trust, three courses of lectures, to be delivered in successive winters, are allowed me for the development of this great subject. When the work was first entrusted to me, I formed the plan of dividing my task into three distinct parts. In the first course of lectures I hoped to cover the whole field of practical religious institutions. In the second I proposed to myself to discuss the nature and origin of the gods of Semitic heathenism, their relations to one another, the myths that surround them, and the whole subject of religious belief, so far as it is not directly involved in the observances of daily religious life. The third winter would thus have been left free for an examination of the part which Semitic religion has played in universal history, and its influence on the general progress of humanity, whether in virtue of the early contact of Semitic faiths with other systems of antique religion, or—what is more important—in virtue of the influence, both positive and negative, that the common type of Semitic religion has exercised on the formulas and structure of the great monotheistic faiths that have gone forth from the Semitic lands. But the first division of the subject has grown under my hands, and I find that it will not be possible in a single winter to cover the whole field of religious institutions in a way at all adequate to the fundamental importance of this part of the enquiry.

It will therefore be necessary to allow the first branch of the subject to run over into the second course, for which I reserve, among other matters of interest, the whole history of religious feasts and also that of the Semitic priesthoods. I hope, however, to give the present course a certain completeness in itself by carrying the investigation to the end of the great subject of sacrifice. The origin and meaning of sacrifice constitute the central problem of ancient religion, and when this problem has been disposed of we may naturally feel that we have reached a point of rest at which both speaker and hearers will be glad to make a pause.

LECTURE II

THE NATURE OF THE RELIGIOUS COMMUNITY, AND THE RELATION OF THE GODS TO THEIR WORSHIPPERS

WE have seen that ancient faiths must be looked on as matters of institution rather than of dogma or formulated belief, and that the system of an antique religion was part of the social order under which its adherents lived; so that the word "system" must here be taken in a practical sense, as when we speak of a political system, and not in the sense of an organised body of ideas or theological opinions. Broadly speaking, religion was made up of a series of acts and observances, the correct performance of which was necessary or desirable to secure the favour of the gods or to avert their anger; and in these observances every member of society had a share, marked out for him either in virtue of his being born within a certain family and community, or in virtue of the station, within the family and community, that he had come to hold in the course of his life. A man did not choose his religion or frame it for himself; it came to him as part of the general scheme of social obligations and ordinances laid upon him, as a matter of course, by his position in the family and in the nation. Individual men were more or less religious, as men now are more or less patriotic; that is, they discharged their religious duties with a greater or less degree of zeal according to their character and temperament; but there was no such thing as an absolutely irreligious man. A certain amount of religion was required of everybody; for the due performance of religious acts was a social obligation in which every one had his appointed share. Of intolerance in the modern sense of the word ancient society knew nothing; it never persecuted a man into particular beliefs for the good of his own soul. Religion did not exist for the saving of souls but for the preservation and welfare of society, and in all that was necessary to this end every man had to take his part, or break with the domestic and political community to which he belonged.

Perhaps the simplest way of putting the state of the case is this. Every human being, without choice on his own part, but simply in virtue of his birth and upbringing, becomes a member of what we call a *natural* society. He belongs, that is, to a certain family and a certain nation, and this membership lays upon him definite obligations and duties which he is called upon to fulfil as a matter of course, and on pain of social penalties and disabilities, while at the same time it confers upon him certain social rights and advantages. In this respect the ancient and modern worlds are alike; but there is this important difference, that the tribal or national societies of the ancient world were not strictly natural in the modern sense of the word, for the gods had their part and place in them equally with men. The circle into which a man was born was not simply a group of kinsfolk and fellow-citizens, but embraced also certain divine beings, the gods of the family and of the state, which to the ancient mind were as much a part of the particular community with which they stood connected as the human members of the social circle. The relation between the gods of antiquity and their worshippers was expressed in the language of human relationship, and this language was not taken in a figurative sense but with strict literality. If a god was spoken of as father and his worshippers as his offspring, the meaning was that the worshippers were literally of his stock, that he and they made up one natural family with reciprocal family duties to one another. Or, again, if the god was addressed as king, and the worshippers called themselves his servants, they meant that the supreme guidance of the state was actually in his hands, and accordingly the organisation of the state included provision for consulting his will and obtaining his direction in all weighty matters, and also provision for approaching him as king with due homage and tribute.

Thus a man was born into a fixed relation to certain gods as surely as he was born into relation to his fellow-men; and his religion, that is, the part of conduct which was determined by his relation to the gods, was simply one side of the general scheme of conduct prescribed for him by his position as a member of society. There was no separation between the spheres of religion and of ordinary life. Every social act had a reference to the gods as well as to men, for the social body was not made up of men only, but of gods and men.

This account of the position of religion in the social system holds good, I believe, for all parts and races of the ancient world in the earlier stages of their history. The causes of so remarkable a uniformity lie hidden in the mists of prehistoric time, but must plainly have been of a general kind, operating on all parts of mankind without distinction of race and local environment; for in every region of the world, as soon as we find a nation or tribe emerging from prehistoric darkness into the light of authentic history, we find also that its religion conforms to the general type which has just been indicated. As time rolls on and society advances, modifications take place. In religion as in other matters the transition from the antique to the modern type of life is not sudden and unprepared, but is gradually led up to by a continuous disintegration of the old structure of society, accompanied by the growth of new ideas and institutions. In Greece, for example, the intimate connection of religion with the organisation of the family and the state was modified and made less exclusive, at a relatively early date, by the Pan-Hellenic conceptions which find their theological expressions in Homer. If the Homeric poems were the Bible of the Greeks, as has so often been said, the true meaning of this phrase is that in these poems utterance was given to ideas about the gods which broke through the limitations of local and tribal worship, and held forth to all Greeks a certain common stock of religious ideas and motives, not hampered by the exclusiveness which in the earlier stages of society allows of no fellowship in religion that is not also a fellowship in the interests of a single kin or a single political group. In Italy there never was anything corresponding to the Pan-Hellenic ideas that operated in Greece, and accordingly the strict union of religion and the state, the solidarity of gods and men as parts of a single society with common interests and common aims, was characteristically exhibited in the institutions of Rome down to quite a late date. But in Greece as well as in Rome the ordinary traditional work-a-day religion of the masses never greatly departed from the primitive type. The final disintegration of antique religion in the countries of Græco-Italian civilisation was the work first of the philosophers and then of Christianity. But Christianity itself, in Southern Europe, has not altogether obliterated the original features of the paganism which it displaced. The Spanish peasants who insult the Madonna of the neighbouring village, and come to blows over the merits of rival local saints, still do homage to the same antique conception of religion which in Egypt animated the feuds of Ombos and Tentyra, and made hatred for each other's gods the formula that summed up all the local jealousies of the two towns.

The principle that the fundamental conception of ancient religion is the solidarity of the gods and their worshippers as part of one organic society, carries with it important consequences, which I propose to examine in some detail, with special reference to the group of religions that forms the proper subject of these lectures. But though my facts and illustrations will be drawn from the Semitic sphere, a great part of what I shall have to say in the present lecture might be applied, with very trifling modifications, to the early religion of any other part of mankind. The differences between Semitic and Aryan religion, for example, are not so primitive or fundamental as is often imagined. Not only in matters of worship, but in social organisation generally—and we have seen that ancient religion is but a part of the general social order which embraces gods and men alike—the two races, Aryans and Semites, began on lines which are so much alike as to be almost indistinguishable, and the divergence between their paths, which becomes more and more apparent in the course of ages, was not altogether an affair of race and innate tendency, but depended in a great measure on the operation of special local and historical causes.

In both races the first steps of social and religious development took place in small communities, which at the dawn of history had a political system based on the principle of kinship, and were mainly held together by the tie of blood, the only social bond which then had absolute and undisputed strength, being enforced by the law of blood revenge. As a rule, however, men of several clans lived side by side, forming communities which did not possess the absolute homogeneity of blood brotherhood, and yet were united by common interests and the habit of friendly association. The origin of such associations, which are found all over the world at a very early stage of society, need not occupy us now. It is enough to note the fact that they existed, and were not maintained by the feeling of kindred, but by habit and community of interests. These local communities of men of different clans, who lived together on a footing of amity, and had often to unite in common action, especially in war, but also in affairs of polity and justice, were the origin of the antique state. There is probably no case in ancient history where a state was simply the development of a single homogeneous clan or gens, although the several clans which united to form a state often came in course of time to suppose themselves to be only branches of one great ancestral brotherhood, and were thus knit together in a closer unity of sentiment and action. But in the beginning, the union of several clans for common political action was not sustained either by an effective sentiment of kinship (the law of blood revenge uniting only members of the same clan) or by any close political organisation, but was produced by the pressure of practical necessity, and always tended towards dissolution when this practical pressure was withdrawn. The only organisation for common action was that the leading men of the clans consulted together in time of need, and their influence led the masses with them. Out of these conferences arose the senates of elders found in the ancient states of Semitic and Aryan antiquity alike. The kingship, again, as we find it in most antique states, appears to have ordinarily arisen in the way which is so well illustrated by the history of Israel. In time of war an individual leader is indispensable; in a time of prolonged danger the temporary authority of an approved captain easily passes into the lifelong leadership at home as well as in the field, which was exercised by such a judge as Gideon; and at length the advantages of having a permanent head, both as a leader of the army and as a restraint on the perennial feuds and jealousies of clans that constantly threaten the solidity of the state, are recognised in the institution of the kingship, which again tends to become hereditary, as in the case of the house of David, simply because the king's house naturally becomes greater and richer than other houses, and so better able to sustain the burden of power.

Up to this point the progress of society was much alike in the East and in the West, and the progress of religion, as we shall see in the sequel, followed that of society in general. But while in Greece and Rome the early period of the kings lies in the far background of tradition, and only forms the starting-point of the long development with which the historian of these countries is mainly occupied, the independent evolution of Semitic society was arrested at an early stage. In the case of the nomadic Arabs, shut up in their wildernesses of rock and sand, Nature herself barred the way of progress. The life of the desert does not furnish the material conditions for permanent advance beyond the tribal system, and we find that the religious development of the Arabs was proportionally retarded, so that at the advent of Islam the ancient heathenism, like the ancient tribal structure of society, had become effete without having ever ceased to be barbarous.

The northern Semites, on the other hand, whose progress up to the eighth century before Christ certainly did not lag behind that of the Greeks, were deprived of political independence, and so cut short in their natural development, by the advance from the Tigris to the Mediterranean of the great Assyrian monarchs, who, drawing from the rich and broad alluvium of the Two Rivers resources which none of their neighbours could rival, went on from conquest to conquest till all the small states of Syria and Palestine had gone down before them. The Assyrians were conquerors of the most brutal and destructive kind, and wherever they came the whole structure of ancient society was dissolved. From this time onwards the difference between the Syrian or Palestinian and the Greek was not one of race alone; it was the difference between a free citizen and a slave of an Oriental despotism. Religion as well as civil society was profoundly affected by the catastrophe of the old free communities of the northern Semitic lands; the society of one and the same religion was no longer identical with the state, and the old solidarity of civil and religious life continued to exist only in a modified form. It is not therefore surprising that from the eighth century onwards the history of Semitic religion runs a very different course from that which we observe on the other side of the Mediterranean.

The ancient Semitic communities were small, and were separated from each other by incessant feuds. Hence, on the principle of solidarity between gods and their worshippers, the particularism characteristic of political society could not but reappear in the sphere of religion. In the same measure as the god of a clan or town had indisputable claim to the reverence and service of the community to which he belonged, he was necessarily an enemy to their enemies and a stranger to those to whom they were strangers. Of this there are sufficient evidences in the way in which the Old Testament speaks about the relation of the nations to their gods. When David in the bitterness of his heart complains of those who "have driven him out from connection with the heritage of Jehovah," he represents them as saying to him, "Go, serve other gods."[1] In driving him to seek refuge in another land and another nationality, they compel him to change his religion, for a man's religion is part of his political connection. "Thy sister," says Naomi to Ruth, "is gone back unto her people and unto her gods"; and Ruth replies, "Thy people shall be my people, and thy God my God":[2] the change of nationality involves a change of cult. Jeremiah, in the full consciousness of the falsehood of all religions except that of Israel, remarks that no nation changes its gods although they be no gods:[3] a nation's worship remains as constant as its political identity. The Book of Deuteronomy, speaking in like manner from the standpoint of monotheism, reconciles the sovereignty of Jehovah with the actual facts of heathenism, by saying that He has "allotted" the various objects of false worship "unto all nations under the whole heaven."[4] The "allotment" of false gods among the nations, as property is allotted, expresses with precision the idea that each god had his own determinate circle of worshippers, to whom he stood in a peculiar and exclusive relation.

The exclusiveness of which I have just spoken naturally finds its most pronounced expression in the share taken by the gods in the feuds and wars of their worshippers. The enemies of the god and the enemies of his people are identical; even in the Old Testament "the enemies of Jehovah" are originally nothing else than the enemies of Israel.[5] In battle each god fights for his own people, and to his aid success is ascribed; Chemosh gives victory to Moab, and Asshur to Assyria;[6] and often the divine

[1] 1 Sam. xxvi. 19.
[2] Ruth i. 14 *sqq.*
[3] Jer. ii. 11.
[4] Deut. iv. 19.
[5] 1 Sam. xxx. 26, "the spoil of the enemies of Jehovah"; Judg. v. 31.
[6] See the inscription of King Mesha on the so-called Moabite Stone, and the Assyrian inscriptions, *passim.*

image or symbol accompanies the host to battle. When the ark was brought into the camp of Israel, the Philistines said, "Gods are come into the camp; who can deliver us from the hand of these mighty gods?"[1] They judged from their own practice, for when David defeated them at Baal-perazim, part of the booty consisted in their idols which had been carried into the field.[2] When the Carthaginians, in their treaty with Philip of Macedon,[3] speak of "the gods that take part in the campaign," they doubtless refer to the inmates of the sacred tent which was pitched in time of war beside the tent of the general, and before which prisoners were sacrificed after a victory.[4] Similarly an Arabic poet says, "Yaghūth went forth with us against Morād";[5] that is, the image of the god Yaghūth was carried into the fray. You observe how literal and realistic was the conception of the part taken by the deity in the wars of his worshippers.

When the gods of the several Semitic communities took part in this way in the ancestral feuds of their worshippers, it was impossible for an individual to change his religion without changing his nationality, and a whole community could hardly change its religion at all without being absorbed into another stock or nation. Religious like political ties were transmitted from father to son; for a man could not choose a new god at will; the gods of his fathers were the only deities on whom he could count as friendly and ready to accept his homage, unless he forswore his own kindred and was received into a new

[1] 1 Sam. iv. 7 *sqq.* [2] 2 Sam. v. 21.

[3] Polybius, vii. 9. [4] Diodorus, xx. 65.

[5] Yācūt, iv. 1023. A survival of the same idea is seen in the portable tabernacle of the Carmathians (Ibn al-Jauzī, *ap.* De Goeje, *Carmathes* [1886], pp. 180 220 *sq.*) from which victory was believed to descend. De Goeje compares the portable sanctuary of Mokhtār (Ṭabari, ii. 702 *sqq.*) and the *'oṭfa* still used by Bedouin tribes (Burckhardt, *Bed. and Wah.* i. 145; Lady Anne Blunt, *Bedouin Tribes*, ii. 146; Doughty, i. 61, ii. 304).

circle of civil as well as religious life. In the old times hardly any but outlaws changed their religion; ceremonies of initiation, by which a man was received into a new religious circle, became important, as we shall see by and by, only after the breaking up of the old political life of the small Semitic commonwealths.

On the other hand, all social fusion between two communities tended to bring about a religious fusion also. This might take place in two ways. Sometimes two gods were themselves fused into one, as when the mass of the Israelites in their local worship of Jehovah identified Him with the Baalim of the Canaanite high places, and carried over into His worship the ritual of the Canaanite shrines, not deeming that in so doing they were less truly Jehovah-worshippers than before. This process was greatly facilitated by the extreme similarity in the attributes ascribed to different local or tribal gods, and the frequent identity of the divine titles.[1] One Baal hardly differed from another, except in being connected with a different kindred or a different place, and when the kindreds were fused by intermarriage, or lived together in one village on a footing of social amity, there was nothing to keep their gods permanently distinct. In other cases, where the several deities brought together by the union of their worshippers into one state were too distinct to lose their individuality, they continued to be worshipped side by side as allied

[1] It will appear in the sequel that the worship of the greater Semitic deities was closely associated with the reverence which all primitive pastoral tribes pay to their flocks and herds. To a tribe whose herds consisted of kine and oxen, the cow and the ox were sacred beings, which in the oldest times were never killed or eaten except sacrificially. The tribal deities themselves were conceived as closely akin to the sacred species of domestic animals, and their images were often made in the likeness of steers or heifers in cow-keeping tribes, or of rams and ewes in shepherd tribes. It is easy to see how this facilitated the fusion of tribal worships, and how deities originally distinct might come to be identified on account of the similarity of their images and of the sacrifices offered to them.

divine powers, and it is to this kind of process that we must apparently ascribe the development of a Semitic pantheon or polytheistic system. A pantheon, or organised commonwealth of gods, such as we find in the state religion of Egypt or in the Homeric poems, is not the primitive type of heathenism, and little trace of such a thing appears in the oldest documents of the religion of the smaller Semitic communities. The old Semites believed in the existence of many gods, for they accepted as real the gods of their enemies as well as their own, but they did not worship the strange gods from whom they had no favour to expect, and on whom their gifts and offerings would have been thrown away. When every small community was on terms of frequent hostility with all its neighbours, the formation of a polytheistic system was impossible. Each group had its own god, or perhaps a god and a goddess, to whom the other gods bore no relation whatever. It was only as the small groups coalesced into larger unities, that a society and kinship of many gods began to be formed, on the model of the alliance or fusion of their respective worshippers; and indeed the chief part in the development of a systematic hierarchy or commonwealth of Semitic deities is due to the Babylonians and Assyrians, among whom the labours of statesmen to build up a consolidated empire out of a multitude of local communities, originally independent, were seconded by the efforts of the priests to give a corresponding unity of scheme to the multiplicity of local worships.[1]

Thus far we have looked only at the general fact, that in a Semitic community men and their gods formed a social and political as well as a religious whole. But to

[1] In the eighth century B.C. some of the Western Semitic states had a considerable pantheon, as appears most clearly from the notices of the "gods of Ya'di" on the inscriptions recently found at Zenjirli in North-West Syria, at the foot of Mount Amanus. Five of these gods are named.

make our conceptions more concrete we must consider what place in this whole was occupied by the divine element of the social partnership. And here we find that the two leading conceptions of the relation of the god to his people are those of fatherhood and of kingship. We have learned to look on Semitic society as built up on two bases—on kinship, which is the foundation of the system of clans or gentes, and on the union of kins, living intermingled or side by side, and bound together by common interests, which is the foundation of the state. We now see that the clan and the state are both represented in religion: as father the god belongs to the family or clan, as king he belongs to the state; and in each sphere of the social order he holds the position of highest dignity. Both these conceptions deserve to be looked at and illustrated in some detail.

The relation of a father to his children has a moral as well as a physical aspect, and each of these must be taken into account in considering what the fatherhood of the tribal deity meant in ancient religion. In the physical aspect the father is the being to whom the child owes his life, and through whom he traces kinship with the other members of his family or clan. The antique conception of kinship is participation in one blood, which passes from parent to child and circulates in the veins of every member of the family. The unity of the family or clan is viewed as a physical unity, for the blood is the life,—an idea familiar to us from the Old Testament,[1]—and it is the same

[1] Gen. ix. 4; Deut. xii. 23. Among the Arabs also *nafs* is used of the life-blood. When a man dies a natural death his life departs through the nostrils (*māta ḥatfa anfihi*), but when he is slain in battle "his life flows on the spear point" (Ḥamāsa, p. 52). Similarly *lā nafsa lahu sāïlatun* means *lā dama lahu yajrī* (*Miṣbāḥ*, *s.v.*). To the use of *nafs* in the sense of blood, the Arabian philologists refer such expressions as *nifās*, childbirth; *nafsā*, puerpera. The use of *nafisat* or *nufisat* in the sense of *ḥāḍat* (Bokhārī, i. 72, l. 10) appears to justify their explanation.

blood and therefore the same life that is shared by every descendant of the common ancestor. The idea that the race has a life of its own, of which individual lives are only parts, is expressed even more clearly by picturing the race as a tree, of which the ancestor is the root or stem and the descendants the branches. This figure is used by all the Semites, and is very common both in the Old Testament and in the Arabian poets.

The moral aspect of fatherhood, again, lies in the social relations and obligations which flow from the physical relationship—in the sanctity of the tie of blood which binds together the whole family, and in the particular modification of this tie in the case of parent and child, the parent protecting and nourishing the child, while the child owes obedience and service to his parent.

In Christianity, and already in the spiritual religion of the Hebrews, the idea of divine fatherhood is entirely dissociated from the physical basis of natural fatherhood. Man was created in the image of God, but he was not begotten; God-sonship is not a thing of nature but a thing of grace. In the Old Testament, Israel is Jehovah's son, and Jehovah is his father who created him;[1] but this creation is not a physical act, it refers to the series of gracious deeds by which Israel was shaped into a nation. And so, though it may be said of the Israelites as a whole, "Ye are the children of Jehovah your God,"[2] this sonship is national, not personal, and the individual Israelite has not the right to call himself Jehovah's son.

But in heathen religions the fatherhood of the gods is physical fatherhood. Among the Greeks, for example, the idea that the gods fashioned men out of clay, as potters fashion images, is relatively modern. The older conception is that the races of men have gods for their ancestors, or

[1] Hos. xi. 1; Deut. xxxii. 6. [2] Deut. xiv. 1.

are the children of the earth, the common mother of gods and men, so that men are really of the stock or kin of the gods.[1] That the same conception was familiar to the older Semites appears from the Bible. Jeremiah describes idolaters as saying to a stock, Thou art my father; and to a stone, Thou hast brought me forth.[2] In the ancient poem, Num. xxi. 29, the Moabites are called the sons and daughters of Chemosh, and at a much more recent date the prophet Malachi calls a heathen woman "the daughter of a strange god."[3] These phrases are doubtless accommodations to the language which the heathen neighbours of Israel used about themselves; they belong to an age when society in Syria and Palestine was still mainly organised on the tribal system, so that each clan, or even each complex of clans forming a small independent people, traced back its origin to a great first father; and they indicate that, just as in Greece, this father or *ἀρχηγέτης* of the race was commonly identified with the god of the race. With this it accords that in the judgment of most modern enquirers several names of deities appear in the old genealogies of nations in the Book of Genesis. Edom, for example, the progenitor of the Edomites, was identified by the Hebrews with Esau the brother of Jacob, but to the heathen he was a god, as appears from the theophorous proper name Obededom, "worshipper of Edom."[4] The remains of such

[1] See details and references in Preller-Robert, *Griechische Mythol.* (1887) i. 78 *sqq.*

[2] Jer. ii. 27.

[3] Mal. ii. 11.

[4] Bäthgen, *Beiträge zur Semitischen Religionsg.* p. 10, objects that not all names compounded with עבד are theophorous. And it is true that on the Nabatæan inscriptions we find names of this form in which the second element is the name of a king; but this is in a state of society where the king was revered as at least quasi-divine, and where the apotheosis of dead kings was not unknown. Cf. Wellh. p. 2 *sq.*; Euting, *Nabat. Inschr.* p. 32 *sq.*; and especially Clermont-Ganneau, *Rec. d'Archéol. Or.* i. 39 *sqq.* It must, however, be admitted that in questions of the history of religion, arguments derived from names are apt to be somewhat inconclusive; it is

mythology are naturally few in records which have come to us through the monotheistic Hebrews. On the other hand, the extant fragments of Phœnician and Babylonian cosmogonies date from a time when tribal religion and the connection of individual gods with particular kindreds was forgotten or had fallen into the background. But in a generalised form the notion that men are the offspring of the gods still held its ground. In the Phœnician cosmogony of Philo Byblius it does so in a confused shape, due to the author's euhemerism, that is, to his theory that deities are nothing more than deified men who had been great benefactors to their species. But euhemerism itself can arise, as an explanation of popular religion, only where the old gods are regarded as akin to men, and where, therefore, the deification of human benefactors does not involve any such patent absurdity as on our way of thinking. Again, in the Chaldæan legend preserved by Berosus,[1] the belief that men are of the blood of the gods is expressed in a form too crude not to be very ancient; for animals as well as men are said to have been formed out of clay mingled with the blood of a decapitated deity. Here we have a blood-kinship

possible, though surely very improbable, that the national name אדום (always written *plene*) means "men," Arabic *anām*, and is different from the god-name אדם; see Nöldeke in *ZDMG*. xlii. 470.

As examples of god-names in the genealogies of Genesis, I have elsewhere adduced Uz (Gen. xxii. 21, xxxvi. 28; LXX, Ωζ, Ωξ, Ως; and in Job i. 1, Αὐσῖτις)='Auḍ (*Kinship*, 261) and Yeush (Gen. xxxvi. 14)=Yaghūth. The second of these identifications is accepted by Nöldeke, but rejected by Lagarde, *Mitth*. ii. 77, *Bildung der Nomina*, p. 124. The other has been criticised by Nöldeke, *ZDMG*. xl. 184, but his remarks do not seem to me to be conclusive. That the Arabian god is a mere personification of Time is a hard saying, and the view that *'auḍo* or *'auḍa* in the line of al-A'shā is derived from the name of the god, which Nöldeke finds to be "doch etwas bizarr," has at least the authority of Ibn al-Kalbī as cited by Jauharī, and more clearly in the *Lisān*. A god קינן bearing the same name as the antediluvian Cainan (Gen. v. 9) appears in Ḥimyaritic inscriptions; *ZDMG*. xxxi. 86; *CIS*. iv. p. 20.

[1] Müller, *Fr. Hist. Gr*. ii. 497 *sq*.

of gods men and beasts, a belief which has points of contact with the lowest forms of savage religion.

It is obvious that the idea of a physical affinity between the gods and men in general is more modern than that of affinity between particular gods and their worshippers; and the survival of the idea in a generalised form, after men's religion had ceased to be strictly dependent on tribal connection, is in itself a proof that belief in their descent from the blood of the gods was not confined to this or that clan, but was a widespread feature in the old tribal religions of the Semites, too deeply interwoven with the whole system of faith and practice to be altogether thrown aside when the community of the same worship ceased to be purely one of kinship.

That this was really the case will be seen more clearly when we come to speak of the common features of Semitic ritual, and especially of the ritual use of blood, which is the primitive symbol of kinship. Meantime let us observe that there is yet another form in which the idea of divine descent survived the breaking up of the tribal system among the northern Semites. When this took place, the worshippers of one god, being now men of different kindreds, united by political bonds instead of bonds of blood, could not be all thought of as children of the god. He was no longer their father but their king. But as the deities of a mixed community were in their origin the old deities of the more influential families, the members of these families might still trace their origin to the family god, and find in this pedigree matter of aristocratic pride. Thus royal and noble houses among the Greeks long continued to trace their stem back to a divine forefather, and the same thing appears among the Semites. We are told by Virgil and Silius Italicus,[1] that the royal house of Tyre

[1] *Æn.* i. 729; *Punica*, i. 87.

and the noblest families of Carthage claimed descent from the Tyrian Baal; among the Aramæan sovereigns of Damascus, mentioned in the Bible, we find more than one Ben-hadad, "son of the god Hadad," and at Zenjirli the king Bar-RKB seems from his name to claim descent from the god RKB-EL.[1] Among the later Aramæans names like Barlāhā, "son of God," Barba'shmīn, "son of the Lord of Heaven," Barate, "son of Ate," are not uncommon. At Palmyra we have Barnebo, "son of Nebo," Barshamsh, "son of the Sun-god"; and in Ezra ii. the eponym of a family of temple slaves is Barkos, "son of the god Caus." Whether any definite idea was attached to such names in later times is doubtful; perhaps their diffusion was due to the constant tendency of the masses to copy aristocratic names, which is as prevalent in the East as among ourselves.[2]

[1] For the god-sonship of Assyrian monarchs, see Tiele, *Babylonisch-Assyr. Gesch.* p. 492.

[2] Among the Hebrews and Phœnicians personal names of this type do not appear; we have, however, the woman's name בתבעל, "daughter of Baal," *CIS.* pt. i. Nos. 469, 727, etc. On the other hand, the worshipper is called brother (that is, kinsman) or sister of the god in such names as the Phœnician חמלך, חמלכת, חרם ; חתמלך, חתמלכת, חתמלקרת, חתלת, חתנת, "sister of Tanith," and the Hebrew חיאל, אחיה. A singular and puzzling class of theophorous names are those which have the form of an Arabic *konya*; as Abibaal, "father of Baal." It has been common to evade the difficulty by rendering "my father is Baal"; but this view breaks down before such a woman's name as אמאשמן (*CIS.* No. 881), mother of the god Eshmun. See Nöldeke in *ZDMG.* xlii. (1888) p. 480, who seems disposed to believe that "father" has here some metaphorical sense, comparing Gen. xlv. 8. For my own part I hazard the conjecture that the *konya* was in practice used as equivalent to the patronymic; the custom of calling the eldest son after the grandfather was so widespread that M, son of N, was pretty sure to be known also as M, father of N, and the latter, as the more polite form of address, might very well come to supersede the patronymic altogether. I think there are some traces of this in Arabic; the poet 'Amr b. Kolthum addresses the king 'Amr b. Hind as Abu Hind (Moall. l. 23). In Hebrew the prefixes אבי, אחי, חמו are used in forming names of women as well as men, and so in Phœnician Abibaal may be a woman's name (*CIS.* No. 387), as אבעלי, אבמלך are in Ḥimyaritic (*CIS.* pt. iv. Nos. 6, 85); but for this linguistic peculiarity Nöldeke has adduced satisfactory analogies.

The belief that all the members of a clan are sons and daughters of its god, might naturally be expected to survive longest in Arabia, where the tribe was never lost in the state, and kinship continued down to the time of Mohammed to be the one sacred bond of social unity. In point of fact many Arabian tribes bear the names of gods, or of celestial bodies worshipped as gods, and their members are styled "sons of Hobal," "sons of the Full Moon," and the like.[1] There is no adequate reason for refusing to explain these names, or at least the older ones among them, on the analogy of the similar clan-names found among the northern Semites; for Arabian ritual, as well as that of Palestine and Syria, involves in its origin a belief in the kinship of the god and his worshippers. In the later ages of Arabian heathenism, however, of which alone we have any full accounts, religion had come to be very much dissociated from tribal feeling, mainly, it would seem, in consequence of the extensive migrations which took place in the first centuries of our era, and carried tribes far away from the fixed sanctuaries of the gods of their fathers.[2] Men forgot their old worship, and as the names of gods were also used as individual proper names, the divine ancestor, even before Islam, had generally sunk to the rank of a mere man. But though the later Arabs worshipped gods that were not the gods of their fathers, and tribes of alien blood were often found gathered together on festival

[1] See *Kinship*, p. 205 *sqq.*, and Wellhausen, *Heidenthum*, p. 4 *sqq.*, who explains all such names as due to omission of the prefix '*Abd* or the like. In some cases this probably is so, but it must not be assumed that because the same tribe is called (for example) 'Auf or 'Abd 'Auf indifferently, Banu 'Auf is a contraction of Banu 'Abd 'Auf. It is quite logical that the sons of 'Auf form the collective body of his worshippers; cf. Mal. iii. 17; and for the collective use of '*abd* cf. *Ḥamāsa*, p. 312, first verse. Personal names indicating god-sonship are lacking in Arabia; see on supposed Sabæan examples *ZDMG.* xxxvii. 15.

[2] See Wellhausen, *ut supra*, p. 182 *sq.*, and compare 1 Sam. xxvi. 19.

occasions at the great pilgrim shrines, there are many evidences that all Arabic deities were originally the gods of particular kins, and that the bond of religion was originally coextensive with the bond of blood.

A main proof of this lies in the fact that the duties of blood were the only duties of absolute and indefeasible sanctity. The Arab warrior in the ages immediately preceding Islam was very deficient in religion in the ordinary sense of the word; he was little occupied with the things of the gods and negligent in matters of ritual worship. But he had a truly religious reverence for his clan, and a kinsman's blood was to him a thing holy and inviolable. This apparent paradox becomes at once intelligible when we view it in the light of the antique conception, that the god and his worshippers make up a society in which the same character of sanctity is impressed on the relations of the worshippers to one another as on their relations to their god. The original religious society was the kindred group, and all the duties of kinship were part of religion. And so even when the clan-god had fallen into the background and was little remembered, the type of a clan-religion was still maintained in the enduring sanctity of the kindred bond.[1]

Again, the primitive connection of religion with kindred is attested by the existence of priesthoods confined to men of one clan or family, which in many cases was of a

[1] When the oracle at Tabāla forbade the poet Imraulcais to make war on the slayers of his father, he broke the lot and dashed the pieces in the face of the god, exclaiming with a gross and insulting expletive, "If it had been thy father that was killed, thou wouldst not have refused me vengeance." The respect for the sanctity of blood overrides respect for a god who, by taking no interest in the poet's blood-feud, has shown that he has no feeling of kindred for the murdered man and his son. Imraulcais's act does not show that he was impious, but only that kinship was the principle of his religion. That with such principles he consulted the oracle of a strange god at all, is perhaps to be explained by the fact that his army was a miscellaneous band of hirelings and broken men of various tribes.

different blood from the class of the worshippers. Cases of this sort are common, not only among the Arabs,[1] but among the other Semites also, and generally throughout the ancient world. In such cases the priestly clan may often represent the original kindred group which was once in exclusive possession of the *sacra* of the god, and continued to administer them after worshippers from without were admitted to the religion.

And further, it will appear when we come to the subject of sacrifice, that when tribes of different blood worshipped at the same sanctuary and adored the same god, they yet held themselves apart from one another and did not engage in any common act that united them in religious fellowship. The circle of worship was still the kin, though the deity worshipped was not of the kin, and the only way in which two kindreds could form a religious fusion was by a covenant ceremony, in which it was symbolically set forth that they were no longer twain, but of one blood. It is clear, therefore, that among the Arabs the circle of religious solidarity was originally the group of kinsmen, and it needs no proof that, this being so, the god himself must have been conceived as united to his worshippers by the bond of blood, as their great kinsman, or more specifically as their great ancestor.

It is often said that the original Semitic conception of the godhead was abstract and transcendental; that while Aryan religion with its poetic mythology drew the gods down into the sphere of nature and of human life, Semitic religion always showed an opposite tendency, that it sought to remove the gods as far as possible from man, and even contained within itself from the first the seeds of an abstract deism. According to this view, the anthropomorphisms of Semitic religion, that is, all expres-

[1] Wellhausen, p. 129.

sions which in their literal sense imply that the gods have a physical nature cognate to that of man, are explained away as mere allegory, and it is urged, in proof of the fundamental distinction between the Aryan and Semitic conceptions of the divine nature, that myths like those of the Aryans, in which gods act like men, mingle with men, and in fact live a common life with mankind, have little or no place in Semitic religion. But all this is mere unfounded assumption. It is true that the remains of ancient Semitic mythology are not very numerous; but mythology cannot be preserved without literature, and an early literature of Semitic heathenism does not exist. The one exception is the cuneiform literature of Babylonia, and in it we find fragments of a copious mythology. It is true, also, that there is not much mythology in the poetry of heathen Arabia; but Arabian poetry has little to do with religion at all: it dates from the extreme decadence of the old heathenism, and is preserved to us only in the collections formed by Mohammedan scholars, who were careful to avoid or obliterate as far as possible the traces of their fathers' idolatry. That the Semites never had a mythological epic poetry comparable to that of the Greeks is admitted; but the character of the Semitic genius, which is deficient in plastic power and in the faculty of sustained and orderly effort, is enough to account for the fact. We cannot draw inferences for religion from the absence of an elaborate mythology; the question is whether there are not traces, in however crude a form, of the mythological point of view. And this question must be answered in the affirmative. I must not turn aside now to speak at large of Semitic myths, but it is to the point to observe that there do exist remains of myths, and not only of myths but of sacred usages, involving a conception of the divine beings and their relation with man which entirely justifies us in taking the kinship of men with gods in its literal and physical sense, exactly as in Greece. In Greece the loves of the gods with the daughters of men were referred to remote antiquity, but in Babylon the god Bel was still, in the time of Herodotus, provided with a human wife, who spent the night in his temple and with whom he was believed to share his couch.[1] In one of the few fragments of old mythology which have been transplanted unaltered into the Hebrew Scriptures, we read of the sons of gods who took wives of the daughters of men, and became the fathers of the renowned heroes of ancient days. Such a hero is the Izdubar of Babylonian myth, to whom the great goddess Ishtar did not disdain to offer her hand. Arabian tradition presents similar legends. The clan of ʿAmr b. Yarbūʿ was descended from a *siʿlāt*, or she-demon, who became the wife of their human father, but suddenly disappeared from him on seeing a flash of lightning.[2] In this connection the distinction between gods and demi-gods is immaterial; the demi-gods are of divine kind, though they have not attained to the full position of deities with a recognised circle of worshippers.[3]

There is then a great variety of evidence to show that the type of religion which is founded on kinship, and in which the deity and his worshippers make up a society united by the bond of blood, was widely prevalent, and

[1] Herod. i. 181 *sq*. This is not more realistic than the custom of providing the Hercules (Baal) of Sanbulos with a horse, on which he rode out to hunt by night (Tac. *Ann*. xii. 13; cf. *Gaz. Archéol*. 1879, p. 178 *sqq*.).

[2] Ibn Doreid, *Kitāb al-ishticāc*, p. 139. It is implied that the demoniac wife was of lightning kind. Elsewhere also the *siʿlāt* seems to be a fiery scorching being. In Ibn Hishām, p. 27, l. 14, the Abyssinian hosts resemble *Saʿālī* because they ravage the country with fire, and the green trees are scorched up before them. See also Rasmussen, *Addit*. p. 71, l. 19 of the Ar. text.

[3] Modern legends of marriage or courtship between men and jinn, Doughty, ii. 191 *sq*.; *ZDPV*. x. 84. Whether such marriages are lawful is solemnly discussed by Mohammedan jurists.

that at an early date, among all the Semitic peoples. But the force of the evidence goes further, and leaves no reasonable doubt that among the Semites this was the original type of religion, out of which all other types grew. That it was so is particularly clear as regards Arabia, where we have found the conception of the circle of worship and the circle of kindred as identical to be so deeply rooted that it dominated the practical side of religion, even after men worshipped deities that were not kindred gods. But among the other branches of the Semites also, the connection between religion and kinship is often manifested in forms that cannot be explained except by reference to a primitive stage of society, in which the circle of blood relations was also the circle of all religious and social unity. Nations, as distinguished from mere clans, are not constructed on the principle of kinship, and yet the Semitic nations habitually feigned themselves to be of one kin, and their national religions are deeply imbued, both in legend and in ritual, with the idea that the god and his worshippers are of one stock. This, I apprehend, is good evidence that the fundamental lines of all Semitic religion were laid down, long before the beginnings of authentic history, in that earliest stage of society when kinship was the only recognised type of permanent friendly relation between man and man, and therefore the only type on which it was possible to frame the conception of a permanent friendly relation between a group of men and a supernatural being. That all human societies have been developed from this stage is now generally recognised; and the evidence shows that amongst the Semites the historical forms of religion can be traced back to such a stage.

Recent researches into the history of the family render

it in the highest degree improbable that the physical kinship between the god and his worshippers, of which traces are found all over the Semitic area, was originally conceived as fatherhood. It was the mother's, not the father's, blood which formed the original bond of kinship among the Semites as among other early peoples, and in this stage of society, if the tribal deity was thought of as the parent of the stock, a goddess, not a god, would necessarily have been the object of worship. In point of fact, goddesses play a great part in Semitic religion, and that not merely in the subordinate *rôle* of wives of the gods; it is also noticeable that in various parts of the Semitic field we find deities originally female changing their sex and becoming gods, as if with the change in the rule of human kinship.[1] So long as kinship was traced through the mother alone, a male deity of common stock with his worshippers could only be their cousin, or, in the language of that stage of society, their brother. This in fact is the relationship between gods and men asserted by Pindar, when he ascribes to both alike a common mother Earth, and among the Semites a trace of the same point of view may be seen in the class of proper names which designate their bearers as "brother" or "sister" of a deity.[2] If this be so, we must distinguish the religious significance belonging to the wider and older conception of kinship between the deity and the race that worshipped him, from the special and more advanced ideas, conformed to a higher stage of social development, that were added when the kindred god came to be revered as a father.

Some of the most notable and constant features of all ancient heathenism, and indeed of all nature-religions,

[1] See *Kinship*, p. 292 *sqq.*, note 8. I hope to return to this subject on a future opportunity.

[2] See above, p. 45, note 2.

from the totemism of savages upward, find their sufficient explanation in the physical kinship that unites the human and superhuman members of the same religious and social community, without reference to the special doctrine of divine fatherhood. From this point of view the natural solidarity of the god and his worshippers, which has been already enlarged upon as characteristic of antique religion, at once becomes intelligible; the indissoluble bond that unites men to their god is the same bond of blood-fellowship which in early society is the one binding link between man and man, and the one sacred principle of moral obligation. And thus we see that even in its rudest forms religion was a moral force; the powers that man reveres were on the side of social order and tribal law; and the fear of the gods was a motive to enforce the laws of society, which were also the laws of morality.

But though the earliest nature-religion was fully identified with the earliest morality, it was not fitted to raise morality towards higher ideals; and instead of leading the way in social and ethical progress, it was often content to follow or even to lag behind. Religious feeling is naturally conservative, for it is bound up with old custom and usage; and the gods, who are approached only in traditional ritual, and invoked as giving sanction to long-established principles of conduct, seem always to be on the side of those who are averse to change. Among the Semites, as among other races, religion often came to work against a higher morality, not because it was in its essence a power for evil, but because it clung to the obsolete ethical standard of a bygone stage of society. To our better judgment, for example, one of the most offensive features in tribal religion is its particularism; a man is held answerable to his god for wrong done to a member of his own kindred or political community, but he may deceive, rob, or kill an alien without offence to religion; the deity cares only for his own kinsfolk. This is a very narrow morality, and we are tempted to call it sheer immorality. But such a judgment would be altogether false from an historical point of view. The larger morality which embraces all mankind has its basis in habits of loyalty, love, and self-sacrifice, which were originally formed and grew strong in the narrower circle of the family or the clan; and the part which the religion of kinship played in the development and maintenance of these habits, is one of the greatest services it has done to human progress. This service it was able to render because the gods were themselves members of the kin, and the man who was untrue to kindred duty had to reckon with them as with his human clansmen.

An eloquent French writer has recently quoted with approval, and applied to the beginnings of Semitic religion, the words of Statius, *Primus in orbe deos fecit timor*,[1] "Man fancied himself surrounded by enemies whom he sought to appease." But however true it is that savage man feels himself to be environed by innumerable dangers which he does not understand, and so personifies as invisible or mysterious enemies of more than human power, it is not true that the attempt to appease these powers is the foundation of religion. From the earliest times, religion, as distinct from magic or sorcery, addresses itself to kindred and friendly beings, who may indeed be angry with their people for a time, but are always placable except to the enemies of their worshippers or to renegade members of the community. It is not with a vague fear of unknown powers, but with a loving reverence for known gods who are knit to their worshippers by strong bonds of kinship, that

[1] Renan, *Hist. d'Israel*, i. 29.

religion in the only true sense of the word begins. Religion in this sense is not the child of terror; and the difference between it and the savage's dread of unseen foes is as absolute and fundamental in the earliest as in the latest stages of development. It is only in times of social dissolution, as in the last age of the small Semitic states, when men and their gods were alike powerless before the advance of the Assyrians, that magical superstitions based on mere terror, or rites designed to conciliate alien gods, invade the sphere of tribal or national religion. In better times the religion of the tribe or state has nothing in common with the private and foreign superstitions or magical rites that savage terror may dictate to the individual. Religion is not an arbitrary relation of the individual man to a supernatural power, it is a relation of all the members of a community to a power that has the good of the community at heart, and protects its law and moral order. This distinction seems to have escaped some modern theorists, but it was plain enough to the common sense of antiquity, in which private and magical superstitions were habitually regarded as offences against morals and the state. It is not only in Israel that we find the suppression of magical rites to be one of the first cares of the founder of the kingdom, or see the introduction of foreign worships treated as a heinous crime. In both respects the law of Israel is the law of every well-ordered ancient community.

In the historical stage of Semitic religion the kinship of the deity with his or her people is specified as fatherhood or motherhood, the former conception predominating, in accordance with the later rule that assigned the son to his father's stock. Under the law of male kinship woman takes a subordinate place; the father is the natural head of the family, and superior to the mother, and accordingly the chief place in religion usually belongs, not to a mother-goddess, but to a father-god. At the same time the conception of the goddess-mother was not unknown, and seems to be attached to cults which go back to the ages of polyandry and female kinship. The Babylonian Ishtar in her oldest form is such a mother-goddess, unmarried, or rather choosing her temporary partners at will, the queen head and firstborn of all gods.[1] She is the mother of the gods and also the mother of men, who, in the Chaldæan flood-legends, mourns over the death of her offspring. In like manner the Carthaginians worshipped a "great mother," who seems to be identical with Tanith-Artemis, the "heavenly virgin,"[2] and the Arabian Lāt was worshipped by the Nabatæans as mother of the gods, and must be identified with the virgin-mother, whose worship at Petra is described by Epiphanius.[3]

[1] Tiele, *Babylonisch-Assyrische Gesch.* p. 528.

[2] אם רבת, *CIS.* Nos. 195, 380; cf. No. 177. The identification of Tanith with Artemis appears from No. 116, where עבדתנת='Αρτεμίδωρος, and is confirmed by the prominence of the *virgo cœlestis* or *numen virginale* in the later cults of Punic Africa. The identification of the mother of the gods with the heavenly virgin, *i.e.* the unmarried goddess, is confirmed if not absolutely demanded by Aug. *Civ. Dei*, ii. 4. At Carthage she seems also to be identical with Dido, of whom as a goddess more in another connection. See Hoffmann, *Ueb. einige Phœn. Inschrr.* p. 32 *sq.* The foul type of worship corresponding to the conception of the goddess as polyandrous prevailed at Sicca Veneria, and Augustin speaks with indignation of the incredible obscenity of the songs that accompanied the worship of the Carthaginian mother-goddess; but perhaps this is not wholly to be set down as of Punic origin, for the general laxity on the point of female chastity in which such a type of worship originates has always been characteristic of North Africa (see Tissot, *La Prov. d'Afrique*, i. 477).

[3] De Vogüé, *Syr. Centr.* Inscr. Nab. No. 8; Epiph., *Panarium* 51 (ii. 483, Dind.), see *Kinship*, p. 292 *sq.* I am not able to follow the argument by which Wellh., pp. 40, 46, seeks to invalidate the evidence as to the worship of a mother-goddess by the Nabatæans. He supposes that the Χααβου, which Epiphanius represents as the virgin-mother of Dusares, is really nothing more than the cippus, or betyl, out of which the god was supposed to have been born, *i.e.* the image of the god himself, not a distinct deity. But from the time of Herodotus downwards, al-Lāt was worshipped in these regions

Originally, since men are of one stock with their gods, the mother of the gods must also have been, like Ishtar, the mother of men; but except in Babylonia and Assyria, where the kings at least continued to speak of themselves as the progeny of Ishtar, it is not clear that this idea was present to the Semitic worshipper when he addressed his goddess as the great mother. But if we may judge from analogy, and even from such modern analogies as are supplied by the cult of the Virgin Mary, we can hardly doubt that the use of a name appropriated to the tenderest and truest of human relationships was associated in acts of worship with feelings of peculiar warmth and trustful devotion. "Can a woman forget her sucking child, that she should not have compassion on the son of her womb? Yea, they may forget, yet will I not forget thee."[1] That such thoughts were not wholly foreign to Semitic heathenism appears, to give a single instance, from the

side by side with a god, and the evidence of De Vogüé's inscription and that of Epiphanius agree in making Lāt the mother and the god her son. Epiphanius implies that the virgin-mother was worshipped also at Elusa; and here Jerome, in his life of S. Hilarion, knows a temple of a goddess whom he calls Venus, and who was worshipped "ob Luciferum," on account of her connection with the morning star. Wellhausen takes this to mean that the goddess of Elusa was identified with the morning star; but that is impossible, for, in his comm. on Amos v., Jerome plainly indicates that the morning star was worshipped as a god, not as a goddess. This is the old Semitic conception; see Isa. xiv. 12, "Lucifer, son of the Dawn"; and in the Arabian poets, also, the planet Venus is masculine, as Wellhausen himself observes. I see no reason to believe that the Arabs of Nilus worshipped the morning star as a goddess; nor perhaps does the worship of this planet as a goddess (Al-'Ozzā) appear anywhere in Arabia, except among the Eastern tribes who came under the influence of the Assyrian Ishtar-worship, as it survived among the Aramæans. This point was not clear to me when I wrote my *Kinship*, and want of attention to it has brought some confusion into the argument. That the goddess of Elusa was Al-'Ozzā, as Wellh., p. 44, supposes, is thus very doubtful. Whether, as Tuch thought, her local name was Khalaṣa is also doubtful, but we must not reject the identification of Elusa with the place still called Khalaṣa; see Palmer, *Desert of the Exodus*, p. 423, compared with p. 550 *sqq.*

[1] Isa. xlix. 15.

language in which Assurbanipal appeals to Ishtar in his time of need, and in the oracle she sends to comfort him.[1]

But in this, as in all its aspects, heathenism shows its fundamental weakness, in its inability to separate the ethical motives of religion from their source in a merely naturalistic conception of the godhead and its relation to man. Divine motherhood, like the kinship of men and gods in general, was to the heathen Semites a physical fact, and the development of the corresponding cults and myths laid more stress on the physical than on the ethical side of maternity, and gave a prominence to sexual ideas which was never edifying, and often repulsive. Especially was this the case when the change in the law of kinship deprived the mother of her old pre-eminence in the family, and transferred to the father the greater part of her authority and dignity. This change, as we know, went hand in hand with the abolition of the old polyandry; and as women lost the right to choose their own partners at will, the wife became subject to her husband's lordship, and her freedom of action was restrained by his jealousy, at the same time that her children became, for all purposes of inheritance and all duties of blood, members of his and not of her kin. So far as religion kept pace with the new laws of social morality due to this development, the independent divine mother necessarily became the subordinate partner of a male deity; and so the old polyandrous Ishtar reappears in Canaan and elsewhere as Astarte, the wife of the supreme Baal. Or if the supremacy of the goddess was too well established to be thus undermined, she might change her sex, as in Southern Arabia, where Ishtar is transformed into the masculine

[1] George Smith, *Assurbanipal*, p. 117 *sqq.; Records of the Past*, ix. 51 *sqq.*

ʿAthtar. But not seldom religious tradition refused to move forward with the progress of society; the goddess retained her old character as a mother who was not a wife bound to fidelity to her husband, and at her sanctuary she protected, under the name of religion, the sexual licence of savage society, or even demanded of the daughters of her worshippers a shameful sacrifice of their chastity, before they were permitted to bind themselves for the rest of their lives to that conjugal fidelity which their goddess despised.

The emotional side of Semitic heathenism was always very much connected with the worship of female deities, partly through the associations of maternity, which appealed to the purest and tenderest feelings, and partly through other associations connected with woman, which too often appealed to the sensuality so strongly developed in the Semitic race. The feelings called forth when the deity was conceived as a father were on the whole of an austerer kind, for the distinctive note of fatherhood, as distinguished from kinship in general, lay mainly in the parental authority, in the father's claim to be honoured and served by his son. The honour which the fifth commandment requires children to pay to their fathers is named in Mal. i. 6 along with that which a servant owes to his master, and the same prophet (iii. 17) speaks of the considerate regard which a father shows for "the son that serveth him." To this day the grown-up son in Arabia serves his father in much the same offices as the domestic slave, and approaches him with much the same degree of reverence and even of constraint. It is only with his little children that the father is effusively affectionate and on quite easy terms. On the other hand, the father's authority had not a despotic character. He had no such power of life and death over his sons as

Roman law recognised,[1] and indeed, after they passed beyond childhood, had no means of enforcing his authority if they refused to respect it. Paradoxical as this may seem, it is quite in harmony with the general spirit of Semitic institutions that authority should exist and be generally acknowledged without having any force behind it except the pressure of public opinion. The authority of an Arab sheikh is in the same position; and when an Arab judge pronounces sentence on a culprit, it is at the option of the latter whether he will pay the fine, which is the invariable form of penalty, or continue in feud with his accuser.

Thus, while the conception of the tribal god as father introduces into religion the idea of divine authority, of reverence and service due from the worshipper to the deity, it does not carry with it any idea of the strict and rigid enforcement of divine commands by supernatural sanctions. The respect paid by the Semite to his father is but the respect which he pays to kindred, focussed upon a single representative person, and the father's authority is only a special manifestation of the authority of the kin, which can go no further than the whole kin is prepared to back it. Thus, in the sphere of religion, the god, as father, stands by the majority of the tribe in enforcing tribal law against refractory members: outlawry, which is the only punishment ordinarily applicable to a clansman, carries with it excommunication from religious communion, and the man who defies tribal law has to fear

[1] See Deut. xxi. 18, where the word "chastened" should rather be "admonished." The powerlessness of Jacob to restrain his grown-up sons is not related as a proof that he was weak, but shows that a father had no means of enforcing his authority. The law of Deuteronomy can hardly have been carried into practice. In Prov. xxx. 17 disobedience to parents is cited as a thing which brings a man to a bad end, not as a thing punished by law. That an Arab father could do no more than argue with his son, and bring tribal opinion to bear on him, appears from *Agh.* xix. 102 *sq.*

the god as well as his fellow-men. But in all minor matters, where outlawry is out of the question, the long-suffering tolerance which tribesmen in early society habitually extend to the offences of their fellow-tribesmen is ascribed also to the god; he does not willingly break with any of his worshippers, and accordingly a bold and wilful man does not hesitate to take considerable liberties with the paternal deity. As regards his worshippers at large, it appears scarcely conceivable, from the point of view of tribal religion, that the god can be so much displeased with anything they do that his anger can go beyond a temporary estrangement, which is readily terminated by their repentance, or even by a mere change of humour on the part of the god, when his permanent affection for his own gets the better of his momentary displeasure, as it is pretty sure to do if he sees them to be in straits, *e.g.* to be hard pressed by their and his enemies. On the whole, men live on very easy terms with their tribal god, and his paternal authority is neither strict nor exacting.

This is a very characteristic feature of heathen religion, and one which does not disappear when the god of the community comes to be thought of as king rather than as father. The inscription of King Mesha, for example, tells us that Chemosh was angry with his people, and suffered Israel to oppress Moab; and then again that Chemosh fought for Moab, and delivered it from the foe. There is no explanation offered of the god's change of mind; it appears to be simply taken for granted that he was tired of seeing his people put to the worse. In like manner the mass of the Hebrews before the exile received with blank incredulity the prophetic teaching, that Jehovah was ready to enforce His law of righteousness even by the destruction of the sinful commonwealth of Israel. To the prophets Jehovah's long-suffering meant the patience with which He offers repeated calls to repentance, and defers punishment while there is hope of amendment; but to the heathen, and to the heathenly-minded in Israel, the long-suffering of the gods meant a disposition to overlook the offences of their worshippers.

To reconcile the forgiving goodness of God with His absolute justice, is one of the highest problems of spiritual religion, which in Christianity is solved by the doctrine of the atonement. It is important to realise that in heathenism this problem never arose in the form in which the New Testament deals with it, not because the gods of the heathen were not conceived as good and gracious, but because they were not absolutely just. This lack of strict justice, however, is not to be taken as meaning that the gods were in their nature unjust, when measured by the existing standards of social righteousness; as a rule they were conceived as sympathising with right conduct, but not as rigidly enforcing it in every case. To us, who are accustomed to take an abstract view of the divine attributes, this is difficult to conceive, but it seemed perfectly natural when the divine sovereignty was conceived as a kingship precisely similar to human kingship.

In its beginnings, human kingship was as little absolute as the authority of the fathers and elders of the clan, for it was not supported by an executive organisation sufficient to carry out the king's sentence of justice or constrain obedience to his decrees. The authority of the prince was moral rather than physical; his business was to guide rather than to dictate the conduct of his free subjects, to declare what was just rather than to enforce it.[1]

[1] In Aramaic the root MLK (from which the common Semitic word for "king" is derived) means "to advise"; and in Arabic the word *Amîr*, "commander," "prince," also means "adviser"; 'Orwa b. al-Ward, i. 16, and *schol.*

Thus the limitations of royal power went on quite an opposite principle from that which underlies a modern limited monarchy. With us the king or his government is armed with the fullest authority to enforce law and justice, and the limitations of his power lie in the independence of the legislature and the judicial courts. The old Semitic king, on the contrary, was supreme judge, and his decrees were laws, but neither his sentences nor his decrees could take effect unless they were supported by forces over which he had very imperfect control. He simply threw his weight into the scale, a weight which was partly due to the moral effect of his sentence, and partly to the material resources which he commanded, not so much *quâ* king as in the character of a great noble and the head of a powerful circle of kinsfolk and clients. An energetic sovereign, who had gained wealth and prestige by successful wars, or inherited the resources accumulated by a line of kingly ancestors, might wield almost despotic power, and in a stable dynasty the tendency was towards the gradual establishment of absolute monarchy, especially if the royal house was able to maintain a standing army devoted to its interests. But a pure despotism of the modern Eastern type probably had not been reached by any of the small kingdoms that were crushed by the Assyrian empire, and certainly the ideas which underlay the conception of divine sovereignty date from an age when the human kingship was still in a rudimentary state, when its executive strength was very limited, and the sovereign was in no way held responsible for the constant maintenance of law and order in all parts of his realm. In most matters of internal order he was not expected to interfere unless directly appealed to by one or other party in a dispute, and even then it was not certain that the party in whose favour he decided would not be left to make good his rights with the aid of his own family connections. So loose a system of administration did not offer a pattern on which to frame the conception of a constant unremitting divine providence, overlooking no injustice and suffering no right to be crushed; the national god might be good and just, but was not continually active or omnipresent in his activity. But we are not to suppose that this remissness was felt to be a defect in the divine character. The Semitic nature is impatient of control, and has no desire to be strictly governed either by human or by divine authority. A god who could be reached when he was wanted, but usually left men pretty much to themselves, was far more acceptable than one whose ever watchful eye can neither be avoided nor deceived. What the Semitic communities asked, and believed themselves to receive, from their god as king lay mainly in three things: help against their enemies, counsel by oracles or soothsayers in matters of national difficulty, and a sentence of justice when a case was too hard for human decision. The valour, the wisdom, and the justice of the nation looked to him as their head, and were strengthened by his support in time of need. For the rest it was not expected that he should always be busy righting human affairs. In ordinary matters it was men's business to help themselves and their own kinsfolk, though the sense that the god was always near, and could be called upon at need, was a moral force continually working in some degree for the maintenance of social righteousness and order. The strength of this moral force was indeed very uncertain, for it was always possible for the evildoer to flatter himself that his offence would be overlooked; but even so uncertain an influence of religion over conduct was of no little use in the slow and difficult process of the consolidation of an orderly society out of barbarism.

As a social and political force, in the earlier stages of Semitic society, antique religion cannot be said to have failed in its mission; but it was too closely modelled on the traditional organisation of the family and the nation to retain a healthful vitality when the social system was violently shattered. Among the northern Semites the age of Assyrian conquest proved as critical for religious as for civil history, for from that time forward the old religion was quite out of touch with the actualities of social life, and became almost wholly mischievous. But apart from the Assyrian catastrophe, there are good reasons to think that in the eighth century B.C. the national religion of the northern Semites had already passed its prime, and was sinking into decadence. The moral springs of conduct which it touched were mainly connected with the first needs of a rude society, with the community's instinct of self-preservation. The enthusiasm of religion was seen only in times of peril, when the nation, under its divine head, was struggling for national existence. In times of peace and prosperity, religion had little force to raise man above sensuality and kindle him to right and noble deeds. Except when the nation was in danger, it called for no self-denial, and rather encouraged an easy sluggish indulgence in the good things that were enjoyed under the protection of the national god. The evils that slowly sap society, the vices that at first sight seem too private to be matters of national concern, the disorders that accompany the increase and unequal distribution of wealth, the relaxation of moral fibre produced by luxury and sensuality, were things that religion hardly touched at all, and that the easy, indulgent god could hardly be thought to take note of. The God who could deal with such evils was the God of the prophets, no mere Oriental king raised to a throne in heaven, but the just and jealous

God, whose eyes are in every place, beholding the evil and the good, who is of purer eyes than to behold evil, and cannot look upon iniquity.[1]

In what precedes I have thought it convenient to assume for the moment, without breaking the argument by pausing to offer proof, that among the Semitic peoples which got beyond the mere tribal stage and developed a tolerably organised state, the supreme deity was habitually thought of as king. The definitive proof that this was really so must be sought in the details of religious practice, to which we shall come by and by, and in which we shall find indicated a most realistic conception of the divine kingship. Meantime some proofs of a different character may be briefly indicated. In the Old Testament the kingship of Jehovah is often set forth as the glory of Israel, but never in such terms as to suggest that the idea of divine kingship was peculiar to the Hebrews. On the contrary, other nations are "the kingdoms of the false gods."[2] In two exceptional cases a pious judge or a prophet appears to express the opinion that Jehovah's sovereignty is inconsistent with human kingship,[3] such as existed in the surrounding nations; but this difficulty was never felt by the mass of the Israelites, nor even by the prophets in the regal period, and it was certainly not felt by Israel's neighbours. If a son could be crowned in the lifetime of his father, as was done in the case of Solomon, or could act for his father as Jotham acted for Uzziah,[4] there was no difficulty in looking on the human king as the viceroy of the divine sovereign, who, as we have seen, was often believed to be the father of the royal race, and so to lend a certain sanctity to the dynasty. Accordingly we find that the Tyrian Baal bears the title of Melcarth, "king of

[1] Prov. xv. 3; Hab. i. 13.
[2] Isa. x. 10.
[3] Judg. viii. 23; 1 Sam. xii. 12.
[4] 1 Kings i. 32 *sqq.*; 2 Kings xv. 5.

the city," or more fully, "our lord Melcarth, the Baal of Tyre,"[1] and this sovereignty was acknowledged by the Carthaginian colonists when they paid tithes at his temple in the mother city; for in the East tithes are the king's due.[2] Similarly the supreme god of the Ammonites was Milkom or Malkam, which is only a variation of Melek, "king." The familiar Moloch or Molech is the same thing in a distorted pronunciation, due to the scruples of the later Jews, who furnished the consonants of the word MLK with the vowels of *bosheth*, "shameful thing," whenever it was to be understood as the title of a false god. In Babylonia and Assyria the application of royal titles to deities is too common to call for special exemplification. Again, we have Malakhbel, "King Bel," as the great god of the Aramæans of Palmyra; but in this and other examples of later date it is perhaps open to suppose that the kingship of the supreme deity means his sovereignty over other gods rather than over his worshippers. On the other hand, a large mass of evidence can be drawn from proper names of religious significance, in which the god of the worshipper is designated as king. Such names were as common among the Phœnicians and Assyrians as they were among the Israelites,[3] and are

[1] *CIS.* No. 122.

[2] Diod. xx. 14; and for the payment of tithes to the king, 1 Sam. viii. 15, 17; Aristotle, *Œcon.* ii. p. 1352 *b* of the Berlin ed., cf. p. 1345 *b*.

[3] אהלמלך, *CIS.* No. 50, cf. אהלבעל, No. 54; יחומלך, King of Byblus, No. 1, cf. יחובעל, No. 69; מלכיתן, Nos. 10, 16, etc., cf. בעליתן, No. 78; רשפיתן, No. 44; עבדמלך, No. 46, cf. עבדאסר, עבדאשמן, etc.; עזמלך, Nos. 189, 219, 386, cf. עזבעל, on a coin of Byblus, Head, p. 668. The title of מלכת, "queen," for Astarte is seen probably in חמלכת, חתמלכת (*supra*, p. 45, note 2), and more certainly in מחמלכת, "handmaid of the queen," cf. מחעשתרת, No. 83, and in נעמלכת, "favour of the queen," No. 41. For Assyrian names of similar type see Schrader in *ZDMG.* xxvi. 140 *sqq.*, where also an Edomite king's name on a cylinder of Sennacherib is read Malik-ramu, "the (divine) king, is exalted."

found even among the Arabs of the Syrian and Egyptian frontier.[1]

Where the god is conceived as a king, he will naturally be addressed as lord, and his worshippers will be spoken of as his subjects, and so we find as divine titles Adōn, "lord" (whence Adonis = the god Tammuz), and Rabbath, "lady" (as a title of Tanith), among the Phœnicians, with corresponding phrases among other nations,[2] while in all parts of the Semitic field the worshipper calls himself the servant or slave (*'abd*, *'ebed*) of his god, just as a subject does in addressing his king. The designation "servant" is much affected by worshippers, and forms the basis of a large number of theophorous proper names—'Abd-Eshmun "servant of Eshmun," 'Abd-Baal, 'Abd-Osir, etc. At first sight this designation seems to point to a more rigid conception of divine kingship than I have presented, for it is only under a strict despotism that the subject is the slave of the monarch; nay, it has been taken as a fundamental distinction between Semitic religion and that of the Greeks, that in the one case the relation of man to his god is servile, while in the other it is not so. But this conclusion rests on the neglect of a nicety of language, a refinement of Semitic politeness. When a man addresses any superior he calls him "my lord," and speaks of himself and others as "thy servants,"[3] and this form of politeness is

[1] *E.g.* Κοσμαλαχος, Ἐλμαλαχος, "Cos, El is king," *Rev. Arch.* 1870, pp. 115, 117; Schrader, *KAT.* p. 257, reads Kausmalak as the name of an Edomite king on an inscription of Tiglathpileser. For the god Caus, or Cos, see Wellhausen, *Heidenthum*, p. 77; cf. *ZDMG.* 1887, p. 714.

[2] *E.g.* Nabatæan *Rab*, "Lord," in the proper name רבאל (Euting, 21. 3, 21. 14; Waddington, 2152, 2189, 2298), and at Gaza the god Marna, that is, "our Lord," both on coins (Head, p. 680), and in M. Diaconus, *Vita Porphyrii*, § 19; also at Kerak, Wadd. 2412 *g*.

[3] This holds good for Hebrew and Aramaic; also for Phœnician (Schröder, *Phön. Spr.* p. 18, n. 5); and even in Arabia an old poet says: "I am the slave of my guest as long as he is with me, but save in this there is no trace of the slave in my nature" (*Ḥamāsa*, p. 727).

naturally *de rigueur* in presence of the king; but where the king is not addressed, his "servants" mean his courtiers that are in personal attendance on him, or such of his subjects as are actually engaged in his service, for example, his soldiers. In the Old Testament this usage is constant, and the king's servants are often distinguished from the people at large. And so the servants of Jehovah are sometimes the prophets, who hold a special commission from Him; at other times, as often in the Psalms, His worshipping people assembled at the temple; and at other times, as in Deutero-Isaiah, His true servants as distinguished from the natural Israel, who are His subjects only in name. In short, both in the political and in the religious sphere, the designation *'abd*, *'ebed*, "servant," is strictly correlated with the verb *'abad*, "to do service, homage, or religious worship," a word which, as we have already seen, is sufficiently elastic to cover the service which a son does for his father, as well as that which a master requires from his slave.[1] Thus, when a man is named the servant of a god, the implication appears to be, not merely that he belongs to the community of which the god is king, but that he is specially devoted to his service and worship. Like other theophorous names, compounds with *'abd* seem to have been originally most common in royal and priestly families, whose members naturally claimed a special interest in religion and a constant nearness to the god; and in later times, when a man's particular worship was not rigidly defined by his national connection, they served to specify the cult to which he was particularly attached, or the patron to whom his parents dedicated him. That the use of such names was not connected with the

[1] *Supra*, p. 60. Primarily עבד is "to work," and in Aramaic "to make, to do." Ancient worship is viewed as work or service, because it consists in material operations (sacrifice). The same connection of ideas appears in the root פלח and in the Greek ῥέζειν θεῷ.

idea of slavery to a divine despot is pretty clear from their frequency among the Arabs, who had very loose ideas of all authority, whether human or divine. Among the Arabs, indeed, as among the old Hebrews, the relation of the subject to his divine chief is often expressed by names of another class. Of King Saul's sons two were named Ishbaal and Meribaal, both meaning "man of Baal," *i.e.* of Jehovah, who in these early days was called Baal without offence; among the Arabs of the Syrian frontier we have Amriel, "man of El," Amrishams, "man of the Sun-god," and others like them;[1] and in Arabia proper Imraulcais, "the man of Cais," Shai' al-Lāt, "follower, comrade of Lāt," Anas al-Lāt, all expressive of the relation of the free warrior to his chief.

That the Arabs, like their northern congeners, thought of deity as lordship or chieftainship is proved not only by such proper names, and by the titles *rab*, *rabbi*, "lord," "lady," given to their gods and goddesses, but especially by the history of the foundation of Islam. In his quality of prophet, Mohammed became a judge, lawgiver, and captain, not of his own initiative, but because the Arabs of different clans were willing to refer to a divine authority questions of right and precedence in which they would not yield to one another.[2] They brought their difficulties to the prophet as the Israelites did to Moses, and his decisions became the law of Islam, as those of Moses were the foundation of the Hebrew Torah. But up to the time of the prophet the practical development of the idea of divine kingship among the nomadic Arabs was very elementary and inadequate, as was to be expected in a society which had never taken kindly to the institution of human king-

[1] Nöldeke, *Sitzungsb. Berl. Ak.* 1880, p. 768; Wellhausen, *Heidenthum*, p. 3.

[2] For the god as giver of decisions, compare the name *farrāḍ*, borne by an idol of the Sa'd al-'ashīra (Ibn Sa'd, ed. Wellh. No. 124 *b*).

ship. In the prosperous days of Arabian commerce, when the precious wares of the far East reached the Mediterranean chiefly by caravan from Southern Arabia, there were settled kingdoms in several parts of the peninsula. But after the sea-route to India was opened, these kingdoms were broken up and almost the whole country fell back into anarchy. The nomads proper often felt the want of a controlling authority that would put an end to the incessant tribal and clan feuds, but their pride and impatience of control never permitted them to be long faithful to the authority of a stranger; while, on the other hand, the exaggerated feeling for kindred made it quite certain that a chief chosen at home would not deal with an even hand between his own kinsman and a person of different blood. Thus, after the fall of the Yemenite and Nabatæan kingdoms, which drew their strength from commerce, there was no permanently successful attempt to consolidate a body of several tribes into a homogeneous state, except under Roman or Persian suzerainty. The decay of the power of religion in the peninsula in the last days of Arab heathenism presents a natural parallel to this condition of political disintegration. The wild tribesmen had lost the feeling of kinship with their tribal gods, and had not learned to yield steady submission and obedience to any power dissociated from kinship. Their religion sat as loose on them as their allegiance to this or that human king whom for a season they might find it convenient to obey, and they were as ready to renounce their deities in a moment of petulance and disgust as to transfer their service from one petty sovereign to another.[1]

[1] Religion had more strength in towns like Mecca and Ṭāif, where there was a sanctuary, and the deity lived in the midst of his people, and was honoured by stated and frequent acts of worship. So under Islam, the Bedouins have never taken kindly to the laws of the Coran, and live in entire neglect of the most simple ordinances of religion, while the townsmen

Up to this point we have considered the conception, or rather the institution, of divine sovereignty as based on the fundamental type of Semitic kingship, when the nation was still made up of free tribesmen, retaining their tribal organisation and possessing the sense of personal dignity and independence engendered by the tribal system, where all clansmen are brothers, and where each man feels that his brethren need him and that he can count on the help of his brethren. There is no principle so levelling as the law of blood-revenge, which is the basis of the tribal system, for here the law is man for man, whether in defence or in offence, without respect of persons. In such a society the king is a guiding and moderating force rather than an imperial power; he is the leader under whom men of several tribes unite for common action, and the arbiter in cases of difficulty or of irreconcilable dispute between two kindreds, when neither will humble itself before the other. The kingship, and therefore the godhead, is not a principle of absolute order and justice, but it is a principle of higher order and more impartial justice than can be realised where there is no other law than the obligation of blood. As the king waxes stronger, and is better able to enforce his will by active interference in his subjects' quarrels, the standard of right is gradually raised above the consideration which disputant has the strongest kin to back him, for it is the glory of the sovereign to vindicate the cause of the weak, if only because by so doing he shows himself to be stronger than the strong. And as the god, though not conceived as omnipotent, is at least conceived as much stronger than man, he becomes in a special measure the champion of right against might, the protector

are in their way very devout. Much of this religion is hypocrisy; but so it was, to judge by the accounts of the conversion of the Thacīf at Ṭāif, even in the time of Mohammed. Religion was a matter of custom, of keeping up appearances.

of the poor, the widow and the fatherless, of the man who has no helper on earth.

Now it is matter of constant observation in early history that the primitive equality of the tribal system tends in progress of time to transform itself into an aristocracy of the more powerful kins, or of the more powerful families within one kin. That is, the smaller and weaker kins are content to place themselves in a position of dependence on their more powerful neighbours in order to secure their protection; or even within one and the same kin men distinguish between their nearer and more distant cousins, and, as wealth begins to be unequally distributed, the great man's distant and poor relation has to be content with a distant and supercilious patronage, and sinks into a position of inferiority. The kingship is the one social force that works against this tendency, for it is the king's interest to maintain a balance of power, and prevent the excessive aggrandisement of noble families that might compete with his own authority. Thus even for selfish reasons the sovereign is more and more brought into the position of the champion of the weak against the strong, of the masses against the aristocracy. Generally speaking, the struggle between king and nobles to which these conditions give rise ended differently in the East and in the West. In Greece and Rome the kingship fell before the aristocracy; in Asia the kingship held its own, till in the larger states it developed into despotism, or in the smaller ones it was crushed by a foreign despotism. This diversity of political fortune is reflected in the diversity of religious development. For as the national god did not at first supersede tribal and family deities any more than the king superseded tribal and family institutions, the tendency of the West, where the kingship succumbed, was towards a divine aristocracy of many gods, only modified by a weak reminiscence of the old kingship in the not very effective sovereignty of Zeus, while in the East the national god tended to acquire a really monarchic sway. What is often described as the natural tendency of Semitic religion towards ethical monotheism, is in the main nothing more than a consequence of the alliance of religion with monarchy. For however corrupt the actual kingships of the East became, the ideal of the kingship as a source of even-handed justice throughout the whole nation, without respect of persons, was higher than the ideal of aristocracy, in which each noble is expected to favour his own family even at the expense of the state or of justice; and it is on the ideal, rather than on the actual, that religious conceptions are based, if not in ordinary minds, at least in the minds of more thoughtful and pious men. At the same time the idea of absolute and ever-watchful divine justice, as we find it in the prophets, is no more natural to the East than to the West, for even the ideal Semitic king is, as we have seen, a very imperfect earthly providence, and moreover he has a different standard of right for his own people and for strangers. The prophetic idea that Jehovah will vindicate the right even in the destruction of His own people of Israel, involves an ethical standard as foreign to Semitic as to Aryan tradition. Thus, as regards their ethical tendency, the difference between Eastern and Western religion is one of degree rather than of principle; all that we can say is that the East was better prepared to receive the idea of a god of absolute righteousness, because its political institutions and history, and, not least, the enormous gulf between the ideal and the reality of human sovereignty, directed men's minds to appreciate the need of righteousness more strongly, and accustomed them to look to a power of monarchic character as its necessary source. A similar judgment must be passed on the supposed monotheistic tendency of the Semitic as opposed to the Hellenic or Aryan system of religion. Neither system, in its natural development, can fairly be said to have come near to monotheism; the difference touched only the equality or subordination of divine powers. But while in Greece the idea of the unity of God was a philosophical speculation, without any definite point of attachment to actual religion, the monotheism of the Hebrew prophets kept touch with the ideas and institutions of the Semitic race by conceiving the one true God as the king of absolute justice, the national God of Israel, who at the same time was, or rather was destined to become, the God of all the earth, not merely because His power was world-wide, but because as the perfect ruler He could not fail to draw all nations to do Him homage (Isa. ii. 2 *sqq.*).

When I speak of the way in which the prophets conceived of Jehovah's sovereignty, as destined to extend itself beyond Israel and over all the earth, I touch on a feature common to all Semitic religions, which must be explained and defined before we can properly understand wherein the prophets transcended the common sphere of Semitic thought, and which indeed is necessary to complete our view of the ultimate development of the Semitic religions as tribal and national institutions.

From a very early date the Semitic communities embraced, in addition to the free tribesmen of pure blood (Heb. *ezrāḥ*, Arab. *ṣarīḥ*) with their families and slaves, a class of men who were personally free but had no political rights, viz. the protected strangers (Heb. *gērīm*, sing. *gēr*; Arab. *jīrān*, sing. *jār*), of whom mention is so often made both in the Old Testament and in early Arabic literature. The *gēr* was a man of another tribe or district, who, coming to sojourn in a place where he was not strengthened by the presence of his own kin, put himself under the protection of a clan or of a powerful chief. From the earliest times of Semitic life the lawlessness of the desert, in which every stranger is an enemy, has been tempered by the principle that the guest is inviolable. A man is safe in the midst of enemies as soon as he enters a tent or even touches the tent rope.[1] To harm a guest, or to refuse him hospitality, is an offence against honour, which covers the perpetrator with indelible shame. The bond of hospitality among the Arabs is temporary; the guest is entertained for a night or at most for three days,[2] and the protection which the host owes to him expires after three days more.[3] But more permanent protection is seldom refused to a stranger who asks for it,[4] and when granted by any tribesman it binds the whole tribe. The obligation thus constituted is one of honour, and not enforced by any human sanction except public opinion, for if the stranger is wronged he has no kinsmen to fight for him. And for this very reason it is a sacred obligation, which among the old Arabs was often confirmed by oath at a sanctuary, and could not be renounced except by a formal act at the same holy place,[5] so that the god himself became the protector of the stranger's cause. The protected stranger did not necessarily give up his old worship any more than he gave up his old kindred, and in the earliest times it is not to be supposed that he was admitted to full communion in the religion of his protectors, for religion went with political rights. But it was natural that he should acknowledge in some degree the god of the land in which he lived, and indeed, since the stated exercises of religion were confined

[1] See further, *Kinship*, p. 41 *sqq.*

[2] This is the space prescribed by the traditions of the prophet, Ḥarīrī (De Sacy's 2nd ed. p. 177; cf. Sharīshī, i. 242). A viaticum sufficient for a day's journey should be added; all beyond this is not duty but alms.

[3] Burckhardt, *Bedouins and Wahábys*, i. 336.

[4] Burckhardt, *op. cit.* i. 174.

[5] Ibn Hishām, p. 243 *sqq.*; *Kinship*, p. 43.

to certain fixed sanctuaries, the man who was far from his old home was also far from his own god, and sooner or later could hardly fail to become a dependent adherent of the cult of his patrons, though not with rights equal to theirs. Sometimes, indeed, the god was the direct patron of the *gēr*, a thing easily understood when we consider that a common motive for seeking foreign protection was the fear of the avenger of blood, and that there was a right of asylum at sanctuaries. From a Phœnician inscription found near Larnaca, which gives the monthly accounts of a temple, we learn that the *gērīm* formed a distinct class in the *personnel* of the sanctuary, and received certain allowances,[1] just as we know from Ezek. xliv. that much of the service of the first temple was done by uncircumcised foreigners. This notion of the temple-client, the man who lives in the precincts of the sanctuary under the special protection of the god, is used in a figurative sense in Ps. xv., "Who shall sojourn (*yāgūr, i.e.* live as a *gēr*) in Thy tabernacle?" and similarly the Arabs give the title of *jār allāh* to one who resides in Mecca beside the Caaba.

The importance of this occasional reception of strangers was not great so long as the old national divisions remained untouched, and the proportion of foreigners in any community was small. But the case became very different when the boundaries of nations were changed by the migration of tribes, or by the wholesale deportations that were part of the policy of the Assyrians towards conquered countries where their arms had met with strenuous resistance. In such circumstances it was natural for the new-comers to seek admission to the sanctuaries of the "god of the land,"[2] which they were able to do by presenting themselves as his clients. In such a case the clients of

[1] *CIS.* No. 86.

[2] 2 Kings xvii. 26.

the god were not necessarily in a position of political dependence on his old worshippers, and the religious sense of the term *gēr* became detached from the idea of social inferiority. But the relation of the new worshippers to the god was no longer the same as on the old purely national system. It was more dependent and less permanent; it was constituted, not by nature and inherited privilege, but by submission on the worshipper's side and free bounty on the side of the god; and in every way it tended to make the relation between man and god more distant, to make men fear the god more and throw more servility into their homage, while at the same time the higher feelings of devotion were quickened by the thought that the protection and favour of the god was a thing of free grace and not of national right. How important this change was may be judged from the Old Testament, where the idea that the Israelites are Jehovah's clients, sojourning in a land where they have no rights of their own, but are absolutely dependent on His bounty, is one of the most characteristic notes of the new and more timid type of piety that distinguishes post-exilic Judaism from the religion of Old Israel.[1] In the old national religions a man felt sure of his standing with the national god, unless he forfeited it by a distinct breach of social law; but the client is accepted, so to speak, on his good behaviour, an idea which precisely accords with the anxious legality of Judaism after the captivity.

In Judaism the spirit of legality was allied with genuine moral earnestness, as we see in the noble description of the character that befits Jehovah's *gēr* drawn in Ps. xv.; but among the heathen Semites we find the same spirit of legalism, the same timid uncertainty as to a man's standing

[1] Lev. xxv. 23; Ps. xxxix. 12 [Heb. 13]; Ps. cxix. 19; 1 Chron. xxix. 15.

with the god whose protection he seeks, while the conception of what is pleasing to the deity has not attained the same ethical elevation. The extent to which, in the disintegration of the old nationalities of the East and the constant movements of population due to political disturbance, men's religion detached itself from their local and national connections, is seen by the prevalence of names in which a man is designated the client of the god. In Phœnician inscriptions we find a whole series of men's names compounded with *Gēr*,—Germelkarth, Gerastart, and so forth,—and the same type recurs among the Arabs of Syria in the name Gairelos or Gerelos, "client of El."[1] In Arabia proper, where the relation of protector and protected had a great development, and whole clans were wont to attach themselves as dependants to a more powerful tribe, the conception of god and worshipper as patron and client appears to have been specially predominant, not merely because dependent clans took up the religion of the patrons with whom they took refuge, but because of the frequent shiftings of the tribes. Wellhausen has noted that the hereditary priesthoods of Arabian sanctuaries were often in the hands of families that did not belong to the tribe of the worshippers, but apparently were descended from older inhabitants;[2] and in such cases the modern worshippers were really only clients of a foreign god. So, in fact, at the great Sabæan pilgrimage shrine of Riyām, the god Ta'lab is adored as "patron," and his worshippers are called his clients.[3] To the same conception may be assigned the proper name Salm, "submission," shortened from such theophorous forms as the Palmyrene Salm al-Lāt, "sub-

[1] See Nöldeke, *Sitzungsb. Berl. Ak.* 1880, p. 765.

[2] Wellhausen, *Heidenthum*, p. 129; cf. p. 183.

[3] Mordtmann u. Müller, *Sab. Denkm.* p. 22, No. 5, l. 2 *sq.* (שימהמו), l. 8 *sq.* (ארמהו) *etc.* Cf. No. 13, l. 12, ארמה, the clients of the goddess Shams.

mission to Lat,"[1] and corresponding to the religious use of the verb *istalama*, "he made his peace," to designate the ceremony of kissing, stroking, or embracing the sacred stone at the Caaba;[2] and perhaps also the numerous names compounded with *taim*, which, if we may judge by the profane use of the word *motayyam*, applied to a deeply attached lover, seems to have some such sense as "devotee."[3] But above all, the prevalence of religion based on clientship and voluntary homage is seen in the growth of the practice of pilgrimage to distant shrines, which is so prominent a feature in later Semitic heathenism. Almost all Arabia met at Mecca, and the shrine at Hierapolis drew visitors from the whole Semitic world. These pilgrims were the guests of the god, and were received as such by the inhabitants of the holy places. They approached the god as strangers, not with the old joyous confidence of national worship, but with atoning ceremonies and rites of self-mortification, and their acts of worship were carefully prescribed for them by qualified instructors,[4] the prototypes of the modern Meccan *Moṭawwif*. The

[1] De Vogüé, No. 54.

[2] Ibn Doraid, *Kit. al-ishticāc*, p. 22. The same idea of a religion accepted by voluntary submission is expressed in the name *Islām*. We shall see later that much the same idea underlies the designation of the Christian religion as a "mystery."

[3] *Taim* is generally taken to be a mere synonym of *'Abd*; but in Arabic the word is quite obsolete, except as an element in old theophorous names, and the other forms derived from the root give no clear insight into its original sense. In the dialect of the Sinaitic inscriptions, where proper names like Taimallāhī, Taimdhūsharā are common, *taim* seems to occur as a common noun in Euting, *Sinaitische Inschriften*, No. 431, where the editor renders תימה by "sein Knecht." But the Arabic uses of the root seem to point to a somewhat more special sense, perhaps "captive," which might be figuratively applied to a devotee, or, when the name compounded with *taim* is a clan-name, as is the usual Arabian case, to a subject tribe that had adopted the worship of their conquerors. On the other hand, *tīma* is a sheep not sent forth to pasture, but kept at the homestead to be milked, and on this analogy *taim* may mean *domestic*.

[4] Lucian, *De Dea Syria*, lvi.

progress of heathenism towards universalism, as it is displayed in these usages, seemed only to widen the gulf between the deity and man, to destroy the naïve trustfulness of the old religion without substituting a better way for man to be at one with his god, to weaken the moral ideas of nationality without bringing in a higher morality of universal obligation, to transform the divine kingship into a mere court pageant of priestly ceremonies without permanent influence on the order of society and daily life. The Hebrew ideal of a divine kingship that must one day draw all men to do it homage offered better things than these, not in virtue of any feature that it possessed in common with the Semitic religions as a whole, but solely through the unique conception of Jehovah as a God whose love for His people was conditioned by a law of absolute righteousness. In other nations individual thinkers rose to lofty conceptions of a supreme deity, but in Israel, and in Israel alone, these conceptions were incorporated in the accepted worship of the national god. And so of all the gods of the nations Jehovah alone was fitted to become the God of the whole earth.

At the end of these remarks on the relations of the gods to their worshippers, it may not be amiss to advert to an objection to the whole course of our investigation that will possibly occur to some readers. Most enquirers into Semitic religion have made it their first business to discuss the nature of the gods, and with this view have sought to determine a particular class of natural phenomena or moral actions over which each deity presides. Persons trained in this school may remark on reading the foregoing pages that they are not a whit the better for knowing that the gods were conceived as parents kings or patrons, since these relationships do not help us to understand what the gods could do for their worshippers. The ancients prayed to their gods for rain and fruitful seasons, for children, for health and long life, for the multiplication of their flocks and herds, and for many other things that no child asked from his father, no subject from his king. Hence it may be argued that fathership and kingship in religion are mere forms of words; the essence of the thing is to know why the gods were deemed able to do for their worshippers things that kings and fathers cannot do. So far as this objection is a general challenge to the method of the present volume, I must leave the sequel to answer it; but the point that the gods did for their worshippers things that human fathers kings and patrons were not expected to do, demands and may receive some elucidation at the present point. And first I will remark that the help of the gods was sought in all matters, without distinction, that were objects of desire and could not certainly be attained by the worshipper's unaided efforts. Further, it appears that help in all these matters was sought by the worshipper from whatever god he had a right to appeal to. If a Semitic worshipper was sick he called upon his national or tribal god, and the same god was addressed if he desired rain or victory over enemies. The power of a god was not conceived as unlimited, but it was very great, and applied to all sorts of things that men could desire. So far as primitive Semitic heathenism is concerned, it is quite a mistake to suppose that a god to whom men prayed for rain was necessarily a god of clouds, while another deity was the god of flocks, and the proper recipient of prayers for increase in the sheepfold. The gods had their physical limitations, as we shall see in the next lecture, but not in the sense that each deity presided over a distinct department of nature; that is a conception much too abstract for the primitive mind, and proper to an advanced stage of polytheism which most of the Semitic nations never fully reached. In early heathenism the really vital question is not what a god has power to do, but whether I can get him to do it for me, and this depends on the relation in which he stands to me. If I have a god who is my king, I ask him for things that I do not ask from a human chief, simply because he is able to do them, and as his subject I have a claim to his help in all matters where my welfare belongs to the welfare of the state over which he presides. And in fact it is by no means true that in asking the god for rain the Semites went quite beyond what could be asked of a human king; for, strange as it may seem to us, almost all primitive peoples believe that rain-making is an art to which men can attain, and some of them expect their kings to exercise it.[1] To peoples in this stage of development a rainmaker is not a cosmical power, but merely a person, human or divine, possessed of a certain art or charm. To say that a god who can make rain is necessarily an elemental power associated with the clouds and the sky, is as absurd as to say that Hera was the goddess of Love when she borrowed the girdle of Aphrodite. This is a very obvious remark, but it knocks on the head a great deal that has been written about Semitic religion.

[1] Frazer, *The Golden Bough*, i. 13 *sqq.* 44 *sqq.*, gives sufficient proofs of this.

LECTURE III

THE RELATIONS OF THE GODS TO NATURAL THINGS—HOLY PLACES—THE JINN

IN the last lecture I endeavoured to sketch in broad outline the general features of the religious institutions of the Semites in so far as they rest on the idea that gods and men, or rather the god and his own proper worshippers, make up a single community, and that the place of the god in the community is interpreted on the analogy of human relationships. We are now to follow out this point of view through the details of sacred rite and observance, and to consider how the various acts and offices of religion stand related to the place assigned to the deity in the community of his worshippers. But as soon as we begin to enter on these details, we find it necessary to take account of a new series of relations connecting man on the one hand, and his god on the other, with physical nature and material objects. All acts of ancient worship have a material embodiment, which is not left to the choice of the worshipper but is limited by fixed rules. They must be performed at certain places and at certain times, with the aid of certain material appliances and according to certain mechanical forms. These rules import that the intercourse between the deity and his worshippers is subject to physical conditions of a definite kind, and this again implies that the relations between gods and men are not independent of the material environment. The relations of a man to his fellow-men are limited by physical conditions, because man, on the side of his bodily organism, is himself a part of the material universe; and when we find that the relations of a man to his god are limited in the same way, we are led to conclude that the gods too are in some sense conceived to be a part of the natural universe, and that this is the reason why men can hold converse with them only by the aid of certain material things. It is true that in some of the higher forms of antique religion the material restrictions imposed on the legitimate intercourse between gods and men were conceived to be not natural but positive, that is they were not held to be dependent on the nature of the gods, but were looked upon as arbitrary rules laid down by the free will of the deity. But in the ordinary forms of heathenism it appears quite plainly that the gods themselves are not exempt from the general limitations of physical existence; indeed, we have already seen that where the relation of the deity to his worshippers is conceived as a relation of kinship, the kinship is taken to have a physical as well as a moral sense, so that the worshipped and the worshippers are parts not only of one social community but of one physical unity of life.

It is important that we should realise to ourselves with some definiteness the primitive view of the universe in which this conception arose, and in which it has its natural place. It dates from a time when men had not learned to draw sharp distinctions between the nature of one thing and another. Savages, we know, are not only incapable of separating in thought between phenomenal and noumenal existence, but habitually ignore the distinctions, which to us seem obvious, between organic and inorganic nature, or within the former region between animals and plants. Arguing altogether by analogy, and concluding from the known to the unknown with the freedom of men who do not know the difference between the imagination and the reason, they ascribe to all material objects a life analogous to that which their own self-consciousness reveals to them. They see that men are liker to one another than beasts are to men, that men are liker to beasts than they are to plants, and to plants than they are to stones; but all things appear to them to live, and the more incomprehensible any form of life seems to them the more wonderful and worthy of reverence do they take it to be. Now this attitude of savage man to the natural things by which he is surrounded is the very attitude attested to us for ancient times by some of the most salient features of antique religion. Among races which have attained to a certain degree of culture, the predominant conception of the gods is anthropomorphic; that is, they are supposed on the whole to resemble men and act like men, and the artistic imagination, whether in poetry or in sculpture and painting, draws them after the similitude of man. But at the same time the list of deities includes a variety of natural objects of all kinds, the sun moon and stars, the heavens and the earth, animals and trees, or even sacred stones. And all these gods, without distinction of their several natures, are conceived as entering into the same kind of relation to man, are approached in ritual of the same type, and excite the same kind of hopes and fears in the breasts of their worshippers. It is of course easy to say that the gods were not identified with these natural objects, that they were only supposed to inhabit them; but for our present purpose this distinction is not valid. A certain crude distinction between soul and body, combined with the idea that the soul may act where the body is not, is suggested to the most savage races by familiar psychical phenomena, particularly by those of dreams; and the unbounded use of analogy characteristic of pre-scientific thought extends this conception to all parts of nature which becomes to the savage mind full of spiritual forces, more or less detached in their movements and action from the material objects to which they are supposed properly to belong. But the detachment of the invisible life from its visible embodiment is never complete. A man after all is not a ghost or phantom, a life or soul without a body, but a body with its life, and in like manner the unseen life that inhabits the plant, tree, or sacred stone makes the sacred object itself be conceived as a living being. And in ritual the sacred object was spoken of and treated as the god himself; it was not merely his symbol but his embodiment, the permanent centre of his activity in the same sense in which the human body is the permanent centre of man's activity. In short, the whole conception belongs in its origin to a stage of thought in which there was no more difficulty in ascribing living powers and personality to a stone tree or animal, than to a being of human or superhuman build.

The same lack of any sharp distinction between the nature of different kinds of visible beings appears in the oldest myths, in which all kinds of objects, animate and inanimate, organic and inorganic, appear as cognate with one another, with men, and with the gods. The kinship between gods and men which we have already discussed is only one part of a larger kinship which embraces the lower creation. In the Babylonian legend beasts as well as man are formed of earth mingled with the life-blood of a god; in Greece the stories of the descent of men from gods stand side by side with ancient legends of men sprung from trees or rocks, or of races whose mother was a tree and their father a god.[1] Similar myths, connecting both men and gods with animals plants and rocks, are found all over the world, and were not lacking among the Semites. To this day the legend of the country explains the name of the Beni Sokhr tribe by making them the offspring of the sandstone rocks about Madāin Ṣāliḥ.[2] To the same stage of thought belong the stories of transformations of men into animals, which are not infrequent in Arabian legend. Mohammed would not eat lizards because he fancied them to be the offspring of a metamorphosed clan of Israelites.[3] Macrīzī relates of the Ṣeiʿar in Ḥadramaut that in time of drought part of the tribe change themselves into ravening were-wolves. They have a magical means of assuming and again casting off the wolf shape.[4] Other Hadramites changed themselves into vultures or kites.[5] In the Sinai Peninsula the hyrax and the panther are believed to have been originally men.[6] Among the northern Semites transformation myths are not uncommon, though they have generally been preserved to us only in Greek forms. The pregnant mother of Adonis was changed into a myrrh tree, and in the tenth month the tree burst open and the infant god came forth.[7] The metamorphosis of Derceto into a fish was related both at Ascalon and at Bambyce, and so forth. In the same spirit is conceived the Assyrian myth which includes the lion, the eagle, and the war-horse among the lovers of

[1] *Odyssey*, xviii. 163; Preller-Robert, i. 79 *sq.*

[2] Doughty, *Travels in Arabia*, i. 17; see Ibn Doraid, p. 329, l. 20. Conversely, many stones and rocks in Arabia were believed to be transformed men, but especially women. Dozy, *Israeliten te Mekka*, p. 201, gives examples. See also Yācūt, i. 123.

[3] Damīrī, ii. 87; cf. Doughty, i. 326. A similar *ḥadīth* about the mouse, Damīrī, ii. 218.

[4] *De valle Hadhramaut* (Bonn 1866), p. 19 *sq.*

[5] *Ibid.* p. 20. See also Ibn Mojāwir in Sprenger, *Post-routen*, p. 142.

[6] See *Kinship*, p. 203 *sq.*, where I give other evidences on the point.

[7] Apollodorus, iii. 14. 3; Servius on *Æn* v. 72.

Ishtar, while in the region of plastic art the absence of any sharp line of distinction between gods and men on the one hand and the lower creation on the other is displayed in the predilection for fantastic monsters, half human half bestial, which began with the oldest Chaldæan engraved cylinders, gave Phœnicia its cherubim griffins and sphinxes,[1] and continued to characterise the sacred art of the Babylonians down to the time of Berosus.[2] Of course most of these things can be explained away as allegories, and are so explained to this day by persons who shut their eyes to the obvious difference between primitive thought, which treats all nature as a kindred unity because it has not yet differentiated things into their kinds, and modern monistic philosophy, in which the universe of things, after having been realised in its multiplicity of kinds, is again brought into unity by a metaphysical synthesis. But by what process of allegory can we explain away the belief in were-wolves? When the same person is believed to be now a man and now a wolf, the difference which we recognise between a man and a wild beast is certainly not yet perceived. And such a belief as this cannot be a mere isolated extravagance of the fancy; it points to a view of nature as a whole which is, in fact, the ordinary view of savages in all parts of the world, and everywhere produces just such a confusion between the several orders of natural and supernatural beings as we find to have existed among the early Semites.

The influence of these ideas on early systems of religion may be considered under two aspects: (1) On the one hand, the range of the supernatural is so wide that no

[1] See Menant, *Glyptique Orientale*, vol. i.

[2] Berosus (*Fr. Hist. Gr.* ii. 497) refers to the images at the temple of Bel which preserved the forms of the strange monsters that lived in the time of chaos. But the peculiar prevalence of such figures on the oldest gems shows that the chaos in question is only the chaotic imagination of early man.

antique religion attempts to deal with all its manifestations. The simplest proof of this is that magic and sorcery, though they lay outside of religion and were forbidden arts in all the civilised states of antiquity, were yet never regarded as mere imposture. It was not denied that there were supernatural agencies at work in the world of which the public religion took no account. Religion dealt only with the gods, *i.e.* with a definite circle of great supernatural powers whose relations to man were established on a regular friendly basis and maintained by stated rites and fixed institutions. Beyond the circle of gods there lay a vast and undetermined mass of minor supernatural agencies, some of which were half-incorporated in religion under the name of demi-gods, while others were altogether ignored except in private popular superstition, or by those who professed the art of constraining demoniac powers to do them service and obey their commands. (2) On the other hand, the gods proper were not sharply marked off, *as regards their nature*, from the lower orders of demoniac beings, or even from such physical objects as were believed to possess demoniac attributes. Their distinctive mark lay in their relations with man, or, more exactly, with a definite circle of men, their habitual worshippers. As these relations were known and stable, they gave rise to an orderly and fixed series of religious institutions. But the forms of religious service were not determined merely by the fact that the god was considered in one case as the father, in another as the king, in yet another as the patron of his worshippers. In determining how the god was to be approached, and how his help could be most fully realised, it was necessary to take account of the fact that he was not an omnipotent and omnipresent being standing wholly outside of nature, but was himself linked to the physical world by a series of affinities connecting him not merely with man but with beasts trees and inanimate things. In antique religion gods as well as men have a physical environment, on and through which they act, and by which their activity is conditioned.

The influence of this idea on ancient religion is very far-reaching and often difficult to analyse. But there is one aspect of it that is both easily grasped and of fundamental importance; I mean the connection of particular gods with particular places. The most general term to express the relation of natural things to the gods which our language affords is the word "holy"; thus when we speak of holy places, holy things, holy persons, holy times, we imply that the places things persons and times stand in some special relation to the godhead or to its manifestation. But the word "holy" has had a long and complicated history, and has various shades of meaning according to the connection in which it is used. It is not possible, by mere analysis of the modern use of the word, to arrive at a single definite conception of the meaning of holiness; nor is it possible to fix on any one of the modern aspects of the conception, and say that it represents the fundamental idea from which all other modifications of the idea can be deduced. The primitive conception of holiness, to which the modern variations of the idea must be traced back, belonged to a habit of thought with which we have lost touch, and we cannot hope to understand it by the aid of logical discussion, but only by studying it on its own ground as it is exhibited in the actual working of early religion. It would be idle, therefore, at this stage to attempt any general definition, or to seek for a comprehensive formula covering all the relations of the gods to natural things. The problem must be attacked in detail, and for many reasons the most suitable point of attack will be found in the connection that ancient religion conceived to exist between particular deities and particular "holy" places. This topic is of fundamental importance, because all complete acts of ancient worship were necessarily performed at a holy place, and thus the local connections of the gods are involved, explicitly or implicitly, in every function of religion.

The local relations of the gods may be considered under two heads. In the first place the activity power and dominion of the gods were conceived as bounded by certain local limits, and in the second place they were conceived as having their residences and homes at certain fixed sanctuaries. These two conceptions are not of course independent, for generally speaking the region of divine authority and influence surrounds the sanctuary which is the god's principal seat; but for convenience of exposition we shall look first at the god's *land* and then at his *sanctuary* or dwelling-place.

Broadly speaking, the land of a god corresponds with the land of his worshippers; Canaan is Jehovah's land as Israel is Jehovah's people.[1] In like manner the land of Assyria (Asshur) has its name from the god Asshur,[2] and in general the deities of the heathen are called indifferently the gods of the nations and the gods of the lands.[3] Our natural impulse is to connect these expressions with the divine kingship, which in modern states of feudal origin is a sovereignty over land as well as men. But the older Semitic kingdoms were not feudal, and before the captivity we shall hardly find an example of a Semitic sovereign being called king of a land.[4] In fact the relations of

[1] Hos. ix. 3; cf. Reland, *Palæstina*, vol. i. p. 16 *sqq.*

[2] Schrader, *KAT.* 2nd ed. p. 35 *sqq.*; cf. Micah v. 6 (Heb. 5), where the "land of Asshur" stands in parallelism with "land of Nimrod." Nimrod is a god, see his article in *Enc. Brit.*, 9th ed., and Wellhausen, *Hexateuch* (2nd ed. 1889), p. 308 *sqq.*

[3] 2 Kings xviii. 33 *sqq.*

[4] The Hebrews say "king of Asshur" (Assyria), Edom, Aram (Syria), etc.,

a god to his land were not merely political, or dependent on his relation to the inhabitants. The Aramæans and Babylonians whom the king of Assyria planted in northern Israel brought their own gods with them, but when they were attacked by lions they felt that they must call in the aid of "the god of the land," who, we must infer, had in his own region power over beasts as well as men.[1] Similarly the Aramæans of Damascus, after their defeat in the hill-country of Samaria, argue that the gods of Israel are gods of the hills and will have no power in the plains; the power of the gods has physical and local limitations. So too the conception that a god cannot be worshipped outside of his own land, which we find applied even to the worship of Jehovah,[2] does not simply mean that there can be no worship of a god where he has no sanctuary, but that the land of a strange god is not a fit place to erect a sanctuary. In the language of the Old Testament foreign countries are unclean,[3] so that Naaman, when he desires to worship the God of Israel at Damascus, has to beg for two mules' burden of the soil of Canaan, to make a sort of enclave of Jehovah's land in his Aramæan dwelling-place.

In Semitic religion the relation of the gods to particular places which are special seats of their power is usually expressed by the title Baal (pl. *Baalim*, fem. *Baalath*).

but these are names of nations, the countries being properly the "land of Asshur," etc. The local designation of a king is taken from his capital, or royal seat. Thus the king of Israel is king of Samaria (1 Kings xxi. 1), Sihon, king of the Amorites, is king of Heshbon (Deut. iii. 6). Hiram, whom the Bible calls king of Tyre, appears on the oldest of Phœnician inscriptions (*CIS.* No. 5) as king of the Sidonians, *i.e.* the Phœnicians (cf. 1 Kings xvi. 31), Nebuchadnezzar is king of Babylon, and so forth. The only exception to this rule in old Hebrew is, I think, Og, king of Bashan (Deut. i. 4; 1 Kings iv. 19), who is a mythical figure, presumably an old god of the region.

[1] 2 Kings xvii. 24 *sqq.*

[2] 1 Sam. xxvi. 19; Hos. ix. 4.

[3] Amos vii. 17; Josh. xxii. 19.

As applied to men *baal* means the master of a house, the owner of a field cattle or the like; or in the plural the *baalim* of a city are its freeholders and full citizens.[1] In a secondary sense, in which alone the word is ordinarily used in Arabic, *baal* means husband; but it is not used of the relation of a master to his slave, or of a superior to his inferior, and it is incorrect to regard it, when employed as a divine title, as a mere synonym of the titles implying lordship over men which came before us in the last lecture. When a god is simply called "the Baal," the meaning is not "the lord of the worshipper" but the possessor of some place or district, and each of the multitude of local Baalim is distinguished by adding the name of his own place.[2] Melcarth is the Baal of Tyre, Astarte the Baalath of Byblus;[3] there was a Baal of Lebanon,[4] of Mount Hermon,[5] of Mount Peor, and so forth. In Southern Arabia Baal constantly occurs in similar local connections, *e.g.* Dhū Samāwī is the Baal of the district Bācir, ʽAthtar the Baal of Gumdān, and the sun-goddess the Baalath of several places or regions.[6]

[1] So often in the Old Testament, and also in Phœnician. *Baalath* is used of a female citizen (*CIS.* No. 120).

[2] Cf. Stade in *ZATW.* 1886, p. 303.

[3] *CIS.* Nos. 1, 122.

[4] *CIS.* No. 5.

[5] See Judg. iii. 3, where this mountain is called the mountain of the Baal of Hermon. Hermon properly means a sacred place. In the Old Testament place-names like Baal-peor, Baal-meon are shortened from Beth Baal Peor, "house or sanctuary of the Baal of Mount Peor," etc.

[6] Hence we read in the Himyaritic inscriptions of sun-goddesses in the plural (*e.g.* אשמסהמו, *CIS.* pt. iv. No. 46), as in Canaan we have a plurality of local Baalim. Special forms of Baal occur which are defined not by the name of a place or region but in some other way, *e.g.* by the name of a sacred object, as Baal-tamar, "lord of the palm-tree," preserved to us only in the name of a town, Judg. xx. 33. So too Baal-ḥammān, on the Carthaginian Tanith inscriptions, may be primarily "lord of the sun-pillar"; yet compare אל חמן, "the divinity of (the place) Hammōn" (*CIS.* No. 8, and the inscr. of Maʽṣūb); see G. Hoffmann in the *Abhandlungen* of the Göttingen Academy, vol. xxxvi. (4 May 1889). Baal-zebub, the god of Ekron, is "owner of flies," rather than Βάαλ Μυῖα, the fly-god. In one or two cases the title of Baal

As the heathen gods are never conceived as ubiquitous, and can act only where they or their ministers are present, the sphere of their permanent authority and influence is naturally regarded as their residence. It will be observed that the local titles which I have cited are generally derived either from towns where the god had a temple, or (as the Semites say) a house, or else from mountains, which are constantly conceived as the dwelling-places of deities. The notion of personal property in land is a thing that grows up gradually in human society, and is first applied to a man's homestead. Pasture land is common property,[1] but a man acquires rights in the soil by building a house, or by "quickening" a waste place, *i.e.* bringing it under cultiva-

seems to be prefixed to the name of a god; thus we have Baal-zephon as a place-name on the frontiers of Egypt, and also a god צפן (*CIS.* Nos. 108, 265). Similarly the second element in Baal-gad, a town at the foot of Mount Hermon, is the name of an ancient Semitic god. The grammatical explanation of these forms is not clear to me. Another peculiar form is Baal-berith at Shechem, which in ordinary Hebrew simply means "possessor of covenant," *i.e.* "covenant ally," but may here signify the Baal who presides over covenants, or rather over the special covenant by which the neighbouring Israelites were bound to the Canaanite inhabitants of the city. Peculiar also is the more modern Baal-marcod, κοίρανος κωμῶν (near Bairūt), known from inscriptions (Wadd. Nos. 1855, 1856; Ganneau, *Rec. d'Arch. Or.* i. 95, 103). The Semitic form is supposed to be בעל מרקד, "lord of dancing," *i.e.* he to whom dancing is due as an act of homage; cf. for the construction, Prov. iii. 27. In later times Baal or Bel became a proper name, especially in connection with the cult of the Babylonian Bel, and entered into compounds of a new kind like the Aglibol and Malakhbel of Palmyra. Baal Shamaim, "the lord of heaven," belongs to the class of titles taken from the region of nature in which the god dwells or has sway. בעל מרפא (*CIS.* No. 41) and בעלת החדרת (*ibid.* No. 177) are of doubtful interpretation. In the Panamu inscription of Zenjirli, l. 22, בעל בית can hardly mean "patron of the royal family," as Sachau takes it, but rather designates RKB-El as the local Baal of the sanctuary, or perhaps of the royal city. On the whole there is nothing in these peculiar forms to shake the general conclusion that Baal is primarily the title of a god as inhabitant or owner of a place.

[1] Common, that is, to a tribe, for the tribes are very jealous of encroachments on their pastures. But, as we have here to do with the personal rights of the Baal within his own community, the question of intertribal rights does not come in.

tion. Originally, that is, private rights over land are a mere consequence of rights over what is produced by private labour upon the land.[1] The ideas of building and cultivation are closely connected—the Arabic *'amara*, like the German *bauen*, covers both—and the word for house or homestead is extended to include the dependent fields or territory. Thus in Syriac "the house of Antioch" is the territory dependent on the town, and in the Old Testament the land of Canaan is called not only Jehovah's land but his house.[2] If the relation of the Baal to his district is to be judged on these analogies, the land is his, first because he inhabits it, and then because he "quickens" it, and makes it productive.

That this is the true account of the relations of the name Baal appears from what Hosea tells us of the religious conceptions of his idolatrous contemporaries, whose nominal Jehovah worship was merged in the numerous local cults of the Canaanite Baalim. To the Baalim they ascribed all the natural gifts of the land, the corn the wine and the oil, the wool and the flax, the vines and fig-trees,[3] and we shall see by and by that the whole ritual of feasts and sacrifices was imbued with this conception. We can, however, go a step further, and trace the idea to an earlier form, by the aid of a fragment of old heathen phraseology which has survived in the language of Jewish and Arabian agriculture. In the system of Mohammedan taxation land irrigated by the water-wheel or other laborious methods pays five per cent. of its produce in the name of charity-tax, whereas land

[1] The law of Islam is that land which has never been cultivated or occupied by houses becomes private property by being "quickened" (*bil-iḥyā*). See Nawawī, *Minhāj*, ed. Van den Berg, ii. 171. This is in accordance with pre-Islamic custom. Cf. Wellhausen, *Heidenthum*, p. 105.

[2] Hos. viii. 1, ix. 15, compared with ix. 3.

[3] Hos. ii. 8 *sqq.*

that does not require laborious irrigation pays a full tithe. The latter, according to Arabian jurists, is of various kinds, which are designated by special names; but all these are summed up in the general expression "what the sky waters and what the Ba'l waters." Similarly the Mishna and Talmud draw a distinction between land artificially irrigated and land naturally moist, calling the latter the "house of Baal" or "field of the house of Baal." It must be remembered that in the East the success of agriculture depends more on the supply of water than on anything else, and the "quickening of dead ground" (*iḥyā al-mawāt*), which, as we have seen, creates ownership, has reference mainly to irrigation.[1] Accordingly what the husbandman irrigates is his own property, but what is naturally watered he regards as irrigated by a god and as the field or property of this god, who is thus looked upon as the Baal or owner of the spot.

It has generally been assumed that Baal's land, in the sense in which it is opposed to irrigated fields, means land watered by the rains of heaven, "the waters of the sky" as the Arabs call them, and from this again it has been inferred that the Baal who gives his name to land naturally moist and fertile is the god of the sky (*Baal-shamaim*), who plays so great a part in later Semitic religion, and is identified by Philo Byblius with the sun. But, strictly regarded, this view, which is natural in our climate and with our meteorological notions, appears to be inconsistent with the conditions of vegetable growth in most parts of the Semitic lands, where the rainfall is precarious or confined to certain seasons, so that the face of the earth is bare and lifeless for the greater part of the year except where it is kept fresh by irrigation or by the natural

[1] See, for example, Abū Yūsuf Ya'cūb, *Kitāb al-Kharāj*, Cairo, A.H. 1302, p. 37.

percolation of underground water. To us, of course, it is plain that all fertility is ultimately due to the rains which feed the springs and watery bottoms, as well as the broad corn-fields; but this is a knowledge beyond the science of the oldest Semites;[1] while on the other hand the distinction between favoured spots that are always green and fruitful and the less favoured fields that are useless during the rainless season, is alike obvious and essential to the most primitive systems of husbandry.

In Arabia the rainfall is all-important for pasture,[2] but except in the far south, which comes within the skirts of the monsoon region, it is too irregular to form a basis for agriculture. An occasional crop of gourds or melons may be raised in certain places after copious showers; and on low-lying plains, where the rain sinks into a heavy soil and cannot flow away, the palm-tree will sometimes live and produce a dry tough fruit of little value.[3] But on the whole the contrast between land naturally productive and land artificially fertilised, as it presents itself to the Arabian husbandman, has no direct connection with rainfall, but depends on the depth of the ground-water. Where the roots of the date-palm can reach the subterranean flow, or where a fountain sends forth a stream whose branches fertilise an oasis without the toil of the

[1] Cf. the remarks of Dillmann in his comm. on Gen. i. 6-8.

[2] Ibn Sa'd, No. 80. Here Wellhausen introduces a reference to agriculture, but in rendering *janābunā*, "our palm gardens," he departs from the traditional interpretation. (See Lane.)

[3] Such palms and the land they grow on are called *'idhy*, pl. *a'dhā*; the dates are *saḥḥ* or *casb*; see Al-Azharī's luminous account of the different kinds of date-palms in the *Lisān*, s.v. *ba'l*. In the traditions that require a whole tithe to be paid on crops watered by rain the *'idhy* seems to be mainly contemplated; for in Ibn Sa'd, No. 68, the prophet exacts no tithe on such precarious crops as cucumbers raised on ground watered by rain. I rode in 1880 through a desolate plain of heavy soil some miles to the S.-E. of Mecca, and was told that after good rain the waste would be covered with patches of melons and the like.

water-wheel, the ground is naturally fertile, and such land is "watered by the Ba'l." The best Arabian authorities say expressly that ba'l palm-trees are such as drink by their roots, without artificial irrigation and without rain, "from the water which God has created beneath the earth,"[1] and in an exact specification of what is liable to the full tithe the *ba'l* and the sky are mentioned together, not used interchangeably.[2]

[1] Al-Aṣma'ī and Al-Azharī in the *Lisān*, s.v. *ba'l*. This article and the materials collected in the Glossary to De Goeje's *Belādhorī* give almost all the evidence. I may add a ref. to Ibn Sa'd, No. 119, compared with No. 73, and Macrīzī *Khiṭaṭ*, ii. 129, and in the next note I will cite some of the leading traditions, which are very inaccurately given by Sprenger in *ZDMG.* xviii.

[2] The fullest expressions are, Bokhārī, ii. 122 (Būlāc vocalised ed.), "what is watered by the sky and the fountains or is *'atharī*"; *Mowaṭṭa* (Tunis ed.), p. 94, "what is watered by the sky and the fountains and the *ba'l*"; *ibid.* p. 95, "what is watered by the sky and the fountains or is *ba'l*." Shorter phrases are, *Belādh.* p. 70, "what is watered by the *ba'l* and what is watered by the sky," with such variants as "the surface flow [*ghail, saiḥ*] and the sky" (*ib.* p. 71), "the fountains and the sky" (B. Hishām, 956), "the rivers and the clouds" (Moslim, ed. of A.H. 1290, i. 268). These variations are intelligible if we bear in mind the aspect of the cultivated patches in such a valley as the Batn Marr. The valley is a great water-course, but for the most part the water flows underground, breaking out in powerful springs where there is a sharp fall in the ground, and sometimes flowing for a few hundred yards in a visible stream, which is soon led off in many branches through the palms and tiny corn-fields and presently disappears again under the sand and stones. Where the hard bottom is level and near the surface, the palms can drink from their roots where there is no visible stream; but where the bottom lies deep (as in the neighbourhood of Ṭāif) cultivation is possible only by the use of the water-wheel, and then the tithe is reduced to 5 per cent. Where irrigation can be effected by gravitation through a pipe or channel, without pumping, the land is still regarded as naturally fertile and pays full tithe; see *Gl. Bel.* and Ibn Sa'd, No. 119. According to one interpretation, the obscure word *'atharī*, which I have not met with in any tradition except that cited above, means land watered by an artificial channel (*'āthūr*). This may be a mere guess, for the oldest and best Arabian scholars seem to have had no clear understanding of the word; but at least it is preferable to the view which identifies *'atharī* and *'idhy*. For a comparison of the traditions given above indicates that *'atharī* is either a synonym for *ba'l* or some species thereof; moreover, the oasis in W. Sirhān which Guarmani (p. 209) calls Etera, and Lady Anne Blunt (*Nejd*, i. 89 *sqq.*) writes Itheri, can hardly be anything else than *'Atharī* in a modern pronunciation. (Huber writes it with initial *alif*, but his ortho-

The Arabian evidence therefore leads us to associate the life-giving operation of the Baʿl or Baal, not with the rains of heaven, but with springs, streams and underground flow. On the other hand it is clear (*e.g.* from Hosea) that among the agricultural peoples of Canaan the Baalim were looked upon as the authors of all fertility, including the corn crops, which are wholly dependent on rain in most parts of Palestine. And it is here that we find the sky-Baal (*Baal-shamaim*) with such local forms as Marna "the lord of rains" at Gaza.[1] Thus the question arises whether the original Semitic conception of the sphere of the Baal's activity has been modified in Arabia to suit its special climate, or whether, on the other hand, the notion of the Baal as lord of rain is of later growth.

It would be easier to answer this question if we knew with certainty whether the use of Baal (Baʿl) as a divine title is indigenous to Arabia or borrowed from the agricultural Semites beyond the peninsula. On the former alternative, which is accepted by some of the first scholars of our day, such as Wellhausen and Nöldeke, Baal-worship must be held to be older than the Semitic dispersion, and

graphy, as the editors warn us, is not greatly to be trusted.) ʿAtharī, for which some good authorities give also ʿ*aththarī* (see *Lisān*), seems to mean "belonging to Athtar," the S. Arabian god, who corresponds in name, but not in sex, to the Babylonian Ishtar, the Phœnician Astarte, and the Aramaic ʿAttar or Athar. Athtar is one of the S. Arabian gods who preside over irrigation (*CIS.* pt. 4; cf. *ZDMG.* xxxvii. 371); cf. also the place ʿAththar, described as a jungly haunt of lions (*Bānat Soʿād*, 46).

The crops dependent on rain are so unimportant in most parts of Arabia that some of the prophet's decrees pass them by altogether, and simply say that the *saiḥ* pays full tithe (Ibn Saʿd, No. 68). Thus it is easy to understand how, in less precise speech, the term *baʿl* is applied *à potiori* to all crops not artificially irrigated; and so, when the empire of Islam was extended to lands of more copious rain, confusion arose and the true meaning of *baʿl* was obscured. The corn crops of Palestine, which strictly speaking are *aʿdhā* (Abulf. ed. Reinaud, p. 227), and those near Alexandria, which are sown on the retiring of the Nile, are alike said by Mocaddasī to be "on the *baʿl*"; but this is not in accordance with the old classical usage.

[1] Procopius of Gaza, iii. 19, in Galland, vol. ix.—"dominus imbrium."

to belong to an age when all the Semites were still nomadic. And in that case it can hardly be doubted that the Arabs, as the nearest representatives of ancient Semitic life, held most closely to the original conception of the Baal. Personally I think it most probable that Baal as a divine title entered Arabia with the date-palm, whose culture is certainly not indigenous to the peninsula. There is direct proof from inscriptions of the worship of "the Baal" among the Nabatæans of the Sinaitic desert to the north, and among the Sabæans and Himyarites in the south of the peninsula; but for central Arabia Baal-worship is only an inference from certain points of language, of which the most important is the phrase we have been considering.[1] Thus, to say the least, it is possible that Baal-worship was never known to the pastoral Bedouins except in so far as they came under the influence of the denizens of the agricultural oases, who had borrowed their art from Syria or Irac, and, according to all analogy, could not have failed to borrow at the same time so much of the foreign religion as was deemed necessary to secure the success of their husbandry. But even on this hypothesis I conceive it to be in the highest degree improbable that Baal on entering Arabia was changed from a god of rain to a god of springs and watery bottoms. We have here to do mainly with the culture of the date-palm, and I find no evidence that this tree was largely grown on land watered by rain alone in any part of the Semitic area. And even in Palestine, which is the typical case of a Semitic country dependent on rain, there is so vast a difference between the productiveness of lands that are watered by rain alone and those which enjoy natural or artificial irrigation, that we can hardly conceive the idea of natural fertility, expressed

[1] See Nöldeke in *ZDMG.* xl. 174; and Wellhausen, p. 176.

by the term Baal's land, to have been originally connected with the former. For my own part I have no doubt that Semitic agriculture began, as it has always most flourished, in places naturally watered by springs and streams, and that the language of agricultural religion was fixed by the conditions prevailing in such places.[1]

I see an important confirmation of this view in the *local character* of the Baalim, which has always been a hopeless puzzle to those who begin with the conception of the Baal as a sky god, but is at once intelligible if the seats of the gods were originally sought in spots of natural fertility, by springs and river-banks, in the groves and tangled thickets and green tree-shaded glades of mountain hollows and deep watercourses. All the Semites, as we shall presently see, attached a certain sanctity to such places quite apart from agriculture; and as agriculture must have begun in naturally productive spots, it is inevitable to infer that agricultural religion took its starting-point from the sanctity already attaching to waters groves and meadows.[2] The difficulty which we

[1] A good conception of the material conditions of Palestinian agriculture may be got from an article by Anderlind in *ZDPV.* ix. (1886). The following illustration from *Belādhorī*, p. 151, may be helpful. The district of Bāho (Baibalissus) was dependent on rain alone, and paid the usual tithes. The inhabitants proposed to Maslama that he should make them an irrigation canal from the Euphrates, and offered to pay him one-third of their crops in addition to the tithe.

[2] In this argument I have not ventured to lay any weight on the Mishnic use of the term, "Baal's field." In Palestine, many centuries before the Mishna was composed, the Baalim were certainly regarded as fertilising the corn crops, and must therefore have been viewed as givers of rain; thus it is only natural that Baal's land, as opposed to land artificially irrigated, should include corn-lands wholly dependent on rain, as it plainly does in *B. B.* iii. 1. On the other hand, there are clear indications that even in Palestine the word was sometimes used in a sense corresponding to the Arabic usage; in other words, that crops which cannot be raised in Palestine except in spots naturally moist or artificially watered are divided into בעל and שקי. This distinction, for example, is applied to such vegetables as onions and cabbages (*Terūm.* x. 11; *Shebī.* ii. 9), and in *Suc.* iii. 3 we read of a water-willow (*populus Euphratica*) grown on the *ba'l.* Moreover, in *Shebī.* ii. 9 there is a

feel in accepting this view arises mainly from the totally different climate in which we live. When a man has journeyed in the Arabian wilderness, traversing day after day stony plateaus, black volcanic fields, or arid sands walled in by hot mountains of bare rock and relieved by no other vegetation than a few grey and thorny acacias or scanty tufts of parched herbage, till suddenly, at a turn of the road, he emerges on a Wady where the ground-water rises to the surface, and passes as if by magic into a new world, where the ground is carpeted with verdure, and a grove of stately palm-trees spreads forth its canopy of shade against the hot and angry heaven, he does not find it difficult to realise that to early man such a spot was verily a garden and habitation of the gods. In Syria the contrasts are less glaring than in the desert; but only in the spring time, and in many parts of the country not even then, is the general fertility such that a fountain or a marshy bottom with its greensward and thicket of natural wood can fail strongly to impress the imagination. Nor are the religious associations of such a scene felt only by heathen barbarians. "The trees of the Lord drink their fill, the cedars of Lebanon which He hath planted: Where the birds make their nests; as for the stork, the fir-trees are her house" (Ps. civ. 16). This might pass for the description of the natural sanctuary of the Baal of Lebanon, but who does not feel its solemn grandeur? Or who will condemn the touch of primitive naturalism

clear statement that vegetables grown on the *ba'l* were irrigated, so that the contrast with שקי can only be maintained by supposing that the latter term, as is the case in Arabia, is restricted to laborious irrigation (*e.g.* by water drawn from a cistern), and that vegetable gardens lying beneath a spring on the hillside, such as still common in Palestine, were reckoned to the *ba'l*. The only vegetables that were and are commonly grown in Palestine on the open field before the summer sun has dried up the ground are those of the gourd and cucumber kind; see *Shebi.* ii. 1; Klein in *ZDPV.* iv. 82, and cf. Isa. i. 8.

that colours the comparison in the first Psalm: "He shall be like a tree planted by watercourses, that bringeth forth his fruit in his season; his leaf also shall not wither, and whatsoever he doeth shall prosper" (Ps. i. 3)?

When the conception of Baal's land is thus narrowed to its oldest form, and limited to certain favoured spots that seem to be planted and watered by the hand of the gods,[1] we are on the point of passing from the idea of the land of the god to that of his homestead and sanctuary. But before we take this step it will be convenient for us to glance rapidly at the way in which the primitive idea was widened and extended. Ultimately, as we see from Hosea, all agricultural produce was regarded as the gift of the Baalim, and all the worshippers who frequented a particular sanctuary brought a tribute of first-fruits to the local god, whether their crops grew on land naturally moist and fertile, or on land laboriously irrigated, or on fields watered by the rain of heaven. The god therefore had acquired certain proprietary rights, or at least certain rights of suzerainty, over the whole district inhabited by his worshippers, far beyond the limits of the original Baal's land.

The first step in this process is easily understood from the fundamental principles of Semitic land-law. Property in water is older and more important than property in land. In nomadic Arabia there is no property, strictly so called, in desert pastures, but certain families or tribes hold the watering-places without which the right of pasture is useless. Or, again, if a man digs a well he has a preferential right to water his camels at it before other camels are admitted; and he has an absolute right to prevent others from using the water for agricultural purposes unless they buy it from him. This is Moslem law; but

[1] To the same circle of ideas belongs the conception of the Garden of Eden, planted by God, and watered not by rain but by rivers.

it is broadly in accordance with old Arabian custom, and indeed with general Semitic custom, as appears from many passages of the Old Testament.[1] On these principles it is clear that even in the nomadic stage of society the god of the waters may be held to exercise certain vague rights over the adjoining pasture lands, the use of which depends on access to the watering-places. And with the introduction of agriculture these rights become definite. All irrigated lands are dependent on him for the water that makes them fertile, and pay him first-fruits or tithes in acknowledgment of his bounty. So far all is clear, and in many parts of the Semitic area—notably in the alluvium of the Euphrates and Tigris, the granary of the ancient East—agriculture is so completely dependent on irrigation that no more than this is needed to bring all habitable land within the domain of the gods who send forth from the storehouse of subterranean waters, fountains and rivers to quicken the dead soil, and so are the authors of all growth and fertility. But in Palestine the corn crops, which form a chief source of agricultural wealth, are mainly grown without irrigation on land watered by rain alone. Yet in Hosea's time the first-fruits of corn were offered at the shrines of the Baalim, who had therefore become, in Canaan, the givers of rain as well as the lords of terrestrial waters. The explanation of this fact must be sought in the uncontrolled use of analogy characteristic of early thought. The idea that the Baalim were the authors of all fertility can only have taken shape among communities whose agriculture was essentially dependent on irrigation. But a little consideration will convince

[1] Gen. xxi. 25 *sqq.*, xxvi. 17 *sqq.*; Judg. i. 15; joint ownership in a well, Gen. xxix. 8; Ex. ii. 16. Traces of a water law stricter than that of Islam appear in Deut. ii. 6, 28; but the Arabian law, that the wayfarer and his beasts were allowed to drink freely, but not to anticipate the owners of the water, must always have been the general rule.

us that even in Palestine the earliest agriculture was necessarily of this type. Cultivation begins in the most fertile spots, which in that climate means the spots watered by streams and fountains. In such places agricultural villages must have existed, each with its worship of the local Baal, while the broad plains of Sharon or Esdraelon were still abandoned to wandering herdsmen. As husbandry spread from these centres and gradually covered the whole land, the worship of the Baalim spread with it; the gods of the springs extended their domain over the lands watered by the sky, and gradually added to their old attributes the new character of "lords of rain." The physical notions of the early Semites lent themselves readily enough to this development. Men saw with their own eyes that clouds rise from the sea (1 Kings xviii. 44) or from "the ends of the earth," *i.e.* the distant horizon (Jer. x. 13; Ps. cxxxv. 7), and so they had no reason to doubt that the rain came from the same storehouse as the fountains and streams of the Baalim.[1] In the oldest poetry of the Hebrews, when Jehovah rides over His land in the thunderstorm, His starting-point is not heaven but Mount Sinai; a natural conception, for in mountainous regions storms gather round the highest summits. And on this analogy we may infer that when the rainclouds lay heavy on the upland glens and wooded crown of Lebanon, where the great Baalim of Phœnicia had their most famous seats at the sources of sacred

[1] I cannot follow Dillmann in regarding the cosmology of Gen. i., with its twofold storehouse of water above and beneath the firmament, as more primitive than the simpler conception of rising clouds (נשיאים). The cosmology of Gen. i. is confined to post-exilic writings (for 2 Kings vii. 2, 19 is not to the point), and involves a certain amount of abstract thought; while the other view merely represents things as they appear to the eye. It is quite a mistake to find a doctrine of evaporation in passages like Jer. x. 13; the epithet *nesī'īm* refers to the visible movements of the clouds; cf. such Arabic epithets as *ḥabī*, "a cloud crouching on the horizon."

streams, their worshippers would see a visible proof that the gods of the fountains and rivers were also the givers of rain. In the latest stage of Phœnician religion, when all deities were habitually thought of as heavenly or astral beings, the holiest sanctuaries were still those of the primitive fountains and river gods, and both ritual and legend continued to bear witness to the original character of these deities. Many examples of this will come before us in due course; for the present, it may suffice to cite the case of Aphaca, where the Urania or heaven goddess was worshipped by casting gifts into the sacred pool, and where it was fabled that once a year the goddess descended into the waters in the shape of a falling star.[1]

Finally the life-giving power of the god was not limited to vegetative nature, but to him also was ascribed the increase of animal life, the multiplication of flocks and herds, and, not least, of the human inhabitants of the land. For the increase of animate nature is obviously conditioned, in the last resort, by the fertility of the soil, and primitive races, which have not learned to differentiate the various kinds of life with precision, think of animate as well as vegetable life as rooted in the earth and sprung from it. The earth is the great mother of all things in most mythological philosophies, and the comparison of the life of mankind, or of a stock of men, with the life of a tree, which is so common in Semitic as in other primitive poetry, is not in its origin a mere figure. Thus where the growth of vegetation is ascribed to a particular divine power, the same power receives the thanks and homage of his worshippers for the increase of cattle and of men. Firstlings as well as first-fruits were offered at the shrines

[1] Sozomen, ii. 5; cf. the fallen star which Astarte is said to have consecrated at the holy isle of Tyre (Philo Byblius in *Fr. Hist. Gr.* iii. 569).

of the Baalim,[1] and one of the commonest classes of personal names given by parents to their sons or daughters designates the child as the gift of the god.[2]

In this rapid sketch of the development of the idea of the local Baalim I have left many things to be confirmed or filled out in detail by subsequent reference to the particulars of their ritual, and I abstain altogether from entering at this stage into the influence which the conception of the Baalim as productive and reproductive powers exercised on the development of a highly sensual mythology, especially when the gods were divided into sexes, and the Baal was conceived as the male principle of reproduction, the husband of the land which he fertilised,[3] for this belongs rather to the discussion of the nature of the gods.

[1] We shall see as we proceed that the sacrifice of firstlings is older than agricultural religion, and was not originally a tribute like the first-fruits. But in religions of the Baal type firstlings and first-fruits were brought under the same general conception.

[2] To this class belong primarily the numerous Hebrew and Phœnician names compounded with forms of the root נתן or יתן, "to give" (Heb. Jonathan, Phœn. Baaljathon; Heb. Mattaniah, Phœn. Mutumbal [masc. and fem.], etc.; Nabatæan, Cosnathan [Euting, No. 12]); and Arabic names formed by adding the god's name to Wahb, Zaid (perhaps also Aus), "gift of." Cognate to these are the names in which the birth of a son is recognised as a proof of the divine favour (Heb. Hananiah, Johanan; Phœn. Hannibal, No'ammilkat [*CIS.* No. 41], etc.; Edomite, Baal-Hanan [Gen. xxxvi. 38]; Ar. Ναμηλη [Wadd. 2143], "favour of El," Auf-el, "[good] augury from El," Ουαδδηλος [Wadd. 2372], "love of El"), or which express the idea that he has helped the parents or heard their prayers (Heb. Azariah, Shemaiah; Phœn. Asdrubal, Eshmunazar, etc.); cf. Gen. xxix. xxx., 1 Sam. i. Finally there is a long series of names such as Yeḥavbaal (*CIS.* No. 69), Kemoshyeḥī (De Vogüé, *Mélanges*, p. 89), "Baal, Chemosh gives life." The great variety of gods referred to in Phœnician names of these forms shows that the gift of children was ascribed to all Baalim, each in his own sphere; cf. Hosea, chap. i.

[3] This conception appears in Hosea and underlies the figure in Isa. lxii. 4, where married land (be'ūlāh) is contrasted with wilderness; Wellhausen, *Heidenthum*, p. 170. It is a conception which might arise naturally enough from the ideas above developed, but was no doubt favoured by the use of *baal* to mean "husband." How *baal* comes to mean husband is not

You will observe also that the sequence of ideas which I have proposed is applicable in its entirety only to agricultural populations, such as those of Canaan, Syria, and Irac on the one hand and of Yemen on the other. It is in these parts of the Semitic field that the conception of the local gods as Baalim is predominant, though traces of Ba'l as a divine title are found in Central Arabia in various forms.[1]

In the central parts of Arabia agriculture was confined to oases, and the vocabulary connected with it is mainly borrowed from the northern Semites.[2] Many centuries before the date of the oldest Arabic literature, when the desert was the great highway of Eastern commerce, colonies of the settled Semites, Yemenites, and Aramæans occupied the oases and watering-places in the desert that were suitable for commercial stations, and to these immigrants must be ascribed the introduction of agriculture and even of the date-palm itself. The most developed cults of Arabia belong not to the pure nomads, but to these agricultural and trading settlements, which the Bedouins visited only as pilgrims, not to pay stated homage to the lord of the land from which they drew their life, but in fulfilment of vows. As most of our knowledge about Arabian cults refers to pilgrimages and the visits of the Bedouins, the impression is produced that all offerings were vows, and that fixed tribute of the fruits of the earth, such as was paid in the settled lands

perfectly clear; the name is certainly associated with monandry and the appropriation of the wife to her husband, but it does not imply a servile relation, for the slave-girl does not call her master *ba'l*. Probably the key is to be found in the notion that the wife is her husband's tillage (Coran ii. 233), in which case private rights over land were older than exclusive marital rights.

[1] For the evidence see Nöldeke in *ZDMG*. vol. xl. (1886) p. 174; and Wellhausen, *Heidenthum*, p. 170.

[2] Fränkel, *Aram. Fremdww.* p. 125.

to local Baalim, was unknown; but this impression is not accurate. From the Coran (vi. 137) and other sources we have sufficient evidence that the settled Arabs paid to the god a regular tribute from their fields, apparently by marking off as his a certain portion of the irrigated and cultivated ground.[1] Thus as regards the settled Arabs the parallelism with the other Semites is complete, and the only question is whether cults of the Baal type and the name of Baal itself were not borrowed, along with agriculture, from the northern Semitic peoples.

This question I am disposed to answer in the affirmative; for I find nothing in the Arabic use of the word *ba'l* and its derivatives which is inconsistent with the view that they had their origin in the cultivated oases, and much that strongly favours such a view. The phrase "land which the Baal waters" has no sense till it is opposed to "land which the hand of man waters," and irrigation is certainly not older than agriculture. It is questionable whether the idea of the godhead as the permanent or immanent source of life and fertility—a very different

[1] All the evidence on this point has been confused by an early misunderstanding of the passage in the Coran: "They set apart for Allāh a portion of the tilth or the cattle he has created, and say, This is Allāh's—as they fancy—and this belongs to our partners (idols); but what is assigned to idols does not reach Allāh, and what is assigned to Allāh really goes to the idols." It is plain that the heathen said indifferently "this belongs to Allāh," meaning the local god (cf. Wellh. *Heid.* p. 185), or this belongs to such and such a deity (naming him), and Mohammed argues, exactly as Hosea does in speaking of the homage paid by his contemporaries to local Baalim, whom they identified with Jehovah, that whether they say "Allah" or "Hobal," the real object of their homage is a false god. But the traditional interpretation of the text is that one part was set aside for the supreme Allah and another for the idols, and this distortion has coloured all accounts of what the Arabs actually did, for of course historical tradition must be corrected by the Coran. Allowance being made for this error, which made the second half of the verse say that Allah was habitually cheated out of his share in favour of the idols, the notices in Ibn Hishām, p. 53, Sprenger, *Leb. Moh.* iii. 358, Pocock, *Specimen*, p. 112, may be accepted as based upon fact. In Pocock's citation from the *Naẓm al-dorr* it appears that irrigated land is referred to.

thing from the belief that the god is the ancestor of his worshippers—had any place in the old tribal religion of the nomadic Arabs. To the nomad, who does not practise irrigation, the source of life and fertility is the rain that quickens the desert pastures, and there is no evidence that rain was ascribed to tribal deities. The Arabs regard rain as depending on the constellations, *i.e.* on the seasons, which affect all tribes alike within a wide range; and so when the showers of heaven are ascribed to a god, that god is Allah, the supreme and non-tribal deity.[1] It is to be noted also that among the Arabs the theophorous proper names that express religious ideas most akin to those of the settled Semites are derived from deities whose worship was widespread and not confined to the nomads. Further it will appear in a later lecture that the fundamental type of Arabian sacrifice does not take the form of a tribute to the god, but is simply an act of communion with him. The gift of firstlings, indeed, which has so prominent a place in Canaanite religion, is not unknown in Arabia. But this aspect of sacrifice has very little prominence; we find no approach to the payment of stated tribute to the gods, and the festal sacrifices at fixed seasons, which are characteristic of religions that regard the gods as the source of the annual renovation of fertility in nature, seem to have been confined to the great sanctuaries at which the nomads appeared only as pilgrims before a foreign god.[2] In these pilgrimages the nomadic Arabs might learn the name of Baal, but they

[1] Wellhausen, *Heid.* p. 175; cf. Ibn Sa'd, No. 80; *Diw. Hodh.*, cxiii. 18. Note also that rain is not one of the boons prayed for at 'Arafa (Agh. iii. 4; cf. xix. 132. 6), though charms to produce rain were used (Wellh. p. 157). These evidences do not prove that the gods were never appealed to as rain-makers, but they render it very improbable that they were habitually thought of as such.

[2] Cf. Wellhausen, p. 116.

could not assimilate the conception of the god as a land-owner and apply it to their own tribal deities, for the simple reason that in the desert private property in land was unknown and the right of water and of pasturage was common to every member of the tribe.[1] But in estimating the influence on Arabian religion of agriculture and the ideas connected with settled life, we must remember how completely, in the centuries before Mohammed, the gods of the *madar* ("glebe," *i.e.* villagers and townsfolk) had superseded the gods of the *wabar* ("hair," *i.e.* dwellers in haircloth tents). Much the most important part of the religious practices of the nomads consisted in pilgrimages to the great shrines of the town Arabs, and even the minor sanctuaries, which were frequented only by particular tribes, seem to have been often fixed at spots where there was some commencement of settled life. Where the god had a house or temple we recognise the work of men who were no longer pure nomads, but had begun to form fixed homes; and indeed modern observation shows that, when an Arab tribe begins to settle down, it acquires the elements of husbandry before it gives up its tents and learns to erect immovable houses. Again there were sanctuaries without temples, but even at these the god had his treasure in a cave, and a priest who took care of his possessions, and there is no reason to think that the priest was an isolated hermit. The presumption is that

[1] We shall see in the next lecture that the institution of the *ḥimā* or sacred pasture-land is not based on the idea of property but on a principle of taboo. A main argument for the antiquity of Baal religion in Arabia is drawn from the denominative verb *ba'ila* = *aliha*, which means "to be in a state of helpless panic and perplexity," literally "to be Baal-struck." But such results are more naturally to be ascribed to the influence of an alien god than of a tribal divinity, and the word may well be supposed to have primarily expressed the confusion and mazed perplexity of the nomad when he finds himself at some great feast at a pilgrim shrine, amidst the strange habits and worship of a settled population; cf. Æthiopic *ba'āl*, "feast."

almost every holy place at the time of Mohammed was a little centre of settled agricultural life, and so also a centre of ideas foreign to the purely nomadic worshippers that frequented it.[1]

The final result of this long discussion is that the conception of the local god as Baal or lord of the land, the source of its fertility and the giver of all the good things of life enjoyed by its inhabitants, is intimately bound up with the growth of agricultural society, and involves a series of ideas unknown to the primitive life of the savage huntsman or the pure pastoral nomad. But we have also seen that the original idea of Baal's land was limited to certain favoured spots that seem to be planted and watered by the hand of the god, and to form, as it were, his homestead. Thus in its beginnings the idea of the land of the god appears to be only a development, in accordance with the type of agricultural life, of the more primitive idea that the god has a special home or haunt on earth. Agricultural habits teach men to look on this home as a garden of God, cultivated and fertilised by the hand of deity, but it was not agriculture that created the conception that certain places were the special haunts of

[1] In Arabia one section of a tribe is often nomadic while another is agricultural, but in spite of their kinship the two sections feel themselves very far apart in life and ways of thought, and a nomad girl often refuses to stay with a village husband. In this connection the traditions of the foreign origin of the cult at Mecca deserve more attention than is generally paid to them, though not in the line of Dozy's speculations. To the tribes of the desert the religion of the towns was foreign in spirit and contrasted in many ways with their old nomadic habits; moreover, as we have seen, it was probably coloured from the first by Syrian and Nabatæan influences. Yet it exercised a great attraction, mainly by appealing to the sensual part of the Bedouin's nature; the feasts were connected with the markets, and at them there was much jollity and good cheer. They began to be looked on as making up the sum of religion, and the cult of the gods came to be almost entirely dissociated from daily life, and from the customs associated with the sanctity of kinship, which at one time made up the chief part of nomad religion. Cf. Wellh., *Heid.* p. 182.

superhuman powers. That the gods are not ubiquitous but subject to limitations of time and space, and that they can act only where they or their messengers are present, is the universal idea of antiquity and needs no explanation. In no region of thought do men begin with transcendental ideas and conceive of existences raised above space and time. Thus whatever the nature of the gods, they were doubtless conceived from the first as having their proper homes or haunts, which they went forth from and returned to, and where they were to be found by the worshippers with whom they had fixed relations. We are not entitled to say *à priori* that this home would necessarily be a spot on the surface of the earth, for, just as there are fowls of the heaven and fish of the sea as well as beasts of the field, there might be, and in fact were, celestial gods and gods of the waters under the earth as well as gods terrestrial. In later times celestial gods predominate, as we see from the prevalence of sacrifice by fire, in which the homage of the worshipper is directed upwards in the pillar of savoury smoke that rises from the altar towards the seat of the godhead in the sky. But all sacrifices are not made by fire. The Greeks, especially in older times, buried the sacrifices devoted to gods of the underworld, and threw into the water gifts destined for the gods of seas and rivers. Both these forms of fireless ritual are found also among the Semites; and indeed among the Arabs sacrifices by fire were almost unknown, and the gift of the worshipper was conveyed to the deity simply by being laid on sacred ground, hung on a sacred tree, or, in the case of liquid offerings and sacrificial blood, poured over a sacred stone. In such cases we have the idea of locality connected with the godhead in the simplest form. There is a fixed place on the earth's surface, marked by a sacred tree or a sacred stone, where the god is wont to be found, and offerings deposited there have reached their address.

In later times the home or sanctuary of a god was a temple, or, as the Semites call it, a "house" or "palace." But as a rule the sanctuary is older than the house, and the god did not take up his residence in a place because a house had been provided for him, but, on the contrary, when men had learned to build houses for themselves, they also set up a house for their god in the place which was already known as his home. Of course, as population increased and temples were multiplied, means were found to evade this rule, and new sanctuaries were constituted in the places most convenient for the worshippers; but even in such cases forms were observed which implied that a temple could not fitly be erected except in a place affected by the deity, and the greatest and holiest sanctuaries were those which, according to undisputed tradition, he had been known to frequent from time immemorial.

That the gods haunted certain spots, which in consequence of this were holy places and fit places of worship, was to the ancients not a theory but a matter of fact, handed down by tradition from one generation to another, and accepted with unquestioning faith. Accordingly we find that new sanctuaries can be formed and new altars or temples erected, only where the godhead has given unmistakable evidence of his presence. All that is necessary to constitute a Semitic sanctuary is a precedent; it is assumed that where the god has once manifested himself and shown favour to his worshippers he will do so again, and when the precedent has been strengthened by frequent repetition the holiness of the place is fully established. Thus in the earlier parts of the Old Testament a theophany is always taken to be a good reason for sacrificing on the spot. The deity has manifested himself either visibly or by some mighty deed, and therefore an act of worship cannot be out of place. Saul builds an altar on the site of his victory over the Philistines,[1] the patriarchs found sanctuaries on the spot where the deity has appeared to them,[2] Gideon and Manoah present an offering where they have received a divine message.[3] Even in the Hebrew religion God is not equally near at all places and all times, and when a man is brought face to face with Him he seizes the opportunity for an act of ritual homage. But the ordinary practices of religion are not dependent on extraordinary manifestations of the divine presence; they proceed on the assumption that there are fixed places where the deity has appeared in the past and may be expected to appear again. When Jacob has his dream of a divine apparition at Bethel, he concludes not merely that Jehovah is present there at the moment, but that the place is "the house of God, the gate of heaven." And accordingly Bethel continued to be regarded as a sanctuary of the first class down to the captivity. In like manner all the places where the patriarchs were recorded to have worshipped or where God appeared to them, figure as traditional holy places in the later history, and at least one of them, that of Mamre, was a notable sanctuary down to Christian times. We are entitled to use these facts as illustrative of Semitic religion in general, and not of the distinctive features of the spiritual religion of the Old Testament; for the worship of Bethel, Shechem, Beersheba, and the other patriarchal holy places, was mingled with Canaanite elements and is regarded as idolatrous by the prophets; and the later ritual at Mamre, which was put down by the Christian emperors, was purely heathenish.[4]

[1] 1 Sam. xiv. 35.

[2] Gen. xii. 7, xxii. 14, xxviii. 18 *sqq.*; cf. Ex. xvii. 15.

[3] Judg. vi. 20, xiii. 19.

[4] The evidence is collected by Reland, *Palæstina*, p. 711 *sqq.*

This law of precedent as forming a safe rule for ritual institutions is common to the Old Testament religion and to the surrounding heathenism; the difference lies in the interpretation put on it. And even in this respect all parts of the Old Testament are not on the same level By a prophet like Isaiah the residence of Jehovah in Zion is almost wholly dematerialised. Isaiah has not risen to the full height of the New Testament conception that God, who is spirit and is to be worshipped spiritually, makes no distinction of spot with regard to His worship, and is equally near to receive men's prayers in every place; but he falls short of this view, not out of regard for ritual tradition, but because, conceiving Jehovah as the king of Israel, the supreme director of its national polity, he necessarily conceives His kingly activity as going forth from the capital of the nation. The ordinary conception of the Old Testament, in the historical books and in the Law, is not so subtle as this. Jehovah is not tied to one place more than another, but He is not to be found except in the places where "He has set a memorial of His name," and in these He "comes to His worshippers and blesses them" (Ex. xx. 24). Even this view rises above the current ideas of the older Hebrews in so far as it represents the establishment of fixed sanctuaries as an accommodation to the necessities of man. It is obvious that in the history of Jacob's vision the idea is not that Jehovah came to Jacob, but that Jacob was unconsciously guided to the place where there already was a ladder set between earth and heaven, and where, therefore, the godhead was peculiarly accessible. Precisely similar to this is the old Hebrew conception of Sinai or Horeb, "the Mount of God." It is clear that in Ex. iii. the ground about the burning bush does not become holy because God has appeared to Moses. On the contrary, the theophany takes place there because it is holy ground, Jehovah's habitual dwelling-place. In Ex. xix. 4, when Jehovah at Sinai says that He has brought the Israelites unto Himself, the meaning is that He has brought them to the Mount of God; and long after the establishment of the Hebrews in Canaan, poets and prophets describe Jehovah, when He comes to help His people, as marching from Sinai in thundercloud and storm.[1]

This point of view, which in the Old Testament appears only as an occasional survival of primitive thought, corresponds to the ordinary ideas of Semitic heathenism. The local relations of the gods are natural relations; men worship at a particular spot because it is the natural home or haunt of the god. Holy places in this sense are older than temples, and even older than the beginnings of settled life. The nomad shepherd or the savage hunter has no fixed home, and cannot think of his god as having one, but he has a district or beat to which his wanderings are usually confined, and within it again he has his favourite lairs or camping-places. And on this analogy he can imagine for himself tracts of sacred ground habitually frequented by the gods, and special points within these tracts which the deity particularly affects. By and by, under the influence of agriculture and settled life, the sacred tract becomes the estate of the god, and the special sacred points within it become his temples; but originally the former is only a mountain or glade in the unenclosed wilderness, and the latter are merely spots in the desert defined by some natural landmark, a cave, a rock, a fountain or a tree.

We have seen that, when a sanctuary was once constituted, the mere force of tradition and precedent, the

[1] Deut. xxxiii. 2; Judg. v. 4 *sqq.*; Hab. iii. 3. That the sanctity of Sinai is derived from the law-giving there is not the primitive idea. This appears most clearly from the critical analysis of the Pentateuch, but is sufficiently evident from the facts cited above.

continuous custom of worshipping at it, were sufficient to maintain its character. At the more developed sanctuaries the temple, the image of the god, the whole apparatus of ritual, the miraculous legends recounted by the priests, and the marvels that were actually displayed before the eyes of the worshippers, were to an uncritical age sufficient confirmation of the belief that the place was indeed a house of God. But in the most primitive sanctuaries there were no such artificial aids to faith, and it is not so easy to realise the process by which the traditional belief that a spot in the wilderness was the sacred ground of a particular deity became firmly established. Ultimately, as we have seen, the proof that the deity frequents a particular place lies in the fact that he manifests himself there, and the proof is cumulative in proportion to the frequency of the manifestations. The difficulty about this line of proof is not that which naturally suggests itself to our minds. We find it hard to think of a visible manifestation of the godhead as an actual occurrence, but all primitive peoples believe in frequent theophanies, or at least in frequent occasions of personal contact between men and superhuman powers. When all nature is mysterious and full of unknown activities, any natural object or occurrence which appeals strongly to the imagination, or excites sentiments of awe and reverence, is readily taken for a manifestation of divine or demoniac life. But a supernatural being as such is not a god, he becomes a god only when he enters into stated relations with man, or rather with a community of men. In the belief of the heathen Arabs, for example, nature is full of living beings of superhuman kind, the *Jinn* or demons.[1] These *jinn* are not pure spirits but

[1] For details as to the *jinn* in ancient times, see Wellhausen, *Heidenthum*, p. 135 *sqq.* The later form of the belief in such beings, much modified by

corporeal beings, more like beasts than men, for they are ordinarily represented as hairy, or have some other animal shape, as that of an ostrich or a snake. Their bodies are not phantasms, for if a *jinnī* is killed a solid carcase remains; but they have certain mysterious powers of appearing and disappearing, or even of changing their aspect and temporarily assuming human form, and when they are offended they can avenge themselves in a supernatural way, *e.g.* by sending disease or madness. Like the wild beasts, they have, for the most part, no friendly or stated relations with men, but are outside the pale of man's society, and frequent savage and deserted places far from the wonted tread of men.[1] It appears from several poetical passages of the Old Testament that the northern Semites believed in demons of a precisely similar kind, hairy beings (*sĕʿīrīm*), nocturnal monsters (*līlīth*), which haunted waste and desolate places, in fellowship with jackals and ostriches and other animals that shun the abodes of man.[2]

In Islam the gods of heathenism are degraded into *jinn*, just as the gods of north Semitic heathenism are called *sĕʿīrīm*[3] in Lev. xvii. 7, or as the gods of Greece and Rome became devils to the early Christians. In all these cases the adherents of a higher faith were not prepared to deny that the heathen gods really existed, and

Islam, is illustrated by Lane in Note 21 of the Introduction to his version of the *Arabian Nights*. In the old translation of the *Arabian Nights* they are called Genii. See also Van Vloten in *Vienna Or. Jour.* 1893, p. 169 *sqq.*, from Al-Jāḥiẓ.

[1] Certain kinds of them, however, frequent trees and even human habitations, and these were identified with the serpents which appear and disappear so mysteriously about walls and the roots of trees. See Nöldeke, *Ztschr. f. Völkerpsych.* 1860, p. 412 *sqq.*; Wellh. *ut sup.* p. 137. For the snake as the form of the *jinn* of trees, see Rasmussen, *Addit.* p. 71, compared with Jauharī and the *Lisān*, *s. rad.* حمط.

[2] Isa. xiii. 21, xxxiv. 14; cf. Luke xi. 24.

[3] "Hairy demons," E.V. "devils," but in Isa. xiii. 21 "satyrs."

did the things recorded of them; the difference between gods and demons lies not in their nature and power—for the heathen themselves did not rate the power of their gods at omnipotence—but in their relations to man. The *jinn* would make very passable gods, for the cruder forms of heathenism, if they only had a circle of human dependants and worshippers; and conversely a god who loses his worshippers falls back into the ranks of the demons, as a being of vague and indeterminate powers who, having no fixed personal relations to men, is on the whole to be regarded as an enemy. The demons, like the gods, have their particular haunts which are regarded as awful and dangerous places. But the haunt of the *jinn* differs from a sanctuary as the *jinn* themselves differ from gods. The one is feared and avoided, the other is approached, not indeed without awe, but yet with hopeful confidence; for though there is no essential physical distinction between demons and gods, there is the fundamental moral difference that the *jinn* are strangers and so, by the law of the desert, enemies, while the god, to the worshippers who frequent his sanctuary, is a known and friendly power. In fact the earth may be said to be parcelled out between demons and wild beasts on the one hand, and gods and men on the other.[1] To the former belong the untrodden wilderness with all its unknown perils, the wastes and jungles that lie outside the familiar tracks and pasture grounds of the tribe, and which only the boldest men venture upon without terror; to the latter belong the regions that man knows and habitually frequents, and within which he has established relations, not only with his human neighbours, but with the super-

[1] The close association between demons and wild beasts is well brought out in a scholion to Ibn Hishām (ii. 9, l. 20, 23), where wild beasts and serpents swarm round a ruin, and every one who seeks to carry anything away from it is stricken by the *jinn*.

natural beings that have their haunts side by side with him. And as man gradually encroaches on the wilderness and drives back the wild beasts before him, so the gods in like manner drive out the demons, and spots that were once feared, as the habitation of mysterious and presumably malignant powers, lose their terrors and either become common ground or are transformed into the seats of friendly deities. From this point of view the recognition of certain spots as haunts of the gods is the religious expression of the gradual subjugation of nature by man. In conquering the earth for himself primitive man has to contend not only with material difficulties but with superstitious terror of the unknown, paralysing his energies and forbidding him freely to put forth his strength to subdue nature to his use. Where the unknown demons reign he is afraid to set his foot and make the good things of nature his own. But where the god has his haunt he is on friendly soil, and has a protector near at hand; the mysterious powers of nature are his allies instead of his enemies, "he is in league with the stones of the field, and the wild beasts of the field are at peace with him."[1]

The triumph of the gods over the demons, like the triumph of man over wild beasts, must have been effected very gradually, and may be regarded as finally sealed and secured only in the agricultural stage, when the god of the community became also the supreme lord of the land and the author of all the good things therein. When this stage was reached the demons—or supernatural beings that have no stated relations to their human neighbours—were either driven out into waste and untrodden places, or were reduced to insignificance as merely subordinate

[1] Job v. 23. The allusion to the wild beasts is characteristic; cf. Hos. ii. 20 (18); 2 Kings xvii. 26. An Arabian parallel in Ibn Sa'd, No. 145, with Wellhausen's note, *Skizzen*, iv. 194.

beings of which private superstition might take account, but with which public religion had nothing to do. Within the region frequented by a community of men the god of the community was supreme; every phenomenon that seemed supernatural was ordinarily referred to his initiative and regarded as a token of his personal presence, or of the presence of his messengers and agents; and in consequence every place that had special supernatural associations was regarded, not as a haunt of unknown demons, but as a holy place of the known god. This is the point of view which prevailed among the ancient Hebrews, and undoubtedly prevailed also among their Canaanite neighbours. Up to a certain point the process involved in all this is not difficult to follow. That the powers that haunt a district in which men live and prosper must be friendly powers is an obvious conclusion. But it is not so easy to see how the vague idea of supernatural but friendly neighbours passes into the precise conception of a definite local god, or how the local power comes to be confidently identified with the tribal god of the community. The tribal god, as we have seen, has very definite and permanent relations to his worshippers, of a kind quite different from the local relations which we have just been speaking of; he is not merely their friendly neighbour, but (at least in most cases) their kinsman and the parent of their race. How does it come about that the parent of a race of men is identified with the superhuman being that haunts a certain spot, and manifests himself there by visible apparitions, or other evidence of his presence satisfactory to the untutored mind? The importance of such an identification is enormous, for it makes a durable alliance between man and certain parts of nature which are not subject to his will and control, and so permanently raises his position in the scale of the universe, setting him free, within a certain range, from the crushing sense of constant insecurity and vague dread of the unknown powers that close him in on every side. So great a step in the emancipation of man from bondage to his natural surroundings cannot have been easily made, and is not to be explained by any slight *à priori* method. The problem is not one to be solved off-hand, but to be carefully kept in mind as we continue our studies.

There is one thing, however, which it may be well to note at once. We have seen that through the local god, who on the one hand has fixed relations to a race of men, and on the other hand has fixed relations to a definite sphere of nature, the worshipper is brought into stated and permanent alliance with certain parts of his material environment which are not subject to his will and control. But within somewhat narrow limits exactly the same thing is effected, in the very earliest stage of savage society, and in a way that does not involve any belief in an individual stock-god, through the institution of totemism. In the totem stage of society each kinship or stock of savages believes itself to be physically akin to some natural kind of animate or inanimate things, most generally to some kind of animal. Every animal of this kind is looked upon as a brother, is treated with the same respect as a human clansman, and is believed to aid his human relations by a variety of friendly services.[1] The importance of such a permanent alliance, based on the indissoluble bond of kinship, with a whole group of natural beings lying outside the sphere of humanity, is not to be measured by our knowledge of what animals can and cannot do. For

[1] See J. G. Frazer, *Totemism* (Edinburgh: A. & C. Black, 1887), p. 20 *sqq.* This little volume is the most convenient summary of the main facts about totemism.

as their nature is imperfectly known, savage imagination clothes them with all sort of marvellous attributes; it is seen that their powers differ from those of man, and it is supposed that they can do many things that are beyond his scope. In fact they are invested with gifts such as we should call supernatural, and of the very same kind which heathenism ascribes to the gods—for example with the power of giving omens and oracles, of healing diseases and the like.

The origin of totemism is as much a problem as the origin of local gods. But it is highly improbable that the two problems are independent; for in both cases the thing to be explained is the emancipation of a society of men from the dread of certain natural agencies, by the establishment of the conception of a physical alliance and affinity between the two parts. It is a strong thing to suppose that a conception so remarkable as this, which is found all over the world, and which among savage races is invariably put in the totem form, had an altogether distinct and independent origin among those races which we know only in a state of society higher than savagery. The belief in local nature-gods that are also clan-gods may not be directly evolved out of an earlier totemism, but there can be no reasonable doubt that it is evolved out of ideas or usages which also find their expression in totemism, and therefore must go back to the most primitive stage of savage society. It is important to bear this in mind, if only that we may be constantly warned against explaining primitive religious institutions by conceptions that belong to a relatively advanced stage of human thought. But the comparison of totemism can do more than this negative service to our enquiry, for it calls our attention to certain habits of very early thought which throw light on several points in the conception of local sanctuaries.

In the system of totemism men have relations not with individual powers of nature, *i.e.* with gods, but with certain classes of natural agents. The idea is that nature, like mankind, is divided into groups or societies of things, analogous to the groups or kindreds of human society. As life analogous to human life is imagined to permeate all parts of the universe, the application of this idea may readily be extended to inanimate as well as to animate things. But the statistics of totemism show that the natural kinds with which the savage mind was most occupied were the various species of animals. It is with them especially that he has permanent relations of kinship or hostility, and round them are gathered in a peculiar degree his superstitious hopes and fears and observances. Keeping these facts before us, let us look back for a moment at the Arabian *jinn*. One difference between gods and *jinn* we have already noted; the gods have worshippers, and the *jinn* have not. But there is another difference that now forces itself on our attention; the gods have individuality, and the *jinn* have not. In the *Arabian Nights* we find *jinn* with individual names and distinctive personalities, but in the old legends the individual *jinnī* who may happen to appear to a man has no more a distinct personality than a beast.[1] He is only one of a group of beings which to man are indistinguishable from

[1] This may be illustrated by reference to a point of grammar which is of some interest and is not made clear in the ordinary books. The Arab says "the *ghūl* appeared," not "a *ghūl* appeared," just as David says "the lion came and the bear" (1 Sam. xvii. 34; Amos iii. 12, v. 19). The definite article is used because in such cases definition cannot be carried beyond the indication of the species. The individuals are numerically different, but qualitatively indistinguishable. This use of the article is sharply to be distinguished from such a case as האיש in 1 Sam. ix. 9, where the article is generic, and a general practice of men is spoken of; and also from cases like הפליט (Gen. xiv. 13), האיב, גאל הדם, etc., where the noun is really a verbal adjective implying an action, and the person is defined by the action ascribed to him.

one another, and which are regarded as making up a nation or clan of superhuman beings,[1] inhabiting a particular locality, and united together by bonds of kinship and by the practice of the blood-feud, so that the whole clan acts together in defending its haunts from intrusion or in avenging on men any injury done to one of its members.[2] This conception of the communities of the *jinn* is precisely identical with the savage conception of the animal creation. Each kind of animal is regarded as an organised kindred, held together by ties of blood and the practice of blood revenge, and so presenting a united front when it is assailed by men in the person of any of its members. Alike in the Arabian superstitions about the *jinn* and in savage superstitions about animals it is this solidarity between all the members of one species, rather than the strength of the individual *jinnī* or animal, that makes it an object of superstitious terror.

These points of similarity between the families of the *jinn* in Arabia and the families of animals among savages are sufficiently striking, but they do not nearly exhaust the case. We have already seen that the *jinn* usually appear to men in animal form, though they can also take the shape of men. This last feature, however, cannot be regarded as constituting a fundamental distinction between

[1] A curious local story about two clans of *jinn*, the B. Mālik and the B. Shaiṣabān may be read in Yācūt, iii. 476 *sqq.* It is a genuine Bedouin tale, but like most later stories of the kind is not strictly mythical, but a free invention on the lines of current superstition. The oldest case of a clan of the *jinn* which is defined by a patronymic and not merely by a local name is perhaps that of the B. Ocaish, Nābigha, xxix. 10; cf. B. Hish. p. 282. But Tha'lab makes the B. Ocaish a human race, and the words of Nābigha are quite consistent with this view. Jinn with personal names appear in several traditions of the prophet, but only, so far as I can see, in such as are manifestly "weak," *i.e.* spurious.

[2] For the blood-feud of the *jinn* the classical example is that in Azracī, p. 261 (see below). But see also Damīrī, *s.v. arcam* (vol. i. p. 23), where we learn that the slayer of a serpent-demon was likely to die or go mad, and this was held to be the revenge of the kin of the slain.

them and ordinary animals in the mind of the Arabs, who believed that there were whole tribes of men who had the power of assuming animal form. On the whole it appears that the supernatural powers of the *jinn* do not differ from those which savages, in the totem stage, ascribe to wild beasts. They appear and disappear mysteriously, and are connected with supernatural voices and warnings, with unexplained sickness or death, just as totem animals are; they occasionally enter into friendly relations or even into marriages with men, but animals do the same in the legends of savages; finally, a madman is possessed by the *jinn* (*majnūn*), but there are a hundred examples of the soul of a beast being held to pass into a man.[1] The accounts of the *jinn* which we possess have come to us from an age when the Arabs were no longer pure savages, and had ceased to ascribe demoniac attributes to most animals; and our narrators, when they repeat tales about animals endowed with speech or supernatural gifts, assume as a matter of course that they are not ordinary animals but a special class of beings. But the stories themselves are just such as savages tell about real animals; the blood-feud between the Banu Sahm and the *jinn* of Dhū Ṭawā is simply a war between men and all creeping things, which, as in the Old Testament, have a common name[2] and are regarded as a single species or kindred; and the "wild beast of the wild beasts of the *jinn*," which Taabbaṭa Sharran slew in a night encounter and carried home under his arm, was as concrete an animal as one can well imagine.[3] The proper form of the *jinn* seems to be

[1] The widespread belief in this form of possession ought to be cited by commentators on Dan. iv. 13.

[2] *Ḥanash*=Heb. שרץ, רמש. For the story see Azracī, p. 261 *sqq.*; Wellh. p. 138.

[3] *Agh.* xviii. 210 *sqq.* Taabbaṭa Sharran is an historical person, and the incident also is probably a fact. From the verses in which he describes his

always that of some kind of lower animal, or a monstrous composition of animal forms, as appears even in later times in the description of the four hundred and twenty species that were marshalled before Solomon.[1] But the tendency to give human shape to creatures that can reason and speak is irresistible as soon as men pass beyond pure savagery, and just as animal gods pass over into anthropomorphic gods, figured as riding on animals or otherwise associated with them, the *jinn* begin to be conceived as manlike in form, and the supernatural animals of the original conception appear as the beasts on which they ride.[2] Ultimately the only animals directly and constantly identified with the *jinn* were snakes and other noxious creeping things. The authority of certain utterances of the prophet had a share in this limitation, but it is

foe it would seem that the supposed *ghūl* was one of the feline carnivora. In Damīrī, ii. 212, last line, a *ghūl* appears in the form of a thieving cat.

[1] Cazwīnī, i. 372 *sq.* Even when they appear in the guise of men they have some animal attribute, *e.g.* a dog's hairy paw in place of a hand, Damīrī, ii. 213, l. 22.

[2] The stories in which the apparition takes this shape are obviously late. When a demon appears riding on a wolf or an ostrich to give his opinion on the merits of the Arabian poets (*Agh.* viii. 78, ix. 163, cited by Wellh. p. 137), we have to do with literary fiction rather than genuine belief; and similarly the story of a *ghūl* who rides on an ostrich in Cazwīnī, i. 373 *sq.*, is only an edifying Moslem tale. These stories stand in marked contrast with the genuine old story in Maidānī, i. 181, where the demon actually is an ostrich. The transition to the anthropomorphic view is seen in the story of Taabbaṭa Sharran, where the monster *ghūl* is called one of the wild beasts of the *jinn*, as if he were only their animal emissary. The riding beasts of the *jinn* are of many species; they include the jackal, the gazelle, the porcupine, and it is mentioned as an exceptional thing that the hare is not one of them (*Ṣiḥāḥ*, *s.v.*; Rasmussen, *Addit.* p. 71, l. 14), for which reason amulets are made from parts of its body (cf. *ZDMG.* xxxix. 329). Prof. De Goeje supplies me with an interesting quotation from Zamakhsharī, *Fāic*, i. 71: "Ignorant people think that wild beasts are the cattle of the *jinn*, and that a man who meets a wild beast is affected by them with mental disorder." The paralysing effect of terror is assigned to supernatural agency. Cf. Arist. *Mir. Ausc.* 145: "In Arabia there is said to be a kind of hyæna, which when it sees a beast first (*i.e.* before being seen, Plato, *Rep.* i. p. 336 D; Theocr. xiv. 22; Virgil, *Ecl.* 9. 54) or treads on a man's shadow, renders it or him incapable of voice and movement."

natural enough that these creatures, of which men everywhere have a peculiar horror and which continue to haunt and molest men's habitations after wild beasts have been driven out into the desert, should be the last to be stripped of their supernatural character.[1]

It appears then that even in modern accounts *jinn* and various kinds of animals are closely associated, while in the older legends they are practically identified, and also that nothing is told of the *jinn* which savages do not tell of animals. Under these circumstances it requires a very exaggerated scepticism to doubt that the *jinn*, with all their mysterious powers, are mainly nothing else than more or less modernised representatives of animal kinds, clothed with the supernatural attributes inseparable from the savage conception of animate nature. A species of *jinn* allied by kinship with a tribe of men would be indistinguishable from a totem kind, and instead of calling the *jinn* gods without worshippers, we may, with greater precision, speak of them as potential totems without human kinsfolk. This view of the nature of the *jinn* helps us to understand the principle on which particular spots were viewed as their haunts. In the vast solitudes of the Arabian desert every strange sound is readily taken to be the murmuring of the *jinn*, and every strange sight to be a demoniac apparition. But when certain spots were fixed on as being pre-eminently haunted places, we must necessarily suppose that the sights and sounds that were deemed supernatural really were more frequent there than elsewhere. Mere fancy might keep the supernatural reputation of a place alive, but in its origin even the uncontrolled

[1] The snake is an object of superstition in all countries. For superstitions connected with "creeping things" in general among the northern Semites, see Ezek. viii. 10. An oath by all the creeping things (*ḥanash*) between the two Ḥarras appears in B. Hish. 10, l. 14, Ṭab. i. 911. 20, in a spurious imitation of the style of the heathen soothsayers.

imagination of the savage must have some point of contact with reality. Now the nocturnal sights and sounds that affray the wayfarer in haunted regions, and the stories of huntsmen who go up into a mountain of evil name and are carried off by the *ghūl*, point distinctly to haunted spots being the places where evil beasts walk by night. Moreover, while the *jinn* frequent waste and desert places in general, their special haunts are just those where wild beasts gather most thickly—not the arid and lifeless desert, but the mountain glades and passes, the neighbourhood of trees and groves, especially the dense untrodden thickets that occupy moist places in the bottoms of the valleys.[1]

These, it is true, are the places where the spontaneous life of nature is most actively exhibited in all its phases, and where therefore it may seem self-evident that man will be most apt to recognise the presence of divine or at least of superhuman powers. But so general an explanation as this is no explanation at all. Primitive religion was not a philosophical pantheism, and the primitive deities were not vague expressions for the principle of life in nature. What we have to explain is that the places where the life of nature is most intense—or rather some of these places—appeared to the primitive Semite to be the habitations, not

[1] All this, and especially the association of the *jinn* with natural thickets, is well brought out by Wellhausen, *Heidenthum*, p. 136, though he offers no explanation of the reason why "the direct impression of divine life present in nature" is associated with so bizarre a conception. In Southern Arabia natural jungles are still avoided as the haunts of wild beasts; no Arab, according to Wrede, willingly spends a night in the Wady Ma'isha, because its jungles are the haunts of many species of dangerous carnivora (Wrede's *Reise in Hadhramaut*, ed. Maltzan, p. 131). The lions of Al-Sharā and of the jungles of the Jordan valley (Zech. xi. 3) may be compared, and it is to be remembered that in savage life, when man's struggle with wild beasts is one of life and death, the awe associated with such places is magnified tenfold. Even in the old Mohammedan literature no sharp line is drawn between danger from wild beasts and danger from *jinn*; see the scholion cited *supra*, p. 121, note.

of abstract divine powers, but of very concrete and tangible beings, with the singular attributes which we have found the *jinn* to possess, and that this belief did not rest on mere general impressions, but was supported by reference to actual demoniac apparitions. The usual vague talk about an instinctive sense of the presence of the deity in the manifestations of natural life does not carry us a whit nearer the comprehension of these beliefs, but it is helpful to note that spots of natural fertility, untouched by man's hand and seldom trodden by his foot, are the favoured haunts of wild beasts, that all savages clothe wild beasts and other animals with the very same supernatural qualities which the Arabs ascribe to the *jinn*, and that the Arabs speak of Baccār as a place famous for its demons in exactly the same matter-of-fact way in which they speak of Al-Sharā and its famous lions.

While the most marked attributes of the *jinn* are plainly derived from animals, it is to be remembered that the savage imagination, which ascribes supernatural powers to all parts of animate nature, extends the sphere of animate life in a very liberal fashion. Totems are not seldom taken from trees, which appear to do everything for their adherents that a totem animal could do. And indeed that trees are animate, and have perceptions, passions and a reasonable soul, was argued even by the early Greek philosophers on such evidence as their movements in the wind and the elasticity of their branches.[1] Thus while the supernatural associations of groves and thickets may appear to be sufficiently explained by the fact that these are the favourite lairs of wild beasts, it appears probable that the association of certain kinds of *jinn* with trees must in many cases be regarded as primary, the trees themselves being conceived as animated demoniac beings.

[1] Aristotle, *De plantis*, i. p. 815; Plutarch, *Plac. Philos.* v. 26.

In Ḥaḍramaut it is still dangerous to touch the sensitive Mimosa, because the spirit that resides in the plant will avenge the injury.[1] The same idea appears in the story of Ḥarb b. Omayya and Mirdās b. Abī 'Amir, historical persons who lived a generation before Mohammed. When these two men set fire to an untrodden and tangled thicket, with the design to bring it under cultivation, the demons of the place flew away with doleful cries in the shape of white serpents, and the intruders died soon afterwards. The *jinn* it was believed slew them "because they had set fire to their dwelling-place."[2] Here the spirits of the trees take serpent form when they leave their natural seats, and similarly in Moslem superstition the *jinn* of the *'oshr* and the *ḥamāṭa* are serpents which frequent trees of these species. But primarily supernatural life and power reside in the trees themselves, which are conceived as animate and even as rational. Moslim b. 'Ocba heard in a dream the voice of the *gharcad* tree designing him to the command of the army of Yazīd against Medina.[3] Or again the value of the gum of the acacia (*samora*) as an amulet is connected wth the idea that it is a clot of menstruous blood (*ḥaiḍ*), *i.e.* that the tree is a woman.[4] And similarly the old Hebrew fables of trees that speak and act like human beings[5] have their original source in the savage personification of vegetable species.

[1] Wrede's *Reise*, ed. Maltzan, p. 131.

[2] *Agh.* vi. 92, xx. 135 *sq.*

[3] *Agh.* i. 14.

[4] Rasmussen, *Add.* p. 71; Zamakhsharī, *Asās*, *s.v.* حيض. New-born children's heads were rubbed with the gum to keep away the *jinn*, just as they used to be daubed with the blood of the sacrifice called *'acīca* (see my *Kinship*, p. 152). The blood of menstruation has supernatural qualities among all races, and the value of the hare's foot as an amulet was connected with the belief that this animal menstruates (Rasm. *ut sup.*). The same thing was affirmed of the hyæna, which has many magical qualities and peculiar affinities to man (*Kinship*, p. 199).

[5] Judg. ix. 8 *sqq.*; 2 Kings xiv. 9.

In brief it is not unjust to say that, wherever the spontaneous life of nature was manifested in an emphatic way, the ancient Semite saw something supernatural. But this is only half the truth; the other half is that the supernatural was conceived in genuinely savage fashion, and identified with the quasi-human life ascribed to the various species of animals or plants or even of inorganic things.

For indeed certain phenomena of inorganic nature directly suggest to the primitive mind the idea of living force, and the presence of a living agent. Thus, to take a trivial example, the mediæval Arabs associate a definite class of demons with sand-whirlwinds and apply the name *zawābi'* indifferently to these phenomena and to the *jinn* that accompany or cause them.[1] More important is the widespread belief that the stars move because they are alive, which underlies the planet and constellation worship of the Semites as of other ancient nations. Volcanic phenomena, in like manner, are taken for manifestations of supernatural life, as we see in the Greek myths of Typhoeus and in the Moslem legend of the crater of Barahūt in Ḥaḍramaut, whose rumblings are held to be the groans of lost souls;[2] probably also in the legend of the "fire of Yemen" in the valley of Ḍarawān which in heathen times is said to have served as an ordeal, devouring the guilty and sparing the innocent;[3] and again,

[1] See the lexx. and also Jāḥiẓ as cited by Vloten, *Vien. Or. J.* vii. 180. In several Arabian legends the eccentric movements of dust-whirlwinds are taken to be the visible signs of a battle between two clans of Jinn (B. Hish. ii. 42, Yācūt, iii. 478; cf. B. Hish. 331 *sq.*).

[2] See Yācūt, i. 598; De Goeje, *Ḥadramaut*, p. 20 (Rev. Col. Intern. 1886). Does this belief rest on an early myth connected with the name of Ḥaḍramaut itself? See Olshausen in *Rhein. Mus.* Ser. 3, vol. viii. p. 322; *Sitzungsb. d. Berliner Ak.* 1879, p. 571 *sqq.*

[3] Ibn Hishām, p. 17, with the scholia; Bekri, p. 621; Yācūt, iii. 470. Yācūt describes the valley as accursed; no plant grew there, no man could traverse it, and no bird fly across it.

mephitic vapours rising from fissures in the earth are taken to be potent spiritual influences.[1] But remote phenomena like the movements of the stars, and exceptional phenomena like volcanoes, influence the savage imagination less than mundane and everyday things, which are not less mysterious to him and touch his common life more closely. It seems to be a mistake to suppose that distant and exceptional things are those from which primitive man forms his general views of the supernatural; on the contrary he interprets the remote by the near, and thinks of heavenly bodies, for example, as men or animals, like the animate denizens of earth.[2] Of all inanimate things that which has the best marked supernatural associations among the Semites is flowing (or, as the Hebrews say, "living") water. In one of the oldest fragments of Hebrew poetry[3] the fountain is addressed as a living being; and sacred wells are among the oldest and most ineradicable objects of reverence among all the Semites, and are credited with oracular powers and a sort of volition by which they receive or reject offerings. Of course these superstitions often take the form of a belief that the sacred spring is the dwelling-place of beings which from time to time emerge from it in human or animal form, but the fundamental

[1] It may be conjectured that the indignation of the *jinn* at the violation of their haunts, as it appears in the story of Harb and Mirdās, would not have been so firmly believed in but for the fact that places such as the *jinn* were thought to frequent are also the haunts of ague, which is particularly active when land is cultivated for the first time. According to a Mohammedan tradition, the Prophet assigned the uplands (*jals*) to the believing jinn, and the deep lowlands (*ghaur*) to the unbelieving. The latter are in Arabia the homes of fever and plague (Damīrī, i. 231).

[2] See Lang, *Myth, Ritual and Religion*, chap. v. Among the Semites the worship of sun, moon and stars does not appear to have had any great vogue in the earliest times. Among the Hebrews there is little trace of it before Assyrian influence became potent, and in Arabia it is by no means so prominent as is sometimes supposed; cf. Wellhausen, p. 173 *sqq*.

[3] Num. xxi. 17, 18: "Spring up, O well! sing ye to it!"

idea is that the water itself is the living organism of a demoniac life, not a mere dead organ.[1]

If now we turn from the haunts of the demons to sanctuaries proper, the seats of known and friendly powers with whom men maintain stated relations, we find that in their physical character the homes of the gods are precisely similar to those of the *jinn*—mountains and thickets, fertile spots beside a spring or stream, or sometimes points defined by the presence of a single notable tree. As man encroaches on the wilderness, and brings these spots within the range of his daily life and walk, they lose their terror but not their supernatural associations, and the friendly deity takes the place of the dreaded demons. The conclusion to be drawn from this is obvious. The physical characters that were held to mark out a holy place are not to be explained by conjectures based on the more developed type of heathenism, but must be regarded as taken over from the primitive beliefs of savage man. The nature of the god did not determine the place of his sanctuary, but conversely the features of the sanctuary had an important share in determining the development of ideas as to the functions of the god. How this was possible we have seen in the conception of the local Baalim. The spontaneous luxuriance of marshy lands already possessed supernatural associations when there was no thought of bringing it under the service of man by cultivation, and when the rich valley bottoms were avoided with superstitious terror as the haunts of formidable natural enemies. How this terror was first broken through, and the transformation of certain groups of hostile demons into friendly and kindred powers was first effected, we cannot tell; we can only say

[1] For the details as to sacred waters among the Semites, see below in Lect. V.

that the same transformation is already effected, by means of totemism, in the most primitive societies of savages, and that there is no record of a stage in human society in which each community of men did not claim kindred and alliance with some group or species of the living powers of nature. But if we take this decisive step for granted, the subsequent development of the relation of the gods to the land follows by a kind of moral necessity, and the transformation of the vague friendly powers that haunt the seats of spontaneous natural life into the beneficent agricultural Baalim, the lords of the land and its waters, the givers of life and fertility to all that dwell on it, goes naturally hand in hand with the development of agriculture and the laws of agricultural society.

I have tried to put this argument in such a way as may not commit us prematurely to the hypothesis that the friendly powers of the Semites were originally totems, *i.e.* that the relations of certain kindred communities of men with certain groups of natural powers were established before these natural powers had ceased to be directly identified with species of plants and animals. But if my analysis of the nature of the *jinn* is correct, the conclusion that the Semites did pass through the totem stage can be avoided only by supposing them to be an exception to the universal rule, that even the most primitive savages have not only enemies but permanent allies (which at so early a stage in society necessarily means kinsfolk) among the non-human or superhuman animate kinds by which the universe is peopled. And this supposition is so extravagant that no one is likely to adopt it. On the other hand, it may be argued with more plausibility that totemism, if it ever did exist, disappeared when the Semites emerged from savagery, and that the religion of the race, in its higher stages, may have rested on altogether independent bases. Whether this hypothesis is or is not admissible must be determined by an actual examination of the higher heathenism. If its rites usages and beliefs really are independent of savage ideas, and of the purely savage conception of nature of which totemism is only one aspect, the hypothesis is legitimate; but it is not legitimate if the higher heathenism itself is permeated in all its parts by savage ideas, and if its ritual and institutions are throughout in the closest contact with savage ritual and institutions of totem type. That the latter is the true state of the case will I believe become overwhelmingly clear as we proceed with our survey of the phenomena of Semitic religion; and a very substantial step towards the proof that it is so has already been taken, when we have found that the sanctuaries of the Semitic world are identical in physical character with the haunts of the *jinn*, so that as regards their local associations the gods must be viewed as simply replacing the plant and animal demons.[1] If this is so we can hardly avoid the conclusion that some of the Semitic gods are of totem origin, and we may expect to find the most distinct traces of this origin at the oldest sanctuaries. But we are not to suppose that every local deity will have totem associations, for new gods as well as new sanctuaries might doubtless spring up at a later stage of human progress than that of which totemism is characteristic. Even holy places that had an old connection with the demons may, in many instances, have come to be looked upon as the abode of friendly powers and fit seats of worship, after the demons had ceased to be directly identified with species of plants and animals, and had

[1] The complete development of this argument as it bears on the nature of the gods must be reserved for a later course of lectures; but a provisional discussion of some points on which a difficulty may arise will be found below: see *Additional Note* A, *Gods, Demons, and Plants or Animals.*

acquired quasi-human forms like the nymph and satyrs of the Greeks. It is one thing to say that the phenomena of Semitic religion carry us back to totemism, and another thing to say that they are all to be explained from totemism.

LECTURE IV

HOLY PLACES IN THEIR RELATION TO MAN

I HAVE spoken hitherto of the physical characters of the sanctuary, as the haunt of divine beings that prove, in the last resort, to be themselves parts of the mundane universe, and so have natural connections with sacred localities; let us now proceed to look at the places of the gods in another aspect, to wit in their relation to men, and the conduct which men are called upon to observe at and towards them. The fundamental principle by which this is regulated is that the sanctuary is holy, and must not be treated as a common place. The distinction between what is *holy* and what is *common* is one of the most important things in ancient religion, but also one which it is very difficult to grasp precisely, because its interpretation varied from age to age with the general progress of religious thought. To us holiness is an ethical idea. God, the perfect being, is the type of holiness; men are holy in proportion as their lives and character are godlike; places and things can be called holy only by a figure, on account of their associations with spiritual things. This conception of holiness goes back to the Hebrew prophets, especially to Isaiah; but it is not the ordinary conception of antique religion, nor does it correspond to the original sense of the Semitic words that we translate by "holy." While it is not easy to fix the exact idea of holiness in ancient Semitic religion, it is quite certain that it has nothing to do with morality and purity of life. Holy persons were such, not in virtue of their character but in virtue of their race, function, or mere material consecration; and at the Canaanite shrines the name of "holy" (masc. *cĕdeshīm*, fem. *cĕdeshōth*) was specially appropriated to a class of degraded wretches, devoted to the most shameful practices of a corrupt religion, whose life, apart from its connection with the sanctuary, would have been disgraceful even from the standpoint of heathenism. But holiness in antique religion is not mainly an attribute of persons. The gods are holy,[1] and their ministers of whatever kind or grade are holy also, but holy seasons holy places and holy things, that is, seasons places and things that stand in a special relation to the godhead and are withdrawn by divine sanction from some or all ordinary uses, are equally to be considered in determining what holiness means. Indeed the holiness of the gods is an expression to which it is hardly possible to attach a definite sense apart from the holiness of their physical surroundings; it shows itself in the sanctity attached to the persons places things and times through which the gods and men come in contact with one another. The holiness of the sanctuary, which is the matter immediately before us, seems also to be on the whole the particular form of sanctity which lends itself most readily to independent investigation. Holy persons things and times, as they are conceived in antiquity, all presuppose the existence of holy places at which the persons minister, the things are preserved, and the times are celebrated. Nay the holiness of the godhead itself is manifest to men, not equally at all places, but specially at those places where the gods are immediately present and from which their activity proceeds. In fact

[1] The Phœnicians speak of the "holy gods" (האלנם הקדשם, *CIS.* No. 3, l. 9, 22), as the Hebrews predicate holiness of Jehovah.

the idea of holiness comes into prominence wherever the gods come into touch with men; it is not so much a thing that characterises the gods and divine things in themselves, as the most general notion that governs their relations with humanity; and, as these relations are concentrated at particular points of the earth's surface, it is at these points that we must expect to find the clearest indications of what holiness means.

At first sight the holiness of the sanctuary may seem to be only the expression of the idea that the sanctuary belongs to the god, that the temple and its precincts are his homestead and domain, reserved for his use and that of his ministers, as a man's house and estate are reserved for himself and his household. In Arabia, for example, where there were great tracts of sacred land, it was forbidden to cut fodder, fell trees, or hunt game;[1] all the

[1] Wellh., *Heidenthum*, p. 102, and refs. there given to the ordinances laid down by Mohammed for the *Ḥaram* of Mecca and the *Ḥimā* of Wajj at Ṭāif. In both cases the ordinance was a confirmation of old usage, and similar rules were laid down by Mohammed for his new *Ḥaram* at Medina (Belādhorī, p. 7 *sq.*). At Mecca the law against killing or chasing animals did not apply to certain noxious creatures. The usually received tradition (Bokhārī, ii. 195, of the Būlāc vocalised ed.) names the raven and the kite, the rat, the scorpion and the "biting dog," which is taken to cover the lion, panther, and wolf, and other carnivora that attack man (Mowaṭṭa, ii. 198). The serpent also was killed without scruple at Minā, which is within the Ḥaram (Bokh. ii. 196, l. 1 *sqq.*). That the protection of the god is not extended to manslaying animals and to the birds of prey that molest the sacred doves is intelligible. The permission to kill vermin is to be compared with the story of the war between the Jinn and the B. Sahm (*supra*, p. 128). From the law against cutting plants the *idhkhir* (*Andropōgon schœnanthus*, or lemon-grass) was excepted by Mohammed with some hesitation, on the demand of Al-Abbās, who pointed out that it was the custom to allow it to be cut for certain purposes. Here unfortunately our texts are obscure and vary greatly, but the variations all depend on the reading of two words of which one is either "smiths" or "graves" and the other "purification" or "roofs" of houses. In the Arabic the variations turn on small graphical points often left out by scribes. I take it that originally the two uses were either both practical, "for the smiths and the (thatching of) house-roofs," or both ceremonial, "for entombment and the purification of houses." As the lemon-grass was valued in antiquity for its perfume, and the fragrant *ḥarmal* was also

natural products of the holy soil were exempt from human appropriation. But it would be rash to conclude that what cannot be the private property of men is therefore the private property of the gods, reserved for the exclusive use of them or their ministers. The positive exercise of legal rights of property on the part of the gods is only possible where they have human representatives to act for them, and no doubt in later times the priests at the greater Semitic sanctuaries did treat the holy reservations as their own domain. But in early times there was no privileged class of sacred persons to assert on their own behalf the doctrine of divine proprietorship, and in these times accordingly the prohibition of private encroachment was consistent with the existence of public or communal rights in holy places and things. In nomadic Arabia sanctuaries are older than any doctrine of property that could possibly be applied to a tract like the *ḥaram* at Mecca or the *ḥimā* of Ṭāif. To constitute private property, according to the ancient doctrine still preserved in Moslem law, a man must build on the soil or cultivate it; there is no property in natural pastures. Every tribe indeed has its own range of plains and valleys, and its own watering-places, by which it habitually encamps at certain seasons and from which it repels aliens by the strong hand. But this does not constitute property, for the boundaries of the tribal land are merely maintained by force against enemies, and not only every tribesman but every covenanted ally has equal and unrestricted right to pitch his tent and drive his cattle where he will. This is still the rule among nomadic tribes, but where there are

used in old Arabia to lay the dead in, and is still used to fumigate houses, the second reading is the better. The lemon-grass might be cut for purposes of a religious or quasi-religious character. Mohammed probably hesitated because these uses were connected with heathen superstition. Cf. *Muh. in Medina*, p. 338.

fixed villages the inhabitants claim an exclusive right to a certain circuit of pasture round the township. Claims of this description are older than Islam, and are guaranteed by Mohammed in several of his treaties with new converts, in varying terms, which evidently follow the variations of customary law in different parts of the peninsula. In such cases we may legitimately speak of *communal* property in pasture-lands, but *private* property in such has never been known to Arabian law.[1]

From this statement it is obvious that the Arabs might indeed conceive the temple to be the personal property of the god, but could not bring the rules affecting sacred pastures under the same category. On the analogies that have just come before us we can readily understand that the haunts of unfriendly demons would be shunned for fear of their enmity, but the friendly god could have no exclusive right to hold waste lands against his worshippers. At Mecca the Coraish built houses or dug wells and enjoyed the full right of property in the work of their hands, and the open Ḥaram was free to every man's cattle like an ordinary tribal or communal pasture-ground. These rules are so obviously in accordance with the whole spirit of ancient Arabian institutions that they can hardly have been peculiar to Mecca. About other sacred tracts, which lost their religious prerogative through the spread of Islam, our information is too scanty to permit a positive statement, yet it seems probable that at most sanctuaries embracing a stretch of pasture-ground, the right of grazing was free to the community of the god, but not to outsiders. It appears to me that this formula covers all the known facts if we make a reasonable allowance for local variations

[1] See Ibn Sa'd, Nos. 21, 23, 121, with Wellhausen's refs. to Doughty, ii. 245, and especially Ibn Hishām, p. 955. In two cases the reserved pasture is called a *ḥimā*, and this is the term still used. Cf. on the law of pasture, Abū Yūsuf, *Kit. al-Kharāj* (Būlāc, A.H. 1302), p. 58 *sq.*

in the definition of outsiders. Where the sacred tract was attached to the sanctuary of a town, it might be an open question whether the privileged religious community was limited to the townsmen or included a wider circle of the surrounding Bedouins who were accustomed to pay occasional homage at the shrine. On the other hand, a sanctuary that lay between the waters of several tribes and was equally visited by all would afford a common pasture-ground where enemies could meet and feed their flocks in security under the peace of the god. And finally, there seem to have been some Arabian sanctuaries that were neither attached to a town nor intertribal, but practically were in the hands of a single family of hereditary priests. At such sanctuaries all worshippers were in some sense outsiders, and the priests might claim the *ḥimā* as a *quasi*-private domain for themselves and the god. All these cases seem to find more or less clear exemplification in the fragmentary details that have come down to us. At the *ḥimā* of Wajj, attached to the sanctuary of al-Lāt at Ṭāif, the rules are practically identical with those at Mecca; and when we observe that Mohammed confirmed these rules, in the interest of the inhabitants,[1] at the same time that he destroyed al-Lāt and did away with the ancient sanctity of the spot, it is natural to infer that in other cases also the *ḥimā* which he allowed to subsist as a communal pasture-ground round a village or town was originally a sacred tract, protected from encroachment by the fear of the god rather than by any civil authority. It is indeed plain that with such a property-law as has been described, and in the absence of any intertribal authority, religion was the only power, other than the high

[1] According to Bekrī, p. 838, the treaty of Mohammed with the Thacīf, or people of Ṭāif, contained the clause *wathacīfun aḥaccu 'n-nāsi biwajjin*, so that the confirmation of the old taboos was clearly meant to benefit them. And so it did; for to cut down the wood is the quickest way to ruin a pasture-ground for camels. See the interesting remarks of Floyer in *Journ. R. A. Soc.*

hand, that could afford any security to a communal pasture, and we are not without evidence as to how this security was effected. The privileges of the Ḥaram at Mecca and Medina are still placed under a religious sanction; on those who violated the latter Mohammed invoked the irrevocable curse of God and the angels and all men.[1] The restrictions on the use of other *ḥimās* have under Islam only a civil sanction, but the punishments appointed by Mohammed for those who violate them are manifestly based on old religious customs exactly parallel to the *taboos* prevalent among savage nations whose notions of property are still imperfectly developed. If a wood-cutter intruded on the *ḥimā* of Wajj or Nacī', he forfeited his hatchet and his clothes; if a man unlawfully grazed his cattle on the *ḥimā* of Jorash, the cattle were forfeit.[2] To us these seem to be arbitrary penalties, attached by the will of the lawgiver to a breach of civil law; but to the Arabs, just emerged from heathenism, this was not so. We shall presently see that the ancient Semites, like other early races, deemed holiness to be propagated by physical contagion, so that common things brought into the sanctuary became holy and could not be safely withdrawn again to common use. Thus the forfeiture of clothes in Islamic law is only a continuation of the old rule, attested for the sanctuary of Mecca, that common raiment worn in the sacred place had to be cast off and left behind;[3] while the forfeiture of cattle at Jorash follows the rule recorded for the sanctuary of Al-Jalsad, that cattle straying from outside into the *ḥimā* become sacred and cannot be reclaimed. By students of primitive society these rules will at once be recognised as belonging to the sphere of *taboo* and not of

[1] Belādhorī, p. 8.
[2] Ibn Hishām, p. 918; Belādhorī, p. 9; Ibn Hishām, p. 955.
[3] For the details on this point see below, *Additional Note* B.

property-law; those who are not familiar with the subject will find it further elucidated at the end of this volume in *Additional Note* B.

Hitherto we have been speaking of a type of sanctuary older than the institution of property in land. But even where the doctrine of property is fully developed, holy places and holy things, except where they have been appropriated to the use of kings and priests, fall under the head of public rather than of private estate. According to ancient conceptions, the interests of the god and his community are too closely identified to admit of a sharp distinction between sacred purposes and public purposes, and as a rule nothing is claimed for the god in which his worshippers have not a right to share. Even the holy dues presented at the sanctuary are not reserved for the private use of the deity, but are used to furnish forth sacrificial feasts in which all who are present partake. So too the sanctuaries of ancient cities served the purpose of public parks and public halls, and the treasures of the gods, accumulated within them, were a kind of state treasure, preserved by religious sanctions against peculation and individual encroachment, but available for public objects in time of need. The Canaanites of Shechem took money from their temple to provide means for Abimelech's enterprise, when they resolved to make him their king; and the sacred treasure of Jerusalem, originally derived from the fruits of David's campaigns, was used by his successors as a reserve fund available in great emergencies. On the whole, then, it is evident that the difference between holy things and common things does not originally turn on ownership, as if common things belonged to men and holy things to the gods. Indeed there are many holy things which are also private property, images, for example, and the other appurtenances of domestic sanctuaries.

Thus far it would appear that the rights of the gods in holy places and things fall short of ownership, because they do not exclude a right of user or even of property by man in the same things. But in other directions the prerogatives of the gods, in respect of that which is holy, go beyond what is involved in ownership. The approach to ancient sanctuaries was surrounded by restrictions which cannot be regarded as designed to protect the property of the gods, but rather fall under the notion that they will not tolerate the vicinity of certain persons (*e.g.* such as are physically unclean) and certain actions (*e.g.* the shedding of blood). Nay, in many cases the assertion of a man's undoubted rights as against a fugitive at the sanctuary is regarded as an encroachment on its holiness; justice cannot strike the criminal, and a master cannot recover his runaway slave, who has found asylum on holy soil. In the Old Testament the legal right of asylum is limited to the case of involuntary homicide;[1] but the wording of the law shows that this was a narrowing of ancient custom, and many heathen sanctuaries of the Phœnicians and Syrians retained even in Roman times what seems to have been an unlimited right of asylum.[2] At certain Arabian

[1] Ex. xxi. 13, 14. Here the right of asylum belongs to all altars, but it was afterwards limited, on the abolition of the local altars, to certain old sanctuaries—the cities of refuge.

[2] This follows especially from the account in Tacitus, *Ann.* iii. 60 *sqq.*, of the inquiry made by Tiberius into abuses of the right of asylum. Among the holy places to which the right was confirmed after due investigation were Paphos and Amathus, both of them Phœnician sanctuaries. The asylum at the temple of Melcarth at Tyre is mentioned by Diodorus, xvii. 41. 8. There was also a right of asylum at Daphne near Antioch (Strabo, xvi. 2. 6; 2 Macc. iv. 33), and many Phœnician and Syrian towns are designated as asylums on their coins; see Head, *Greek Num.*, Index iv., under ΑΣΥΛΟΣ and ΙΕΡΑΣ ΑΣΥΛΟΥ. The Heracleum at the fishcuring station near the Canobic mouth of the Nile (Herod. ii. 113) may also be cited, for its name and place leave little doubt that it was a Phœnician temple. Here the fugitive slave was dedicated by being tattooed with sacred marks—a Semitic custom; cf. Lucian, *Dea Syria*, lix., and *Aghānī*,

sanctuaries the god gave shelter to all fugitives without distinction, and even stray or stolen cattle that reached the holy ground could not be reclaimed by their owners.[1] What was done with these animals is not stated; possibly they enjoyed the same liberty as the consecrated camels which the Arabs, for various reasons, were accustomed to release from service and suffer to roam at large. These camels seem to be sometimes spoken of as the property of the deity,[2] but they were not used for his service. Their consecration was simply a limitation of man's right to use them.[3]

We have here another indication that the relations of holiness to the institution of property are mainly negative. Holy places and things are not so much reserved for the use of the god as surrounded by a network of restrictions and disabilities which forbid them to be used by men except in particular ways, and in certain cases forbid them to be used at all. As a rule the restrictions are such as to prevent the appropriation of holy things by men, and

vii. 110, l. 26, where an Arab patron stamps his clients with his camel mark. I owe the last reference to Prof. de Goeje.

[1] Yācūt, *s.v. Jalsad* and *Fals*; Wellhausen, pp. 48, 50.

[2] See the verse from Ibn Hishām, p. 58, explained by Wellh. p. 103. The grounds on which Wellhausen concludes that these consecrated camels formed a sacred herd grazing on the holy pasture of the god are not quite satisfactory. The story in Mofaḍḍal, *Amthāl*, p. 19, shows that sometimes at least they remained with their old herd; and this agrees best with the statement of the Arabian philologists.

[3] *E.g.* their milk might be drunk only by guests (Ibn Hishām, p. 58). Similarly, consecration sometimes meant no more than that men might eat the flesh but not women, or that only particular persons might eat of it (Sura, vi. 139 *sq.*). Above all, the consecrated camel might not be ridden, whence the name *ḥāmī*. It is recorded on the authority of Laith (Lisān, xix. 341) that in certain cases the back of the camel was so injured that it could not be ridden; but this certainly was not the universal rule, for in an emergency a man mounts a sacred camel to pursue robbers (Mofaḍḍal, *Amthāl*, p. 19; Freytag, *Ar. Provv.* i. 352). The *immissio hirudinum in tergum*, Rasmussen, *Add.* p. 70; Wellhausen, p. 111, is only a corruption of what Laith tells. In Rasmussen's text read اغلاق for اعلاق, and سناسن for سنامن.

sometimes they cancel existing rights of property. But they do so only by limiting the right of user, and in the case of objects like idols, which no one would propose to use except for sacred purposes, a thing may be holy and still be private property. From this point of view it would appear that common things are such as men have licence to use freely at their own good pleasure without fear of supernatural penalties, while holy things may be used only in prescribed ways and under definite restrictions, on pain of the anger of the gods. That holiness is essentially a restriction on the licence of man in the free use of natural things, seems to be confirmed by the Semitic roots used to express the idea. No stress can be laid on the root קדש, which is that commonly used by the northern Semites, for of this the original meaning is very uncertain, though there is some probability that it implies "separation" or "withdrawal." But the root חרם, which is mainly employed in Arabic but runs through the whole Semitic field, undoubtedly conveys the notion of prohibition, so that a sacred thing is one which, whether absolutely or in certain relations, is prohibited to human use.[1] The same idea of prohibition or interdiction associated with that of protection from encroachment is found in the root חמי, from which is derived the word *ḥimā*, denoting a sacred enclosure or *temenos*.[2]

We have already found reason to think that in Arabia

[1] In Hebrew this root is mainly applied to such consecration as implies absolute separation from human use and association, *i.e.* the total destruction of an accursed thing, or in more modern times excommunication. Somewhat similar is the sense of *ḥarām* in the Arabic form of oath "*ana ḥarāmum in . . .*," *Agh.* xix. 27. 18.

[2] Hence perhaps the name of Hamath on the Orontes; Lagarde, *Bildung der Nomina*, p. 156. The primary sense of the root, as Nöldeke has remarked, is "to watch over," whence in Palestinian Aramaic it comes to be the usual word for "to see," while in Hebrew again the word חומה, "a wall," is derived from it.

the holiness of places is older than the institution of property in land, and the view of holiness that has just been set forth enables us to understand why it should be so. We have found that from the earliest times of savagery certain spots were dreaded and shunned as the haunts of supernatural beings. These, however, are not holy places any more than an enemy's ground is holy; they are not hedged round by definite restrictions, but altogether avoided as full of indefinite dangers. But when men establish relations with the powers that haunt a spot, it is at once necessary that there should be rules of conduct towards them and their surroundings. These rules moreover have two aspects. On the one hand, the god and his worshippers form a single community—primarily, let us suppose, a community of kinship—and so all the social laws that regulate men's conduct towards a clansman are applicable to their relations to the god. But, on the other hand, the god has natural relations to certain physical things, and these must be respected also; he has himself a natural life and natural habits in which he must not be molested. Moreover the mysterious superhuman powers of the god—the powers which we call supernatural—are manifested, according to primitive ideas, in and through his physical life, so that every place and thing which has natural associations with the god is regarded, if I may borrow a metaphor from electricity, as charged with divine energy and ready at any moment to discharge itself to the destruction of the man who presumes to approach it unduly. Hence in all their dealings with natural things men must be on their guard to respect the divine prerogative, and this they are able to do by knowing and observing the rules of holiness, which prescribe definite restrictions and limitations in their dealings with the god and all natural things that in any way pertain to the god. Thus we see that holiness is not necessarily limited to things that are the property of the deity to the exclusion of men; it applies equally to things in which both gods and men have an interest, and in the latter case the rules of holiness are directed to regulate man's use of the holy thing in such a way that the godhead may not be offended or wronged.

Rules of holiness in the sense just explained, *i.e.* a system of restrictions on man's arbitrary use of natural things, enforced by the dread of supernatural penalties,[1] are found among all primitive peoples. It is convenient to have a distinct name for this primitive institution, to mark it off from the later developments of the idea of holiness in advanced religions, and for this purpose the Polynesian term *taboo* has been selected.[2] The field covered by taboos among savage and half-savage races is very wide, for there is no part of life in which the savage does not feel himself to be surrounded by mysterious agencies and recognise the need of walking warily. Moreover all taboos do not belong to religion proper, that is, they are not always rules of conduct for the regulation of man's contact with deities that, when taken in the right way, may be counted on as friendly, but rather appear in many cases to be precautions against the approach of malignant enemies—against contact with evil spirits and the like. Thus alongside of taboos that exactly correspond to rules of holiness, protecting the inviolability of idols and sanctuaries, priests and chiefs, and generally of all persons and things pertaining to the gods and their worship, we find another kind of taboo which in

[1] Sometimes by civil penalties also. For in virtue of its solidarity the whole community is compromised by the impiety of any one of its members, and is concerned to purge away the offence.

[2] A good account of taboo, with references to the best sources of information on the subject, is given by Mr. J. G. Frazer in the 9th ed. of the *Encycl. Britan*, vol. xxiii. p. 15 *sqq.*

the Semitic field has its parallel in rules of uncleanness. Women after child-birth, men who have touched a dead body and so forth, are temporarily taboo and separated from human society, just as the same persons are unclean in Semitic religion. In these cases the person under taboo is not regarded as holy, for he is separated from approach to the sanctuary as well as from contact with men; but his act or condition is somehow associated with supernatural dangers, arising, according to the common savage explanation, from the presence of formidable spirits which are shunned like an infectious disease. In most savage societies no sharp line seems to be drawn between the two kinds of taboo just indicated, and even in more advanced nations the notions of holiness and uncleanness often touch. Among the Syrians, for example, swine's flesh was taboo, but it was an open question whether this was because the animal was holy or because it was unclean.[1] But though not precise, the distinction between what is holy and what is unclean is real; in rules of holiness the motive is respect for the gods, in rules of uncleanness it is primarily fear of an unknown or hostile power, though ultimately, as we see in the Levitical legislation, the law of clean and unclean may be brought within the sphere of divine ordinances, on the view that uncleanness is hateful to God and must be avoided by all that have to do with Him.

The fact that all the Semites have rules of uncleanness as well as rules of holiness, that the boundary between the two is often vague, and that the former as well as the latter present the most startling agreement in point of detail with savage *taboos*,[2] leaves no reasonable doubt as to the origin and ultimate relations of the idea of holiness.

[1] Lucian, *Dea Syr.* liv.; cf. Antiphanes, *ap.* Athen. iii. p. 95 [Meineke, *Fr. Com. Gr.* iii. 68].

[2] See *Additional Note* B, *Holiness, Uncleanness, and Taboo.*

On the other hand, the fact that the Semites—or at least the northern Semites—distinguish between the holy and the unclean, marks a real advance above savagery. All taboos are inspired by awe of the supernatural, but there is a great moral difference between precautions against the invasion of mysterious hostile powers and precautions founded on respect for the prerogative of a friendly god. The former belong to magical superstition—the barrenest of all aberrations of the savage imagination—which, being founded only on fear, acts merely as a bar to progress and an impediment to the free use of nature by human energy and industry. But the restrictions on individual licence which are due to respect for a known and friendly power allied to man, however trivial and absurd they may appear to us in their details, contain within them germinant principles of social progress and moral order. To know that one has the mysterious powers of nature on one's side so long as one acts in conformity with certain rules, gives a man strength and courage to pursue the task of the subjugation of nature to his service. To restrain one's individual licence, not out of slavish fear, but from respect for a higher and beneficent power, is a moral discipline of which the value does not altogether depend on the reasonableness of the sacred restrictions; an English schoolboy is subject to many unreasonable taboos, which are not without value in the formation of character. But finally, and above all, the very association of the idea of holiness with a beneficent deity, whose own interests are bound up with the interests of the community, makes it inevitable that the laws of social and moral order, as well as mere external precepts of physical observance, shall be placed under the sanction of the god of the community. Breaches of social order are recognised as offences against the holiness of the deity, and the development of law and morals is made possible, at a stage when human sanctions are still wanting, or too imperfectly administered to have much power, by the belief that the restrictions on human licence which are necessary to social well-being are conditions imposed by the god for the maintenance of a good understanding between himself and his worshippers.

As every sanctuary was protected by rigid taboos it was important that its site and limits should be clearly marked. From the account already given of the origin of holy places, it follows that in very many cases the natural features of the spot were sufficient to distinguish it. A fountain with its margin of rich vegetation, a covert of jungle haunted by lions, a shaggy glade on the mountain-side, a solitary eminence rising from the desert, where toppling blocks of weather-beaten granite concealed the dens of the hyæna and the bear, needed only the support of tradition to bear witness for themselves to their own sanctity. In such cases it was natural to draw the border of the holy ground somewhat widely, and to allow an ample verge on all sides of the sacred centre. In Arabia, as we have seen, the *ḥimā* sometimes enclosed a great tract of pasture land roughly marked off by pillars or cairns, and the *ḥaram* or sacred territory of Mecca extends for some hours' journey on almost every side of the city. The whole mountain of Horeb was sacred ground, and so probably was Mount Hermon, for its name means "holy," and the summit and slopes still bear the ruins of many temples.[1] In like manner Renan concludes from the multitude of sacred remains along the course of the Adonis, in the Lebanon, that the whole valley was a kind of sacred territory of the god from whom the river had its name.[2] In a cultivated and thickly-peopled land

[1] For the sanctity of Hermon see further Reland, *Palæstina*, p. 323.
[2] Renan, *Mission de Phénicie* (1864), p. 295.

it was difficult to maintain a rigid rule of sanctity over a wide area, and strict taboos were necessarily limited to the temples and their immediate enclosures, while in a looser sense the whole city or land of the god's worshippers was held to be the god's land and to participate in his holiness. Yet some remains of the old sanctity of whole regions survived even in Syria to a late date. Iamblichus, in the last days of heathenism, still speaks of Mount Carmel as "sacred above all mountains and forbidden of access to the vulgar," and here Vespasian worshipped at the solitary altar, embowered in inviolable thickets, to which ancient tradition forbade the adjuncts of temple and image.[1]

The taboos or restrictions applicable within the wide limits of these greater sacred tracts have already been touched upon. The most universal of them was that men were not allowed to interfere with the natural life of the spot. No blood might be shed and no tree cut down; an obvious rule whether these living things are regarded as the protected associates of the god, or—which perhaps was the earlier conception—as participating in the divine life. In some cases all access to the Arabian *ḥimā* was forbidden, as at the sacred tract marked off round the grave of Ibn Ṭofail.[2] For with the Arabs grave and sanctuary were

[1] Iamblicus, *Vit. Pyth.* iii. (15); Tacitus, *Hist.* ii. 78. From 1 Kings xviii. it would be clear, apart from the classical testimonies, that Carmel was a sacred mountain of the Phœnicians. It had also an altar of Jehovah, and this made it the fit place for the contest between Jehovah-worship and Baal-worship. Carmel is still clothed with thickets as it was in Old Testament times (Amos i. 2; Mic. vii. 14; Cant. vii. 5); and Amos ix. 3, Mic. vii. 14, where its woods appear as a place of refuge, do not receive their full force till we combine them with Iamblichus's notice that the mountain was an *ἄβατον*, where the flocks, driven up into the forest in autumn to feed on the leaves (as is still done, Thomson, *Land and Book* [1860], pp. 204 *sq.*, 485), were inviolable, and where the fugitive found a sure asylum. The sanctity of Carmel is even now not extinct, and the scene at the Festival of Elijah, described by Seetzen, ii. 96 *sq.*, is exactly like an old Canaanite feast.

[2] *Agh.* xv. 139; Wellh. p. 163. This is not the place to go into the

kindred ideas, and famous chiefs and heroes were honoured by the consecration of their resting-place. But an absolute exclusion of human visitors, while not unintelligible at a tomb, could hardly be maintained at a sanctuary which contained a place of worship, and we have seen that some *ḥimās* were open pastures, while the *ḥaram* at Mecca even contained a large permanent population.[1] The tendency was evidently to a gradual relaxation of burdensome restrictions, not necessarily because religious reverence declined, but from an increasing confidence that the god was his servants' well-wisher and did not press his prerogative unduly. Yet the "jealousy" of the deity—an idea familiar to us from the Old Testament—was never lost sight of in Semitic worship. In the higher forms of religion this quality, which nearly corresponds to self-respect and the sense of personal dignity in a man, readily lent itself to an ethical interpretation, so that the jealousy of the deity was mainly conceived to be indignation against wrong-doing, as an offence against the honour of the divine sovereign;[2] but in savage times the personal

general question of the worship of ancestors. See Wellhausen, *ut supra*; Goldziher, *Culte des Ancêtres chez les Arabes* (Paris, 1885), and *Muh. Studien*, p. 229 *sqq.*; and some remarks, perhaps too sceptical, in my *Kinship*, p. 18 *sqq.*

[1] Yācūt, iii. 790 (cf. Wellh. p. 102), says that marks, called "scarecrows" (*akhyila*), were set up to show that a place was a *ḥimā*, and must not be approached. But to "approach" a forbidden thing (*cariba*) is the general word for violating a taboo, so the expression ought not perhaps to be pressed too closely. The Greek ἄβατον is also used simply in the sense of inviolable (along with ἄσυλον). It is notable, however, that in the same passage Yācūt tells us that two of the marks that defined the *ḥimā* of Faid were called "the twin sacrificial stones" (*gharīyān*). He did not know the ritual meaning of *gharīy*, and may therefore include them among the *akhyila* by mere inadvertence. But if the place of sacrifice really stood on the border of the sacred ground, the inevitable inference is that the worshippers were not allowed to enter the enclosure. This would be parallel to the sacrifice in Ex. xxiv. 4, where the altar is built outside the limits of Sinai, and the people are not allowed to approach the mountain.

[2] This, it will be remembered, is the idea on which Anselm's theory of the atonement is based.

diginity of the god, like that of a great chief, asserts itself mainly in punctilious insistence on a complicated etiquette that surrounds his place and person. Naturally the strictness of the etiquette admits of gradations. When the god and his worshippers live side by side, as in the case of Mecca, or still more in cases where the idea of holiness has been extended to cover the whole land of a particular religion, the general laws of sacred observance, applicable in all parts of the holy land, are modified by practical considerations. Strict taboos are limited to the sanctuary (in the narrower sense) or to special seasons and occasions, such as religious festivals or the time of war; in ordinary life necessary actions that constitute a breach of ceremonial holiness merely involve temporary uncleanness and some ceremonial act of purification, or else are condoned altogether provided they are done in a particular way. Thus in Canaan, where the whole land was holy, the hunter was allowed to kill game if he returned the life to the god by pouring it on the ground; or again the intercourse of the sexes, which was strictly forbidden at temples and to warriors on an expedition, entailed in ordinary life only a temporary impurity, purged by ablution or fumigation.[1] But in all this care was taken not to presume on the prerogative of the gods, or trench without permission on the sanctity of their domain; and in particular, fresh encroachments on untouched parts of nature—the breaking up of waste lands, the foundation of new cities, or even the annual cutting down of corn or gathering in of the vintage—were not undertaken without special precautions to propitiate the divine powers. It was felt that such encroachments were not without grave danger, and it was often thought necessary to accompany them with expiatory

[1] See *Additional Note C, Taboos on the Intercourse of the Sexes.*

ceremonies of the most solemn kind.[1] Within the god's holy land all parts of life are regulated with constant regard to his sanctity, and so among the settled Semites, who live on Baal's ground, religion entered far more deeply into common life than was the case among the Arabs, where only special tracts were consecrated land and the wide desert was as yet unclaimed either by gods or by men.

Some of the restrictions enforced at ancient sanctuaries have already been touched upon; but it will repay us to look at them again more closely under the new light which falls upon the subject as soon as we recognise that all such restrictions are ultimately of the nature of taboos. The simplest and most universal of these taboos is that which protects the trees of the *temenos* or *ḥimā*, and all the natural life of the spot. In the more advanced forms of Semitic religion the natural wood of the sanctuary is sometimes represented as planted by the god,[2] which would

[1] The details, so far as they are concerned with the yearly recurring ritual of harvest and vintage, belong to the subject of Agricultural Feasts, and must be reserved for a future course of lectures. The danger connected with the breaking up of waste lands is illustrated for Arabia by the story of Ḥarb and Mirdās (*supra*, p. 133). Here the danger still comes from the *jinn* of the place, but even where the whole land already belongs to a friendly deity, precautions are necessary when man lays his hand for the first time on any of the good things of nature. Thus the Hebrews ate the fruit of new trees only in the fifth year; in the fourth year the fruit was consecrated to Jehovah, but the produce of the first three years was "uncircumcised," *i.e.* taboo, and might not be eaten at all (Lev. xix. 23 *sqq.*). A similar idea underlies the Syrian traditions of human sacrifice at the foundation of cities (Malalas, Bonn ed. pp. 37, 200, 203), which are not the less instructive that they are not historically true. In Arabia the local *jinn* or earth-demons (*ahl al-arḍ*) are still propitiated by sprinkling the blood of a sacrifice when new land is broken up, a new house built, or a new well opened (Doughty, i. 136, ii. 100, 198). Kremer, *Studien*, p. 48, cites a passage from Abū 'Obaida, *ap.* Damīrī, i. 241, which shows that such sacrifices to the *jinn* follow an ancient custom, forbidden by the prophet.

[2] The cypresses at Daphne were planted by Heracles (Malalas, p. 204); cf. Ps. civ. 16.

of course give him a right of property in it. But for the most part the phenomena of tree and grove worship, of which we shall learn more in Lect. V., point to a more ancient conception, in which the vegetation of the sanctuary is conceived as actually instinct with a particle of divine life. Equally widespread, and to all appearance equally primitive, is the rule exempting the birds, deer and other game of the sanctuary from molestation.[1] These wild creatures must have been regarded as the guests or clients rather than the property of the god, for Semitic law recognises no property in *feræ naturæ.* But in the oldest law the client is only an artificial kinsman, whose rights are constituted by a ceremony importing that he and his patron are henceforth of one blood; and thus it is probable that, in the beginning, the beasts and birds of the sanctuary, as well as its vegetation, were conceived as holy because they partook of the pervasive divine life. We may conceive the oldest sanctuaries as charged in all their parts and pertinents with a certain supernatural energy. This is the usual savage idea about things that are *taboo*, and even in the higher religions the process of subsuming all taboos under the conception of the holiness of the personal god is always slow and often imperfectly carried out. In particular there is one main element in the doctrine of *taboo*, perfectly irrational from the standpoint of any religion that has clear views as to the

[1] The cases of Mecca and Wajj have already been cited; for the former compare the verses in Ibn Hishām, p. 74, ll. 10, 11. Birds found sanctuary at the temple of Jerusalem (Ps. lxxxiv. 3). At Curium in Cyprus, where religion is full of Semitic elements, dogs did not venture to follow game into the sacred grove, but stood outside barking (Aelian, *N. A.* xi. 7), and the same belief prevailed in the Middle Ages with regard to the mosque and tomb of Ṣiddīcā (Al-Shajara) in the mountains E. of Sidon (Mocaddasī, p. 188). In the sacred island of Icarus in the Persian Gulf the wild goats and gazelles might be taken for sacrifice only (Arrian, vii. 20); or, according to Aelian (*N. A.* xi. 9), the huntsman had to ask permission of the goddess; otherwise the hunt proved vain and a penalty was incurred.

personality of the gods, which was never eliminated from the Semitic conception of holiness, and figures even in the ritual parts of the Old Testament. Holiness, like taboo, is conceived as infectious, propagating itself by physical contact. To avoid complicating the present argument by a multitude of details, I reserve the full illustration of this matter for a note,[1] and confine myself to the observation that even in Hebrew ritual common things brought into contact with things very sacred are themselves "sanctified," so that they can be no longer used for common purposes. In some cases it is provided that this inconvenient sanctity may be washed out and purged away by a ceremonial process; in others the consecration is indelible, and the thing has to be destroyed. In the Old Testament these are mere fragmentary survivals of old rules of sanctity; and the details are to some extent peculiar. The idea that things which fall under a taboo, and so are withdrawn from common use, must be destroyed, is far more prominent among the Hebrews than among other Semites; but the general principle applies to all Semitic religions, and at once explains most of the special taboos applicable to sanctuaries, *e.g.* the right of asylum, the forfeiture of camels that stray on holy ground, and the Meccan rule that strangers who worship at the Caaba in their common dress must leave it behind them at the door of the sanctuary. All such rules are governed by the principle that common things brought into contact with the holy place become holy and inviolable, like the original pertinents of the sanctuary. Naturally this principle admits of many varieties in detail. Holiness acquired by contact is not so indelible as inborn sanctity. In many rituals it can be removed from clothes by washing them, and from the person of a worshipper by ablution. As a rule the con-

[1] See *Additional Note* B, *Holiness, Uncleanness, and Taboo.*

secration of persons by holy things is only temporary; thus the Syrian who touched a dove, the holiest of birds, was taboo for a single day, and at most ancient asylums the fugitive was no longer inviolable when he left the sacred precincts (Num. xxxv. 26 *sq.*).

The ultimate sanction of these rules lay in the intrinsic power of holy things to vindicate themselves against encroachment; or according to the higher heathenism in the jealousy of the personal god, who resents all undue violation of his environment. But when the rules were once established, they tended to maintain themselves without the constant intervention of supernatural sanctions by the action of ordinary social forces. A bold man might venture to violate a taboo and take his risk of supernatural danger; but if his comrades were not equally bold they would immediately shun him lest the danger should spread to them.[1] On this principle most ancient societies attached the penalty of outlawry or death to impious offences, such as the violation of holy things, without waiting for the god to vindicate his own cause.[2] The argument of Joash, "If he be a god, let him plead for himself, because one hath cast down his altar," does not commend itself to a firm faith. The deity is not put to such a proof till his power begins to be doubted.[3] The

[1] Cf. the case of Achan, Josh. vi. 18, vii. 1, 11 *sq.*, where Achan's breach of a taboo involves the whole host.

[2] Cf. Lev. xx. 4, 5; if the people of the land do not slay the impious person, Jehovah will destroy him and all his clan. In the Pentateuch it is sometimes difficult to decide whether the penalty invoked on impious offences is civil or supernatural, *e.g.* Lev. xvii. 4, xix. 8.

[3] Judg. vi. 31. An Arabian parallel in Ibn Hishām, p. 303 *sq.*—'Amr's domestic idol has been repeatedly defiled by unknown Moslems. At length the owner girds the god with a sword, and bids him defend himself if he is good for anything. Of course conversion follows. Similarly in Yācūt, iii. 912 *sq.*, a daring man reclaims a stolen camel from the sanctuary of Al-Fals. A bystander exclaims, "Wait and see what will happen to him this very day!"; when several days pass and nothing happens, he renounces

principle that it is not safe to wait till the god vindicates his own holiness, has enormous historical importance as one of the chief bases of early criminal law. In the oldest type of society impious acts or breaches of taboo were the only offences treated as crimes; *e.g.* there is no such crime as theft, but a man can save his property from invasion by placing it under a taboo, when it becomes an act of impiety to touch it.[1] Among the Hebrews such taboos are created by means of a curse (Judg. xvii. 2), and by the same means a king can give validity to the most unreasonable decrees (1 Sam. xiv. 24 *sqq.*). But unreasonable taboos, as we see in the case of Saul and Jonathan, are sure to be evaded in the long run because public opinion goes against them, whereas taboos that make for the general good and check wrong-doing are supported and enforced by the community, and ultimately pass into laws with a civil sanction. But no ancient society deemed its good order to be sufficiently secured by civil sanctions alone; there was always a last recourse to the curse, the ordeal, the oath of probation at the sanctuary—all of them means to stamp an offender with the guilt of impiety and

idols and becomes a Christian. I suspect that in Judg. vi. the original text expressed a similar belief that the god's vengeance must fall on the very day of the offence. The clause אשר יריב לו יומת עד הבקר gives a very unsuitable sense. But the true Septuagint text (which in this book is better represented by A than by B) indicates a reading בו for לו. Accepting this and reading ימות (which in the old orthography is not distinguished for יומת) we get good sense: "The man who strives with the Baal dies before (the next) morning." The common belief was that supernatural judgments came swiftly on the offence, or not at all. That Jehovah does not overlook sin because He is long-suffering and gives time for repentance (Ex. xxxiv. 6, 7), is one of the distinctive points of O. T. doctrine which the prophets had special difficulty in impressing on their hearers.

[1] I believe that in early society (and not merely in the very earliest) we may safely affirm that every offence to which death or outlawry is attached was primarily viewed as a breach of holiness; *e.g.* murder within the kin, and incest, are breaches of the holiness of tribal blood, which would be supernaturally avenged if men overlooked them.

bring him under the direct judgment of the supernatural powers.

Very noteworthy, in this connection, is the representation in Deut. xxvii., Josh. ix. 30 *sqq.*, according to which the Israelites, on their first entry into Canaan, placed a number of the chief heads of public morality under the protection of a solemn taboo by a great act of public cursing. I use the word taboo deliberately as implying a more mechanical sequence of sin and punishment than we associate with the idea of divine judgment; see the description of the operation of the curse in Zech. v. 1–4.[1]

[1] Among the Arabs the operation of a curse is purely mechanical; if a man falls on his face it may pass over him; see Wellhausen, p. 126. For the oath of purgation among the Arabs, see *Kinship*, pp. 53, 263; among the Hebrews, Deut. xxi. 7 and Num. v. 11 *sq.*, where the connection with very primitive ideas of taboo is unmistakable (cf. p. 180, *infra*). A late Syriac survival of the use of a curse to protect (or perhaps to create) an exclusive right of property (as in Judg. xvii. 2) is found in Jacob of Edessa, *Qu.* 47, "concerning a priest who writes a curse and hangs it on a tree that no man may eat of the fruit." Various examples of the operation of a curse to vindicate rights of property, etc., in the lawless society of Arabia before Islam are collected in *Div. Hodh.* No. 245, in the form of anecdotes of the Times of Ignorance related to the Caliph 'Omar I. 'Omar observes that God granted temporal judgments, in answer to prayer, when there was no knowledge of a future state; but in Islam divine retribution is reserved for the day of judgment.

LECTURE V

SANCTUARIES, NATURAL AND ARTIFICIAL.—HOLY WATERS, TREES, CAVES, AND STONES

We have seen that holiness admits of degrees, and that within a sacred land or tract it is natural to mark off an inner circle of intenser holiness, where all ritual restrictions are stringently enforced, and where man feels himself to be nearer to his god than on other parts even of holy ground. Such a spot of intenser holiness becomes the sanctuary or place of sacrifice, where the worshipper approaches the god with prayers and gifts, and seeks guidance for life from the divine oracle. As holy tracts in general are the regions haunted by divine powers, so the site of the sanctuary *par excellence*, or place of worship, is a spot where the god is constantly present in some visible embodiment, or which has received a special consecration by some extraordinary manifestation of deity. For the more developed forms of cultus a mere vague *ḥimā* does not suffice; men require a special point at which they may come together and do sacrifice with the assurance that the god is present at the act. In Arabia, indeed, it seems to be not incredible that certain sacrifices were simply laid on sacred ground to be devoured by wild beasts. But even in Arabia the *ḥimā* usually, probably always, contained a fixed point where the blood of the offering was directly presented to the deity by being applied to sacred stones, or where a sacred tree was hung with gifts. In the ordinary forms of heathenism, at any rate, it was essential that the worshipper should bring his offering into the actual presence of the god, or into contact with the symbol of that presence.[1]

The symbol or permanent visible object, at and through which the worshipper came into direct contact with the god, was not lacking in any Semitic place of worship, but had not always the same form, and was sometimes a natural object, sometimes an artificial erection. The usual natural symbols are a fountain or a tree, while the ordinary artificial symbol is a pillar or pile of stones; but very often all three are found together, and this was the rule in the more developed sanctuaries, particular sacred observances being connected with each.

The choice of the natural symbols, the fountain and the tree, is no doubt due in part to the fact that the favourite haunts of animate life, to which a superstitious reverence was attached, are mainly found beside wood and running water. But besides this we have found evidence of the direct ascription to trees and living waters of a life analogous to man's, but mysterious and therefore awful.[2] To us this may seem to be quite another point of view; in the one case the fountain or the tree merely marks the spot which the deity frequents, in the other it is the visible embodiment of the divine presence. But the primitive imagination has no difficulty in combining different ideas about the same holy place or thing. The gods are not tied to one form of embodiment or manifestation; for, as has already been observed,[3] some sort of distinction between life and the material embodiment

[1] This rule is observed even when the god is a heavenly body. The sacrifices of the Saracens to the morning star, described by Nilus, were celebrated when that star rose, and could not be made after it was lost to sight on the rising of the sun (*Nili op. quædam* [Paris, 1639], pp. 28, 117).

[2] *Supra*, p. 135 *sqq.*

[3] *Supra*, pp. 86, 87.

of life is suggested to the rudest peoples by phenomena like those of dreams. Even men, it is supposed, can change their embodiment, and assume for a time the shape of wolves or birds;[1] and of course the gods with their superior powers have a still greater range, and the same deity may quite well manifest himself in the life of a tree or a spring, and yet emerge from time to time in human or animal form. All manifestations of life at or about a holy place readily assume a divine character and form a religious unity, contributing as they do to create and nourish the same religious emotion; and in all of them the godhead is felt to be present in the same direct way. The permanent manifestations of his presence, however, the sacred fountain and the sacred tree, are likely to hold the first place in acts of worship, simply because they are permanent and so attach to themselves a fixed sacred tradition. These considerations apply equally to the sanctuaries of nomadic and of settled peoples, but among the latter the religious importance of water and wood could not fail to be greatly reinforced by the growth of the ideas of Baal-worship, in which the deity as the giver of life is specially connected with quickening waters and vegetative growth.

With this it agrees that sacred wells, in connection with sanctuaries, are found in all parts of the Semitic area, but are less prominent among the nomadic Arabs than among the agricultural peoples of Syria and Palestine. There is mention of fountains or streams at a good many Arabian sanctuaries, but little direct evidence that these waters were holy, or played any definite part in the ritual. The clearest case is that of Mecca, where the holiness of the well Zamzam is certainly pre-Islamic. It would even seem that in old time gifts were cast into it, as they were

[1] *Supra*, pp. 87, 88.

cast into the sacred wells of the northern Semites.[1] Some kind of ritual holiness seems also to have attached to the pool beneath a waterfall at the Dausite sanctuary of Dusares.[2] Again, as healing springs and sacred springs are everywhere identified, it is noteworthy that the south Arabs regard medicinal waters as inhabited by *jinn*, usually of serpent form,[3] and that the water of the sanctuary at the Palmetum was thought to be health-giving, and was carried home by pilgrims[4] as Zamzam water now is. In like manner the custom of pilgrims carrying away water from the well of ʿOrwa[5] is probably a relic of ancient sanctity. Further, on the borders of the Arabian field, we have the sacred fountain of Ephca at Palmyra, with which a legend of a demon in serpent form is still connected. This is a sulphurous spring, which had a guardian

[1] So Wellhausen, p. 101, concludes with probability from the story that when the well was rediscovered and cleaned out by the grandfather of Mohammed, two golden gazelles and a number of swords were found in it. Everything told of the prophet's ancestors must be received with caution, but this does not look like invention. The two golden gazelles are parallel to the golden camels of Sabæan and Nabatæan inscriptions (*ZDMG*. xxxviii. 143 *sq*.).

[2] Ibn Hishām, p. 253; Wellhausen, p. 45. A woman who adopts Islam breaks with the heathen god by "purifying herself" in this pool. This implies that her act was a breach of the ritual of the spot; presumably a woman who required purification (viz. from her courses) was not admitted to the sacred water; cf. Yācūt, i. 657, l. 2 *sqq*., iv. 651, l. 4 *sqq*.; Ibn Hishām, p. 15 ult. In Ṭabarī, i. 271 *sq*., we read that the water of Beersheba shrank when a woman in her courses drew from it. Cf. also Bērūnī, *Chron*. p. 246, l. 8 *sqq*. Under ordinary circumstances to bathe in the sacred spring would be an act of homage to the heathen god: so at least it was in Syria.

[3] Mordtmann in *ZDMG*. xxxviii. 587, cites a modern instance from Maltzan, *Reise in Südarabien*, p. 304, and others from Hamdānī's *Iklīl*, *ap*. Müller, *Burgen*, i. 34. Maltzan's spring, the hot well of Msaʿide, has every feature of an ancient sanctuary except that the serpent-god, who is invoked as Msaʿud, and sends hot or cold water at the prayer of the worshipper, has been degraded to the rank of a demon. There is an annual pilgrimage to the spot in the month Rajab, the ancient sacred month of Arabia, which is accompanied by festivities and lasts for several days.

[4] Agatharchides, *ap*. Diod. Sic. iii. 43.

[5] Yācūt, i. 434; Cazwīnī, i. 200.

appointed by the god Yarhibol, and on an inscription is called the "blessed fountain."[1] Again, in the desert beyond Bostra, we find the Stygian waters, where a great cleft received a lofty cataract. The waters had the power to swallow up or cast forth the gifts flung into them, as a sign that the god was or was not propitious, and the oath by the spot and its stream was the most horrible known to the inhabitants of the region.[2] The last two cases belong to a region in which religion was not purely Arabian in character, but the Stygian waters recall the waterfall in the Dausite sanctuary of Dusares, and Ptolemy twice mentions a Stygian fountain in Arabia proper.

Among the northern Semites, the agricultural Canaanites and Syrians, sacred waters hold a much more prominent place. Where all ground watered by fountains and streams, without the aid of man's hand, was regarded as the Baal's land, a certain sanctity could hardly fail to be ascribed to every source of living water; and where the divine activity was looked upon as mainly displaying itself in the quickening of the soil, the waters which gave fertility to the land, and so life to its inhabitants, would appear to be the direct embodiment of divine energies. Accordingly we find that Hannibal, in his covenant with Philip of Macedon, when he swears before all the deities of Carthage and of Hellas, includes among the divine powers to which his oath appeals "the sun the moon and the earth, rivers meadows (?) and waters."[3] Thus when we find that temples were so often erected near springs and

[1] Wadd., No. 2571 *c*; De Vog., No. 95. For the modern serpent myth see Mordtmann, *ut supra*; Blunt, *Pilgr. to Nejd*, ii. 67.

[2] Damascius, *Vita Isidori*, § 199.

[3] Polybius, vii. 9. The word "meadows" is uncertain, resting on a conjecture of Casaubon: λειμώνων for δαιμόνων. Reiske conjectured λιμνῶν. In Palestine to this day all springs are viewed as the seats of spirits, and the

rivers, we must consider not only that such a position was convenient, inasmuch as pure water was indispensable for ablutions and other ritual purposes, but that the presence of living water in itself gave consecration to the place.[1] The fountain or stream was not a mere adjunct to the temple, but was itself one of the principal *sacra* of the spot, to which special legends and a special ritual were often attached, and to which the temple in many instances owed its celebrity and even its name. This is particularly the case with perennial streams and their sources, which in a country like Palestine, where rain is confined to the winter months, are not very numerous, and form striking features in the topography of the region. From Hannibal's oath we may conclude that among the Phœnicians and Carthaginians all such waters were held to be divine, and what we know in detail of the waters of the Phœnician coast goes far to confirm the conclusion.[2] Of the eminent sanctity of certain rivers, such as the Belus and the Adonis, we have direct evidence, and the grove and pool of Aphaca at the source of the latter stream was the most famous of all Phœnician holy places.[3] These rivers are named from gods, and so also, on the same coast, are the Asclepius, near Sidon, the Ares (perhaps identical with the Lycus), and presumably the Kishon.[4] The river of Tripolis, which descends from the famous cedars, is still called the Cadīsha

peasant women, whether Moslem or Christian, ask their permission before drawing water (*ZDPV*. x. 180); cf. Num. xxi. 17.

[1] For the choice of a place beside a pool as the site of a chapel, see Waddington, No 2015, εὐσεβίης τόπος οὗτος ὃν ἔκτισεν ἐγγύθι λίμνης.

[2] The authorities for the details, so far as they are not cited below, will be found in Baudissin, *Studien*, ii. 161.

[3] Euseb., *Vit. Const.* iii. 55; Sozomen, ii. 5.

[4] River of קיש, Ar. Cais. Prof. De Goeje, referring to Hamdānī, p. 3, l. 9, and perhaps p. 221, l. 14, suggests to me by letter that Cais is a title, "dominus."

or holy stream, and the grove at its source is sacred to Christians and Moslems alike.[1]

In Hellenic and Roman times the source of the Jordan at Paneas with its grotto was sacred to Pan, and in ancient days the great Israelite sanctuary of Dan occupied the same site, or that of the twin source at Tell al-Cāḍi. It is evident that Naaman's indignation when he was told to bathe in the Jordan, and his confidence that the rivers of Damascus were better than all the waters of Israel, sprang from the idea that the Jordan was the sacred healing stream of the Hebrews, as Abana and Pharpar were the sacred rivers of the Syrians, and in this he probably did no injustice to the belief of the mass of the Israelites. The sanctity of the Barada, the chief river of Damascus, was concentrated at its nominal source, the fountain of El-Fiji, that is, *πηγαί*. The river-gods Chrysorrhoa and Pegai often appear on Damascene coins, and evidently had a great part in the religion of the city. That the thermal waters of Gadara were originally sacred may be inferred from the peculiar ceremonies that were still observed by the patients in the time of Antoninus Martyr (*De locis Sanctis*, vii.). The baths were used by night; there were lights and incense, and the patient saw visions during the pernoctation. To this day a patient at the natural bath of Tiberias must not offend the spirits by pronouncing the name of God (*ZDPV.* x. 179).

The river of Cœle-Syria, the Orontes, was carved out, according to local tradition, by a great dragon, which disappeared in the earth at its source.[2] The connection

[1] Robinson, iii. 590. On Carthaginian soil, it is not impossible that the Bagradas or Majerda, Macaros or Macros in MSS. of Polybius, bears the name of the Tyrian Baal-Melcarth.

[2] Strabo, xvi. 2. 7. Other sacred traditions about the Orontes are given by Malalas, p. 38, from Pausanias of Damascus.

of *jinn* in the form of dragons or serpents with sacred or healing springs has already come before us in Arabian superstition, and the lake of Cadas near Emesa, which is regarded as the source of the river (Yācūt, iii. 588), bears a name which implies its ancient sanctity. Among Syrian waters those of the Euphrates played an important part in the ritual of Hierapolis, and from them the great goddess was thought to have been born; while the source of its chief Mesopotamian tributary, the Aborrhas or Chaboras, was reverenced as the place where Hera (Atargatis) bathed after her marriage with Zeus (Bel). It gave out a sweet odour, and was full of tame, that is sacred, fishes.[1]

The sacredness of living waters was by no means confined to such great streams and sources as have just been spoken of. But in cultivated districts fountains could not ordinarily be reserved for purposes exclusively sacred. Each town or village had as a rule its own well, and its own high place or little temple, but in Canaan the well was not generally within the precincts of the high place. Towns were built on rising ground, and the well lay outside the gate, usually below the town, while the high place stood on the higher ground overlooking the human habitations.[2] Thus any idea of sanctity that might be connected with the fountain was dissociated from the temple ritual, and would necessarily become vague and attenuated.[3] Sacred springs in the full sense of the word

[1] Ælian, *Nat. Ann.* xii. 30; Pliny, *H. N.* xxxi. 37, xxxii. 16.

[2] Gen. xxiv. 11; 1 Sam. ix. 11; 2 Sam. ii. 13, xxiii. 16; 2 Kings ii. 21; 1 Kings xxi. 13, 19, compared with chap. xxii. 38.

[3] There are, however, indications that in some cases the original sanctuary was at a well beneath the town. In 1 Kings i. 9, 38, the fountains of En-rogel, where Adonijah held his sacrificial feast, and of Gihon, where Solomon was crowned, are plainly the original sanctuaries of Jerusalem. The former was by the "serpent's stone," and may perhaps be identified with the "dragon well" of Neh. ii. 13. Here again, as in Arabia and at the Orontes, the dragon or serpent has a sacred significance.

are generally found, not at the ordinary local sanctuaries, but at remote pilgrimage shrines like Aphaca, Beersheba, Mamre, or within the enclosure of great and spacious temples like that at Ascalon, where the pool of Atargatis was shown and her sacred fishes were fed. Sometimes, as at Daphne near Antioch, the water and its surrounding groves formed a sort of public park near a city, where religion and pleasure were combined in the characteristic Syriac fashion.[1]

The myths attached to holy sources and streams, and put forth to worshippers as accounting for their sanctity, were of various types; but the practical beliefs and ritual usages connected with sacred waters were much the same everywhere. The one general principle which runs through all the varieties of the legends, and which also lies at the basis of the ritual, is that the sacred waters are instinct with divine life and energy. The legends explain this in diverse ways, and bring the divine quality of the waters into connection with various deities or supernatural powers, but they all agree in this, that their main object is to show how the fountain or stream comes to be impregnated, so to speak, with the vital energy of the deity to which it is sacred.

Among the ancients blood is generally conceived as the principle or vehicle of life, and so the account often given of sacred waters is that the blood of the deity flows in them. Thus as Milton writes—

> Smooth Adonis from his native rock
> Ran purple to the sea, supposed with blood
> Of Thammuz yearly wounded.[2]

---

[1] A similar example, Wadd., No. 2370. A sacred fountain of Eshmun "in the mountain" seems to appear in *CIS.* No. 3, l. 17; cf. G. Hoffmann, *Ueber einige Phœn. Inschrr.* p. 52 *sq.*

[2] *Paradise Lost*, i. 450, following Lucian, *Dea Syria*, viii.

The ruddy colour which the swollen river derived from the soil at a certain season[1] was ascribed to the blood of the god who received his death-wound in Lebanon at that time of the year, and lay buried beside the sacred source.[2] Similarily a tawny fountain near Joppa was thought to derive its colour from the blood of the sea-monster slain by Perseus,[3] and Philo Byblius says that the fountains and rivers sacred to the heaven-god (Baalshamaim) were those which received his blood when he was mutilated by his son.[4] In another class of legends, specially connected with the worship of Atargatis, the divine life of the waters resides in the sacred fish that inhabit them. Atargatis and her son, according to a legend common to Hierapolis and Ascalon, plunged into the waters—in the first case the Euphrates, in the second the sacred pool at the temple near the town—and were changed into fishes.[5] This is only another form of the idea expressed in the first class of legend, where a god dies, that is ceases to exist in human form, but his life passes into the waters where he is buried; and this again is merely a theory to bring the divine water or the divine fish into harmony with anthro-

[1] The reddening of the Adonis was observed by Maundrell on March $\frac{17}{27}$, 169$\frac{6}{7}$, and by Renan early in February.

[2] Melito in Cureton, *Spic. Syr.* p. 25, l. 7. That the grave of Adonis was also shown at the mouth of the river has been inferred from *Dea Syr.* vi. vii. The river Belus also had its Memnonion or Adonis tomb (Josephus, *B. J.* ii. 10. 2.) In modern Syria cisterns are always found beside the graves of saints, and are believed to be inhabited by a sort of fairy. A pining child is thought to be a fairy changeling, and must be lowered into the cistern. The fairy will then take it back, and the true child is drawn up in its room. This is in the region of Sidon (*ZDPV.* vol. vii. p. 84; cf. *ib.* p. 106).

[3] Pausanias, iv. 35. 9.

[4] Euseb. *Præp. Ev.* i. 10. 22 (*Fr. Hist. Gr.* iii. 568). The fountain of the Chabōras, where Hera μετὰ τοὺς γάμους . . ἀπελούσατο, belongs to the same class.

[5] Hyginus, *Astr.* ii. 30; Manilius, iv. 580 *sqq.*; Xanthus in Athenæus, viii. 37. I have discussed these legends at length in the *English Hist. Review*, April 1887, to which the reader is referred for details.

pomorphic ideas.[1] The same thing was sometimes effected in another way by saying that the anthropomorphic deity was born from the water, as Aphrodite sprang from the sea-foam, or as Atargatis, in another form of the Euphrates legend, given by the scholiast on Germanicus's Aratus, was born of an egg which the sacred fishes found in the Euphrates and pushed ashore. Here, we see, it was left to the choice of the worshippers whether they would think of the deity as arising from or disappearing in the water, and in the ritual of the Syrian goddess at Hierapolis both ideas were combined at the solemn feasts, when her image was carried down to the river and back again to the temple. Where the legend is so elastic we can hardly doubt that the sacred waters and sacred fish were worshipped for their own sake before the anthropomorphic goddess came into the religion, and in fact the sacred fish at the source of the Chaboras are connected with an altogether different myth. Fish were *taboo*, and sacred fish were found in rivers or in pools at sanctuaries, all over Syria.[2] This superstition has proved one of the

[1] The idea that the godhead consecrates waters by descending into them appears at Aphaca in a peculiar form associated with the astral character which, at least in later times, was ascribed to the goddess Astarte. It was believed that the goddess on a certain day of the year descended into the river in the form of a fiery star from the top of Lebanon. So Sozomen, *H. E.* ii. 4, 5. Zosimus, i. 58, says only that fireballs appeared at the temple and the places about it, on the occasion of solemn feasts, and does not connect the apparition with the sacred waters. There is nothing improbable in the frequent occurrence of striking electrical phenomena in a mountain sanctuary. We shall presently find fiery apparitions connected also with sacred trees (*infra*, p. 193). "Thunders, lightnings and light flashing in the heavens," appear as objects of veneration among the Syrians (Jacob of Edessa, *Qu.* 43); cf. also the fiery globe of the Heliopolitan Lion-god, whose fall from heaven is described by Damascius, *Vit. Is.* § 203, and what Pausanias of Damascus relates of the fireball that checked the flood of the Orontes (Malalas, p. 38).

[2] Xenophon, *Anab.* i. 4. 9, who found such fish in the Chalus near Aleppo, expressly says that they were regarded as gods. Lucian, *Dea Syr.* xlv., relates that at the lake of Atargatis at Hierapolis the sacred fish

most durable parts of ancient heathenism; sacred fish are still kept in pools at the mosques of Tripolis and Edessa. At the latter place it is believed that death or other evil consequences would befall the man who dared to eat them.[1]

The living power that inhabits sacred waters and gives them their miraculous or healing quality is very often held to be a serpent, as in the Arabian and Hebrew cases which have been already cited,[2] or a huge dragon or water monster, such as that which in the Antiochene legend hollowed out the winding bed of the Orontes and disappeared beneath its source.[3] In such cases the serpents are of course supernatural serpents or *jinn*, and the dragon of Orontes was identified in the Greek period with Typhon, the enemy of the gods.[4] But the demon may also have other forms; thus at Rāmallāh in Palestine there are two springs, of which one is inhabited by a camel, the other by a bride; while the spring at 'Artās is guarded by a white and a black ram.[5]

In all their various forms the point of the legends is that the sacred source is either inhabited by a demoniac being or imbued with demoniac life. The same notion appears with great distinctness in the ritual of sacred

wore gold ornaments, as did also the eels at the sanctuary of the war-god Zeus, amidst the sacred plane-trees (Herod. v. 119) at Labraunda in Caria (Pliny, *H. N.* xxxii. 16, 17; Ælian, *N. A.* xii. 30). Caria was thoroughly permeated by Phœnician influence.

[1] Sachau, *Reise*, p. 197.

[2] *Supra*, p. 168 *sqq.*

[3] The Leviathan (תַּנִּין) of Scripture, like the Arabian *tinnīn*, is probably a personification of the waterspout (Mas'ūdī, i. 263, 266; Ps. cxlviii. 7). Thus we see how readily the Eastern imagination clothes aquatic phenomena with an animal form.

[4] Hence perhaps the modern name of the river Nahr al-'Âṣī, "the rebel's stream"; the explanation in Yācūt, iii. 588, does not commend itself. The burial of the Typhonic dragon at the source of the Orontes may be compared with the Moslem legend of the well at Babylon, where the rebel angels Hārūt and Mārūt were entombed (Cazwīnī, i. 197).

[5] *ZDPV.* x. 180; *PEF. Qu. St.* 1893, p. 204.

waters. Though such waters are often associated with temples, altars, and the usual apparatus of a cultus addressed to heavenly deities, the service paid to the holy well retained a form which implies that the divine power addressed was in the water. We have seen that at Mecca, and at the Stygian waters in the Syrian desert, gifts were cast into the holy source. But even at Aphaca, where, in the times to which our accounts refer, the goddess of the spot was held to be the Urania or celestial Astarte, the pilgrims cast into the pool jewels of gold and silver, webs of linen and byssus and other precious stuffs, and the obvious contradiction between the celestial character of the goddess and the earthward destination of the gifts was explained by the fiction that at the season of the feast she descended into the pool in the form of a fiery star. Similarly, at the annual fair and feast of the Terebinth, or tree and well of Abraham at Mamre, the heathen visitors, who reverenced the spot as a haunt of "angels,"[1] not only offered sacrifices beside the tree, but illuminated the well with lamps, and cast into it libations of wine, cakes, coins, myrrh, and incense.[2] On the other hand, at the sacred waters of Karwa and Sāwid in S. Arabia, described by Hamdānī in the *Iklīl* (Müller, *Burgen*, p. 69), offerings of bread, fruit or other food were deposited beside the fountain. In the former case they were believed to be eaten by the serpent denizen of the water, in the latter they were consumed by beasts and birds. At Gaza bread is still thrown into the sea by way of offering.[3]

[1] *I.e.* demons. Sozomen says "angels," and not "devils," because the sanctity of the place was acknowledged by Christians also.

[2] Sozomen, *H. E.* ii. 4.—As all "living waters" seem to have had a certain sanctity in N. Semitic religion, the custom of throwing the Ἀδώνιδος κῆποι into springs (Zenobius, *Cent.* i. 49) may probably belong to this chapter.

[3] *PEF. Qu. St.* 1893, p. 216.

In ancient religion offerings are the proper vehicle of prayer and supplication, and the worshipper when he presents his gift looks for a visible indication whether his prayer is accepted.[1] At Aphaca and at the Stygian fountain the accepted gift sank into the depths, the unacceptable offering was cast forth by the eddies. It was taken as an omen of the impending fall of Palmyra that the gifts sent from that city at an annual festival were cast up again in the following year.[2] In this example we see that the holy well, by declaring the favourable or unfavourable disposition of the divine power, becomes a place of oracle and divination. In Greece, also, holy wells are connected with oracles, but mainly in the form of a belief that the water gives prophetic inspiration to those who drink of it. At the Semitic oracle of Aphaca the method is more primitive, for the answer is given directly by the water itself, but its range is limited to what can be inferred from the acceptance or rejection of the worshipper and his petition.

The oracle of Daphne near Antioch, which was obtained by dipping a laurel leaf into the water, was presumably of the same class, for we cannot take seriously the statement that the response appeared written on the leaf.[3] The choice of the laurel leaf as the offering cast into the water must be due to Greek influence, but Daphne was a sanctuary of Heracles, *i.e.* of the Semitic Baal, before the temple of Apollo was built.[4]

[1] Cf. Gen. iv. 4, 5.

[2] Zosimus, i. 58. At Aphaca, as at the Stygian fountain, the waters fall down a cataract into a deep gorge.

[3] Sozomen, v. 19. 11. Cf. the ordeal by casting a tablet into the water at Palici in Sicily. The tablet sank if what was written on it was false (*Mir. Ausc.* § 57).

[4] Malalas, p. 204. A variant of this form of oracle occurs at Myra in Lycia, where the omen is from the sacred fish accepting or rejecting the food offered to them (Pliny, *H. N.* xxxii. 17; Ælian, *N. A.* viii. 5; Athenæus,

An oracle that speaks by receiving or rejecting the worshipper and his homage may very readily pass into an ordeal, where the person who is accused of a crime, or is suspected of having perjured himself in a suit, is presented at the sanctuary, to be accepted or rejected by the deity, in accordance with the principle that no impious person can come before God with impunity.[1] A rude form of this ordeal seems to survive even in modern times in the widespread form of trial of witches by water. In Ḥaḍramaut, according to Macrīzī,[2] when a man was injured by enchantment, he brought all the witches suspect to the sea or to a deep pool, tied stones to their backs and threw them into the water. She who did not sink was the guilty person, the meaning evidently being that the sacred element rejects the criminal.[3] That an impure person dare not approach sacred waters is a general principle—whether the impurity is moral or physical is not a distinction made by ancient religion. Thus in Arabia we have found that a woman in her uncleanness was afraid, for her children's sake, to bathe in the water of Dusares; and to this day among the Yezīdīs no one may enter the valley of Sheik Adi, with its sacred fountain, unless he has first purified his body and clothes.[4] The sacred oil-spring of the Carthaginian sanctuary, described in the book of *Wonderful Stories* that passes under the name of Aristotle,[5] would not flow except for persons ceremonially pure. An ordeal at a sacred spring based on

viii. 8, p. 333). How far Lycian worship was influenced by the Semites is not clear.

[1] Cf. Job xiii. 16; Isa. xxxiii. 14.

[2] *De Valle Ḥadhramaut*, p. 26 *sq.*

[3] The story about Mojammi' and Al-Ahwaṣ (*Agh.* iv. 48), cited by Wellhausen, *Heid.* p. 152, refers to this kind of ordeal, not to a form of magic. A very curious story of the water test for witches in India is told by Ibn Batuta, iv. 37.

[4] Layard, *Nineveh*, i. 280.

[5] *Mir. Ausc.* § 113.

this principle might be worked in several ways,[1] but the usual Semitic method seems to have been by drinking the water. Evidently, if it is dangerous for the impious person to come into contact with the holy element, the danger must be intensified if he ventures to take it into his system, and it was believed that in such a case the draught produced disease and death. At the Asbamæan lake and springs near Tyana the water was sweet and kindly to those that swore truly, but the perjured man was at once smitten in his eyes, feet and hands, seized with dropsy and wasting.[2] In like manner he who swore falsely by the Stygian waters in the Syrian desert died of dropsy within a year. In the latter case it would seem that the oath by the waters sufficed; but primarily, as we see in the other case, the essential thing is the draught of water at the holy place, the oath simply taking the place of the petition which ordinarily accompanies a ritual act. Among the Hebrews this ordeal by drinking holy water is preserved even in the pentateuchal legislation in the case of a woman suspected of infidelity to her husband.[3] Here also the belief was that the holy water, which was mingled with the dust of the sanctuary, and administered with an oath, produced dropsy and wasting; and the antiquity of the

[1] See, for example, the Sicilian oracle of the Palic lake, where the oath of the accused was written on a tablet and cast into the water to sink or swim (*Mir. Ausc.* § 57).

[2] *Mir. Ausc.* § 152; Philostr., *Vit. Apollonii*, i. 6. That the sanctuary was Semitic I infer from its name; see below, p. 182.

[3] Num. v. 11 *sqq.* In *Agh.* i. 156, l. 3 *sqq.*, a suspected wife swears seventy oaths at the Caaba, to which she is conducted with circumstances of ignominy—seated on a camel between two sacks of dung. This was under Islam, but is evidently an old custom. In heathen Arabia the decision in such a case was sometimes referred to a diviner, as we see from the story of Hind bint 'Otba (*'Icd*, iii. 273; *Agh.* viii. 50). An ordeal for virgins accused of unchastity existed at the Stygian water near Ephesus. The accused swore that she was innocent; her oath was written and tied round her neck. She then entered the shallow pool, and if she was guilty the water rose till it covered the writing (Achilles Tatius, viii. 12).

ceremony is evident not only from its whole character, but because the expression "holy water" (ver. 17) is unique in the language of Hebrew ritual, and must be taken as an isolated survival of an obsolete expression. Unique though the expression be, it is not difficult to assign its original meaning; the analogies already before us indicate that we must think of water from a holy spring, and this conclusion is certainly correct. Wellhausen has shown that the oldest Hebrew tradition refers the origin of the Torah to the divine sentences taught by Moses at the sanctuary of Kadesh or Meribah,[1] beside the holy fountain which in Gen. xiv. 7 is also called "the fountain of judgment." The principle underlying the administration of justice at the sanctuary is that cases too hard for man are referred to the decision of God. Among the Hebrews in Canaan this was ordinarily done by an appeal to the sacred lot, but the survival of even one case of ordeal by holy water leaves no doubt as to the sense of the "fountain of judgment" (En-Mishpaṭ) or "waters of controversy" (Meribah).

With this evidence before us as to the early importance of holy waters among the Hebrews, we cannot but attach significance to the fact that the two chief places of pilgrimage of the northern Israelites in the time of Amos were Dan and Beersheba.[2] We have already seen that there was a sacred fountain at Dan, and the sanctuary of Beersheba properly consisted of the "Seven Wells," which gave the place its name. It is notable that among the Semites a special sanctity was attached to groups of seven wells.[3] In the canons of Jacob of Edessa (Qu. 43) we read of nominally Christian Syrians who bewail their diseases to

[1] *Prolegomena*, viii. 3 (Eng. trans. p. 343).

[2] Amos viii. 14; cf. 1 Kings xii. 30.

[3] See Nöldeke in *Litt. Centralblatt*, 22 Mar. 1879, p. 363.

the stars, or turn for help to a solitary tree or a fountain or *seven springs* or water of the sea, etc. Among the Mandæans, also, we read of mysteries performed at seven wells, and among the Arabs a place called "the seven wells" is mentioned by Strabo, xvi. 4. 24.[1] The name of the Asbamæan waters seems also to mean "seven waters" (Syr. *shab'ā mayā*); the spot is a lake where a number of sources bubble up above the surface of the water. Seven is a sacred number among the Semites, particularly affected in matters of ritual, and the Hebrew verb "to swear" means literally "to come under the influence of seven things." Thus seven ewe lambs figure in the oath between Abraham and Abimelech at Beersheba, and in the Arabian oath of covenant described by Herodotus (iii. 8), seven stones are smeared with blood. The oath of purgation at seven wells would therefore have peculiar force.[2]

It is the part of a divine power to grant to his worshippers not only oracles and judgment, but help in trouble and blessing in daily life. The kind of blessing which it is most obvious to expect from a sacred spring is the quickening and fertilisation of the soil and all that depends on it. That fruitful seasons were the chief object of petition at the sacred springs requires no special proof, for this object holds the first place in all the great religious occasions of the settled Semites, and everywhere we find that the festal cycle is regulated by the seasons of the

[1] Cf. also the seven marvellous wells at Tiberias (Cazwīnī, i. 193), and the Thorayyā or "Pleiad waters" at Ḍarīya (Yācūt, i. 924, iii. 588; Bekrī, 214, 627); also the modern Syrian custom of making a sick child that is thought to be bewitched drink from seven wells or cisterns (*ZDPV.* vii. 106).

[2] In Amos viii. 14 there is mention of an oath by the way (ritual?) of Beersheba. The pilgrims at Mamre would not drink of the water of the well. Sozomen supposes that the gifts cast in made it undrinkable; but at an Oriental market, where every bargain is accompanied by false oaths and protestations, the precaution is rather to be explained by fear of the divine ordeal.

agricultural year.[1] Beyond doubt the first and best gift of the sacred spring to the worshipper was its own life-giving water, and the first object of the religion addressed to it was to encourage its benignant flow.[2] But the life-giving power of the holy stream was by no means confined to the quickening of vegetation. Sacred waters are also healing waters, as we have already seen in various examples, particularly in that of the Syrians, who sought to them for help in disease. I may here add one instance which, though it lies a little outside of the proper Semitic region, is connected with a holy river of the Syrians. In the Middle Ages it was still believed that he who bathed in the spring-time in the source of the Euphrates would be free from sickness for the whole year.[3] This healing power was not confined to the water itself, but extended to the vegetation that surrounded it. By the sacred river Belus grew the colocasium plants by which Heracles was healed after his conflict with the Hydra, and the roots continued to be used as a cure for bad sores.[4] At Paneas an herb that healed all diseases grew at the base of a statue which was supposed to represent Christ, evidently a relic of the old heathenism of the place.[5] Thus when Ezekiel describes

[1] A myth of the connection of sacred waters with the origin of agriculture seems to survive in modernised form in the mediæval legend of 'Ain al-bacar, "the oxen's well," at Acre. It was visited by Christian, Jewish and Moslem pilgrims, because the oxen with which Adam ploughed issued from it (Cazwīnī, Yācūt). There was a *mashhed*, or sacred tomb, beside it, perhaps the modern representative of the ancient Memnonium.

[2] In Num. xxi. 17 we find a song addressed to the well exhorting it to rise, which in its origin is hardly a mere poetic figure. We may compare what Cazwīnī, i. 189, records of the well of Ilābistān. When the water failed, a feast was held at the source, with music and dancing, to induce it to flow again. See also the modern Palestinian usage cited above, p. 169, n. 3.

[3] Cazwīnī, i. 194. I may also cite the numerous fables of amulets, to be found in the Tigris and other rivers, which protected their wearers against wild beasts, demons and other dangers (*Mir. Ausc.* § 159 *sq.*).

[4] Claudius Iolaus, *ap.* Steph. Byz. *s.v.* Ἄκη.

[5] Theophanes, quoted by Reland, ii. 922.

the sacred waters that issue from the New Jerusalem as giving life wherever they come, and the leaves of the trees on their banks as supplying medicine, his imagery is in full touch with common Semitic ideas (Ezek. xlvii. 9, 12).

The healing power of sacred water is closely connected with its purifying and consecrating power, for the primary conception of uncleanness is that of a dangerous infection. Washings and purifications play a great part in Semitic ritual, and were performed with living water, which was as such sacred in some degree. Whether specially sacred springs were used for purification, and if so under what restrictions I cannot make out; in most cases, I apprehend, they were deemed too holy to be approached by a person technically impure. It appears, however, from Ephræm Syrus that the practice of bathing in fountains was one of the heathen customs to which the Syrians of his time were much addicted, and he seems to regard this as a sort of heathen consecration.[1] Unfortunately the rhetoric of the Syrian fathers seldom condescends to precise details on such matters.

From this account of the ritual of sacred wells it will, I think, be clear that the usages and ceremonies are all intelligible on general principles, without reference to particular legends or the worship of the particular deities associated with special waters. The fountain is treated as a living thing, those properties of its waters which we call natural are regarded as manifestations of a divine life, and the source itself is honoured as a divine being, I had almost said a divine animal. When religion takes a form decidedly anthropomorphic or astral, myths are devised to reconcile the new point of view with the old usage, but the substance of the ritual remains unchanged.

[1] *Opp.* iii. 670 *sq.*; *H. et S.*, ed. Lamy, ii. 395, 411.

Let us now pass on from the worship of sacred waters to the cults connected with sacred trees.[1]

That the conception of trees as demoniac beings was familiar to the Semites has been already shown by many examples,[2] and there is also abundant evidence that in all parts of the Semitic area trees were adored as divine.

Tree worship pure and simple, where the tree is in all respects treated as a god, is attested for Arabia (but not on the best authority) in the case of the sacred date-palm at Nejrān.[3] It was adored at an annual feast, when it was all hung with fine clothes and women's ornaments. A similar tree, to which the people of Mecca resorted annually, and hung upon it weapons, garments, ostrich eggs and other gifts, is spoken of in the traditions of the prophet under the vague name of a *dhāt anwāṭ*, or "tree to hang things on." It seems to be identical with the sacred acacia at Nakhla in which the goddess Al-ʿOzzā was believed to reside.[4] The tree at Ḥodaibiya, mentioned in Sura xlviii. 18, was frequented by pilgrims who thought to derive a blessing from it, till it was cut down by the Caliph ʿOmar lest it should be worshipped like Al-Lāt and Al-ʿOzzā.[5] By the modern Arabs sacred trees are called *manāhil*, places where angels or *jinn* descend and are heard dancing and singing. It is deadly danger to pluck

[1] On sacred trees among the Semites, see Baudissin, *Studien*, ii. 184 *sqq.*; for Arabia, Wellhausen, *Heid.* p. 101. Compare Bötticher, *Baumcultus der Hellenen* (Berl. 1856), and Mannhardt, *Wald- und Feld-Culte* (Berl. 1875, 77).

[2] *Supra*, p. 133.

[3] Tabarī, i. 922 (Nöldeke's trans. p. 181); B. Hish. 22. The authority is Wahb b. Monabbih, who, I fear, was little better than a plausible liar.

[4] Wellhausen, p. 30 *sqq.*, p. 35.

[5] Yācūt, iii. 261. At Ḥodaibiya there was also a well whose waters were miraculously increased by the prophet (B. Hish. 742; *Moh. in Med.* 247). I suspect that the sanctity of tree and well are older than Mohammed, for the place is reckoned to the Ḥaram but juts out beyond the line of its border (Yācūt, ii. 222).

so much as a bough from such a tree; they are honoured with sacrifices, and parts of the flesh are hung on them, as well as shreds of calico, beads, etc. The sick man who sleeps under them receives counsel in a dream for the restoration of his health.[1]

Among the heathen Syrians tree worship must have had a large place, for this is one of the superstitions which Christianity itself was powerless to eradicate. We have already met with nominal Christians of Syria who in their sicknesses turned for help to a solitary tree, while zealous Christians were at pains to hew down the "trees of the demons."[2] As regards the Phœnicians and Canaanites we have the testimony of Philo Byblius that the plants of the earth were in ancient times esteemed as gods and honoured with libations and sacrifices, because from them the successive generations of men drew the support of their life. To this day the traveller in Palestine frequently meets with holy trees hung like an Arabian *dhāt anwāṭ* with rags as tokens of homage.

What place the cult of trees held in the more developed forms of Semitic religion it is not easy to determine. In later times the groves at the greater sanctuaries do not seem to have been direct objects of worship, though they shared in the inviolability that belonged to all the surroundings of the deity, and were sometimes—like the ancient cypresses of Heracles at Daphne—believed to have been planted by the god himself.[3] It was not at the great sanctuaries of cities but in the open field, where the rural population had continued from age to age to practise primitive rites without modification, that the worship of "solitary

[1] Doughty, *Arabia Deserta*, i. 448 *sqq*.

[2] See the citations in Kayser, *Jacob v. Edessa*, p. 141.

[3] Similarly the tamarisk at Beersheba was believed to have been planted by Abraham (Gen. xxi. 33).

trees" survived the fall of the great gods of Semitic heathenism.[1]

There is no reason to think that any of the greater Semitic cults was developed out of tree worship. In all of them the main place is given to altar service, and we shall see by and by that the beginnings of this form of worship, so far as they can be traced back to a time when the gods were not yet anthropomorphic, point to the cult of animals rather than of trees. That trees are habitually found at sanctuaries is by no means inconsistent with this view, for where the tree is merely conceived as planted by the god or as marking his favourite haunt, it receives no direct homage.

When, however, we find that no Canaanite high place was complete without its sacred tree standing beside the altar, and when we take along with this the undoubted fact that the direct cult of trees was familiar to all the Semites, it is hardly possible to avoid the conclusion that some elements of tree worship entered into the ritual even of such deities as in their origin were not tree-gods. The local sanctuaries of the Hebrews, which the prophets regard as purely heathenish, and which certainly were modelled in all points on Canaanite usage, were altar-sanctuaries. But the altars were habitually set up "under green trees," and, what is more, the altar was incomplete unless an *ashera* stood beside it. The meaning of this word, which the Authorised Version wrongly renders "grove," has given rise to a good deal of controversy. What kind of object the *ashera* was appears from Deut. xvi. 21: "Thou shalt not plant an *ashera* of any kind of

[1] The solitary tree may in certain cases be the last relic of a ruined heathen sanctuary. What Mocaddasi relates about the place called Al-Shajara ("the Tree"; *supra*, p. 160) points to something of this kind; for here there was an annual feast or fair. At the Terebinth of Mamre in like manner an altar at least can hardly have been lacking in heathen times.

wood (or, an *ashera*, any kind of tree) beside the altar of Jehovah"; it must therefore have been either a living tree or a tree-like post, and in all probability either form was originally admissible. The oldest altars, as we gather from the accounts of patriarchal sanctuaries, stood under actual trees; but this rule could not always be followed, and in the period of the kings it would seem that the place of the living tree was taken by a dead post or pole, planted in the ground like an English Maypole.[1] The *ashera* undoubtedly was an object of worship; for the prophets put it on the same line with other sacred symbols, images cippi and Baal-pillars (Isa. xvii. 8; Micah v. 12 *sqq.*), and the Phœnician inscription of Maṣ'ūb speaks of "the Astarte in the Ashera of the divinity of Hammon." The *ashera* therefore is a sacred symbol, the seat of the deity, and perhaps the name itself, as G. Hoffmann has suggested, means nothing more than the "mark" of the divine presence. But the opinion that there was a Canaanite goddess called Ashera, and that the trees or poles of the same name were her particular symbols, is not tenable; every altar had its *ashera*, even such altars as in the popular, pre-prophetic forms of Hebrew religion were dedicated to Jehovah.[2] This is

[1] It is a thing made by man's hands; Isa. xvii. 8, cf. 1 Kings xvi. 33, etc. In 2 Kings xxi. 7 (cf. xxiii. 6) we read of the Ashera-image. Similarly in 1 Kings xv. 13 there is mention of a "grisly object" which Queen Maacah made for an Ashera. These expressions may imply that the sacred pole was sometimes carved into a kind of image. That the sacred tree should degenerate first into a mere Maypole, and then into a rude wooden idol, is in accordance with analogies found elsewhere, *e.g.* in Greece; but it seems quite as likely that the *ashera* is described as a kind of idol simply because it was used in idolatrous cultus. An Assyrian monument from Khorsābād, figured by Botta and Layard, and reproduced in Rawlinson, *Monarchies*, ii. 37, and Stade, *Gesch. Isr.* i. 461, shows an ornamental pole planted beside a portable altar. Priests stand before it engaged in an act of worship, and touch the pole with their hands, or perhaps anoint it with some liquid substance.

[2] The prohibition in Deut. xvi. 21 is good evidence of the previous practice of the thing prohibited. See also 2 Kings xiii. 6.

not consistent with the idea that the sacred pole was the symbol of a distinct divinity; it seems rather to show that in early times tree worship had such a vogue in Canaan that the sacred tree, or the pole its surrogate, had come to be viewed as a general symbol of deity which might fittingly stand beside the altar of any god.[1]

[1] If a god and a goddess were worshipped together at the same sanctuary, as was the case, for example, at Aphaca and Hierapolis, and if the two sacred symbols at the sanctuary were a pole and a pillar of stone, it might naturally enough come about that the pole was identified with the goddess and the pillar with the god. The worship of Tammuz or Adonis was known at Jerusalem in the time of Ezekiel (viii. 14), and with Adonis the goddess Astarte must also have been worshipped, probably as the "queen of heaven" (Jer. vii., xliv.; cf. on this worship Kuenen in the *Verslagen*, etc., of the Royal Acad. of Amsterdam, 1888). It is not therefore surprising that in one or two late passages, written at a time when all the worship of the high places was regarded as entirely foreign to the religion of Jehovah, the Asherim seem to be regarded as the female partners of the Baalim; *i.e.* that the *ashera* is taken as a symbol of Astarte (Judg. iii. 7). The prophets of the *ashera* in 1 Kings xviii. 19, who appear along with the prophets of the Tyrian Baal as ministers of the foreign religion introduced by Jezebel, must have been prophets of Astarte. They form part of the Tyrian queen's court, and eat of her table, so that they have nothing to do with Hebrew religion. And conversely the old Hebrew sacred poles can have had nothing to do with the Tyrian goddess, for Jehu left the *ashera* at Samaria standing when he abolished all trace of Tyrian worship (2 Kings xiii. 6). There is no evidence of the worship of a divine pair among the older Hebrews; in the time of Solomon Astarte worship was a foreign religion (1 Kings xi. 5), and it is plain from Jer. ii. 27 that in ordinary Hebrew idolatry the tree or stock was the symbol not of a goddess but of a god. Even among the Phœnicians the association of sacred trees with goddesses rather than with gods is not so clear as is often supposed. From all this it follows that the "prophets of the Ashera" in 1 Kings, *l.c.*, are very misty personages, and that the mention of them implies a confusion between Astarte and the Ashera, which no Israelite in Elijah's time, or indeed so long as the northern kingdom stood, could have fallen into. In fact they do not reappear either in ver. 22 or in ver. 40, and the mention of them seems to be due to a late interpolation (Wellh., *Hexateuch*, 2nd ed. (1889), p. 281).

The evidence offered by Assyriologists that Ashrat = Ashera was a goddess (see Schrader in *Zeitschr. f. Assyriologie*, iii. 363 *sq.*) cannot overrule the plain sense of the Hebrew texts. Whether it suffices to show that in some places the general symbol of deity had become a special goddess is a question on which I do not offer an opinion; but see G. Hoffmann, *Ueber einige Phœn. Inschrr.* (1889), p. 26 *sqq.*, whose whole remarks are noteworthy. In *Cit.* 51 (*ZDMG.* xxxv. 424) the goddess seems to be called the

The general adoption of tree symbols at Canaanite sanctuaries must be connected with the fact that all Canaanite Baalim, whatever their original character, were associated with naturally fertile spots (Baal's land), and were worshipped as the givers of vegetable increase. We have seen already in the case of sacred streams how the life-blood of the god was conceived as diffused through the sacred waters, which thus became themselves impregnated with divine life and energy. And it was an easy extension of this idea to suppose that the tree which overshadowed the sacred fountain, and drew perennial strength and freshness from the moisture at its roots, was itself instinct with a particle of divine life. With the ancients the conception of life, whether divine or human, was not so much individualised as it is with us; thus, for example, all the members of one kin were conceived as having a common life embodied in the common blood which flowed through their veins. Similarly one and the same divine life might be shared by a number of objects, if all of them were nourished from a common vital source, and the elasticity of this conception made it very easy to bring natural holy things of different kinds into the cult of one and the same god. Elements of water tree and animal worship could all be combined in the ritual of a single anthropomorphic deity, by the simple supposition that the life of the god flowed in the sacred waters and fed the sacred tree.

As regards the connection of holy waters and holy trees, it must be remembered that in most Semitic lands self-sown wood can flourish only where there is underground water, and where therefore springs or wells exist beside the trees. Hence the idea that the same life is

mother of the sacred pole (אם האשרת), but the editors of the *CIS.* (No. 13) read האזרת.

manifested in the water and in the surrounding vegetation could hardly fail to suggest itself, and, broadly speaking, the holiness of fountains and that of trees, at least among the northern Semites, appear to be parts of the same religious conception, for it is only in exceptional cases that the one is found apart from the other.[1]

Where a tree was worshipped as the symbol of an anthropomorphic god we sometimes find a transformation legend directly connecting the life of the god with the vegetative life of the tree. This kind of myth, in which a god is transformed into a tree or a tree springs from the blood of a god, plays a large part in the sacred lore of Phrygia, where tree worship had peculiar prominence, and is also common in Greece. The Semitic examples are not numerous, and are neither so early nor so well attested as to inspire confidence that they are genuine old legends independent of Greek influence.[2] The most important of them is the myth told at Byblus in the time of Plutarch, of the sacred *erica* which was worshipped in the temple of Isis, and was said to have grown round the dead body of Osiris. At Byblus, Isis and Osiris are really Astarte and Adonis, so this may possibly be an original Semitic legend of a holy tree growing from the grave of a god.[3]

[1] An interesting example of the combination may here be added to those cited above. The Syriac text of Epiphanius, *De pond. et mens.* § 62 (Lagarde, *V. T. Fragm.* p. 65 ; *Symmicta*, ii. 203), tells us that Atad of Gen. l. 11 was identified with the spring and thorn-bush of Beth-haglā near Jericho, and the explanation offered of the name Beth-haglā seems to be based on a local tradition of a ritual procession round the sacred objects. See also the *Onomastica*, *s.v.* Area Atath. In Greece also it is an exception to find a sacred tree without its fountain ; Bötticher, p. 47.

[2] Cf. Baudissin, *op. cit.* p. 214.

[3] Plut. *Is. et Os.* §§ 15, 16. One or two features in the story are noteworthy. The sacred erica was a mere dead stump, for it was cut down by Isis and presented to the Byblians wrapped in a linen cloth and anointed with myrrh like a corpse. It therefore represented the dead god. But as a mere stump it also resembles the Hebrew *ashera*. Can it be that the rite of draping and anointing a sacred stump supplies the answer to the unsolved

I apprehend, however, that the physical link between trees and anthropomorphic gods was generally sought in the sacred water from which the trees drew their life. This is probable from the use of the term *ba'l* to denote trees that need neither rain nor irrigation, and indeed from the whole circle of ideas connected with Baal's land. A tree belonged to a particular deity, not because it was of a particular species, but simply because it was the natural wood of the place where the god was worshipped and sent forth his quickening streams to fertilise the earth. The sacred trees of the Semites include every prominent species of natural wood—the pines and cedars of Lebanon, the evergreen oaks of the Palestinian hills, the tamarisks of the Syrian jungles, the acacias of the Arabian wadies, and so forth.[1] So far as these natural woods are concerned, the attempts that have been made to connect individual species of trees with the worship of a single deity break down altogether; it cannot, for example, be said that the cypress belongs to Astarte more than to Melcarth, who planted the cypress trees at Daphne.

Cultivated trees, on the other hand, such as the palm, the olive and the vine, might *à priori* be expected, among the Semites as among the Greeks, to be connected with the special worship of the deity of the spot from which their culture was diffused; for religion and agricultural

question of the nature of the ritual practices connected with the Ashera? Some sort of drapery for the *ashera* is spoken of in 2 Kings xxiii. 7, and the Assyrian representation cited on p. 188, note 1, perhaps represents the anointing of the sacred pole.

[1] In modern Palestine the carob tree is peculiarly demoniac, the reddish hue of the wood suggesting blood (*ZDPV.* x. 181). According to *PEF. Qu. St.* 1893, p. 203 *sq.*, fig, carob and sycamore trees are haunted by devils, and it is dangerous to sleep under them, whereas the lotus tree (*sidr*) and the tamarisk appear to be inhabited by a *wely* (saint). But a tree of any species may be sacred if it grows at a Macām or sacred spot.

arts spread together and the one carried the other with it. Yet even of this there is little evidence; the palm was a familiar symbol of Astarte, but we also find a "Baal of the palm-tree" (Baal-tamar) in a place-name in Judg. xx. 33. The only clear Semitic case of the association of a particular deity with a fruit tree is, I believe, that of the Nabatæan Dusares, who was the god of the vine. But the vine came to the Nabatæans only in the period of Hellenic culture,[1] and Dusares as the wine-god seems simply to have borrowed the traits of Dionysus.

At Aphaca at the annual feast the goddess appeared in the form of a fiery meteor, which descended from the mountain-top and plunged into the water, while according to another account fire played about the temple, presumably, since an electrical phenomenon must have lain at the foundation of this belief, in the tree-tops of the sacred grove.[2] Similarly it was believed that fire played about the branches of the sacred olive tree between the Ambrosian rocks at Tyre, without scorching its leaves.[3] In like manner Jehovah appeared to Moses in the bush in flames of fire, so that the bush seemed to burn yet not to be consumed. The same phenomenon, according to Africanus[4] and Eustathius,[5] was seen at the terebinth of Mamre; the whole tree seemed to be aflame, but when the fire sank again remained unharmed. As lights were set by the well under the tree, and the festival was a nocturnal one, this was probably nothing more than an optical delusion exaggerated by the superstitious imagination, a mere artificial contrivance to keep up an ancient belief which must once have had wide currency in connection with

[1] Diodorus, xix. 94. 3. [2] *Supra*, p. 175, note 1.

[3] Achilles Tatius, ii. 14; Nonnus, xl. 474; cf. the representation on a coin of Gordian III. figured in Pietschmann, *Phœnizier*, p. 295.

[4] Georg. Syncellus, Bonn ed. p. 202.

[5] Cited by Reland, p. 712.

sacred trees, and is remarkable because it shows how a tree might become holy apart from all relation to agriculture and fertility. Jehovah, "who dwells in the bush" (Deut. xxxiii. 16), in the arid desert of Sinai, was the God of the Hebrews while they were still nomads ignorant of agriculture; and indeed the original seat of a conception like the burning bush, which must have its physical basis in electrical phenomena, must probably be sought in the clear dry air of the desert or of lofty mountains. The apparition of Jehovah in the burning bush belongs to the same circle of ideas as His apparition in the thunders and lightnings of Sinai.

When the divine manifestation takes such a form as the flames in the bush, the connection between the god and the material symbol is evidently much looser than in the Baal type of religion, where the divine life is immanent in the life of the tree; and the transition is comparatively easy from the conception of Deut. xxxiii. 16, where Jehovah inhabits (not visits) the bush, as elsewhere He is said to inhabit the temple, to the view prevalent in most parts of the Old Testament, that the tree or the pillar at a sanctuary is merely a memorial of the divine name, the mark of a place where He has been found in the past and may be found again. The separation between Jehovah and physical nature, which is so sharply drawn by the prophets and constitutes one of the chief points of distinction between their faith and that of the masses, whose Jehovah worship had all the characters of Baal worship, may be justly considered as a development of the older type of Hebrew religion. It has sometimes been supposed that the conception of a God immanent in nature is Aryan, and that of a transcendental God Semitic; but the former view is quite as characteristic of the Baal worship of the agricultural Semites as of the early faiths of the agricultural Aryans. It is true that the higher developments of Semitic religion took a different line, but they did not grow out of Baal worship.

As regards the special forms of cultus addressed to sacred trees, I can add nothing certain to the very scanty indications that have already come before us. Prayers were addressed to them, particularly for help in sickness, but doubtless also for fertile seasons and the like, and they were hung with votive gifts, especially garments and ornaments, perhaps also anointed with unguents as if they had been real persons. More could be said about the use of branches, leaves or other parts of sacred trees in lustrations, as medicine, and for other ritual purposes. But these things do not directly concern us at present; they are simply to be noted as supplying additional evidence, if such be necessary, that a sacred energy, that is, a divine life, resided even in the parts of holy trees.

The only other aspect of the subject which seems to call for notice at the present stage is the connection of sacred trees with oracles and divination. Oracles and omens from trees and at tree sanctuaries are of the commonest among all races,[1] and are derived in very various ways, either from observation of phenomena connected with the trees themselves, and interpreted as manifestations of divine life, or from ordinary processes of divination performed in the presence of the sacred object. Sometimes the tree is believed to speak with an articulate voice, as the *gharcad* did in a dream to Moslim;[2] but except in a dream it is obvious that the voice of the tree can only be some rustling sound, as of wind in the branches, like that which was given to David as a token

[1] Cf. Bötticher, *op. cit.* chap. xi.

[2] *Supra*, p. 133. The same belief in trees from which a spirit speaks oracles occurs in a modern legend given by Doughty, *Ar. Des.* ii. 209.

of the right moment to attack the Philistines,[1] and requires a soothsayer to interpret it. The famous holy tree near Shechem, called the tree of soothsayers in Judg. ix. 37,[2] and the "tree of the revealer" in Gen. xii. 6, must have been the seat of a Canaanite tree oracle.[3] We have no hint as to the nature of the physical indications that guided the soothsayers, nor have I found any other case of a Semitic tree oracle where the mode of procedure is described. But the belief in trees as places of divine revelation must have been widespread in Canaan. The prophetess Deborah gave her responses under a palm near Bethel, which according to sacred tradition marked the grave of the nurse of Rebekah.[4] That the artificial sacred tree or *ashera* was used in divination would follow from 1 Kings xviii. 19, were it not that there are good grounds for holding that in this passage the prophets of the *ashera* are simply the prophets of the Tyrian Astarte. But in Hos. iv. 12 the "stock" of which the prophet's contemporaries sought counsel can hardly be anything else than the *ashera*.[5] Soothsayers who draw their inspiration

[1] 2 Sam. v. 24.

[2] A.V. "plain of Meonenim."

[3] It was perhaps only one tree of a sacred grove, for Deut. xi. 30 speaks of the "trees of the revealer" in the plural.

[4] Gen. xxxv. 8. There indeed the tree is called an *allōn*, a word generally rendered oak. But *allōn*, like *ēlāh* and *ēlōn*, seems to be a name applicable to any sacred tree, perhaps to any great tree. Stade, *Gesch. Is.* i. 455, would even connect these words with *ēl*, god, and the Phœnician *alonīm*.

[5] As the next clause says, "and their rod declareth to them," it is commonly supposed that rhabdomancy is alluded to, *i.e.* the use of divining rods. And no doubt the divining rod, in which a spirit of life is supposed to reside, so that it moves and gives indications apart from the will of the man who holds it, is a superstition cognate to the belief in sacred trees; but when "their rod" occurs in parallelism with "their stock" or tree, it lies nearer to cite Philo Byblius, *ap.* Eus. *Pr. Ev.* i. 10. 11, who speaks of rods and pillars consecrated by the Phœnicians and worshipped by annual feasts. On this view the rod is only a smaller *ashera*. Drusius therefore seems to hit the mark in comparing Festus's note on *delubrum*, where the

from plants are found in Semitic legend even in the Middle Ages.[1]

To the two great natural marks of a place of worship, the fountain and the tree, ought perhaps to be added grottoes and caves of the earth. At the present day almost every sacred site in Palestine has its grotto, and that this is no new thing is plain from the numerous symbols of Astarte worship found on the walls of caves in Phœnicia. There can be little doubt that the oldest Phœnician temples were natural or artificial grottoes, and that the sacred as well as the profane monuments of Phœnicia, with their marked preference for monolithic forms, point to the rock-hewn cavern as the original type that dominated the architecture of the region.[2] But if this be so, the use of grottoes as temples in later times does not prove that caverns as such had any primitive religious significance. Religious practice is always conservative, and rock-hewn temples would naturally be used after men had ceased to live like troglodytes in caves and holes of the earth. Moreover, ancient temples are in most instances not so much houses where the gods live, as storehouses for the vessels and treasures of the sanctuary. The altar, the sacred tree, and the other divine symbols to which acts of worship are addressed, stand outside in front of the temple, and the whole service is carried on in the open air. Now all over the Semitic world caves and pits are the primitive storehouses, and we know that in Arabia

Romans are said to have worshipped pilled rods as gods. See more on rod worship in Bötticher, *op. cit.* xvi. 5. Was the omen derived from the rod flourishing or withering? We have such an omen in Aaron's rod (Num. xvii.); and Adonis rods, set as slips to grow or wither, seem to be referred to in Isa. xvii. 10 *sqq.*, a passage which would certainly gain force if the withering of the slips was an ill omen. Divination from the flourishing and withering of sacred trees is very common in antiquity (Bötticher, chap. xi.).

[1] Chwolsohn, *Ssabier*, ii. 914.

[2] Renan, *Phénicie*, p. 822 *sq.*

a pit called the *ghabghab*, in which the sacred treasure was stored, was a usual adjunct to sanctuaries.[1] But there are weighty reasons for doubting whether this is the whole explanation of cave sacrifices. In other parts of the world, *e.g.* in Greece, there are many examples of caves associated with the worship of chthonic deities, and also with the oracles of gods like Apollo who are not usually regarded as chthonic or subterranean; and the acts performed in these caves imply that they were regarded as the peculiar seats of divine energy. The common opinion seems to be that Semitic gods were never chthonic, in the sense that their seats and the source of their influence were sought underground. But we know that all branches of the Semites believed in chthonic demons, the Hebrew *ōb*, the Syrian *zakkūrē*, the Arabian *ahl al-arḍ* or "earth-folk,"[2] with whom wizards hold fellowship. Again, the ordinary usages of Semitic religion have many points of contact with the chthonic rites of the Greeks. The Arabian *ghabghab* is not a mere treasury, for the victim is said to be brought to it, and the sacrificial blood flows into the pit.[3] Similarly the annual human sacrifice at Dumætha (Duma) was buried under the altar-idol.[4] As regards the northern Semites the chthonic associations of the Baalim as gods of the subterranean waters are unquestionable, particularly at sanctuaries like Aphaca, where the tomb of the Baal was shown beside his sacred stream;[5] for a buried god is a god that dwells underground. The whole N. Semitic area was dotted over with sacred tombs, Memnonia, Semiramis

[1] Wellhausen, p. 100.

[2] For the *ōb* see especially Isa. xxix. 4; for the *zakkūrē*, *Julianos*, ed. Hoffmann, p. 247, and *ZDMG.* xxviii. 666. For the *ahl al-arḍ* the oldest passage I know is Ibn Hishām, p. 258, l. 19, where these demons appear in connection with witchcraft, exactly like the *ōb* and the *zakkūrē*.

[3] Yācūt, iii. 772 *sq.*; B. Hishām, p. 55, l. 18; cf. Wellhausen, *ut supra*.

[4] Porphyry, *De Abst.* ii. 56.

[5] *Supra*, p. 174, note.

mounds and the like, and at every such spot a god or demigod had his subterranean abode.[1] No part of old Semitic belief was more deeply graven on the popular imagination than this, which still holds its ground among the peasantry, in spite of Christianity and Islam, with the merely nominal modification that the ancient god has been transformed into a wonder-working *sheikh* or *wely*. In view of these facts it can hardly be doubted that remarkable caves or passages, leading into the bowels of the earth, were as likely to be clothed with supernatural associations among the Semites as among the Greeks. And there is at least one great Semitic temple whose legends distinctly indicate that the original sanctuary was a chasm in the ground. According to Lucian, this chasm swallowed up the waters of the Flood (Deucalion's flood, as the Hellenised form of the legend has it), and the temple with its altars and special ritual of pouring water into the gulf was erected in commemoration of this deliverance.[2] According to the Christian Melito, the chasm, or "well," as he calls it, was haunted by a demon and the water-pouring was designed to prevent him from coming up to injure men.[3] Here the primitive sanctity of the chasm is the one fixed point amidst the variations and distortions of later legend; and on this analogy I am disposed to conjecture that in other cases also a cavern or cleft in the earth may have been chosen as a primæval sanctuary because it marked the spot where a chthonic god went up and down between the outer world and his subterranean home, and where he

[1] That the Semiramis mounds were really tomb-sanctuaries appears from the testimony of Ctesias cited by Syncellus, i. 119 (Bonn), and John of Antioch (*Fr. Hist. Gr.* iv. 589), compared with Langlois, *Chron. de Michel le Grand* (Venice, 1868), p. 40. See also my article on "Ctesias and the Semiramis legend" in *Eng. Hist. Rev.* April 1887.

[2] *De Dea Syria*, § 13, cf. § 48.

[3] Melito, *Spic. Syr.* p. 25.

could be best approached with prayers and offerings. What seems particularly to strengthen this conjecture is that the adytum, or dark inner chamber, found in many temples both among the Semites and in Greece, was almost certainly in its origin a cave; indeed in Greece it was often wholly or partially subterranean and is called *μέγαρον*—a word which in this application can hardly be true Greek, and mean "hall," but is rather to be identified with the Semitic מערה, "a cave." The adytum is not a constant feature in Greek temples, and the name *μέγαρον* seems to indicate that it was borrowed from the Semites.[1] Where it does exist it is a place of oracle, as the Holy of Holies was at Jerusalem, and therefore cannot be looked upon in any other light than as the part of the sanctuary where the god is most immediately present.

From this obscure topic we pass at once into clearer light when we turn to consider the ordinary artificial mark of a Semitic sanctuary, viz. the sacrificial pillar, cairn or rude altar. The sacred fountain and the sacred tree are common symbols at sanctuaries, but they are not invariably found, and in most cases they have but a secondary relation to the ordinary ritual. In the more advanced type of sanctuary the real meeting-place between man and his god is the altar. The altar in its developed form is a raised structure upon which sacrifices are presented to the god. Most commonly the sacrifices are fire-offerings, and the altar is the place where they are burned; but in another type of ritual, of which the Roman *lectisternium* and the Hebrew oblation of shewbread are familiar examples, the altar is simply a table on which a meal is spread before the deity. Whether fire is used or not is a

[1] The possibility of this can hardly be disputed when we think of the temple of Apollo at Delos, where the holy cave is the original sanctuary. For this was a place of worship which the Greeks took over from the Phœnicians.

detail in the mode of presentation and does not affect the essence of the sacrificial act. In either case the offering consists of food, "the bread of God" as it is called in the Hebrew ritual,[1] and there is no real difference between a table and altar. Indeed the Hebrew altar of burnt-offering is called the table of the Lord, while conversely the table of shewbread is called an altar.[2]

The table is not a very primitive article of furniture,[3] and this circumstance alone is enough to lead us to suspect that the altar was not originally a raised platform on which a sacrificial meal could be set forth. In Arabia, where sacrifice by fire is almost unknown, we find no proper altar, but in its place a rude pillar or heap of stones, beside which the victim is slain, the blood being poured out over the stone or at its base.[4] This ritual of the blood is the essence of the offering; no part of the flesh falls as a rule to the god, but the whole is distributed among the men who assist at the sacrifice. The sacred stones, which are already mentioned by Herodotus, are called *anṣāb* (sing. *noṣb*), *i.e.* stones set up, pillars. We also find the name *gharīy*, "blood-bedaubed," with reference to the ritual just described. The meaning of this ritual will occupy us later; meantime the thing to be noted is that the altar is only a modification of the *noṣb*, and that the rude Arabian usage is the primitive type out of which all the elaborate altar ceremonies of the more cultivated Semites grew. Whatever else was done in connection with a sacrifice, the primitive rite of sprinkling

[1] Lev. xxi. 8, 17, etc.; cf. Lev. iii. 11.

[2] Mal. i. 7, 12; Ezek. xli. 22; cf. Wellhausen, *Prolegomena*, p. 69. The same word (ערך) is used of setting a table and disposing the pieces of the sacrifice on the fire-altar.

[3] The old Arabian *sofra* is merely a skin spread on the ground, not a raised table.

[4] Wellhausen, *Heid.* p. 113; cf. *ibid.* pp. 39 *sq.* 99.

or dashing the blood against the altar, or allowing it to flow down on the ground at its base, was hardly ever omitted;[1] and this practice was not peculiar to the Semites, but was equally the rule with the Greeks and Romans, and indeed with the ancient nations generally.

As regards fire sacrifices, we shall find reason to doubt whether the hearth on which the sacred flesh was consumed was originally identical with the sacred stone or cairn over which the sacrificial blood was allowed to flow. It seems probable, for reasons that cannot be stated at this point, that the more modern form of altar, which could be used both for the ritual of the blood and as a sacred hearth, was reached by combining two operations which originally took place apart. But in any case it is certain that the original altar among the northern Semites, as well as among the Arabs, was a great stone or cairn at which the blood of the victim was shed. At Jacob's covenant with Laban no other altar appears than the cairn of stones beside which the parties to the compact ate together; in the ancient law of Ex. xx. 24, 25, it is prescribed that the altar must be of earth or of unhewn stone; and that a single stone sufficed appears from 1 Sam. xiv. 32 *sqq.*, where the first altar built by Saul is simply the great stone which he caused to be rolled unto him after the battle of Michmash, that the people might slay their booty of sheep and cattle at it, and not eat the flesh with the blood. The simple shedding of the blood by

[1] There were indeed altars at which no animal sacrifices were presented. Such are, among the Hebrews, the altar of incense and the table of shew-bread, and among the Phœnicians the altar at Paphos (Tac., *Hist.* ii. 3); perhaps also the "altar of the pious" at Delos (Porph., *De Abst.* ii. 28) was of Phœnician origin. In later times certain exceptional sacrifices were burned alive or slain without effusion of blood, but this does not touch the general principle.

the stone or altar consecrated the slaughter and made it a legitimate sacrifice. Here, therefore, there is no difference between the Hebrew altar and the Arabian *noṣb* or *gharīy*.

Monolithic pillars or cairns of stone are frequently mentioned in the more ancient parts of the Old Testament as standing at sanctuaries,[1] generally in connection with a sacred legend about the occasion on which they were set up by some famous patriarch or hero. In the biblical story they usually appear as mere memorial structures without any definite ritual significance; but the pentateuchal law looks on the use of sacred pillars (*maṣṣēbōth*) as idolatrous.[2] This is the best evidence that such pillars had an important place among the appurtenances of Canaanite temples, and as Hosea (iii. 4) speaks of the *maṣṣēba* as an indispensable feature in the sanctuaries of northern Israel in his time, we may be sure that by the mass of the Hebrews the pillars of Shechem, Bethel, Gilgal and other shrines were looked upon not as mere memorials of historical events, but as necessary parts of the ritual apparatus of a place of worship. That the special ritual acts connected with the Canaanite *maṣṣēba* were essentially the same as in the case of the Arabian *noṣb* may be gathered from Philo Byblius, who, in his pseudo-historical manner, speaks of a certain Usous who consecrated two pillars to fire and wind, and paid worship to them, pouring out libations to them of the blood of beasts taken in hunting.[3] From these evidences, and especially from the fact that libations of the same kind

[1] At Shechem, Josh. xxiv. 26; Bethel, Gen. xxviii. 18 *sqq.*; Gilead, (Ramoth-gilead), Gen. xxxi. 45 *sqq.*; Gilgal, Josh. iv. 5; Mizpeh, 1 Sam. vii. 12; Gibeon, 2 Sam. xx. 8; En-rogel, 1 Kings i. 9.

[2] Ex. xxxiv. 13; Deut. xii. 3; cf. Mic. v. 13 (12). For pillars A.V. generally gives, incorrectly, 'images."

[3] Euseb. *Præp. Ev.* i. 10. 10. Libations of blood are mentioned as a heathenish rite in Ps. xvi. 4.

are applied to both, it seems clear that the altar is a differentiated form of the primitive rude stone pillar, the *noṣb* or *maṣṣēba*.[1] But the sacred stone is more than an altar, for in Hebrew and Canaanite sanctuaries the altar, in its developed form as a table or hearth, does not supersede the pillar; the two are found side by side at the same sanctuary, the altar as a piece of sacrificial apparatus, and the pillar as a visible symbol or embodiment of the presence of the deity, which in process of time comes to be fashioned and carved in various ways, till ultimately it becomes a statue or anthropomorphic idol of stone, just as the sacred tree or post was ultimately developed into an image of wood.[2]

It has been disputed whether the sacred stone at Semitic sanctuaries was from the first an object of worship, a sort of rude idol in which the divinity was somehow supposed to be present. It is urged that in the narratives of Genesis the *maṣṣēba* is a mere mark without intrinsic religious significance. But the original significance of the patriarchal symbols cannot be concluded from the sense put on them by writers who lived many centuries after those ancient sanctuaries were first founded; and at the time when the oldest of the pentateuchal narratives were written, the Canaanites and the great mass of the Hebrews certainly treated the *maṣṣēba* as a sort of idol or embodiment of the divine presence. Moreover Jacob's pillar is more than a mere landmark, for it is anointed, just as idols were in antiquity, and the pillar itself, not the spot on which it stood, is called

[1] *Noṣb* and *maṣṣēba* are derived from the same root (NṢB, "set up"). Another name for the pillar or cairn is נציב, which occurs in place-names, both in Canaan and among the Aramæans (Nisibis, "the pillars").

[2] From this point of view the prohibition of a graven image (פסל) in the second commandment stands on one line with the prohibition of an altar of hewn stone (Ex. xx. 25).

"the house of God,"[1] as if the deity were conceived actually to dwell in the stone, or manifest himself therein to his worshippers. And this is the conception which appears to have been associated with sacred stones everywhere. When the Arab daubed blood on the *noṣb* his object was to bring the offering into direct contact with the deity, and in like manner the practice of stroking the sacred stone with the hand is identical with the practice of touching or stroking the garments or beard of a man in acts of supplication before him.[2] Here, therefore, the sacred stone is altar and idol in one; and so Porphyry (*De Abst.* ii. 56) in his account of the worship of Duma in Arabia expressly speaks of "the altar which they use as an idol."[3] The same conception must have prevailed among the Canaanites before altar and pillar were differentiated from one another, otherwise the pillar would have been simply changed into the more convenient form of an altar, and there could have been no reason for retaining both. So far as the evidence from tradition and ritual goes, we can only think of the sacred stone as consecrated by the actual presence of the godhead, so that whatever touched it was brought into immediate contact with the deity. How such a conception first obtained currency is a matter for which no direct evidence is available, and which if settled at all can be settled only by inference and conjecture. At the present stage of our inquiry it is not possible to touch on this subject except in a provisional

[1] Gen. xxviii. 22.

[2] Wellhausen, p. 105; *ibid.* p. 52. Conversely a holy person conveys a blessing by the touch of his hand (Ibn Sa'd, Nos. 90, 130), or even by touching something which others touch after him (B. Hishām, 338. 15).

[3] So in the well-known line of Al-A'shā the god to whom the sacred stone belongs is himself said to be *manṣūb*, "set up" (B. Hish. 256, 8; *Morg. Forsch.* p. 258). The Arabian gods are expressly called "gods of stone" in a verse cited by Ibn Sa'd, No. 118.

way. But some things may be said which will at least tend to make the problem more definite.

Let us note then that there are two distinct points to be considered—(1) how men came to look on an artificial structure as the symbol or abode of the god, (2) why the particular artificial structure is a stone or a cairn of stones.

(1.) In tree worship and in the worship of fountains adoration is paid to a thing which man did not make, which has an independent life, and properties such as to the savage imagination may well appear to be divine. On the same analogy one can understand how natural rocks and boulders, suited by their size and aspect to affect the savage imagination, have acquired in various parts of the world the reputation of being animated objects with power to help and hurt man, and so have come to receive religious worship. But the worship of artificial pillars and cairns of stones, chosen at random and set up by man's hand, is a very different thing from this. Of course not the rudest savage believes that in setting up a sacred stone he is making a new god; what he does believe is that the god comes into the stone, dwells in it or animates it, so that for practical purposes the stone is thenceforth an embodiment of the god, and may be spoken of and dealt with as if it were the god himself. But there is an enormous difference between worshipping the god in his natural embodiment, such as a tree or some notable rock, and persuading him to come and take for his embodiment a structure set up for him by the worshipper. From the metaphysical point of view, which we are always tempted to apply to ancient religion, the worship of stocks and stones prepared by man's hand seems to be a much cruder thing than the worship of natural life as displayed in a fountain or a secular tree; but practically the idea that the godhead consents to be present in a structure set for him by his worshippers implies a degree of intimacy and permanency in the relations between man and the being he adores which marks an advance on the worship of natural objects. It is true that the rule of Semitic worship is that the artificial symbol can only be set up in a place already consecrated by tokens of the divine presence; but the sacred stone is not merely a token that the place is frequented by a god, it is also a permanent pledge that in this place he consents to enter into stated relations with men and accept their service.

(2.) That deities like those of ancient heathenism, which were not supposed to be omnipresent, and which were commonly thought of as having some sort of corporeal nature, could enter into a stone for the convenience of their worshippers, seems to us a fundamental difficulty, but was hardly a difficulty that would be felt by primitive man, who has most elastic conceptions of what is possible. When we speak of an idol we generally think of an image presenting a likeness of the god, because our knowledge of heathenism is mainly drawn from races which had made some advance in the plastic arts, and used idols shaped in such a way as to suggest the appearance and attributes which legend ascribed to each particular deity. But there is no reason in the nature of things why the physical embodiment which the deity assumes for the convenience of his worshipper should be a copy of his proper form, and in the earliest times to which the worship of sacred stones goes back there was evidently no attempt to make the idol a simulacrum. A cairn or rude stone pillar is not a portrait of anything, and I take it that we shall go on altogether false lines if we try to explain its selection as a divine symbol by any consideration of what it looks like. Even when the arts had made considerable progress the Semites felt no need to fashion their sacred symbols into likenesses of the gods. Melcarth was worshipped at Tyre in the form of two pillars,[1] and at the great temple of Paphos, down to Roman times, the idol was not an anthropomorphic image of Astarte, but a conical stone.[2] These antique forms were not retained from want of plastic skill, or because there were not well-known types on which images of the various gods could be and often were constructed; for we see from the second commandment that likenesses of things celestial terrestrial and aquatic were objects of worship in Canaan from a very early date. It was simply not thought necessary that the symbol in which the divinity was present should be like the god.

Phœnician votive cippi were often adorned with rude figures of men, animals and the like, as may be seen in the series of such monuments dedicated to Tanith and Baal Hammān which are depicted in the *Corpus Inscr. Sem.* These figures, which are often little better than hieroglyphics, served, like the accompanying inscriptions, to indicate the meaning of the cippus and the deity to which it was devoted. An image in like manner declares its own meaning better than a mere pillar, but the chief idol of a great sanctuary did not require to be explained in this way; its position showed what it was without either figure or inscription. It is probable that among the Phœnicians and Hebrews, as among the Arabs at the time of Mohammed, portrait images, such as are spoken of in the second com-

[1] Herod. ii. 44. Twin pillars stood also before the temples of Paphos and Hierapolis, and Solomon set up two brazen pillars before his temple at Jerusalem (1 Kings vii. 15, 21). As he named them "The stablisher" and "In him is strength," they were doubtless symbols of Jehovah.

[2] Tac., *Hist.* ii. 2. Other examples are the cone of Elagabalus at Emesa (Herodian, v. 3. 5) and that of Zeus Casius. More in Zoega, *De obeliscis*, p. 203. The cone at Emesa was believed to have fallen from heaven, like the idol of Artemis at Ephesus and other ancient and very sacred idols.

mandment, were mainly small gods for private use.[1] For public sanctuaries the second pillar or *ashera* sufficed.

The worship of sacred stones is often spoken of as if it belonged to a distinctly lower type of religion than the worship of images. It is called fetichism—a merely popular term, which conveys no precise idea, but is vaguely supposed to mean something very savage and contemptible. And no doubt the worship of unshapen blocks is from the artistic point of view a very poor thing, but from a purely religious point of view its inferiority to image worship is not so evident. The host in the mass is artistically as much inferior to the Venus of Milo as a Semitic *maṣṣēba* was, but no one will say that mediæval Christianity is a lower form of religion than Aphrodite worship. What seems to be implied when sacred stones are spoken of as fetiches is that they date from a time when stones were regarded as the natural embodiment and proper form of the gods, not merely as the embodiment which they took up in order to receive the homage of their worshippers. Such a view, I venture to think, is entirely without foundation. Sacred stones are found in all parts of the world and in the worship of gods of the most various kinds, so that their use must rest on some cause which was operative in all primitive religions. But that all or most ancient gods were originally gods of stones, inhabiting natural rocks or boulders, and that artificial cairns or pillars are imitations of these natural objects, is against evidence and quite incredible. Among the Semites the sacred pillar is universal, but the instances of the worship of rocks and stones *in situ* are neither numerous

[1] Of the common use of such gods every museum supplies evidence, in the shape of portable idols and amulets with pictured carving. Compare 2 Macc. xii. 40, where we read that many of the army of Judas Maccabæus—Jews fighting against heathenism—wore under their shirts ἱερώματα τῶν ἀπὸ Ἰαμνείας εἰδώλων.

nor prominent, and the idea of founding a theory of the origin of sacred stones in general upon them could hardly occur to any one, except on the perfectly gratuitous supposition that the idol or symbol must necessarily be like the god.[1]

The notion that the sacred stone is a simulacrum of the god seems also to be excluded by the observation that several pillars may stand together as representatives of a single deity. Here, indeed, the evidence must be sifted with some care, for a god and a goddess were often worshipped together, and then each would have a pillar.[2] But this kind of explanation does not cover all the cases. In the Arabian rite described in Herod. iii. 8, two deities are invoked, but seven sacred stones are anointed with

[1] The stone of al-Lāt at Ṭāïf, in which the goddess was supposed to dwell, is identified by local tradition with a mass which seems to be a natural block *in situ*, though not one of unusual size or form. See my *Kinship*, p. 293, and Doughty, ii. 515. At 'Okāz the sacred circle was performed round rocks (*ṣokhūr*, Yācūt, iii. 705), presumably the remarkable group which I described in 1880 in a letter to the *Scotsman* newspaper. "In the S.E. corner of the small plain, which is barely two miles across, rises a hill of loose granite blocks, crowned by an enormous pillar standing quite erect and flanked by lower masses. I do not think that this pillar can be less than 50 or 60 feet in height, and its extraordinary aspect, standing between two lesser guards on either side, is the first thing that strikes the eye on nearing the plain." The rock of Dusares, referred to by Steph. Byz., is perhaps the cliff with a waterfall which has been already mentioned (*supra*, p. 168), and so may be compared with the rock at Kadesh from which the fountain gushed. The sanctity of rocks from which water flows, or of rocks that form a sacred grotto, plainly cannot be used to explain the origin of sacred cairns and pillars which have neither water nor cavern.

That the phrase "Rock of Israel," applied to Jehovah, has anything to do with stone worship may legitimately be doubted. The use of baetylia, or small portable stones to which magical life was ascribed, hardly belongs to the present argument. The idol Abnīl at Nisibis is simply "the cippus of El" (Assem. i. 27).

[2] Cf. *Kinship*, p. 293 *sqq*. p. 262. Whether the two gharī at Ḥira and Faid (Wellh. p. 40) belong to a pair of gods, or are a double image of one deity, like the twin pillars of Heracles-Melcarth at Tyre, cannot be decided. Wellhausen inclines to the latter view, citing *Ḥamāsa*, 190. 15. But in Arabic idiom the two 'Ozzās may mean al-'Ozzā and her companion goddess al-Lāt. Mr. C. Lyall suggests the reading *gharīyaini*.

blood, and a plurality of sacred stones round which the worshippers circled in a single act of worship are frequently spoken of in Arabian poetry.[1] Similarly in Canaan the place-name Anathoth means images of 'Anath in the plural; and at Gilgal there were twelve sacred pillars according to the number of the twelve tribes,[2] as at Sinai twelve pillars were erected at the covenant sacrifice.[3] Twin pillars of Melcarth have already been noticed at Tyre, and are familiar to us as the "pillars of Hercules" in connection with the Straits of Gibraltar.

Another view taken of sacred pillars and cippi is that they are images, not of the deity, but of bodily organs taken as emblems of particular powers or attributes of deity, especially of life-giving and reproductive power. I will say something of this theory in a note; but as an explanation of the origin of sacred stones it has not even a show of plausibility. Men did not begin by worshipping emblems of divine powers, they brought their homage and offerings to the god himself. If the god was already conceived as present in the stone, it was a natural exercise of the artistic faculty to put something on the stone to indicate the fact; and this something, if the god was anthropomorphically conceived, might either be a human figure, or merely an indication of important parts of the human figure. At Tabāla in Arabia, for

[1] Wellh., *Heid.* p. 99. The poets often seem to identify the god with one of the stones, as al-'Ozzā was identified with one of the three trees at Nakhla. The *anṣāb* stand beside the god (*Tāj*, iii. 560, l. 1) or round him, which probably means that the idol proper stood in the midst. In the verse of al-Farazdac, *Agh.* 3, xix. l. 30, to which Wellhausen calls attention, the Oxford MS. of the Nacāiḍ and that of the late Spitta-Bey read, *'alā ḥini lā tuḥyā 'l-banātu wa-idh humū 'ukūfun 'alā 'l-anṣābi ḥawla 'l-mudawwari*, and the scholia explain *al-mudawwar* as *ṣanam yadūrūna ḥawlahu.* It is impossible to believe that this distinction between one stone and the rest is primitive.

[2] Josh. iv. 20. These stones are probably identical with the stone-idols (A.V. "quarries") of Judg. iii. 19, 26.

[3] Ex. xxiv. 4.

instance, a sort of crown was sculptured on the stone of al-Lāt to mark her head. In like manner other parts of the body may be rudely designated, particularly such as distinguish sex. But that the sacred cippus, as such, is not a sexual emblem, is plain from the fact that exactly the same kind of pillar or cone is used to represent gods and goddesses indifferently.[1]

On a review of all these theories it seems most probable that the choice of a pillar or cairn as the primitive idol was not dictated by any other consideration than convenience for ritual purposes. The stone or stone-heap was a convenient mark of the proper place of sacrifice, and at the same time, if the deity consented to be present at it, provided the means for carrying out the ritual of the sacrificial blood. Further than this it does not seem possible to go, till we know why it was thought so essential to bring the blood into immediate contact with the god adored. This question belongs to the subject of sacrifice, which I propose to commence in the next lecture.[2]

[1] See *Additional Note* D, *Phallic Symbols*.

[2] One or two isolated statements about sacred stones, not sufficiently important or well attested to be mentioned in the text, may deserve citation in a note. Pliny, *H. N.* xxxvii. 161, speaks of an ordeal at the temple of Melcarth at Tyre by sitting on a stone seat, *ex qua pii facile surgebant.*—Yācūt, iii. 760, has a very curious account of a stone like a landmark near Aleppo. When it was thrown down the women of the adjoining villages were seized by a shameful frenzy, which ceased when it was set up again. Yācūt had this by very formal written attestation from persons he names; but failed to obtain confirmation of the story on making personal inquiry at Aleppo.

LECTURE VI

SACRIFICE—PRELIMINARY SURVEY

WE have seen in the course of the last lecture that the practices of ancient religion required a fixed meeting-place between the worshippers and their god. The choice of such a place is determined in the first instance by the consideration that certain spots are the natural haunts of a deity, and therefore holy ground. But for most rituals it is not sufficient that the worshipper should present his service on holy ground: it is necessary that he should come into contact with the god himself, and this he believes himself to do when he directs his homage to a natural object, like a tree or a sacred fountain, which is believed to be the actual seat of the god and embodiment of a divine life, or when he draws near to an artificial mark of the immediate presence of the deity. In the oldest forms of Semitic religion this mark is a sacred stone, which is at once idol and altar; in later times the idol and the altar stand side by side, and the original functions of the sacred stone are divided between them; the idol represents the presence of the god, and the altar serves to receive the gifts of the worshipper. Both are necessary to constitute a complete sanctuary, because a complete act of worship implies not merely that the worshipper comes into the presence of his god with gestures of homage and words of prayer, but also that he lays before the deity some material oblation. In antiquity an act of worship was a formal operation in which certain prescribed rites and ceremonies must be duly observed. And among these the oblation at the altar had so central a place that among the Greeks and Romans the words ἱερουργία and *sacrificium*, which in their primary application denote any action within the sphere of things sacred to the gods, and so cover the whole field of ritual, were habitually used, like our English word sacrifice, of those oblations at the altar round which all other parts of ritual turned. In English idiom there is a further tendency to narrow the word sacrifice to such oblations as involve the slaughter of a victim. In the Authorised Version of the Bible "sacrifice and offering" is the usual translation of the Hebrew *zébaḥ uminḥa*, that is, "bloody and bloodless oblations." For the purposes of the present discussion, however, it seems best to include both kinds of oblation under the term "sacrifice"; for a comprehensive term is necessary, and the word "offering," which naturally suggests itself as an alternative, is somewhat too wide, as it may properly include not only sacrifices but votive offerings, of treasure images and the like, which form a distinct class from offerings at the altar.

Why sacrifice is the typical form of all complete acts of worship in the antique religions, and what the sacrificial act means, is an involved and difficult problem. The problem does not belong to any one religion, for sacrifice is equally important among all early peoples in all parts of the world where religious ritual has reached any considerable development. Here, therefore, we have to deal with an institution that must have been shaped by the action of general causes, operating very widely and under conditions that were common in primitive times to all races of mankind. To construct a theory of sacrifice exclusively on the Semitic evidence would be unscientific and misleading, but for the present purpose it is right to put the facts attested for the Semitic peoples in the foreground, and to call in the sacrifices of other nations to confirm or modify the conclusions to which we are led. For some of the main aspects of the subject the Semitic evidence is very full and clear, for others it is fragmentary and unintelligible without help from what is known about other rituals.

Unfortunately the only system of Semitic sacrifice of which we possess a full account is that of the second temple at Jerusalem;[1] and though the ritual of Jerusalem as described in the Book of Leviticus is undoubtedly based on very ancient tradition, going back to a time when there was no substantial difference, in point of form, between Hebrew sacrifices and those of the surrounding nations, the system as we have it dates from a time when sacrifice was no longer the sum and substance of worship. In the long years of Babylonian exile the Israelites who remained true to the faith of Jehovah had learned to draw nigh to their God without the aid of sacrifice and offering, and, when they returned to Canaan, they did not return to the old

[1] The detailed ritual laws of the Pentateuch belong to the post-exilic document commonly called the Priestly Code, which was adopted as the law of Israel's religion at Ezra's reformation (444 B.C.). To the Priestly Code belong the Book of Leviticus, together with the cognate parts of the adjacent Books, Ex. xxv.–xxxi., xxxv.–xl., and Num. i.–x., xv.–xix., xxv.–xxxvi. (with some inconsiderable exceptions). With the Code is associated an account of the sacred history from Adam to Joshua, and some ritual matter is found in the historical sections of the work, especially in Ex. xii., where the law of the Passover is mainly priestly, and represents post-exilic usage. The law of Deuteronomy (seventh cent. B.C.) and the older codes of Ex. xx.–xxiii., xxxiv., have little to say about the rules of ritual, which in old times were matters of priestly tradition and not incorporated in a law-book. A just view of the sequence and dates of the several parts of the Pentateuch is essential to the historical study of Hebrew religion. Readers to whom this subject is new may refer to Wellhausen's *Prolegomena* (Eng. trans., Edin. 1883), to the article "Pentateuch," *Encycl. Brit.*, 9th ed., to my *Old Test. in the Jewish Church* (2nd ed. 1892), or to Professor Driver's *Introduction*.

type of religion. They built an altar, indeed, and restored its ritual on the lines of old tradition, so far as these could be reconciled with the teaching of the prophets and the Deuteronomic law—especially with the principle that there was but one sanctuary at which sacrifice could be acceptably offered. But this principle itself was entirely destructive of the old importance of sacrifice, as the stated means of converse between God and man. In the old time every town had its altar, and a visit to the local sanctuary was the easy and obvious way of consecrating every important act of life. No such interweaving of sacrificial service with everyday religion was possible under the new law, nor was anything of the kind attempted. The worship of the second temple was an antiquarian resuscitation of forms which had lost their intimate connection with the national life, and therefore had lost the greater part of their original significance. The Book of Leviticus, with all its fulness of ritual detail, does not furnish any clear idea of the place which each kind of altar service held in the old religion, when all worship took the form of sacrifice. And in some particulars there is reason to believe that the desire to avoid all heathenism, the necessity for giving expression to new religious ideas, and the growing tendency to keep the people as far as possible from the altar and make sacrifice the business of a priestly caste, had introduced into the ritual features unknown to more ancient practice.

The three main types of sacrifice recognised by the Levitical law are the whole burnt-offering (*'ōla*), the sacrifice followed by a meal of which the flesh of the victim formed the staple (*shélem, zébaḥ*), and the sin-offering (*ḥaṭṭāth*), with an obscure variety of the last named called *asham* (A.V. "trespass-offering"). Of these *'ōla* and *zébaḥ* are frequently mentioned in the older literature, and they are often spoken of together, as if all animal sacrifices fell under one or the other head. The use of sacrifice as an atonement for sin is also recognised in the old literature, especially in the case of the burnt-offering, but there is little or no trace of a special kind of offering appropriated for this purpose before the time of Ezekiel.[1] The formal distinctions with regard to Hebrew sacrifices that can be clearly made out from the pre-exilic literature are—

(1) The distinction between animal and vegetable oblations, *zébaḥ* and *minḥa*).

(2) The distinction between offerings that were consumed by fire and such as were merely set forth on the sacred table (the shewbread).

(3) The distinction between sacrifices in which the consecrated gift is wholly made over to the god, to be consumed on the altar or otherwise disposed of in his service, and those at which the god and his worshippers partake together in the consecrated thing. To the latter class belong the *zebaḥīm*, or ordinary animal sacrifices, in which a victim is slain, its blood poured out at the altar, and the fat of the intestines with certain other pieces burned, while the greater part of the flesh is left to the offerer to form the material of a sacrificial banquet.

These three distinctions, which are undoubtedly ancient, and applicable to the sacrifices of other Semitic nations, suggest three heads under which a preliminary survey of the subject may be conveniently arranged. But not till we reach the third head shall we find ourselves brought face to face with the deeper aspects of the problem of the origin and significance of sacrificial worship.

[1] See Wellhausen, *Prolegomena*, chap. ii. The Hebrew designations of the species of sacrifices are to be compared with those on the Carthaginian tables of fees paid to priests for the various kinds of offerings, *CIS.* Nos. 165, 164 *sqq.*, but the information given in these is so fragmentary that it is difficult to make much of it. See below, p. 237 n.

1. *The material of sacrifice.* The division of sacrifices into animal and vegetable offerings involves the principle that sacrifices—as distinct from votive offerings of garments, weapons, treasure and the like—are drawn from edible substances, and indeed from such substances as form the ordinary staple of human food. The last statement is strictly true of the Levitical ritual; but, so far as the flesh of animals is concerned, it was subject, even in the later heathen rituals, to certain rare but important exceptions, unclean or sacred animals, whose flesh was ordinarily forbidden to men, being offered and eaten sacramentally on very solemn occasions. We shall see by and by that in the earliest times these extraordinary sacrifices had a very great importance in ritual, and that on them depends the theory of the oldest sacrificial meals; but, as regards later times, the Hebrew sacrifices are sufficiently typical of the ordinary usage of the Semites generally. The four-footed animals from which the Levitical law allows victims to be selected are the ox the sheep and the goat, that is, the "clean" domestic quadrupeds which men were allowed to eat. The same quadrupeds are named upon the Carthaginian inscriptions that give the tariff of sacrificial fees to be paid at the temple,[1] and in Lucian's account of the Syrian ritual at Hierapolis.[2] The Israelites neither ate nor sacrificed camels, but among the Arabs the camel was common food and a common offering. The swine, on the other hand, which was commonly sacrificed and eaten in Greece, was forbidden food to all the Semites,[3] and occurs as a sacrifice only in certain exceptional rites of the kind already alluded to. Deer, gazelles and other kinds of game were eaten by the Hebrews, but not sacrificed, and from Deut. xii. 16 we may conclude that this was an

[1] *CIS.* Nos. 165, 167. [2] *Dea Syria*, liv.
[3] Lucian, *ut sup.* (Syrians); Sozomen, vi. 38 (all Saracens).

ancient rule. Among the Arabs, in like manner, a gazelle was regarded as an imperfect oblation, a shabby substitute for a sheep.[1] As regards birds, the Levitical law admits pigeons and turtle-doves, but only as holocausts and in certain purificatory ceremonies.[2] Birds seem also to be mentioned in the Carthaginian sacrificial lists; what is said of them is very obscure, but it would appear that they might be used either for ordinary sacrifices (*shelem kalīl*) or for special purposes piacular and oracular. That the quail was sacrificed to the Tyrian Baal appears from Athenæus, ix. 47, p. 392*d.*

Fish were eaten by the Israelites, but not sacrificed; among their heathen neighbours, on the contrary, fish—or certain kinds of fish—were forbidden food, and were sacrificed only in exceptional cases.[3]

Among the Hebrew offerings from the vegetable kingdom, meal wine and oil take the chief place,[4] and these were also the chief vegetable constituents of man's daily food.[5]

[1] Wellh. p. 112; Hārith, *Mo'all.* 69; especially *Lisān*, vi. 211. The reason of this rule, and certain exceptions, will appear in the sequel.

[2] Lev. i. 14, xii. 6, 8, xiv. 22, xv. 14, 29; Num. vi. 10. Two birds, of which one is slain and its blood used for lustration, appear also in the ritual for cleansing a leper, or a house that has been affected with leprosy (Lev. xiv. 4 *sq.*, 49 *sq.*). Further, the turtle-dove and nestling (pigeon) appear in an ancient covenant ceremony (Gen. xv. 9 *sqq.*). The fact that the dove was not used by the Hebrews for any ordinary sacrifice, involving a sacrificial meal, can hardly be, in its origin, independent of the sacrosanct character ascribed to this bird in the religion of the heathen Semites. The Syrians would not eat doves, and their very touch made a man unclean for a day (*Dea Syria*, liv.). In Palestine also the dove was sacred with the Phœnicians and Philistines, and on this superstition is based the common Jewish accusation against the Samaritans, that they were worshippers of the dove (see for all this Bochart, *Hierozoicon*, II. i. 1). Nay, sacred doves that may not be harmed are found even at Mecca. In legal times the dove was of course a "clean" bird to the Hebrews, but it is somewhat remarkable that we never read of it in the Old Testament as an article of diet—not even in 1 Kings v. 2 *sqq.* (A.V. iv. 22 *sqq.*)—though it is now one of the commonest table-birds all over the East.

[3] See below, p. 292 *sq.*

[4] Cf. Mic. vi. 7 with Lev. ii. 1 *sqq.*

[5] Ps. civ. 14 *sq.*

In the lands of the olive, oil takes the place that butter and other animal fats hold among northern nations, and accordingly among the Hebrews, and seemingly also among the Phœnicians,[1] it was customary to mingle oil with the cereal oblation before it was placed upon the altar, in conformity with the usage at ordinary meals. In like manner no cereal offering was complete without salt,[2] which, for physiological reasons, is a necessary of life to all who use a cereal diet, though among nations that live exclusively on flesh and milk it is not indispensable and is often dispensed with. Wine, which as Jotham's parable has it, "cheereth gods and men,"[3] was added to whole burnt-offerings and to the oblation of victims of whose flesh the worshippers partook.[4] The sacrificial use of wine, without which no feast was complete, seems to have been well-nigh universal wherever the grape was known,[5] and even penetrated to Arabia, where wine was a scarce and costly luxury imported from abroad. Milk, on the other hand, though one of the commonest articles of food among the Israelites, has no place in Hebrew sacrifice, but libations of milk were offered by the Arabs, and also at Carthage.[6] Their absence among the Hebrews may perhaps be explained by the rule of Ex. xxiii. 18, Lev. ii. 11, which excludes all ferments from presentation at the altar; for in hot climates milk ferments rapidly and is generally eaten sour.[7] The same principle covers the

[1] In *CIS.* No. 165, l. 14, the בלל is to be interpreted by the aid of Lev. vii. 10, and understood of bread or meal moistened with oil.

[2] Lev. ii. 13. [3] Judg. ix. 13. [4] Num. xv. 5.

[5] For some exceptions see Aesch., *Eum.* 107; Soph., *Oed. Col.* 100, with Schol.; Paus. ii. 11. 4; v. 15. 10 (Greek libations to the Eumenides and to the Nymphs); and Athen. xv. 48 (libations to the sun at Emesa).

[6] Wellh. p. 111 *sq.*; *CIS.* No. 165, l. 14; No. 167, l. 10.

[7] The rule against offering fermented things on the altar was not observed in northern Israel in all forms of sacrifice (Amos iv. 5), and traces of greater freedom in this respect appear also in Lev. vii. 13, xxiii. 17. It seems strange that wine should be admitted in sacrifice and leaven excluded, for

prohibition of "honey,"[1] which term, like the modern Arabic *dibs*, appears to include fruit juice inspissated by boiling—a very important article of food in modern and presumably in ancient Palestine. Fruit in its natural state, however, was offered at Carthage,[2] and was probably admitted by the Hebrews in ancient times.[3] Among the

leaven is a product of vinous fermentation, and leavened bread equally with wine is to the nomad a foreign luxury (*al-khamr wal-khamîr*, *Agh.* xix. 25), so that both alike must have been wanting in the oldest type of Hebrew sacrifices. Thus the continued prohibition of leaven in sacrifice, after wine was admitted, can hardly be regarded as a mere piece of religious conservatism, but must have some further significance. It is possible that in its oldest form the legal prohibition of leaven applied only to the Passover, to which Ex. xxiii. 18, xxxiv. 25, specially refer. In this connection the prohibition of leaven is closely associated with the rule that the fat and flesh must not remain over till the morning. For we shall find by and by that a similar rule applied to certain Saracen sacrifices nearly akin to the Passover, which were even eaten raw, and had to be entirely consumed before the sun rose. In this case the idea was that the efficacy of the sacrifice lay in the living flesh and blood of the victim. Everything of the nature of putrefaction was therefore to be avoided, and the connection between leaven and putrefaction is obvious.

The only positive law against the sacrificial use of milk is that in Ex. xxiii. 19, xxxiv. 26: "Thou shalt not seethe a kid in its mother's milk." Mother's milk is simply goat's milk, which was that generally used (Prov. xxvii. 27), and flesh seethed in milk is still a common Arabian dish; sour milk is specified as the kind employed in *PEF. Qu. St.* 1888, p. 188. The context of the passages in Exodus shows that some ancient form of sacrifice is referred to; cf. Judg. vi. 19, where we have a holocaust of sodden flesh. A sacrificial gift sodden in sour milk would evidently be of the nature of fermented food; but I do not feel sure that this goes to the root of the matter. Many primitive peoples regard milk as a kind of equivalent for blood, and thus to eat a kid seethed in its mother's milk might be taken as equivalent to eating "with the blood," and be forbidden to the Hebrews along with the bloody sacraments of the heathen, of which more hereafter.

[1] Lev. ii. 11. [2] *CIS.* No. 166.

[3] The term *hillûlîm*, applied in Lev. xix. 24 to the consecrated fruit borne by a new tree in its fourth year, is applied in Judg. ix. 27 to the Canaanite vintage feast at the sanctuary. The Carthaginian fruit-offering consisted of a branch bearing fruit, like the "ethrog" of the modern Jewish feast of Tabernacles. The use of "goodly fruits" at this festival is ordained in Lev. xxiii. 40, but their destination is not specified. In Carthage, though the inscription that speaks of the rite is fragmentary, it seems to be clear that the fruit was offered at the altar, for incense is mentioned with it; and this, no doubt, is the original sense of the Hebrew rite also.

Hebrews vegetable or cereal oblations were sometimes presented by themselves, especially in the form of first-fruits, but the commonest use of them was as an accompaniment to an animal sacrifice. When the Hebrew ate flesh, he ate bread with it and drank wine, and when he offered flesh on the table of his God, it was natural that he should add to it the same concomitants which were necessary to make up a comfortable and generous meal.

Of these various oblations animal sacrifices are by far the most important in all the Semitic countries. They are in fact the typical sacrifice, so that among the Phœnicians the word *zébaḥ*, which properly means a slaughtered victim, is applied even to offerings of bread and oil.[1] That cereal offerings have but a secondary place in ritual is not unintelligible in connection with the history of the Semitic race. For all the Semites were originally nomadic, and the ritual of the nomad Arabs and the settled Canaanites has so many points in common that there can be no question that the main lines of sacrificial worship were fixed before any part of the Semitic stock had learned agriculture and adopted cereal food as its ordinary diet. It must be observed, however, that animal food—or at least the flesh of domestic animals, which are the only class of victims admitted among the Semites as ordinary and regular sacrifices—was not a common article of diet even among the nomad Arabs. The everyday food of the nomad consisted of milk, of game, when he could get it, and to a limited extent of dates and meal—the latter for the most part being attainable only by purchase or robbery. Flesh

Cf. the raisin-cakes (A.V. "flagons of wine"), Hos. iii. 1, which from the context appear to be connected with the worship of the Baalim.

[1] *CIS.* No. 165, l. 12; 167, l. 9. In the context צד can hardly mean game, but must be taken, as in Josh. ix. 11 *sqq.*, of cereal food, the ordinary "provision" of agricultural peoples.

of domestic animals was eaten only as a luxury or in times of famine.[1] If therefore the sole principle that governed the choice of the material of sacrifices had been that they must consist of human food, milk and not flesh would have had the leading place in nomad ritual, whereas its real place is exceedingly subordinate. To remove this difficulty it may be urged that, as sacrifice is food offered to the gods, it ought naturally to be of the best and most luxurious kind that can be attained; but on this principle it is not easy to see why game should be excluded, for a gazelle is not worse food than an old camel.[2] The true solution of the matter lies in another direction. Among the Hebrews no sacrificial meal was provided for the worshippers unless a victim was sacrificed; if the oblation was purely cereal it was wholly consumed either on the altar or by the priests, in the holy place, *i.e.* by the representatives of the deity.[3] In like manner the only Arabian meal-offering about which we have particulars, that of the god Ocaiṣir,[4] was laid before the idol in handfuls. The poor, however, were allowed to partake of it, being viewed no doubt as the guests of the deity.

[1] See the old narratives, *passim*, and compare Doughty, i. 325 *sq.* The statement of Fränkel, *Fremdwörter*, p. 31, that the Arabs lived mainly on flesh, overlooks the importance of milk as an article of diet among all the pastoral tribes, and must also be taken with the qualification that the flesh used as ordinary food was that of wild beasts taken in hunting. On this point the evidence is clear; Pliny, *H. N.* vi. 161, "nomadas lacte et ferina carne uesci"; Agatharchides, *ap.* Diod. Sic. iii. 44. 2; Ammianus, xiv. 4, 6, "uictus uniuersis caro ferina est lactisque abundans copia qua sustentantur"; Nilus, p. 27. By these express statements we must interpret the vaguer utterances of Diodorus (xix. 94. 9) and Agatharchides (*ap.* Diod. iii. 43. 5) about the ancient diet of the Nabatæans: the "nourishment supplied by their herds" was mainly milk. Certain Arab tribes, like the modern Sleyb, had no herds and lived wholly by hunting, and these perhaps are referred to in what Agatharchides says of the Banizomenes, and in the Syriac life of Simeon Stylites (Assemani, *Mart.* ii. 345), where, at any rate, *besrā d'ḥaiwāthā* means game.

[2] Cf. Gen. xxvii. 7.

[3] Lev. ii. 3, v. 11, vi. 16 (E.V. 22).

[4] Yācūt, *s.v.*; Wellh. p. 58 *sq.*

The cereal offering therefore has strictly the character of a tribute paid by the worshipper to his god, as indeed is expressed by the name *minḥa*, whereas when an animal is sacrificed, the sacrificer and the deity feast together, part of the victim going to each. The predominance assigned in ancient ritual to animal sacrifice corresponds to the predominance of the type of sacrifice which is not a mere payment of tribute but an act of social fellowship between the deity and his worshippers. Why this social meal always includes the flesh of a victim will be considered in a subsequent lecture.

All sacrifices laid upon the altar were taken by the ancients as being literally the food of the gods. The Homeric deities "feast on hecatombs,"[1] nay, particular Greek gods have special epithets designating them as the goat-eater, the ram-eater, the bull-eater, even "the cannibal," with allusion to human sacrifices.[2] Among the Hebrews the conception that Jehovah eats the flesh of bulls and drinks the blood of goats, against which the author of Ps. l. protests so strongly, was never eliminated from the ancient technical language of the priestly ritual, in which the sacrifices are called לחם אלהים, "the food of the deity." In its origin this phrase must belong to the same circle of ideas as Jotham's "wine which cheereth gods and men." But in the higher forms of heathenism the crass materialism of this conception was modified, in the case of fire-offerings, by the doctrine that man's food must be etherealised or sublimated into fragrant smoke before the gods partake of it. This observation brings us to the second of the points which we have noted in connection with Hebrew sacrifice, viz. the distinction between sacrifices that are merely set forth on the sacred table before the deity, and such as are consumed by fire upon the altar.

[1] *Iliad*, ix. 531. [2] αἰγοφάγος, κριοφάγος, ταυροφάγος, Διόνυσος ὠμηστής.

2. The table of shewbread has its closest parallel in the *lectisternia* of ancient heathenism, when a table laden with meats was spread beside the idol. Such tables were set in the great temple of Bel at Babylon,[1] and, if any weight is to be given to the apocryphal story of Bel and the Dragon in the Greek Book of Daniel, it was popularly believed that the god actually consumed the meal provided for him,[2] a superstition that might easily hold its ground by priestly connivance where the table was spread inside a temple. A more primitive form of the same kind of offering appears in Arabia, where the meal-offering to Ocaiṣir is cast by handfuls at the foot of the idol mingled with the hair of the worshipper,[3] and milk is poured over the sacred stones. A narrative of somewhat apocryphal colour, given without reference to his authority by Sprenger,[4] has it that in the worship of 'Amm-anas in Southern Arabia, whole hecatombs were slaughtered and left to be devoured by wild beasts. Apart from the exaggeration, there may be something in this; for the idea that sacred animals are the guests or clients of the god is not alien to Arabian thought,[5] and to feed them is an act of religion

[1] Herod. i. 181, 183; Diod. Sic. ii. 9. 7.

[2] The story, so far as it has a basis in actual superstition, is probably drawn from Egyptian beliefs; but in such matters Egypt and Babylon were much alike; Herod. i. 182.

[3] The same thing probably applies to other Arabian meal-offerings, *e.g.* the wheat and barley offered to Al-Kholaṣa (Azraḳī, p. 78). As the dove was the sacred bird at Mecca, the epithet *Moṭ'im al-ṭair*, "he who feeds the birds," applied to the idol that stood upon Marwa (*ibid.*), seems to point to similar meal-offerings rather than to animal victims left lying before the god. The "idol" made of *ḥais*, *i.e.* a mass of dates kneaded up with butter and sour milk, which the B. Ḥanīfa ate up in time of famine (see the *Lexx.* *s.v.* تباعة; Ibn Coteiba, ed. Wüst. p. 299; Bīrūnī, *Chron.* p. 210), probably belonged to the widespread class of cereal offerings, shaped as rude idols and eaten sacramentally (Liebrecht, *Zur Volkskunde*, p. 436; *ZDMG.* xxx. 539).

[4] *Leb. Moh.* iii. 457.

[5] See above, p. 142 *sqq.*, and the god-name Mot'im al-ṭair in the last

in many heathen systems, especially where, as in Egypt,[1] the gods themselves are totem-deities, *i.e.* personifications or individual representations of the sacred character and attributes which, in the purely totem stage of religion, were ascribed without distinction to all animals of the holy kind. Thus at Cynopolis in Egypt, where dogs were honoured and fed with sacred food, the local deity was the divine dog Anubis, and similarly in Greece, at the sanctuary of the Wolf Apollo (Apollo Lycius) of Sicyon, an old tradition preserved—though in a distorted form—the memory of a time when flesh used to be set forth for the wolves.[2] It is by no means impossible that something of the same sort took place at certain Arabian shrines, for we have already learned how closely the gods were related to the *jinn* and the *jinn* to wild animals, and the list of Arabian deities includes a Lion-god (Yaghūth) and a Vulture-god (Nasr),[3] to whose worship rites like those described by Sprenger would be altogether appropriate.

But while it cannot be thought impossible that sacrificial victims were presented on holy ground and left to be devoured by wild beasts as the guests or congeners of the gods, I confess that there seems to me to be no sufficient evidence that such a practice had any considerable place in Arabian ritual. The leading idea in the animal sacrifices of the Semites, as we shall see by and by, was not that of a gift made over to the god, but of an act of communion,

note but one; also Hamdānī's account of the offerings at Sāwid, *supra*, p. 177.

[1] Strabo, xvii. 1. 39 *sq.* (p. 812).

[2] Pausanias, ii. 9. 7. The later rationalism which changed the Wolf-god into a Wolf-slayer gave the story a corresponding twist by relating that the flesh was poisoned, under the god's directions, with the leaves of a tree whose trunk was preserved in the temple, like the sacred erica at Byblus.

[3] See *Kinship*, pp. 192, 309; Nöldeke, *ZDMG.* 1886, p. 186. See also, for the Himyarite Vulture-god, *ZDMG.* xxix. 600, and compare the eagle standard of Morra, Nābigha, iv. 7, Ahlw. = xxi. 7, Der.

in which the god and his worshippers unite by partaking together of the flesh and blood of a sacred victim. It is true that in the case of certain very solemn sacrifices, especially of *piacula*, to which class the sacrifices cited by Sprenger appear to belong, the victim sometimes came to be regarded as so sacred that the worshippers did not venture to eat of it at all, but that the flesh was burned or buried or otherwise disposed of in a way that secured it from profanation; and among the Arabs, who did not use burning except in the case of human sacrifices, we can quite well understand that one way of disposing of holy flesh might be to leave it to be eaten by the sacred animals of the god. Or again, when a sacrifice is expressly offered as a ransom, as in the case of the hundred camels with which ʿAbd-al-Moṭṭalib redeemed his vow to sacrifice his son, it is intelligible that the offerer reserves no part of the flesh, but leaves it to anyone who chooses to help himself; or even (according to another reading) leaves it free to man and beast.[1] On the whole, however, all the well-authenticated accounts of Arabian sacrifice seem to indicate that the original principle, that the worshippers must actually eat of the sacred flesh, was very rigorously held to.[2] Wellhausen indeed is disposed to think that the practice of slaughtering animals and leaving them beside the altar to be devoured by wild beasts was not confined to certain exceptional cults, but prevailed generally in the case of the *ʿatāïr* (sing. *ʿatīra*) or annual sacrifices presented by the Arabs in the month Rajab, which originally corresponded to the Hebrew Passover-month (Abib, Nisan).[3]

[1] B. Hish. p. 100, l. 7; Ṭabarī, i. 1078, l. 4.

[2] The evidence of Nilus is very important in this connection; for the interval between his time and that of the oldest native traditions is scarcely sufficient to allow for the development of an extensive system of sacrifice without a sacrificial meal; *infra*, p. 338.

[3] Cf. Wellhausen, p. 94 *sq*. To complete the parallelism of the Passover

"It is remarkable," says Wellhausen, "how often we hear of the *'atāïr* lying round the altar-idol, and sometimes in poetical comparisons the slain are said to be left lying on the battlefield like *'atāïr*."[1] But on the Arabian method of sacrifice the carcases of the victims naturally lie on the ground, beside the sacred stone, till the blood, which is the god's portion, has drained into the *ghabghab*, or pit, at its foot, and till all the other ritual prescriptions have been fulfilled. Thus at a great feast when many victims were offered together, the scene would resemble a battle-field; indeed, it is impossible to imagine a more disgusting scene of carnage than is still presented every year at Minā on the great day of sacrifice, when the ground is literally covered with innumerable carcases. It is not therefore necessary to suppose that the *'atāïr* at Rajab were left to the hyæna and the vulture; and, as the name *'atīra* seems to be also used in a more general sense of any victim whose blood is applied to the sacred stones at the sanctuary, it is hardly to be thought that there was anything very exceptional in the form of the Rajab ceremony.

In the higher forms of Semitic heathenism offerings of the shewbread type are not very conspicuous; in truth the idea that the gods actually consume the solid food deposited

with the Rajab offerings, Wellhausen desiderates evidence connecting the *'atāïr* of Rajab with the sacrifice of firstlings. The traditionists, *e.g.* Bokhārī, vi. 207 (at the close of the *Kit. al-'acīca*), distinguish between firstlings (*fara'*) and *'atīra*, but the line of distinction is not sharp. The lexicons apply the name *fara'*, not only to firstlings sacrificed while their flesh was still like glue (*Lisān*, x. 120), but also to the sacrifice of one beast in a hundred, which is what the scholiast on Ḥarith's *Moall.* 69 understands by the *'atīra*. Conversely the *Lisān*, vi. 210, defines the *'atīra* as a firstling (*awwal mā yuntaj*) which was sacrificed to the gods. If we could accept this statement without reserve, in the general confusion of the later Arabs on the subject, it would supply what Wellhausen desiderates.

[1] Wellh. p. 115; cf. the verses cited *ibid.* pp. 16, 56; and, for the poetical comparisons, Ibn Hishām, 534. 4; Alcama, vi. 3, Soc.

at their shrines is too crude to subsist without modification beyond the savage state of society; the ritual may survive, but the sacrificial gifts, which the god is evidently unable to dispose of himself, will come to be the perquisite of the priests, as in the case of the shewbread, or of the poor, as in the meal sacrifice to Ocaiṣir. In such cases the actual eating is done by the guests of the deity, but the god himself may still be supposed to partake of food in a subtle and supersensuous way. It is interesting to note the gradations of ritual that correspond to this modification of the original idea.

In the more primitive forms of Semitic religion the difficulty of conceiving that the gods actually partake of food is partly got over by a predominant use of liquid oblations; for fluid substances, which sink in and disappear, are more easily believed to be consumed by the deity than obstinate masses of solid matter.

The libation, which holds quite a secondary place in the more advanced Semitic rituals, and is generally a mere accessory to a fire offering, has great prominence among the Arabs, to whom sacrifices by fire were practically unknown except, as we shall see by and by, in the case of human sacrifice. Its typical form is the libation of blood, the subtle vehicle of the life of the sacrifice; but milk, which was used in ritual both by the Arabs and by the Phœnicians, is also no doubt a very ancient Semitic libation. In ordinary Arabian sacrifices the blood which was poured over the sacred stone was all that fell to the god's part, the whole flesh being consumed by the worshippers and their guests; and the early prevalence of this kind of oblation appears from the fact that the word נסך, "to pour," which in Hebrew means to pour out a drink-offering, is in Arabic the general term for an act of worship.

In the North Semitic ritual the most notable feature in

the libation, which ordinarily consisted of wine, is that it was not consumed by fire, even when it went with a fire-offering. The Greeks and Romans poured the sacrificial wine over the flesh, but the Hebrews treated it like the blood, pouring it out at the base of the altar.[1] In Ecclesiasticus the wine so treated is even called "the blood of the grape,"[2] from which one is tempted to conclude that here also blood is the typical form of libation, and that wine is a surrogate for it, as fruit-juice seems to have been in certain Arabian rites.[3] It is true that the blood of the sacrifice is not called a libation in Hebrew ritual, and in Ps. xvi. 4 "drink-offerings of blood" are spoken of as something heathenish. But this proves that such libations were known; and that the Hebrew altar ritual of the blood is essentially a drink-offering appears from Ps. l. 13, where Jehovah asks, "Will I eat the flesh of bulls or drink the blood of goats?" and also from 2 Sam. xxiii. 17, where David pours out as a drink-offering the water from the well of Bethlehem, refusing to drink "the blood of the men that fetched it in jeopardy of their lives." Putting all this together, and noting also that libations were retained as a chief part of ritual in the domestic heathenism of the Hebrew women in the time of Jeremiah,[4] and that private service is often more conservative than

[1] Ecclus. l. 15; Jos. *Antt.* iii. 9. 4. Num. xv. 7 is sometimes cited as proving that in older times the wine was poured over the sacrificial flesh, but see against this interpretation Num. xxviii. 7.

[2] The term αἷμα βοτρύων occurs in the Tyrian legend of the invention of wine, Ach. Tatius, ii. 2, and may possibly be the translation of an old Phœnician phrase.

[3] *Kinship*, p. 261 *sq.*; Wellh. p. 121.

[4] Jer. xix. 13, xxxii. 29, xliv. 17, 18. With this worship on the house-tops, cf. what Strabo, xvi. 4. 26, tells of the daily offerings of libations and incense presented to the sun by the Nabatæans at an altar erected on the house-tops. The sacrificial act must be done in the presence of the deity (cf. Nilus, pp. 30, 117), and if the sun or the queen of heaven is worshipped, a place open to the sky must be chosen.

public worship, we are led to conclude (1) that the libation of blood is a common Semitic practice, older than fire-sacrifices, and (2) that the libation of wine is in some sense an imitation of, and a surrogate for, the primitive blood-offering.

Whether libations of water can properly be reckoned among the drink-offerings of the Semites is very doubtful. David's libation is plainly exceptional, and in the Levitical ritual offerings of water have no place. In the actual practice of later Judaism, however, water drawn from the fountain of Siloam, and carried into the Temple amidst the blare of trumpets, was solemnly poured out upon the altar on seven days of the Feast of Tabernacles.[1] According to the Rabbins, the object of this ceremony was to secure fertilising rains in the following year. The explanation is doubtless correct, for it is a common belief all over the world that pouring out water is a potent rain-charm.[2] This being so, we can well understand that the rite derives no countenance from the law; in truth it does not belong to the sphere of religion at all, but falls under the category of sympathetic magic in which natural phenomena are thought to be produced by imitating them on a small scale. In some forms of this charm thunder is imitated as well as rain;[3] and perhaps the trumpet-blowing at the Temple is to be explained in this way.

The closest parallel to the water-pouring of the Feast

[1] See *Succa*, iv. 9; Lightfoot on John vii. 37; Reland, *Ant. Heb.* p. 448 *sq.*, with the refs. there given. The water was poured into a special channel in the altar.

[2] Numerous examples are given by Frazer, *Golden Bough*, i. 13 *sqq.*, to which I may add the annual "water-pouring" at Ispahan (Bīrūnī, *Chron.* p. 228 *sqq.*; Cazwīnī, i. 84).

[3] Frazer, *ut supra*; a very curious Arabian rain-charm, where cattle (or perhaps antelopes) are driven into the mountains with firebrands attached to their tails, seems to be an imitation of lightning. See Wellhausen, p. 157; *Lisān*, v. 140; Rāghib, i. 94.

of Tabernacles is found in the rite of Hierapolis, described by Lucian.[1] Twice a year a great concourse of worshippers assembled at the Temple bearing water from "the sea" (*i.e.* the Euphrates [2]), which was poured out in the Temple and flowed away into a cleft which, according to tradition, absorbed the waters of Deucalion's flood, and so gave occasion to the erection of a sanctuary, with commemorative services on the spot.[3]

In Hebrew ritual oil is not a libation, but when used in sacrifice serves to moisten and enrich a cereal offering. The ancient custom of pouring oil on sacred stones[4] was presumably maintained at Bethel according to the precedent set by Jacob; and even in the fourth Christian century the Bordeaux pilgrim speaks of the "lapis pertusus" at Jerusalem "ad quem ueniunt Iudæi singulis annis et ungunt eum"; but, as oil by itself was not an article of food, the natural analogy to this act of ritual is to be sought in the application of unguents to the hair and skin. The use of unguents was a luxury proper to feasts and gala days, when men wore their best clothes and made merry; and from Ps. xlv. 8 (E.V. 7) compared with Isa. lxi. 3, we may con-

[1] *Dea Syria*, § 13, cf. § 48. The same rite is alluded to by Melito in Cureton, *Spic. Syr.* p. 25.

[2] To the dwellers in Mesopotamia the Euphrates was "the sea"; Philostratus, *Vita Apollonii*, i. 20.

[3] The ritual of pouring water into the cleft has its parallel in the modern practice at the fountain of water before the gates of Tyre, when in September the water becomes red and troubled, and the natives gather for a great feast and restore its limpidity by pouring a pitcher of sea-water into the source (Volney, *État pol. de la Syrie*, chap. viii.; Mariti, ii. 269). Here the ceremony takes place at the end of the dry season when the water is low, and may therefore be compared with the legend that Mohammed made the empty well of Ḥodaibiya to overflow by causing it to be stirred with one of his arrows after a pitcher of water had been poured into it (*Moh. in Med.* p. 247). As a rule the pouring out of water in early superstition is, as we have already seen, a rain-charm, and possibly the rite of Hierapolis was really designed to procure rain, but only in due measure.

[4] Gen. xxviii. 18, xxxv. 14.

clude that the anointing of kings at their coronation is part of the ceremony of investing them in the festal dress and ornaments appropriate to their dignity on that joyous day (cf. Cant. iii. 11). To anoint the head of a guest was a hospitable act and a sign of honour; it was the completion of the toilet appropriate to a feast. Thus the sacred stone or rude idol described by Pausanias (x. 24. 6) had oil poured on it daily, and was crowned with wool at every feast. We have seen that the Semites on festal occasions dressed up their sacred poles, and they did the same with their idols.[1] With all this the ritual of anointing goes quite naturally; thus at Medīna in the last days of heathenism we find a man washing his domestic idol, which had been defiled by Moslems, and then anointing it.[2] But apart from this, the very act of applying ointment to the sacred symbol had a religious significance. The Hebrew word meaning to anoint (*mashaḥ*) means properly to wipe or stroke with the hand, which was used to spread the unguent over the skin. Thus the anointing of the sacred symbol is associated with the simpler form of homage common in Arabia, in which the hand was passed over the idol (*tamassoḥ*). In the oath described by Ibn Hishām, p. 85, the parties dip their hands in unguent and then wipe them on the Caaba. The ultimate source of the use of unguents in religion will be discussed by and by in connection with animal sacrifice.

The sacrificial use of blood, as we shall see hereafter, is connected with a series of very important ritual ideas, turning on the conception that the blood is a special seat of the life. But primarily, when the blood is offered at the altar, it is conceived to be drunk by the deity. Apart from Ps. l. 13 the direct evidence for this is somewhat scanty, so far as the Semites are concerned; the authority usually

[1] Ezek. xvi. 18.

[2] Ibn Hishām, p. 303.

appealed to is Maimonides, who states that the Ṣabians looked on blood as the nourishment of the gods. So late a witness would have little value if he stood alone, but the expression in the Psalm cannot be mere rhetoric, and the same belief appears among early nations in all parts of the globe.[1] Nor does this oblation form an exception to the rule that the offerings of the gods consist of human food, for many savages drink fresh blood by way of nourishment, and esteem it a special delicacy.[2]

Among the Arabs, down to the age of Mohammed, blood drawn from the veins of a living camel was eaten—in a kind of blood pudding—in seasons of hunger, and perhaps also at other times.[3] We shall find, however, as we proceed, that sacrificial blood, which contained the life, gradually came to be considered as something too sacred to be eaten, and that in most sacrifices it was entirely made over to the god at the altar. As all slaughter of domestic animals for food was originally sacrificial among the Arabs as well as among the Hebrews, this carried with it the disuse of blood as an article of ordinary food; and

[1] See Tylor, *Primitive Culture*, ii. 346. The story told by Yācūt, ii. 882, of the demon at the temple of Riām to whom bowls of sacrificial blood were presented, of which he partook, seems to have a Jewish origin. According to one version this demon had the form of a black dog (cf. B. Hish. p. 18, l. 3).

[2] See, for America, Bancroft, *Native Races*, i. 55, 492, ii. 344. In Africa fresh blood is held as a dainty by all the negroes of the White Nile (Marno, *Reise*, p. 79); it is largely drunk by Masai warriors (Thomson, p. 430); and also by the Gallas, as various travellers attest. Among the Hottentots the pure blood of beasts is forbidden to women but not to men; Kolben, *State of the Cape*, i. 205, cf. 203. In the last case we see that the blood is sacred food. For blood-drinking among the Tartars, see Yule's *Marco Polo*, i. 254, and the editor's note. Where mineral salt is not used for food, the drinking of blood supplies, as Thomson remarks, an important constituent to the system.

[3] Maidānī, ii. 119; *Ḥamāsa*, p. 645, last verse. From *Agh.* xvi. 107. 20, one is led to doubt whether the practice was confined to seasons of famine, or whether this kind of food was used more regularly, as was done, on the other side of the Red Sea, by the Troglodytes (Agatharchides in *Fr. Geog. Gr.* i. 153). See further the *Lexx. s.vv. faṣada, 'ilhiz, bajja, musawwad.*

even when slaughter ceased to involve a formal sacrifice, it was still thought necessary to slay the victim in the name of a god and pour the blood on the ground.[1] Among the Hebrews this practice soon gave rise to an absolute prohibition of blood-eating; among the Arabs the rule was made absolute only by Mohammed's legislation.[2]

The idea that the gods partake only of the liquid parts of the sacrifice appears, as has been already said, to indicate a modification of the most crassly materialistic conception of the divine nature. The direction which this modification took may, I think, be judged of by comparing the sacrifices of the gods with the oblations offered to the dead. In the famous *νέκυια* of the *Odyssey*[3] the ghosts drink greedily of the sacrificial blood, and libations of gore form a special feature in Greek offerings to heroes. Among the Arabs, too, the dead are thirsty rather than hungry; water and wine are poured upon their graves.[4] Thirst is a subtler appetite than hunger, and therefore more appropriate to the disembodied shades, just as it is from thirst rather than from hunger that the Hebrews and many other nations borrow metaphors for spiritual longings and intellectual desires. Thus the idea that the gods drink, but do not eat, seems to mark the feeling that they must be thought of as having a less solid material nature than men.

[1] Wellh. p. 114. In an Arab encampment slaves sleep beside "the blood and the dung" (*Agh.* viii. 74. 29); cf. 1 Sam. ii. 8.

[2] Whether the blood of game was prohibited to the Hebrews before the law of Lev. xvii. 13 is not quite clear; Deut. xii. 16 is ambiguous. In Islām as in Judaism the prohibition of blood-eating and the rule that carrion must not be eaten go together (Lev. xvii. 15; B. Hish. p. 206, l. 7).

[3] Bk. xi.; cf. Pindar, *Ol.* i. 90, where the word αἱμακουρίαι is explained by Hesychius as τὰ ἐναγίσματα τῶν κατοιχομένων; Pausan. v. 13, § 2; Plut., *Aristides*, 21.

[4] Wellhausen, p. 161.

A farther step in the same direction is associated with the introduction of fire sacrifices; for, though there are valid reasons for thinking that the practice of burning the flesh or fat of victims originated in a different line of thought (as we shall by and by see), the fire ritual readily lent itself to the idea that the burnt flesh is simply a food-offering etherealised into fragrant smoke, and that the gods regale themselves on the odour instead of the substance of the sacrifice. Here again the analogy of gifts to the dead helps us to comprehend the point of view; among the Greeks of the seventh century B.C. it was, as we learn from the story of Periander and Melissa, a new idea that the dead could make no use of the gifts buried with them, unless they were etherealised by fire.[1] A similar notion seems to have attached itself to the custom of sacrifice by fire, combined probably at an early date with the idea that the gods, as ethereal beings, lived in the upper air, towards which the sacrificial smoke ascended in savoury clouds. Thus the prevalence among the settled Semites of fire sacrifices, which were interpreted as offerings of fragrant smoke, marks the firm establishment of a conception of the divine nature which, though not purely spiritual, is at least stripped of the crassest aspects of materialism.

3. The distinction between sacrifices which are wholly made over to the god and sacrifices of which the god and the worshipper partake together requires careful handling. In the later form of Hebrew ritual laid down in the Levitical law, the distinction is clearly marked. To the former class belong all cereal oblations (Heb. *minḥa*; A.V. "offering" or "meat-offering"), which so far as they are not burned on the altar are assigned to the priests, and among

[1] Herodotus, v. 92; cf. Joannes Lydus, *Mens.* iii. 27, where the object of burning the dead is said to be to etherealise the body along with the soul.

animal sacrifices the sin-offering and the burnt-offering or holocaust. Most sin-offerings were not holocausts, but the part of the flesh that was not burned fell to the priests. To the latter class, again, belong the *zebaḥīm* or *shelamīm* (sing. *zébaḥ*, *shélem*, Amos v. 22), that is, all the ordinary festal sacrifices, vows and freewill offerings, of which the share of the deity was the blood and the fat of the intestines, the rest of the carcase (subject to the payment of certain dues to the officiating priest) being left to the worshipper to form a social feast.[1] In judging of the original scope and meaning of these two classes of sacrifice, it will be convenient, in the first instance, to confine our attention to the simplest and most common forms of offering. In the last days of the kingdom of Judah, and still more after the Exile, piacular sacrifices and holocausts acquired a prominence which they did not possess in ancient times. The old history knows nothing of the Levitical sin-offering; the atoning function of sacrifice is not confined to a particular class of oblation, but belongs to

[1] In the English Bible *zebaḥīm* is rendered "sacrifices," and *shelamīm* "peace-offerings." The latter rendering is not plausible, and the term *shelamīm* can hardly be separated from the verb *shillem*, to pay or discharge, *e.g.* a vow. *Zébaḥ* is the more general word, including (like the Arabic *dhibḥ*) all animals slain for food, agreeably with the fact that in old times all slaughter was sacrificial. In later times, when slaughter and sacrifice were no longer identical, *zébaḥ* was not precise enough to be used as a technical term of ritual, and so the term *shelamīm* came to be more largely used than in the earlier literature.

On the sacrificial lists of the Carthaginians the terms corresponding to עלה and זבח seem to be כלל and צועת. The former is the old Hebrew כליל (Deut. xxxiii. 10; 1 Sam. vii. 9), the latter is etymologically quite obscure. In the Carthaginian burnt-sacrifice a certain weight of the flesh was apparently not consumed on the altar, but given to the priests (*CIS.* 165), as in the case of the Hebrew sin-offering, which was probably a modification of the holocaust. The שלם כלל, which appears along with כלל and צועת in *CIS.* 165 (but not in *CIS.* 167), is hardly a third co-ordinate species of sacrifice. The editors of the *Corpus* regard it as a variety of the holocaust (*hol. eucharisticum*), which is not easily reconciled with their own restitution of l. 11 or with the Hebrew sense of שלם. Perhaps it is an ordinary sacrifice accompanying a holocaust.

all sacrifices.[1] The holocaust, again, although ancient, is not in ancient times a common form of sacrifice, and unless on very exceptional occasions occurs only in great public feasts and in association with *zebaḥīm*. The distressful times that preceded the end of Hebrew independence drove men to seek exceptional religious means to conciliate the favour of a deity who seemed to have turned his back on his people. Piacular rites and costly holocausts became, therefore, more usual, and after the abolition of the local high places this new importance was still further accentuated by contrast with the decline of the more common forms of sacrifice. When each local community had its own high place, it was the rule that every animal slain for food should be presented at the altar, and every meal at which flesh was served had the character of a sacrificial feast.[2] As men ordinarily lived on bread fruit and milk, and ate flesh only on feast days and holidays, this rule was easily observed as long as the local sanctuaries stood. But when there was no altar left except at Jerusalem, the identity of slaughter and sacrifice could no longer be maintained, and accordingly the law of Deuteronomy allows men to slay and eat domestic animals everywhere, provided only that the blood—the ancient share of the god—is poured out upon the ground.[3] When this new rule came into force men ceased to feel that the eating of flesh was essentially a sacred act, and though strictly religious meals were still maintained at Jerusalem on the great feast days, the sacrificial meal necessarily lost much of its old signifi-

[1] To *zébaḥ* and *minḥa*, 1 Sam. iii. 14, xxvi. 19, and still more to the holocaust, Mic. vi. 6, 7.

[2] Hos. ix. 4.

[3] Deut. xii. 15, 16; cf. Lev. xvii. 10 *sq*. The fat of the intestines was also from ancient times reserved for the deity (1 Sam. ii. 16), and therefore it also was forbidden food (Lev. iii. 17). The prohibition did not extend to the fat distributed through other parts of the body.

cance, and the holocaust seemed to have a more purely sacred character than the *zébaḥ*, in which men ate and drank just as they might do at home.

But in ancient times the preponderance was all the other way, and the *zébaḥ* was not only much more frequent than the holocaust, but much more intimately bound up with the prevailing religious ideas and feelings of the Hebrews. On this point the evidence of the older literature is decisive; *zébaḥ* and *minḥa*, sacrifices slain to provide a religious feast, and vegetable oblations presented at the altar, make up the sum of the ordinary religious practices of the older Hebrews, and we must try to understand these ordinary rites before we attack the harder problem of exceptional forms of sacrifice.

Now, if we put aside the *piacula* and whole burnt-offerings, it appears that, according to the Levitical ritual, the distinction between oblations in which the worshipper shared, and oblations which were wholly given over to the deity to be consumed on the altar or by the priests, corresponds to the distinction between animal and vegetable offerings. The animal victim was presented at the altar and devoted by the imposition of hands, but the greater part of the flesh was returned to the worshipper, to be eaten by him under special rules. It could be eaten only by persons ceremonially clean, *i.e.* fit to approach the deity; and if the food was not consumed on the same day, or in certain cases within two days, the remainder had to be burned.[1] The plain meaning of these rules is that the flesh is not common but holy,[2] and that the act of eating it is a part of the service, which is to be completed before men break up from the sanctuary.[3] The *zébaḥ*, therefore, is

[1] Lev. vii. 15 *sqq.*, xix. 6, xxii. 30.

[2] Hag. ii. 12; cf. Jer. xi. 15, LXX.

[3] The old sacrificial feasts occupy but a single day (1 Sam. ix.), or at most two days (1 Sam. xx. 27).

not a mere attenuated offering, in which man grudges to give up the whole victim to his God. On the contrary, the central significance of the rite lies in the act of communion between God and man, when the worshipper is admitted to eat of the same holy flesh of which a part is laid upon the altar as "the food of the deity." But with the *minḥa* nothing of this kind occurs; the whole consecrated offering is retained by the deity, and the worshipper's part in the service is completed as soon as he has made over his gift. In short, while the *zébaḥ* turns on an act of communion between the deity and his worshippers, the *minḥa* (as its name denotes) is simply a tribute.

I will not undertake to say that the distinction so clearly laid down in the Levitical law was observed before the Exile in all cases of cereal sacrifices. Probably it was not, for in most ancient religions we find that cereal offerings come to be accepted in certain cases as substitutes for animal sacrifices, and that in this way the difference between the two kinds of offering gradually gets to be obliterated.[1] But in such matters great weight is to be attached to priestly tradition, such as underlies the Levitical ritual. The priests were not likely to invent a distinction of the kind which has been described, and in point of fact there is good evidence that they did not invent it. For there is no doubt that in ancient times the ordinary source of the *minḥa* was the offering of first-fruits—this is, of a small but choice portion of the annual produce of the ground, which in fact is the only cereal oblation prescribed in the oldest laws.[2] So far as can be seen, the first-fruits were always a tribute wholly made

[1] So at Rome models in wax or dough often took the place of animals. The same thing took place at Athens: Hesychius, *s.vv.* βοῦς and ἕβδομος βοῦς; cf. Thucyd. i. 126 and *schol.* At Carthage we have found the name *zébaḥ* applied to vegetable offerings.

[2] Ex. xxii. 29, xxiii. 19, xxxiv. 26.

over to the deity at the sanctuary. They were brought by the peasant in a basket and deposited at the altar,[1] and so far as they were not actually burned on the altar, they were assigned to the priests[2]—not to the ministrant as a reward for his service, but to the priests as a body, as the household of the sanctuary.[3]

Among the Hebrews, as among many other agricultural peoples, the offering of first-fruits was connected with the idea that it is not lawful or safe to eat of the new fruit until the god has received his due.[4] The offering makes the whole crop lawful food, but it does not make it holy food; nothing is consecrated except the small portion offered at the altar, and of the remaining store clean persons and unclean eat alike throughout the year. This, therefore, is quite a different thing from the consecration of animal sacrifices, for in the latter case the whole flesh is holy, and only those who are clean can eat of it.[5]

In old Israel all slaughter was sacrifice,[6] and a man could never eat beef or mutton except as a religious act, but cereal food had no such sacred associations; as soon as God had received His due of first-fruits, the whole domestic store was common. The difference between cereal and animal food was therefore deeply marked, and though bread was of course brought to the sanctuary to be

[1] Deut. xxvi. 1 *sqq.*

[2] Lev. xxiii. 17; Deut. xviii. 4. For the purpose of this argument it is not necessary to advert to the distinction recognised by post-Biblical tradition between *rēshīth* and *bikkūrīm*, on which see Wellh., *Prolegomena*, 3rd ed., p. 161 *sq.*

[3] This follows from 2 Kings xxiii. 9. The tribute was sometimes paid to a man of God (2 Kings iv. 42), which is another way of making it over to the deity. In the Levitical law also the *minḥa* belongs to the priests as a whole (Lev. vii. 10). This is an important point. What the ministrant receives as a fee comes from the worshipper, what the priests as a whole receive is given them by the deity.

[4] Lev. xxiii. 14; cf. Pliny, *H. N.* xviii. 8.

[5] Hos. ix. 4 refers only to animal food.

[6] The same thing is true of Old Arabia; Wellh. p. 114.

eaten with the *zebaḥīm*, it had not and could not have the same religious meaning as the holy flesh. It appears from Amos iv. 4 that it was the custom in northern Israel to lay a portion of the worshipper's provision of ordinary leavened bread on the altar with the sacrificial flesh, and this custom was natural enough ; for why should not the deity's share of the sacrificial meal have the same cereal accompaniments as man's share? But there is no indication that this oblation consecrated the part of the bread retained by the worshipper and made it holy bread. The only holy bread of which we read is such as belonged to the priests, not to the offerer.[1] In Lev. vii. 14, Num. vi. 15, the cake of common bread is given to the priest instead of being laid on the altar, but it is carefully distinguished from the *minḥa*. In old times the priests had no altar dues of this kind. They had only the first-fruits and a claim to a piece of the sacrificial flesh,[2] from which it may be presumed that the custom of offering bread with the *zébaḥ* was not primitive. Indeed Amos seems to mention it with some surprise as a thing not familiar to Judæan practice. At all events no sacrificial meal could consist of bread alone. All through the old history it is taken for granted that a religious feast necessarily implies a victim slain.[3]

[1] 1 Sam. xxi. 4.

[2] Deut. xviii. 3, 4 ; 1 Sam. ii. 13 *sqq.*

[3] What has been said above of the contrast between cereal sacrificial gifts and the sacrificial feast seems to me to hold good also for Greece and Rome, with some modification in the case of domestic meals, which among the Semites had no religious character, but at Rome were consecrated by a portion being offered to the household gods. This, however, has nothing to do with public religion, in which the law holds good that there is no sacred feast without a victim, and that consecrated *aparchæ* are wholly given over to the sanctuary. The same thing holds good for many other peoples, and seems, so far as my reading goes, to be the general rule. But there are exceptions. My friend Mr. J. G. Frazer, to whose wide reading I never appeal without profit, refers me to Wilken's *Alfoeren van het eiland Beroe*, p. 26, where a true sacrificial feast is made of the first-fruits of rice. This

The distinction which we are thus led to draw between the cereal oblation, in which the dominant idea is that of a tribute paid to the god, and animal sacrifices, which are essentially acts of communion between the god and his worshippers, deserves to be followed out in more detail. But this task must be reserved for another lecture.

is called "eating the soul of the rice," so that the rice is viewed as a living creature. In such a case it is not unreasonable to say that the rice may be regarded as really an animate victim. Agricultural religions seem often to have borrowed ideas from the older cults of pastoral times.

LECTURE VII

FIRST-FRUITS, TITHES, AND SACRIFICIAL MEALS

It became apparent to us towards the close of the last lecture that the Levitical distinction between *minḥa* and *zĕbaḥ*, or cereal oblation and animal sacrifice, rests upon an ancient principle; that the idea of communion with the deity in a sacrificial meal of holy food was primarily confined to the *zĕbaḥ* or animal victim, and that the proper significance of the cereal offering is that of a tribute paid by the worshipper from the produce of the soil. Now we have already seen that the conception of the national deity as the Baal, or lord of the land, was developed in connection with the growth of agriculture and agricultural law. Spots of natural fertility were the Baal's land, because they were productive without the labour of man's hands, which, according to Eastern ideas, is the only basis of private property in the soil; and land which required irrigation was also liable to the payment of a sacred tribute, because it was fertilised by streams which belonged to the god or even were conceived as instinct with divine energy. This whole circle of ideas belongs to a condition of society in which agriculture and the laws that regulate it have made considerable progress, and is foreign to the sphere of thought in which the purely nomadic Semites moved. That the *minḥa* is not so ancient a form of sacrifice as the *zĕbaḥ* will not be doubted, for nomadic life is older than agriculture. But if the foregoing argument is correct, we can say more than this; we can affirm that the idea of the sacrificial meal as an act of communion is older than sacrifice in the sense of tribute, and that the latter notion grew up with the development of agricultural life and the conception of the deity as Baal of the land. Among the nomadic Arabs the idea of sacrificial tribute has little or no place; all sacrifices are free-will offerings, and except in some rare forms of piacular oblation—particularly human sacrifice—and perhaps in some very simple offerings such as the libation of milk, the object of the sacrifice is to provide the material for an act of sacrificial communion with the god.[1]

In most ancient nations the idea of sacrificial tribute is most clearly marked in the institution of the sacred tithe, which was paid to the gods from the produce of the soil, and sometimes also from other sources of revenue.[2] In antiquity tithe and tribute are practically identical, nor is the name of tithe strictly limited to tributes of one-tenth, the term being used to cover any impost paid in kind upon a fixed scale. Such taxes play a great part in the revenues of Eastern sovereigns, and have done so from a very early date. The Babylonian kings drew a tithe from imports,[3] and the tithe of the fruits of the soil had the first place among the revenues of the Persian satraps.[4] The Hebrew kings in like manner took tithes of their subjects, and the tribute in kind which Solomon drew from the provinces for the support of his household may

[1] Some points connected with this statement which invite attention, but cannot be fully discussed at the present stage of the argument, will be considered in *Additional Note* E, *Sacred Tribute in Arabia.*

[2] See the instances collected by Spencer, Lib. iii. cap. 10, § 1; Hermann, *Gottesdienstliche Alterth. d. Griechen*, 2nd ed., § 20, note 4; Wyttenbach in the index to his edition of Plutarch's *Moralia*, *s.v.* Ἡρακλῆς.

[3] Aristotle, *Œcon.* p. 1352*b* of the Berlin edition. A tithe on imports is found also at Mecca (Azracī, p. 107; B. Hish. p. 72).

[4] Aristotle, *Œcon.* p. 1345*b*.

be regarded as an impost of this sort.[1] Thus the institution of a sacred tithe corresponds to the conception of the national god as a king, and so at Tyre tithes were paid to Melcarth, "the king of the city." The Carthaginians, as Diodorus[2] tells us, sent the tithe of produce to Tyre annually from the time of the foundation of their city. This is the earliest example of a Semitic sacred tithe of which we have any exact account, and it is to be noted that it is as much a political as a religious tribute; for the temple of Melcarth was the state treasury of Tyre, and it is impossible to draw a distinction between the sacred tithe paid by the Carthaginians and the political tribute paid by other colonies, such as Utica.[3]

The oldest Hebrew laws require the payment of first-fruits, but know nothing of a tithe due at the sanctuary. And indeed the Hebrew sanctuaries in old time had not such a splendid establishment as called for the imposition of sacred tributes on a large scale. When Solomon erected his temple, in emulation of Hiram's great buildings at Tyre, a more lavish ritual expenditure became necessary; but, as the temple at Jerusalem was attached to the palace, this was part of the household expenditure of the sovereign, and doubtless was met out of the imposts *in natura* levied for the maintenance of the court.[4] In other words, the maintenance of the royal sanctuary was a charge on the king's tithes; and so we find that a tenth directly paid to the sanctuary forms no part of the temple revenues

[1] 1 Sam. viii. 15, 17; 1 Kings iv. 7 *sqq.* The "king's mowings" (Amos vii. 1) belong to the same class of imposts, being a tribute in kind levied on the spring herbage to feed the horses of the king (cf. 1 Kings xviii. 5). Similarly the Romans in Syria levied a tax on pasture-land in the month Nisan for the food of their horses: see Bruns and Sachau, *Syrisch-Röm. Rechtsbuch*, Text L, § 121; and Wright, *Notulæ Syriacæ* (1887), p. 6.

[2] Lib. xx. cap. 14.

[3] Jos., *Antt.* viii. 5. 3, as read by Niese after Gutschmid.

[4] Cf. 2 Kings xvi. 15; Ezek. xlv. 9 *sqq.*

referred to in 2 Kings xii. 4. In northern Israel the royal sanctuaries, of which Bethel was the chief,[1] were originally maintained, in the same way, by the king himself; but as Bethel was not the ordinary seat of the court, so that the usual stated sacrifices there could not be combined with the maintenance of the king's table, some special provision must have been made for them. As the new and elaborate type of sanctuary was due to Phœnician influence, it was Phœnicia, where the religious tithe was an ancient institution, which would naturally suggest the source from which a more splendid worship should be defrayed; the service of the god of the land ought to be a burden on the land. And the general analogy of fiscal arrangements in the East makes it probable that this would be done by assigning to the sanctuary the taxes in kind levied on the surrounding district;[2] it is therefore noteworthy that the only pre-Deuteronomic references to a tithe paid at the sanctuary refer to the "royal chapel" of Bethel.[3]

The tithes paid to ancient sanctuaries were spent in various ways, and were by no means, what the Hebrew tithes ultimately became under the hierocracy, a revenue appropriated to the maintenance of the priests; thus in South Arabia we find tithes devoted to the erection of sacred monuments.[4] One of the chief objects, however, for which they were expended was the maintenance of feasts and sacrifices of a public character, at which the worshippers were entertained free of charge.[5] This element

[1] Amos vii. 13.

[2] Cf. the grant of the village of Bætocæce for the maintenance of the sanctuary of the place, Waddington, No. 2720*a*.

[3] Gen. xxviii. 22; Amos iv. 4.

[4] Mordtm. und Müller, *Sab. Denkm.* No. 11.

[5] Xen., *Anab.* v. 3. 9; Waddington, *ut supra.* Similarly the tithes of incense paid to the priests at Sabota in South Arabia were spent on the feast which the god spread for his guests for a certain number of days (Pliny,

cannot have been lacking at the royal sanctuaries of the Hebrews, for a splendid hospitality to all and sundry who assembled at the great religious feasts was recognised as the duty of the king even in the time of David.[1] And so we find that Amos enumerates the tithe at Bethel as one of the chief elements that contributed to the jovial luxurious worship maintained at that holy place.

If this account of the matter is correct, the tithes collected at Bethel were strictly of the nature of a tribute gathered from certain lands, and payment of them was doubtless enforced by royal authority. They were not used by each man to make a private religious feast for himself and his family, but were devoted to the maintenance of the public or royal sacrifices. This, it ought to be said, is not the view commonly taken by modern critics. The old festivities at Hebrew sanctuaries before the regal period were maintained, not out of any public revenue, but by each man bringing up to the sanctuary his own victim and all else that was necessary to make up a hearty feast, with the sacrificial flesh as its *pièce de resistance*.[2] It is generally assumed that this description was still applicable to the feasts at Bethel in Amos's time, and that the tithes were the provision that each farmer brought with him to feast his domestic circle and friends. At first sight this view looks plausible enough, especially when we find that the Book of Deuteronomy, written a century after Amos prophesied, actually prescribes that the annual tithes should be used by each householder to furnish forth a family feast before Jehovah. But it is not safe to argue back from the reforming ordinances of Deuteronomy to the practices of the northern sanctuaries, without checking the

H. N. xii. 63). M. R. Duval (*Rev. d'Assyriologie*, etc., 1888, p. 1 *sq.*) argues that at Taimā, in N. Arabia, there was a tithe on palm trees from which grants were made to the priest. But this is very doubtful.

[1] 2 Sam. vi. 19.

[2] 1 Sam. i. 21, 24, x. 3.

inference at every point. The connection between tithe and tribute is too close and too ancient to allow us to admit without hesitation that the Deuteronomic annual tithe, which retains nothing of the character of a tribute, is the primitive type of the institution. And this difficulty is not diminished when we observe that the Book of Deuteronomy recognises also another tithe, payable once in three years, which really is of the nature of a sacred tribute, although it is devoted not to the altar but to charity. It is arbitrary to say that the first tithe of Deuteronomy corresponds to ancient usage, and that the second is an innovation of the author; indeed, some indications of the Book of Deuteronomy itself point all the other way. In Deut. xxvi. 12, the third year, in which the charity tithe is to be paid, is called *par excellence* "the year of tithing," and in the following verse the charity tithe is reckoned in the list of "holy things," while the annual tithe, to be spent on family festivities at the sanctuary, is not so reckoned. In the face of these difficulties it is not safe to assume that either of the Deuteronomic tithes exactly corresponds to old usage. And if we look at Amos's account of the worship at Bethel as a whole, a feature which cannot fail to strike us is that the luxurious feasts beside the altars which he describes are entirely different in kind from the old rustic festivities at Shiloh described in 1 Samuel. They are not simple agricultural merry-makings of a popular character, but mainly feasts of the rich, enjoying themselves at the expense of the poor. The keynote struck in chap. ii. 7, 8, where the sanctuary itself is designated as the seat of oppression and extortion, is re-echoed all through the book; Amos's charge against the nobles is not merely that they are professedly religious and yet oppressors, but that their luxurious religion is founded on oppression, on the gains of corruption at the sacred tribunal and other forms of extortion. This is not the association in which we can look for the idyllic simplicity of the Deuteronomic family feast of tithes. But it is the very association in which one expects to find the tithe as I have supposed it to be; the revenues of the state religion, originally designed to maintain a public hospitality at the altar, and enable rich and poor alike to rejoice before their God, were monopolised by a privileged class.

This being understood, the innovations in the law of tithes proposed in the Book of Deuteronomy become sufficiently intelligible. In the kingdom of Judah there was no royal sanctuary except that at Jerusalem, the maintenance of which was part of the king's household charges, and it is hardly probable that any part of the royal tithes was assigned to the maintenance of the local sanctuaries. But as early as the time of Samuel we find religious feasts of clans or of towns, which are not a mere agglomeration of private sacrifices, and so must have been defrayed out of communal funds; from this germ, as religion became more luxurious, a fixed impost on land for the maintenance of the public services, such as was collected among the Phœnicians, would naturally grow. Such an impost would be in the hands, not of the priests, but of the heads of clans and communes, *i.e.* of the rich, and would necessarily be liable to the same abuses as prevailed in the northern kingdom. The remedy which Deuteronomy proposes for these abuses is to leave each farmer to spend his own tithes as he pleases at the central sanctuary. But this provision, if it had stood alone, would have amounted to the total abolition of a communal fund, which, however much abused in practice, was theoretically designed for the maintenance of a public table, where every one had a right to claim a portion, and which was doubtless of some service to the landless proletariate, however hardly its collection might press on the poorer farmer.[1] This difficulty was met by the triennial tithe devoted to charity, to the landless poor and to the landless Levite. Strictly speaking, this triennial due was the only real tithe left—the only impost for a religious purpose which a man was actually bound to pay away—and to it the whole subsequent history of Hebrew tithes attaches itself. The other tithe, which was not a due but of a mere voluntary character, disappears altogether in the Levitical legislation.

If this account of the Hebrew tithe is correct, that institution is of relatively modern origin—as indeed is indicated by the silence of the most ancient laws—and throws very little light on the original principles of Semitic sacrifice. The principle that the god of the land claims a tribute on the increase of the soil was originally expressed in the offering of first-fruits, at a time when sanctuaries and their service were too simple to need any elaborate provision for their support. The tithe originated when worship became more complex and ritual more splendid, so that a fixed tribute was necessary for its maintenance. The tribute took the shape of an impost on the produce of land, partly because this was an ordinary source of revenue for all public purposes, partly because such an impost could be justified from the religious point of view, as agreeing in principle with the oblation of first-fruits, and constituting a tribute to the god from the agricultural blessings he bestowed. But here the similarity between tithes and first-fruits ends. The first-fruits constituted a private sacrifice of the worshipper, who brought

[1] The same principle was acknowledged in Greece, *ἀπὸ τῶν ἱερῶν γὰρ οἱ πτωχοὶ ζῶσιν* (*Schol.* on Aristoph. *Plutus*, 596, in Hermann *op. cit.* § 15, note 16). So too in the Arabian meal-offering to Ocaiṣir (*supra*, p. 223).

them himself to the altar and was answerable for the payment only to God and his own conscience. The tithe, on the contrary, was a public burden enforced by the community for the maintenance of public religion. In principle there was no reason why it should not be employed for any purpose, connected with the public exercises of religion, for which money or money's worth was required; the way in which it should be spent depended not on the individual tithe-payer but on the sovereign or the commune. In later times, after the exile, it was entirely appropriated to the support of the clergy. But in old Israel it seems to have been mainly, if not exclusively, used to furnish forth public feasts at the sanctuary. In this respect it entirely differed from the first-fruits, which might be, and generally were, offered at a public festival, but did not supply any part of the material of the feast. The sacred feast, at which men and their god ate together, was originally quite unconnected with the cereal oblations paid in tribute to the deity, and its staple was the *zébaḥ*—the sacrificial victim. We shall see by and by that in its origin the *zébaḥ* was not the private offering of an individual householder but the sacrifice of a clan, and so the sacrificial meal had pre-eminently the character of a public feast. Now when public feasts are organised on a considerable scale, and furnished not merely with store of sacrificial flesh, but—as was the wont in Israel under the kings—with all manner of luxurious accessories, they come to be costly affairs, which can only be defrayed out of public moneys. The Israel of the time of the kings was not a simple society of peasants, all living in the same way, who could simply club together to maintain a rustic feast by what each man brought to the sanctuary from his own farm. Splendid festivals like those of Bethel were evidently not furnished in this way, but were mainly banquets of the upper classes in which the poor had a very subordinate share. The source of these festivals was the tithe, but it was not the poor tithe-payer who figured as host at the banquet. The organisation of the feast was in the hands of the ruling classes, who received the tithes and spent them on the service in a way that gave the lion's share of the good things to themselves; though no doubt, as in other ancient countries, the principle of a public feast was not wholly ignored, and every one present had something to eat and drink, so that the whole populace was kept in good humour.[1] Of course it is not to be supposed that the whole service was of this public character. Private persons still brought up their own vows and free-will offerings, and arranged their own family parties. But these, I conceive, were quite independent of the tithes, which were a public tax devoted to what was regarded as the public part of religion. On the whole, therefore, the tithe system has nothing to do with primitive Hebrew religion; the only point about it which casts a light backwards on the earlier stages of worship is that it could hardly have sprung up except in connection with the idea that the maintenance of sacrifice was a public duty, and that the sacrificial feast had essentially a public character. This point, however, is of the highest importance, and must be kept clearly before us as we proceed.

Long before any public revenue was set apart for the maintenance of sacrificial ritual, the ordinary type of Hebrew worship was essentially social, for in antiquity all religion was the affair of the community rather than of the

[1] The only way of escape from this conclusion is to suppose that the rich nobles paid out of their own pockets for the more expensive parts of the public sacrifices; and no one who knows the East and reads the Book of Amos will believe that. Nathan's parable about the poor man's one lamb, which his rich neighbour took to make a feast (necessarily at that date sacrificial), is an apposite illustration.

individual. A sacrifice was a public ceremony of a township or of a clan,[1] and private householders were accustomed to reserve their offerings for the annual feasts, satisfying their religious feelings in the interval by vows to be discharged when the festal season came round.[2] Then the crowds streamed into the sanctuary from all sides, dressed in their gayest attire,[3] marching joyfully to the sound of music,[4] and bearing with them not only the victims appointed for sacrifice, but store of bread and wine to set forth the feast.[5] The law of the feast was open-handed hospitality; no sacrifice was complete without guests, and portions were freely distributed to rich and poor within the circle of a man's acquaintance.[6] Universal hilarity prevailed, men ate drank and were merry together, rejoicing before their God.

The picture which I have drawn of the dominant type of Hebrew worship contains nothing peculiar to the religion of Jehovah. It is clear from the Old Testament that the ritual observances at a Hebrew and at a Canaanite sanctuary were so similar that to the mass of the people Jehovah worship and Baal worship were not separated by any well-marked line, and that in both cases the prevailing

[1] 1 Sam. ix. 12, xx. 6. In the latter passage "family" means "clan," not "domestic circle." See below, p. 276, note.

[2] 1 Sam. i. 3, 21.

[3] Hos. ii. 15 (E.V. 13).

[4] Isa. xxx. 29.

[5] 1 Sam. x. 3.

[6] 1 Sam. ix. 13; 2 Sam. vi. 19, xv. 11; Neh. viii. 10. The guests of the sacrifice supply a figure to the prophets (Ezek. xxxix. 17 *sqq.*; Zeph. i. 7). Nabal's refusal to allow David to share in his sheep-shearing feast was not only churlish but a breach of religious custom; from Amos iv. 5 it would appear that with a free-will offering there was a free invitation to all to come and partake. For the Arabian usuage in like cases, see Wellhausen, p. 114 *sq.* A banqueting hall for the communal sacrifice is mentioned as early as 1 Sam. ix. 22, and the name given to it (*lishka*) seems to be identical with the Greek λέσχη, from which it may be gathered that the Phœnicians had similar halls from an early date; cf. Judg. ix. 27, xvi. 23 *sqq.* For the communal feasts of the Syrians in later times, see Posidon. Apam. *ap.* Athen. xii. 527 (*Fr. Hist. Gr.* iii. 258).

tone and temper of the worshippers were determined by the festive character of the service. Nor is the prevalence of the sacrificial feast, as the established type of ordinary religion, confined to the Semitic peoples; the same kind of worship ruled in ancient Greece and Italy, and seems to be the universal type of the local cults of the small agricultural communities out of which all the nations of ancient civilisation grew. Everywhere we find that a sacrifice ordinarily involves a feast, and that a feast cannot be provided without a sacrifice. For a feast is not complete without flesh, and in early times the rule that all slaughter is sacrifice was not confined to the Semites.[1] The identity of religious occasions and festal seasons may indeed be taken as the determining characteristic of the type of ancient religion generally; when men meet their god they feast and are glad together, and whenever they feast and are glad they desire that the god should be of the party. This view is proper to religions in which the habitual temper of the worshippers is one of joyous confidence in their god, untroubled by any habitual sense of human guilt, and resting on the firm conviction that they and the deity they adore are good friends, who understand each other perfectly and are united by bonds not easily broken. The basis of this confidence lies of course in the view that the gods are part and parcel of the same natural community with their worshippers. The divine father or king claims the same kind of respect and service as a human father or king, and practical religion is simply a branch of social duty, an understood part of the conduct

[1] It is Indian (Manu, v. 31 *sqq.*) and Persian (Sprenger, *Eranische Alterth.* iii. 578; cf. Herod. i. 132; Strabo, xv. 3. 13, p. 732). Among the Romans and the older Greeks there was something sacrificial about every feast, or even about every social meal; in the latter case the Romans paid tribute to the household gods. On the identity of feast and sacrifice in Greece, see Athenæus, v. 19; Buchholz, *Hom. Realien*, II. ii. 202, 213 *sqq.*

of daily life, governed by fixed rules to which every one has been trained from his infancy. No man who is a good citizen, living up to the ordinary standard of civil morality in his dealings with his neighbours, and accurately following the ritual tradition in his worship of the gods, is oppressed with the fear that the deity may set a higher standard of conduct and find him wanting. Civil and religious morality have one and the same measure, and the conduct which suffices to secure the esteem of men suffices also to make a man perfectly easy as to his standing with the gods. It must be remembered that all antique morality is an affair of social custom and customary law, and that in the more primitive forms of ancient life the force of custom is so strong that there is hardly any middle course between living well up to the standard of social duty which it prescribes, and falling altogether outside the pale of the civil and religious community. A man who deliberately sets himself against the rules of the society in which he lives must expect to be outlawed; but minor offences are readily condoned as mere mistakes, which may expose the offender to a fine but do not permanently lower his social status or his self-respect. So too a man may offend his god, and be called upon to make reparation to him. But in such a case he knows, or can learn from a competent priestly authority, exactly what he ought to do to set matters right, and then everything goes on as before. In a religion of this kind there is no room for an abiding sense of sin and unworthiness, or for acts of worship that express the struggle after an unattained righteousness, the longing for uncertain forgiveness. It is only when the old religions begin to break down that these feelings come in. The older national and tribal religions work with the smoothness of a machine. Men are satisfied with their gods, and they feel that the gods are satisfied with them.

Or if at any time famine, pestilence or disaster in war appears to shew that the gods are angry, this casts no doubt on the adequacy of the religious system as such, but is merely held to prove that a grave fault has been committed by some one for whom the community is responsible, and that they are bound to put it right by an appropriate reparation. That they can put it right, and stand as well with the god as they ever did, is not doubted; and when rain falls, or the pestilence is checked, or the defeat is retrieved, they at once recover their old easy confidence, and go on eating and drinking and rejoicing before their god with the assurance that he and they are on the best of jovial good terms.

The kind of religion which finds its proper æsthetic expression in the merry sacrificial feast implies a habit of mind, a way of taking the world as well as a way of regarding the gods, which we have some difficulty in realising. Human life is never perfectly happy and satisfactory, yet ancient religion assumes that through the help of the gods it is so happy and satisfactory that ordinary acts of worship are all brightness and hilarity, expressing no other idea than that the worshippers are well content with themselves and with their divine sovereign. This implies a measure of *insouciance*, a power of casting off the past and living in the impression of the moment, which belongs to the childhood of humanity, and can exist only along with a childish unconsciousness of the inexorable laws that connect the present and the future with the past. Accordingly the more developed nations of antiquity, in proportion as they emerged from national childhood, began to find the old religious forms inadequate, and either became less concerned to associate all their happiness with the worship of the gods, and, in a word, less religious, or else were unable to think of the divine powers as habitually well pleased and favourable, and so were driven to look on the anger of the gods as much more frequent and permanent than their fathers had supposed, and to give to atoning rites a stated and important place in ritual, which went far to change the whole attitude characteristic of early worship, and substitute for the old joyous confidence a painful and scrupulous anxiety in all approach to the gods. Among the Semites the Arabs furnish an example of the general decay of religion, while the nations of Palestine in the seventh century B.C. afford an excellent illustration of the development of a gloomier type of worship under the pressure of accumulated political disasters. On the whole, however, what strikes the modern thinker as surprising is not that the old joyous type of worship ultimately broke down, but that it lasted so long as it did, or even that it ever attained a paramount place among nations so advanced as the Greeks and the Syrians. This is a matter which well deserves attentive consideration.

First of all, then, it is to be observed that the frame of mind in which men are well pleased with themselves, with their gods, and with the world, could not have dominated antique religion as it did, unless religion had been essentially the affair of the community rather than of individuals. It was not the business of the gods of heathenism to watch, by a series of special providences, over the welfare of every individual. It is true that individuals laid their private affairs before the gods, and asked with prayers and vows for strictly personal blessings. But they did this just as they might crave a personal boon from a king, or as a son craves a boon from a father, without expecting to get all that was asked. What the gods might do in this way was done as a matter of personal favour, and was no part of their proper function as heads of the community. The benefits which were expected from the gods were of a public character, affecting the whole community, especially fruitful seasons, increase of flocks and herds, and success in war. So long as the community flourished the fact that an individual was miserable reflected no discredit on divine providence, but was rather taken to prove that the sufferer was an evil-doer, justly hateful to the gods. Such a man was out of place among the happy and prosperous crowd that assembled on feast days before the altar; even in Israel, Hannah, with her sad face and silent petition, was a strange figure at the sanctuary of Shiloh, and the unhappy leper, in his lifelong affliction, was shut out from the exercises of religion as well as from the privileges of social life. So too the mourner was unclean, and his food was not brought into the house of God; the very occasions of life in which spiritual things are nearest to the Christian, and the comfort of religion is most fervently sought, were in the ancient world the times when a man was forbidden to approach the seat of God's presence. To us, whose habit it is to look at religion in its influence on the life and happiness of individuals, this seems a cruel law; nay, our sense of justice is offended by a system in which misfortunes set up a barrier between a man and his God. But whether in civil or in profane matters, the habit of the old world was to think much of the community and little of the individual life, and no one felt this to be unjust even though it bore hardly on himself. The god was the god of the nation or of the tribe, and he knew and cared for the individual only as a member of the community. Why, then, should private misfortune be allowed to mar by its ill-omened presence the public gladness of the sanctuary?

Accordingly the air of habitual satisfaction with themselves, their gods and the world, which characterises the worship of ancient communities, must be explained without reference to the vicissitudes of individual life. And so far as the thing requires any other explanation than the general *insouciance* and absorption in the feelings of the moment characteristic of the childhood of society, I apprehend that the key to the joyful character of the antique religions known to us lies in the fact that they took their shape in communities that were progressive and on the whole prosperous. If we realise to ourselves the conditions of early society, whether in Europe or in Asia, at the first daybreak of history, we cannot fail to see that a tribe or nation that could not hold its own and make headway must soon have been crushed out of existence in the incessant feuds it had to wage with all its neighbours. The communities of ancient civilisation were formed by the survival of the fittest, and they had all the self-confidence and elasticity that are engendered by success in the struggle for life. These characters, therefore, are reflected in the religious system that grew up with the growth of the state, and the type of worship that corresponded to them was not felt to be inadequate till the political system was undermined from within or shattered by blows from without.

These considerations sufficiently account for the development of the habitually joyous temper of ancient sacrificial worship. But it is also to be observed that when the type was once formed it would not at once disappear, even when a change in social conditions made it no longer an adequate expression of the habitual tone of national life. The most important functions of ancient worship were reserved for public occasions, when the whole community was stirred by a common emotion; and among agricultural nations the stated occasions of sacrifice were the natural seasons of festivity, at harvest and vintage. At such times every one was ready to cast off his cares and rejoice before his god, and so the coincidence of religious and agricultural gladness helped to keep the old form of worship alive, long after it had ceased to be in full harmony with men's permanent view of the world. Moreover it must be remembered that the spirit of boisterous mirth which characterised the oldest religious festivals was nourished by the act of worship itself. The sacrificial feast was not only an expression of gladness but a means of driving away care, for it was set forth with every circumstance of gaiety, with garlands, perfumes and music, as well as with store of meat and wine. The sensuous Oriental nature responds to such physical stimulus with a readiness foreign to our more sluggish temperament; to the Arab it is an excitement and a delight of the highest order merely to have flesh to eat.[1] From the earliest times, therefore, the religious gladness of the Semites tended to assume an orgiastic character and become a sort of intoxication of the senses, in which anxiety and sorrow were drowned for the moment. This is apparent in the old Canaanite festivals, such as the vintage feast at Shechem described in Judg. ix. 27, and not less in the service of the Hebrew high places, as it is characterised by the prophets. Even at Jerusalem the worship must have been boisterous indeed, when Lam. ii. 7 compares the shouts of the storming party of the Chaldæans in the courts of the temple with the noise of a solemn feast. Among the Nabatæans and elsewhere the orgiastic character of the worship often led in later times to the identification of Semitic gods, especially of Dusares, with

[1] A current Arabic saying which I have somewhere seen ascribed to Taäbbata Sharran, reckons the eating of flesh as one of the three great delights of life. In Maidānī, ii. 22, flesh and wine are classed together as seductive luxuries.

the Greek Dionysus. It is plain that a religion of this sort would not necessarily cease to be powerful when it ceased to express a habitually joyous view of the world and the divine governance; in evil times, when men's thoughts were habitually sombre, they betook themselves to the physical excitement of religion, as men now take refuge in wine. That this is not a fancy picture is clear from Isaiah's description of the conduct of his contemporaries during the approach of the Assyrians to Jerusalem,[1] when the multiplied sacrifices that were offered to avert the disaster degenerated into a drunken carnival—"Let us eat and drink, for to-morrow we die." And so in general when an act of Semitic worship began with sorrow and lamentation—as in the mourning for Adonis, or in the great atoning ceremonies which became common in later times—a swift revulsion of feeling followed, and the gloomy part of the service was presently succeeded by a burst of hilarious revelry, which, in later times at least, was not a purely spontaneous expression of the conviction that man is reconciled with the powers that govern his life and rule the universe, but in great measure a mere orgiastic excitement. The nerves were strung to the utmost tension in the sombre part of the ceremony, and the natural reaction was fed by the physical stimulus of the revelry that followed.

This, however, is not a picture of what Semitic religion was from the first, and in its ordinary exercises, but of the shape it tended to assume in extraordinary times of national calamity, and still more under the habitual pressure of grinding despotism, when the general tone of social life was no longer bright and hopeful, but stood in painful contrast to the joyous temper proper to the traditional forms of worship. Ancient heathenism was not made for such times, but for seasons of national prosperity, when its

[1] Isa. xxii. 12, 13, compared with i. 11 *sqq.*

joyous rites were the appropriate expression for the happy fellowship that united the god and his worshippers to the satisfaction of both parties. Then the enthusiasm of the worshipping throng was genuine. Men came to the sanctuary to give free vent to habitual feelings of thankful confidence in their god, and warmed themselves into excitement in a perfectly natural way by feasting together, as people still do when they rejoice together.

In acts of worship we expect to find the religious ideal expressed in its purest form, and we cannot easily think well of a type of religion whose ritual culminates in a jovial feast. It seems that such a faith sought nothing higher than a condition of physical *bien être*, and in one sense this judgment is just. The good things desired of the gods were the blessings of earthly life, not spiritual but carnal things. But Semitic heathenism was redeemed from mere materialism by the fact that religion was not the affair of the individual but of the community. The ideal was earthly, but it was not selfish. In rejoicing before his god a man rejoiced with and for the welfare of his kindred, his neighbours and his country, and, in renewing by a solemn act of worship the bond that united him to his god, he also renewed the bonds of family social and national obligation. We have seen that the compact between the god and the community of his worshippers was not held to pledge the deity to make the private cares of each member of the community his own. The gods had their favourites no doubt, for whom they were prepared to do many things that they were not bound to do; but no man could approach his god in a purely personal matter with that spirit of absolute confidence which I have described as characteristic of antique religions; it was the community, and not the individual, that was sure of the permanent and unfailing help of its deity. It was a national not a personal providence that was taught by ancient religion. So much was this the case that in purely personal concerns the ancients were very apt to turn, not to the recognised religion of the family or of the state, but to magical superstitions. The gods watched over a man's civic life, they gave him his share in public benefits, the annual largess of the harvest and the vintage, national peace or victory over enemies, and so forth, but they were not sure helpers in every private need, and above all they would not help him in matters that were against the interests of the community as a whole. There was therefore a whole region of possible needs and desires for which religion could and would do nothing; and if supernatural help was sought in such things it had to be sought through magical ceremonies, designed to purchase or constrain the favour of demoniac powers with which the public religion had nothing to do. Not only did these magical superstitions lie outside religion, but in all well-ordered states they were regarded as illicit. A man had no right to enter into private relations with supernatural powers that might help him at the expense of the community to which he belonged. In his relations to the unseen he was bound always to think and act with and for the community, and not for himself alone.

With this it accords that every complete act of worship —for a mere vow was not a complete act till it was fulfilled by presenting a sacrifice—had a public or quasi-public character. Most sacrifices were offered on fixed occasions, at the great communal or national feasts, but even a private offering was not complete without guests, and the surplus of sacrificial flesh was not sold but distributed with an open hand.[1] Thus every act of

[1] See above, p. 254. In Greece, in later times, sacrificial flesh was exposed for sale (1 Cor. x. 25).

worship expressed the idea that man does not live for himself only but for his fellows, and that this partnership of social interests is the sphere over which the gods preside and on which they bestow their assured blessing.

The ethical significance which thus appertains to the sacrificial meal, viewed as a social act, received particular emphasis from certain ancient customs and ideas connected with eating and drinking. According to antique ideas, those who eat and drink together are by this very act tied to one another by a bond of friendship and mutual obligation. Hence when we find that in ancient religions all the ordinary functions of worship are summed up in the sacrificial meal, and that the ordinary intercourse between gods and men has no other form, we are to remember that the act of eating and drinking together is the solemn and stated expression of the fact that all who share the meal are brethren, and that the duties of friendship and brotherhood are implicitly acknowledged in their common act. By admitting man to his table the god admits him to his friendship; but this favour is extended to no man in his mere private capacity; he is received as one of a community, to eat and drink along with his fellows, and in the same measure as the act of worship cements the bond between him and his god, it cements also the bond between him and his brethren in the common faith.

We have now reached a point in our discussion at which it is possible to form some general estimate of the ethical value of the type of religion which has been described. The power of religion over life is twofold, lying partly in its association with particular precepts of conduct, to which it supplies a supernatural sanction, but mainly in its influence on the general tone and temper of men's minds, which it elevates to higher courage and purpose, and raises above a brutal servitude to the physical wants of the moment, by teaching men that their lives and happiness are not the mere sport of the blind forces of nature, but are watched over and cared for by a higher power. As a spring of action this influence is more potent than the fear of supernatural sanctions, for it is stimulative, while the other is only regulative. But to produce a moral effect on life the two must go together; a man's actions must be not only supported by the feeling that the divine help is with him, but regulated by the conviction that that help will not accompany him except on the right path. In ancient religion, as it appears among the Semites, the confident assurance of divine help belongs, not to each man in his private concerns, but to the community in its public functions and public aims; and it is this assurance that is expressed in public acts of worship, where all the members of the community meet together to eat and drink at the table of their god, and so renew the sense that he and they are altogether at one. Now, if we look at the whole community of worshippers as absolutely one, personify them and think of them as a single individual, it is plain that the effect of this type of religion must be regarded as merely stimulative and not regulative. When the community is at one with itself and at one with its god, it may, for anything that religion has to say, do exactly what it pleases towards all who are outside it. Its friends are the god's friends, its enemies the god's enemies; it takes its god with it in whatever it chooses to do. As the ancient communities of religion are tribes or nations, this is as much as to say that, properly speaking, ancient religion has no influence on intertribal or international morality—in such matters the god simply goes with his own nation or his own tribe.

So long as we consider the tribe or nation of common religion as a single subject, the influence of religion is limited to an increase of the national self-confidence—a quality very useful in the continual struggle for life that was waged between ancient communities, but which beyond this has no moral value.

But the case is very different when we look at the religious community as made up of a multitude of individuals, each of whom has private as well as public purposes and desires. In this aspect it is the regulative influence of ancient religion that is predominant, for the good things which religion holds forth are promised to the individual only in so far as he lives in and for the community. The conception of man's chief good set forth in the social act of sacrificial worship is the happiness of the individual in the happiness of the community, and thus the whole force of ancient religion is directed, so far as the individual is concerned, to maintain the civil virtues of loyalty and devotion to a man's fellows at a pitch of confident enthusiasm, to teach him to set his highest good in the prosperity of the society of which he is a member, not doubting that in so doing he has the divine power on his side and has given his life to a cause that cannot fail. This devotion to the common weal was, as every one knows, the mainspring of ancient morality and the source of all the heroic virtues of which ancient history presents so many illustrious examples. In ancient society, therefore, the religious ideal expressed in the act of social worship and the ethical ideal which governed the conduct of daily life were wholly at one, and all morality—as morality was then understood—was consecrated and enforced by religious motives and sanctions.

These observations are fully applicable only to the typical form of ancient religion, when it was still strictly tribal or national. When nationality and religion began to fall apart, certain worships assumed a character more or less cosmopolitan. Even in heathenism, therefore, in its more advanced forms, the gods, or at least certain gods, are in some measure the guardians of universal morality, and not merely of communal loyalty. But what was thus gained in comprehensiveness was lost in intensity and strength of religious feeling, and the advance towards ethical universalism, which was made with feeble and uncertain steps, was never sufficient to make up for the decline of the old heroic virtues that were fostered by the narrower type of national faith.

LECTURE VIII

THE ORIGINAL SIGNIFICANCE OF ANIMAL SACRIFICE

ENOUGH has been said as to the significance of the sacrificial feast as we find it among ancient nations no longer barbarous. But to understand the matter fully we must trace it back to its origin in a state of society much more primitive than that of the agricultural Semites or Greeks.

The sacrificial meal was an appropriate expression of the antique ideal of religious life, not merely because it was a social act and an act in which the god and his worshippers were conceived as partaking together, but because, as has already been said, the very act of eating and drinking with a man was a symbol and a confirmation of fellowship and mutual social obligations. The one thing directly expressed in the sacrificial meal is that the god and his worshippers are *commensals*, but every other point in their mutual relations is included in what this involves. Those who sit at meat together are united for all social effects; those who do not eat together are aliens to one another, without fellowship in religion and without reciprocal social duties. The extent to which this view prevailed among the ancient Semites, and still prevails among the Arabs, may be brought out most clearly by reference to the law of hospitality. Among the Arabs every stranger whom one meets in the desert is a natural enemy, and has no protection against violence except his own strong hand or the fear that his tribe will avenge him if his blood be spilt.[1] But if I have eaten the smallest morsel of food with a man, I have nothing further to fear from him; "there is salt between us," and he is bound not only to do me no harm, but to help and defend me as if I were his brother.[2] So far was this principle carried by the old Arabs, that Zaid al-Khail, a famous warrior in the days of Mohammed, refused to slay a vagabond who carried off his camels, because the thief had surreptitiously drunk from his father's milk bowl before committing the theft.[3] It does not indeed follow as a matter of course that because I have eaten once with a man I am permanently his friend, for the bond of union is conceived in a very realistic way, and strictly speaking lasts no longer than the food may be supposed to remain in my system.[4] But the temporary bond is confirmed by repetition,[5] and readily passes into a permanent tie confirmed by an oath. "There was a sworn alliance between the Liḥyān and the Moṣṭalic, they were

[1] This is the meaning of Gen. iv. 14 *sq.* Cain is "driven out from the face of the cultivated land" into the desert, where his only protection is the law of blood revenge.

[2] The *milḥa*, or bond of salt, is not dependent on the actual use of mineral salt with the food by which the bond is constituted. Milk, for example, will serve the purpose. Cf. Burckhardt, *Bedouins and Wahabys*, i. 329, and *Kāmil*, p. 284, especially the verse of Abu 'l-Ṭamaḥān there cited, where salt is interpreted to mean "milk."

[3] *Agh.* xvi. 51; cf. *Kinship*, p. 149 *sq.*

[4] Burton, *Pilgrimage*, iii. 84 (1st ed.), says that some tribes "require to renew the bond every twenty-four hours," as otherwise, to use their own phrase, "the salt is not in their stomachs" (almost the same phrase is used in the verse of Abu 'l-Ṭamaḥān referred to above). But usually the protection extended to a guest lasts three days and a third after his departure (Burckhardt, *op. cit.* i. 136); or, according to Doughty, i. 228, two nights and the day between. A curious example of the degree to which these notions might be pushed is given in the *Amthāl* of Mofaḍḍal al-Ḍabbī, Const. A. H. 1300, p. 46, where a man claims and obtains the help of Al-Ḥārith in recovering his stolen camels, because the water that was still in their stomachs when they were taken from him had been drawn with the help of a rope borrowed from Al-Ḥārith's herdsmen.

[5] "O enemy of God, wilt thou slay this Jew? Much of the fat on thy paunch is of his substance" (Ibn Hishām, p. 553 *sq.*).

wont to eat and drink together."[1] This phrase of an Arab narrator supplies exactly what is wanted to define the significance of the sacrificial meal. The god and his worshippers are wont to eat and drink together, and by this token their fellowship is declared and sealed.

The ethical significance of the common meal can be most adequately illustrated from Arabian usage, but it was not confined to the Arabs. The Old Testament records many cases where a covenant was sealed by the parties eating and drinking together. In most of these indeed the meal is sacrificial, so that it is not at once clear that two men are bound to each other merely by partaking of the same dish, unless the deity is taken in as a third party to the covenant. The value of the Arabian evidence is that it supplies proof that the bond of food is valid of itself, that religion may be called in to confirm and strengthen it, but that the essence of the thing lies in the physical act of eating together. That this was also the case among the Hebrews and Canaanites may be safely concluded from analogy, and appears to receive direct confirmation from Josh. ix. 14, where the Israelites enter into alliance with the Gibeonites by taking of their victuals, without consulting Jehovah. A formal league confirmed by an oath follows, but by accepting the proffered food the Israelites are already committed to the alliance.

But we have not yet got to the root of the matter. What is the ultimate nature of the fellowship which is constituted or declared when men eat and drink together? In our complicated society fellowship has many types and many degrees; men may be united by bonds of duty and honour for certain purposes, and stand quite apart in all

[1] *Diw. Hodh.* No. 87 (Kosegarten's ed. p. 170). In Sukkarī's account of the battle of Coshāwa (Wright, *Arabic Reading Book*, p. 21) a captive refuses to eat the food of his captor who has slain his son, and thus apparently keeps his right of blood revenge alive.

other things. Even in ancient times—for example, in the Old Testament—we find the sacrament of a common meal introduced to seal engagements of various kinds. But in every case the engagement is absolute and inviolable; it constitutes what in the language of ethics is called a duty of perfect obligation. Now in the most primitive society there is only one kind of fellowship which is absolute and inviolable. To the primitive man all other men fall under two classes, those to whom his life is sacred and those to whom it is not sacred. The former are his fellows; the latter are strangers and potential foemen, with whom it is absurd to think of forming any inviolable tie unless they are first brought into the circle within which each man's life is sacred to all his comrades.

But that circle again corresponds to the circle of kinship, for the practical test of kinship is that the whole kin is answerable for the life of each of its members. By the rules of early society, if I slay my kinsman, whether voluntarily or involuntarily, the act is murder, and is punished by expulsion from the kin;[1] if my kinsman is slain by an outsider I and every other member of my kin are bound to avenge his death by killing the manslayer or some member of his kin. It is obvious that under such a system there can be no inviolable fellowship except between men of the same blood. For the duty of blood revenge is paramount, and every other obligation is dissolved as soon as it comes into conflict with the claims of blood. I cannot bind myself absolutely to a man, even for a temporary purpose, unless during the time of our engagement he is put into a kinsman's place. And this is as much as to say that a

[1] Even in Homeric society no bloodwit can be accepted for slaughter within the kin; a point which is commonly overlooked, *e.g.* by Buchholz, *Hom. Real.* II. i. 76.

stranger cannot become bound to me, unless at the same time he becomes bound to all my kinsmen in exactly the same way. Such is, in fact, the law of the desert; when any member of a clan receives an outsider through the bond of salt, the whole clan is bound by his act, and must, while the engagement lasts, receive the stranger as one of themselves.[1]

The idea that kinship is not purely an affair of birth, but may be acquired, has quite fallen out of our circle of ideas; but so, for that matter, has the primitive conception of kindred itself. To us kinship has no absolute value, but is measured by degrees, and means much or little, or nothing at all, according to its degree and other circumstances. In ancient times, on the contrary, the fundamental obligations of kinship had nothing to do with degrees of relationship, but rested with absolute and identical force on every member of the clan. To know that a man's life was sacred to me, and that every blood-feud that touched him involved me also, it was not necessary for me to count cousinship with him by reckoning up to our common ancestor; it was enough that we belonged to the same clan and bore the same clan-name. What was my clan was determined by customary law, which was not the same in all stages of society; in the earliest Semitic communities a man was of his mother's clan, in later times he belonged to the clan of his father. But the essential idea of kinship was independent of the particular form of the law. A kin was a group of persons whose lives were so bound up together, in what must be called a physical unity, that they could be treated as parts

[1] This of course is to be understood only of the fundamental rights and duties which turn on the sanctity of kindred blood. The secondary privileges of kinship, in matters of inheritance and the like, lie outside of the present argument, and with regard to them the covenanted ally had not the full rights of a kinsman (*Kinship*, p. 47).

of one common life. The members of one kindred looked on themselves as one living whole, a single animated mass of blood, flesh and bones, of which no member could be touched without all the members suffering. This point of view is expressed in the Semitic tongues in many familiar forms of speech. In a case of homicide Arabian tribesmen do not say, "The blood of M. or N. has been spilt," naming the man; they say, "Our blood has been spilt." In Hebrew the phrase by which one claims kinship is "I am your bone and your flesh."[1] Both in Hebrew and in Arabic "flesh" is synonymous with "clan" or kindred group.[2] To us all this seems mere metaphor, from which no practical consequences can follow. But in early thought there is no sharp line between the metaphorical and the literal, between the way of expressing a thing and the way of conceiving it; phrases and symbols are treated as realities. Now, if kinship means participation in a common mass of flesh blood and bones, it is natural that it should be regarded as dependent, not merely on the fact that a man was born of his mother's body, and so was from his birth a part of her flesh, but also on the not less significant fact that he was nourished by her milk. And so we find that among the Arabs there is a tie of milk, as well as of blood, which unites the foster-child to his foster-mother and her kin. Again, after the child is weaned, his flesh and blood continue to be nourished and renewed by the food which he shares with his commensals, so that commensality can be thought of (1) as confirming or even (2) as constituting kinship in a very real sense.[3]

Judg. ix. 2; 2 Sam. v. 1. Conversely in acknowledging kinship the phrase is "Thou art my bone and my flesh" (Gen. xxix. 14; 2 Sam. xix. 12); cf. Gen. xxxvii. 27, "our brother and our flesh."

[2] Lev. xxv. 49; *Kinship*, p. 149.

[3] Cf. *Kinship*, p. 149 *sqq.*

As regards their bearing on the doctrine of sacrifice it will conduce to clearness if we keep these two points distinct. Primarily the circle of common religion and of common social duties was identical with that of natural kinship,[1] and the god himself was conceived as a being of the same stock with his worshippers. It was natural, therefore, that the kinsmen and their kindred god should seal and strengthen their fellowship by meeting together from time to time to nourish their common life by a common meal, to which those outside the kin were not admitted. A good example of this kind of clan sacrifice, in which a whole kinship periodically joins, is afforded by the Roman *sacra gentilicia*. As in primitive society no man can belong to more than one kindred, so among the Romans no one could share in the *sacra* of two gentes—to do so was to confound the ritual and contaminate the purity of the gens. The *sacra* consisted in common anniversary sacrifices, in which the clansmen honoured the gods of the clan and after them the "demons" of their ancestors, so that the whole kin living and dead were brought together in the service.[2] That the earliest sacrificial feasts among the Semites were of the nature of *sacra gentilicia* is matter of inference rather than of direct evidence, but is not on that account less certain. For that the Semites form no exception to the general rule that the circle of religion and of kinship were originally identical, has been shown in Lecture II. The only thing, therefore, for which additional proof is needed is that the sacrificial ritual of the Semites already existed in this primitive form of society. That this was so is morally certain on general grounds; for an institution like the

[1] *Supra*, p. 50.

[2] For proofs and further details see the evidence collected by Marquardt, *Röm. Staatsverwaltung*, 2nd ed., iii. 130 *sq*.

sacrificial meal, which occurs with the same general features all over the world, and is found among the most primitive peoples, must, in the nature of things, date from the earliest stage of social organisation. And the general argument is confirmed by the fact that after several clans had begun to frequent the same sanctuary and worship the same god, the worshippers still grouped themselves for sacrificial purposes on the principle of kinship. In the days of Saul and David all the tribes of Israel had long been united in the worship of Jehovah, yet the clans still maintained their annual gentile sacrifice, at which every member of the group was bound to be present.[1] But evidence more decisive comes to us from Arabia, where, as we have seen, men would not eat together at all unless they were united by kinship or by a covenant that had the same effect as natural kinship. Under such a rule the sacrificial feast must have been confined to kinsmen, and the clan was the largest circle that could unite in a sacrificial act. And so, though the great sanctuaries of heathen Arabia were frequented at the pilgrimage feasts by men of different tribes, who met peaceably for a season under the protection of the truce of God, we find that their participation in the worship of the same holy place did not bind alien clans together in any religious unity; they worshipped side by side, but not together. It is only under Islam that the pilgrimage

[1] 1 Sam. xx. 6, 29. The word *mishpaḥa*, which the English Bible here and elsewhere renders "family," denotes not a household but a clan. In verse 29 the true reading is indicated by the Septuagint, and has been restored by Wellhausen (הֵאּ צִוּוּ לִי אַחַי). It was not David's brother, but his brethren, that is his clansmen, that enjoined his presence. The annual festivity, the duty of all clansmen to attend, the expectation that this sacred duty would be accepted as a valid excuse for absence from court even at the king's new-moon sacrifice, are so many points of correspondence with the Roman gentile worship; cf. Gellius, xvi. 4. 3, and the other passages cited by Marquardt, *Röm. Staatsverwaltung*, 2nd ed., iii. 132, note 4.

becomes a bond of religious fellowship, whereas in the times of heathenism it was the correct usage that the different tribes, before they broke up from the feast, should engage in a rivalry of self-exaltation and mutual abuse, which sent them home with all their old jealousies freshly inflamed.[1]

That the sacrificial meal was originally a feast of kinsmen, is apt to suggest to modern minds the idea that its primitive type is to be sought in the household circle, and that public sacrifices, in which the whole clan united, are merely an extension of such an act of domestic worship as in ancient Rome accompanied every family meal. The Roman family never rose from supper till a portion of food had been laid on the burning hearth as an offering to the Lares, and the current opinion, which regards the gens as nothing more than an enlarged household, naturally looks on the gentile sacrifice as an enlargement of this domestic rite. But the notion that the clan is only a larger household is not consistent with the results of modern research. Kinship is an older thing than family life, and in the most primitive societies known to us the family or household group was not a subdivision of the clan, but contained members of more than one kindred. As a rule the savage

[1] See Goldziher, *Muh. Stud.* i. 56. The prayer and exhortation of the leader of the procession of tribes from ʿArafa (*Agh.* iii. 4; Wellh. p. 191) seems to me to be meant for his own tribe alone. The prayer for "peace among our women, a continuous range of pasture occupied by our herdsmen, wealth placed in the hands of our most generous men," asks only blessings for the tribe, and indeed occurs elsewhere as a form of blessing addressed to a tribe (*Agh.* xix. 132. 6). And the admonition to observe treaties, honour clients, and be hospitable to guests, contains nothing that was not a point of tribal morality. The *ijāza*, or right to give the signal for dissolving the worshipping assembly, belonged to a particular tribe; it was the right to start first. The man who gave the sign to this tribe closed the service for them by a prayer and admonition. This is all that I can gather from the passage, and it does not prove that the tribes had any other religious communion than was involved in their being in one place at one time.

man may not marry a clanswoman, and the children are of the mother's kin, and therefore have no communion of blood religion with their father. In such a society there is hardly any family life, and there can be no sacred household meal. Before the family meal can acquire the religious significance that it possessed in Rome, one of two things must take place: either the primitive association of religion with kinship must be dissolved, or means must have been found to make the whole household of one blood, as was done in Rome by the rule that the wife upon her marriage was adopted into her husband's gens.[1] The rudest nations have religious rules about food, based on the principle of kinship, viz. that a man may not eat the totem animal of his clan; and they generally have some rites of the nature of the sacrificial feast of kinsmen; but it is not the custom of savages to take their ordinary daily food in a social way, in regular domestic meals. Their habit is to eat irregularly and apart, and this habit is strengthened by the religious rules, which often forbid to one member of a household the food which is permitted to another.

We have no direct evidence as to the rules and habits of the Semites in the state of primitive savagery, though there is ample proof of an indirect kind that they originally reckoned kinship through the mother, and that men often, if not always, took their wives from strange kins. It is to be presumed that at this stage of society the Semite did not eat with his wife and children, and it is certain that if he did so the meal could not have had a religious character, as an acknowledgment and seal of kinship and adherence

[1] In Greece, according to the testimony of Theophrastus, *ap.* Porph., *De Abst.* ii. 20 (Bernays, p. 68), it was customary to pay to the gods an *aparche* of every meal. The term ἀπάρχεσθαι seems to place this offering under the head of gifts rather than of sacrificial communion, and the gods to whom the offering was made were not, as at Rome, family gods.

to a kindred god. But in fact the family meal never became a fixed institution among the Semites generally. In Egypt, down to the present day, many persons hardly ever eat with their wives and children,[1] and, among the Arabs, boys who are not of full age do not presume to eat in the presence of their parents, but take their meals separately or with the women of the house.[2] No doubt the seclusion of women has retarded the development of family life in Mohammedan countries; but for most purposes this seclusion has never taken much hold on the desert, and yet in northern Arabia no woman will eat before men.[3] I apprehend that these customs were originally formed at a time when a man and his wife and family were not usually of one kin, and when only kinsmen would eat together.[4] But be this as it may, the fact remains that in Arabia the daily family meal has never been an established institution with such a religious significance as attaches to the Roman supper.[5]

The sacrificial feast, therefore, cannot be traced back to the domestic meal, but must be considered as having been

[1] Lane, *Mod. Egyptians*, 5th ed., i. 179; cf. *Arabian Nights*, chap. ii. note 17.

[2] Burckhardt, *Bed. and Wah.* i. 355; Doughty, ii. 142.

[3] Burckhardt, *op. cit.* i. 349. Conversely Ibn Mojāwir, *ap.* Sprenger, *Postrouten*, p. 151, tells of southern Arabs who would rather die than accept food at the hand of a woman.

[4] In Arabia, even in historical times, the wife was not adopted into her husband's kin. The children in historical times were generally reckoned to the father's stock; but there is much reason to think that this new rule of kinship, when it first came in, did not mean that the infant was born into his father's clan, but that he was adopted into it by a formal act, which did not always take place in infancy. We find that young children follow their mother (*Kinship*, p. 114), and that the law of blood revenge did not prevent fathers from killing their young daughters (*ibid.* p. 277 *sqq.*). Of this more hereafter.

[5] The naming of God, by which every meal is consecrated according to Mohammed's precept, seems in ancient times to have been practised only when a victim was slaughtered; cf. Wellh. p. 114. Here the *tahlīl* corresponds to the blessing of the sacrifice, 1 Sam. ix. 13.

from the first a public feast of clansmen. That this is true not only for Arabia but for the Semites as a whole might be inferred on general grounds, inasmuch as all Semitic worship manifestly springs from a common origin, and the inference is confirmed by the observation that even among the agricultural Semites there is no trace of a sacrificial character being attached to ordinary household meals. The domestic hearth among the Semites was not an altar as it was at Rome.[1]

Almost all varieties of human food were offered to the gods, and any kind of food suffices, according to the laws of Arabian hospitality, to establish that bond between two men which in the last resort rests on the principle that only kinsmen eat together. It may seem, therefore, that in the abstract any sort of meal publicly partaken of by a company of kinsmen may constitute a sacrificial feast. The distinction between the feast and an ordinary meal lies, it may seem, not in the material or the copiousness of the repast, but in its public character. When men eat alone they do not invite the god to share their food, but when the clan eats together as a kindred unity the kindred god must also be of the party.

Practically, however, there is no sacrificial feast according to Semitic usage except where a victim is slaughtered. The rule of the Levitical law, that a cereal oblation, when offered alone, belongs wholly to the god and gives no occasion for a feast of the worshippers, agrees with the older history, in which we never find a sacrificial meal of which flesh does not form part. Among the Arabs the usage is the same; a religious banquet implies a victim. It appears, therefore, to look at the matter from its merely human side, that the slaughter of a victim must have been

[1] The passover became a sort of household sacrifice after the exile, but was not so originally. See Wellhausen, *Prolegomena*, chap. iii.

in early times the only thing that brought the clan together for a stated meal. Conversely, every slaughter was a clan sacrifice, that is, a domestic animal was not slain except to procure the material for a public meal of kinsmen. This last proposition seems startling, but it is confirmed by the direct evidence of Nilus as to the habits of the Arabs of the Sinaitic desert towards the close of the fourth Christian century. The ordinary sustenance of these Saracens was derived from pillage or from hunting, to which, no doubt, must be added, as a main element, the milk of their herds. When these supplies failed they fell back on the flesh of their camels, one of which was slain for each clan (συγγένεια) or for each group which habitually pitched their tents together (συσκηνία)—which according to known Arab usage would always be a fraction of a clan—and the flesh was hastily devoured by the kinsmen in dog-like fashion, half raw and merely softened over the fire.[1]

To grasp the force of this evidence we must remember that, beyond question, there was at this time among the Saracens private property in camels, and that therefore, so far as the law of property went, there could be no reason why a man should not kill a beast for the use of his own family. And though a whole camel might be too much for a single household to eat fresh, the Arabs knew and practised the art of preserving flesh by cutting it into strips and drying them in the sun. Under these circumstances private slaughter could not have failed to be customary, unless it was absolutely forbidden by tribal usage. In short, it appears that while milk, game, the fruits of pillage were private food which might be eaten in any way, the

[1] *Nili opera quædam nondum edita* (Paris, 1639), p. 27.—The συγγένεια answers to the Arabic *baṭn*, the συσκηνία to the Arabic *ḥayy*, in the sense of encampment.

camel was not allowed to be killed and eaten except in a public rite, at which all the kinsmen assisted.

This evidence is all the more remarkable because, among the Saracens of whom Nilus speaks, the slaughter of a camel in times of hunger does not seem to have been considered as a sacrifice to the gods. For a couple of pages later he speaks expressly of the sacrifices which these Arabs offered to the morning star, the sole deity that they acknowledged. These could be performed only when the star was visible, and the whole victim—flesh, skin and bones—had to be devoured before the sun rose upon it, and the day-star disappeared. As this form of sacrifice was necessarily confined to seasons when the planet Venus was a morning star, while the necessity for slaughtering a camel as food might arise at any season, it is to be inferred that in the latter case the victim was not recognised as having a sacrificial character. The Saracens, in fact, had outlived the stage in which no necessity can justify slaughter that is not sacrificial. The principle that the god claims his share in every slaughter has its origin in the religion of kinship, and dates from a time when the tribal god was himself a member of the tribal stock, so that his participation in the sacrificial feast was only one aspect of the rule that no kinsman must be excluded from a share in the victim. But the Saracens of Nilus, like the Arabs generally in the last ages of heathenism, had ceased to do sacrifice to the tribal or clan gods with whose worship the feast of kinsmen was originally connected. The planet Venus, or Lucifer, was not a tribal deity, but, as we know from a variety of sources, was worshipped by all the northern Arabs, to whatever kin they belonged. It is not therefore surprising that in case of necessity we should meet with a slaughter in which the non-tribal deity had no part; but it is noteworthy that, after the victim had lost its sacrificial character, it was still deemed necessary that the slaughter should be the affair of the whole kindred. That this was so, while among the Hebrews, on the other hand, the rule that all legitimate slaughter is sacrifice survived long after householders were permitted to make private sacrifices on their own account, is characteristic of the peculiar development of Arabia, where, as Wellhausen has justly remarked, religious feeling was quite put in the shade by the feeling for the sanctity of kindred blood. Elsewhere among the Semites we see the old religion surviving the tribal system on which it was based, and accommodating itself to the new forms of national life; but in Arabia the rules and customs of the kin retained the sanctity which they originally derived from their connection with the religion of the kin, long after the kindred god had been forgotten or had sunk into quite a subordinate place. I take it, however, that the eating of camels' flesh continued to be regarded by the Arabs as in some sense a religious act, even when it was no longer associated with a formal act of sacrifice; for abstinence from the flesh of camels and wild asses was prescribed by Symeon Stylites to his Saracen converts,[1] and traces of an idolatrous significance in feasts of camels' flesh appear in Mohammedan tradition.[2]

The persistence among the Arabs of the scruple against private slaughter for a man's own personal use may, I think, be traced in a modified form in other parts of Arabia and long after the time of Nilus. Even in modern times,

[1] Theodoret, ed. Nösselt, iii. 1274 *sq.*

[2] Wellh. p. 114; *Kinship*, p. 262. These traces are the more worthy of notice because we also find indications that, down to the time of the prophet, or even later, the idea prevailed that camels, or at all events certain breeds of camels, were of demoniac origin; see Cazwīnī, ii. 42, and other authorities cited by Vloten in the *Vienna Oriental Journal*, vii. 239.

when a sheep or camel is slain in honour of a guest, the good old custom is that the host keeps open house for his neighbours, or at least distributes portions of the flesh as far as it will go. To do otherwise is still deemed churlish, though not illegal, and the old Arabic literature leaves the impression that in ancient times this feeling was still stronger than it is now, and that the whole encampment was considered when a beast was slain for food.[1] But be this as it may, it is highly significant to find that, even in one branch of the Arabian race, the doctrine that hunger itself does not justify slaughter, except as the act of the clan, was so deeply rooted as to survive the doctrine that all slaughter is sacrifice. This fact is sufficient to remove the last doubt as to the proposition that all sacrifice was originally clan sacrifice, and at the same time it puts the slaughter of a victim in a new light, by classing it among the acts which, in primitive society, are illegal to an individual, and can only be justified when the whole clan shares the responsibility of the deed. So far as I know, there is only one class of actions recognised by early nations to which this description applies, viz. actions which involve an invasion of the sanctity of the tribal blood. In fact, a life which no single tribesman is allowed to invade, and which can be sacrificed only by the consent and common action of the kin, stands on the same footing with the life of the fellow-tribesman. Neither may be taken away by private violence, but only by the consent of the kindred

[1] Compare especially the story of Māwia's courtship (*Aghānī*, xvi. 104; Caussin de Perceval, ii. 613). The beggar's claim to a share in the feast is doubtless ultimately based on religious and tribal usage rather than on personal generosity. Cf. Deut. xxvi. 13. Similarly among the Zulus, "when a man kills a cow—which, however, is seldom and reluctantly done, unless it happens to be stolen property—the whole population of the hamlet assemble to eat it without invitation; and people living at a distance of ten miles will also come to partake of the feast" (Shaw, *Memorials of South Africa*, p. 59).

and the kindred god. And the parallelism between the two cases is curiously marked in detail by what I may call a similarity between the ritual of sacrifice and of the execution of a tribesman. In both cases it is required that, as far as possible, every member of the kindred should be not only a consenting party but a partaker in the act, so that whatever responsibility it involves may be equally distributed over the whole clan. This is the meaning of the ancient Hebrew form of execution, where the culprit is stoned by the whole congregation.

The idea that the life of a brute animal may be protected by the same kind of religious scruple as the life of a fellow-man is one which we have a difficulty in grasping, or which at any rate we are apt to regard as more proper to a late and sentimental age than to the rude life of primitive times. But this difficulty mainly comes from our taking up a false point of view. Early man had certainly no conception of the sacredness of animal life as such, but neither had he any conception of the sacredness of human life as such. The life of his clansman was sacred to him, not because he was a man, but because he was a kinsman; and, in like manner, the life of an animal of his totem kind is sacred to the savage, not because it is animate, but because he and it are sprung from the same stock and are cousins to one another.

It is clear that the scruple of Nilus's Saracens about killing the camel was of this restricted kind; for they had no objection to kill and eat game. But the camel they would not kill except under the same circumstances as make it lawful for many savages to kill their totem, *i.e.* under the pressure of hunger or in connection with exceptional religious rites.[1] The parallelism between the Arabian custom and totemism is therefore complete except

[1] Frazer, *Totemism*, pp. 19, 48.

in one point. There is no direct evidence that the scruple against the private slaughter of a camel had its origin in feelings of kinship. But, as we have seen, there is this indirect evidence, that the consent and participation of the clan, which was required to make the slaughter of a camel legitimate, is the very thing that is needed to make the death of a kinsman legitimate. And direct evidence we cannot expect to find, for it is most improbable that the Arabs of Nilus's time retained any clear ideas about the original significance of rules inherited by tradition from a more primitive state of society.

The presumption thus created that the regard paid by the Saracens for the life of the camel sprang from the same principle of kinship between men and certain kinds of animals which is the prime factor in totemism, would not be worth much if it rested only on an isolated statement about a particular branch of the Arab race. But it is to be observed that the same kind of restriction on the private slaughter of animals must have existed in ancient times among all the Semites. We have found reason to believe that among the early Semites generally no slaughter was legitimate except for sacrifice, and we have also found reason, apart from Nilus's evidence, for believing that all Semitic sacrifice was originally the act of the community. If these two propositions are true, it follows that all the Semites at one time protected the lives of animals proper for sacrifice, and forbade them to be slain except by the act of the clan, that is, except under such circumstances as would justify or excuse the death of a kinsman. Now, if it thus appears that the scruple against private slaughter of an animal proper for sacrifice was no mere individual peculiarity of Nilus's Saracens, but must at an early period have extended to all the Semites, it is obvious that the conjecture which connects the scruple with a feeling of kinship between the worshippers and the victim gains greatly in plausibility. For the origin of the scruple must now be sought in some widespread and very primitive habit of thought, and it is therefore apposite to point out that among primitive peoples there are no binding precepts of conduct except those that rest on the principle of kinship.[1] This is the general rule which is found in operation wherever we have an opportunity of observing rude societies, and that it prevailed among the early Semites is not to be doubted. Indeed among the Arabs the rule held good without substantial modification down to the time of Mohammed. No life and no obligation was sacred unless it was brought within the charmed circle of the kindred blood.

Thus the *prima facie* presumption, that the scruple in question had to do with the notion that certain animals were akin to men, becomes very strong indeed, and can hardly be set aside unless those who reject it are prepared to show that the idea of kinship between men and beasts, as it is found in most primitive nations, was altogether foreign to Semitic thought, or at least had no substantial place in the ancient religious ideas of that race. But I do not propose to throw the burden of proof on the antagonist.

I have already had occasion in another connection to shew by a variety of evidences that the earliest Semites, like primitive men of other races, drew no sharp line of distinction between the nature of gods, of men, and of beasts, and had no difficulty in admitting a real kinship between (*a*) gods and men, (*b*) gods and sacred animals, (*c*) families of men and families of beasts.[2] As regards

[1] In religions based on kinship, where the god and his worshippers are of one stock, precepts of sanctity are, of course, covered by the principle of kinship.

[2] *Supra*, pp. 41 *sqq.* 85 *sqq.*

the third of these points, the direct evidence is fragmentary and sporadic; it is sufficient to prove that the idea of kinship between races of men and races of beasts was not foreign to the Semites, but it is not sufficient to prove that such a belief was widely prevalent, or to justify us in taking it as one of the fundamental principles on which Semitic ritual was founded. But it must be remembered that the three points are so connected that if any two of them are established, the third necessarily follows. Now, as regards (*a*), it is not disputed that the kinship of gods with their worshippers is a fundamental doctrine of Semitic religion; it appears so widely and in so many forms and applications, that we cannot look upon it otherwise than as one of the first and most universal principles of ancient faith. Again, as regards (*b*), a belief in sacred animals, which are treated with the reverence due to divine beings, is an essential element in the most widespread and important Semitic cults. All the great deities of the northern Semites had their sacred animals, and were themselves worshipped in animal form, or in association with animal symbols, down to a late date; and that this association implied a veritable unity of kind between animals and gods is placed beyond doubt, on the one hand, by the fact that the sacred animals, *e.g.* the doves and fish of Atargatis, were reverenced with divine honours; and, on the other hand, by theogonic myths, such as that which makes the dove-goddess be born from an egg, and transformation myths, such as that of Bambyce, where it was believed that the fish-goddess and her son had actually been transformed into fish.[1]

[1] Examples of the evidence on this head have been given above; a fuller account of it will fall to be given in a future course of lectures. Meantime the reader may refer to *Kinship*, chap. vii. I may here, however, add a general argument which seems to deserve attention. We have seen (*supra*, p. 142 *sqq.*) that holiness is not based on the idea of property. Holy

Now if kinship between the gods and their worshippers, on the one hand, and kinship between the gods and certain kinds of animals, on the other, are deep-seated principles of Semitic religion, manifesting themselves in all parts of the sacred institutions of the race, we must necessarily conclude that kinship between families of men and animal kinds was an idea equally deep-seated, and we shall expect to find that sacred animals, wherever they occur, will be treated with the regard which men pay to their kinsfolk.

Indeed in a religion based on kinship, where the god and his worshippers are of one stock, the principle of sanctity and that of kinship are identical. The sanctity of a kinsman's life and the sanctity of the godhead are not two things, but one; for ultimately the only thing that is sacred is the common tribal life, or the common blood which is identified with the life. Whatever being partakes in this life is holy, and its holiness may be described indifferently, as participation in the divine life and nature, or as participation in the kindred blood.

Thus the conjecture that sacrificial animals were originally treated as kinsmen, is simply equivalent to the conjecture that sacrifices were drawn from animals of a holy kind, whose lives were ordinarily protected by religious scruples and sanctions; and in support of this position a great mass of evidence can be adduced, not merely for Semitic sacrifice, but for ancient sacrifice generally.

In the later days of heathenism, when animal food

animals, and holy things generally, are primarily conceived, not as belonging to the deity, but as being themselves instinct with divine power or life. Thus a holy animal is one which has a divine life; and if it be holy to a particular god, the meaning must be that its life and his are somehow bound up together. From what is known of primitive ways of thought we may infer that this means that the sacred animal is akin to the god, for all valid and permanent relation between individuals is conceived as kinship.

was commonly eaten, and the rule that all legitimate slaughter must be sacrificial was no longer insisted on, sacrifices were divided into two classes; ordinary sacrifices, where the victims were sheep, oxen or other beasts habitually used for food, and extraordinary sacrifices, where the victims were animals whose flesh was regarded as forbidden meat. The Emperor Julian[1] tells us that in the cities of the Roman Empire such extraordinary sacrifices were celebrated once or twice a year in mystical ceremonies, and he gives as an example the sacrifice of the dog to Hecate. In this case the victim was the sacred animal of the goddess to which it was offered; Hecate is represented in mythology as accompanied by demoniac dogs, and in her worship she loved to be addressed by the name of Dog.[2] Here, therefore, the victim is not only a sacred animal, but an animal kindred to the deity to which it is sacrificed. The same principle seems to lie at the root of all exceptional sacrifices of unclean animals, *i.e.* animals that were not ordinarily eaten, for we have already seen that the idea of uncleanness and holiness meet in the primitive conception of taboo. I leave it to classical scholars to follow this out in its application to Greek and Roman sacrifice; but as regards the Semites it is worth while to establish the point by going in detail through the sacrifices of unclean beasts that are known to us.

1. *The swine.* According to Al-Nadīm the heathen Harranians sacrificed the swine and ate swine's flesh once a year.[3] This ceremony is ancient, for it appears in Cyprus in connection with the worship of the Semitic Aphrodite and Adonis. In the ordinary worship of

[1] *Orat.* v. p. 176.

[2] Porph., *De Abst.* iii. 17, iv. 16. Mr. Bury has suggested that etymologically Ἑκάτη = Hund hound, as ἑκατόν = hundert, hundred.

[3] *Fihrist*, p. 326, l. 3 *sq.*

Aphrodite swine were not admitted, but in Cyprus wild boars were sacrificed once a year on April 2.[1] The same sacrifice is alluded to in the Book of Isaiah as a heathen abomination,[2] with which the prophet associates the sacrifice of two other unclean animals, the dog and the mouse. We know from Lucian that the swine was esteemed sacrosanct by the Syrians,[3] and that it was specially sacred to Aphrodite or Astarte is affirmed by Antiphanes, *ap.* Athen. iii. 49.[4]

2. *The dog.* This sacrifice, as we have seen, is mentioned in the Book of Isaiah, and it seems also to be alluded to as a Punic rite in Justin, xviii. 1. 10, where we read that Darius sent a message to the Carthaginians forbidding them to sacrifice human victims and to eat the flesh of dogs: in the connection a religious meal must be understood. In this case the accounts do not connect the rite with any particular deity to whom the dog was sacred,[5] but we know from Al-Nadīm that the dog was sacred among the Harranians. They offered sacrificial gifts to it, and in certain mysteries dogs were solemnly declared to be the brothers of the mystæ.[6] A hint as to the identity of the god to whom the dog was sacred may perhaps be got from Jacob of Sarug, who mentions "the Lord with the dogs" as one of the deities of Carrhæ.[7] This god again may be compared with the huntsman

[1] Lydus, *De Mensibus*, Bonn ed., p. 80. Exceptional sacrifices of swine to Aphrodite also took place at Argos (Athen. iii. 49) and in Pamphylia (Strabo, ix. 5. 17), but the Semitic origin of these rites is not so certain as in the case of the Cyprian goddess. The sacrifice of a sow is represented on the rock sculptures of J'rapta (Renan, *Phén.* pl. 31; cf. Pietschmann, p. 219).

[2] Isa. lxv. 4, lxvi. 3, 17.

[3] *Dea Syria*, liv.

[4] In a modern Syrian superstition we find that a demoniac swine haunts houses where there is a marriageable maiden, *ZDPG.* vii. 107.

[5] Movers, *Phoenizier*, i. 404, is quite unsatisfactory.

[6] *Fihrist*, p. 326, l. 27; cf. p. 323, l. 28; p. 324, l. 2.

[7] *ZDMG.* xxix. 110; cf. vol. xlii. p. 473.

Heracles of the Assyrians mentioned by Tacitus.[1] The Tyrian Heracles or Melcarth also appears accompanied by a dog in the legend of the invention of the purple dye preserved by Pollux (i. 46) and Malalas (p. 32).[2] In Mohammedan tradition a demoniac character is ascribed to black dogs, which probably implies that in heathenism they had a certain sanctity.[3]

3. *Fish*, or at least certain species of fish, were sacred to Atargatis and forbidden food to all the Syrians, her worshippers, who believed—as totem peoples do—that if they ate the sacred flesh they would be visited by ulcers.[4]

[1] Tacitus, *Ann.* xii. 13. A huntsman god accompanied by a dog is figured on cylinders (*Gazette Archéol.* 1879, p. 178 *sqq.*), but Assyriologists seem not to be agreed as to his identity. There were probably more divine huntsmen than one.

[2] Whether the Sicilian god Adranus, whose sacred dogs are mentioned by Ælian, *Nat. An.* xi. 20 (confirmed by monumental evidence; Ganneau, *Rec. de Arch. Or.* i. 236) is of Semitic origin is very uncertain. He is generally identified with Adar (the Adrammelech of the Bible); see Holm, *Gesch. Sic.* i. 95, 377. But the very existence of an Assyrian god Adar is problematical, and the Hadran of Melito (*Spic. Syr.* p. 25), who is taken by others as the Semitic equivalent of Adranus, is a figure equally obscure.

If the conjecture that the Heracles worshipped by the νόθοι in the Cynosarges at Athens was really the Phœnician Heracles can be made out, the connection of this deity with the dog will receive further confirmation. For Cynosarges means "the dog's yard" (Wachsmuth, *Athen.* i. 461). Steph. Byz. *s.v.* explains the name by a legend that while Diomos was sacrificing to Heracles, a white dog snatched the sacrificial pieces and laid them down on the spot where the sanctuary afterwards stood. The dog is here the sacred messenger who declares the will of the god, like the eagle of Zeus in Malalas, p. 199; cf. Steph. Byz. *s.v.* γαλιῶται. The sanctity of the dog among the Phœnicians seems also to be confirmed by the proper names כלבא, כלבאלים, and by the existence of a class of sacred ministers called "dogs" (*CIS.* No. 86, cf. Deut. xxiii. 18 [19]). Reinach and G. Hoffmann, *op. cit.* p. 17, are hardly right in thinking of literal dogs; but in any case that would only strengthen the argument.

[3] Damīrī, ii. 223; Vloten in *Vienna Or. Journ.* vii. 240. See also the legend of the dog-demon of Riām, B. Hish. p. 18. In Moslem countries dogs are still regarded with a curious mixture of respect and contempt. They are unclean, but it is an act of piety to feed them, and especially to give them drink (Moslim, ii. 196, ed. of A. H. 1290); and to kill a dog, as I have observed at Jeddah, is an act that excites a good deal of feeling. See also *ZDPV.* vii. 93.

[4] See the evidence collected by Selden, *de Diis Syris*, *Synt.* ii. cap. 3.

Yet Mnaseas (*ap.* Athen. viii. 37) tells us that fish were daily cooked and presented on the table of the goddess, being afterwards consumed by the priests; and Assyrian cylinders display the fish laid on the altar or presented before it, while, in one example, a figure which stands by in an attitude of adoration is clothed, or rather disguised, in a gigantic fish skin.[1] The meaning of such a disguise is well known from many savage rituals; it implies that the worshipper presents himself as a fish, *i.e.* as a being kindred to his sacrifice, and doubtless also to the deity to which it is consecrated.

4. *The mouse* appears as an abominable sacrifice in Isa. lxvi. 17, along with the swine and the "abomination" (שקץ). The last word is applied in the Levitical law[2] to creeping vermin generally (שרץ = Arab. *ḥanash*), a term which included the mouse and other such small quadrupeds as we also call vermin. All such creatures were unclean in an intense degree, and had the power to communicate uncleanness to whatever they touched. So strict a taboo is hardly to be explained except by supposing that, like the Arabian *ḥanash*,[3] they had supernatural and demoniac qualities. And in fact, in Ezek. viii. 10, we find them as objects of superstitious adoration. On what authority Maimonides says that the Harranians sacrificed field-mice I do not know,[4] but the biblical evidence is sufficient for our purpose.

5. *The horse* was sacred to the Sun-god, for 2 Kings xxiii. 11 speaks of the horses which the kings of Judah had consecrated to this deity—a superstition to which Josiah put an end. At Rhodes, where religion is throughout of a Semitic type, four horses were cast into the sea as a sacrifice at the annual feast of the sun.[5] The

[1] Menant, *Glyptique*, ii. 53. [2] Lev. xi. 41. [3] *Supra*, p. 129.

[4] Ed. Munk, vol. iii. p. 64, or Chwolsohn, *Ssabier*, ii. 456.

[5] Festus, *s.v.* "October equus"; cf. Pausanias, iii. 20. 4 (sacrifice of horses to the Sun at Taygetus); *Kinship*, p. 208 *sq.*

winged horse (Pegasus) is a sacred symbol of the Carthaginians.

6. *The dove*, which the Semites would neither eat nor touch, was sacrificed by the Romans to Venus;[1] and as the Roman Venus-worship of later times was largely derived from the Phœnician sanctuary of Eryx, where the dove had peculiar honour as the companion of Astarte,[2] it is very possible that this was a Semitic rite, though I have not found any conclusive evidence that it was so. It must certainly have been a very rare sacrifice; for the dove among the Semites had a quite peculiar sanctity, and Al-Nadīm says expressly that it was not sacrificed by the Harranians.[3] It was, however, offered by the Hebrews, in sacrifices which we shall by and by see reason to regard as closely analogous to mystical rites; and in Juvenal, vi. 459 *sqq.*, the superstitious matrons of Rome are represented as calling in an Armenian or Syrian (Commagenian) haruspex to perform the sacrifice of a dove, a chicken, a dog, or even a child. In this association an exceptional and mystic sacrifice is necessarily implied.[4]

The evidence of these examples is unambiguous. When an unclean animal is sacrificed it is also a sacred animal. If the deity to which it is devoted is named, it is the deity which ordinarily protects the sanctity of the victim, and, in some cases, the worshippers either in words or by symbolic disguise claim kinship with the victim and the god. Further, the sacrifice is generally limited to certain solemn occasions, usually annual, and so has the character of a public celebration. In several cases the worshippers partake of the sacred flesh, which at other times it would

[1] Propertius, iv. 5. 62.

[2] Ælian, *Nat. An.* iv. 2.

[3] *Fihrist*, p. 319, l. 21.

[4] Cf. the חזית, *CIS.* No. 165, l. 11. Some other sacrifices of wild animals, which present analogies to these mystic rites, will be considered in *Additional Note* F, *Sacrifices of Sacred Animals.*

be impious to touch. All this is exactly what we find among totem peoples. Here also the sacred animal is forbidden food, it is akin to the men who acknowledge its sanctity, and if there is a god it is akin to the god. And, finally, the totem is sometimes sacrificed at an annual feast, with special and solemn ritual. In such cases the flesh may be buried or cast into a river, as the horses of the sun were cast into the sea,[1] but at other times it is eaten as a mystic sacrament.[2] These points of contact with the most primitive superstition cannot be accidental; they show that the mystical sacrifices, as Julian calls them, the sacrifices of animals not ordinarily eaten, are not the invention of later times, but have preserved with great accuracy the features of a sacrificial ritual of extreme antiquity.

To a superficial view the ordinary sacrifices of domestic animals, such as were commonly used for food, seem to stand on quite another footing; yet we have been led, by an independent line of reasoning, based on the evidence that all sacrifice was originally the act of the

[1] Bancroft, iii. 168; Frazer, *Totemism*, p. 48.

[2] The proof of this has to be put together out of the fragmentary evidence which is generally all that we possess on such matters. As regards America the most conclusive evidence comes from Mexico, where the gods, though certainly of totem origin, had become anthropomorphic, and the victim, who was regarded as the representative of the god, was human. At other times paste idols of the god were eaten sacramentally. But that the ruder Americans attached a sacramental virtue to the eating of the totem appears from what is related of the Bear clan of the Ouataouaks (*Lettres édif. et cur.* vi. 171), who when they kill a bear make him a feast of his own flesh, and tell him not to resent being killed; "tu as de l'esprit, tu vois que nos enfants souffrent la faim, ils t'aiment, ils veulent te faire entrer dans leur corps, n'est il pas glorieux d'être mangé par des enfans de Captaine?" The bear feast of the Ainos of Japan (fully described by Scheube in *Mitth. Deutsch. Gesellsch. S. und S. O. Asiens*, No. 22, p. 44 *sq.*) is a sacrificial feast on the flesh of the bear, which is honoured as divine, and slain with many apologies to the gods, on the pretext of necessity. The eating of the totem as medicine (Frazer, p. 23) belongs to the same circle of ideas. See also *infra*, p. 314.

clan, to surmise that they also in their origin were rare and solemn offerings of victims whose lives were ordinarily deemed sacred, because, like the unclean sacred animals, they were of the kin of the worshippers and of their god.[1]

And in point of fact precisely this kind of respect and reverence is paid to domestic animals among many pastoral peoples in various parts of the globe. They are regarded on the one hand as the friends and kinsmen of men, and on the other hand as sacred beings of a nature akin to the gods; their slaughter is permitted only under exceptional circumstances, and in such cases is never used to provide a private meal, but necessarily forms the occasion of a public feast, if not of a public sacrifice. The clearest case is that of Africa. Agatharchides,[2] describing the Troglodyte nomads of East Africa, a primitive pastoral people in the polyandrous stage of society, tells us that their whole sustenance was derived from their flocks and herds. When pasture abounded, after the rainy season, they lived on milk mingled with blood (drawn apparently, as in Arabia, from the living animal), and in the dry season they had recourse to the flesh of aged or weakly beasts. But the butchers were regarded as unclean. Further, "they gave the name of parent to no human being, but only to the ox and cow, the ram and ewe, from whom they had their nourishment."[3] Here we have all the features which our theory requires: the beasts are sacred and kindred beings,

[1] Strictly speaking the thing is much more than a surmise, even on the evidence already before us. But I prefer to understate rather than overstate the case in a matter of such complexity.

[2] The extracts of Photius and Diodorus are printed together in *Fr. Geog, Gr.* i. 153. The former has some points which the latter omits. See also Artemidorus, *ap.* Strabo, xvi. 4. 17.

[3] This reminds us of the peculiar form of covenant among the Gallas, in which a sheep is introduced as the mother of the parties (Lobo in Pinkerton's *Collection*; *Africa*, i. 8).

for they are the source of human life and subsistence. They are killed only in time of need, and the butchers are unclean, which implies that the slaughter was an impious act.

Similar institutions are found among all the purely pastoral African peoples, and have persisted with more or less modification or attenuation down to our own time.[1] The common food of these races is milk or game;[2] cattle are seldom killed for food, and only on exceptional occasions, such as the proclamation of a war, the circumcision of a youth, or a wedding,[3] or in order to obtain a skin for clothing, or because the creature is maimed or old.[4]

In such cases the feast is public, as among Nilus's Saracens,[5] all blood relations and even all neighbours having a right to partake. Further, the herd and its members are objects of affectionate and personal regard,[6] and are surrounded by sacred scruples and taboos. Among the Caffres the cattle kraal is sacred; women may not enter

[1] For the evidence of the sanctity of cattle among modern rude peoples, I am largely indebted to Mr. Frazer.

[2] Sallust, *Jugurtha*, 89 (Numidians); Alberti, *De Kaffers* (Amst. 1810), p. 37; Lichtenstein, *Reisen*, i. 144. Out of a multitude of proofs I cite these, as being drawn from the parts of the continent most remote from one another.

[3] So among the Caffres (Fleming, *Southern Africa*, p. 260; Lichtenstein, *Reisen*, i. 442). The Dinkas hardly kill cattle except for a funeral feast (Stanley, *Darkest Africa*, i. 424).

[4] Alberti, p. 163 (Caffres); cf. Gen. iii. 21, and Herod. iv. 189. The religious significance of the dress of skin, which appears in the last cited passage, will occupy us later.

[5] So among the Zulus (*supra*, p. 284, note) and among the Caffres (Alberti, *ut supra*).

[6] See in particular the general remarks of Munzinger on the pastoral peoples of East Africa, *Ostafr. Studien* (2nd ed., 1883), p. 547: "The nomad values his cow above all things, and weeps for its death as for that of a child." Again: "They have an incredible attachment to the old breed of cattle, which they have inherited from father and grandfather, and keep a record of their descent"—a trace of the feeling of kinship between the herd and the tribe, as in Agatharchides. See also Schweinfurth, *Heart of Africa*, i. 59 (3rd ed., 1878), and compare 2 Sam. xii. 3.

it,[1] and to defile it is a capital offence.[2] Finally, the notion that cattle are the parents of men, which we find in Agatharchides, survives in the Zulu myth that men, especially great chiefs, "were belched up by a cow."[3]

These instances may suffice to show how universally the attitude towards domestic animals, described by Agatharchides, is diffused among the pastoral peoples of Africa. But I must still notice one peculiar variation of the view that the life of cattle is sacred, which occurs both in Africa and among the Semites. Herodotus[4] tells us that the Libyans, though they ate oxen, would not touch the flesh of the cow. In the circle of ideas which we have found to prevail throughout Africa, this distinction must be connected, on the one hand, with the prevalence of kinship through women, which necessarily made the cow more sacred than the ox, and, on the other, with the fact that it is the cow that fosters man with her milk. The same rule prevailed in Egypt, where the cow was sacred to Hathor-Isis, and also among the Phœnicians, who both ate and sacrificed bulls, but would as soon have eaten human flesh as that of the cow.[5]

The importance of this evidence for our enquiry is all the greater because there is a growing disposition among scholars to recognise an ethnological connection of a somewhat close kind between the Semitic and African races. But the ideas which I have attempted to unfold are not

[1] Fleming, p. 214.

[2] Lichtenstein, i. 479, who adds that the punishment will not seem severe if we consider how holy their cattle are to them.

[3] Lang, *Myth, Ritual*, etc. i. 179.

[4] Bk. iv. chap. 186.

[5] See Porphyry, *De Abst.* ii. 11, for both nations; and, for the Egyptians, Herod. ii. 41. The Phœnician usage can hardly be ascribed to Egyptian influence, for at least a preference for male victims is found among the Semites generally, even where the deity is a goddess. See what Chwolsohn, *Ssabier*, ii. 77 *sqq.*, adduces in illustration of the statement of the *Fihrist*, that the Harranians sacrificed only male victims.

the property of a single race. How far the ancient holiness of cattle, and especially of the cow, among the Iranians, presents details analogous to those which have come before us, is a question which I must leave to the professed students of a very obscure literature; it seems at least to be admitted that the thing is not an innovation of Zoroastrianism, but common to the Iranians with their Indian cousins, so that the origin of the sacred regard paid to the cow must be sought in the primitive nomadic life of the Indo-European race. But to show that exactly such notions as we have found in Africa appear among pastoral peoples of quite different race, I will cite the case of the Todas of South India. Here the domestic animal, the milk-giver and the main source of subsistence, is the buffalo. "The buffalo is treated with great kindness, even with a degree of adoration,"[1] and certain cows, the descendants from mother to daughter of some remote sacred ancestor, are hung with ancient cattle bells and invoked as divinities.[2] Further, "there is good reason for believing the Todas' assertion that they have never at any time eaten the flesh of the female buffalo," and the male they eat only once a year, when all the adult males in the village join in the ceremony of killing and eating a young bull calf, which is killed with special ceremonies and roasted by a sacred fire. Venison, on the other hand, they eat with pleasure.[3] At a funeral one or two buffaloes are killed:[4] "as each animal falls, men,

[1] Marshall, *Travels among the Todas* (1873), p. 130.

[2] *Ibid.* p. 131.

[3] *Ibid.* p. 81. The sacrifice is eaten only by males. So among the Caffres certain holy parts of an ox must not be eaten by women; and in Hebrew law the duty of festal worship was confined to males, though women were not excluded. Among the Todas men and women habitually eat apart, as the Spartans did; and the Spartan blood-broth may be compared with the Toda animal sacrifice.

[4] *Ibid.* p. 176.

women and children group themselves round its head, and fondle, caress, and kiss its face, then sitting in groups of pairs . . . give way to wailing and lamentation." These victims are not eaten, but left on the ground.

These examples may suffice to show the wide diffusion among rude pastoral peoples of a way of regarding sacred animals with which the Semitic facts and the inferences I have drawn from them exactly correspond; let us now enquire how far similar ideas can be shown to have prevailed among the higher races of antiquity. In this connection I would first of all direct your attention to the wide prevalence among all these nations of a belief that the habit of slaughtering animals and eating flesh is a departure from the laws of primitive piety. Except in certain ascetic circles, priestly or philosophical, this opinion bore no practical fruit; men ate flesh freely when they could obtain it, but in their legends of the Golden Age it was told how in the earliest and happiest days of the race, when man was at peace with the gods and with nature, and the hard struggle of daily toil had not begun, animal food was unknown, and all man's wants were supplied by the spontaneous produce of the bounteous earth. This, of course, is not true, for even on anatomical grounds it is certain that our remote ancestors were carnivorous, and it is matter of observation that primitive nations do not eschew the use of animal food in general, though certain kinds of flesh are forbidden on grounds of piety. But, on the other hand, the idea of the Golden Age cannot be a mere abstract speculation without any basis in tradition. The legend in which it is embodied is part of the ancient folk-lore of the Greeks,[1] and the practical application of the idea in the form of a

[1] Hesiod, *Works and Days*, 109 *sqq.* Cf. Preller-Robert, I. i. p. 87 *sqq.*, for the other literature of the subject.

precept of abstinence from flesh, as a rule of perfection or of ceremonial holiness, is first found, not among innovating and speculative philosophers, but in priestly circles, *e.g.* in Egypt and India—whose lore is entirely based on tradition, or in such philosophic schools as that of Pythagoras, all whose ideas are characterised by an extraordinary regard for ancient usage and superstition.

In the case of the Egyptian priests the facts set forth by Porphyry in his book *De Abstinentia*, iv. 6 *sqq.*, on the authority of Chæremon,[1] enable us to make out distinctly the connection between the abstinence imposed on the priests and the primitive beliefs and practice of the mass of the people.

From ancient times every Egyptian had, according to the nome he lived in, his own particular kind of forbidden flesh, venerating a particular species of sacred animal, exactly as totemistic savages still do. The priests extended this precept, being in fact the ministers of a national religion, which gathered into one system the worships of the various nomes; but only some of them went so far as to eat no flesh at all, while others, who were attached to particular cults, ordinarily observed abstinence only from certain kinds of flesh, though they were obliged to confine themselves to a strictly vegetable diet at certain religious seasons, when they were specially engaged in holy functions. It is, however, obvious that the multitude of local prohibitions could not have resulted in a general doctrine of the superior piety of vegetarianism, unless the list of animals which were sacred in one or other part of the country had included those domestic animals which in a highly cultivated country like Egypt must always form the chief source of animal food.

[1] The authority is good; see Bernays, *Theophrastos' Schrift Ueber Frömmigkeit* (Breslau, 1866), p. 21.

In Egypt this was the case, and indeed the greatest and most widely recognised deities were those that had associations with domesticated animals. In this respect Egyptian civilisation declares its affinity to the primitive usages and superstitions of the pastoral populations of Africa generally; the Calf-god Apis, who was supposed to be incarnate in an actual calf at Memphis, and the Cow-goddess Isis-Hathor, who is either represented in the form of a cow, or at least wears a cow's horns, directly connect the dominant cults of Egypt with the sanctity ascribed to the bovine species by the ruder races of Eastern Africa, with whom the ox is the most important domestic animal; and it is not therefore surprising to learn that even in later times the eating of cow's flesh seemed to the Egyptians a practice as horrible as cannibalism. Cows were never sacrificed; and though bulls were offered on the altar, and part of the flesh eaten in a sacrificial feast, the sacrifice was only permitted as a *piaculum*, was preceded by a solemn fast, and was accompanied by public lamentation as at the death of a kinsman.[1] In like manner, at the annual sacrifice at Thebes to the Ram-god Amen, the worshippers bewailed the victim, thus declaring its kinship with themselves; while, on the other hand, its kinship or identity with the god was expressed in a twofold way, for the image of Amen was draped in the skin of the sacrifice, while the body was buried in a sacred coffin.[2]

In Egypt, the doctrine that the highest degree of holiness can only be attained by abstinence from all animal food, was the result of the political fusion of a number of local cults in one national religion, with a national priesthood that represented imperial ideas. Nothing of this sort took place in Greece or in most of the Semitic lands,[3] and

[1] Herod. ii. 39 *sq.*
[2] Herod. ii. 42.
[3] Babylonia is perhaps an exception.

in these accordingly we find no developed doctrine of priestly asceticism in the matter of food.[1]

Among the Greeks and Semites, therefore, the idea of a Golden Age, and the trait that in that age man was vegetarian in his diet, must be of popular not of priestly origin. Now in itself the notion that ancient times were better than modern, that the earth was more productive, men more pious and their lives less vexed with toil and sickness, needs no special explanation; it is the natural result of psychological laws which apply equally to the memory of individuals and the memory of nations. But the particular trait of primitive vegetarianism, as a characteristic feature of the good old times, does not fall under this general explanation, and can only have arisen at a time when there was still some active feeling of pious scruple about killing and eating flesh. This scruple cannot have applied to all kinds of flesh, *e.g.* to game, but it must have covered the very kinds of flesh that were ordinarily eaten in the agricultural stage of society, to which the origin of the legend of the Golden Age undoubtedly belongs. Flesh, therefore, in the legend means the flesh of domestic animals, and the legend expresses a feeling of respect for the lives of these animals, and an idea that their slaughter for food was an innovation not consistent with pristine piety.

When we look into the details of the traditions which later writers cite in support of the doctrine of primæval vegetarianism, we see that in effect this, and no more than

[1] On the supposed case of the Essenes see Lucius's books on the Essenes and Therapeutæ, and Schürer, *Gesch. des Jüd. Volkes*, ii. 478. The Therapeutæ, whether Jews or Christian monks, appear in Egypt, and most probably they were Egyptian Christians. Later developments of Semitic asceticism almost certainly stood under foreign influences, among which Buddhism seems to have had a larger and earlier share than it has been usual to admit. In old Semitic practice, as among the modern Jews and Moslems, religious fasting meant abstinence from all food, not merely from flesh.

this, is contained in them. The general statement that early man respected all animal life is mere inference, but popular tradition and ancient ritual alike bore testimony that the life of the swine and the sheep,[1] but above all of the ox,[2] was of old regarded as sacred, and might not be taken away except for religious purposes, and even then only with special precautions to clear the worshippers from the guilt of murder.

To make this quite plain, it may be well to go in some detail into the most important case of all, that of the ox. That it was once a capital offence to kill an ox, both in Attica and in the Peloponnesus, is attested by Varro.[3] So far as Athens is concerned, this statement seems to be drawn from the legend that was told in connection with the annual sacrifice of the Diipolia, where the victim was a bull, and its death was followed by a solemn enquiry as to who was responsible for the act.[4] In this trial every one who had anything to do with the slaughter was called as a party: the maidens who drew water to sharpen the axe and knife threw the blame on the sharpeners, they put it on the man who handed the axe, he on the man who struck down the victim, and he again on the one who cut its throat, who finally fixed the responsibility on the knife, which was accordingly found guilty of murder and cast into the sea. According to the legend, this act was a mere dramatic imitation of a piacular sacrifice devised to expiate the offence of one Sopatros, who killed an ox that he saw eating the cereal gifts from the table of the gods. This impious offence was followed by famine, but the oracle

[1] Porph., *De Abst.* ii. 9.

[2] *Ibid.* ii. 10, 29 *sq.*; Plato, *Leges*, vi. p. 782; Pausanias, viii. 2. 1 *sqq.* compared with i. 28. 10 (bloodless sacrifices under Cecrops, sacrifice of an ox in the time of Erechtheus).

[3] *R. R.* ii. 5.

[4] Pausanias, i. 24. 4; Theophrastus, *ap.* Porph., *De Abst.* ii. 30.

declared that the guilt might be expiated if the slayer were punished and the victim raised up again in connection with the same sacrifice in which it died, and that it would then go well with them if they tasted of the flesh and did not hold back. Sopatros himself, who had fled to Crete, undertook to return and devise a means of carrying out these injunctions, provided that the whole city would share the responsibility of the murder that weighed on his conscience; and so the ceremonial was devised, which continued to be observed down to a late date.[1] Of course the legend as such has no value; it is derived from the ritual, and not *vice versâ*; but the ritual itself shows clearly that the slaughter was viewed as a murder, and that it was felt to be necessary, not only to go through the form of throwing the guilt on the knife, but to distribute the responsibility as widely as possible, by employing a number of sacrificial ministers—who, it may be observed, were chosen from different kindreds—and making it a public duty to taste of the flesh. Here, therefore, we have a well-marked case of the principle that sacrifice is not to be excused except by the participation of the whole community.[2] This rite does not stand alone. At Tenedos the priest who offered a bull-calf to Dionysus *ἀνθρωπορραίστης* was attacked with stones and had to flee for his life;[3] and at Corinth, in the annual sacrifice of a goat to Hera Acræa, care was taken to shift the responsibility of the death off the shoulders of the community by employing hirelings as

[1] Aristophanes alludes to it as a very old-world rite (*Nubes*, 985), but the observance was still kept up in the days of Theophrastus in all its old quaintness. In Pausanias's time it had undergone some simplification, unless his account is inaccurate.

[2] The further feature that the ox chooses itself as victim, by approaching the altar and eating the gifts laid on it, is noticeable, both because a similar rite recurs at Eryx, as will be mentioned presently, and because in this way the victim eats of the table of the gods, *i.e.* is acknowledged as divine.

[3] Ælian, *Nat. An.* xii. 34.

ministers. Even they did no more than hide the knife in such a way that the goat, scraping with its feet, procured its own death.[1] But indeed the idea that the slaughter of a bull was properly a murder, and only to be justified on exceptional sacrificial occasions, must once have been general in Greece; for *βουφόνια* (*βουφονεῖν, βουφόνος*) or "ox-murder," which in Athens was the name of the peculiar sacrifice of the Diipolia, is in older Greek a general term for the slaughter of oxen for a sacrificial feast.[2] And that the "ox-murder" must be taken quite literally appears in the sacrifice at Tenedos, where the bull-calf wears the cothurnus and its dam is treated like a woman in childbed. Here the kinship of the victim with man is clearly expressed, but so also is his kinship with the "man-slaying" god to whom the sacrifice is offered, for the cothurnus is proper to Bacchus, and that god was often represented and invoked as a bull.[3]

The same combination of ideas appears in the Hebrew and Phœnician traditions of primitive abstinence from flesh and of the origin of sacrifice. The evidence in this case requires to be handled with some caution, for the Phœnician traditions come to us from late authors, who are gravely suspected of tampering with the legends they record, and the Hebrew records in the Book of Genesis, though they are undoubtedly based on ancient popular lore, have been recast under the influence of a higher faith, and purged of such elements as were manifestly inconsistent

[1] Hesychius, *s.v.* αἶξ αἶγα; Zenobius on the same proverb; *Schol.* on Eurip., *Medea.*

[2] See *Iliad,* vii. 466; the Homeric hymn to Mercury, 436, in a story which seems to be one of the many legends about the origin of sacrifice; Æsch., *Prom.* 530.

[3] See especially Plutarch, *Qu. Gr.* 36. Another example to the same effect is that of the goat dressed up as a maiden, which was offered to Artemis Munychia (*Parœmiogr. Gr.* i. 402, and Eustathius as there cited by the editors).

with Old Testament monotheism. As regards the Hebrew accounts, a distinction must be drawn between the earlier Jahvistic story and the post-exile narrative of the priestly historian. In the older account, just as in the Greek fable of the Golden Age, man, in his pristine state of innocence, lived at peace with all animals,[1] eating the spontaneous fruits of the earth; but after the Fall he was sentenced to earn his bread by agricultural toil. At the same time his war with hurtful creatures (the serpent) began, and domestic animals began to be slain sacrificially, and their skins used for clothing.[2] In the priestly history, on the other hand, man's dominion over animals, and seemingly also the agricultural life, in which animals serve man in the work of tillage, are instituted at the creation.[3] In this narrative there is no Garden of Eden, and no Fall, except the growing corruption that precedes the Flood. After the Flood man receives the right to kill and eat animals, if their blood is poured upon the ground,[4] but sacrifice begins only with the Mosaic dispensation. Now, as sacrifice and slaughter were never separated, in the case of domestic animals, till the time of Deuteronomy, this form of the story cannot be ancient; it rests on the post-Deuteronomic law of sacrifice, and especially on Lev. xvii. 10 *sq.* The original Hebrew tradition is that of the Jahvistic story, which agrees with Greek legend in connecting the sacrifice of domestic animals with a fall from the state of pristine innocence.[5] This, of course, is not the main feature in the

[1] Cf. Isa. xi. 6 *sq.*

[2] Gen. ii. 16 *sqq.*, iii. 15, 21, iv. 4. I am disposed to agree with Budde (*Bibl. Urgeschichte*, p. 83), that the words of ii. 15, "to dress it and to keep it," are by a later hand. They agree with Gen. i. 26 *sqq.* (priestly), but not with iii. 17 (Jahvistic).

[3] Gen. i. 28, 29, where the use of corn as well as of the fruit of trees is implied.

[4] Gen. ix. 1 *sq.*

[5] The Greek legend in the *Works and Days* agrees with the Jahvistic

biblical story of the Fall, nor is it one on which the narrator lays stress, or to which he seems to attach any special significance. But for that very reason it is to be presumed that this feature in the story is primitive, and that it must be explained, like the corresponding Greek legend, not by the aid of principles peculiar to the Old Testament revelation, but by considerations of a more general kind. There are other features in the story of the Garden of Eden—especially the tree of life—which prove that the original basis of the narrative is derived from the common stock of North Semitic folk-lore; and that this common stock included the idea of primitive vegetarianism is confirmed by Philo Byblius,[1] whose legend of the primitive men, who lived only on the fruits of the soil and paid divine honour to these, has too peculiar a form to be regarded as a mere transcript either from the Bible or from Greek literature.

It is highly improbable that among the ancient Semites the story of a Golden Age of primitive fruit-eating can have had its rise in any other class of ideas than those which led to the formation of a precisely similar legend in Greece. The Greeks concluded that primitive man did not eat the flesh of domestic animals, because their sacrificial ritual regarded the death of a victim as a kind of murder, only to be justified under special circumstances, and when it was accompanied by special precautions, for which a definite historical origin was assigned. And just in the same way the Cypro-Phœnician legend which Porphyry[2] quotes from Asclepiades, to prove that the early Phœnicians did not eat

story also in ascribing the Fall to the fault of a woman. But this trait does not seem to appear in all forms of the Greek story (see Preller-Robert, i. 94 *sq.*), and the estrangement between gods and men is sometimes ascribed to Prometheus, who is also regarded as the inventor of fire and of animal sacrifice.

[1] *Ap.* Eus., *Pr. Ev.* i. 106 (*Fr. Hist. Gr.* iii. 565).

[2] *De Abst.* iv. 15.

flesh, turns on the idea that the death of a victim was originally a surrogate for human sacrifice, and that the first man who dared to taste flesh was punished with death. The details of this story, which exactly agree with Lamb's humorous account of the discovery of the merits of roast sucking pig, are puerile and cannot be regarded as part of an ancient tradition, but the main idea does not seem to be mere invention. We have already seen that the Phœnicians would no more eat cow-beef than human flesh; it can hardly, therefore, be questioned that in ancient times the whole bovine race had such a measure of sanctity as would give even to the sacrifice of a bull the very character that our theory requires. And when Asclepiades states that every victim was originally regarded as a surrogate for a human sacrifice, he is confirmed in a remarkable way by the Elohistic account of the origin of burnt-sacrifice in Gen. xxii., where a ram is accepted in lieu of Isaac. This narrative presents another remarkable point of contact with Phœnician belief. Abraham says that God Himself will provide the sacrifice (ver. 8), and at ver. 13 the ram presents itself unsought as an offering. Exactly this principle was observed down to late times at the great Astarte temple at Eryx, where the victims were drawn from the sacred herds nourished at the sanctuary, and were believed to offer themselves spontaneously at the altar.[1] This is quite analogous to the usage at the Diipolia, where a number of cattle were driven round the sacred table, and the bull was selected for slaughter that approached it and ate of the sacred *popana*, and must be regarded as one of the many forms and fictions adopted to free the worshippers

[1] Ælian, *Nat. An.* x. 50; cf. Isa. liii. 7; Jer. xi. 19 (R.V.); but especially 1 Sam. vi. 14, where the kine halt at the sacrificial stone (Diog. Laert. i. 10. 3); also B. Hishām, p. 293, l. 14. That the victim presents itself spontaneously or comes to the altar willingly is a feature in many worships (*Mir. Ausc.* 137; Porph., *De Abst.* i. 25).

of responsibility for the death of the victim. All this goes to show that the animal sacrifices of the Phœnicians were regarded as quasi-human. But that the sacrificial kinds were also viewed as kindred to the gods may be concluded from the way in which the gods were represented. The idolatrous Israelites worshipped Jehovah under the form of a steer, and the second commandment implies that idols were made in the shape of many animals. So too the bull of Europa, Zeus Asterius, is, as his epithet implies, the male counterpart of Astarte, with whom Europa was identified at Sidon.[1] Astarte herself was figured crowned with a bull's head,[2] and the place name Ashteroth Karnaim [3] is probably derived from the sanctuary of a horned Astarte. It may indeed be questioned whether this last is identical with the cow-Astarte of Sidon, or is rather a sheep-goddess; for in Deut. vii. 13 the produce of the flock is called the "Ashtaroth of the sheep"—an antique expression that must have a religious origin. This sheep-Aphrodite was specially worshipped in Cyprus, where her annual mystic or piacular sacrifice was a sheep, and was presented by worshippers clad in sheepskins, thus declaring their kinship at once with the victim and with the deity.[4]

It is well to observe that in the most ancient nomadic

[1] *De Dea Syria*, iv.; *Kinship*, p. 306.

[2] Philo Byb., *fr.* 24 (*Fr. Hist. Gr.* iii. 569).

[3] Gen. xiv. 5. Kuenen, in his paper on *De Melecheth des Hemels*, p. 37, thinks it possible that the true reading is "Ashteroth and Karnaim." But the identity of the later Carnain or Carnion with Ashtaroth or בעשתרה, "the temple of Astarte" (Josh. xxi. 27), is confirmed by the fact that there was a τέμενος or sacred enclosure there (1 Macc. v. 43). See further *ZDMG.* xxix. 431, note 1. The ancient sanctity of the Astarte-shrine has been transferred to the sepulchre of Job; cf. *S. Silviæ Peregrinatio* (Rome, 1887), 56 *sqq.* A Punic Baal-Carnaim has lately been discovered in the sanctuary of Saturnus Balcaranensis on Jebel Bū Curnein near Tunis. This, however, may probably be a local designation derived from the ancient name of the double-topped mountain (*Mélanges d'Archéol. etc.*, Rome, 1892, p. 1 *sq.*).

[4] See *Additional Note* G, *The Sacrifice of a Sheep to the Cyprian Aphrodite.*

times, to which the sanctity of domestic animals must be referred, the same clan or community will not generally be found to breed more than one kind of domestic animal. Thus in Arabia, though the lines of separation are not so sharp as we must suppose them to have formerly been, there is still a broad distinction between the camel-breeding tribes of the upland plains and the shepherd tribes of the mountains; and in like manner sheep and goats are the flocks appropriate to the steppes of Eastern Palestine, while kine and oxen are more suitable for the well-watered Phœnician mountains. Thus in the one place we may expect to find a sheep-Astarte, and in another a cow-goddess, and the Hebrew idiom in Deut. vii. 13 agrees with the fact that before the conquest of agricultural Palestine, the Hebrews, like their kinsmen of Moab, must have been mainly shepherds, not cowherds.[1]

I have now, I think, said enough about the sanctity of domestic animals; the application to the doctrine of sacrifice must be left for another lecture.

[1] The great ancestress of the house of Joseph is Rachel, "the ewe." For the Moabites see 2 Kings iii. 4.

LECTURE IX

THE SACRAMENTAL EFFICACY OF ANIMAL SACRIFICE, AND COGNATE ACTS OF RITUAL—THE BLOOD COVENANT—BLOOD AND HAIR OFFERINGS

In the course of the last lecture we were led to look with some exactness into the distinction drawn in the later ages of ancient paganism between ordinary sacrifices, where the victim is one of the animals commonly used for human food, and extraordinary or mystical sacrifices, where the significance of the rite lies in an exceptional act of communion with the godhead, by participation in holy flesh which is ordinarily forbidden to man. Analysing this distinction, and carrying back our examination of the evidence to the primitive stage of society in which sacrificial ritual first took shape, we were led to conclude that in the most ancient times all sacrificial animals had a sacrosanct character, and that no kind of beast was offered to the gods which was not too holy to be slain and eaten without a religious purpose, and without the consent and active participation of the whole clan.

For the most primitive times, therefore, the distinction drawn by later paganism between ordinary and extraordinary sacrifices disappears. In both cases the sacred function is the act of the whole community, which is conceived as a circle of brethren, united with one another and with their god by participation in one life or life-blood. The same blood is supposed to flow also in the veins of the victim, so that its death is at once a shedding of the tribal blood and a violation of the sanctity of the divine life that is transfused through every member, human or irrational, of the sacred circle. Nevertheless the slaughter of such a victim is permitted or required on solemn occasions, and all the tribesmen partake of its flesh, that they may thereby cement and seal their mystic unity with one another and with their god. In later times we find the conception current that any food which two men partake of together, so that the same substance enters into their flesh and blood, is enough to establish some sacred unity of life between them; but in ancient times this significance seems to be always attached to participation in the flesh of a sacrosanct victim, and the solemn mystery of its death is justified by the consideration that only in this way can the sacred cement be procured which creates or keeps alive a living bond of union between the worshippers and their god. This cement is nothing else than the actual life of the sacred and kindred animal, which is conceived as residing in its flesh, but especially in its blood, and so, in the sacred meal, is actually distributed among all the participants, each of whom incorporates a particle of it with his own individual life.

The notion that, by eating the flesh, or particularly by drinking the blood, of another living being, a man absorbs its nature or life into his own, is one which appears among primitive peoples in many forms. It lies at the root of the widespread practice of drinking the fresh blood of enemies—a practice which was familiar to certain tribes of the Arabs before Mohammed, and which tradition still ascribes to the wild race of Caḥṭān [1]—and also of the

[1] See the evidence in *Kinship*, p. 284; and cf. Doughty, ii. 41, where the better accounts seem to limit the drinking of human blood by the Caḥṭān to the blood covenant.

habit observed by many savage huntsmen of eating some part (*e.g.* the liver) of dangerous carnivora, in order that the courage of the animal may pass into them. And in some parts of the world, where men have the privilege of choosing a special kind of sacred animal either in lieu of, or in addition to, the clan totem, we find that the compact between the man and the species that he is thenceforth to regard as sacred is sealed by killing and eating an animal of the species, which from that time forth becomes forbidden food to him.[1]

But the most notable application of the idea is in the rite of blood brotherhood, examples of which are found all over the world.[2] In the simplest form of this rite, two men become brothers by opening their veins and sucking one another's blood. Thenceforth their lives are not two but one. This form of covenant is still known in the Lebanon[3] and in some parts of Arabia.[4] In ancient Arabic literature there are many references to the blood covenant, but instead of human blood that of a victim slain at the sanctuary is employed. The ritual in this case is that all who share in the compact must dip their hands into the gore, which at the same time is applied to the sacred stone that symbolises the deity, or is poured forth at its base. The dipping of the hands into the dish

[1] Frazer (*Totemism*, p. 54) has collected evidence of the killing, but not of the eating. For the latter he refers me to Cruickshank, *Gold Coast* (1853), p. 133 *sq.*

[2] See the collection of evidence in Trumbull, *The Blood Covenant* (New York, 1885); and compare, for the Arabs, *Kinship*, pp. 48 *sqq.*, 261; Wellhausen, p. 120; Goldziher, *Literaturbl. f. or. Phil.* 1886, p. 24, *Muh. Stud.* p. 67. In what follows I do not quote examples in detail for things sufficiently exemplified in the books just cited.

[3] Trumbull, p. 5 *sq.*

[4] Doughty, ii. 41. The value of the evidence is quite independent of the accuracy of the statement that the Caḥṭān still practise the rite; at least the tradition of such a rite subsists. See also Trumbull, p. 9.

implies communion in an act of eating,[1] and so the members of the bond are called "blood-lickers." There seems to be no example in the old histories and poems of a covenant in which the parties lick one another's blood. But we have seen that even in modern times the use of human blood in covenants is not unknown to the Semites, and the same thing appears for very early times from Herodotus's account of the form of covenant used by the Arabs on the borders of Egypt.[2] Blood was drawn with a sharp stone from the thumbs of each party, and smeared on seven sacred stones with invocations of the gods. The smearing makes the gods parties to the covenant, but evidently the symbolical act is not complete unless at the same time the human parties taste each other's blood. It is probable that this was actually done, though Herodotus does not say so. But it is also possible that in course of time the ritual had been so far modified that it was deemed sufficient that the two bloods should meet on the sacred stone.[3] The rite described by Herodotus has for its object the admission of an individual stranger[4] to fellowship with an Arab clansman and his kin; the compact is primarily between two individuals, but the obligation contracted by the single clansman is binding on all his "friends," *i.e.* on the other members of the kin. The reason why it is so binding is that he who has drunk a clansman's blood is no longer a stranger but a brother, and included in the mystic circle of those who have a share in the life-blood that is common to all the clan. Primarily the covenant is not a

[1] Matt. xxvi. 23.

[2] Herod. iii. 8.

[3] Some further remarks on the various modifications of covenant ceremonies among the Semites will be found in *Additional Note* H.

[4] The ceremony might also take place between an Arab and his "townsman" (ἀστός), which, I apprehend, must mean another Arab, but one of a different clan. For if a special contract between two clansmen were meant, there would be no meaning in the introduction to the "friends" who agree to share the covenant obligation.

special engagement to this or that particular effect, but a bond of troth and life-fellowship to all the effects for which kinsmen are permanently bound together. And this being so, it is a matter of course that the engagement has a religious side as well as a social, for there can be no brotherhood without community of *sacra*, and the sanction of brotherhood is the jealousy of the tribal deity, who sedulously protects the holiness of kindred blood. This thought is expressed symbolically by the smearing of the two bloods, which have now become one, upon the sacred stones, which is as much as to say that the god himself is a third blood-licker, and a member of the bond of brotherhood.[1] It is transparent that in ancient times the deity so brought into the compact must have been the kindred god of the clan to which the stranger was admitted; but even in the days of Herodotus the old clan religion had already been in great measure broken down; all the Arabs of the Egyptian frontier, whatever their clan, worshipped the same pair of deities, Orotal and Alilat (Al-Lāt), and these were the gods invoked in the covenant ceremony. If, therefore, both the contracting parties were Arabs, of different clans but of the same religion, neither could feel that the covenant introduced him to the *sacra* of a new god, and the meaning of the ceremony would simply be that the gods whom both adored took the compact under their protection. This is the ordinary sense of covenant with sacrifice in later times, *e.g.* among the Hebrews, but also among the Arabs, where the deity invoked is ordinarily Allah at the Caaba or some other great deity of more than tribal consideration. But that the appeal to a god already acknowledged by both parties is a departure from

[1] Compare the blood covenant which a Mosquito Indian used to form with the animal kind he chose as his protectors; Bancroft, i. 740 *sq.* (Frazer, p. 55).

the original sense of the rite, is apparent from the application of the blood, not only to the human contractors, but to the altar or sacred stone, which continued to be an invariable feature in covenant sacrifice; for this part of the rite has its full and natural meaning only in a ceremony of initiation, where the new tribesman has to be introduced to the god for the first time and brought into life-fellowship with him, or else in a periodical clan sacrifice held for the purpose of refreshing and renewing a bond between the tribesmen and their god, which by lapse of time may seem to have been worn out.

In Herodotus the blood of the covenant is that of the human parties; in the cases known from Arabic literature it is the blood of an animal sacrifice. At first sight this seems to imply a progress in refinement and an aversion to taste human blood. But it may well be doubted whether such an assumption is justified by the social history of the Arabs,[1] and we have already seen that the primitive form of the blood covenant has survived into modern times. Rather, I think, we ought to consider that the ceremony described by Herodotus is a covenant between individuals, without that direct participation of the whole kin, which, even in the time of Nilus, many centuries later, was essential in those parts of Arabia to an act of sacrifice involving the death of a victim. The covenants made by sacrifice are generally if not always compacts between whole kins, so that here sacrifice was appropriate, while at the same time a larger supply of blood was necessary than could well be obtained without slaughter. That the blood of an animal was accepted in lieu of the tribesmen's own blood, is generally passed over by modern writers without explanation. But an explanation is certainly required,

[1] See the examples of cannibalism and the drinking of human blood cited in *Kinship*, p. 284 *sq*.

and is fully supplied only by the consideration that, the victim being itself included in the sacred circle of the kin, whose life was to be communicated to the new-comers, its blood served quite the same purpose as man's blood. On this view the rationale of covenant sacrifice is perfectly clear.

I do not, however, believe that the origin of sacrifice can possibly be sought in the covenant between whole kins—a kind of compact which in the nature of things cannot have become common till the tribal system was weak, and which in primitive times was probably unknown. Even the adoption of individuals into a new clan, so that they renounced their old kin and *sacra*, is held by the most exact students of early legal custom to be, comparatively speaking, a modern innovation on the rigid rules of the ancient blood-fellowship; much more, then, must this be true of the adoption or fusion of whole clans. I apprehend, therefore, that the use of blood drawn from a living man for the initiation of an individual into new *sacra*, and the use of the blood of a victim for the similar initiation of a whole clan, must both rest in the last resort on practices that were originally observed within the bosom of a single kin.

To such sacrifice the idea of a covenant, whether between the worshippers mutually or between the worshippers and their god, is not applicable, for a covenant means artificial brotherhood, and has no place where the natural brotherhood of which it is an imitation already subsists. The Hebrews, indeed, who had risen above the conception that the relation between Jehovah and Israel was that of natural kinship, thought of the national religion as constituted by a formal covenant-sacrifice at Mount Sinai, where the blood of the victims was applied to the altar on the one hand, and to the people on the other,[1] or even

[1] Ex. xxiv. 4 *sqq.*

by a still earlier covenant rite in which the parties were Jehovah and Abraham.[1] And by a further development of the same idea, every sacrifice is regarded in Ps. l. 5 as a covenant between God and the worshipper.[2] But in purely natural religions, where the god and his community are looked upon as forming a physical unity, the idea that religion rests on a compact is out of place, and acts of religious communion can only be directed to quicken and confirm the life-bond that already subsists between the parties. Some provision of this sort may well seem to be necessary where kinship is conceived in the very realistic way of which we have had so many illustrations. Physical unity of life, regarded as an actual participation in one common mass of flesh and blood, is obviously subject to modification by every accident that affects the physical system, and especially by anything that concerns the nourishment of the body and the blood. On this ground alone it might well seem reasonable to reinforce the sacred life from time to time by a physical process. And this merely material line of thought naturally combines itself with considerations of another kind, which contain the germ of an ethical idea. If the physical oneness of the

[1] Gen. xv. 8 *sqq.*

[2] That Jehovah's relation to Israel is not natural but ethical, is the doctrine of the prophets, and is emphasised, in dependence on their teaching, in the Book of Deuteronomy. But the passages cited show that the idea has its foundation in pre-prophetic times; and indeed the prophets, though they give it fresh and powerful application, plainly do not regard the conception as an innovation. In fact, a nation like Israel is not a natural unity like a clan, and Jehovah as the national God was, from the time of Moses downward, no mere natural clan god, but the god of a confederation, so that here the idea of a covenant religion is entirely justified. The worship of Jehovah throughout all the tribes of Israel and Judah is probably older than the genealogical system that derives all the Hebrews from one natural parent; cf. *Kinship*, p. 257. Mohammed's conception of heathen religion as resting on alliance (Wellh. p. 123) is also to be explained by the fact that the great gods of Arabia in his time were not the gods of single clans.

deity and his community is impaired or attenuated, the help of the god can no longer be confidently looked for. And conversely, when famine, plague or other disaster shows that the god is no longer active on behalf of his own, it is natural to infer that the bond of kinship with him has been broken or relaxed, and that it is necessary to retie it by a solemn ceremony, in which the sacred life is again distributed to every member of the community. From this point of view the sacramental rite is also an atoning rite, which brings the community again into harmony with its alienated god, and the idea of sacrificial communion includes within it the rudimentary conception of a piacular ceremony. In all the older forms of Semitic ritual the notions of communion and atonement are bound up together, atonement being simply an act of communion designed to wipe out all memory of previous estrangement.

The actual working of these ideas may be seen in two different groups of ritual observance. Where the whole community is involved, the act of communion and atonement takes the shape of sacrifice. But, besides this communal act, we find what may be called private acts of worship, in which an individual seeks to establish a physical link of union between himself and the deity, apart from the sacrifice of a victim, either by the use of his own blood in a rite analogous to the blood covenant between private individuals, or by other acts involving an identical principle. Observances of this kind are peculiarly instructive, because they exhibit in a simple form the same ideas that lie at the root of the complex system of ancient sacrifice; and it will be profitable to devote some attention to them before we proceed further with the subject of sacrifice proper. By so doing we shall indeed be carried into a considerable digression, but I hope that we shall return to our main subject with a firmer grasp of the fundamental principles involved.[1]

In the ritual of the Semites and other nations, both ancient and modern, we find many cases in which the worshipper sheds his own blood at the altar, as a means of recommending himself and his prayers to the deity.[2] A classical instance is that of the priests of Baal at the contest between the god of Tyre and the God of Israel (1 Kings xviii. 28). Similarly at the feast of the Syrian goddess at Mabbog, the Galli and devotees made gashes in their arms, or offered their backs to one another to beat,[3] exactly as is now done by Persian devotees at the annual commemoration of the martyrdom of Hasan and Hosain.[4] I have elsewhere argued that the general diffusion of this usage among the Aramæans is attested by the Syriac word *ethkashshaph*, "make supplication," literally "cut oneself." [5]

The current view about such rites in modern as in ancient times has been that the effusion of blood without taking away life is a substitute for human sacrifice,[6] an explanation which recommends itself by its simplicity, and probably hits the truth with regard to certain cases. But,

[1] For the subject discussed in the following paragraphs, compare especially the copious collection of materials by Dr. G. A. Wilken, *Ueber das Haaropfer, etc.*, Amsterdam, 1886–7.

[2] Cf. Spencer, *Leg. Rit. Heb.* ii. 13. 2.

[3] *Dea Syria*, 1.

[4] This seems to be a modern survival of the old rites of Anaitis-worship, for the similar observances in the worship of Bellona at Rome under the empire were borrowed from Cappadocia, and apparently from a form of the cult of Anaitis (see the refs. in Roscher, *s.v.*). The latter, again, was closely akin to the worship of the Syrian goddess, and appears to have been developed to a great extent under Semitic influence. See my paper on "Ctesias and the Semiramis Legend," *English Hist. Rev.*, April 1887.

[5] *Journ. Phil.* xiv. 125; cf. Nöldeke in *ZDMG.* xl. 723.

[6] See Pausanias, iii. 16. 10, where this is the account given of the bloody flagellation of the Spartan ephebi at the altar of Artemis Orthia. Similarly Euripides, *Iph. Taur.* 1458 *sqq.*; cf. also Bourke, *Snake Dance of the Moquis of Arizona*, p. 196; and especially Wilken, *op. cit.* p. 68 *sqq.*

as a general explanation of the offering of his own blood by a suppliant, it is not quite satisfactory. Human sacrifice is offered, not on behoof of the victim, but at the expense of the victim on behoof of the sacrificing community, while the shedding of one's own blood is in many cases a means of recommending oneself to the godhead. Further, there is an extensive class of rites prevalent among savage and barbarous peoples in which blood-shedding forms part of an initiatory ceremony, by which youths, at or after the age of puberty, are admitted to the status of a man, and to a full share in the social privileges and *sacra* of the community. In both cases the object of the ceremony must be to tie, or to confirm, a blood-bond between the worshipper and the god by a means more potent than the ordinary forms of stroking, embracing or kissing the sacred stone. To this effect the blood of the man is shed at the altar, or applied to the image of the god, and has exactly the same efficacy as in the forms of blood covenant that have been already discussed.[1] And that this is so receives strong confirmation from the identical practices observed among so many nations in mourning for deceased kinsmen. The Hebrew law forbade mourners to gash or puncture themselves in honour of the dead,[2] evidently associating this practice, which nevertheless was common down to the close of the old kingdom,[3] with heathenish rites. Among the Arabs

[1] That the blood must fall on the altar, or at its foot, is expressly attested in certain cases, *e.g.* in the Spartan worship of Artemis Orthia, and in various Mexican rites of the same kind; see Sahagun, *Nouvelle Espagne* (French Tr., 1880), p. 185. In Tibullus's account of Bellona worship (Lib. i. El. 6, vv. 45 *sqq.*) the blood is sprinkled on the idol; the church-fathers add that those who shared in the rite drank one another's blood.

[2] Lev. xix. 28, xxi. 5; Deut. xiv. 1.

[3] Jer. xvi. 6. The funeral feast which Jeremiah mentions in the following verse (see the Revised Version, and compare Hos. ix. 4), and which has for its object to comfort the mourners, is, I apprehend, in its origin a feast of communion with the dead; cf. Tylor, *Primitive Culture*, ii. 26 *sqq.* This

in like manner, as among the Greeks and other ancient nations, it was customary in mourning to scratch the face to the effusion of blood.[1] The original meaning of this practice appears in the form which it has retained among certain rude nations. In New South Wales, "several men stand by the open grave and cut each other's heads with a boomerang, and hold their heads over the grave so that the blood from the wound falls on the corpse."[2] Similarly in Otaheite the blood as well as the tears shed in mourning were received on pieces of linen, which were thrown on the bier.[3] Here the application of blood and tears to the dead is a pledge of enduring affection; and in Australia the ceremony is completed by cutting a piece of flesh from the corpse, which is dried, cut up and distributed among the relatives and friends of the deceased; some suck their portion "to get strength and courage." The twosided nature of the rite in this case puts it beyond question that the object is to make an enduring covenant with the dead.

Among the Hebrews and Arabs, and indeed among many other peoples both ancient and modern, the laceration of the flesh in mourning is associated with the practice of shaving the head or cutting off part of the hair and

act of communion consoles the survivors; but in the oldest times the consolation has a physical basis; thus the Arabian *solwān*, or draught that makes the mourner forget his grief, consists of water with which is mingled dust from the grave (Wellh. p. 142), a form of communion precisely similar in principle to the Australian usage of eating a small piece of the corpse. There is a tendency at present, in one school of anthropologists, to explain all death customs as due to fear of ghosts. But among the Semites, at any rate, almost all death customs, from the kissing of the corpse (Gen. l. 1) onwards, are dictated by an affection that endures beyond the grave.

[1] Wellh. p. 160, gives the necessary citations. Cf. on the rites of mourning in general, Bokhārī, ii. 75 *sq.*, and Freytag in his Latin version of the *Ḥamāsa*, i. 430 *sq.*

[2] F. Bonney in *Journ. Anthrop. Inst.* xiii. (1884) p. 134. For this and the following reference I am indebted to Mr. Frazer.

[3] *Cook's First Voyage*, Bk. i. chap. 19.

depositing it in the tomb or on the funeral pyre.[1] Here also a comparison of the usage of more primitive races shows that the rite was originally two-sided, and had exactly the same sense as the offering of the mourner's blood. For among the Australians it is permitted to pull some hair from the corpse in lieu of a part of its flesh. The hair, in fact, is regarded by primitive peoples as a living and important part of the body, and as such is the object of many taboos and superstitions.[2]

[1] See for the Arabs (among whom the practice was confined to women) the authorities referred to above; also Krehl, *Rel. der Araber*, p. 33, and Goldziher, *Muh. Stud.* i. 248; note also the epithet *ḥalāc* = *ḥālica*, "death." For the Hebrews—whose custom was not to shave the whole head but only the front of it—see Jer. xvi. 6; Amos viii. 10; Ezek. vii. 18; and the legal prohibitions, Lev. xix. 27; Deut. xiv. 1; cf. also Lev. xxi. 5; Ezek. xliv. 20. In the Hebrew case it is not expressly said that the hair was laid on the tomb, but in Arabia this was done in the times of heathenism, and is still done by some Bedouin tribes, according to the testimony of modern travellers. A notable feature in the Arabian custom is that after shaving her head the mourner wrapped it in the *sicāb*, a cloth stained with her own blood. See the verse ascribed to the poetess Al-Khansā in *Tāj*, *s.v.*

[2] *Enc. Brit.* article "Taboo." Wilken (*op. cit.* p. 78 *sqq.*, and "De Simsonsage," *Gids*, 1888, No. 5) has collected many instances to show that the hair is often regarded as the special seat of life and strength. It may be conjectured that this idea is connected with the fact that the hair continues to grow, and so to manifest life, even in mature age, and this conjecture is supported by the fact that the nails are among many peoples the object of similar superstitious regard. The practice of cutting off the hair of the head, or a part of it, is pretty widely diffused; see Wilken, *Haaropfer*, p. 74, and for the Arabs an isolated statement of a Mahūby Arab in Doughty, i. 450, to which Mr. Doughty does not appear to attach much weight. Yet it seems to me that a custom of cutting off the hair of the dead is implied when we read that the Bekrites before the desperate battle of Ciḍḍa shaved their heads as devoting themselves to death (*Ham.* 253, l. 17), and perhaps also in B. Hishām, p. 254, l. 16 *sq.*, where a man dreams that his head is shaven and accepts this as an omen of death. Wilken supposes that the hair was originally cut away from the corpse, or from the dying man, to facilitate the escape of the soul from the body. This notion might very well recommend itself to the savage mind, inasmuch as the hair continues to grow for some time after death. But when we find the hair of the dead used as a means of divination, or as a charm, as is done among many peoples (Wilken, *Haaropfer*, Anh. ii.), we are led to think that the main object in cutting it off must be to preserve it as a means of continued connection with the dead. The possession of hair from a man's head or of a shaving from his nails is, in

Thus, when the hair of the living is deposited with the dead, and the hair of the dead remains with the living, a permanent bond of connection unites the two.

Now among the Semites and other ancient peoples the hair-offering is common, not only in mourning but in the worship of the gods, and the details of the ritual in the two cases are so exactly similar that we cannot doubt that a single principle is involved in both. The hair of Achilles was dedicated to the river-god Spercheus, in whose honour it was to be shorn on his safe return from Troy; but, knowing that he should never return, the hero transferred the offering to the dead Patroclus, and laid his yellow locks in the hand of the corpse. Arab women laid their hair on the tomb of the dead; young men and maidens in Syria cut off their flowing tresses and deposited them in caskets of gold and silver in the temples.[1] The Hebrews shaved the fore part of the head in mourning; the Arabs of Herodotus habitually adopted a like tonsure in honour of their god Orotal, who was supposed to wear his hair in the same way.[2] To argue from these parallels

primitive magic, a potent means of getting and retaining a hold over him. This, I suppose, is the reason why an Arab before releasing a captive cut off his hair and put it in his quiver; see the authorities cited by Wilken, p. 111, and add Rasmussen, *Addit.* p. 70 *sq.*, *Agh.* xii. 128. 1. On the same principle Mohammed's hair was preserved by his followers and worn on their persons (*Muh. in Med.* 429, *Agh.* xv. 12. 13). One such hair is the famous relic in the mosque of the Companion at Cairawān.

[1] *Dea Syria*, lx., where modern editors, by a totally inadmissible conjecture, make it appear that maidens offered their locks, and youths only their beard. Cf. Ephraem Syrus, *Op. Syr.* i. 246; the Syriac version of Lev. xix. 27 renders "ye shall not let your hair grow long," and Ephraem explains that it was the custom of the heathen to let their hair grow for a certain time, and then on a fixed day to shave the head in a temple or beside a sacred fountain.

[2] The peculiar Arab tonsure is already referred to in Jer. xxv. 23, R.V. It is found elsewhere in antiquity, *e.g.* in Eubœa and in some parts of Asia Minor (*Iliad*, ii. 542; Plut. *Thes.* 5; Strabo, x. 3. 6; Chœrilus, *ap.* Jos., *c. Ap.* i. 22; Pollux, ii. 28). At Delphi, where Greek ephebi were wont to offer the long hair of their childhood, this peculiar cut was called *θησηίς*, for

between customs of mourning and of religion that the worship of the gods is based on the cult of the dead, would be to go beyond the evidence; what does appear is that the same means which were deemed efficacious to maintain an enduring covenant between the living and the dead were used to serve the religious purpose of binding together in close union the worshipper and his god.

Starting from this general principle, we can explain without difficulty the two main varieties of the hair-offering as it occurs in religion. In its nature the offering is a personal one, made on behalf of an individual, not of a community. It does not therefore naturally find a place in the stated and periodical exercises of local or tribal religion, where a group of men is gathered together in an ordinary act of communal worship. Its proper object is to create or to emphasise the relation between an individual and a god, and so it is in place either in ceremonies of initiation, by which a new member is incorporated into the circle of a particular religion, or in connection with special vows and special acts of devotion, by which a worshipper seeks to knit more closely the bond between himself and his god. Thus in Greek religion the hair-offering occurs either at the moment when a youth enters on manhood, and so takes up a full share in the religious as well as the political responsibilities of a citizen, or else in fulfilment of a vow made at some moment when a man is in special need of divine succour. The same thing is true of Semitic religion, but to make this clear requires some explanation.

Theseus was said to have shorn only his front locks at the temple. Among the Curetes this was the way in which warriors wore their hair; presumably, therefore, children let the front locks grow long, and sacrificed them on entering manhood, just as among the Arabs the two side locks are the distinguishing mark of an immature lad.

In early societies a man is destined by his birth to become a member of a particular political and social circle, which is at the same time a distinct religious community. But in many cases this destination has to be confirmed by a formal act of admission to the community. The child or immature stripling has not yet full civil privileges and responsibilities, and in general, on the principle that civil and religious status are inseparable, he has no full part either in the rights or in the duties of the communal religion. He is excluded from many religious ceremonies, and conversely he can do without offence things which on religious grounds are strictly forbidden to the full tribesman. Among rude nations the transition from civil and religious immaturity to maturity is frequently preceded by certain probationary tests of courage and endurance; for the full tribesman must above all things be a warrior. In any case the step from childhood to manhood is too important to take place without a formal ceremony and public rites of initiation, importing the full and final incorporation of the neophyte into the civil and religious fellowship of his tribe or community.[1] It is clear from what has already been said, that the application of the blood of the youth to the sacred symbol, or the depositing of his hair at the shrine of his people's god, might form a significant feature in such a ritual; and among very many rude peoples one or other of these ceremonies is actually observed in connection with the rites which every young man must pass through before he attains the position of a warrior, and is allowed to marry and exercise the other prerogatives of perfect manhood. Among wholly barbarous races these initiation ceremonies have great importance,

[1] In some cases the rite seems to be connected with the transference of the lad from the mother's to the father's kin. But for the present argument it is not necessary to discuss this aspect of the matter.

and are often extremely repulsive in character. The blood-offering in particular frequently takes a form which makes it a severe test of the neophyte's courage—as in the cruel flagellation of Spartan ephebi at the altar of Artemis Orthia, or in the frightful ordeal which takes the place of simple circumcision in some of the wilder mountain tribes of Arabia.[1] As manners become less fierce, and society ceases to be organised mainly for war, the ferocity of primitive ritual is naturally softened, and the initiation ceremony gradually loses importance, till at last it becomes a mere domestic celebration, which in its social aspect may be compared to the private festivities of a modern family when a son comes of age, and in its religious aspect to the first communion of a youthful Catholic. When the rite loses political significance, and becomes purely religious, it is not necessary that it should be deferred to the age of full manhood; indeed, the natural tendency of pious parents will be to dedicate their child as early as possible to the god who is to be his protector through life. Thus circumcision, which was originally a preliminary to marriage, and so a ceremony of introduction to the full prerogative of manhood, is now generally undergone by Mohammedan boys before they reach maturity, while, among the Hebrews, infants were circumcised on the eighth day from birth. Similar variations of usage apply to the Semitic hair-offering. Among the Arabs in the time of Mohammed it was common to sacrifice a sheep on the birth of a child, and then to shave the head of the infant and daub the scalp with the blood of the victim. This ceremony—callek *'acīca*, or "the cutting off of the hair"—was designed to "avert evil from the child," and was evidently an act of dedication by which the infant was brought under the

[1] The connection between circumcision and the initiatory blood-offering will be considered more fully in another place.

protection of the god of the community.[1] Among Lucian's Syrians, on the other hand, the hair of boys and girls was allowed to grow unshorn as a consecrated thing from birth to adolescence, and was cut off and dedicated at the sanctuary as a necessary preliminary to marriage. In other words, the hair-offering of youths and maidens was a ceremony of religious initiation, through which they had to pass before they were admitted to the status of social maturity. The same thing appears to have occurred, at least in the case of maidens, at Phœnician sanctuaries; for the female worshippers at the Adonis feast of Byblus, who, according to the author just cited, were required to sacrifice either their hair or their chastity,[2] appear from other accounts to have been generally maidens, of whom this act of devotion was exacted as a preliminary to marriage.[3] I apprehend that

[1] That the hair was regarded as an offering appears from the Moslem practice, referred by tradition to the example of Fāṭima, of bestowing in alms its weight of silver. Alms are a religious oblation, and in the similar custom which Herod. ii. 65, Diod. i. 83, attest for ancient Egypt, the silver was paid to the sanctuary. See for further details *Kinship*, p. 152 *sqq.*, where I have dwelt on the way in which such a ceremony would facilitate the change of the child's kin, when the rule that the son followed the father and not the mother began to be established. I still think that this point is worthy of notice, and that the desire to fix the child's religion, and with it his tribal connection, at the earliest possible moment, may have been one cause for performing the ceremony in infancy. But Nöldeke's remarks in *ZDMG.* xl. 184, and a fuller consideration of the whole subject of the hair-offering, have convinced me that the name *'acīca* is not connected with the idea of change of kin, but is derived from the cutting away of the first hair. In this, however, I see a confirmation of the view that among the Arabs, as among the Syrians, the old usage was to defer the cutting of the first hair till adolescence, for *'acca* is a very strong term to apply to the shaving of the scanty hair of a new-born infant, while it is quite appropriate to the sacrifice of the long locks characteristic of boyhood. Cf. also the use of the same verb in the phrases *'occat tamīmatuhu* (*Kāmil*, 405, l. 19), *'acca 'l-shabābu tamīmati* (*Tāj*, *s.v.*), used of the cutting away, when manhood was reached, of the amulet worn during childhood. In modern Syria (Sidon district) a child's hair must not be cut till it is a year old (*ZDPV.* vii. 85).

[2] *Dea Syria*, vi.

[3] Sozomen, v. 10. 7. Cf. Socrates, i. 18, and the similar usage in

among the Arabs, in like manner, the *'acîca* was originally a ceremony of initiation into manhood, and that the transference of the ceremony to infancy was a later innovation, for among the Arabs, as among the Syrians, young lads let their hair grow long, and the sign of immaturity was the retention of the side locks, which adult warriors did not wear.[1] The cutting of the side locks was therefore a formal mark of admission into manhood, and in the time of Herodotus it must also have been a formal initiation into the worship of Orotal, for otherwise the religious significance which the Greek historian attaches to the shorn forehead of the Arabs is unintelligible. At that time, therefore, we must conclude that a hair-offering, precisely equivalent to the *'acîca*, took place upon entry into manhood, and thereafter the front hair was habitually worn short as a permanent memorial of this dedicatory sacrifice. It is by no means clear that even in later times the initiatory ceremony was invariably performed in infancy, for the name *'acîca*, which in Arabic denotes the first hair as well as the religious ceremony of cutting it off, is sometimes applied to the ruddy locks of a lad approaching manhood,[2] and figuratively to the plumage of a swift young ostrich or the tufts of an ass's hair, neither of which has much resemblance to the scanty down on the head of a new-born babe.[3]

It would seem, therefore, that the oldest Semitic usage, both in Arabia and in Syria, was to sacrifice the hair of

Babylon, Herod. i. 199. We are not to suppose that participation in these rites was confined to maidens before marriage (Euseb. *Vit. Const.* iii. 58. 1), but it appears that it was obligatory on them.

[1] See Wellh., *Heid.* p. 119.

[2] Imraulcais, 3. 1; see also *Lisān*, xii. 129, l. 18, and Dozy, *s.v.*

[3] Zohair, 1. 17; *Diw. Hodh.* 232. 9. The sense of "down," which Nöldeke, *ut supra*, gives to the word in these passages, is hardly appropriate.

childhood upon admission to the religious and social status of manhood.

The bond between the worshipper and his god which was established by means of the hair-offering had an enduring character, but it was natural to renew it from time to time, when there was any reason to fear that the interest of the deity in his votary might have been relaxed. Thus it was customary for the inhabitants of Ṭāïf in Arabia to shave their heads at the sanctuary of the town whenever they returned from a journey.[1] Here the idea seems to be that absence from the holy place might have loosened the religious tie, and that it was proper to bind it fast again. In like manner the hair-offering formed part of the ritual in every Arabian pilgrimage,[2] and also at the great feasts of Byblus and Bambyce,[3] which were not mere local celebrations, but drew worshippers from distant parts. The worshipper in these cases desired to attach himself as firmly as possible to a deity and a shrine with which he could not hope to keep up frequent and regular connection, and thus it was fitting that, when he went forth from the holy place, he should leave part of himself behind, as a permanent link of union with the temple and the god that inhabited it.

The Arabian and Syrian pilgrimages with which the hair-offering was associated were exceptional services; in many cases their object was to place the worshipper under the protection of a foreign god, whose cult had no place in the pilgrim's local and natural religion, and in any case

[1] *Muh. in Med.* p. 381.

[2] Wellh. p. 117; Goldziher, *op. cit.* p. 249. That the hair was shaved as an offering appears most clearly in the worship of Ocaiṣir, where it was mixed with an oblation of meal.

[3] *Dea Syria*, vi., lv. In the latter case the eyebrows also were shaved, and the sacrifice of hair from the eyebrow reappears in Peru, in the laws of the Incas. On the painted inscription of Citium (*CIS.* No. 86) barbers (גלבם) are enumerated among the stated ministers of the temple.

the service was not part of a man's ordinary religious duties, but was spontaneously undertaken as a work of special piety, or under the pressure of circumstances that made the pilgrim feel the need of coming into closer touch with the divine powers. Among the Hebrews, at least in later times, when stated pilgrimages to Jerusalem were among the ordinary and imperative exercises of every man's religion, the pilgrimage did not involve a hair-offering, nor is it probable that in any part of antiquity this form of service was required in connection with ordinary visits to one's own local temple. The Pentateuchal law recognises the hair-offering only in the case of the peculiar vow of the Nazarite, the ritual of which is described in Num. vi. The details there given do not help us to understand what part the Nazirate held in the actual religious life of the Jews under the law, but from Josephus[1] we gather that the vow was generally taken in times of sickness or other trouble, and that it was therefore exactly parallel to the ordinary Greek vow to offer the hair on deliverance from urgent danger. From the antique point of view, the fact that a man is in straits or peril is a proof that the divine powers on which his life is dependent are estranged or indifferent, and a warning to bring himself into closer relation with the god from whom he is estranged. The hair-offering affords the natural means towards this end, and, if the offering cannot be accomplished at the moment, it ought to be made the subject of a vow, for a vow is the recognised way of antedating a future act of service and making its efficacy begin at once. A vow of this kind, aiming at the redintegration of normal relations with the deity, is naturally more than a bare promise; it is a promise for the performance of which one at once begins to make active

[1] *B. J.* ii. 15. 1.

preparation, so that the life of the votary from the time when he assumes the engagement is taken out of the ordinary sphere of secular existence, and becomes one continuous act of religion.[1] As soon as a man takes the vow to poll his locks at the sanctuary, the hair is a consecrated thing, and as such, inviolable till the moment for discharging the vow arrives; and so the flowing locks of the Hebrew Nazarite or of a Greek votary like Achilles are the visible marks of his consecration. In like manner the Arabian pilgrim, whose resolution to visit a distant shrine was practically a vow,[2] was not allowed to poll or even to comb and wash his locks till the pilgrimage was accomplished; and on the same principle the whole course of his journey, from the day when he first set his face towards the temple with the resolution to do homage there, was a period of consecration (*iḥrām*),[3] during which he was subject to a number of other ceremonial restrictions or taboos, of the same kind with those imposed by actual presence in the sanctuary.

The taboos connected with pilgrimages and other vows require some further elucidation, but to go into the matter now would carry us too far from the point immediately before us. I will therefore reserve what I have still to say on this subject for an additional note.[4] What has been said already covers all the main examples of the hair-offering among the Semites.[5] They present considerable variety

[1] Of course, if the vow is conditional on something to happen in the future, the engagement does not necessarily come into force till the condition is fulfilled.

[2] In Mohammedan law it is expressly reckoned as a vow.

[3] Under Islam the consecration of the pilgrim need not begin till he reaches the boundaries of the sacred territory. But it is permitted, and according to many authorities preferable, to assume the *iḥrām* on leaving one's home; and this was the ancient practice.

[4] See *Additional Note* I, *The Taboos incident to Pilgrimages and Vows.*

[5] Quite distinct from the hair-offering are the cases in which the hair is shaved off (but not consecrated) as a means of purification after pollution;

of aspect, but the result of our discussion is that they can be referred to a single principle. In their origin the hair-offering and the offering of one's own blood are precisely similar in meaning. But the blood-offering, while it presents the idea of life-union with the god in the strongest possible form, is too barbarous to be long retained as an ordinary act of religion. It continued to be practised among the civilised Semites, by certain priesthoods and societies of devotees; but in the habitual worship of lay-men it either fell out of use or was retained in a very attenuated form, in the custom of tatooing the flesh with punctures in honour of the deity.[1] The hair-offering, on the other hand, which involved nothing offensive to civilised

e.g. Lev. xiv. 9 (purification of leper); *Dea Syria*, liii. (after defilement by the dead); Deut. xxi. 12. In such cases the hair is cut off because defilement is specially likely to cling to it.

[1] For the στίγματα on the wrists and necks of the heathen Syrians the classical passage is *Dea Syria*, lix.; compare for further evidence the discussion in Spencer, *Leg. Rit. Heb.* ii. 14; and see also *Kinship*, p. 213 *sqq.* The tattooed marks were the sign that the worshipper belonged to the god; thus at the temple of Heracles at the Canobic mouth of the Nile, the fugitive slave who had been marked with the sacred stigmata could not be reclaimed by his master (Herod. ii. 113). The practice therefore stands on one line with the branding or tattooing of cattle, slaves and prisoners of war. But in Lev. xix. 28, where tattooing is condemned as a heathenish practice, it is immediately associated with incisions in the flesh made in mourning or in honour of the dead, and this suggests that in their ultimate origin the *stigmata* are nothing more than the permanent scars of punctures made to draw blood for a ceremony of self-dedication to the deity. Among the Arabs I find no direct evidence of a religious significance attached to tattooing, and the practice appears to have been confined to women, as was also the habitual use of amulets in mature life. The presumption is that this coincidence is not accidental, but that the tattooed marks were originally sacred stigmata like those of the Syrians, and so were conceived to have the force of a charm. Pietro della Valle (ed. 1843), i. 395, describes the Arabian tattooing, and says that it is practised all over the East by men as well as by women. But so far as I have observed, it is only Christian men that tattoo in Syria, and with them the pattern chosen is a sacred symbol, which has been shown to me as a proof that a man was exempt from the military service to which Moslems are liable. In Farazdac, ed. Boucher, p. 232, l. 9, a tattooed hand is the mark of a foreigner. In Egypt men of the peasant class are sometimes tattooed.

feelings, continued to play an important part in religion to the close of paganism, and even entered into Christian ritual in the tonsure of priests and nuns.[1]

Closely allied to the practice of leaving part of oneself —whether blood or hair—in contact with the god at the sanctuary, are offerings of part of one's clothes or other things that one has worn, such as ornaments or weapons. In the *Iliad*, Glaucus and Diomede exchange armour in token of their ancestral friendship; and when Jonathan makes a covenant of love and brotherhood with David, he invests him with his garments, even to his sword, his bow, and his girdle.[2] Among the Arabs, he who seeks protection lays hold of the garments of the man to whom he appeals, or more formally ties a knot in the head-shawl of his protector.[3] In the old literature, "pluck away my garments from thine" means "put an end to our attachment."[4] The clothes are so far part of a man that they can serve as a vehicle of personal connection. Hence the religious significance of suspending on an idol or *Dhāt Anwāt*, not only weapons, ornaments and complete garments, but mere shreds from one's raiment. These rag-offerings are still to be seen hanging on the sacred

[1] The latter was practised in Jerome's time in the monasteries of Egypt and Syria (*Ep.* 147 ad Sabinianum).

[2] 1 Sam. xviii. 3 *sq.* I presume that by ancient law Saul was bound to acknowledge the formal covenant thus made between David and his son, and that this ought to be taken into account in judging of the subsequent relations between the three.

[3] Wellhausen, *Heidenthum*, p. 105, note 3; Burckhardt, *Bed. and Wah.* i. 130 *sq.*; Blunt, *Bedouin Tribes of the Euphrates*, i. 42. The knot, says Burckhardt, is tied that the protector may look out for witnesses to prove the act, and "the same custom is observed when any transaction is to be witnessed." But primarily, I apprehend, the knot is the symbolic sign of the engagement that the witnesses are called to prove, and I was told in the Ḥijāz that the suppliant gets a fragment of the fringe of the shawl to keep as his token of the transaction. In the covenant sacrifice, Herod. iii. 8, the blood is applied to the sacred stones with threads from the garments of the two contracting parties.

[4] Imraulc., *Moall.* l. 21

trees of Syria and on the tombs of Mohammedan saints; they are not gifts in the ordinary sense, but pledges of attachment.[1] It is possible that the rending of garments in mourning was originally designed to procure such an offering for the dead, just as the tearing of the hair on the like occasion is not a natural sign of mourning, but a relic of the hair-offering. Natural signs of mourning must not be postulated lightly; in all such matters habit is a second nature.[2]

Finally, I may note in a single word that the counterpart of the custom of leaving part of oneself or of one's clothes with the deity at the sanctuary, is the custom of wearing sacred relics as charms, so that something belonging to the god remains always in contact with one's person.[3]

The peculiar instructiveness of the series of usages which we have been considering, and the justification for the long digression from the subject of sacrifice into which they have led us, is that the ceremonies designed to establish a life-bond between the worshipper and his god are here dissociated from the death of a victim and from every idea of penal satisfaction to the deity. They have

[1] A masterful man, in the early days of Islam, reserves a water for his own use by hanging pieces of fringe of his red blanket on a tree beside it, or by throwing them into the pool; Farazdac, p. 195, *Agh.* viii. 159. 10 *sqq.*

[2] It is to be noted that most of the standing methods of expressing sorrow and distress are derived from the formal usages employed in primitive times in mourning for the dead. These usages, however, are not all to be derived from one principle. While the rudest nations seek to keep up their connection with the beloved dead, they also believe that very dangerous influences hover round death-beds, corpses, and graves, and many funeral ceremonies are observed as safeguards against these, as has been well shown by Mr. Frazer, *Journ. Anthr. Inst.* xv. 64 *sqq.*; though I think he has not sufficiently allowed for another principle that underlies many such customs, namely, the affectionate desire of even the rudest peoples to keep up a friendly intercourse with their dead friends and relations. Compare below, p. 370.

[3] Thus in Palestine, at the present time, the man who hangs a rag on a sacred tree takes with him in return, as a preservative against evil, one of the rags that have been sanctified by hanging there for some time before (*PEF. Qu. St.* 1893, p. 204).

indeed an atoning force, whenever they are used to renew relations with a god who is temporarily estranged, but this is merely a consequence of the conception that the physical link which they establish between the divine and human parties in the rite binds the god to the man as well as the man to the god. Even in the case of the blood-offering there is no reason to hold that the pain of the self-inflicted wounds had originally any significant place in the ceremony. But no doubt, as time went on, the barbarous and painful sacrifice of one's own blood came to be regarded as more efficacious than the simpler and commoner hair-offering; for in religion what is unusual always appears to be more potent, and more fitted to reconcile an offended deity.

The use of the Syriac word *ethkashshaph* seems to show that the sacrifice of one's own blood was mainly associated among the Aramæans with deprecation or supplication to an angry god, and though I cannot point among the Semites to any formal atoning ceremony devised on this principle, the idea involved can be well illustrated by a rite still sometimes practised in Arabia, as a means of making atonement to a man for offences short of murder. With bare and shaven head the offender appears at the door of the injured person, holding a knife in each hand, and, reciting a formula provided for the purpose, strikes his head several times with the sharp blades. Then, drawing his hands over his bloody scalp, he wipes them on the doorpost. The other must then come out and cover the suppliant's head with a shawl, after which he kills a sheep, and they sit down together at a feast of reconciliation. The characteristic point in this rite is the application of the blood to the doorpost, which, as in the passover service, is equivalent to applying it to the person of the inmates. Here, therefore, we still see the old idea at work, that the reconciling value of the rite lies, not in the self-inflicted wounds, but in the application of the blood to make a life-bond between the two parties.

On the same analogy, when we turn to those blood-rites in which a whole community takes part, and in which therefore a victim has to be slaughtered to provide the material for the ceremony, we may expect to find that, at least in old times, the significant part of the ceremony does not lie in the death of the victim, but in the application of its life or life-blood; and in this expectation we shall not be disappointed.

Of all Semitic sacrifices those of the Arabs have the rudest and most visibly primitive character; and among the Arabs, where there was no complicated fire-ceremony at the altar, the sacramental meal stands out in full relief as the very essence of the ritual. Now, in the oldest known form of Arabian sacrifice, as described by Nilus, the camel chosen as the victim is bound upon a rude altar of stones piled together, and when the leader of the band has thrice led the worshippers round the altar in a solemn procession accompanied with chants, he inflicts the first wound, while the last words of the hymn are still upon the lips of the congregation, and in all haste drinks of the blood that gushes forth. Forthwith the whole company fall on the victim with their swords, hacking off pieces of the quivering flesh and devouring them raw with such wild haste, that in the short interval between the rise of the day star which marked the hour for the service to begin, and the disappearance of its rays before the rising sun, the entire camel, body and bones, skin, blood and entrails, is wholly devoured.[1] The plain meaning of this is that the victim was

[1] This must not be regarded as incredible. According to Artemidorus, *ap.* Strabo, xvi. 4. 17, the Troglodytes ate the bones and skin as well as the flesh of cattle.

devoured before its life had left the still warm blood and flesh,—raw flesh is called "living" flesh in Hebrew and Syriac,—and that thus in the most literal way all those who shared in the ceremony absorbed part of the victim's life into themselves. One sees how much more forcibly than any ordinary meal such a rite expresses the establishment or confirmation of a bond of common life between the worshippers, and also, since the blood is shed upon the altar itself, between the worshippers and their god.

In this sacrifice, then, the significant factors are two: the conveyance of the living blood to the godhead, and the absorption of the living flesh and blood into the flesh and blood of the worshippers. Each of these is effected in the simplest and most direct manner, so that the meaning of the ritual is perfectly transparent. In later Arabian sacrifices, and still more in the sacrifices of the more civilised Semitic nations, the primitive crudity of the ceremonial was modified, and the meaning of the act is therefore more or less disguised, but the essential type of the ritual remains the same.

In all Arabian sacrifices except the holocaust—which occurs only in the case of human victims—the godward side of the ritual is summed up in the shedding of the victim's blood, so that it flows over the sacred symbol, or gathers in a pit (*ghabghab*) at the foot of the altar idol. An application of the blood to the summit of the sacred stone may be added, but that is all.[1] What enters the *ghabghab* is held to be conveyed to the deity; thus at certain Arabian shrines the pit under the altar was the place where votive treasures were deposited. A pit to receive the blood existed also at Jerusalem under the altar of burnt-offering, and similarly in certain Syrian sacrifices the blood was collected in a hollow, which

[1] Zohair, x. 24.

apparently bore the name of *mashkan*, and thus was designated as the habitation of the godhead.[1]

In Arabia, accordingly, the most solemn act in the ritual is the shedding of the blood, which in Nilus's narrative takes place at the moment when the sacred chant comes to an end. This, therefore, is the crisis of the service, to which the choral procession round the altar leads up.[2] In later Arabia, the *ṭawāf*, or act of circling the sacred stone, was still a principal part of religion; but even before Mohammed's time it had begun to be dissociated from sacrifice, and become a meaningless ceremony. Again, the original significance of the *wocūf*, or "standing," which in the ritual of the post-Mohammedan pilgrimage has in like manner become an unmeaning ceremony, is doubtless correctly explained by Wellhausen, who compares it with the scene described by more than one old poet, where the worshippers stand round the altar idol, at a respectful distance, gazing with rapt attention, while the slaughtered victims lie stretched on the ground. The moment of this act of adoration must be that when the slaughter of the victims is just over, or still in progress, and their blood is draining into the *ghabghab*, or being applied by the priest to the head of the *noṣb*.[3]

In the developed forms of North Semitic worship, where fire-sacrifices prevail, the slaughter of the victim loses its importance as the critical point in the ritual.

[1] See the text published by Dozy and De Goeje in the *Actes* of the Leyden Congress of Orientalists, 1883, vol. iii. pp. 337, 363. For the *ghabghab*, see p. 198 *supra*, and Wellhausen, p. 100. Compare also the Persian ritual, Strabo, xv. 3. 14, and that of certain Greek sacrifices, Plutarch, *Aristides*, xxi.: τὸν ταῦρον εἰς τὴν πυρὰν σφάξας.

[2] The festal song of praise (הלל, *tahlīl*) properly goes with the dance round the altar (cf. Ps. xxvi. 6 *sq.*), for in primitive times song and dance are inseparable.

[3] Wellh. p. 56 *sq.*; Yācūt, iii. 94, l. 13 *sq.* (cf. Nöldeke in *ZDMG.* 1887, p. 721); *ibid.* p. 182, l. 2 *sq.* (*supra*, p. 228).

The altar is above all things a hearth, and the burning of the sacrificial fat is the most solemn part of the service.

This, however, is certainly not primitive; for even in the period of fire-sacrifice the Hebrew altar is called מזבח, that is, "the place of slaughter,"[1] and in ancient times the victim was slain on or beside the altar, just as among the Arabs, as appears from the account of the sacrifice of Isaac, and from 1 Sam. xiv. 34.[2] The latter passage proves that in the time of Saul the Hebrews still knew a form of sacrifice in which the offering was completed in the oblation of the blood. And even in the case of fire-sacrifice the blood was not cast upon the flames, but dashed against the sides of the altar or poured out at its foot; the new ritual was not able wholly to displace the old. Nay, the sprinkling of the blood continued to be regarded as the principal point of the ritual down to the last days of Jewish ritual; for on it the atoning efficacy of the sacrifice depended.[3]

As regards the manward part of the ritual, the revolting details given by Nilus have naturally no complete parallel in the worship of the more civilised Semites, or even of the later Arabs. In lieu of the scramble described by Nilus—the wild rush to cut gobbets of flesh from the still quivering victim—we find among the later Arabs a partition of the sacrificial flesh among all who are present at the ceremony. Yet it seems possible that the *ijāza*, or "permission," that is, the word of command that terminates the *wocūf*, was originally the permission to fall upon the

[1] Aram. *madbaḥ*, Arab. *madhbaḥ*; the latter means also a trench in the ground, which is intelligible from what has been said about the *ghabghab*.

[2] *Supra*, p. 202. In Ps. cxviii. 27 the festal victim is bound with cords to the horns of the altar, a relic of ancient usage which was no longer intelligible to the Septuagint translators or to the Jewish traditional expositors. Cf. the sacrificial stake to which the victim is bound in Vedic sacrifices.

[3] Heb. ix. 22; Reland, *Ant. Heb.* p. 300.

slaughtered victim. In the Meccan pilgrimage the *ijāza* which terminates the *wocūf* at ʿArafa was the signal for a hot race to the neighbouring sanctuary of Mozdalifa, where the sacred fire of the god Cozaḥ burned; it was, in fact, not so much the permission to leave ʿArafa as to draw near to Cozaḥ. The race itself is called *ifāḍa*, which may mean either "dispersion" or "distribution." It cannot well mean the former, for ʿArafa is not holy ground, but merely the point of assemblage, just outside the Ḥaram, at which the ceremonies began, and the station at ʿArafa is only the preparation for the vigil at Mozdalifa. On the other hand, if the meaning is "distribution," the *ifāḍa* answers to the rush of Nilus's Saracens to partake of the sacrifice. The only difference is that at Mozdalifa the crowd is not allowed to assemble close to the altar, but has to watch the performance of the solemn rites from afar; compare Ex. xix. 10–13.[1]

The substitution of an orderly division of the victim for the scramble described by Nilus does not touch the meaning of the ceremonial. Much more important, from its effect in disguising an essential feature in the ritual, is the modification by which, in most Semitic sacrifices, the flesh is not eaten "alive" or raw, but sodden or roasted. It is obvious that this change could not fail to establish itself with the progress of civilisation; but it was still possible to express the idea of communion in the actual life of the victim by eating its flesh "with the blood."

[1] It may be noted that the ceremonies at Mozdalifa lay wholly between sunset and sunrise, and that there was apparently one sacrifice just at or after sunset and another before sunrise,—another point of contact with the ritual described by Nilus. The *wocūf* corresponding to the morning sacrifice was of course held at Mozdalifa within the Ḥaram, for the pilgrims were already consecrated by the previous service. Nābigha in two places speaks of a race of pilgrims to a place called Ilāl. If the reference is to the Meccan *ḥajj*, Ilāl must be Mozdalifa not, as the geographers suppose, a place at ʿArafa.

That bloody morsels were consumed by the heathen in Palestine, and also by the less orthodox Israelites, is apparent from Zech. ix. 7; Ezek. xxxiii. 25;[1] Lev. xix. 26; and the context of these passages, with the penalty of excommunication attached to the eating of blood in Lev. vii. 27, justify us in assuming that this practice had a directly religious significance, and occurred in connection with sacrifice. That it was in fact an act of communion with heathen deities, is affirmed by Maimonides, not as a mere inference from the biblical texts, but on the basis of Arabic accounts of the religion of the Harranians.[2] It would seem, however, that in the northern Semitic lands the ritual of blood-eating must already have been rare in the times to which our oldest documents belong; presumably, indeed, it was confined to certain mystic initiations, and did not extend to ordinary sacrifices.[3]

[1] I cannot comprehend why Cornill corrects Ezek. xxxiii. 25 by Ezek. xviii. 6, xxii. 9, and not conversely; cf. LXX. on Lev. xix. 26, where the same mistake occurs.

[2] *Dalālat al-Ḥāïrīn*, iii. 46, vol. iii. p. 104 of Munk's ed. (Paris, 1866) and p. 371 of his translation. That Maimonides had actual accounts of the Harranians to go on appears by comparing the passage with that quoted above from an Arabic source in the *Actes* of the Leyden Congress; but there may be a doubt whether his authorities attested blood-eating among the Harranians, or only supplied hints by which he interpreted the biblical evidence.

[3] For the mystic sacrifices of the heathen Semites, see above, p. 290 *sqq.* That these sacrifices were eaten with the blood appears from a comparison of Isa. lxv. 4, lxvi. 3, 17. All these passages refer to the same circle of rites, in which the victims chosen were such animals as were strictly taboo in ordinary life—the swine, the dog, the mouse and vermin (שקץ) generally. To such sacrifices, as we learn from lxvi. 17, a peculiar consecrating and purifying efficacy was attached, which must be ascribed to the sacramental participation in the sacrosanct flesh. The flesh was eaten in the form of broth, which in lxv. 4 is called broth of *piggūlīm*, *i.e.* of carrion, or flesh so killed as to retain the blood in it (Ezek. iv. 14; cf. Zech ix. 7). We are to think, therefore, of a broth made with the blood, like the black broth of the Spartans, which seems also to have been originally a sacred food, reserved for warriors. The dog-sacrifice in lxvi. 3 is killed by breaking its neck, which agrees with this conclusion. Similarly in the mysteries of the Ainos, the sacred bear, which forms the sacrifice, is killed

In the legal sacrifices of the Hebrews blood was never eaten, but in the covenant sacrifice of Ex. xxiv. it is sprinkled on the worshippers, which, as we have already learned by a comparison of the various forms of the blood covenant between men, has the same meaning. In later forms of sacrifice this feature disappears, and the communion between god and man, which is still the main thing in ordinary sacrifices, is expressed by burning part of the flesh on the altar, while the rest is cooked and eaten by the worshippers. But the application of the living blood to the worshipper is retained in certain special cases—at the consecration of priests and the purification of the leper [1]—where it is proper to express in the strongest way the establishment of a special bond between the god and his servant,[2] or the restitution of one who has been cut off from religious fellowship with the deity and the community of his worshippers. In like manner, in the forms of sin-offering described in Lev. iv., it is at least required that the priest should dip his finger in the blood of the victim; and in this kind of ritual, as is expressly stated in Lev. x. 17, the priest acts as the representative of the sinner or bears his sin. Again, the blood of the Paschal lamb is applied to the doorposts, and so extends its efficacy to all within the dwelling—the "house" in all the Semitic languages standing for the household or family.[3]

without effusion of blood; cf. the Indian rite, Strabo, xv. 1. 54 (Satapatha Brahmana, tr. Eggeling, ii. 190), and the Cappadocian, *ibid.* xv. 3. 15; also the Finnish sacrifice, Mannhardt, *Ant. Wald- u. Feldkulte*, p. 160, and other cases of the same kind, *Journ. R. Geog. Soc.* vol. iii. p. 283, vol. xl. p. 171. Spencer compares the πνικτά of Acts xv. 20.

[1] Lev. viii. 23, xiv. 6, 14.

[2] The relation between God and His priests rests on a covenant (Deut. xxxiii. 9; Mal. ii. 4 *sqq.*).

[3] In modern Arabia "it is the custom to slaughter at the tent door and sprinkle the camels with the blood" (Blunt, *Nejd*, i. 203; also Doughty, i. 499). This protects the camels from sickness. Also the live booty from a foray is sprinkled with sacrificial blood—presumably to incorporate it with the tribal

The express provision that the flesh of the lamb must not be eaten raw seems to be directed against a practice similar to what Nilus describes; and so also the precept that the passover must be eaten in haste, in ordinary outdoor attire, and that no part of it must remain till the morning, becomes intelligible if we regard it as having come down from a time when the living flesh was hastily devoured beside the altar before the sun rose.[1] From all this it is apparent that the ritual described by Nilus is by no means an isolated invention of the religious fancy, in one of the most barbarous corners of the Semitic world, but a very typical embodiment of the main ideas that underlie the sacrifices of the Semites generally. Even in its details it probably comes nearer to the primitive form of Semitic worship than any other sacrifice of which we have a description.

We may now take it as made out that, throughout the Semitic field, the fundamental idea of sacrifice is not that of a sacred tribute, but of communion between the god and his worshippers by joint participation in the living flesh and blood of a sacred victim. We see, however, that in the more advanced forms of ritual this idea becomes attenuated and tends to disappear, at least in the commoner kinds of sacrifice. When men cease to eat raw or living flesh, the blood, to the exclusion of the solid parts of the body, comes to be regarded as the vehicle of life and the true *res sacramenti*. And the nature of the sacrifice as a sacramental act is still further disguised when—for reasons

cattle (*tilād*); Doughty, i. 452. An obscure reference to the smearing of a camel with blood is found in Azraqī, p. 53, l. 13, *Agh.* xiii. 110, l. 6, but the variations between the two texts make it hazardous to attempt an explanation. Cp. on the whole subject of blood-sprinkling, Kremer, *Studien*, p. 45 *sqq.*

[1] There is so much that is antique about the Paschal ritual, that one is tempted to think that the law of Ex. xii. 46, "neither shall ye break a bone thereof," may be a prohibition of some usage descended from the rule, given by Nilus, that the bones as well as the flesh must be consumed.

that will by and by appear more clearly—the sacramental blood is no longer drunk by the worshippers but only sprinkled on their persons, or finally finds no manward application at all, but is wholly poured out at the altar, so that it becomes the proper share of the deity, while the flesh is left to be eaten by man. This is the common form of Arabian sacrifice, and among the Hebrews the same form is attested by 1 Sam. xiv. 34. At this stage, at least among the Hebrews, the original sanctity of the life of domestic animals is still recognised in a modified form, inasmuch as it is held unlawful to use their flesh for food except in a sacrificial meal. But this rule is not strict enough to prevent flesh from becoming a familiar luxury. Sacrifices are multiplied on trivial occasions of religious gladness or social festivity, and the rite of eating at the sanctuary loses the character of an exceptional sacrament, and means no more than that men are invited to feast and be merry at the table of their god, or that no feast is complete in which the god has not his share.

This stage in the evolution of ritual is represented by the worship of the Hebrew high places, or, beyond the Semitic field, by the religion of the agricultural communities of Greece. Historically, therefore, it coincides with the stage of religious development in which the deity is conceived as the king of his people and the lord of the land, and as such is habitually approached with gifts and tribute. It was the rule of antiquity, and still is the rule in the East, that the inferior must not present himself before his superior without a gift "to smooth his face" and make him gracious.[1] The same phrase is habitually applied in the Old Testament to acts of sacrificial worship, and in Ex.

[1] חִלָּה פניו, Prov. xix. 6; Ps. xlv. 13 (12), E.V., "intreat his favour." In the Old Testament the phrase is much oftener used of acts of worship addressed to the deity, *e.g.* 1 Sam. xiii. 12, of the burnt-offering.

xxiii. 15 the rule is formulated that no one shall appear before Jehovah empty-handed. *Δῶρα θεοὺς πείθει, δῶρ' αἰδοίους βασιλῆας.*

As the commonest gifts in a simple agricultural state of society necessarily consisted of grain, fruits and cattle, which served to maintain the open hospitality that prevailed at the courts of kings and great chiefs, it was natural that animal sacrifices, as soon as their sacramental significance fell into the background, should be mainly regarded as gifts of homage presented at the court of the divine king, out of which he maintained a public table for his worshippers. In part they were summed up along with the cereal oblations of first-fruits as stated tributes, which everyone who desired to retain the favour of the god was expected to present at fixed seasons; in part they were special offerings with which the worshipper associated special petitions, or with which he approached the deity to present his excuses for a fault and request forgiveness.[1] In the case where it is the business of the worshipper to make satisfaction for an offence, the gift may assume rather the character of a fine payable at the sanctuary; for in the oldest free communities personal chastisement is reserved for slaves, and the offences of freemen are habitually wiped out by the payment of an amercement.[2] But in the older Hebrew custom the fines paid to the sanctuary do not appear to have taken the form of victims for sacrifice, but rather of payments in money to the priest,[3] and the atoning effect ascribed to gifts

[1] 1 Sam. xxvi. 19: "If Jehovah hath stirred thee up against me, let Him be gratified by an oblation."

[2] The reason of this is that not even a chief can strike or mutilate a freeman without exposing himself to retaliation. This is still the case among the Bedouins, and so it was also in ancient Israel; see *The Old Testament in the Jewish Church*, 2nd ed., p. 368.

[3] 2 Kings xii. 16; cf. Amos ii. 8; Hos. iv. 8.

and sacrifices of all kinds seems simply to rest on the general principle that a gift smooths the face and pacifies anger.

It has sometimes been supposed that this is the oldest form of the idea of atoning sacrifice, and that the elaborate piacula, which begin to take the chief place in the altar ritual of the Semites from the seventh century onwards, are all developed out of it. The chief argument that appears to support this view is that the whole burnt-offering, which is entirely made over to the deity, the worshipper retaining no part for his own use, is prominent among piacular sacrifices, and may even be regarded as the piacular sacrifice *par excellence*. In the later forms of Syrian heathenism the sacrificial meal practically disappears, and almost the whole altar service consists of piacular holocausts,[1] and among the Jews the highest sin-offerings, whose blood was brought into the inner sanctuary, were wholly consumed, but not upon the altar,[2] while the flesh of other sin-offerings was at least withdrawn from the offerer and eaten by the priests.

We have seen, however, that a different and profounder conception of atonement, as the creation of a life-bond between the worshipper and his god, appears in the most primitive type of Semitic sacrifices, and that traces of it can still be found in many parts of the later ritual. Forms of consecration and atonement in which the blood of the victim is applied to the worshipper, or the blood of the worshipper conveyed to the symbol of godhead, occur in all stages of heathen religion, not only among the Semites but among the Greeks and other races; and even on *à priori* grounds it seems probable that when the Northern Semites,

[1] That the Harranians never ate sacrificial flesh seems to be an exaggeration, but one based on the prevalent character of their ritual; see Chwolsohn ii. 89 *sq.*

[2] Lev. vi. 23 (30), xvi. 27, iv. 11, 20.

in the distress and terror produced by the political convulsions of the seventh century, began to cast about for rites of extraordinary potency to conjure the anger of the gods, they were guided by the principle that ancient and half obsolete forms of ritual are more efficacious than the everyday practices of religion.

Further, it is to be observed that in the Hebrew ritual both of the holocaust and of the sin-offering, the victim is slain at the altar "before Jehovah," a phrase which is wanting in the rule about ordinary sacrifices, and implies that the act of slaughter and the effusion of the blood beside the altar have a special significance, as in the ancient Arabian ritual. Moreover, in the sin-offering there is still—although in a very attenuated form—a trace of the manward application of the blood, when the priest dips his finger in it, and so applies it to the horns of the altar, instead of merely dashing it against the sides of the altar from a bowl;[1] and also, as regards the destination of the flesh, which is eaten by the priests in the holy place, it is clear from Lev. x. 17 that the flesh is given to the priests because they minister as the representatives of the sinful people, and that the act of eating it is an essential part of the ceremony, exactly as in the old ritual of communion. In fact the law expressly recognises that the flesh and blood of the sin-offering is a sanctifying medium of extraordinary potency; whosoever touches the flesh becomes holy, the garment on which the blood falls must be washed in a holy place, and even the vessel in which the flesh is sodden must be broken or scoured to remove the infection of its sanctity.[2] That this is the reason why none but the priests are allowed

[1] Lev. iv. 6, 17, 34, compared with chap. iii. 2. זרק is to sprinkle or dash from the bowl, מזרק

[2] Lev. vi. 20 (27).

to eat of it has been rightly discerned by Ewald;[1] the flesh, like the sacramental cup in the Roman Catholic Church, was too sacred to be touched by the laity. Thus the Levitical sin-offering is essentially identical with the ancient sacrament of communion in a sacred life; only the communion is restricted to the priests, in accordance with the general principle of the priestly legislation, which surrounds the holy things of Israël by fence within fence, and makes all access to God pass through the mediation of the priesthood.

I am not aware that anything quite parallel to the ordinary Hebrew sin-offering occurs among the other Semites; and indeed no other Semitic religion appears to have developed to the same extent the doctrine of the consuming holiness of God, and the consequent need for priestly intervention between the laity and the most holy things. But among the Romans the flesh of certain piacula was eaten by the priests, and in the piacular sacrifice of the Arval Brothers the ministrants also partook of the blood.[2] Among the Greeks, again, piacular victims —like the highest forms of the Hebrew sin-offering— were not eaten at all, but either burned, or buried, or cast into the sea, or carried up into some desert mountain far from the foot of man.[3] It is commonly supposed that this was done because they were unclean, being laden with the sins of the guilty worshippers; but this explanation is excluded, not only by the analogy of the Hebrew sin-offering, which is a *códesh codashīm*, or holy thing of the first class, but by various indications in Greek myth and ritual. For to the Greeks earth and sea are not impure but holy, and at Trœzen a sacred laurel was

[1] *Alterthümer*, 3rd ed., p. 87 *sq.*; cf. the Syrian fish-sacrifices of which only the priests partook, *supra*, p. 293.

[2] Marquardt, *Sacralwesen*, p. 185; Servius on Æn. iii. 231.

[3] Hippocrates, ed. Littré, vi. 362.

believed to have grown from the buried carcase of the victim used in the atonement for Orestes.[1] Further, the favourite piacular victims were sacred animals, *e.g.* the swine of Demeter and the dog of Hecate, and the essential part of the lustration consisted in the application of the blood of the offering to the guilty person, which is only intelligible if the victim was a holy sacrament. The blood was indeed too holy to be left in permanent contact with a man who was presently to return to common life, and therefore it was washed off again with water.[2] According to Porphyry, the man who touched a sacrifice designed to avert the anger of the gods was required to bathe and wash his clothes in running water before entering the city or his house,[3] an ordinance which recurs in the case of such Hebrew sin-offerings as were not eaten, and of the red heifer whose ashes were used in lustrations. These were burnt "without the camp," and both the ministrant priest and the man who disposed of the body had to bathe and wash their clothes exactly as in the Greek ritual.[4]

From all this it would appear that the sin-offering and other forms of piacula, including the holocaust, in which there is no sacrificial meal of which the sacrificer himself partakes, are yet lineally descended from the ancient ritual of sacrificial communion between the worshippers and their god, and at bottom rest on the same principle with those ordinary sacrifices in which the sacrificial meal played a chief part. But the development of this part of our

[1] Pausanias, ii. 31. 8.

[2] Apoll. Rhod., *Argon.* iv. 702 *sqq.* Cf. Schoemann, *Gr. Alterth.* II. v. 13.

[3] *De Abst.* ii. 44.

[4] Lev. xvi. 24, 28 ; Num. xix. 7–10. In the *Fihrist*, p. 319, l. 12, after it has been explained that the sacrifices of the Harranians were not eaten but burned, it is added, "and the temple is not entered on that day."

subject must be reserved for another lecture, in which I will try to explain how the original form of sacrifice came to be differentiated into two distinct types of worship, and gave rise on the one hand to the "honorific" or ordinary, and on the other to the "piacular" or exceptional sacrifices of later times.

LECTURE X

THE DEVELOPMENT OF SACRIFICIAL RITUAL—FIRE-SACRIFICES AND PIACULA

WE have come to see that the sin-offering as well as the ordinary sacrificial meal is lineally descended from the primitive sacrifice of communion, in which the victim is a sacred animal that may not ordinarily be killed or used for food. But while in the one case the notion of the special holiness and inviolable character of the victim has gradually faded away, in the other this aspect of the sacrifice has been intensified, till even a religious participation in the flesh is regarded as an impiety. Each of these opposite processes can to a certain extent be traced from stage to stage. As regards the sacrificial meal, we find, both in the case of Nilus's Saracens and in that of African peoples, with whom the ox has a sanctity similar to that which the Arabs ascribed to the camel, that the sacramental flesh begins to be eaten as food under the pressure of necessity; and when this is done, it also begins to be cooked like other food. Then we have the stage, represented by the early Hebrew religion, in which domestic animals are freely eaten, but only on condition that they are presented as sacrifices at the altar and consumed in a sacred feast. And, finally, a stage is reached in which, as in Greece in the time of the Apostle Paul, sacrificial meat is freely sold in the shambles, or, as in Arabia before Mohammed, nothing more is required than that the beast designed for food shall be slain in the name of a god. In piacular sacrifices, on the other hand, we find, in a variety of expressions, a struggle between the feeling that the victim is too holy to be eaten or even touched, and the principle that its atoning efficacy depends on the participation of the worshippers in its life, flesh and blood. In one rite the flesh may be eaten, or the blood drunk, but only by consecrated priests; in another, the flesh is burned, but the blood is poured on the hands or body of the sinner; in another, the lustration is effected with the ashes of the victim (the red heifer of the Jewish law); or, finally, it is enough that the worshipper should lay his hands on the head of the victim before its slaughter, and that then its life-blood should be presented at the altar.

The reasons for the gradual degradation of ordinary sacrifice are not far to seek; they are to be found, on the one hand, in the general causes which make it impossible for men above the state of savagery to retain a literal faith in the consanguinity of animal kinds with gods and men, and, on the other hand, in the pressure of hunger, and afterwards in the taste for animal food, which in a settled country could not generally be gratified except by eating domestic animals. But it is not so easy to understand, *first*, why in spite of these influences certain sacrifices retained their old sacrosanct character, and in many cases became so holy that men were forbidden to touch or eat of them at all; and, *second*, why it is to this particular class of sacrifices that a special piacular efficacy is assigned.

In looking further into this matter, we must distinguish between the sacred domestic animals of pastoral tribes—the milk-givers, whose kinship with men rests on the principle of fosterage—and those other sacred animals of wild or half-domesticated kinds, such as the dove and the swine, which even in the later days of Semitic heathenism were surrounded by strict taboos, and looked upon as in some sense partakers of a divine nature. The latter are undoubtedly the older class of sacred beings; for observation of savage life in all parts of the world shows that the belief in sacred animals, akin to families of men, attains its highest development in tribes which have not yet learned to breed cattle and live on their milk. Totemism pure and simple has its home among races like the Australians and the North American Indians, and seems always to lose ground after the introduction of pastoral life. It would appear that the notion of kinship with milk-giving animals through fosterage has been one of the most powerful agencies in breaking up the old totem-religions, just as a systematic practice of adoption between men was a potent agency in breaking up the old exclusive system of clans. As the various totem clans began to breed cattle and live on their milk, they transferred to their herds the notions of sanctity and kinship which formerly belonged to species of wild animals, and thus the way was at once opened for the formation of religious and political communities larger than the old totem kins. In almost all ancient nations in the pastoral and agricultural stage, the chief associations of the great deities are with the milk-giving animals; and it is these animals, the ox, the sheep, the goat, or in Arabia the camel, that appear as victims in the public and national worship. But experience shows that primitive religious beliefs are practically indestructible, except by the destruction of the race in which they are ingrained, and thus we find that the new ideas of what I may call pastoral religion overlaid the old notions, but did not extinguish them. For example, the Astarte of the Northern Semites is essentially a goddess of flocks and herds, whose symbol and sacred animal is the cow, or (among the sheep-rearing tribes of the Syro-

Arabian desert) the ewe.[1] But this pastoral worship appears to have come on the top of certain older faiths, in which the goddess of one kindred of men was associated with fish, and that of another kindred with the dove. These creatures, accordingly, though no longer prominent in ritual, were still held sacred and surrounded by taboos, implying that they were of divine nature and akin to the goddess herself. The very fact that they were not regularly sacrificed, and therefore not regularly eaten even in religious feasts, tended to preserve their antique sanctity long after the sacrificial flesh of beeves and sheep had sunk almost to the rank of ordinary food; and thus, as we have seen in considering the case of the mystic sacrifices of the Roman Empire, the rare and exceptional rites, in which the victim was chosen from a class of animals ordinarily tabooed as human food, retained even in later paganism a sacramental significance, almost absolutely identical with that which belonged to the oldest sacrifices. It was still felt that the victim was of a divine kind, and that, in partaking of its flesh and blood, the worshippers enjoyed a veritable communion with the divine life. That to such sacrifices there was ascribed a special cathartic and consecrating virtue requires no explanation, for how can the impurity of sin be better expelled than by a draught of sacred life? and how can man be brought nearer to his god than by physically absorbing a particle of the divine nature?

It is, however, to be noted that piacula of this kind, in which atonement is effected by the use of an exceptional victim of sacred kind, do not rise into prominence till the national religions of the Semites fall into decay. The public piacular sacrifices of the independent Semitic states appear, so far as our scanty information goes, to

[1] *Supra*, p. 310.

have been mainly drawn from the same kinds of domestic animals as supplied the ordinary sacrifices, except where an exceptional emergency demanded a human victim. Among the Hebrews, in particular, there is no trace of anything answering to the later mystic sacrifices up to the time of the captivity. At this epoch, when the national religion appeared to have utterly broken down, and the judgment of those who were not upheld by the faith of the prophets was that "Jehovah had forsaken His land,"[1] all manner of strange sacrifices of unclean creatures—the swine, the dog, the mouse and other vermin—began to become popular, and were deemed to have a peculiar purifying and consecrating power.[2] The creatures chosen for these sacrifices are such as were unclean in the first degree, and surrounded by strong taboos of the kind which in heathenism imply that the animal is regarded as divine; and in fact the sacrifices of vermin described in the Book of Isaiah have their counterpart in the contemporary worship of all kinds of vermin described by Ezekiel.[3] Both rites are evidently part of a single superstition, the sacrifice being a mystical communion in the body and blood of a divine animal. Here, therefore, we have a clear case of the re-emergence into the light of day of a cult of the most primitive totem type, which had been banished for centuries from public religion, but must have been kept alive in obscure circles of private or local superstition, and sprang up again on the ruins of the national faith, like some noxious weed in the courts of a deserted temple. But while the ritual and its interpretation are still quite primitive, the resuscitated totem mysteries have this great difference from their ancient

[1] Ezek. viii. 12.
[2] Isa. lxv. 3 *sqq.*, lxvi. 3, 17; see above, p. 291 *sq.*, p. 343, note 3.
[3] Ezek. viii. 10.

models, that they are no longer the exclusive possession of particular kins, but are practised, by men who desert the religion of their birth, as means of initiation into a new religious brotherhood, no longer based on natural kinship, but on mystical participation in the divine life held forth in the sacramental sacrifice. From this point of view the obscure rites described by the prophets have a vastly greater importance than has been commonly recognised; they mark the first appearance in Semitic history of the tendency to found religious societies on voluntary association and mystic initiation, instead of natural kinship and nationality. This tendency was not confined to the Hebrews, nor did it reach its chief development among them. The causes which produced a resuscitation of obsolete mysteries among the Jews were at work at the same period among all the Northern Semites; for everywhere the old national deities had shown themselves powerless to resist the gods of Assyria and Babylon. And among these nations the tendency to fall back for help on primitive superstitions was not held in check, as it was among the Hebrews, by the counter-influence of the Prophets and the Law. From this period, therefore, we may date with great probability the first rise of the mystical cults which played so large a part in the later developments of ancient paganism, and spread their influence over the whole Græco-Roman world. Most of these cults appear to have begun among the Northern Semites, or in the parts of Asia Minor that fell under the empire of the Assyrians and Babylonians. The leading feature that distinguishes them from the old public cults with which they entered into competition, is that they were not based on the principle of nationality, but sought recruits from men of every race who were willing to accept initiation through the mystic sacraments; and in pursuance of this object they carried on a missionary propaganda in all parts of the Roman Empire, in a way quite alien to the spirit of national religion. The nature of their sacramental sacrifices, so far as it is known to us, indicates that they were of a like origin with the Hebrew superstitions described by Isaiah; they used strange victims, invoked the gods by animal names, and taught the initiated to acknowledge kinship with the same animals.[1] To pursue this subject further would carry us beyond the limits of our present task; for a full discussion of mystical sacrifices cannot be confined to the Semitic field. These sacrifices, as we have seen, lie aside from the main development of the national religions of the Semites, and they acquire public importance only after the collapse of the national systems. In later times they were much sought after, and were held to have a peculiar efficacy in purging away sin, and bringing man into living union with the gods. But their atoning efficacy proceeds on quite different lines from that of the recognised piacular rites of national religion. In the latter the sinner seeks reconciliation with the national god whom he has offended, but in mystic religion he takes refuge from the divine wrath by incorporating himself in a new religious community. Something of the same kind takes place in more primitive society, when an outlaw, who has been banished from the social and religious fellowship of his clan for shedding kindred blood, is received by the covenant of adoption into another clan. Here also the act of adoption, which is a religious as well as a civil rite, is in so far an act of atonement, that the outlaw has again a god to receive his worship and his prayers; but he is not reconciled to the god of his former worship, for it is only in a somewhat advanced stage of polytheism that acceptance by one

[1] Porph., *De Abst.* iv. 16, compared with *Fihrist*, p. 326, l. 25 *sq.*

god puts a man right with the gods as a whole. Among the Greeks, where the gods formed a sort of family circle, and were accessible to one another's influence, the outlaw, like Orestes, wanders about in exile, till he can find a god willing to receive him and act as his sponsor with the other deities; and here, therefore, as in the mystical rites of the Semites, the ceremony of purification from bloodshed is essentially a ceremony of initiation into the cult of some god who, like the Apollo of Trœzen, makes it his business to receive suppliants. But among the older Semites there was no kinship or friendship between the gods of adjacent tribes or nations, and there was no way of reconciliation with the national god through the mediation of a third party, so that all atoning sacrifices were necessarily offered to the national god himself, and drawn, like ordinary sacrifices, from the class of domestic animals appropriated to his worship.

In the oldest stage of pastoral religion, when the tribal herd possessed inviolate sanctity, and every sheep or camel —according as the tribe consisted of shepherds or camelherds—was regarded as a kinsman, there was no occasion and no place for a special class of atoning sacrifices. The relations between the god and his worshippers were naturally as good and intimate as possible, for they were based on the strongest of all ties, the tie of kinship. To secure that this natural good understanding should continue unimpaired, it was only necessary that the congenital bond of kinship should not wear out, but continue strong and fresh. And this was provided for by periodical sacrifices, of the type described by Nilus, in which a particle of the sacred life of the tribe was distributed, between the god and his worshippers, in the sacramental flesh and blood of an animal of the holy stock of the clan. To make the sacrifice effective, it was only necessary that the victim should be perfect and without fault—a point which is strongly insisted upon in all ancient sacrifice—*i.e.*, that the sacred life should be completely and normally embodied in it. In the later ages of antiquity there was a very general belief—the origin of which will be explained as we proceed—that in strictness the oldest rituals demanded a human victim, and that animal sacrifices were substitutes for the life of a man. But in the oldest times there could be no reason for thinking a man's life better than that of a camel or a sheep as a vehicle of sacramental communion; indeed, if we may judge from modern examples of that primitive habit of thought which lies at the root of Semitic sacrifice, the animal life would probably be deemed purer and more perfect than that of man.

On the other hand, there is every reason to think that even at this early stage certain impious crimes, notably murder within the kin, were expiated by the death of the offender. But the death of such a criminal cannot with any justice be called a sacrifice. Its object was simply to eliminate the impious person from the society whose sanctity he had violated, and outlawry was accepted as an alternative to execution.

As time went on, the idea of the full kinship of men with their cattle began to break down. The Saracens of Nilus killed and ate their camels in time of hunger, but we may be sure that they would not in similar circumstances have eaten one another. Thus even in a society where the flesh of the tribal camel was not ordinary food, and where private slaughter was forbidden, a camel's life was no longer as sacred as that of a man; it had begun to be recognised that human life, or rather the life of a tribesman, was a thing of unique sanctity. At the same time the old forms of sacrifice were retained, and the tradition of their old meaning cannot have been lost, for the ritual forms were too plainly significant to be misinterpreted. In short, the life of a camel, which no longer had the full value of a tribesman's life for ordinary purposes, was treated as a tribesman's life when it was presented at the altar; so that here we have already a beginning of the idea that the victim *quâ* victim possesses a sacrosanct character which does not belong to it merely in virtue of its natural kind. But now also, let it be noted, it is expressly attested that the sacrificial camel is regarded as the substitute for a human victim. The favourite victims of the Saracens were young and beautiful captives,[1] but if these were not to be had they contented themselves with a white and faultless camel. As to the veracity of this account there is no question: Nilus's own son, Theodulus, when a captive in the hands of these barbarians, escaped being sacrificed only by the accident that, on the appointed morning, his captors did not awake till the sun rose, and the lawful hour for the rite was past; and there are well-authenticated instances of the sacrifice of captives to Al-ʿOzzā by the Lakhmite king of Al-Ḥīra at least a century later.[2]

It is true that in these cases the victims are aliens and not tribesmen, as in strictness the sense of the ritual requires; but the older Semites, when they had recourse to human sacrifice, were more strictly logical, and held with rigour to the fundamental principle that the life of the victim must be a kindred life.[3] The modification accepted

[1] The sacrifice of choice captives occurs also among the Carthaginians (Diod. xx. 65), and perhaps a trace of the same thing appears among the Hebrews in the slaying of Agag "before the LORD, at the sanctuary of Gilgal" (1 Sam. xv. 33).

[2] Nöldeke's *Tabari*, p. 171 (Procop., *Pers.* ii. 28; Land, *Anecd.* iii. 247); Isaac of Antioch, i. 220.

[3] See, for the Hebrews, Gen. xxii.; 2 Kings xxi. 6; Micah vi. 7: for the Moabites, 2 Kings iii. 27: for the Phœnicians, Philo Byblius in *Fr. Hist.*

by the Saracens was one for which there was the strongest motive, and accordingly all over the world we find cases of human sacrifice in which an alien is substituted for a tribesman. This was not done in accordance with any change in the meaning of the ritual, for originally the substitution was felt to be a fraud on the deity; thus Diodorus tells us that the Carthaginians, in a time of trouble, felt that their god was angry because slave boys had been privily substituted for the children of their best families; and elsewhere we find that it is considered necessary to make believe that the victim is a tribesman, or even, as in the human sacrifices of the Mexicans, to dress and treat him as the representative of the deity to whom he is to be offered. Perhaps something of this kind was in the mind of Nilus's Saracens when they drank with prisoners destined to death, and so admitted them to boon fellowship.[1]

Gr. iii. 570 (Eus., *Pr. Ev.* 156 D); Porph., *De Abst.* ii. 56: for the Carthaginians, Porph., *ibid.* ii. 27; Diodorus, xx. 14; Plutarch, *De Superst.* 13: for the Syrians, *Dea Syr.* lviii.; Lampridius, *Vita Heliog.* 8, "pueri nobiles et decori . . . patrimi et matrimi": for the Babylonians, 2 Kings xvii. 31. For the Arabs the well-known story of 'Abd al-Moṭṭalib's vow (B. Hish. p. 97), though of doubtful authenticity, may probably be accepted as based on actual custom. Another example of a vow to sacrifice a son is given in Mālik's Mowaṭṭa, Tunis ed., p. 176 (Kremer, *Stud. z. vergl. Culturg.* p. 44).

[1] Nilus, p. 66, where, however, the slaughter is not formally a sacrifice. The narrative represents the offer of drink as mere mockery, but it is difficult to reconcile this with known Arabian custom; see above, p. 270. A more serious attempt to adopt Theodulus into the Saracen community seems to have been made after his providential escape from death; he was invited to eat unclean things and sport with the women (p. 117). The combination is significant, and as μιαροφαγεῖν must refer to the eating of idolatrous meats, presumably camel's flesh,—which Symeon Stylites forbade to his Arab converts,—the question arises whether γυναιξὶ προσπαίζειν has not also a reference to some religious practice, and whether Wellhausen, p. 40, has not been too hasty in supposing that the orgies of the Arabian Venus renounced by the converts just mentioned are mere rhetorical orgies; cf. *Kinship*, p. 295.

It has been suggested to me by an eminent scholar that the sacrifice of choice captives after a victory may be a form of *nacī'a* and properly a thank-offering from the spoil; cf. the slaying of Agag. This is not impossible, for

From a purely abstract point of view it seems plausible enough that the Saracens, who accepted an alien as a substitute for a tribesman, might also accept a camel as a substitute for a man. The plan of substituting an offering which can be more readily procured or better spared, for the more costly victim which traditional ritual demands, was largely applied throughout antiquity, and belongs to the general system of make-believe by which early nations, while entirely governed by regard for precedents, habitually get over difficulties in the strict carrying out of traditional rules. If a Roman rite called for a stag as victim, and a stag could not be had, a sheep was substituted and feigned to be a stag (*cervaria ovis*), and so forth. The thing was really a fraud, but one to which the gods were polite enough to shut their eyes rather than see the whole ceremony fail. But in the particular case before us it is difficult to believe that the camel was substituted for a man, and ultimately for a tribesman. In that case the ritual of the camel-sacrifice would have been copied from human sacrifice, but in reality this was not so. The camel was eaten, but the human victim was burned, after the blood had been poured out as a libation,[1] and there can be no

different ideas often find their embodiment in identical ceremonies; but the case of Jephthah's daughter and the express testimony of Diodorus appear to me to weigh strongly against such a view.

[1] This appears from what we read of the preparations for the sacrifice of Theodulus, among which are mentioned frankincense (the accompaniment of fire-offerings) and a bowl for the libation, p. 110; and, at p. 113, Theodulus prays: "Let not my blood be made a libation to demons, nor let unclean spirits be made glad with the sweet smoke of my flesh." See Wellhausen, p. 113, who conjectures that in Arabia human sacrifices were generally burned, citing Yācūt, iv. 425, who tells that every clan of Rabī'a gave a son to the god Moḥarric, "the burner," at Salmān (in 'Irāc, on the pilgrim road from Cufa). Nöldeke, in *ZDMG.* xli. 712, doubts whether the reference is to human sacrifice; for Yācūt (*i.e.* Ibn al-Kalbī) presently cites examples of men of different clans called "sons of Moḥarric," which may imply that the sons were not sacrificed, but consecrated as children of the god. This,

question that the former is the more primitive rite. I apprehend, therefore, that human sacrifice is not more ancient than the sacrifice of sacred animals, and that the prevalent belief of ancient heathenism, that animal victims are an imperfect substitute for a human life, arose by a false inference from traditional forms of ritual that had ceased to be understood. In the oldest rituals the victim's life is manifestly treated as sacred, and in some rites, as we have seen in our examination of the Attic *Buphonia*, the idea that the slaughter is really a murder, *i.e.* a shedding of kindred blood, was expressed down to quite a late date. When the full kinship of animals with men was no longer recognised in ordinary life, all this became unintelligible, and was explained by the doctrine that at the altar the victim took the place of a man.

This doctrine appears all over the ancient world in connection with atoning sacrifices, and indeed the false inference on which it rests was one that could not fail to be drawn wherever the old forms of sacrifice had been shaped at a time when cattle were revered as kindred

however, is so peculiar an institution for Arabia that it still remains probable that the consecration was a substitute for sacrifice. At Salmān, in the neighbourhood of Al-Ḥīra, we are in the region of the human sacrifices of the Lakhmite kings. And these were probably burnt-offerings; cf. the legend of the holocaust of one hundred prisoners by 'Amr b. Hind, *Kāmil*, p. 97; *Agh.* xix. 129. Hence this king is said to have been called Moḥarric, or, according to another tradition, because he burned Yemāma (Mofaḍḍal al-Ḍabbī, *Amthāl*, p. 68); but, as Nöldeke observes (*Ghassan. Fürsten* [1887], p. 7), Moḥarric without the article is hardly a mere epithet (*lacab*), and I apprehend that the Lakhmite family was called "the family of Moḥarric" after their god, presumably Lucifer, the morning star, who afterwards became feminine as al-'Ozzā (*supra*, p. 56, note 3). The Ghassanid princes of the house of Jafna were also called "the family of Moḥarric," Ibn Cot. p. 314; Ibn Dor. p. 259, and here the tradition is that their ancestor was the first Arab who burned his enemies in their encampment. This, however, is obviously a form of *ḥérem*, and must, I take it, be a religious act. For the "family" (*āl*) of a god, as meaning his worshippers, see *Kinship*, p. 258.

beings. And this appears to have been the case in the beginnings of every pastoral society. Accordingly, to cite but a few instances, the notion that animal sacrifice is accepted in lieu of an older sacrifice of the life of a man appears among the Hebrews, in the story of Isaac's sacrifice,[1] among the Phœnicians,[2] among the Egyptians, where the victim was marked with a seal bearing the image of a man bound, and with a sword at his throat,[3] and also among the Greeks, the Romans, and many other nations.[4] As soon, however, as it came to be held that cattle were merely substitutes, and that the full sense of the sacrifice was not brought out without an actual human victim, it was naturally inferred that the original form of offering was more potent, and was indicated on all occasions of special gravity. Wherever we find the doctrine of substitution of animal life for that of man, we find also examples of actual human sacrifice, sometimes confined to seasons of extreme peril, and sometimes practised periodically at solemn annual rites.[5]

[1] Gen. xxii. 13; cf. Lev. xvii. 11.

[2] Porph., *De Abst.* iv. 15.

[3] Plut., *Is. et Os.* xxxi. According to Wiedemann, *Herodots Zweites Buch*, p. 182, these symbols are simply the hieroglyphic determinant of the word *sema*, "slay."

[4] See the examples in Porph., *De Abst.* ii. 54 *sqq.*, and for the Romans, Ovid, *Fasti*, vi. 162. We have had before us Greek rites where the victim is disguised as a man; but conversely human sacrifices are often dressed up as animals, or said to represent animals: an example, from the worship at Hierapolis-Bambyce, is found in *Dea Syria*, lviii., where fathers sacrificing their children say that they are not children but beeves.

[5] Examples of human sacrifices, many of which subsisted within the Roman Empire down to the time of Hadrian, are collected by Porphyry, *ut supra*, on whom Eusebius, *Præp. Ev.* iv. 16, *Laus Const.* xiii. 7, depends. See also Clem. Alex., *Coh. ad Gentes*, p. 27 (p. 36, Potter); cf. Hermann, *Gr. Alth.* ii. § 27. In what follows I confine myself to the Semites; it may therefore be noted that, in antiquity generally, human victims were buried, burned, or cast into the sea or into a river (cf. Mannhardt's essay on the Lityerses legend). Yet indications survive that they were originally sacrifices of communion, and as such were tasted by the worshippers: notably in the most famous case of all, the human sacrifice offered in Arcadia to Zeus Lycæus—the wolf-god—where a fragment of the *exta* was

I apprehend that this is the point from which the special development of piacular sacrifices, and the distinction between them and ordinary sacrifices, takes its start. It was impossible that the sacrificial customs should continue unmodified where the victim was held to represent a man and a tribesman, for even savages commonly refuse to eat their own kinsfolk, and to growing civilisation the idea that the gods had ordained meals of human flesh, or of flesh that was as sacred as that of a man, was too repulsive to be long retained. But when I say "repulsive," I put the matter rather in the light in which it appears to us, than in that wherein it presented itself to the first men who had scruples about cannibalism. Primarily the horror of eating human flesh was no doubt superstitious; it was felt to be dangerous to eat so sacrosanct a thing, even with all the precautions of religious ceremonial. Accordingly, in human sacrifices, and also in such other offerings as continued to be performed with a ritual simulating human sacrifice, the sacrificial meal tended to fall out of use; while, on the other hand, where the sacrificial meal was retained, the tendency was to drop such features in the ritual as suggested the disgusting idea of cannibalism.[1] And so the apparent paradox is explained, that precisely in those sacrifices in which the victim most fully retained its original theanthropic character, and was therefore most efficacious as a vehicle of atonement, the primitive idea of

placed among the portions of sacrificial flesh derived from other victims that were offered along with the human sacrifice, and the man who tasted it was believed to become a were-wolf (Plato, *Rep.* viii. 15, p. 565 D; Pausanias, viii. 2).

Of the human sacrifices of rude peoples those of the Mexicans are perhaps the most instructive, for in them the theanthropic character of the victim comes out most clearly.

[1] Of course neither tendency was consistently carried out in every detail of ritual; there remains enough that is common to honorific and piacular sacrifice to enable us to trace them back to a common source.

atonement by communion in the sacred flesh and blood was most completely disguised. The modifications in the form of ritual that ensued when sacrifices of a certain class were no longer eaten, can be best observed by taking the case of actual human sacrifice and noting how other sacrifices of equivalent significance follow its model.

Whether the custom of actually eating the flesh survived in historical times in any case of human sacrifice is more than doubtful,[1] and even in the case of animal piacula—apart from those of mystic type, in which the idea of initiation into a new religion was involved—the sacrificial meal is generally wanting or confined to the priests. The custom of drinking the blood, or at least of sprinkling it on the worshippers, may have been kept up longer; there is some probability that it was observed in the human sacrifices of Nilus's Saracens;[2] and the common Arabian

[1] According to Mohammedan accounts, the Harranians in the Middle Ages annually sacrificed an infant, and, boiling down its flesh, baked it into cakes, of which only freeborn men were allowed to partake (*Fihrist*, p. 323, l. 6 *sqq.*; cf. Chwolsohn's *Excursus on Human Sacrifice*, vol. ii. p. 142). But in regard to the secret mysteries of a forbidden religion, such as Syrian heathenism was in Arabian times, it is always doubtful how far we can trust a hostile narrator, who, even if he did not merely reproduce popular fictions, might easily take for a real human sacrifice what was only the mystic offering of a theanthropic animal. The new-born infant corresponds to the Arabian *fara'*, offered while its flesh was still like glue, and to the Hebrew piaculum of a sucking lamb in 1 Sam. vii. 9.

[2] The reason for thinking this is that on the Arabian mode of sacrifice a bowl was not required to convey the blood to the deity, while it would be necessary if the blood was drunk by the worshippers or sprinkled upon them. It is true that the narrative speaks also of the preparation of a libation,—whether of water or of wine does not appear,—but this in the Arabian ritual can hardly be more than a vehicle for the more potent blood, just as the blood was mixed with water in Greek sacrifices to heroes. Water as a vehicle for sacrificial ashes appears in the Hebrew ritual of the red heifer (Num. xix. 9), and is prescribed as a vehicle for the blood of lustration in Lev. xiv. 5 *sq.* In the legends cited in the next note we find the notion that if the blood of a human victim touches the ground, vengeance will be taken for it. That the drinking of human blood, *e.g.* from an enemy slain in battle, was a Saracen practice, is attested by Ammianus and Procopius

belief that the blood of kings, and perhaps also of other men of noble descent, is a cure for hydrophobia and demoniacal possession, seems to be a reminiscence of blood-drinking in connection with human sacrifice, for the Greeks in like manner, who ascribed epilepsy to demoniacal possession, sought to cure it by piacular offerings and purifications with blood.[1]

When the sacrosanct victim ceased to be eaten, it was necessary to find some other way of disposing of its flesh. It will be remembered that, in the sacrificial meals of Nilus's Saracens, it was a point of religion that the whole carcase should be consumed before the sun rose; the victim was so holy that no part of it could be treated as mere waste. The problem of disposing of the sacred carcase was in fact analogous to that which occurs whenever a kinsman dies. Here, too, the point is to find a way of dealing with the body consistent with the respect due to the dead—a respect which does not rest on sentimental grounds, but on the belief that the corpse is taboo, a source

(see *Kinship*, p. 284 *sqq.*); and the anecdote given by Wellh. p. 120, from *Agh.* xii. 144, where a husband, unable to save his wife from the enemy, kills her, anoints himself with her blood, and fights till he is slain, illustrates the significance which the Arabs attached to human blood as a vehicle of communion.

[1] Hippocrates, ed. Littré, vi. 362. The evidence for this Arabian superstition is collected by Freytag in his notes to the *Ḥamāsa*, ii. 583, and by Wellh. p. 142. It consists in poetical and proverbial allusions, to which may be added a verse in Mas'ūdī, iii. 193, and in a legend from the mythical story of Queen Zabbā (*Agh.* xiv. 74; Ṭabari, i. 760; Maidānī, i. 205 *sqq.*), where a king is slain by opening the veins of his arms, and the blood, to be used as a magical medicine, is gathered in a bowl. Not a drop must fall on the ground, otherwise there will be blood-revenge for it. I cannot but suspect that the legend is based on an old form of sacrifice applied to captive chiefs (cf. the case of Agag); it is described as the habitual way of killing kings; cf. *Agh.* xv. 75. 4, where 'Abd Yaghūth is killed by opening his veins. The rule that not a drop of the blood must fall on the ground appears also in Caffre sacrifice; Maclean, *Caffre Laws*, p. 81. According to later authorities, cited in the *Tāj al-'Arūs* (i. 3. 181 of the old edition), it was enough for this cure to draw a drop of blood from the finger of a noble, and drink it mixed with water.

of very dangerous supernatural influences of an infectious kind. In later times this infectiousness is expressed as uncleanness; but in the primitive taboo, as we know, sanctity and uncleanness meet and are indistinguishable. Now, as regards the kindred dead generally, we find a great range of funeral customs, all directed to make sure that the corpse is properly disposed of, and can no longer be a source of danger to the living, but rather of blessing.[1] In certain cases it is the duty of the survivors to eat up their dead, just as in Nilus's sacrifice. This was the use of the Issedones, according to Herodotus (iv. 26). At other times the dead are thrown outside the kraal, to be eaten by wild beasts (Masai land), or are deposited in a desert place which men must not approach; but more commonly the body is buried or burned. All these practices reappear in the case of such sacrifices as may not be eaten. Mere exposure on the soil of the sanctuary was perhaps the use in certain Arabian cults;[2] but this, it is plain, could not suffice unless the sacred enclosure was an adyton forbidden to the foot of man. Hence at Duma the annual human victim is buried at the foot of the altar idol,[3] and elsewhere, perhaps, the corpse is hung up between earth and heaven before the deity.[4] Or else the sacrosanct flesh is carried

[1] This subject has been fully handled by Mr. J. G. Frazer in *Journ. Anthrop. Inst.* xv. 64 *sqq.*, to which I refer for details. I think Mr. Frazer goes too far in supposing that mere fear of ghosts rules in all these observances. Not seldom we find also a desire for continued fellowship with the dead, under such conditions as make the fellowship free from danger. In the language of physics, sanctity is a *polar* force, it both attracts and repels.

[2] *Supra*, p. 225 *sqq.*

[3] Porph., *De Abst.* ii. 56. In old Arabia little girls were often buried alive by their fathers, apparently as sacrifices to the goddesses; see *Kinship*, p. 281. A similar form of human sacrifice probably lies at the root of the legend about the tombs of the lovers whom Semiramis buried alive (Syncellus, i. 119, from John of Antioch), for though these lovers are gods, all myths of the death of gods seem to be derived from sacrifices of theanthropic victims.

[4] Deut. xxi. 21; cf. 1 Sam. xxxi. 10. The execution of criminals con-

away into a desert place in the mountains, as was done in the Greek piacula of which Hippocrates speaks, or is simply flung down (a precipice) from the vestibule of the temple, as was the use of Hierapolis.[1] Among the Hebrews, on the same principle, the heifer offered in atonement for an untraced murder was sacrificed by breaking (or, perhaps, severing) its neck in a barren ravine.[2]

Most commonly, however, human sacrifices, and in general all such sacrifices as were not eaten, were burned; and this usage is found not only among the Hebrews and Phœnicians, with whom fire-sacrifices were common, but among the Arabs, who seem to have admitted the fire-offering in no other case. In the more advanced rituals the use of fire corresponds with the conception of the gods as subtle beings, moving in the air, whose proper nourishment is the fragrant smoke of the burning flesh, so that the burnt-offering, like the fat of the vitals in ordinary victims, is the food of the gods, and falls under the head of sacrificial gifts. But in the Levitical ritual this explanation is sedulously excluded in the case of the sin-offering; the fat is burned on the altar, but the rest of the flesh, so far as it is not eaten by the priests, is burned outside the camp, *i.e.* outside the walls of Jerusalem, so that in fact the burning is merely an additional precaution added to

stantly assumes sacrificial forms, for the tribesman's life is sacred even if he be a criminal, and he must not be killed in a common way. This principle is finally extended to all religious executions, in which, as the Hebrews and Moabites say, the victim is devoted, as a *ḥerem*, to the god (Stele of Mesha, l. 17). In one peculiar sacrifice at Hierapolis (*Dea Syr.* xlix.) the victims were suspended alive from trees, and the trees were then set on fire. The fire is perhaps a later addition, and the original rite may have consisted in suspension alone. The story of a human victim hung up in the temple at Carrhæ by the Emperor Julian (Theod., *H. E.* iii. 21), and the similar stories in the Syriac Julian-romances (ed. Hoffm. p. 247, etc.), are too apocryphal to be used, though they probably reflect some obsolete popular superstition.

[1] *Dea Syria*, lviii.

[2] Deut. xxi. 4.

the older rule that the sacred flesh must not be left exposed to human contact. Now the Levitical sin-offering is only a special development of the old piacular holocaust, and thus the question at once suggests itself whether in its first origin the holocaust was a subtle way of conveying a gift of food to the god; or whether rather the victim was burned, because it was too sacred to be eaten and yet must not be left undisposed of. In the case of the Arabian holocaust, which is confined to human victims, this is certainly the easiest explanation; and even among the Hebrews and their neighbours it would seem that human sacrifices were not ordinarily burned on the altar or even within the precincts of the sanctuary, but rather outside the city. It is plain from various passages of the prophets, that the sacrifices of children among the Jews before the captivity, which are commonly known as sacrifices to Moloch, were regarded by the worshippers as oblations to Jehovah, under the title of king,[1] yet they were not presented at the temple, but consumed outside the town at the Tophet in the ravine below the temple.[2] From Isa. xxx. 33 it appears that Tophet means a pyre, such as is prepared for a king. But the Hebrews themselves did not burn their dead, unless in very exceptional cases,[3] and

[1] Jer. vii. 31, xix. 5, xxxii. 35; Ezek. xxiii. 39; Mic. vi. 7. The form Moloch (LXX.), or rather Molech (Heb.), is nothing but *Melech*, "king," read with the vowels of *bosheth*, "shameful thing"; see Hoffmann in Stade's *Zeitschr.* iii. (1883) p. 124. In Jer. xix. 5 delete עלות לבעל with LXX.

[2] The valley of Hinnom is the Tyropœon; see *Enc. Brit.*, arts. "Jerusalem" and "Temple."

[3] Saul's body was burned (1 Sam. xxxi. 12), possibly to save it from the risk of exhumation by the Philistines, but perhaps rather with a religious intention, and almost as an act of worship, since his bones were buried under the sacred tamarisk at Jabesh. In Amos vi. 10 the victims of a plague are burned, which is to be understood by comparing Lev. xx. 14, xxi. 9; Amos ii. 1, and remembering that plague was a special mark of divine wrath (2 Sam. xxiv.), so that its victims might well be regarded as intensely taboo.

burial was equally the rule among their Phœnician neighbours, as is plain from researches in their cemeteries,[1] and apparently among all the Semites. Thus, when the prophet describes the deep and wide pyre "prepared for the king," he does not draw his figure from ordinary life, nor is it conceivable that he is thinking of the human sacrifices in the valley of Hinnom, a reference which would bring an utterly discordant strain into the imagery. What he does refer to is a rite well known to Semitic religion, which was practised at Tarsus down to the time of Dio Chrysostom, and the memory of which survives in the Greek legend of Heracles-Melcarth,[2] in the story of Sardanapalus, and in the myth of Queen Dido. At Tarsus there was an annual feast at which a very fair pyre was erected, and the local Heracles or Baal burned on it in effigy.[3] This annual commemoration of the death of the god in fire must have its origin in an older rite, in which the victim was not a mere effigy but a theanthropic sacrifice, *i.e.* an actual man or sacred animal, whose life, according to the antique conception now familiar to us, was an embodiment of the divine-human life.

The significance of the death of the god in Semitic religion is a subject on which I must not enter in this connection; we are here concerned with it only in so far as the details, scenic or mythical, of the death of the god throw light on the ritual of human sacrifice. And for

[1] This is true also of Carthage; Tissot, *La Prov. d'Afrique*, i. 612; Justin, xix. 1. But at Hadrumetum in the second century B.C. the dead were burned; see Berger in *Revue archéol.*, Juillet–Décembre, 1889, p. 375.

[2] For the burning of the Tyrian Heracles, cf. *Clem. Recog.* x. 24, where we read that the sepulchre of the god was shown "apud Tyrum, ubi igni crematus est." It is a plausible conjecture, very generally accepted, that in Herod. vii. 167 the legend of the self-immolation of Melcarth has got mixed up with the story of the death of Hamilcar.

[3] See O. Müller, "Sandon und Sardanapal," in *Rhein. Mus.*, Ser. i. Bd. iii.

this purpose it is well to cite also the legend of the death of Dido as it is related by Timæus,[1] where the pyre is erected outside the walls of the palace, *i.e.* of the temple of the goddess, and she leaps into it from the height of the edifice. According to Justin, the pyre stood "at the end of the town"; in fact the sanctuary of Cœlestis, which seems to represent the temple of Dido, stood a little way outside the citadel or original city of Carthage, on lower ground, and, at the beginning of the fourth century of our era, was surrounded by a thorny jungle, which the popular imagination pictured as inhabited by asps and dragons, the guardians of the sanctuary.[2] It can hardly be doubted that the spot at which legend placed the self-sacrifice of Dido to her husband Sicharbas was that at which the later Carthaginian human sacrifices were performed.[3]

We have therefore a series of examples all pointing to human sacrifice beneath and outside the city. At Hierapolis the victims are cast down from the temple, but we do not read that they are burned; at Jerusalem they are burned in the ravine below the temple, but not cast down. At Carthage the two rites meet, the sacrifice is outside the city and outside the walls of the temple; but the divine victim leaps into the pyre, and later victims, as Diodorus tells us,[4] were allowed to roll into a fiery pit from a sort of scaffold in the shape of an image of the god with outstretched arms. In this last shape of the rite the object plainly is to free the worshippers from the guilt of

[1] *Fr. Hist. Gr.* i. 197; cf. Justin, xviii. 6. On Dido as identical with Tanith (Tont), ἡ δαίμων τῆς Καρχηδόνος, see the ingenious conjectures of G. Hoffmann, *Phœn. Inschr.* p. 32 *sq.*

[2] Tissot, i. 653. Silius Ital., i. 81 *sqq.*, also describes the temple of Dido as enclosed in a thick grove, and surrounded by awful mystery.

[3] The name Sichar-bas, סכר־בעל, "commemoration of Baal," is not a divine title, but is to be understood from Ex. xx. 24. סכר is the Phœnician form of Heb. זכר.

[4] Diod. xx. 14.

bloodshed; the child was delivered alive to the god, and he committed it to the flames. For the same reason, at the so-called sacrifice of the pyre at Hierapolis, the holocausts were burned alive,[1] and so was the Harranian sacrifice of a bull to the planet Saturn described by Dimashcī.[2] This last sacrifice is the lineal descendant of the older human sacrifices of which we have been speaking; for the Carthaginian Baal or Moloch was identified with Saturn, and at Hierapolis the sacrificed children are called oxen. But in the more ancient Hebrew rite the children offered to Moloch were slaughtered before they were burned.[3] And that the burning is secondary, and was not the original substance of the rite, appears also from the use of Hierapolis, where the sacrifice is simply flung from the temple. So, too, although Dido in Timæus flings herself into the fire, there are other forms of the legend of the sacrifice of a Semite goddess, in which she simply casts herself down into water.[4]

When the burning came to be the essence of the rite, the spot outside the city where it was performed might naturally become itself a sanctuary, though it is plain from the descriptions of the temple of Dido that the sanctuary was of a very peculiar and awful kind, and separated from contact with man in a way not usual in the shrines of ordinary worship. And when this is so, the deity of this awful sanctuary naturally comes to be regarded as a separate divinity, rejoicing in a cult which

[1] *Dea Syria*, xlix. [2] Ed. Mehren, p. 40 (Fr. trans. p. 42).

[3] Ezek. xvi. 20, xxiii. 39; Gen. xxii. 10. The inscriptions in Gesenius, *Mon. Phœn.* p. 448 *sq.*, which have sometimes been cited in this connection, are now known to have nothing to do with human sacrifice.

[4] The Semiramis legend at Hierapolis and Ascalon; the legend of the death of Astarte at Aphaca (Meliton), which must be identified with the falling of the star into the water at the annual feast, just as in another legend Aphrodite after the death of Adonis throws herself from the Leucadian promontory (Ptol., *Nov. Hist.* vii. p. 198, West.).

the other gods abhor. But originally, we see, the human sacrifice is offered to the ordinary god of the community, only it is not consumed on the altar in the sanctuary, but cast down into a ravine outside, or burned outside. This rule appears to be universal, and I may note one or two other instances that confirm it. Mesha burns his son as a holocaust to Chemosh, not at the temple of Chemosh, but on the wall of his beleaguered city;[1] being under blockade, he could not go outside the wall. Again, at Amathus the human sacrifices offered to Jupiter Hospes were sacrificed "before the gates,"[2] and here the Jupiter Hospes of the Roman narrator can be none other than the Amathusian Heracles or Malika, whose name, preserved by Hesychius, identifies him with the Tyrian Melcarth. Or, again, Malalas[3] tells us that the 22nd of May was kept as the anniversary of a virgin sacrificed at the foundation of Antioch, at sunrise, "half-way between the city and the river," and afterwards worshipped like Dido as the Fortune of the town.

All this is so closely parallel to the burning of the flesh of the Hebrew sin-offerings outside the camp, that it seems hardly doubtful that originally, as in the Hebrew sin-offering, the true sacrifice, *i.e.* the shedding of the blood, took place at the temple, and the burning was a distinct act. An intermediate stage is exhibited in the sacrifice of the red heifer, where the whole ceremony takes place outside the camp, but the blood is sprinkled in the direction of the sanctuary (Num. xix. 4). And in support of this view let me press one more point that has come out in our evidence. The human holocaust is not burned on an altar, but on a pyre or fire-pit constructed for the occasion. This appears both in the myths of Dido and Heracles and

[1] 2 Kings iii. 27. [2] Ovid, *Metaph.* x. 224; cf. Movers, i. 408 *sq.*
[3] P. 200 of the Bonn ed.

in actual usage. At Tarsus a very fair pyre is erected yearly for the burning of Heracles; in the Carthaginian sacrifice of boys the victims fall into a pit of flame, and in the Harranian ox-sacrifice the victim is fastened to a grating placed over a vault filled with burning fuel; finally, Isaiah's Tophet is a broad and deep excavation filled with wood exactly like the fiery trench in which, according to Arabic tradition, the victims of 'Amr b. Hind and the martyrs of Nejrān found their end.[1] All these arrangements are totally unlike the old Semitic altar or sacred stone, and are mere developments of the primitive fireplace, made by scooping a hollow in the ground.[2] It appears, then, that in the ritual of human sacrifice, and therefore by necessary inference in the ritual of the holocaust generally, the burning was originally no integral part of the ceremony, and did not take place on the altar or even within the sanctuary, but in a place apart, away from the habitations of man. For human sacrifices and for solemn

[1] *Aghānī*, xix. 129; B. Hishām, p. 24 (Ṭab. i. 925; Sūra, 85, 4 *sqq.*).

[2] It seems to me that תפת is properly an Aramaic name for a fireplace, or for the framework set on the fire to support the victim, which appears in the Harranian sacrifice and, in a modified form, at Carthage. For we are not to think of the brazen Saturn as a shapely statue, but as a development of the dogs of a primitive fireplace. I figure it to myself as a pillar or cone with a rude head and arms, something like the divine symbol so often figured on Carthaginian Tanith cippi. Now the name for the stones on which a pot is set, and then for any stand or tripod set upon a fire, is in Arabic أثفية *Othfiyā*, in Syriac ܛܦܝܐ, *Tfāyā*, of which we might, according to known analogies, have a variant *tfāth*. The corresponding Hebrew word is אַשְׁפֹּת (for *shfāth*), which means an ashpit or dunghill, but primarily must have denoted the fireplace, since the denonominative verb שפת is "to set on a pot." In nomad life the fireplace of one day is the ash-heap of the next. Now, at the time when the word תפת first appears in Hebrew, the chief foreign influence in Judæan religion was that of Damascus (2 Kings xvi.), and there is therefore no improbability in the hypothesis that תפת is an Aramaic word. The pronunciation *tofeth* is quite precarious, for LXX. has ταφεθ, and the Massorets seem to have given the loathsome thing the points of *bosheth*.

piacula this rule continued to be observed even to a late date, but for ordinary animal holocausts the custom of burning the flesh in the court of the sanctuary must have established itself pretty early. Thus, as regards the Hebrews, both the early narrators of the Pentateuch (the Jahvist and the Elohist) presuppose the custom of burning holocausts and other sacrifices on the altar,[1] so that the fusion is already complete between the sacred stone to receive the blood, and the hearth on which the flesh was burned. But the oldest history still preserves traces of a different custom. The burnt-sacrifices of Gideon and Manoah are not offered on an altar, but on the bare rock;[2] and even at the opening of Solomon's temple the fire-offerings were not burned on the altar, but in the middle of the court in front of the *naos*, as was done many centuries later at Hierapolis on the day of the Pyre-sacrifice. It is true that in 1 Kings viii. 64 this is said to have been done only because "the brazen altar that was before the Lord" was not large enough for so great an occasion; but, according to 1 Kings ix. 25, the holocausts and ordinary sacrifices which Solomon offered three times in the year were in like manner offered (not on the brazen altar, but) on an altar "built" by the king, *i.e.* a structure of stones; and indeed we have no unambiguous notice of a permanent altar of burnt-offering in the temple of Jerusalem till the reign of Ahaz, who had one constructed on the model of the altar of Damascus. This altar, and not the brazen altar, was again the model for the altar of the second temple, which was of stone, not of brass, and it is plain from the narrative of 2 Kings xvi., especially in the form of the text which has been preserved by the Septuagint,

[1] Gen. viii. 20, xxii. 9. Ex. xx. 24 makes the holocaust be slaughtered on the altar, but does not expressly say that it was burned on it.

[2] Judg. vi. 20, xiii. 19; Judg. vi. 26, the more modern story of Gideon's offering, gives the modern ritual.

that Ahaz's innovation was not merely the introduction of a new architectural pattern, but involved a modification of the whole ritual.[1]

We may now pass on to the case of ordinary fire-offerings, in which only the fat of the vitals is consumed on the altar. It is easy to see that when men began to shrink from the eating of sacrificial flesh, they would not necessarily at once take refuge in entire abstinence. The alternative was to abstain from partaking of those parts in which the sacred life especially centred. Accordingly we find that in ordinary Hebrew sacrifices the whole blood is poured out at the altar as a thing too sacred to be eaten.[2] Again, the head is by many nations regarded as a special seat of the soul, and so, in Egyptian sacrifice, the head was not eaten, but thrown into the Nile,[3] while among the Iranians the head of the victim was dedicated to Haoma, that the immortal part of the animal might return to him. But a not less important seat of life, according to Semitic ideas, lay in the viscera, especially in the kidneys and the liver, which in the Semitic dialects are continually named as the seats of emotion, or more broadly in the fat of the omentum and the organs that lie in and near it.[4] Now it is precisely this part of the

[1] See *Additional Note* K, *The Altar at Jerusalem*. I may add that, in 1 Kings xviii., Elijah's altar does not seem to be a raised structure, but simply a circle marked out by twelve standing stones and a trench.

[2] Among the Hottentots blood is allowed to men but not to women; the female sex being among savages excluded from many holy privileges. Similarly the flesh of the Hebrew sin-offering must be eaten only by males (Lev. vi. 22 [29]), and among the Caffres the head, breast and heart are man's part (Lichtenstein, p. 451).

[3] Herod. ii. 39. The objection to eating the head is very widely spread; *e.g.*, in Bavaria, as late as the fifteenth century (Usener, *Religionsgesch. Untersuchungen*, ii. 84). Some Arabs objected to eating the heart (Wustenfeld, *Reg.* p. 407).

[4] The Arabic *Khilb* (Heb. חֵלֶב, Syr. *ḥelbā*) primarily denotes the omentum or midriff, but includes the fat or suet connected therewith; see Lev. iii. 3. An Arab says of a woman who has inspired him with passion,

victim, the fat of the omentum with the kidneys and the lobe of the liver, which the Hebrews were forbidden to eat, and, in the case of sacrifice, burned on the altar.

The ideas connected with the kidney fat and its appurtenances may be illustrated by the usages of primitive peoples in modern times. When the Australians kill an enemy in blood revenge, "they always abstract the kidney fat, and also take off a piece of the skin of the thigh" [or a piece of the flank].[1] "These are carried home as trophies. . . . The caul fat is carefully kept by the assassin, and used to lubricate himself"; he thinks, we are told, that thus the strength of the victim enters into him.[2] When the Basutos offer a sacrifice to heal the sick, as soon as the victim is dead, "they hasten to take the epiploon or intestinal covering, which is considered the most sacred

"she has overturned my heart and torn my midriff" (Lane, p. 782). So in Ps. xvi. 10 the sense is not "they have closed their fat (unfeeling) heart," but "they have shut up their midriff," and thus are insensible to pity. From this complex of fat parts the fat of the kidneys is particularly selected by the Arabs, and by most savages, as the special seat of life. One says, "I found him with his kidney fat," meaning I found him brisk and all alive (Lane, p. 1513). In Egypt, according to Burckhardt (*Ar. Prov.* No. 301), "when a sheep is killed by a private person, some of the bystanders often take away the kidneys, or at least the fat that incloses them, as due to the public from him who slaughters the sheep." This, I take it, is a relic of old sacrificial usage; what used to be given to the god is now given in charity. For Greek ideas about the kidney fat see Mr. Platt's note on *Iliad*, φ. 204, in *Journ. Phil.* xix. (1890) 46.

[1] The thigh is a seat of life and especially of procreative power, as appears very clearly in the idiom of the Semites (*Kinship*, p. 34). From this may be explained the sacredness of the *nervus ischiadicus* among the Hebrews (Gen. xxxii. 33), and similar superstitions among other nations. Is this also the reason why the "fat thigh bones" are an altar-portion among the Greeks? The nature of the lameness produced by injury to the sinew of the thigh socket is explained by the Arabic lexx., *s.v.* حارقة; the man can only walk on the tips of his toes. This seems to have been a common affection, for poetical metaphors are taken from it.

[2] Brough Smyth, ii. 289, i. 102; cf. Lumholtz, *Among Cannibals* (Lond. 1889), p. 272.

part, and put it round the patient's neck. . . . The gall is then poured on the head of the patient. After a sacrifice the gall bladder is invariably fastened to the hair of the individual for whom the victim has been slain, and becomes a sign of purification."[1]

The importance attached by various nations to these vital parts of the body is very ancient, and extends to regions where sacrifice by fire is unknown. The point of view from which we are to regard the reluctance to eat of them is that, being more vital, they are more holy than other parts, and therefore at once more potent and more dangerous. All sacrificial flesh is charged with an awful virtue, and all *sacra* are dangerous to the unclean or to those who are not duly prepared; but these are so holy and so awful that they are not eaten at all, but dealt with in special ways, and in particular are used as powerful charms.[2]

We see from the case of the Basuto sacrifice that it is by no means true that all that man does not eat must be given to the god, and the same thing appears in other examples. The Hebrews pour out the blood at the altar, but the Greeks use it for lustration and the old Arabs as a cure for madness. The Persians restore the head and with it the life to Haoma, while the Tauri, according to Herodotus (iv. 103), in their human sacrifices, bury the body or cast it down from the cliff on which the temple stands, but fix the head on a pole above their houses as a sacred guardian. Among the Semites, too, the magical use of a dried head had great vogue. This sort of charm

[1] Casalis, p. 250.

[2] This may be illustrated by the case of the blood of sacrificial victims. Among the Greeks bull's blood was regarded as a poison; but for this belief there is no physiological basis: the danger lay in its sacred nature. But conversely it was used under divine direction as a medicine; Ælian, *N. A.* xi. 35. On blood as a medicine see also Pliny, *H. N.* xxviii. 43, xxvi. 8; and Adams's *Paulus Ægineta*, iii. 25 *sq.*

is mentioned by Jacob of Edessa,[1] and hares' heads were worn as amulets by Arab women.[2] So, too, when we find bones, and especially dead men's bones, used as charms,[3] we must think primarily of the bones of sacrifices. Nilus's Saracens at least broke up the bones and ate the marrow, but the solid osseous tissue must from the first have defied most teeth unless it was pounded, and so it was particularly likely to be kept and used as a charm. Of course the sacred bones may have been often buried, and when fire was introduced they were likely to be burned, as is the rule with the Caffres.[4] As the sacrifices of the Caffres are not fire-sacrifices, it is clear that in this case the bones are burned to dispose of the holy substance, not to provide food for the gods. But even when the bones or the whole carcase of a sacrosanct victim are burned, the sacred virtue is not necessarily destroyed. The ashes of sacrifice are used, like the blood, for lustrations of various kinds, as we see in the case of the red heifer among the Hebrews; and in agricultural religions such ashes are very commonly used to give fertility to the land. That is, the sacred elements, after they cease to be eaten, are still used in varied forms as a means of communicating the divine life and life-giving or protective virtue to the worshippers, their houses, their lands, and all things connected with them.

In the later fire-rituals, the fat of the victim, with its blood, is quite specially the altar food of the gods. But between the practice which this view represents and the

[1] Qu. 43; see more examples in Kayser's notes, p. 142, and in a paper by Jahn, *Ber. d. sächs-Ges. d. Wiss.* 1854, p. 48. For the magical human head, of which we read so much in the latest forms of Semitic heathenism, see Chwolsohn, ii. 150 *sqq.*, and the *Actes* of the Leyden Congress, ii. 365 *sq.*

[2] *Diw. Hudh.* clxxx. 9; *ZDMG.* xxxix. 329.

[3] Examples, *infra*, *Additional Note* B, p. 448. The very dung of cattle was a charm in Syria (Jacob of Edessa, Qu. 42), to which many parallels exist, not only in Africa, but among the Aryans of India.

[4] Maclean, p. 81.

primitive practice, in which the whole body was eaten, we must, I think, in accordance with what has just been said, insert an intermediate stage, which can still be seen and studied in the usage of primitive peoples. Among the Damaras the fat of particular animals "is supposed to possess certain virtues, and is carefully collected and kept in vessels of a particular kind. A small portion dissolved in water is given to persons who return home safely after a lengthened absence; . . . the chief makes use of it as an unguent for his body."[1] So too "dried flesh and fat" are used as amulets by the Namaquas.[2] Among the Bechuanas lubrication with grease is part of the ceremony of admission of girls into womanhood, and among the Hottentots young men on their initiation into manhood are daubed with fat and soot.[3] Grease is the usual unguent all over Africa, and from these examples we see that its use is not merely hygienic, but has a sacred meaning. Indeed, the use of various kinds of fat, especially human fat, as a charm, is common all over the world, and we learn from the Australian superstition, quoted above, that the reason of this is that the fat, as a special seat of life, is a vehicle of the living virtue of the being from which it is taken. Now we have seen, in speaking of the use of unguents in Semitic religion,[4] that this particular medium has in some way an equivalent value to blood, for which it may be substituted in the covenant ceremony, and also in the ceremony of bedaubing the sacred stone as an act of homage. If, now, we remember that the oldest unguents are animal fats, and that vegetable oil was unknown to the Semitic nomads,[5] we are plainly led to the conclusion

[1] Anderson, *Lake Ngami*, p. 223.

[2] *Ibid.* p. 330. The dried flesh reminds us of the Arabian custom of drying strips of sacrificial flesh on the days of Minā (Wellh. p. 79).

[3] *Ibid.* p. 465; Kolben, i. 121.

[4] *Supra*, p. 233.

[5] Fränkel, *Fremdwörter*, p. 147.

that unction is primarily an application of the sacrificial fat, with its living virtues, to the persons of the worshippers. On this view the anointing of kings, and the use of unguents on visiting the sanctuary, are at once intelligible.[1]

The agricultural Semites anointed themselves with olive oil, and burned the sacrificial fat on the altar. This could be done without any fundamental modification of the old type of sacred stone or altar pillar, simply by making a hollow on the top to receive the grease; and there is some reason to think that fire-altars of this simple kind, which in certain Phœnician types are developed into altar candlesticks, are older than the broad platform-altar proper for receiving a burnt-offering.[2] But there are evidences even in the Old Testament that it was only gradually that the burning of the fat came to be an integral part of the altar ritual. In 1 Sam. ii. 15 we find a controversy between the priests and the people on this very topic. The worshippers maintain that the priest has no claim to his fee of flesh till the fat is burned; but the priests assert their right to have a share of raw flesh at once. It is assumed in the argument that if the priests held back their claim till they had burned the fat, the flesh would be already cooked—so the worshippers at least did not wait to see the fat burned. And probably the priests had precedent on their side, for the old law of Ex. xxiii. 18 only requires that the fat of a festal sacrifice shall be burned before daybreak—the sacrifice itself having taken place in the evening.

I fear that these details may seem tedious, but the cumulative evidence which they afford that the burning of

[1] The use of unguents by witches when they desire to transform themselves into animal shape,—as we find it, for example, in Apuleius's novel,—belongs to the same region of superstition, and to that most primitive form of the superstition which turns on the kinship of men with animals.

[2] See below, *Additional Note* K.

the flesh or fat held quite a secondary place in ancient sacrifice, and was originally no integral part of the oblation at the altar, is of the greatest importance for the history of sacrificial ideas. They show how impossible it is to regard animal sacrifices as primarily consisting in a gift of food to the gods, and how long it was before this notion superseded the original notion of communion between men and their gods in the life of the sacrifice.

I do not suppose that it is possible, on the basis of the evidences that have come before us, to reconstruct from step to step the whole history of the development of fire-sacrifices. But we can at least see in a general way how the chief modifications of sacrificial ritual and idea came in.

Originally neither the flesh nor the life of the victim could be regarded as a gift or tribute—*i.e.* as something which belonged to the worshipper, and of which he divested himself in order to make it over to the object of his worship. It is probable that sacrifice is older than the idea of private property, and it is certain that its beginnings go back to a time when the owner of a sheep, an ox, or a camel had no right to dispose of its life according to his own good pleasure. Such an animal could only be slain in order that its life might be distributed between all the kin and the kindred god. At this stage the details of the ritual are shaped by the rule that no part of the life must be lost, and that therefore the whole body, which is the vehicle of the life, must be distributed and used up in the holy ritual. In the first instance, therefore, everything must be eaten up, and eaten while it is still alive—fresh and raw. Gradually this rule is modified, partly because it is difficult to insist, in the face of growing civilisation, on the rule that even bones, skin and offal must be devoured, and partly because there is increasing reluctance to partake of the holy life. This reluctance again is connected with the growth of the distinction between degrees of holiness. Not every man is holy enough to partake of the most sacred sacraments without danger. What is safe for a consecrated chief or priest is not safe for the mass of the people. Or even it is better that the most sacred parts of the victim should not be eaten at all; the blood and the fat are medicines too powerful to be taken internally, but they may be sprinkled or daubed on the worshippers, while the sacrificial meal is confined to the parts of the flesh in which the sacred life is less intensely present. Or, finally, it is most seemly and most safe to withdraw the holiest things from man's use altogether, to pour out the whole blood at the altar, and to burn the fat. All this applies to ordinary sacrifices, in which the gradual concentration of the holiness of the victim in its fat and blood tends to make the rest of the flesh appear less and less holy, till ultimately it becomes almost a common thing. But, on special occasions, where the old ritual is naturally observed with antique rigidity, and where, therefore, the victim is treated at the altar as if it were a tribesman, the feeling of sacred horror against too close an approach to things most holy extends to the whole flesh, and develops itself, especially in connection with actual human sacrifice, into the rule that no part of such victims may be eaten, but that the whole must be reverently burned.

If we may generalise from the case of Arabia, where the holocaust was confined to human victims and the fat of ordinary sacrifices was not burned, it would appear that it was human sacrifice that first gave rise to the use of fire as a safe means of disposing of the bodies of the holiest victims. From this practice that of burning the fat in common sacrifices may very well have been derived. But the evidence is not sufficient to justify a positive conclusion on the matter, and it is quite possible that the use of fire began among the Northern Semites in connection with ordinary sacrifices, simply as a means of dealing with such parts of the victim as were not or could not be eaten, and yet were too holy to be left undisposed of. The Hebrew ritual of ordinary sacrifices is careful to prescribe that what is not eaten on the first or second day shall be burned.[1] This is evidently a mere softening of the old rule that the flesh of the victim must be consumed without delay, while it is still alive and quivering, into the rule that it must not be allowed to putrefy and decompose; and this again, since the close connection between putrefaction and fermentation is patent even to the unscientific observer, seems also to be the principle on which ferments are excluded from the altar. The use of fire in sacrifice, as the most complete and thorough means of avoiding putrefaction in whatever part of the victim cannot or may not be eaten, must have suggested itself so naturally wherever fire was known, that no other reason is necessary to explain its wide adoption. The burial of the sacrificial flesh, of which we have found one or two examples, does not appear to have met with so much favour, and indeed was not so satisfactory from the point of view indicated by the rules of Hebrew ritual.[2]

The use of fire in this sense does not involve any fundamental modification in the ideas connected with sacrifice. The critical point in the development is when the fat of ordinary victims, or still more, the whole flesh of the holocaust, is burned within the sanctuary or on the altar, and is regarded as being thus made over to the deity. This point claims to be examined more fully, and must be reserved for consideration at our next meeting.

[1] Lev. vii. 15 *sqq.*

[2] See *Additional Note* L, *High Places.*

LECTURE XI

SACRIFICIAL GIFTS AND PIACULAR SACRIFICES—THE SPECIAL IDEAS INVOLVED IN THE LATTER

IN connection with the later Semitic sacrifices, fire is employed for two purposes, apparently quite independent of one another. Its ordinary use is upon the altar, where it serves to sublimate, and so to convey to deities of an ethereal nature, gifts of solid flesh, which are regarded as the food of the gods. But in certain Hebrew piacula the sacrificial flesh is burned without the camp, and is not regarded as the food of the gods. The parts of the victim which in the highest form of piacula are burned outside the camp are the same which in lower forms of the sin-offering were eaten by the priests as representatives of the worshippers, or which in ordinary sacrifices would have been eaten by the worshippers themselves. Here, therefore, the fire seems to play the same part that is assigned to it under the rule that, if an ordinary sacrifice is not eaten up within one or two days, the remnant must be burned. All sacrificial flesh is holy, and must be dealt with according to fixed ritual rules, one of which is that it must not be allowed to putrefy. Ordinary sacrificial flesh may be either eaten or burned, but sin-offerings are too holy to be eaten except by the priests, and in certain cases are too holy to be eaten even by them, and therefore must be burned, not as a way of conveying them to the deity, but simply as a way of fitly disposing of them.

It is commonly supposed that the first use of fire was upon the altar, and that the burning outside the camp is a later invention, expressing the idea that, in the case of a sacrifice for sin, the deity does not desire a material gift, but only the death of the offender. The ritual of the Hebrew sin-offering lends itself to such an interpretation readily enough, but it is impossible to believe that its origin is to be explained on any such view. If the sin-offering is merely a symbolical representation of a penal execution, why is the flesh of the victim holy in the first degree? and why are the blood and fat offered upon the altar? But it is unnecessary to press these minor objections to the common view, which is refuted more conclusively by a series of facts that have come before us in the course of the last lecture. There is a variety of evidence that fire was applied to sacrifices, or to parts of sacrifices, as an alternative to their consumption by the worshippers, before the altar became a hearth, and before it came to be thought that what was burned was conveyed, as etherealised food, to the deity. The Hebrew piacula that were burned outside the camp represent an older form of ritual than the holocaust on the altar, and the thing that really needs explanation is the origin of the latter.

Originally all sacrifices were eaten up by the worshippers. By and by certain portions of ordinary sacrifices, and the whole flesh of extraordinary sacrifices, ceased to be eaten. What was not eaten was burned, and in process of time it came to be burned on the altar and regarded as made over to the god. Exactly the same change took place with the sacrificial blood, except that here there is no use of fire. In the oldest sacrifices the blood was drunk by the worshippers, and after it ceased to be drunk it was all poured out at the altar. The tendency evidently was to convey directly to the godhead every portion of a sacrifice that was not consumed by the worshipper; but how did this tendency arise?

I daresay that some of you will be inclined to say that I am making a difficulty of a matter that needs no explanation. Is it not obvious that a sacrifice is a consecrated thing, that consecrated things belong to the god, and that the altar is their proper place? No doubt this seems to be obvious, but it is precisely the things that seem obvious which in a subject like ours require the most careful scrutiny. You say that consecrated things belong to the god, but we saw long ago that this is not the primitive idea of holiness. A holy thing is taboo, *i.e.* man's contact with it and use of it are subject to certain restrictions, but this idea does not in early society rest on the belief that it is the property of the gods. Again, you say that a sacrifice is a consecrated thing, but what do you mean by this? If you mean that the victim became holy by being selected for sacrifice and presented at the altar, you have not correctly apprehended the nature of the oldest rites. For in them the victim was naturally holy, not in virtue of its sacrificial destination, but because it was an animal of holy kind. So long as the natural holiness of certain animal species was a living element in popular faith, it was by no means obvious that holy things belong to the god, and should find their ultimate destination at the altar.

In later heathenism the conception of holy kinds and the old ideas of taboo generally had become obsolete, and the ritual observances founded upon them were no longer understood. And, on the other hand, the comparatively modern idea of property had taken shape, and began to play a leading part both in religion and in social life. The victim was no longer a naturally sacred thing, over which man had very limited rights, and which he was required to treat as a useful friend rather than a chattel, but was drawn from the absolute property of the worshipper, of which he had a right to dispose as he pleased. Before its presentation the victim was a common thing, and it was only by being selected for sacrifice that it became holy. If, therefore, by presenting his sheep or ox at the altar, the owner lost the right to eat or sell its flesh, the explanation could no longer be sought in any other way than by the assumption that he had surrendered his right of property to another party, viz. to the god. Consecration was interpreted to mean a gift of man's property to the god, and everything that was withdrawn by consecration from the free use of man was conceived to have changed its owner. The blood and fat of ordinary sacrifices, or the whole flesh in the case of the holocaust, were withdrawn from human use; it was held, therefore, that they had become the property of the god, and were reserved for his use. This being so, it was inevitable that the burning of the flesh and fat should come to be regarded as a method of conveying them to the god; and as soon as this conclusion was drawn, the way was open for the introduction of the modern practice, in which the burning took place on the altar. The transformation of the altar into the hearth, on which the sacrificial flesh was consumed, marks the final establishment of a new view of holiness, based on the doctrine of property, in which the inviolability of holy things is no longer made to rest on their intrinsic supernatural quality, but upon their appropriation to the use and service of the gods. The success of this new view is not surprising, for in every department of early society we find that as soon as the notion of property, and of transfers of property from one person to another, gets firm footing, it begins to swallow up all earlier formulas for the relations of persons and things. But the adaptation of old institutions to new ideas can seldom be effected without leaving internal contradictions between the old and the new, which ultimately bring about the complete dissolution of the incongruous system. The new wine bursts the old bottles, and the new patch tears the old garment asunder.

In the case of ordinary sacrifices, the theory that holy things are the property of the deity, and that the consecration of things naturally common implies a gift from man to his god, was carried out with little difficulty. It was understood that at the altar the whole victim is made over to the deity and accepted by him, but that the main part of the flesh is returned to the worshipper, to be eaten sacrificially as a holy thing at the table of the god. This explanation went well enough with the conception of the deity as a king or great lord, whose temple was the court at which he sat to receive the homage of his subjects and tenants, and to entertain them with princely hospitality. But it did not satisfactorily account for the most characteristic feature in sacrifice, the application of the blood to the altar, and the burning of the fat on the sacred hearth. For these, according to the received interpretation, were the food of the deity; and so it appeared that the god was dependent on man for his daily nourishment, although, on the other hand, all the good things that man enjoyed he owed to the gift and favour of his god. This is the weak point in the current view of sacrifice which roused the indignation of the author of Psalm l., and afforded so much merriment to later satirists like Lucian. The difficulty might be explained away by a spiritualising interpretation, which treated the material altar gift as a mere symbol, and urged that the true value of the offering lay in the homage of the worshipper's heart, expressed in the traditional oblation. But the religion of the masses never took so subtle a view as this, and to the majority of the worshippers even in Israel, before the exile, the dominant idea in the ritual was that the material oblation afforded a physical satisfaction to the god, and that copious offerings were an infallible means of keeping him in good humour. So long as sacrifice was exclusively or mainly a social service, performed by the community, the crassness of this conception found its counterpoise in the ideas of religious fellowship that have been expounded in Lecture VII.[1] But in private sacrifice there was little or nothing to raise the transaction above the level of a mere bargain, in which no ethical consideration was involved, but the good understanding between the worshipper and his god was maintained by reciprocal friendly offices of a purely material kind. This superficial view of religion served very well in times of prosperity, but it could not stand the strain of serious and prolonged adversity, when it became plain that religion had to reckon with the sustained displeasure of the gods. In such circumstances men were forced to conclude that it was useless to attempt to appease the divine wrath by gifts of things which the gods, as lords of the earth, already possessed in abundance. It was not only Jehovah who could say, "I will take no bullock out of thy house, nor he-goats from thy folds; for every beast of the forest is Mine, and the cattle on a thousand hills." The Baalim too were in their way lords of nature, and even from the standpoint of heathenism it was absurd to suppose that they were really dependent on the tribute of their worshippers. In short, the gift-theory of sacrifice was not enough to account for the rule that sacrifice is the sole and sufficient form of every act of worship, even in religions which had not realised, with the Hebrew prophets, that what the true God requires of

[1] *Supra*, p. 263 *sqq.*

His worshippers is not a material oblation, but "to do justice, and love mercy, and walk humbly with thy God."

If the theory of sacrifice as a gift or tribute, taken from man's property and conveyed to the deity, was inadequate even as applied to ordinary oblations, it was evidently still more inadequate as applied to the holocaust, and especially to human sacrifice. It is commonly supposed that the holocaust was more powerful than ordinary sacrifices, because the gift to the god was greater. But even in ordinary sacrifices the whole victim was consecrated and made over to the god; only in the holocaust the god kept everything to himself, while in ordinary sacrifices he invited the worshipper to dine with him. It does not appear that there is any good reason, on the doctrine of sacrificial tribute, why this difference should be to the advantage of the holocaust. In the case of human sacrifices the gift-theory led to results which were not only absurd but revolting—absurd, since it does not follow that because a man's firstborn son is dearer to himself than all his wealth, the life of that son is the most valuable gift that he can offer to his god; and revolting, when it came to be supposed that the sacrifice of children as fire-offerings was a gift of food to a deity who delighted in human flesh.[1] So detestable a view of the nature of the gods cannot fairly be said to correspond to the general character of the old Semitic religions, which ought to be judged of by the ordinary forms of worship and not by exceptional rites. If the gods had been habitually conceived as cannibal monsters, the general type of ritual would have been gloomy and timorous, whereas really it was full of joyous and even careless confidence. I conclude, therefore, that the child-devouring King of the later Moloch-worship owes his cannibal attributes, not to

[1] Ezek. xvi. 20, xxiii. 37.

the fundamental principles of Semitic religion, but to false logic, straining the gift-theory of sacrifice to cover rites to which it had no legitimate application. And this conclusion is justified when we find that, though human sacrifices were not unknown in older times, the ancient ritual was to burn them without the camp—a clear proof that their flesh was not originally regarded as a food-offering to the deity.[1]

On the whole, then, the introduction of ideas of property into the relations between men and their gods seems to have been one of the most fatal aberrations in the development of ancient religion. In the beginnings of human thought, the natural and the supernatural, the material and the spiritual, were confounded, and this confusion gave rise to the old notion of holiness, which turned on the idea that supernatural influences emanated, like an infection, from certain material things. It was necessary to human progress that this crude conception should be superseded, and at first sight we are disposed to see nothing but good in the introduction of the notion that holy things are forbidden to man because they are reserved for the use of the gods, and that the danger associated with illegitimate invasion of them is not due to any deadly supernatural influence, directly proceeding from the holy object, but to the wrath of a personal god, who will not suffer his property to be tampered with. In one direction this modification was undoubtedly beneficial, for the vague dread of the unknown supernatural, which in savage society is so strong that it paralyses progress of every kind, and turns man aside from his legitimate task of subduing nature to his use, receives a fatal blow as soon as all supernatural processes are referred to the will and

[1] Compare the remarks on the sacrifice of the firstborn, *infra*, *Additional Note* E.

powers of known deities, whose converse with man is guided by fixed laws. But it was in the last degree unfortunate that these fixed laws were taken to be largely based on the principle of property; for the notion of property materialises everything that it touches, and its introduction into religion made it impossible to rise to spiritual conceptions of the deity and his relations to man on the basis of traditional religion. On the other hand, the more ancient idea of living communion between the god and his worshippers, which fell more and more into the background under the theory of sacrificial gifts, contained an element of permanent truth wrapped up in a very crude embodiment, and to it therefore all the efforts of ancient heathenism towards a better way of converse with the divine powers attach themselves, taking hold of those forms and features of sacrifice which evidently involved something more than the mere presentation to the deity of a material tribute. And as the need for something more than the ordinary altar gifts supplied was not habitually present to men's minds, but forced itself upon them in grave crises of life, and particularly in times of danger, when the god seemed to be angry with his people, or when at any rate it was of importance to make sure that he was not angry, all the aspects of worship that go beyond the payment of gifts and tribute came to be looked upon as having a special atoning character, that is, as being directed not so much to maintain a good understanding with the deity, as to renew it when it was interrupted.

When the idea of atonement is taken in this very general form, there is obviously no sharp line between atoning and ordinary sacrifices; for in ordinary life the means that are used to keep a man in good humour will often suffice to restore him to good humour, if they are sedulously employed. On this analogy a mere gift, presented at a suitable moment, or of greater value than usual, was often thought sufficient to appease the divine wrath; a general atoning force was ascribed to all sacrifices, and the value of special piacula was often estimated simply by the consideration that they cost the worshipper more than an everyday offering. We have seen that even human sacrifices were sometimes considered from this point of view; and in general the idea that every offence against the deity can be appraised, and made good by a payment of a certain value, was not inconsistent with the principles of ancient law, which deals with offences against persons on the doctrine of retaliation, but admits to an almost unlimited extent the doctrine that the injured party may waive his right of retaliation in consideration of a payment by the offender. But it is not the doctrine of ancient law that an injured party can be compelled to accept material compensation for an offence; and therefore, even on ordinary human analogies, no religious system could be regarded as complete which had not more powerful means of conjuring the divine displeasure than were afforded by the mere offer of a gift or payment. In point of fact, all ancient religions had sacrificial ceremonies of this more powerful kind, in which the notion of pleasing the god by a gift either found no expression at all, or evidently did not exhaust the significance of the ritual; and these are the sacrifices to which the distinctive name of *piacula* is properly applied.

It is sometimes supposed that special piacula did not exist in the older Semitic religions, and were invented for the first time when the gift-theory of sacrifice began to break down. But this supposition is incredible in itself, and is not consistent with the historical evidence. It is incredible that a gift should have been the oldest known way of reconciling an offended god, for in ordinary life atonement by fine came in at a relatively late date, and never entirely superseded the *lex talionis*; and it is certain, from what we have learned by observing the old form of piacular holocausts, that these sacrifices were not originally regarded as payments to the god, but arose on quite different lines, as an independent development of the primitive sacrifice of communion, whose atoning efficacy rested on the persuasion that those in whose veins the same life-blood circulates cannot be other than friends, bound to serve each other in all the offices of brotherhood.

It has appeared in the course of our inquiry that two kinds of sacrifice, which present features inconsistent with the gift-theory, continued to be practised by the ancient Semites; and to both kinds there was ascribed a special efficacy in persuading or constraining the favour of the gods. The first kind is the mystic sacrifice, represented by a small class of exceptional rites, in which the victim was drawn from some species of animals that retained even in modern times their ancient repute of natural holiness. Sacrifices of this sort could never fall under the gift-theory, for creatures naturally holy are not man's property, but, so far as they have an owner at all, are the property of the god. The significance attached to these sacrifices and the nature of their peculiar efficacy, has already received sufficient attention. The other kind of offering which was thought of as something more than a mere gift, consisted of holocausts, and other sacrifices, whose flesh was not conveyed to the god and eaten at his table, but burned without the camp, or buried, or cast away in a desert place. This kind of service we have already studied from a formal point of view, considering the way in which its ritual was differentiated from the old communion sacrifice, and also the way in which most sacrifices of the kind were ultimately brought under the class of sacrificial gifts, by the introduction of the practice of burning the flesh on the altar or burying it in the *ghabghab*; but we have not yet considered how these successive modifications of ritual were interpreted and made to fit into the general progress of social institutions and ideas. Some notice of this side of the subject is necessary to complete our study of the principles of ancient sacrifice, and to it the remainder of the present lecture will be devoted.

It must, however, be remembered that in ancient religion there was no authoritative interpretation of ritual. It was imperative that certain things should be done, but every man was free to put his own meaning on what was done. Now the more complicated ritual prestations, to which the elaborate piacular services of later times must be reckoned, were not forms invented, once for all, to express a definite system of ideas, but natural growths, which were slowly developed through many centuries, and in their final form bore the imprint of a variety of influences, to which they had been subjected from age to age under the changing conditions of human life and social order. Every rite therefore lent itself to more than one interpretation, according as this or that aspect of it was seized upon as the key to its meaning. Under such circumstances we must not attempt to fix a definite interpretation on any of the developments of ancient ritual; all that we can hope to do is to trace in the ceremonial the influence of successive phases of thought, the presence of which is attested to us by other movements in the structure of ancient society, or conversely to show how features in ritual, of which the historical origin had been forgotten, were accounted for on more modern principles, and used to give support to new ideas that were struggling for practical recognition.

From the analysis of the ritual of holocausts and other piacula given in the last two lectures, it appears that through all the varieties of atoning ceremony there runs a common principle: the victim is sacrosanct, and the peculiar value of the ceremony lies in the operation performed on its life, whether that life is merely conveyed to the god on the altar, or is also applied to the worshippers by the sprinkling of the blood, or some other lustral ceremony. Both these features are nothing more than inheritances from the most primitive form of sacramental communion; and in the oldest sacrifices their meaning is perfectly transparent and unambiguous, for the ritual exactly corresponds with the primitive ideas, that holiness means kinship to the worshippers and their god, that all sacred relations and all moral obligations depend on physical unity of life, and that unity of physical life can be created or reinforced by common participation in living flesh and blood. At this earliest stage the atoning force of sacrifice is purely physical, and consists in the redintegration of the congenital physical bond of kinship, on which the good understanding between the god and his worshippers ultimately rests. But in the later stage of religion, in which sacrifices of sacrosanct victims and purificatory offerings are exceptional rites, these antique ideas were no longer intelligible; and in ordinary sacrifices those features of the old ritual were dropped or modified which gave expression to obsolete notions, and implied a physical transfer of holy life from the victim to the worshippers. Here, therefore, the question arises why that which had ceased to be intelligible was still preserved in a peculiar class of sacrifices. The obvious answer is that it was preserved by the force of use and precedent.

It is common, in discussions of the significance of

piacular ritual, to begin with the consideration that piacula are atonements for sin, and to assume that the ritual was devised with a view to the purchase of divine forgiveness. But this is to take the thing by the wrong handle. The characteristic features in piacular sacrifice are not the invention of a later age, in which the sense of sin and divine wrath was strong, but are features carried over from a very primitive type of religion, in which the sense of sin, in any proper sense of the word, did not exist at all, and the whole object of ritual was to maintain the bond of physical holiness that kept the religious community together. What we have to explain is not the origin of the sacrificial forms that later ages called piacular, but the way in which the old type of sacrifice came to branch off into two distinct types. And here we must consider that, even in tolerably advanced societies, the distinction between piacular and ordinary offerings long continued to be mainly one of ritual, and that the former were not so much sacrifices for sin, as sacrifices in which the ceremonial forms, observed at the altar, continued to express the original idea that the victim's life was sacrosanct, and in some way cognate to the life of the god and his worshippers. Thus, among the Hebrews of the pre-prophetic period, it certainly appears that a peculiar potency was assigned to holocausts and other exceptional sacrifices, as a means of conjuring the divine displeasure; but a certain atoning force was ascribed to all sacrifices; and, on the other hand, sacrifices of piacular form and force were offered on many occasions when we cannot suppose the sense of sin or of divine anger to have been present in any extraordinary degree. For example, it was the custom to open a campaign with a burnt-offering, which in old Israel was the most solemn piaculum; but this did not imply any feeling that war was a divine judgment and a sign of the anger of Jehovah.[1] It appears rather that the sacrifice was properly the consecration of the warriors; for the Hebrew phrase for opening war is "to consecrate war" (קדש מלחמה), and warriors are consecrated persons, subject to special taboos.[2] Here, therefore, it lies near at hand to suppose that the holocaust is simply the modification, on lines which have been already explained, of an ancient form of sacramental communion.[3] The Greeks in like manner commenced their wars with piacular sacrifices of the most solemn kind; indeed, according to Phylarchus,[4] a human victim was at one time customary, which is certainly not true for historical times; but I have no doubt that the statement of Phylarchus corresponds to a wide-spread tradition such as might easily arise if the offerings made on occasion of war were of the exceptional and sacrosanct character with which legends of actual human sacrifice are so frequently associated.[5] One illus-

[1] The burnt-offering at the opening of a campaign appears in Judg. vi. 20 (cf. ver. 26), xx. 26; 1 Sam. vii. 9, xiii. 10. In Judg. xi. 31 we have, instead of a sacrifice before the war, a vow to offer a holocaust on its successful termination. The view taken by the last redactor of the historical books (Judg., Sam., Kings), that the wars of Israel with its neighbours were always chastisements for sin, is not ancient; cf. Gen. xxvii. 29, xlix. 8; Num. xxiv. 24; Deut. xxxiii. 29.

[2] Isa. xiii. 3; Jer. vi. 4, li. 28; Joel iv. [iii.] 9; Mic. iii. 5. See *supra*, p. 158, and *Additional Note* C.

[3] I conjecture that the form of gathering warriors together by sending round portions of a victim that has been hewn into pieces (1 Sam. xi. 7; cf. Judg. xix. 29) had originally a sacramental sense, similar to that expressed by the covenant form in which the victim is cut in twain; cf. *Additional Note* H, and the Scythian custom noticed by Lucian, *Toxaris*, § 48. A covenant by hewing an ox into small pieces was also in use among the Molossians; Zenobius, ii. 83.

[4] *Ap.* Porph., *De Abst.* ii. 56.

[5] Even in the palmy days of Hellenic civilisation we find evidence of a deeply-rooted belief in the potency of human sacrifice to ensure victory in war. So late as the time of Pelopidas, the propriety of such sacrifice was formally discussed, and upheld by historical as well as mythical precedents (Plutarch, *Pelopidas*, 21). But the historical precedents reduce themselves, on closer examination, to the single and wholly exceptional case of the sacrifice of three captives before the battle of Salamis. On the other hand,

tration of Phylarchus's statement will occur to everyone, viz. the sacrifice of Iphigenia; and here it is to be noted that, while all forms of the legend are agreed that Agamemnon must have committed some deadly sin before so terrible an offering was required of him, there is no agreement as to what his sin was. It is not therefore unreasonable to think that in the original story the piaculum was simply the ordinary preliminary to a campaign, and that later ages could not understand why such a sacrifice should be made, except to atone for mortal guilt.[1]

If, now, it be asked why the ordinary preliminary to a campaign was a sacrifice of the exceptionally solemn kind which in later times was deemed to have a special reference to sin, the answer must be that the ritual was fixed by immemorial precedent, going back to the time when all sacrifices were of the sacramental type, and involved the shedding of a sacrosanct life. At that time every sacrifice was an awful mystery, and not to be performed except on great occasions, when it was most necessary that the bond of kindred obligation between every member of the community, divine and human, should be as strong and fresh as possible. The outbreak of war was plainly such an occasion, and it is no hazardous conjecture that the rule of commencing a campaign with sacrifice dates from the most primitive times.[2] Accordingly the ceremonial to be observed in sacrifice on such an occasion would be protected by well-established tradition, and the victim would

additions might easily be made to the list of legendary precedents, *e.g.* the case of Bombus (Zenobius, ii. 84).

[1] The opening of a campaign appears also in Africa as one of the rare occasions that justify the slaughter of a victim from the tribal herds; see above, p. 297.

[2] There is also some reason to think that in very ancient times a sacrifice was appointed to be offered after a victory. See *Additional Note* M, *Sacrifice by Victorious Warriors.*

continue to be treated at the altar with all the old ritual forms which implied that its blood was holy and akin to man's, long after the general sanctity of all animals of sacrificial kind had ceased to be acknowledged in daily life. And in the same way sacrifices of exceptional form, in which the victim was treated as a human being, or its blood was applied in a primitive ceremonial to the persons of the worshippers, or its flesh was regarded as too sacred to be eaten, would continue to be offered on all occasions which were marked out as demanding a sacrifice, by some very ancient rule, dating from the time when the natural sanctity of sacrificial kinds was still recognised. In such cases the ancient ceremonial would be protected by immemorial custom; while, on the other hand, there would be nothing to prevent a more modern type of ritual from coming into use on occasions for which there was no ancient sacrificial precedent, *e.g.* on such occasions as arose for the first time under the conditions of agricultural life, when the old sanctity of domestic animals was very much broken down. Sacrifices were vastly more frequent with the agricultural than with the pastoral nations of antiquity, but, among the older agricultural Semites, the occasions that called for sacrifices of exceptional or piacular form were not numerous, and may fairly be regarded as corresponding in the main to the rare occasions for which the death of a victim was already prescribed by the rules of their nomadic ancestors.

This, it may be said, is no more than a hypothesis, but it satisfies the conditions of a legitimate hypothesis, by postulating the operation of no unknown or uncertain cause, but only of that force of precedent which in all times has been so strong to keep alive religious forms of which the original meaning is lost. And in certain cases, at any rate, it is very evident that rites of exceptional form, which later ages generally connected with ideas of sin and atonement, were merely the modern representatives of primitive sacraments, kept up through sheer force of habit, without any deeper meaning corresponding to the peculiar solemnity of their form. Thus the annual piacula that were celebrated, with exceptional rites, by most nations of antiquity, are not necessarily to be regarded as having their first origin in a growing sense of sin or fear of divine wrath,—although these reasons operated in later times to multiply such acts of service and increase the importance attached to them,—but are often nothing more than survivals of ancient annual sacrifices of communion in the body and blood of a sacred animal. For in some of these rites, as we have seen in Lecture VIII.,[1] the form of communion in flesh too holy to be eaten except in a sacred mystery is retained; and where this is not the case, there is at least some feature in the annual piaculum which reveals its connection with the oldest type of sacrifice. It is a mistake to suppose that annual religious feasts date only from the beginnings of agricultural life, with its yearly round of seed-time and harvest; for in all parts of the world annual sacraments are found, and that not merely among pastoral races, but even in rude hunting tribes that have not emerged from the totem stage.[2] And though some of these totem sacraments involve actual communion in the flesh and blood of the sacred animal, the commoner case, even in this primitive stage of society, is that the theanthropic victim is deemed too holy to be eaten, and therefore, as in the majority of Semitic piacula, is burned, buried, or cast into a stream.[3] It is certainly

[1] *Supra*, p. 290 *sqq*.

[2] For examples of annual sacraments by sacrifice of the totem, see Frazer, *Totemism*, p. 48, and *supra*, p. 295, note 2.

[3] I apprehend that in most climates the vicissitudes of the seasons are certainly not less important to the savage huntsman or to the pastoral

illegitimate to connect these very primitive piacula with any explicit ideas of sin and forgiveness; they have their origin in a purely naturalistic conception of holiness, and mean nothing more than that the mystic unity of life in the religious community is liable to wear out, and must be revived and strengthened from time to time.

Among the annual piacula of the more advanced Semites which, though they are not mystical sacrifices of an "unclean" animal, yet bear on their face the marks of extreme antiquity, the first place belongs to the Hebrew Passover, held in the spring month Nisan, where the primitive character of the offering appears not only from the details of the ritual,[1] but from the coincidence of its season with that of the Arabian sacrifices in the month Rajab. Similarly in Cyprus, on the first of April, a sheep was offered to Astarte (Aphrodite) with ritual of a character evidently piacular.[2] At Hierapolis, in like manner, the chief feast of the year was the vernal ceremony of the Pyre, in which animals were burned alive—an antique ritual which has been illustrated in the last lecture. And again, among the Harranians, the first half of Nisan was

barbarian than to the more civilised tiller of the soil. From Doughty's account of the pastoral tribes of the Arabian desert, and also from what Agatharchides tells us of the herdsmen by the Red Sea, we perceive that in the purely pastoral life the seasons when pasture fails are annual periods of semi-starvation for man and beast. Among still ruder races, like the Australians, who have no domestic animals, the difference of the seasons is yet more painfully felt; so much so, indeed, that in some parts of Australia children are not born except at one season of the year; the annual changes of nature have impressed themselves on the life of man to a degree hardly conceivable to us. In pastoral Arabia domestic cattle habitually yean in the brief season of the spring pasture (Doughty, i. 429), and this would serve to fix an annual season of sacrifice. Camels calve in February and early March; Blunt, *Bed. Tribes*, ii. 166.

[1] *Supra*, p. 344. Note also that the head and the inwards have to be eaten, *i.e.* the special seats of life (Ex. xii. 9).

[2] Lydus, *De Mens.* iv. 45; cf. *Additional Note* G. The κώδιον marks the sacrifice as piacular, whether my conjecture κωδίῳ ἐσκεπασμένοι for κωδίῳ ἐσκεπασμένον is accepted or not.

marked by a series of exceptional sacrifices of piacular colour.[1]

So remarkable a concurrence in the season of the great annual piacular rites of Semitic communities leaves little doubt as to the extreme antiquity of the institution. Otherwise the season of the annual piacula is not material to our present purpose, except in so far as its coincidence with the yeaning time appears to be connected with the frequent use of sucking lambs and other very young animals as piacular victims. This point, however, seems to be of some importance as an indirect evidence of the antiquity of annual piacula. The reason often given for the sacrifice of very young animals, that a man thus got rid of a sacred obligation at the very cheapest rate, is not one that can be seriously maintained; while, on the other hand, the analogy of infanticide, which in many savage countries is not regarded as murder if it be performed immediately after birth, makes it very intelligible that, in those primitive times when a domestic animal had a life as sacred as that of a tribesman, new-born calves or lambs should be selected for sacrifice. The selection of an annual season of sacrifice coincident with the yeaning-time may therefore be plausibly referred to the time when sacrificial slaughter was still a rare and awful event, involving responsibilities which the worshippers were anxious to reduce, by every device, within the narrowest possible limits.

The point which I took a little time ago, that sacrifices of piacular form are not necessarily associated with a sense of sin, comes out very clearly in the case of annual piacula. Among the Hebrews, under the Law, the annual expiation

[1] *Fihrist*, p. 322. Traces of the sacredness of the month Nisan are found also at Palmyra (*Enc. Brit.* xviii. 199, note 2), and among the Nabatæans, as Berger has inferred from a study of the inscriptions of Madāïn-Ṣāliḥ.

on the great Day of Atonement was directed to cleanse the people from all their sins,[1] *i.e.* according to the Mishnic interpretation, to purge away the guilt of all sins, committed during the year, that had not been already expiated by penitence, or by the special piacula appointed for particular offences;[2] but there is little trace of any such view in connection with the annual piacula of the heathen Semites; and even in the Old Testament this interpretation appears to be modern. The Day of Atonement is a much less ancient institution than the Passover; and in the Passover, though the sprinkled blood has a protecting efficacy, the law prescribes no forms of humiliation and contrition, such as are enjoined for the more modern rite. Again, the prophet Ezekiel, whose sketch of a legislation for Israel, on its restoration from captivity, is older than the law of Leviticus, does indeed provide for two annual atoning ceremonies, in the first and in the seventh month;[3] but the point of these ceremonies lies in an elaborate application of the blood to various parts of the temple, with the object of "reconciling the house." This reference of the sacrifice reappears also in Lev. xvi.; the sprinkling of the blood on the great Day of Atonement "cleanses the altar, and makes it holy from all the uncleanness of the children of Israel."[4] Here an older and merely physical conception of the ritual breaks through, which has nothing to do with the forgiveness of sin; for uncleanness in the Levitical ritual is not an ethical conception. It seems that the holiness of the altar is liable to be impaired, and requires to be annually refreshed by an application of holy blood—a conception which it would be hard to justify from the higher teaching of the Old Testa-

[1] Lev. xvi. 30. [2] *Yoma*, viii. 8, 9.

[3] Ezek. xlv. 19, 20 (LXX.).

[4] Lev. xvi. 19; cf. ver. 33, where the atonement extends to the whole sanctuary.

ment, but which is perfectly intelligible as an inheritance from primitive ideas about sacrifice, in which the altar-idol on its part, as well as the worshippers on theirs, is periodically reconsecrated by the sprinkling of holy (*i.e.* kindred) blood, in order that the life-bond between the god it represents and his kindred worshippers may be kept fresh. This is the ultimate meaning of the yearly sprinkling with a tribesman's blood, which, as Theophrastus tells us, was demanded by so many altars of antiquity,[1] and also of the yearly sprinkling where the victim was not a man, but a sacrosanct or theanthropic animal.

Of all this, however, the later ages of antique religion understood no more than that ancient tradition prescribed certain annual rites of peculiar and sometimes of awful character as indispensable to the maintenance of normal relations between the gods and the worshipping community. The neglect of these rites, it was believed, entailed the wrath of the gods; the Carthaginians, for example, in their distress in the war with Agathocles, believed that Cronus was angry because slaves had been substituted for the noble boys that were his proper victims. But it does not appear that they looked behind this and concluded that the god could not demand periodical sacrifices of such price except as an atonement for the ever-recurring sins of the nation. Ancient religion was so entirely ruled by precedent, that men did not deem it necessary to have an adequate moral explanation even of the most exorbitant demands of traditional ritual; they were content to explain them by some legend that told how the ritual first came to be set up. Thus Diodorus,

[1] Examples of annual human sacrifice in the Semitic field at Carthage, Porph., *De Abst.* ii. 27 (from Theophrastus), Pliny, *H. N.* xxxvi. 29 ; at Dumætha, or Duma, in Arabia, *De Abst.* ii. 56. At Laodicea in Syria the annual sacrifice of a deer was held to be a substitute for the more ancient sacrifice of a virgin. (See below, *Additional Note* G.)

when he mentions the Carthaginian human sacrifices, suggests the probability that they preserve the memory of Cronus devouring his children;[1] and the Phœnicians themselves appear, from the fragments of Philo Byblius, to have traced back the custom of sacrificing children to a precedent set by the God El, whom the Greeks identify with Cronus.[2]

Indeed, among the Semites the most current view of annual piacula seems to have been that they commemorate a divine tragedy—the death of some god or goddess.[3] The origin of such myths is easily explained from the nature of the ritual. Originally the death of the god was nothing else than the death of the theanthropic victim; but when this ceased to be understood it was thought that the piacular sacrifice represented an historical tragedy in which the god was killed. Thus at Laodicea the annual sacrifice of a deer in lieu of a maiden, which was offered to the goddess of the city, is associated with a legend that the goddess was a maiden who had been sacrificed to consecrate the foundation of the town, and was thenceforth worshipped as its Fortune, like Dido at Carthage; it was therefore the death of the goddess herself that was annually renewed in the piacular rite. The same explanation applies to such scenic representations as were spoken of in the last lecture,[4] where the deity is annually burned in effigy, since the substitution of an effigy for a

[1] Diod. xx. 14.

[2] Euseb., *Præp. Ev.* i. 10. 21, 33. Thus it would seem that even the unenlightened Israelites addressed in Mic. vi. 7 had a profounder sense of sin than was current among the heathen Semites.

[3] I have not noted any Semitic example of another type of explanatory legend of which there are various instances in Greece, viz. that the annual piaculum was appointed as the punishment of an ancient crime for which satisfaction had to be made from generation to generation: Pausan. ix. 8. 2 (at Potniæ), vii. 19 *sq.* (at Patræ in Achaia). In both cases, according to the legend, the sacrifice was originally human.

[4] *Supra*, p. 364 *sqq.*

human sacrifice, or for a victim representing a god, is very common in antique and barbarous religions.[1] And in like manner the annual mourning for Tammuz or Adonis, which supplies the closest parallel in point of form to the fasting and humiliation on the Hebrew Day of Atonement, is the scenic commemoration of a divine tragedy in which the worshippers take part with appropriate wailing and lamentation. That the rites of the Semitic Adonia[2] were connected with a great sacrificial act, may safely be inferred on general principles; and that the sacrifice was piacular in form, follows from Lucian's account of the ritual of Byblus: "When they have done wailing they first burn a sacrifice[3] to Adonis as to one dead"—the offering therefore was a holocaust as in other annual piacula, and probably corresponds to the annual sacrifice of swine on April 2, at Cyprus, which Joannes Lydus connects with the Adonis legend.[4]

The Adonia therefore seem to me to be only a special form of annual piaculum, in which the sacrifice has come to be overshadowed by its popular and dramatic accompaniments.[5] The legend, the exhibition of the dead god in effigy,[6] the formal act of wailing, which filled all the streets

[1] Thus the Romans substituted puppets of rushes or wool for human offerings in the Argea and the worship of Mania. In Mexico, again, human victims were habitually regarded as incarnations of the deity, but also paste images of the gods were made and eaten sacramentally.

[2] I use this word as a convenient general term describing a particular type of ritual, without committing myself to the opinion that all rites of the type were in connection with the worship of the same god. It is not even certain that there was a god Adonis. What the Greeks took for a proper name is perhaps no more than a title, *Adon*, "lord," applicable to various deities, *CIL.* viii. 1211.

[3] Καταγίζουσι; for the sense of the word compare Lucian, *De Luctu*, 19.

[4] *Supra*, p. 290 *sq.* If this be so, the Cyprian Adonis was originally the Swine-god, and in this as in many other cases the sacred victim has been changed by false interpretation into the enemy of the god. Cf. Frazer, *The Golden Bough*, ii. 50.

[5] In Greece, where the Adonia were no part of the State religion, the celebration seems to have been limited to these.

[6] This is part of the genuine Semitic ritual, not merely Greek or

and was not confined to the sanctuary, took much greater hold of the imagination than the antique piaculum at the temple, and became one of the most deeply rooted parts of popular religion.[1] Late in the Middle Ages, in A.D 1064 and again in 1204, the Arabic historian Ibn al-Athīr[2] records sporadic revivals, on a great scale, of the ancient lament for the dead god. In the former case a mysterious threat was circulated from Armenia to Chuzistan, that every town which did not lament the dead "king of the Jinn" should utterly perish; in the latter a fatal disease raged in the parts of Mosul and Irac, "and it was divulged that a woman of the Jinn called Umm ʿUncūd (Mother of the Grape-cluster) had lost her son, and that everyone who would not make lamentation for him would fall a victim to the epidemic." In this case the form of the lamentation is recorded: "O Umm ʿUncūd, excuse us, ʿUncūd is dead, we knew it not."

It seems to me that one characteristic feature in these late observances is entirely true to the spirit of the old Semitic heathenism. The mourning is not a spontaneous expression of sympathy with the divine tragedy, but obligatory and enforced by fear of supernatural anger. And a chief object of the mourners is to disclaim responsibility for the god's death—a point which has already come before us in connection with theanthropic sacrifices, such as the "ox-murder at Athens."

When the original meaning of the theanthropic ritual was forgotten, and the death of the god was explained by

Alexandrian; see Lampridius, *Heliog.* vii.: "Salambonam etiam omni planctu et iactatione Syriaci cultus exhibuit." As it is not disputed that Salambo or Salambas = צלם בעל, "the image of Baal," it is strange that scholars should have been misled by Hesychius and the *Etym. Magn.* into making Salambo a name of the Oriental Aphrodite.

[1] *Dea Syria*, 6 (Byblus); Ammianus, xx. 9. 15 (Antioch).

[2] Ed. Tornberg, x. 27; cf. Bar Hebræus, *Chron. Syr.* ed. Bedjan, p. 242.

legendary history as a thing of the far past, the obligatory mourning at the annual piaculum was continued by force of usage, and presumably gave rise to various speculations which can only be matter of conjecture to us. But it is reasonable to suppose that ceremonies which were currently interpreted as the commemoration of a mythical tragedy could not suggest to the mass of the worshippers any ethical ideas transcending those embodied in the myth. The legends of the deaths of Semitic gods that have come down to us are singularly devoid of moral significance, and it is difficult to believe that they could excite any deeper feeling than a vague sentimental sympathy, or a melancholy conviction that the gods themselves were not exempt from the universal law of suffering and death. And with the common crowd I apprehend that the main feeling involved was generally that which we have seen to survive in the latest manifestations of heathen sentiment—the feeling that a bereaved deity is an angry deity, who may strike blindly all round at those who are not careful to free themselves from the suspicion of blame.

Among the agricultural Semites, where the Baal was mainly worshipped as the giver of vegetative increase and the quickening spirit of vegetative life, the annual mourning for the dead god seems often to have been brought into relation to agriculture and the cycle of agricultural feasts. In the Baal religion all agricultural operations, but particularly the harvest and vintage, are necessarily viewed as in some degree trenching on the holy things of the god, and must be conducted with special religious precautions.[1] Thus among the Hebrews the spring piaculum of the Passover, which in its origin belongs to the pre-agricultural stage of Semitic society, was connected in the Pentateuchal system with the opening of the corn-harvest,

[1] *Supra*, p. 158.

and in like manner the great Day of Atonement precedes the vintage feast. Mr. Frazer has brought together a good deal of evidence connecting the Adonia—or rather certain forms of the Adonia [1]—with the corn-harvest; the death of the god being held to be annually repeated in the cutting of the divine grain.[2] Similarly the wailing for ʻUncūd, the divine Grape-cluster, seems to be the last survival of an old vintage piaculum. I can only touch on this point here, since the developments of religion connected with agriculture lie beyond the scope of the present volume. The dread of the worshippers, that the neglect of the usual ritual would be followed by disaster, is particularly intelligible if they regarded the necessary operations of agriculture as involving the violent extinction of a particle of divine life. Here, in fact, the horror attending the service is much the same as in the case of the original theanthropic sacrifice, only it is a holy fruit that suffers instead of a holy animal.

In the brighter days of Semitic heathenism, the annual celebration of the god's death hardly suggested any serious thought that was not presently drowned in an outburst of mirth saluting the resurrection of the Baal on the following morning; and in more distressful times, when the gloomier aspects of religion were those most in sympathy with the prevailing hopelessness of a decadent nation,—such times as those in which Ezekiel found the women of Jerusalem

[1] The rites of Byblus cannot be connected either with vintage or harvest, for both of these fall in the dry season, and the Byblian god died when his sacred river was swollen with rain. Here the pre-agricultural spring piaculum seems to have retained its old place in the yearly religious cycle.

[2] *The Golden Bough*, chap. iii. § 4. The evidence adduced by Mr. Frazer is not all applicable without limitation to the Semitic Adonia—Greek and Alexandrian forms of the mourning were probably coloured by Greek and Egyptian influence. The Semitic evidence points to Babylonia as the source of the Semitic corn piaculum; it is therefore worth noting that Bezold finds Tammuz and the following month Ab designated as the harvest months of N. Babylonia in the fifteenth century B.C. (*Tell el-Amarna Tablets*, Brit. Mus. 1892, p. xxix.).

mourning for Tammuz,—the idea that the gods themselves were not exempt from the universal law of death, and had ordered this truth to be commemorated in their temples by bloody, or even human sacrifices, could only favour the belief that religion was as cruel as the relentless march of adverse fate, and that man's life was ruled by powers that were not to be touched by love or pity, but, if they could be moved at all, would only be satisfied by the sacrifice of man's happiness and the surrender of his dearest treasures. The close psychological connection between sensuality and cruelty, which is familiar to students of the human mind, displays itself in ghastly fashion in the sterner aspects of Semitic heathenism; and the same sanctuaries which, in prosperous times, resounded with licentious mirth and carnal gaiety, were filled in times of distress with the cowardly lamentations of worshippers, who to save their own lives were ready to give up everything they held dear, even to the sacrifice of a firstborn or only child.

On the whole the annual piacula of Semitic heathenism appear theatrical and unreal, when they are not cruel and repulsive. The stated occurrence of gloomy rites at fixed seasons, and without any direct relation to human conduct, gave the whole ceremony a mechanical character, and so made it inevitable that it should be either accepted as a mere scenic tragedy, whose meaning was summed up in a myth, or interpreted as a proof that the divine powers were never thoroughly reconciled to man, and only tolerated their worshippers in consideration of costly atonements constantly renewed. I apprehend that even in Israel the annual piacula, which were observed from an early date, had little or no share in the development of the higher sense of sin and responsibility which characterises the religion of the Old Testament. The Passover is a rite of the most primæval antiquity; and in the local cults, annual mournings, like the lamentation for Jephthah's daughter, — which undoubtedly was connected with an annual sacrifice, like that which at Laodicea commemorated the mythical death of the virgin goddess,—had been yearly repeated from very ancient times. Yet, only after the exile, and then only by a sort of afterthought, which does not override the priestly idea that the annual atonement is above all a reconsecration of the altar and the sanctuary, do we find the annual piaculum of the Day of Atonement interpreted as a general atonement for the sins of Israel during the past year. In the older literature, when exceptional and piacular rites are interpreted as satisfactions for sin, the offence is always a definite one, and the piacular rite has not a stated and periodical character, but is directly addressed to the atonement of a particular sin or course of sinful life.

The conception of piacular rites as a satisfaction for sin appears to have arisen after the original sense of the theanthropic sacrifice of a kindred animal was forgotten, and mainly in connection with the view that the life of the victim was the equivalent of the life of a human member of the religious community. We have seen that when the victim was no longer regarded as naturally holy, and equally akin to the god and his worshippers, the ceremony of its death was still performed with solemn circumstances, not appropriate to the slaughter of a mere common beast. It was thus inevitable that the victim should be regarded either as a representative of the god, or as the representative of a tribesman, whose life was sacred to his fellows. The former interpretation predominated in the annual piacula of the Baal religions, but the latter was that naturally indicated in such atoning sacrifices as were offered on special emergencies and did not lend themselves to a mythical interpretation. For in old times the circumstances of the slaughter were those of a death which could only be justified by the consent, and even by the active participation, of the whole community, *i.e.* of the judicial execution of a kinsman.[1] In later times this rule was modified, and in ordinary sacrifices the victim was slain either by the offerer, or by professional slaughterers, who formed a class of inferior ministers at the greater sanctuaries.[2] But communal holocausts and piacula continued to be slain by the chief priests, or by the heads of the community or by their chosen representatives, so that the slaughter retained the character of a solemn public act.[3] Again, the feeling that the slaying involves a grave responsibility, and must be justified by divine permission, was expressed by the Arabs, even in ordinary slaughter, by the use of the *bismillah, i.e.* by the slaughterer striking the victim in the name of his god.[4] But in many piacula this feeling was carried much further, and care was taken to slay the victim without bloodshed, or to make believe that it had killed itself.[5] Certain

[1] *Supra*, p. 284 *sq.*

[2] In *CIS.* No. 86, the ministers of the temple include a class of slaughterers (זבחם), and so it was at Hierapolis (*Dea Syria*, xliii.). Among the Jews, at the second temple, the Levites often acted as slaughterers; but before the captivity the temple slaughterers were uncircumcised foreigners (Ezek. xliv. 6 *sqq.*; cf. *O.T. in J. Ch.* 2nd ed., p. 260 *sqq.*).

[3] Thus in the Old Testament we find young men as sacrificers in Ex. xxiv. 5; the elders in Lev. iv. 15, Deut. xxi. 4; Aaron in Lev. xvi. 15; cf. *Yoma*, iv. 3. All sacrifices, except the last named, might, according to the Rabbins, be killed by any Israelite.

The choice of "young men," or rather "lads," as sacrificers in Ex. xxiv. is curiously analogous to the choice of lads as executioners. Judg. viii. 20 is not an isolated case, for Nilus also (p. 67) says that the Saracens charged lads with the execution of their captives.

[4] The same feeling is expressed in Lev. xvii. 11; Gen. viii. 3 *sqq.*

[5] The blood that calls for vengeance is blood that falls on the ground (Gen. iv. 10). Hence blood to which vengeance is refused is said to be trodden under foot (Ibn Hishām, p. 79, *ult.*, p. 861, l. 5), and forgotten blood is covered by the earth (Job xvi. 18). And so we often find the idea that a death in which no blood is shed, or none falls upon the ground, does not call for vengeance; while, on the other hand, a simple blow calls for

holocausts, like those of the Pyre-festival at Hierapolis, were burned alive; and other piacula were simply pushed over a height, so that they might seem to kill themselves by their fall. This was done at Hierapolis, both with animals and with human victims; and, according to the Mishna, the Hebrew scapegoat was not allowed to go free in the wilderness, but was killed by being pushed over a precipice.[1] The same kind of sacrifice occurs in Egypt, in a rite which is possibly of Semitic origin,[2] and in Greece, in more than one case where the victims were human.[3]

All such forms of sacrifice are precisely parallel to those which were employed in sacred executions, *i.e.* in the judicial slaying of members of the community. The criminal in ancient times was either stoned by the whole congregation, as was the usual form of the execution among the ancient Hebrews; or strangled, as was commonly done among the later Jews; or drowned, as in the Roman punishment for parricide, where the kin in the narrower sense is called on to execute justice on one of its own members; or otherwise disposed of in some way which either avoids bloodshed or prevents the guilt of blood from being fixed on an individual. These coincidences between the ritual of sacrifice and of execution are not accidental; in each case they had their origin in the scruple against shedding

blood-revenge, if it happens to draw blood through the accident of its falling on a sore (Moffaḍḍal al-Ḍabbī, *Amthāl*, p. 10, ed. Constant. AH. 1300). Infanticide in Arabia was effected by burying the child alive; captive kings were slain by bleeding them into a cup, and if one drop touched the ground it was thought that their death would be revenged (*supra*, p. 369, note 1). Applications of this principle to sacrifices of sacrosanct and kindred animals are frequent; they are strangled or killed with a blunt instrument (*supra*, p. 343; note also the club or mallet that appears in sacrificial scenes on ancient Chaldean cylinders, Menant, *Glyptique*, i. 151), or at least no drop of their blood must fall on the ground (Bancroft, iii. 168).

[1] *Dea Syria*, lviii.; *Yoma*, vi. 6.

[2] Plutarch, *Is. et Os.* § 30; cf. *Additional Note* F.

[3] At the Thargelia, and in the Leucadian ceremony.

kindred blood; and, when the old ideas of the kinship of man and beast became unintelligible, they helped to establish the view that the victim whose life was treated as equivalent to that of a man was a sacrifice to justice, accepted in atonement for the guilt of the worshippers. The parallelism between piacular sacrifice and execution came out with particular clearness where the victim was wholly burnt, or where it was cast down a precipice; for burning was the punishment appointed among the Hebrews and other ancient nations for impious offences,[1] and casting from a cliff is one of the commonest forms of execution.[2]

The idea originally connected with the execution of a tribesman is not exactly penal in our sense of the word; the object is not to punish the offender, but to rid the community of an impious member—ordinarily a man who has shed the sacred tribal blood. Murder and incest, or offences of a like kind against the sacred laws of blood, are in primitive society the only crimes of which the community as such takes cognisance; the offences of man against man are matters of private law, to be settled between the parties on the principle of retaliation or by the payment of damages. But murder, to which as the typical form of crime we may confine our attention, is an inexpiable offence, for which no compensation can be taken; the man who has killed his kinsman or his covenant ally, whether of design or by chance, is impious,

[1] Gen. xxxviii. 24; Lev. xx. 14, xxi. 9; Josh. vii. 15.

[2] The Tarpeian rock at Rome will occur to everyone. Among the Hebrews we find captives so killed (2 Chron. xxv. 12), and in our own days the Sinai Arabs killed Prof. Palmer by making him leap from a rock; cf. also 2 Kings viii. 12, Hos. x. 14, from which it would seem that this was the usual way of killing non-combatants. I apprehend that the obscure form of execution "before the Lord," mentioned in 2 Sam. xxi. 9 (and also Num. xxv. 4), is of the same sort, for the victims fall and are killed; הוקע will answer to أوقع. Note that this religious execution takes place at the season of the Paschal piaculum.

and must be cut off from his community by death or outlawry. And in such a case the execution or banishment of the culprit is a religious duty, for if it is not performed the anger of the deity rests on the whole kin or community of the murderers.

In the oldest state of society the punishment of a murderer is not on all fours with a case of blood-revenge. Blood-revenge applies to manslaughter, *i.e.* to the killing of a stranger. And in that case the dead man's kin make no effort to discover and punish the individual slayer; they hold his whole kin responsible for his act, and take vengeance on the first of them on whom they can lay hands. In the case of murder, on the other hand, the point is to rid the kin of an impious person, who has violated the sanctity of the tribal blood, and here therefore it is important to discover and punish the criminal himself. But if he cannot be discovered, some other means must be taken to blot out the impiety and restore the harmony between the community and its god, and for this purpose a sacramental sacrifice is obviously indicated, such as Deut. xxi. provides for the purging of the community from the guilt of an untraced murder.[1] In such a case it was inevitable that the sacrifice, performed as it was with circumstances closely akin to those of an execution, should come to be regarded as a surrogate for the death of the true culprit. And this interpretation was all the more readily established because, from an early date, the alliance of different kins had begun to give rise to cases of homicide in which the line of distinction was no longer clear between murder and manslaughter, between the case where the culprit himself must die, and the case where any life

[1] Here the responsibility for the bloodshed falls on the nearest town (ver. 2); cf. *Agh.* ix. 178, l. 26 *sq.*, where the blood-wit for a man slain is charged to the nearest homestead.

kindred to his may suffice. Thus in the time of David[1] the Israelites admit that a crime calling for expiation was committed by Saul when he slew the Gibeonites, who were the sworn allies of Israel. But, on the other hand, the Gibeonites claim satisfaction under the law of blood-revenge, and ask that in lieu of Saul himself certain members of his house shall be given up to them. And in this way the idea of substitution is brought in, even in a case which is, strictly speaking, one of murder.

In all discussion of the doctrine of substitution as applied to sacrifice, it must be remembered that private sacrifice is a younger thing than clan sacrifice, and that private piacula offered by an individual for his own sins are of comparatively modern institution. The mortal sin of an individual—and it is only mortal sin that has to be considered in this connection—was a thing that affected the whole community, or the whole kin of the offender. Thus the inexpiable sin of the sons of Eli is visited on his whole clan from generation to generation;[2] the sin of Achan is the sin of Israel, and as such is punished by the defeat of the national army;[3] and the sin of Saul and "his bloody house" (*i.e.* the house involved in the bloodshed) leads to a three years' famine. Accordingly it is the business of the community to narrow the responsibility for the crime, and to free itself of the contagious taint by fixing the guilt either on a single individual, or at least on his immediate kin, as in the case of Achan, who was stoned and then buried with his whole family. Hence, when a tribesman is executed for an impious offence, he dies on behalf of the community, to restore normal relations between them and their god; so that the analogy with sacrifice is very close in purpose as well as in form. And so the cases in which the anger of the god can be traced

[1] 2 Sam. xxi. [2] 1 Sam. ii. 27 *sqq.* [3] Josh. vii. 1, 11.

to the crime of a particular individual, and atoned for by his death, are very naturally seized upon to explain the cases in which the sin of the community cannot be thus individualised, but where, nevertheless, according to ancient custom, reconciliation is sought through the sacrifice of a theanthropic victim. The old explanation, that the life of the sacrosanct animal is used to retie the life-bond between the god and his worshippers, fell out of date when the kinship of races of men with animal kinds was forgotten. A new explanation had to be sought; and none lay nearer than that the sin of the community was concentrated on the victim, and that its death was accepted as a sacrifice to divine justice. This explanation was natural, and appears to have been widely adopted, though it hardly became a formal dogma, for ancient religion had no official dogmas, but contented itself with continuing to practise antique rites, and letting everyone interpret them as he would. Even in the Levitical law the imposition of hands on the head of the victim is not formally interpreted as a laying of the sins of the people on its head, except in the case of the scape-goat.[1] And here the carrying away of the people's guilt to an isolated and desert region (ארץ גזרה) has its nearest analogies, not in ordinary atoning sacrifices, but in those physical methods of getting rid of an infectious taboo which characterise the lowest forms of superstition. The same form of disinfection recurs in the Levitical legislation, where a live bird is made to fly away with the contagion of leprosy,[2] and in Arabian custom, when a widow before remarriage makes a bird fly away with the uncleanness of her widowhood.[3] In ordinary burnt-

[1] Lev. xvi. 21.

[2] Lev. xiv. 7, 53; cf. Zech. v. 5 *sqq.*

[3] *Tāj al-'Arūs*, *s.v.* فضّ, VIII. (Lane, *s.v.; O. T. in J. Ch.*, 1st ed., p. 439; Wellh. p. 156). An Assyrian parallel in *Records of the Past*, ix. 151. It is indeed probable that in the oldest times the outlawry of a

offerings and sin-offerings the imposition of hands is not officially interpreted by the Law as a transference of sin to the victim, but rather has the same sense as in acts of blessing or consecration,[1] where the idea no doubt is that the physical contact between the parties serves to identify them, but not specially to transfer guilt from the one to the other.

In the Levitical ritual, all piacula, both public and private, refer only to sins committed unwittingly. As regards the sin-offering for the people this is quite intelligible, in accordance with what has just been said; for if the national sin can be brought home to an individual, he of course must be punished for it. But the private sin-offerings presented by an individual, for sins committed unwittingly, and subsequently brought to his knowledge, appear to be a modern innovation; before the exile the private offences for which satisfaction had to be made at the sanctuary were not mortal sins, and gave no room for the application of the doctrine of life for life, but were atoned for by a money payment, on the analogy of the satisfaction given by payment of a fine for the offences of man against man (2 Kings xii. 16). And, on the whole, while there can be no doubt that public piacula were often regarded as surrogates for the execution of an offender, who either was not known or whom the community hesitated to bring to justice, I very much doubt whether private offerings were often viewed in this light; even the sacrifice of a child, as we have already seen, was conceived rather as the greatest and most exorbitant gift that a man can offer.[2] The very idea of an execution implies a

criminal meant nothing more than freeing the community, just in this way, from a deadly contagion.

[1] Gen. xlviii. 14; Num. viii. 10; Deut. xxxiv. 9; cf. 2 Kings ii. 13 *sqq.*

[2] The Greek piacula for murder were certainly not regarded as executions, but as cathartic rites.

public function, and not a private prestation, and so I apprehend that the conception of a satisfaction paid to divine justice could not well be connected with any but public piacula. In these the death of the victim might very well pass for the scenic representation of an execution, and so represent the community as exonerating itself from all complicity in the crime to be atoned for. Looked at in this view, atoning rites no doubt served in some measure to keep alive a sense of divine justice and of the imperative duty of righteousness within the community. But the moral value of such scenic representation was probably not very great; and where an actual human victim was offered, so that the sacrifice practically became an execution, and was interpreted as a punishment laid on the community by its god, the ceremony was so wholly deficient in distributive justice that it was calculated to perplex, rather than to educate, the growing sense of morality.

Christian theologians, looking on the sacrifices of the Old Testament as a type of the sacrifice on the cross, and interpreting the latter as a satisfaction to divine justice, have undoubtedly over-estimated the ethical lessons embodied in the Jewish sacrificial system; as may be inferred even from the fact that, for many centuries, the official theology of the Church was content to interpret the death of Christ as a ransom for mankind paid to the devil, or as a satisfaction to the divine honour (Anselm), rather than as a recognition of the sovereignty of the moral law of justice. If Christian theology shows such variations in the interpretation of the doctrine of substitution, it is obviously absurd to expect to find a consistent doctrine on this head in connection with ancient sacrifice;[1]

[1] Jewish theology has a great deal to say about the acceptance of the merits of the righteous on behalf of the wicked, but very little about atonement through sacrifice.

and it may safely be affirmed that the influence of piacular sacrifices, in keeping the idea of divine justice before the minds of ancient nations, was very slight compared with the influence of the vastly more important idea that the gods, primarily as the vindicators of the duties of kinship, and then also of the wider morality which ultimately grew up on the basis of kinship, preside over the public exercise of justice, give oracles for the detection of hidden offences, and sanction or demand the execution of guilty tribesmen. Of these very real functions of divine justice the piacular sacrifice, when interpreted as a scenic execution, is at best only an empty shadow.

Another interpretation of piacular sacrifice, which has great prominence in antiquity, is that it purges away guilt. The cleansing effect of piacula is mainly associated with the application to the persons of the worshippers of sacrificial blood or ashes, or of holy water and other things of sacred virtue, including holy herbs and even the fragrant smoke of incense. This is a topic which it would be easy to illustrate at great length and with a variety of curious particulars; but the principle involved is so simple that little would be gained by the enumeration of all the different substances to which a cathartic value was ascribed, either by themselves or as accessories to an atoning sacrifice. A main point to be noted is that ritual purity has in principle nothing to do with physical cleanliness, though such a connection was ultimately established by the common use of water as a means of lustration. Primarily, purification means the application to the person of some medium which removes a taboo, and enables the person purified to mingle freely in the ordinary life of his fellows. It is not therefore identical with consecration, for the latter often brings special taboos with it. And so we find that the ancients used purificatory rites after as well as before holy functions.[1] But as the normal life of the member of a religious community is in a broad sense a holy life, lived in accordance with certain standing precepts of sanctity, and in a constant relation to the deity of the community, the main use of purificatory rites is not to tone down, to the level of ordinary life, the excessive holiness conveyed by contact with sacrosanct things, but rather to impart to one who has lost it the measure of sanctity that puts him on the level of ordinary social life. So much indeed does this view of the matter predominate, that among the Hebrews all purifications are ordinarily reckoned as purification from uncleanness; thus the man who has burned the red heifer or carried its ashes, becomes ceremonially unclean, though in reality the thing that he has been in contact with was not impure but most holy;[2] and similarly the handling of the Scriptures, according to the Rabbins, defiles the hands, *i.e.* entails a ceremonial washing. Purifications, therefore, are performed by the use of any of the physical means that re-establish normal relations with the deity and the congregation of his worshippers—in short, by contact with something that contains and can impart a divine virtue. For ordinary purposes the use of living water may suffice, for, as we know, there is a sacred principle in such water. But the most powerful cleansing media are necessarily derived from the body and blood of sacrosanct victims, and the forms of purification embrace such rites as the sprinkling of sacrificial blood or ashes on the person, anointing with holy unguents, or fumigation with the smoke of incense, which from early times was a favourite accessory to sacrifices. It seems probable, however, that the religious value of incense was

[1] See *infra*, *Additional Note* B, p. 446 *sq.*, and *supra*, p. 351 *sq.*
[2] Num. xix. 8, 10.

originally independent of animal sacrifice, for frankincense was the gum of a very holy species of tree, which was collected with religious precautions.[1] Whether, therefore, the sacred odour was used in unguents or burned like an altar sacrifice, it appears to have owed its virtue, like the gum of the *samora* tree,[2] to the idea that it was the blood of an animate and divine plant.

It is easy to understand that cathartic media, like holiness itself, were of various degrees of intensity, and were sometimes used, one after another, in an ascending scale. All contact with holy things has a dangerous side; and so, before a man ventures to approach the holiest sacraments, he prepares himself by ablutions and other less potent cathartic applications. On this principle ancient religions developed very complicated schemes of purificatory ceremonial, but in all grave cases these culminated in piacular sacrifice; "without shedding of blood there is no remission of sin."[3]

In the most primitive form of the sacrificial idea the blood of the sacrifice is not employed to wash away an impurity, but to convey to the worshipper a particle of holy life. The conception of piacular media as purificatory, however, involves the notion that the holy medium not only adds something to the worshipper's life, and refreshes its sanctity, but expels from him something that is impure. The two views are obviously not inconsistent, if we conceive impurity as the wrong kind of life, which is dispossessed by inoculation with the right kind. Some idea of this sort is, in fact, that which savages associate with the uncleanness of taboo, which they commonly

[1] Pliny, xii. 54. The right even to see the trees was reserved to certain holy families, who, when engaged in harvesting the gum, had to abstain from all contact with women and from participation in funerals.

[2] *Supra*, p. 133.

[3] Heb. ix. 22.

ascribe to the presence, in or about the man, of "spirits" or living agencies; and the same idea occurs in much higher forms of religion, as when, in mediæval Christianity, exorcisms to expel devils from the catechumen are regarded as a necessary preliminary to baptism.

Among the Semites the impurities which were thought of as cleaving to a man, and making him unfit to mingle freely in the social and religious life of his community, were of very various kinds, and often of a nature that we should regard as merely physical, *e.g.* uncleanness from contact with the dead, from leprosy, from eating forbidden food, and so forth. All these are mere survivals of savage taboos, and present nothing instructive for the higher developments of Semitic religion. They were dealt with, where the uncleanness was of a mild form, mainly by ablutions; or where the uncleanness was more intense, by more elaborate ceremonies involving the use of sacrificial blood,[1] of sacrificial ashes,[2] or the like. Sometimes, as we have seen, the Hebrews and Arabs conveyed the impurity to a bird, and allowed it to fly away with it.[3]

There is, however, one form of impurity, viz. that of bloodshed, with which important ethical ideas connected themselves. Here also the impurity is primarily a physical one; it is the actual blood of the murdered man, staining the hands of the slayer, or lying unatoned and unburied on the ground, that defiles the murderer and his whole community, and has to be cleansed away. We have

[1] Lev. xiv. 17, 51. [2] Num. xix. 17.

[3] *Supra*, p. 422. In the Arabian case the woman also threw away a piece of camel's dung, which must also be supposed to have become the receptacle for her impurity; or she cut her nails or plucked out part of her hair (cf. Deut. xxi. 12), in which, as specially important parts of the body (*supra*, p. 324, note 2), the impure life might be supposed to be concentrated; or she anointed herself with perfume, *i.e.* with a holy medium, or rubbed herself against an ass, sheep or goat, presumably in order to transfer her uncleanness to the animal.

already seen[1] that the Semitic religions provide no atonement for the murderer himself, that can restore him to his original place in his tribe, and this principle survives in the Hebrew law, which does not admit piacula for mortal sins. The ritual idea of cleansing from the guilt of blood is only applicable to the community, which disavows the act of its impious member, and seeks the restoration of its injured holiness by a public sacrificial act. Thus in Semitic antiquity the whole ritual conception of the purging away of sin is bound up with the notion of the solidarity of the body of worshippers—the same notion which makes the pious Hebrews confess and lament not only their own sins, but the sins of their fathers.[2] When the conception that the community, as such, is responsible for the maintenance of holiness in all its parts, is combined with the thought that holiness is specially compromised by crime,—for in early society bloodshed within the kin is the typical form, to the analogy of which all other crimes are referred,—a solid basis is laid for the conception of the religious community as a kingdom of righteousness, which lies at the root of the spiritual teaching of the Hebrew prophets. The stricter view of divine righteousness which distinguishes Hebrew religion from that of the Greeks even before the prophetic period, is mainly connected with the idea that, so far as individuals are concerned, there is no atonement for mortal sin.[3] This principle indeed is common to all races in the earliest stages of law and religion; but among the Greeks it was early broken down, for reasons that have been already explained,[4] while among the Hebrews it subsisted, without change, till a date when the conception of sin was sufficiently developed to

[1] *Supra*, pp. 359 *sq.*, 423.
[2] Hos. x. 9; Jer. iii. 25; Ezra ix. 7; Ps. cvi. 6.
[3] Ex. xxi. 14.
[4] *Supra*, p. 360

permit of its being interpreted, as was done by the prophets, in a way that raised the religion of Israel altogether out of the region of physical ideas with which primitive conceptions of holiness are bound up.

We had occasion a moment ago to glance at the subject of confession of sin and lamentation over it. The connection of this part of religion with piacular sacrifice is important enough to deserve a separate consideration.

Among the Jews the great Day of Expiation was a day of humiliation and penitent sorrow for sin, for which a strict fast and all the outward signs of deep mourning were prescribed.[1] Similar forms of grief were observed in all solemn supplications at the sanctuary, not only by the Hebrews,[2] but by their neighbours.[3] On such occasions, where the mourners assemble at a temple or high place, we must, according to the standing rules of ancient religion, assume that a piacular sacrifice formed the culminating point of the service;[4] and conversely it appears probable that forms of mourning, more or less accentuated, habitually went with piacular rites, not only when they were called for by some great public calamity, but on other occasions too. For we have already seen that in the annual piacula of the Baal religion there was also a formal act of mourning, which, however, was not an expression of penitence for sin, but a lament over the dead god. In this last case the origin and primary significance of the obligatory lamentation is sufficiently transparent; for the death of the god is originally nothing else than

[1] According to *Yoma*, viii. 1, washing, unguents, and the use of shoes were forbidden.

[2] 1 Sam. vii. 6; Isa. xxxvii. 1; Joel ii. 12 *sqq.*

[3] Isa. xv. 2 *sqq.*

[4] In Hos. vii. 14 the mourners who howl upon their beds are engaged in a religious function. And as ordinary mourners lie on the ground, I take it that the beds are the couches on which men reclined at a sacrificial banquet (Amos ii. 8, vi. 4), which here has the character, not of a joyous feast, but of an atoning rite.

the death of the theanthropic victim, which is bewailed by those who assist at the ceremony, exactly as the Todas bewail the slaughter of the sacred buffalo.[1] On the same principle the Egyptians of Thebes bewailed the death of the ram that was annually sacrificed to the god Amen, and then clothed the idol in its skin and buried the carcase in a sacred coffin.[2] Here the mourning is for the death of the sacrosanct victim, which, as the use of the skin indicates, represents the god himself. But an act of lamentation was not less appropriate in cases where the victim was thought of rather as representing a man of the kindred of the worshippers; and primarily, as we know, the theanthropic victim was equally akin to the god and to the sacrificers.

I think it can be made probable that a form of lamentation over the victim was part of the oldest sacrificial ritual, and that this is the explanation of such rites as the howling (ὀλολυγή) which accompanied Greek sacrifices, and in which, as in acts of mourning for the dead, women took the chief part. Herodotus (iv. 189) was struck with the resemblance between the Greek practice and that of the Libyans, a race among whom the sacredness of domestic animals was very marked. The Libyans killed their sacrifices without bloodshed, by throwing them over their huts[3] and then twisting their necks. Where bloodshed is avoided in a sacrifice, we may be sure that the life of the victim is regarded as human or theanthropic, and the howling can be nothing else than an act of mourning. Among the Semites, in like manner, the shouting (*hallel*, *tahlīl*) that accompanied

[1] *Supra*, p. 299 *sq.*

[2] Herod. ii. 42. In Egypt an act of mourning went also with other sacrifices, notably in the great feast at Busiris; Herod. ii. 40, 61.

[3] This is analogous to the Paschal sprinkling of blood on the lintel and doorposts.

sacrifice may probably, in its oldest shape, have been a wail over the death of the victim, though it ultimately took the form of a chant of praise (Hallelujah), or, among the Arabs, degenerated into a meaningless repetition of the word *labbaika*. For it is scarcely legitimate to separate the Semitic *tahlīl* from the Greek and Libyan ὀλολυγή, and indeed the roots הלל and ילל (Ar. ولول), "to chant praises" and "to howl," are closely connected.[1]

Another rite which admits of a twofold interpretation is the sacrificial dance. Dancing is a common expression of religious joy, as appears from many passages of the Old Testament, but the limping dance of the priests of Baal in 1 Kings xviii. 26 is associated with forms of mournful supplication, and in Syriac the same verb, in different conjugations, means "to dance" and "to mourn."

In ordinary sacrificial service, the ancient attitude of awe at the death of the victim was transformed into one of gladness, and the shouting underwent a corresponding change of meaning.[2] But piacular rites continued

[1] On this topic consult, but with caution, Movers, *Phoen.* i. 246 *sq.* The Arabic *ahalla, tahlīl*, is primarily connected with the slaughter of the victim (*supra*, p. 340). Meat that has been killed in the name of an idol is *mā ohilla lighairi 'llāh*, and the *tahlīl* includes (1) the *bismillāh* of the sacrificer, (2) the shouts of the congregation accompanying this act, (3) by a natural extension, all religious shouting. If, now, we note that the *bismillāh* is the form by which the sacrificer excuses his bold act, and that *tahlīl* also means "shrinking back in terror" (see Nöldeke in *ZDMG.* xli. 723), we can hardly doubt that the shouting was originally not joyous, but an expression of awe and anguish. The derivation of اهلّ from هلال, the new moon (Lagarde, *Orientalia*, ii. 19; Snouck-Hurgronje, *Het mekkaansche Feest*, p. 75), is tempting, but must be given up. Compare on the whole matter, Wellh. p. 107 *sqq.*

[2] This transition was probably much easier than it seems to us; for shouting in mourning and shouting in joy seem both to be primarily directed to drive away evil influences. Of course, men, like children, are noisy when they are glad, but the conventional shrill cries of women in the East (*zaghārīt*) are not natural expressions of joy, and do not differ materially from the sound made in wailing. The Hebrew word *rinna* is used both of shouts of joy and of the cry of suppliants at a religious fast (Jer.

to be conducted with signs of mourning, which were interpreted, as we have seen, sometimes as a lamentation for the death of the god, and sometimes as forms of penitent supplication, and deprecation of divine wrath.

That feelings of contrition find an expression in acts of mourning, is an idea so familiar to us that at first sight it seems to need no explanation; but a little reflection will correct this impression, and make it appear by no means unreasonable to suppose that the forms of mourning observed in supplicatory rites were not primarily expressions of sorrow for sin, or lamentable appeals to the compassion of the deity, but simply the obligatory wailing for the death of a kindred victim. The forms prescribed are identical with those used in mourning for the dead; and if it be urged that this is merely an expression of the most pungent grief, I reply that we have already found reason to be chary in assuming that certain acts are natural expressions of sorrow, and to recognise that the customs observed in lamentation for the dead had originally a very definite meaning, and could not become general expressions of grief till that meaning was forgotten.[1] And it is surely easier to suppose that the ancient rites of lamentation for the victim changed their sense, when men fell out of touch with the original meaning of them, than that they were altogether dropped for a time, and then resumed with a new meaning.

Again, the idea that the gods have a kindred feeling with their worshippers, and are touched with compassion when they see them to be miserable, is no doubt familiar even to early religions. But formal acts of worship in antiquity,

xiv. 12). In Arabic the root is used mainly of plaintive cries, as of mourning women.

[1] *Supra*, p. 322 *sq.*, p. 336 *sq.*

as we have seen from our analysis of sacrificial rites, are directed, not merely to appeal to the sentiment of the deity, but to lay him under a social obligation. Even in the theology of the Rabbins, penitence atones only for light offences, all grave offences demanding also a material prestation.[1] If this is the view of later Judaism, after all that had been taught by the prophets as to the worthlessness of material offerings, in the eyes of a God who looks at the heart, it is hardly to be thought that in heathen religions elaborate forms of mourning and supplication were nothing more than appeals to divine compassion. And, in fact, there is no doubt that some of the forms which we are apt to take as expressions of intense grief or self-abasement before the god, had originally quite another meaning. For example, when the worshippers gash their own flesh in rites of supplication, this is not an appeal to the divine compassion, but a purely physical means of establishing a blood-bond with the god.[2] Again, the usage of religious fasting is commonly taken as a sign of sorrow, the worshippers being so distressed at the alienation of their god that they cannot eat; but there are very strong reasons for believing that, in the strict Oriental form in which total abstinence from meat and drink is prescribed, fasting is primarily nothing more than a preparation for the sacramental eating of holy flesh. Some savage nations not only fast, but use strong purges before venturing to eat holy meat;[3] similarly the Harranians fasted on the eighth of Nisan, and then broke their fast on mutton, at the same time offering sheep as holocausts;[4] the modern Jews fast from ten in the morning before eating the Passover; and

[1] *Yoma*, viii. 8, תשובה מכפרת על עבירות קלות.

[2] *Supra*, p. 321 *sqq.*

[3] Thomson, *Masai Land*, p. 430.

[4] *Fihrist*, p. 322. In Egypt a fast preceded the sacrificial meal at the great feast of Busiris, where the victim is clearly theanthropic, Herod. ii. 40, 61.

even a modern Catholic must come to the communion with an empty stomach. On the whole, then, the conclusion seems to be legitimate, that the ritual of penitent confession and humiliation for sin follows the same law that we have found to hold good in other departments of ritual observance; the original interpretation turns on a physical conception of holiness, and it is only gradually and incompletely that physical ideas give way to ethical interpretation.

To the account that has been given of various aspects of the atoning efficacy of sacrifice, and of ritual observances that go with sacrifice, I have still to add some notice of a very remarkable series of ceremonies, in which the skin of the sacrosanct victim plays the chief part. In Nilus's sacrifice the skin and hair of the victim are eaten up like the rest of the carcase, and in some piacula, *e.g.* the Levitical red heifer, the victim is burned skin and all. Usually, however, it is flayed; and in later rituals, where rules are laid down determining whether the skin shall belong to the sacrificer or be part of the priest's fee, the hide is treated merely as an article of some commercial value which has no sacred significance.[1] But we have seen that in old times all parts of the sacrosanct victim were intensely holy, even down to the offal and excrement, and whatever was not eaten or burned was used for other sacred purposes, and had the force of a charm. The skin, in particular, is used in antique rituals either to clothe the idol or to clothe the worshippers. The meaning

[1] By the Levitical law (Lev. vii. 8) the skin of the holocaust goes to the ministrant priest; in other cases it must be inferred that it was retained by the owner. In the Carthaginian tariffs the usage varies, one temple giving the hides of victims to the priests and another to the owner of the sacrifice (*CIS.* Nos. 165, 167). At Sippar in Babylonia the sacrificial dues paid to the priest included the hide (*Beiträge zur Assyriologie*, vol. i. (1890) pp. 274, 286).

of both these rites was sufficiently perspicuous at the stage of religious development in which the god, his worshippers, and the victim were all members of one kindred.

As regards the draping of the idol or sacred stone in the skin, it will be remembered that in Lecture V. we came to the conclusion that in most cases sacred stones are not naturally holy, but are arbitrary erections which become holy because the god consents to dwell in them. We also find a widespread idea, persisting even in the ritual of the Jewish Day of Atonement, that the altar (which is only a more modern form of the sacred stone) requires to be consecrated with blood, and periodically reconsecrated in the same way.[1] In fact it is the sacred blood that makes the stone holy and a habitation of divine life; as in all the other parts of ritual, man does not begin by persuading his god to dwell in the stone, but by a theurgic process he actually brings divine life to the stone. All sanctuaries are consecrated by a theophany; but in the earliest times the sacrifice is itself a rudimentary theophany, and the place where sacred blood has once been shed is the fittest place to shed it again. From this point of view it is natural, not only to pour blood upon the altar-idol, but to anoint it with sacred fat, to fix upon it the heads and horns of sacrifices, and so forth. All these things are done in various parts of the world,[2] and when the sacred stone is on the way to become an idol, and primarily an animal-idol, it is peculiarly appropriate to dress it in the skin of the divine victim.

On the other hand, it is equally appropriate that the

[1] Ezek. xliii. 18 *sqq.*; Lev. viii. 15; Ezek. xlv. 18 *sqq.*; Lev. xvi. 33.

[2] The heads of oxen are common symbols on Greek altars, and this is only a modern surrogate for the actual heads of victims. The horns of the Semitic altar have perhaps the same origin.

worshipper should dress himself in the skin of a victim, and so, as it were, envelop himself in its sanctity. To rude nations dress is not merely a physical comfort, but a fixed part of social religion, a thing by which a man constantly bears on his body the token of his religion, and which is itself a charm and a means of divine protection. Among African nations, where the sacredness of domestic animals is still acknowledged, one of the few purposes for which a beast may be killed is to get its skin as a cloak; and in the Book of Genesis (iii. 21) the primitive coat of skin is given to the first men by the Deity Himself. Similarly Herodotus, when he speaks of the sacrifices and worship of the Libyans,[1] is at once led on to observe that the ægis or goat-skin, worn by the statues of Athena, is nothing else than the goat-skin, fringed with thongs, which was worn by the Libyan women; the inference implies that it was a sacred dress.[2] When the dress of sacrificial skin, which at once declared a man's religion and his sacred kindred, ceased to be used in ordinary life, it was still retained in holy and especially in piacular functions. We have several examples of this within the Semitic field: the Assyrian Dagon-worshipper who offers the mystic fish-sacrifice to the Fish-god draped in a fish-skin; the old Phœnician sacrifice of game by men clothed in the skin of

[1] Herod. iv. 188 *sqq.*; that the victims were goats is suggested by the context, but becomes certain by comparison of Hippocrates, ed. Littré, vi. 356.

[2] The thongs correspond to the fringes on the garment prescribed by Jewish law, which had a sacred significance (Num. xv. 38 *sqq.*). One of the oldest forms of the fringed garment is probably the *rahṭ* or *ḥauf*, a girdle or short kilt of skin slashed into thongs, which was worn by Arab girls, by women in their courses, and also, it is said, by worshippers at the Caaba. From this primitive garment are derived the thongs and girdles with lappets that appear as amulets among the Arabs (*barīm, morassa'a*; the latter is pierced, and another thong passed through it); compare the magical thongs of the Luperci, cut from the skin of the piaculum, whose touch cured sterility.

their prey; the Cyprian sacrifice of a sheep to the Sheep-goddess, in which sheep-skins are worn.[1] Similar examples are afforded by the Dionysiac mysteries and other Greek rites, and by almost every rude religion; while in later cults the old rite survives at least in the religious use of animal masks.[2] When worshippers present themselves at the sanctuary, already dressed in skins of the sacred kind, the meaning of the ceremony is that they come to worship as kinsmen of the victim, and so also of the god. But when the fresh skin of the victim is applied to the worshipper in the sacrifice, the idea is rather an imparting to him of the sacred virtue of its life. Thus in piacular and cathartic rites the skin of the sacrifice is used in a way quite similar to the use of the blood, but dramatically more expressive of the identification of the worshipper's life with that of the victim. In Greek piacula the man on whose behalf the sacrifice was performed simply put his foot on the skin (κώδιον); at Hierapolis the pilgrim put the head and feet over his own head while he knelt on the skin;[3] in certain late Syrian rites a boy is initiated by a sacrifice in which his feet are clothed in slippers made of the skin of the sacrifice.[4] These rites do not appear to have suggested any idea, as to the meaning of piacular sacrifice, different from those that have already come before us; but as the skin of a sacrifice is the oldest form of a sacred garment, appropriate to the performance of holy functions, the figure of a "robe of righteousness," which is found both in the Old Testa-

[1] *Supra*, pp. 293, 310; and *Additional Notes* F and G. Note also that the hereditary priests of the Palmetum were dressed in skins (Strabo, xvi. 4. 18). Cf. the "girdle," or rather "kilt of skin," worn by the prophet Elijah (2 Kings i. 8).

[2] Such masks were used by the Arabs of Nejrān in rites which the Bishop Gregentius, in the laws he made for his flock (chap. xxxiv.), denounces as heathenish (Boissonade, *Anecd. Gr.* vol. v.).

[3] *Dea Syria*, lv. [4] *Actes* of the Leyden Congress, ii. 1. 336 (361).

ment and in the New, and still supplies one of the commonest theological metaphors, may be ultimately traced back to this source.

On the whole it is apparent, from the somewhat tedious discussion which I have now brought to a close, that the various aspects in which atoning rites presented themselves to ancient worshippers have supplied a variety of religious images which passed into Christianity, and still have currency. Redemption, substitution, purification, atoning blood, the garment of righteousness, are all terms which in some sense go back to antique ritual. But in ancient religion all these terms are very vaguely defined; they indicate impressions produced on the mind of the worshipper by features of the ritual, rather than formulated ethico-dogmatical ideas; and the attempt to find in them anything as precise and definite as the notions attached to the same words by Christian theologians is altogether illegitimate. The one point that comes out clear and strong is that the fundamental idea of ancient sacrifice is sacramental communion, and that all atoning rites are ultimately to be regarded as owing their efficacy to a communication of divine life to the worshippers, and to the establishment or confirmation of a living bond between them and their god. In primitive ritual this conception is grasped in a merely physical and mechanical shape, as indeed, in primitive life, all spiritual and ethical ideas are still wrapped up in the husk of a material embodiment. To free the spiritual truth from the husk was the great task that lay before the ancient religions, if they were to maintain the right to continue to rule the minds of men. That some progress in this direction was made, especially in Israel, appears from our examination. But on the whole it is manifest that none of the ritual systems of antiquity was able by mere natural development to shake itself free from the congenital defect inherent in every attempt to embody spiritual truth in material forms. A ritual system must always remain materialistic, even if its materialism is disguised under the cloak of mysticism.

ADDITIONAL NOTES

ADDITIONAL NOTE A (p. 138)

GODS, DEMONS, AND PLANTS OR ANIMALS

THE object of this note is to consider some difficulties that may be felt with regard to the argument in the text.

1. The importance which I have attached to Arabian superstitions about the *jinn*, as affording a clue to the origin of local sanctuaries, may appear to be excessive when it is observed that the facts are almost all drawn from one part of the Semitic field. What evidence is there, it may be asked, that these Arabian superstitions are part of the common belief of the Semitic race? To this I reply, in the first place, that the Arabian conception proves upon analysis to have nothing peculiar about it. It is the ordinary conception of all primitive savages, and involves ideas that only belong to the savage mind. To suppose that it originated in Arabia, for special and local reasons, after the separation of the other Semites, is therefore to run in the teeth of all probability. Again, the little we do know about the goblins of the Northern Semites is in full agreement with the Arabian facts. The demons were banished from Hebrew religion, and hardly appear in the Old Testament except in poetic imagery. But the שְׂעִירִים or hairy ones, the לִילִית or nocturnal goblin, are exactly like the Arabian *jinn* (Wellhausen, p. 135).

The main point, however, is that the savage view of nature, which ascribes to plants and animals discourse of reason, and supernatural or demoniac attributes, can be shown to have prevailed among the Northern Semites as well as the Arabs. The savage point of view is constantly found to survive, in connection with practices of magic, after it has been superseded in religion proper; and the superstitions of the vulgar in modern civilised countries are not much more advanced than those of the rudest nations. So too among the Semites, magical rites and vulgar superstitions are not so much survivals from the higher official heathenism of the great sanctuaries as from a lower and more primitive stage of belief, which the higher forms of heathen worship overshadowed but did not extinguish. And the view of nature that pervades Semitic magic is precisely that savage view which we have found to underlie the Arabian belief in the *jinn*. Of the magical practices of the ancient Syrians, which persisted long after the introduction of Christianity, some specimens are preserved in the *Canons* of Jacob of Edessa, edited in Syriac by Lagarde, *Rel. iur. eccl. ant.* (Leipz. 1856), and translated by Kayser, *Die Canones Jacob's von Edessa* (Leipz. 1886). One of these, used in cases of sickness, was to dig up the root of a certain kind of thorn called "ischiac," and make an offering to it, eating and drinking beside the root, which was treated as a guest at the feast (Qu. 38). Another demoniac plant of the Northern Semites is the Baaras, described by Josephus, *B. J.* vii. 6. 3, which flees from those who try to grasp it, and whose touch is death so long as it is rooted in the ground. This plant seems to be the mandrake (Ar. *yabrūh*), about which the Arabs tell similar stories, and which even the ancient Germans thought to be inhabited by a spirit. When the plants in Jotham's parable speak and act like men, this is mere personification; but the dispute of the mallow and the mandrake, which Maimonides relates from the forged *Nabatæan Agriculture* (Chwolsohn, *Ssabier*, ii. 459, 914), and which prevents the mallow from supplying her prophet with responses, is a genuine piece of old Semitic superstition. In matters of this sort we cannot doubt that even a forger correctly represents popular beliefs. As regards animals, the demoniac character of the serpent in the Garden of Eden is unmistakable; the serpent is not a mere temporary disguise of Satan, otherwise its punishment would be meaningless.[1] The practice of serpent charming, repeatedly referred to in the Old Testament, is also connected with the demoniac character of the creature; and in general the idea that animals can be constrained by spells, *e.g.* prevented from injuring flocks and vineyards (Jacob of Ed., Qu. 46), rests on the same

[1] So in the legends of Syriac saints, the proper form of Satan, which he is compelled to resume when met with the name of Christ or the sign of the cross, is that of a black snake (*Mar Ḳardagh*, ed. Abbeloos, p. 39; Hoffmann, *Syr. Akten*, p. 76).

view, for the power of wizards is over demons and beings that are subject to the demons.

One of the most curious of the Syrian superstitions is as follows:—When caterpillars infest a garden, the maidens are assembled; a single caterpillar is taken, and one of the girls is constituted its mother. The insect is then bewailed and buried, and the mother is conducted to the place where the other caterpillars are, amidst lamentations for her bereavement. The whole of the caterpillars will then disappear (*op. cit.* Qu. 44). Here it is clearly assumed that the insects understand and are impressed by the tragedy got up for their benefit. The Syriac legends of Tūr 'Abdīn, collected by Prym and Socin (Gött. 1881), are full of beasts with demoniac powers. In these stories each kind of beast forms a separate organised community; they speak and act like men, but have supernatural powers, and close relations to the *jinn* that also occur in the legends. In conclusion, it may be observed that the universal Semitic belief in omens and guidance given by animals belongs to the same range of ideas. Omens are not blind tokens; the animals know what they tell to men.

2. If the argument in the text is correct, it may be asked why there are not direct and convincing evidences of Semitic totemism. You argue, it may be said, that traces of the old savage view of nature, which corresponds to totemism, are still clearly visible in the Semitic view of demons. But in savage nations that view is habitually conjoined with the belief that one kind of demon—or, more correctly, one kind of plants or animals endowed with demoniac qualities—is allied by kinship with each kindred of men. How does this square with the Arabian facts, in which all demons or demoniac animals habitually appear as man's enemies? The general answer to this difficulty is that totems, or friendly demoniac beings, rapidly develop into gods when men rise above pure savagery; whereas unfriendly beings, lying outside the circle of man's organised life, are not directly influenced by the social progress, and retain their primitive characteristics unchanged. When men deem themselves to be of the same blood with a particular animal kind, every advance in their way of thinking about themselves reacts on their ideas about the sacred animals. When they come to think of their god as the ancestor of their race, they must also think of him as the ancestor of their totem animals, and, so far as our observation goes, they tend to figure him as having animal form. The animal god concentrates on his

own person the respect that used to be paid to all animals of the totem kind, or at least the respect paid to them is made to depend on the worship he receives. Finally, the animal god, who, as a demoniac being, has many human attributes, is transformed into an anthropomorphic god, and his animal connections fall quite into the background. But nothing of this sort can happen to the demoniac animals that are left outside, and not brought into fellowship with men. They remain as they were, till the progress of enlightenment—a slow progress among the mass of any race—gradually strips them of their supernatural attributes. Thus it is natural that the belief in hostile demons of plant or animal kinds should survive long after the friendly kinds have given way to individual gods, whose original totem associations are in great measure obliterated. At the stage which even the rudest Semitic peoples had reached when they first become known to us, it would be absurd to expect to find examples of totemism pure and simple. What we may expect to find is the fragmentary survival of totem ideas, in the shape of special associations between certain kinds of animals on the one hand, and certain tribes or religious communities and their gods on the other hand. And of evidence of this kind there is, we shall see, no lack in Semitic antiquity. For the present I will only cite some direct evidences of kinship or brotherhood between human communities and animal kinds. Ibn al-Mojāwir relates that when the B. Hārith, a tribe of South Arabia, find a dead gazelle, they wash it, wrap it in cerecloths and bury it, and the whole tribe mourns for it seven days (Sprenger, *Postrouten*, p. 151). The animal is buried like a man, and mourned for as a kinsman.[1] Among the Arabs of Sinai the *wabr* (the coney of the Bible) is the brother of man, and it is said that he who eats his flesh will never see father and mother again. In the Harranian mysteries the worshippers acknowledged dogs, ravens and ants as their brothers (*Fihrist*, p. 326, l. 27). At Baalbek, the γενναῖος, or ancestral god of the town, was worshipped in the form of a lion (Damascius, *Vit. Isid.* § 203; cf. גר בעל, "leontopodion," Löw, *Aram. Pflanzennamen*, p. 406; G. Hoffmann, *Phoen.*

[1] Similarly we are told by Sohailī in his com. on B. Hishām (ed. Wüst. ii. 41 *sq.*) of more than one instance in which an orthodox Muslim wrapped a dead snake in a piece of his cloak and buried it. 'Omar II. is said to have done so. In this case the snake was "a believing Jinnī," an explanation that seems to be devised to justify an act of primitive superstition; cf. Damīrī, i. 233.

Inschr. 1889, p. 27). On the banks of the Euphrates, according to *Mir. Ausc.* 149 *sq.*, there was found a species of small serpents that attacked foreigners, but did not molest natives, which is just what a totem animal is supposed to do.

3. If the oldest sanctuaries of the gods were originally haunts of a multiplicity of *jinn*, or of animals to which demoniac attributes were ascribed, we should expect to find, even in later times, some trace of the idea that the holy place is not inhabited by a single god, but by a plurality of sacred denizens. If the relation between the worshipping community and the sanctuary was formed in the totem state of thought, when the sacred denizens were still veritable animals, all animals of the sacred species would multiply unmolested in the holy precincts, and the individual god of the sanctuary, when such a being came to be singled out from the indeterminate plurality of totem creatures, would still be the father and protector of all animals of his own kind. And accordingly we do find that Semitic sanctuaries gave shelter to various species of sacred animals,—the doves of Astarte, the gazelles of Tabāla and Mecca, and so forth. But, apart from this, we may expect to find traces of vague plurality in the conception of the godhead as associated with special spots, to hear not so much of the god as of the gods of a place, and that not in the sense of a definite number of clearly individualised deities, but with the same indefiniteness as characterises the conception of the *jinn*. I am inclined to think that this is the idea which underlies the Hebrew use of the plural אלהים, and the Phœnician use of אלם, in a singular sense, on which cf. Hoffmann, *op. cit.* p. 17 *sqq.* Merely to refer this to primitive polytheism, as is sometimes done, does not explain how the plural form is habitually used to designate a single deity. But if the *Elōhīm* of a place originally meant all its sacred denizens, viewed collectively as an indeterminate sum of indistinguishable beings, the transition to the use of the plural in a singular sense would follow naturally, as soon as this indeterminate conception gave way to the conception of an individual god of the sanctuary. Further, the original indeterminate plurality of the *Elōhīm* appears in the conception of angels as *Bnē Elōhīm*, "sons of Elohim," which, according to linguistic analogy, means "beings of the Elohim kind." In the Old Testament the "sons of God" form the heavenly court, and ordinarily when an angel appears on earth he appears alone and on a special mission. But, in some of the oldest Hebrew traditions, angels

frequent holy places, such as Bethel and Mahanaim, when they have no message to deliver (Gen. xxviii. 12, xxxii. 2). That the angels, as "sons of God," form part of the old Semitic mythology, is clear from Gen. vi. 2, 4, for the sons of God who contract marriages with the daughters of men are out of place in the religion of the Old Testament, and the legend must have been taken over from a lower form of faith; perhaps it was a local legend connected with Mount Hermon (B. Enoch vi. 6; Hilary on Ps. cxxxiii.). Ewald (*Lehre der Bibel*, ii. 283) rightly observes that in Gen. xxxii. 28-30 the meaning is that an angel has no name, *i.e.* no distinctive individuality; he is simply one of a class; cf. p. 126, note, *supra*. Yet in wrestling with him Jacob wrestles with אלהים (cf. Hos. xii. 4).

That the Arabic *jinn* is not a loan-word, as has sometimes been supposed, is shown by Nöldeke, *ZDMG.* xli. 717.

ADDITIONAL NOTE B (p. 153)

HOLINESS, UNCLEANNESS AND TABOO

VARIOUS parallels between savage taboos, and Semitic rules of holiness and uncleanness, will come before us from time to time; but it may be useful to bring together at this point some detailed evidences that the two are in their origin indistinguishable.

Holy and unclean things have this in common, that in both cases certain restrictions lie on men's use of and contact with them, and that the breach of these restrictions involves supernatural dangers. The difference between the two appears, not in their relation to man's ordinary life, but in their relation to the gods. Holy things are not free to man, because they pertain to the gods; uncleanness is shunned, according to the view taken in the higher Semitic religions, because it is hateful to the god, and therefore not to be tolerated in his sanctuary, his worshippers, or his land. But that this explanation is not primitive can hardly be doubted, when we consider that the acts that cause uncleanness are exactly the same which among savage nations place a man under taboo, and that these acts are often involuntary, and often innocent, or even necessary to society. The savage, accordingly, imposes a taboo on a woman in childbed, or during her courses, and on the man who touches a corpse, not out of any regard for the gods, but simply because birth and everything connected with the propagation of the species on the one hand, and disease and death on the other, seem to him to involve the action of superhuman agencies of a dangerous kind. If he attempts to explain, he does so by supposing that on these occasions spirits of deadly power are present; at all events the persons involved seem to him to be sources of mysterious danger, which has all the characters of an infection, and may extend to other people unless due precautions are observed. This is not scientific, but it is perfectly intelligible, and forms the basis of a consistent system of practice; whereas, when the rules of uncleanness are made to rest on the will of the gods, they appear altogether arbitrary and meaningless. The affinity of such taboos with laws of uncleanness comes out most clearly when we observe that uncleanness is treated like a contagion, which has to be washed away or otherwise eliminated by physical means. Take the rules about the uncleanness produced by the carcases of vermin in Lev. xi. 32 *sqq.*; whatever they touch must be washed; the water itself is then unclean, and can propagate the contagion; nay, if the defilement affect an (unglazed) earthen pot, it is supposed to sink into the pores, and cannot be washed out, so that the pot must be broken. Rules like this have nothing in common with the spirit of Hebrew religion; they can only be remains of a primitive superstition, like that of the savage who shuns the blood of uncleanness, and such like things, as a supernatural and deadly virus. The antiquity of the Hebrew taboos, for such they are, is shown by the way in which many of them reappear in Arabia; cf. for example Deut. xxi. 12, 13, with the Arabian ceremonies for removing the impurity of widowhood (*supra*, pp. 422, 428, n.). In the Arabian form the ritual is of purely savage type; the danger to life that made it unsafe for a man to marry the woman was transferred in the most materialistic way to an animal, which it was believed generally died in consequence, or to a bird. So too in the law for cleansing the leper (Lev. xiv. 4 *sqq.*) the impurity is transferred to a bird, which flies away with it; compare also the ritual of the scape-goat. So, again, the impurity of menstruation was recognised by all the Semites,[1] as in fact it is by all primitive

[1] The precept of the Coran, ii. 222, rests on ancient practice; see Baiḍāwī on the passage, *Ḥamāsa*, p. 107, last verse, and *Agh.* xvi. 27, 31.

and ancient peoples. Now among savages this impurity is distinctly connected with the idea that the blood of the *menses* is dangerous to man, and even the Romans held that "nihil facile reperiatur mulierum profluuio magis mirificum," or more full of deadly qualities (Pliny, *H. N.* vii. 64). Similar superstitions are current with the Arabs, a great variety of supernatural powers attaching themselves to a woman in this condition (Cazwīnī, i. 365). Obviously, therefore, in this case the Semitic taboo is exactly like the savage one; it has nothing to do with respect for the gods, but springs from mere terror of the supernatural influences associated with the woman's physical condition. That unclean things are tabooed on account of their inherent supernatural powers or associations, appears further from the fact that just these things are most powerful in magic; menstruous blood in particular is one of the strongest of charms in most countries, and so it was among the Arabs (Cazwīnī, *ut supra*). Wellhausen has shown how closely the ideas of amulet and ornament are connected (*Heid.* p. 143), but has not brought out the equally characteristic fact that unclean things are not less potent. Such amulets are called by the Arabs *tanjīs*, *monajjasa*; and it is explained that the heathen Arabs used to tie unclean things, dead men's bones and menstruous rags, upon children, to avert the *jinn* and the evil eye (*Cāmūs*, *s.v.*); cf. Jacob of Edessa, *op. cit.* Qu. 43.

We have seen, in the example of the swine, that prohibitions against using, and especially eating, certain animals belong in the higher Semitic religions to a sort of doubtful ground between the unclean and the holy. This topic cannot be fully elucidated till we come to speak of sacrifice, when it will appear probable that most of these restrictions, if not all of them, are parallel to the taboos which totemism lays on the use of sacred animals as food. Meantime it may be observed that such prohibitions, like those

For the Syrian heathen, *Fihrist*, p. 319, l. 18. According to Wāḥidī, *Asbāb*, women in their courses were not allowed to remain in the house, which is a common savage rule. According to Mofaḍḍal al-Ḍabbī, *Amthāl*, p. 24, l. 20, the *'ārik* was isolated from her people in a hut, which, as may be inferred from the story, was on the outskirts of the hamlet or encampment. The same custom is indicated in the legend of the fall of Ḥaṭra, Ṭab. i. 829. 3. Girls at their first menstruation seem to have been strictly confined to a hut or tent; see the *Lisān* on the term *mo'ṣir*. This is also common all over the world. Widows were similarly confined; see the Lexx. *s.v.* حفش.

that have been already considered, manifest their savage origin by the nature of the supernatural sanction attached to them. As the elk clan of the Omahas believe that they cannot eat the elk without boils breaking out on their bodies, so the Syrians, with whom fish were sacred to Atargatis, thought that if they ate a sprat or an anchovy they were visited with ulcers, swellings and wasting disease.[1] In both cases the punishment of the impious act is not a divine judgment, in our sense of that word, but flows directly from the malignant influences resident in the forbidden thing, which, so to speak, avenges itself on the offender. With this it agrees that the more notable unclean animals possess magical powers; the swine, for example, which the Saracens as well as the Hebrews and Syrians refused to eat (Sozomen, vi. 38), supplies many charms and magical medicines (Cazwīnī, i. 393).

The irrationality of laws of uncleanness, from the standpoint of spiritual religion or even of the higher heathenism, is so manifest, that they must necessarily be looked on as having survived from an earlier form of faith and of society. And this being so, I do not see how any historical student can refuse to class them with savage taboos. The attempts to explain them otherwise, which are still occasionally met with, seem to be confined to speculative writers, who have no knowledge of the general features of thought and belief in rude societies. As regards holy things in the proper sense of the word, *i.e.* such as are directly connected with the worship and service of the gods, more difficulty may reasonably be felt; for many of the laws of holiness may seem to have a good and reasonable sense even in the higher forms of religion, and to find their sufficient explanation in the habits and institutions of advanced societies. At present the most current view of the meaning of restrictions on man's free use of holy things is that holy things are the god's property, and I have therefore sought (*supra*, p. 142 *sqq.*) to show that the idea of property does not suffice to explain the facts of the case. A man's property consists of things to which he has an exclusive right; but in holy things the worshippers have rights as well as the gods, though their rights are subject to definite restrictions. Again, an owner is bound to respect other people's property while he preserves his own; but

[1] Menander, *ap.* Porph., *De Abst.* iv. 15; Plut., *De Superst.* x.; Selden, *De Diis Syris*, Synt. ii. Cap. 3. For savage parallels, see Frazer, *Totemism*, p. 16 *sqq.*

the principle of holiness, as appears in the law of asylum, can be used to override the privileges of human ownership. In this respect holiness exactly resembles taboo. The notion that certain things are taboo to a god or a chief means only that he, as the stronger person, and not only stronger but invested with supernatural power, and so very dangerous to offend, will not allow anyone else to meddle with them. To bring the taboo into force it is not necessary that there should be prior possession on the part of god or chief; other people's goods may become taboo, and be lost to their original owner, merely by contact with the sacred person or with sacred things. Even the ground on which a king of Tahiti trod became taboo, just as the place of a theophany was thenceforth holy among the Semites. Nor does it follow that because a thing is taboo from the use of man, it is therefore in any real sense appropriated to the use of a god or sacred person; the fundamental notion is merely that it is not safe for ordinary people to use it; it has, so to speak, been touched by the infection of holiness, and so becomes a new source of supernatural danger. In this respect, again, the rules of Semitic holiness show clear marks of their origin in a system of taboo; the distinction that holy things are employed for the use of the gods, while unclean things are simply forbidden to man's use, is not consistently carried out, and there remain many traces of the view that holiness is contagious, just as uncleanness is, and that things which are to be retained for ordinary use must be kept out of the way of the sacred infection. Of things undoubtedly holy, but not in any way used for the divine service, the consecrated camels of the Arabs afford a good example. But in old Israel also we find something of the same kind. By the later law (Lev. xxvii. 27) the firstling of a domestic animal that could not be sacrificed, and which the owner did not care to redeem, was sold for the benefit of the sanctuary, but by the old law (Ex. xiii. 13, xxxiv. 20) its neck was broken—a less humane rule than that of Arabia, where animals tabooed from human use were allowed to run free.[1]

Of the contagiousness of holiness there are many traces exactly similar to taboo. Among the Syrians the dove was most holy, and he who touched it became taboo for a day (*Dea Syria*, liv.). In Isa. lxv. 5 the heathen *mystæ* warn the bystander not to

[1] This parallel shows that the Arabian institution is not a mere degenerate form of an older consecration to positive sacred uses.

approach them lest he become taboo.[1] The flesh of the Hebrew sin-offering, which is holy in the first degree, conveys a taboo to everyone who touches it, and if a drop of the blood falls on a garment, this must be washed, *i.e.* the sanctity must be washed out, in a holy place, while the earthen pot in which the sacrifice is sodden must be broken, as in the case where dead vermin falls in a vessel and renders it unclean (Lev. vi. 27 *sq.* [Heb. ver. 20 *sq.*]; cf. Lev. xvi. 26, 28). At Mecca, in the times of heathenism, the sacred circuit of the Caaba was made by the Bedouins either naked, or in clothes borrowed from one of the *Ḥoms*, or religious community of the sacred city. Wellhausen has shown that this usage was not peculiar to Mecca, for at the sanctuary of Al-Jalsad also it was customary for the sacrificer to borrow a suit from the priest; and the same custom appears in the worship of the Tyrian Baal (2 Kings x. 22), to which it may be added that, in 2 Sam. vi. 14, David wears the priestly ephod at the festival of the in-bringing of the ark. He had put off his usual clothes, for Michal calls his conduct a shameless exposure of his person; see also 1 Sam. xix. 24. The Meccan custom is explained by saying that they would not perform the sacred rite in garments stained with sin, but the real reason is quite different. It appears that sometimes a man did make the circuit in his own clothes, but in that case he could neither wear them again nor sell them, but had to leave them at the gate of the sanctuary (Azracī, p. 125; B. Hishām, p. 128 *sq.*). They became taboo (*ḥarīm*, as the verse cited by Ibn Hishām has it) through contact with the holy place and function. If any doubt remains as to the correctness of this explanation, it will, I trust, be dispelled by a quotation from Shortland's *Southern Districts of New Zealand* (p. 293 *sq.*), which has been given to me by Mr. Frazer. "A slave or other person not sacred would not enter a 'wahi tapu,' or sacred place, without having first stripped off his clothes; for the clothes, having become sacred the instant they entered the precincts of the 'wahi tapu,' would ever after be useless to him in the ordinary business of his life."[2]

[1] The suffix shows that the verb is transitive; not "for I am holier than thou," but "for I would sanctify thee." We should therefore point it as *Piel*, and compare Ezek. xliv. 19, xlvi. 12, where precautions are laid down to prevent the people from being consecrated by approach to holy garments and holy flesh.

[2] It is perhaps on this principle that a man found encroaching on a *ḥimā* is punished by being stripped of his clothes, etc.; *Muḥ in Med.* p. 385

In the case of the garment stained by the blood of the sin-offering, we see that taboos produced by contact with holy things, like those due to uncleanness, can be removed by washing. In like manner, among the Jews the contact of a sacred volume or a phylactery "defiled the hands," and called for an ablution, and the high priest on the Day of Atonement washed his flesh with water, not only when he put on the holy garments of the day, but when he put them off (Lev. xvi. 24; cf. Mishna, *Yōmā*, viii. 4). In savage countries such ablutions are taken to be a literal physical removal of the contagious principle of the taboo, and all symbolical interpretations of them are nothing more than an attempt, in higher stages of religious development, to justify adhesion to traditional ritual.

These examples may suffice to show that it is impossible to separate the Semitic doctrine of holiness and uncleanness from the system of taboo. If anyone is not convinced by them, I am satisfied that he will not be convinced by an accumulation of evidence. But as the subject is curious in itself, and may possibly be found to throw light on some obscure customs, I will conclude this part of the subject by some additional remarks, of a more conjectural character, on the costume worn at the sanctuary.

The use of special vestments by priestly celebrants at religious functions is very widespread, and has relations which cannot be illustrated till we come to speak of sacrifice.[1] But it is certain that originally every man was his own priest, and the ritual observed in later times by the priests is only a development of what was originally observed by all worshippers. As regards the matter of vestments, it was an early and widespread custom to make a difference between the dress of ordinary life and that donned on sacred occasions. The ancient Hebrews, on approaching the presence of the Deity, either washed their clothes (Ex. xix. 10) or changed them (Gen. xxxv. 2), that is, put on their best clothes, and the women also wore their jewels (Hos. ii. 13 [15]; cf. Sozomen's account of the feast at Mamre, *H. E.* ii. 4).

The washing is undoubtedly to remove possible uncleanness,

(Wajj), Belādhorī, p. 9 (Naci'). The story that 'Amr Mozaiciā tore his clothes every night, that no one else might wear them (Ibn Doraid, p. 258), is perhaps a reminiscence of an old taboo attached to royalty.

[1] See what is said of the skin of the victim as furnishing a sacred dress, *supra*, p. 437 *sq.*

and in Gen. xxxv. 2 the change of garments has the same association. But the instances given above show that, if it was important not to carry impurity into the sanctuary, it was equally necessary not to carry into ordinary life the marks of contact with holy places and things. As all festive occasions in antiquity were sacred occasions, it may be presumed that best clothes were also holy clothes, reserved for festal purposes. They were perfumed (Gen. xxvii. 15, 27), and perfume among the Semites is a very holy thing (Pliny, xii. 54), used in purifications (Herod. i. 198), and applied, according to Phœnician ritual, to all those who stood before the altar, clad in the long byssus robes, with a single purple stripe, which were appropriated to religious offices (Silius, iii. 23 *sqq.*; cf. Herodian, v. 5. 10). Jewels, too, such as women wore in the sanctuary, had a sacred character; the Syriac word for an earring is *c'dāshā*, "the holy thing,"[1] and generally speaking jewels serve as amulets.[2] On the whole, therefore, holy dress and gala dress are one and the same thing, and it seems, therefore, legitimate to suppose that in early times best clothes meant clothes that were taboo for the purposes of ordinary life. But of course the great mass of people in a poor society could not keep a special suit for sacred occasions. Such persons would either wash their clothes after as well as before any specially sacred function (Lev. vi. 27, xvi. 26, 28), or would have to borrow sacred garments. Shoes could not well be washed, unless they were mere linen stockings, as in the Phœnician sacred dress described by Herodian; they were therefore put off before treading on holy ground (Ex. iii. 5; Josh. v. 15, etc.).[3]

Another Hebrew usage that may be noted here is the ban (Heb. *ḥérem*), by which impious sinners, or enemies of the com-

[1] The Arabic *codās* is doubtless an ancient loanword from this; but *cadīs*, an old Yemenite name for pearls (see *Tāj*, *s.v.*), is probably an independent expression of the same idea.

[2] As amulets, jewels are mainly worn to protect the chief organs of action (the hands and the feet), but especially the orifices of the body (ear-rings; nose-rings, hanging over the mouth; jewels on the forehead, hanging down and protecting the eyes). In Doughty, ii. 199, a man stuffs his ears with cotton before venturing to descend a well haunted by *jinn*. Similarly the lower orifices of the trunk are protected by clothing, which has a sacred meaning (*supra*, p. 437, note 2). Similar remarks apply to tattooing, staining with stibium and henna, etc.

[3] [A person about to consult the oracle of Trophonius, after being washed and anointed, put on a linen shirt and *shoes of the country*, ὑποδησάμενος ἐπιχωρίας κρηπῖδας (Pausanias, ix. 39).—J. G. Frazer.]

munity and its god, were devoted to utter destruction. The ban is a form of devotion to the deity, and so the verb "to ban" is sometimes rendered "consecrate" (Micah iv. 13) or "devote" (Lev. xxvii. 28 *sq.*). But in the oldest Hebrew times it involved the utter destruction, not only of the persons involved, but of their property; and only metals, after they had passed through the fire, were added to the treasure of the sanctuary (Josh. vi. 24, vii. 24; 1 Sam. xv.). Even cattle were not sacrificed, but simply slain, and the devoted city must not be rebuilt (Deut. xiii. 16; Josh. vi. 26).[1] Such a ban is a taboo, enforced by the fear of supernatural penalties (1 Kings xvi. 34), and, as with taboo, the danger arising from it is contagious (Deut. vii. 26; Josh. vii.); he that brings a devoted thing into his house falls under the same ban himself.

ADDITIONAL NOTE C (p. 158)

TABOOS ON THE INTERCOURSE OF THE SEXES

According to Herodotus, ii. 64, almost all peoples, except the Greeks and Egyptians, *μίσγονται ἐν ἱροῖσι καὶ ἀπὸ γυναικῶν ἀνιστάμενοι ἄλουτοι ἐσέρχονται ἐς ἱρόν.* This is good evidence of what the Greeks and Egyptians practised; but the assertion about other nations is incorrect, at least as regards the Semites and parts of Asia Minor,[2] whose religion had much in common with theirs. As regards the evidence, it comes to the same thing whether we are told that certain acts were forbidden at the sanctuary, or to pilgrims bound for the sanctuary, or that no one could enter the sanctuary without purification after committing them. We find that among the Arabs sexual intercourse was forbidden to pilgrims to Mecca. The same rule obtained among

[1] In Judg. ix. 45 the site is sown with salt, which is ordinarily explained with reference to the infertility of saline ground. But the strewing of salt has elsewhere a religious meaning (Ezek. xliii. 24), and is a symbol of consecration. Similarly Hesychius explains the phrase, *ἁρὰς ἐπισπεῖραι· ἔθος Κυπρίων σπειρόντων κριθὰς μεθ' ἁλὸς καταρᾶσθαί τισιν.*

[2] See the inscription of Apollo Lermenus, *Journ. Hell. Studies*, viii. 380 *sqq.*; this was not a Greek cult.

the Minæans in connection with the sacred office of collecting frankincense (Pliny, *H. N.* xii. 54). Among the Hebrews we find the restriction in connection with the theophany at Sinai (Ex. xix. 15) and the use of consecrated bread (1 Sam. xxi. 5); Sozomen, ii. 4, attests it for the heathen feast at Mamre; and Herodotus himself tells us that among the Babylonians and Arabs every conjugal act was immediately followed, not only by an ablution, but by such a fumigation as is still practised in the Sūdān (Herod. i. 198). This restriction is not directed against immorality, for it applies to spouses; nor does it spring from asceticism, for the temples of the Semitic deities were thronged with sacred prostitutes; who, however, were careful to retire with their partners outside the sacred precincts (Herod. i. 199, *ἔξω τοῦ ἱροῦ*; cf. Hos. iv. 14, which curiously agrees in expression with *Ḥam.* p. 599, second verse, where the reference is to the love-making of the Arabs just outside the *ḥimā*).

The extension of this kind of taboo to warriors on an expedition is common among rude peoples, and we know that it had place among the Arabs, and was not wholly obsolete as late as the second century of Islām; see *Agh.* xiv. 67 (Ṭabarī, ed. Kosegarten, i. 144), xv. 161; Al-Akhṭal, *Dīw.* p. 120, l. 2; cf. Mas'ūdī, vi. 63–65, *Fr. Hist. Ar.* p. 247 *sq.* See also Note I, *infra*, p. 481 *sqq.* In the Old Testament, war and warriors are often spoken of as consecrated,—a phrase which seems to be connected, not merely with the use of sacred ceremonies at the opening of a campaign, but with the idea that war is a holy function, and the camp a holy place (Deut. xxiii. 10–15). That the taboo on sexual intercourse applied to warriors in old Israel cannot be positively affirmed, but is probable from Deut. xxiii. 10, 11, compared with 1 Sam. xxi. 5, 6 [E.V. 4, 5]; 2 Sam. xi. 11. The passage in 1 Sam., which has always been a *crux interpretum*, calls for some remark. It seems to me that the text can be translated as it stands, if only we take יקדש as a plural, which is possible without adding ו. David says, "Nay, but women are forbidden to us, as has always been my rule when I go on an expedition, so that the gear (clothes, arms, etc.) of the young men is holy even when it is a common (not a sacred) journey; how much more so when [Prov. xxi. 27] to-day they will be consecrated, gear and all." David distinguishes between expeditions of a common kind, and campaigns which were opened by the consecration of the warriors and their gear. He hints that his present excursion is of the second kind, and that the ceremony of consecration will take place as soon as he joins his men; but he reminds the priest that his custom has been to enforce the rules of sanctity even on ordinary expeditions. יקדש should perhaps be pointed as *Pual.* The word עצרה might more exactly be rendered "taboo," for it is evidently a technical expression. So in Jer. xxxvi. 5, "I am עצור, I cannot go into the temple," does not mean "I am imprisoned" (cf. ver. 19), but "I am restrained from entering the sanctuary by a ceremonial impurity." It seems to me that the proverbial עצור ועזוב, one of those phrases which name two categories, under one or other of which everybody is included, means "he who is under taboo, and he who is free"; cf. also נעצר, 1 Sam. xxi. 7 [8], and עצרה, "tempus clausum." The same sense appears in Arabic *mo'sir*, applied to a girl who is shut up under the taboo which, in almost all early nations, affects girls at the age of puberty.

ADDITIONAL NOTE D (p. 212)

THE SUPPOSED PHALLIC SIGNIFICANCE OF SACRED POSTS AND PILLARS

THAT sacred posts and pillars among the Semites are phallic symbols is an opinion which enjoys a certain currency, mainly through the influence of Movers; but, as is so often the case with the theories of that author, the evidence in its favour is of the slenderest. For the pre-Hellenistic period Movers relies on 1 Kings xv. 13, 2 Chron. xv. 16, taking מפלצת, after the Vulgate, to mean *simulacrum Priapi*; but this is a mere guess, not supported by the other ancient versions. He also appeals to Ezek. xvi. 17, which clearly does not refer to phallic worship, but to images of the Baalim; the passage is imitated from Hos. ii. Many recent commentators suppose that יד, "hand," in Isa. lvii. 8, means the phallus. This is the merest conjecture, and even if it were certain, the use of יד in the sense of cippus, sign-post, would still have to be explained, not by supposing that every monument or road mark was a phallic pillar, but from the obvious symbolism which gives us the word finger-post. The Phœnician cippi dedicated to Tanith and Baal Hamman often have a hand figured on them, but a real hand, not a phallus.

In ancient times obscene symbols were used without offence to denote sex, and female symbols of this kind are found in many Phœnician grottoes scratched upon the rock. Herodotus, ii. 106, says that he saw in Syria Palæstina stelæ engraved with γυναικὸς αἰδοῖα, presumably *massēboth* dedicated to female deities; but how this can support the view that the *massēba* represents ἀνδρὸς αἰδοῖον I am at a loss to see. Indeed, the whole phallic theory seems to be wrecked on the fact that the *massēba* represents male and female deities indifferently. At a later date the two great pillars that stood in the Propylæa of the temple of Hierapolis are called *phalli* by Lucian (*Dea Syr.* xvi.). Such twin pillars are very common at Semitic temples; even the temple at Jerusalem had them, and they are shown on coins representing the temple at Paphos; so that Lucian's evidence seems important, especially as he tells us that they bore an inscription to the effect that "these phalli were set up by Dionysus to his mother Hera." But the inscription appears to have been in Greek, and proves only that the Greeks, who were accustomed to phallic symbols in Dionysus-worship, and habitually regarded the licentious sacred feasts of the Semites as Dionysiac, put their own interpretation on the pillars. In § xxviii. of Lucian's work it clearly appears that the meaning and use of the pillars was an open question. Men were accustomed to ascend them, and spend a week on the top—like the Christian Stylites of the same region. Lucian thinks that this too was done because of Dionysus, but the natives said either that at the immense height (which is stated at 30 fathoms) they held near converse with the gods and prayed for the good of all Syria, or that the practice was a memorial of the Flood, when men were driven by fear to ascend trees and mountains. It is not easy to extract anything phallic out of these statements.

Besides this, Movers (i. 680) cites the statement of Arnobius, *Adv. Gentes*, v. 19 (p. 212), that phalli, as signs of the grace of the deity, were presented to the *mystæ* of the Cyprian Venus; but the use of the phallus as an amulet—which was very wide-spread in antiquity—can throw no light on the origin of sacred pillars. Everything else that he adduces is purely fantastic, and without a particle of evidence, and I have not found anything in more recent writers to strengthen his argument.

ADDITIONAL NOTE E (p. 245)

SACRED TRIBUTE IN ARABIA—THE GIFT OF FIRSTLINGS

I HAVE stated in the text that the idea of sacred tribute has little or no place among the nomadic Arabs, and it will hardly be disputed that, broadly speaking, this statement accords with the facts. But it is important to determine, with as much precision as possible, whether the conception of tribute and gifts of homage paid to the deity had any place at all in the old religion of the purely nomadic Semites, and if it had, to define that place with exactness. As the full discussion of this question touches on matters which go beyond the subject of Lecture VII., I have reserved the topic for an Additional Note.

Among the agricultural Semites the idea of a sacred tribute appears mainly in connection with first-fruits and tithes of agricultural produce. Animal sacrifices were ultimately brought under the category of gifts of homage; and so, when they were not presented as freewill offerings, but in accordance with ritual laws that demanded certain definite oblations for definite occasions, they also came to be looked upon as a kind of tribute. But we have seen that, even in the later rituals, there was a clear distinction between cereal oblations, which were simply payments to the god, and animal sacrifices, which were used to furnish a feast for the god and his worshippers together. The explanation that the victim is wholly given up to the god, who then gives back part of it to the worshipper, that he may feast at the temple as the guest of his deity, is manifestly too artificial to be regarded as primitive; and if, on the other hand, we look on a sacrifice simply as a feast provided by the worshipper, at which the god is the chief guest, it does not appear that, according to ancient ideas, any payment of tribute, or even any gift, is involved. Hospitality is not placed by early nations under the category of a gift; when a man slaughters an animal, everyone who is present has his share in the feast as a matter of course, and those who eat do not feel that any present has been made to them. And in like manner it seems very doubtful whether the oblations of milk which were poured out before certain Arabian idols can in any proper sense be called gifts,—*i.e.* transfers of valuable property,—for in the desert it is still a shame to sell milk (Doughty, i. 215, ii. 443), and a draught from the milk-bowl is never refused to anyone. In a society where milk and meat are never sold, and where only a churl refuses to share these articles of food with every by-passer, we must not look to the sacrificial meal as a proof that the Arabs paid tribute to their gods.

The agricultural tribute of first-fruits and tithes is a charge on the produce of the land, paid to the gods as Baalim or landlords. In this form tribute cannot appear among pure nomads. But tribute is also paid to kings who are not landlords, by subjects who are not their tenants. An example of such a tribute is the royal tithe in Israel, which was paid by the free landowners; and on this analogy it seems quite conceivable that a sacred tribute paid to the god, as king or chief of his worshippers, might arise in a purely nomadic community. In examining this possibility, however, we must have regard to the actual constitution of Arabian society.

Among the free tribes of the Arabian desert there is no taxation, and the chiefs derive no revenue from their tribesmen, but, on the contrary, are expected to use their wealth with generosity for the public benefit. A modern sheikh or emir, according to Burckhardt's description (*Bed. and Wah.* i. 118), is expected to treat strangers in a better style than any other member of the tribe, to maintain the poor, and to divide among his friends whatever presents he may receive. "His means of defraying these expenses are the tribute he exacts from the Syrian villages, and his emoluments from the Mecca pilgrim caravan,"—in short, black-mail. Black-mail is merely a regulated form of pillage, and the gains derived from it correspond to those which in earlier times came directly from the plundering of enemies and strangers. In ancient Arabia the chief took the fourth part of the spoils of war (*Ḥam.* p. 336, last verse; Wācidī, ed. Kremer, p. 10), and had also certain other perquisites, particularly the right to select for himself, before the division, some special gift, such as a damsel or a sword (the so-called *ṣafāyā*, *Ḥam.* p. 458, last verse, and Abū 'Obaida, *ap.* Reiske, *An. Musl.* i. 26 *sqq.* of the notes).[1] Among the Hebrews, in like manner, the chief received a liberal share of the booty (1 Sam. xxx. 20), including some choice gift corresponding to the *ṣafāyā* (Judg. v. 30, viii. 24). In the

[1] Among the Arabs, a sacrifice (*nacī'a*) preceded the division of the spoil; see below, *Additional Note* M.

Levitical law a fixed share of the spoil is assigned to the sanctuary (Num. xxxi. 28 *sqq.*), just as in the Moslem theocracy the chief's fourth is changed to a fifth, payable to Allah and his prophet, but partly used for the discharge of burdens of charity and the like, such as in old times fell upon the chiefs (Sura viii. 42). These fixed sacred tributes are modern, both in Arabia and in Israel; but even in old times the spoils of war were a chief source of votive offerings. The votive offerings of the Arabs frequently consisted of weapons (Wellh. p. 110; cf. 1 Sam. xxi. 9); and, among the Hebrews, part of the chief's booty was generally consecrated (Judg. viii. 27; 2 Sam. viii. 10 *sq.*; Micah iv. 13). Similarly, Mesha of Moab dedicates part of his spoil to Chemosh; and in Greece the sacred tithe occurs mainly in the form of a percentage on the spoils of war. It is obvious, however, that the apportionment of a share of booty to the chief or to the god does not properly fall under the category of tribute. And on the general Arabian principle that a chief must not tax his own tribesmen, it does not appear that there was any room for the development of a system of sacred dues, so long as the gods were tribal deities worshipped only by their own tribe. Among the Arabs tribute is a payment to an alien tribe or to its chiefs, either by way of black-mail, or in return for protection. A king who receives gifts and tribute is a king reigning over subjects who are not of his own clan, and whom, therefore, he is not bound to help and protect at his own expense. I apprehend that the oldest Hebrew taxation rested on this principle; for even Solomon seems to have excluded the tribe of Judah from his division of the kingdom for fiscal purposes (1 Kings iv. 7 *sqq.*), while David, as a prosperous warrior, who drew vast sums from conquered nations, probably raised no revenue from his Israelite subjects. As regards Saul, we know nothing more than that he enriched his own tribesmen (1 Sam. xxii. 7). The system of taxation described in 1 Sam. viii. can hardly have been in full force till the time of Solomon at the earliest, and its details seem to indicate that, in fiscal as in other matters, the developed Hebrew kingship took a lesson from its neighbours of Phœnicia, and possibly of Egypt.

To return, however, to the Arabs: the tributes which chiefs and kings received from foreigners were partly transit dues from traders (Pliny, *H. N.* xii. 63 *sqq.*). In such tribute the gods had their share, as Pliny expressly relates for the case of the incense traffic, and as Azracī (p. 107) appears to imply for the case of Greek merchants at Mecca. Commerce and religion were closely connected in all the Semitic lands; the greatest and richest temples are almost always found at cities which owed their importance to trade.

Of the other kind of tribute, paid by a subject tribe to a prince of alien kin, a lively picture is afforded by *Agh.* x. 12, where we find Zohair b. Jadhīma sitting in person at the fair of 'Okāẓ to collect from the Hawāzin, who frequented this annual market, their gifts of ghee, curds and small cattle. In like manner the tribute of the pastoral Moabites to the kings of the house of 'Omri was paid in sheep (2 Kings iii. 4); and on such analogies we can very well conceive that sacrificial oblations of food might be regarded as tribute, wherever the worshippers were not the tribesmen but the clients of their god. But to suppose that sacrifices generally were regarded by the ancient Semitic nomads as tributes and gifts of homage, is to suppose that the typical form of Semitic religion is clientship, a position which is altogether untenable.

Thus it would seem that all we know of the social institutions of the Arabs is in complete accordance with the results, obtained in the text of these lectures, with regard to the original meaning of sacrifice. The conclusion to which the ritual points, viz. that the sacrifice was in no sense a payment to the god, but simply an act of communion of the worshippers with one another and their god, is in accord with the relations that actually subsisted between chiefs and their tribesmen; and when we read that in the time of Mohammed the ordinary worship of household gods consisted in stroking them with the hand as one went out and in (*Muh. in Med.* p. 350), we are to remember that reverent salutation was all that, in ordinary circumstances, a great chieftain would expect from the meanest member of his tribe. At the pilgrimage feasts of the Arabs, as of the Hebrews, no man appeared without a gift; but this was in the worship of alien gods.

In a payment of tribute two things are involved—(1) a transfer of property, and (2) an obligation, not necessarily to pay on a fixed scale, but at least to pay something. That an Arabian sacrifice cannot without straining be conceived as a transfer of property, has appeared in the course of this note, and is shown from another point of view in Lecture XI. (*supra*, p. 390 *sqq.*). And in most sacrifices the second condition is also unfulfilled, for in Arabia it is left to a man's free will whether he will appear before the god and do sacrifice, even in the sacred month of Rajab.

It seems, however, to be probable that the absolute freedom of the individual will in matters of religious duty, as it appears among the Arabs in the generations immediately preceding Islam, was in part due to the breaking up of the old religion. There can, for example, be hardly a doubt that the ascetic observances during a war of blood-revenge, which in the time of the prophet were assumed by a voluntary vow, were at one time imperatively demanded by religious custom (*infra, Note* K). Again, there were certain religious restrictions on the use of a man's property which, even in later times, do not seem to have been purely optional, *e.g.* the prohibition of using for common work a camel which had produced ten female foals. But, in older times at least, such a camel was not given over in property to the god; the restriction was simply a taboo (*supra*, p. 149).

There is, however, one Arabian sacrifice which has very much the aspect of a fixed due payable to the god, viz. the sacrifice of firstlings (فرع, *fara'*). It has already been remarked (*supra*, p. 227, note 3) that the accounts which have been handed down to us about the *fara'* are confused and uncertain; but although the word seems to have been extended to cover other customary sacrifices, it appears properly to denote "the foal or lamb which is first cast." This is the definition given in the *ḥadīth*, which in such matters has always great weight, and it is confirmed by the proverb in Maidānī, ii. 20 (Freytag, *Ar. Pr.* ii. 212). As we also learn from the *ḥadīth* (*Lisān, s.v.*) that the custom was to sacrifice the *fara'* when it was still so young that the flesh was like glue and stuck to the skin, it would seem that this sacrifice must be connected with the Hebrew sacrifice of the firstborn of kine and sheep, which according to the oldest law (Ex. xxii. 30) was to be offered on the eighth day from birth. There is an unfortunate ambiguity about the definition of the Arabian *fara'*, for the first birth may mean either the first birth of the dam, or the first birth of the year, and Maidānī takes it in the latter sense, making *fara'* a synonym of *roba'*, *i.e.* a foal which, being born in the *rabī'*, or season of abundant grass, when the mother was well fed, naturally grew up stronger and better than foals born later (cf. Gen. iv. 4). But apart from the analogy of the Hebrew firstlings, which are quite unambiguously explained as firstborn (פטר רחם, Ex.

xxxiv. 19), there are other uses of the Arabic word *fara'* which make Maidānī's interpretation improbable; and the presumption is that, however the rule may have been relaxed or modified in later times, there was a very ancient Semitic custom, anterior to the separation of the Arabs and Hebrews, of sacrificing the first-born of domestic animals. The conclusion that this offering was, for nomadic life, what the offering of first-fruits was among agricultural peoples, viz. a tribute paid to the gods, seems so obvious that it requires some courage to resist it. Yet, from what has been already said, it seems absolutely impossible that, at the very early date when the Hebrews and Arabs lived together, any tribute could have been paid to the god as chief or king; and, even in the form of the sacrifice of firstlings which is found among the Hebrews, there seem to be indications that the parallelism with the offering of first-fruits is less complete than at first sight it seems to be.

The first-fruits are an annual gift of the earliest and choicest fruits of the year, but the firstlings are the first offspring of an animal. Their proper parallel in the vegetable kingdom is therefore found in the law of Lev. xix. 23 *sqq.*, which ordains that for three years the fruit of a new orchard shall be treated as "uncircumcised," and not eaten, that the fourth year's fruit shall be consecrated to Jehovah, and that thereafter the fruit shall be common. The characteristic feature in this ordinance, from which its original meaning must be deduced, is the taboo on the produce of the first three years, not the offering at the temple paid in the fourth year. And that some form of taboo lies also at the bottom of the sacrifice of firstlings, appears from the provision of the older Hebrew law that, if a firstling ass is not redeemed by its owner, its neck shall be broken (Ex. xxxiv. 20). We see, however, that the tendency was to bring all such offerings under the category of sacred tribute; for by the later law (Lev. xxvii. 27) the ass that is not redeemed is to be sold for the benefit of the sanctuary, and even in the older law all the firstborn of men must be redeemed.

Primarily, a thing that is taboo is one that has supernatural qualities or associations, of a kind that forbid it to be used for common purposes. This is all that is involved, under the older law, in the holiness of the firstling ass; it is such an animal as the Arabs would have allowed to go free, instead of killing it. But in the very earliest times all domestic animals had a certain measure of holiness, and were protected by certain taboos which prevented them from being used by man as mere chattels; and so it would appear that the holiness of the firstborn, which is congenital (Lev. xxvii. 26), is only a higher form of the original sanctity of domestic animals. The correctness of this conclusion can be verified by a practical test; for if firstlings are animals of special intrinsic holiness, the sacrifices to which they are appropriate will be special acts of communion, piacular holocausts or the like, and not mere common sacrificial meals. And this is actually the case in the oldest Hebrew times; for the Passover, which is the sacrifice of firstlings *par excellence*, is an atoning rite of a quite exceptional kind (*supra*, p. 406).[1]

Further, there is a close connection between the firstlings and the piacular holocaust; both are limited to males, and the holocaust of Samuel (1 Sam. vii. 9) is a sucking lamb, while from Ex. xx. 30 we see that firstlings were offered on the eighth day (or, probably, as soon after it as was practicable; cf. Lev. xxii. 27).

The consecration of first-born male children (Ex. xiii. 13, xxii. 28, xxxiv. 20) has always created a difficulty. The legal usage was to redeem the human firstlings, and in Num. iii. this redemption is further connected in a very complicated way with the consecration of the tribe of Levi. It appears, however, that in the period immediately before the exile, when sacrifices of first-born children became common, these grisly offerings were supposed to fall under the law of firstlings (Jer. vii. 31, xix. 5; Ezek. xx. 25). To conclude from this that at one time the Hebrews actually sacrificed all their first born sons is absurd; but, on the other hand, there must have been some point of attachment in ancient custom for the belief that the deity asked for such a sacrifice. In point of fact, even in old times, when exceptional circumstances called for a human victim, it was a child, and by preference a first-born or only child, that was selected by the peoples in and around Palestine.[2] This is

[1] That the paschal sacrifice was originally a sacrifice of firstlings is clearly brought out by Wellhausen, *Prolegomena*, chap. iii. § 1, 1. Ultimately the paschal lamb and the firstlings fell apart; the former was retained, with much of its old and characteristic ritual, as a domestic sacrifice, while the latter continued to be presented at the sanctuary and offered on the altar, the whole flesh being the perquisite of the priest (Num. xviii. 18). But in the law of Deuteronomy (xii. 17 *sqq.*, xv. 19 *sqq.*) the firstlings have not yet assumed the character of a sacred tribute.

[2] 2 Kings iii. 27; Philo Byblius in *Fr. Hist. Gr.* iii. 571; cf. Porph., *De Abst.* ii. 56, τῶν φιλτάτων τινά.

commonly explained as the most costly offering a man can make; but it is rather to be regarded as the choice, for a special purpose, of the most sacred kind of victim. I apprehend that all the prerogatives of the firstborn among Semitic peoples are originally prerogatives of sanctity; the sacred blood of the kin flows purest and strongest in him (Gen. xlix. 3; Deut. xxi. 17). Neither in the case of children, nor in that of cattle, did the congenital holiness of the first-born originally imply that they must be sacrificed or given to the deity on the altar, but only that if sacrifice was to be made they were the best and fittest, because the holiest, victims. But when the old ideas of holiness became unintelligible, and holy beasts came to mean beasts set aside for sacrifice, an obvious extension of this new view of holiness demanded that the human first-born should be redeemed, by the substitution of an animal victim (Gen. xxii.); and from this usage, again, the Moloch sacrifices were easily developed in the seventh century, when ordinary means seemed too weak to conjure the divine anger.

In the Passover we find the sacrifice of firstlings assuming the form of an annual feast, in the spring season. Such a combination is possible only when the yeaning time falls in spring. So far as sheep are concerned, there were two lambing times in ancient Italy, some sheep yeaning in spring, others in autumn. That the same thing was true of Palestine may perhaps be inferred from the old versions of Gen. xxx. 41, 42.[1] But in Arabia all cattle, small and great, yean in the season of the spring pasture, so that here we have the necessary condition for a spring sacrifice of firstlings,[2] and also a reason, more conclusive than the assertion of the *Lisān* (*supra*, p. 228), for identifying the Arabian Rajab sacrifices with the sacrifice of firstlings.

[1] Not from the text itself; cf. Bochart, Pars I. Lib. ii. cap. 46.

[2] Doughty, *Arabia Deserta*, i. 429; Blunt, *Bedouin Tribes*, ii. 166: "The calving time for camels is in February and early March." Of course there are exceptions to this rule; but the *ṣaifī* or summer foal is held by the Arabs to be a weakling (*Ḥamāsa*, p. 389, l. 25).

ADDITIONAL NOTE F (p. 294)

SACRIFICES OF SACRED ANIMALS

In the text I have spoken only of animals corresponding to Julian's definition of the creatures suited for mystical piacula, viz. that they were such as were ordinarily excluded from human diet. But there are other animals which, though not strictly forbidden food in the times of which we have record, retained a certain reputation of natural holiness, which gave them a peculiar virtue when used in sacrifice. Of course, when the sacredness of an animal species ceases to be marked by the definite taboos that we find in the case of the swine, the dog, or the dove, the proof that it was once held to be holy in a particular religious circle becomes dependent on circumstantial evidence, and more or less vague. But it seems worth while to cite one or two examples in which the point can be fairly well made out, or at least made sufficiently probable to deserve further examination.

1. Deer and antelopes of various kinds were sacred animals in several parts of the Semitic field; see *Kinship*, p. 194 *sq.* They were not, indeed, forbidden food, but they had special relations to various deities. Troops of sacred gazelles occur down to a late date at sanctuaries, *e.g.* at Mecca and Tabāla (Wellh. p. 102), and in the island spoken of by Arrian, vii. 20. Moreover, stags or gazelles occur as sacred symbols in South Arabia, in connection with 'Athtar-worship; at Mecca, probably in connection with the worship of Al-'Ozzā; and in Phœnicia, both on gems and on coins of Laodicea ad Mare. Further, Ibn Mojāwir speaks of a South Arab tribe which, when a gazelle was found dead, solemnly buried it and mourned for seven days (see p. 444).

No kind of wild quadruped was an ordinary sacrificial animal among the Semites, and even the Arabs regard a gazelle as a mean substitute for a sheep; but in certain rituals we find the stag or gazelle as an exceptional sacrifice. The most notable case is the annual stag sacrifice at Laodicea on the Phœnician coast, which was regarded as a substitute for a more ancient sacrifice of a maiden, and was offered to a goddess whom Porphyry calls Athena (*De Abst.* ii. 56), while Pausanias (iii. 16. 8) identifies her with the Brauronian Artemis, and supposes that the cult was introduced by Seleucus. But the town (Ramitha in Phœnician, according to Philo, *ap.* Steph. Byz.) is much older than its re-christening by Seleucus, and if the goddess had really been Greek, she would not have been identified with Athena as well as with Artemis. She was, in fact, a form of Astarte, the ancient Tyche of the city, who, according to the usual manner of the later euhemeristic Syrians, was supposed to have been a virgin, immolated when the city was founded, and thereafter worshipped as a deity (Malalas, p. 203). Here, therefore, we have one of the many legends of the death of a deity which are grafted on a rite of annual human sacrifice, or on the annual sacrifice of a sacred animal, under circumstances that showed its life to be taken as having the value of a human life on the one hand, or of the life of the deity on the other. The stag, whose death has such significance, is a theanthropic victim, exactly as in the mystic sacrifices discussed in the text.

Of the stag or gazelle as a Phœnician sacrifice we have further evidence from Philo Byblius (Euseb., *Pr. Ev.* i. 10. 10) in the legend of the god Usous, who first taught men to clothe themselves in the skins of beasts taken in hunting, and to pour out their blood sacrificially before sacred stones. This god was worshipped at the sanctuary he instituted, at an annual feast, and doubtless with the ceremonies he himself devised, *i.e.* with libations of the blood of a deer or antelope—for these are the important kinds of game in the district of the Lebanon—presented by worshippers clad in deer-skins. The wearing of the skin of the victim, as we have seen at p. 438, is characteristic of mystical and piacular rites. Most scholars, from Scaliger downwards, have compared Usous with Esau; but it has not been observed that the scene of Isaac's blessing, where his son must first approach him with the savoury flesh of a gazelle, has all the air of a sacrificial scene. Moreover, Jacob, who substitutes kids for gazelles, wears their skin upon his arms and neck. The goat, which here appears as a substitute for the game offered by the huntsman Esau, was one of the chief Hebrew piacula, if not the chief of all. In Babylonia and Assyria also it has an exceptional place among sacrifices; see the representation in Menant, *Glyptique*, vol. i. p. 146 *sqq.*, vol. ii. p. 68. What is obsolete in common life often survives in poetic phrase and metaphor, and I am tempted to see in the opening words of David's dirge on Saul ("The gazelle, O Israel, is slain on thy high places," 2 Sam. i. 19) an allusion to some ancient sacrifice of similar type to that which so long survived at Laodicea. The sacred deer of Icarus, according to Arrian, could only be taken for sacrifice.

2. The wild ass was eaten by the Arabs, and must have been eaten with a religious intention, since its flesh was forbidden to his converts by Symeon the Stylite. Conversely, among the Harranians the ass was forbidden food, like the swine and the dog; but there is no evidence that, like these animals, it was sacrificed or eaten in exceptional mysteries. Yet when we find one section of Semites forbidden to eat the ass, while another section eats it in a way which to Christians appears idolatrous, the presumption that the animal was anciently sacred becomes very strong. An actual ass-sacrifice appears in Egypt in the worship of Typhon (Set or Sutech), who was the chief god of the Semites in Egypt, though Egyptologists doubt whether he was originally a Semitic god. The ass was a Typhonic animal, and in certain religious ceremonies the people of Coptus sacrificed asses by casting them down a precipice, while those of Lycopolis, in two of their annual feasts, stamped the figure of a bound ass on their sacrificial cakes (Plut., *Is. et Os.* § 30); see, for the meaning of these cakes, *supra*, pp. 225, note 3, 240, note 1; and for sacrifice by casting from a precipice, *supra*, pp. 374, 418. Both forms indicate a mystic or piacular rite, and stand on one line with the holocausts of living men to Typhon mentioned by Manetho (*ibid.* § 73). If it could be made out that these rites were really of Semitic origin, the ass would be a clear case of an ancient mystic piaculum within our field; but meantime the matter must rest doubtful. It may, however, be noted that the old clan name Hamor ("he-ass") among the Canaanites in Shechem, seems to confirm the view that the ass was sacred with some of the Semites; and the fables of ass-worship among the Jews (on which compare Bochart, *Hierozoicon*, Pars I. Lib. ii. cap. 18) probably took their rise, like so many other false statements of a similar kind, in a confusion between the Jews and their heathen neighbours. As regards the eating of wild asses' flesh by the Arabs, I have not found evidence in Arabic literature that in the times before Mohammed it had any religious meaning, though Cazwīnī tells us that its flesh and hoofs supplied powerful charms, and this is generally a relic of sacrificial use. On the religious associations of the ass in classical antiquity, and the uses of the ass's head as a charm, see the *Compte-rendu de la*

Comm. Imp. Archéol. (St. Petersburg) for 1863, and the *Berichte d. sächs. Ges. d. Wiss.*, 1854, p. 48.

It has been supposed that the "golden" Set, worshipped by the Semitic Hyksos in the Delta, was a Sun-god (E. Meyer, *Gesch. des Alt.* i. p. 135). If this be so, the horses of the sun may have succeeded to the older sanctity of the ass; for the ass is much more ancient than the horse in the Semitic lands.

3. To these two examples of sacred quadrupeds I am inclined to add one of a sacred bird. The quail sacrifice of the Phœnicians is said by Eudoxus (*ap.* Athen. ix. 47) to commemorate the resurrection of Heracles. But this was an annual festival at Tyre, in the month Peritius (February—March), *i.e.* just at the time when the quail returns to Palestine, immense crowds appearing in a single night (Jos., *Ant.* viii. 5. 3, compared with Tristram, *Fauna*, p. 124). An annual sacrifice of this sort, connected with a myth of the death of the god, can hardly be other than the mystical sacrifice of a sacred animal; and it is to be noted that the ancients regard quail's flesh as dangerous food, producing vertigo and tetanus, while on the other hand an ointment made from the brain is a cure for epilepsy (Bochart, II. i. 15). Lagarde (*Gr. Uebers. der Provv.* p. 81) once proposed to connect the Arabic سُمَانَى, "quail," with the god Eshmun-Iolaos, who restored Heracles to life by giving him a quail to smell at; if this be right, the god-name must be derived from that of the bird, and not *vice versâ*.

ADDITIONAL NOTE G (p. 310)

THE SACRIFICE OF A SHEEP TO THE CYPRIAN APHRODITE

Instead of a note on this subject, I here print a paper read before the Cambridge Philological Society in 1888, of which only a brief abstract has hitherto been published:—

The peculiar rite which forms the subject of the present paper is known to us from a passage in Joannes Lydus, *De Mensibus*, iv. 45, which has been often referred to by writers on ancient religion, but, so far as my reading goes, without any notice being taken of a most serious difficulty, which it seems impossible to overcome without a change of the text. Lydus in the chapter in question begins by describing the practices by which women of the higher and lower classes respectively did honour to Venus on the Calends of April. Here, of course, he is speaking of Roman usage, as is plain from the general plan of his book and from the ceremonies he specifies. The honourable women did service to Venus ὑπὲρ ὁμονοίας καὶ βίου σώφρονος. This agrees with the worship of Venus *verticordia*, the patroness of female virtue, whose worship Ovid connects with the Calends of April (*Fasti*, iv. 155 *sq.*), and Mommsen conjectures to have been mentioned under that day in the *Fasti Præn.* Again, Lydus says that the women of the common sort bathed in the men's baths, crowned with myrtle, which agrees with Ovid (*ibid.* 139 *sq.*), Plutarch (*Numa*, c. 19), and the service of *Fortuna virilis* in the *Fast. Præn.* The transition from this Roman worship of Venus to the Cyprian ritual of the same day, is made by a remark as to the victims proper to the goddess. Venus, he says, was worshipped with the same sacrifices as Juno, but in Cyprus πρόβατον κωδίῳ ἐσκεπασμένον συνέθυον τῇ Ἀφροδίτῃ· ὁ δὲ τρόπος τῆς ἱερατείας ἐν τῇ Κύπρῳ ἀπὸ τῆς Κορίνθου παρῆλθέ ποτε. As Lydus goes on to say that thereafter (εἶτα δέ), on the second of April, they sacrificed wild boars to the goddess, on account of the attack of that animal on Adonis, it is clear that the sacrifice of a sheep took place on the first of April, and that Engel (*Kypros*, ii. 155) entirely overlooks the context when he says that, according to Lydus, the ordinary sacrifices of Aphrodite were the same as those of Hera, but that in Cyprus a favourite sacrifice to the former goddess was a sheep with a woolly fleece. Lydus does not say that a sheep was a favourite Cyprian sacrifice to Aphrodite, but that it was the sacrifice appropriated to the first of April. The very point of the passage is that the Roman feast of the first of April appears in Cyprus with variations in detail.

This coincidence cannot be accidental, and the explanation is not far to seek. The Cyprian Aphrodite is the Semitic Astarte, and her ritual is throughout marked with a Semitic stamp. It is to Semitic ritual, therefore, that we must look for the origin of the April feast. Now, among the Syrians, Nisan is the month corresponding to April, and on the first three days of Nisan, as we learn from the *Fihrist*, the Syrians of Harran, who clung to the ancient Astarte-worship far into the Middle Ages, visited the temple of the goddess in groups (Lydus's *συνέθυον*), offered sacrifices, and burned living animals. The burning of living animals answers to the ceremonies observed at Hierapolis in the great feast of the Syrian goddess at the incoming of spring, when, as we read in Lucian, goats, sheep and other living creatures were suspended on a pyre, and the whole was consumed. The feast, therefore, is an annual spring feast of Semitic origin. The Roman observance was less solemn, and of a popular kind rather than part of the State religion. Macrobius (*Sat.* i. 12. 12–15) tells us, indeed, that at Rome this festival was not ancient, but was introduced for an historical reason which he omits to record. Now, a new ritual at Rome was almost certainly a borrowed one, and there is ample evidence (for which it is enough to refer to Preller's *Römische Mythologie*) that the most influential centre of Venus-worship in the West, and that which had most to do with the development of her cult in Italy, was the great temple at Eryx, the ארך of the Carthaginians. From Phœnician inscriptions it is certain that the goddess of Eryx (עשתרת ארך, *CIS.* No. 140, cf. No. 135) was Astarte; and thus it is easily understood that the Asiatic festival found its way to Rome. A festival so widespread, and one which held its ground so long, is well worthy of careful examination.

When Lydus, in passing from the Roman to the Cyprian rite, says *ἐτιμᾶτο δὲ ἡ Ἀφροδίτη τοῖς αὐτοῖς οἷς καὶ ἡ Ἥρα*, I cannot find with Engel that he makes any general statement that, as a rule, the same sacrifices were appropriate to Venus and to Juno. Oriental worships allowed a far greater range in the choice of victims for a single deity or temple than was customary in Greece or Rome. For the Carthaginian temples of Baal this appears from extant inscriptions; and as regards Astarte-Aphrodite, Tacitus (*Hist.* iii. 2) tells us that at Paphos, and Ælian (*Nat. An.* x. 50) that at Eryx, the worshipper chose any kind of sacrifice he pleased. This liberty, which was evidently surprising to the Romans and the Greeks, was probably due to the syncretism which established itself at an early date at all the great Semitic sanctuaries; one deity, as we see in the case of Hierapolis, combining a number of characters which originally belonged to different gods, and uniting at a single temple a corresponding variety of ancient rituals. Such syncretism was probably very ancient among the cosmopolitan Phœnicians; and throughout the Semitic world it received a great impulse by the breaking up of the old small States through Assyrian, Babylonian and Persian conquests. The political and religious cosmopolitanism of the East under the Macedonians rested on a basis which had been prepared centuries before.

In the West no such powerful political agencies were at work to develop an early tendency to syncretism, nor was it so easy to confound the well-marked individualities of the Western Pantheon as to combine the hazy personalities of different Baals or Astartes. When the need for cosmopolitan forms of worship arose, Eastern gods and rituals were borrowed, as in the case of Sarapis; and the old acknowledged worships still retained their individual peculiarities. It is known that neither Juno nor Hera admitted such a free choice of victims for her shrine as was permitted at Eryx and Paphos. Their ordinary sacrifice was a cow; for, like other goddesses, they preferred victims of their own sex (Arnobius, vii. 19). But, so far as the Oriental Aphrodite had a preference, it was for male victims. So Tacitus tells us for Paphos, and Plautus also in the *Pœnulus* has "sex agnos immolavi Veneri." This preference was presumably connected with the androgynous character ascribed to the Eastern goddess in Cyprus and elsewhere, and of itself is sufficient to separate her sacrifices, as a whole, from those of Juno and Hera.[1] Besides, the favourite victim of Aphrodite was the goat (Tac. *Hist.* iii. 2), which, except at Sparta (Pausanias, iii. 15. 9) and in the annual piacular sacrifice of Hera Acræa at Corinth (Hesychius, *s.v.* αἶξ αἶγα; Zenobius on the same proverb; Schol. on Eurip., *Medea*), was excluded from the altars of Hera. Juno has relations to the goat at Lanuvium, but at Rome her cultus was closely related to that of Jupiter, from whose offerings the goat was strictly excluded (Arnobius, vii. 21).

I have perhaps spent too much time on this argument, for surely the context itself is sufficient to show that Lydus is not speaking of Venus-worship in general. What he says is that on the Calends of April—a special occasion—Venus was worshipped at Rome with the sacrifices of Juno. And as he is speaking of a ritual in which the worshippers were women, I think we may go a step further, and recall the fact that the Calends of every month were sacred to Juno Lucina, to whom on that day the *regina*

[1] The preference for male victims seems, however, to have other connections also; see p. 299, *supra*.

sacrorum offered in the Regia a sow or ewe-lamb (Macrob. i. 15. 19). The functions of Lucina, as the patroness of virtuous matrons and the family life of women, were so nearly identical with those of Venus *verticordia*, that their sacrifices might well be the same. And if this be so, it was natural for Lydus to pass on as he does to a remark on the Cyprian ritual, where the same sacrifices occur with characteristic variations. The sex of the victims is different, for a reason already explained, and the sacrifices are divided between two days. But the victims are still the sheep and the pig, so that the fundamental identity of the Roman and the Eastern service of the day receives fresh confirmation.

So far all is plain; but now we come to the unsolved difficulty. It lies in the phrase πρόβατον κωδίῳ ἐσκεπασμένον. These words describe the characteristic peculiarity, for the sake of which our author turns aside to mention the Cyprian rite, and it seems to be in relation to this feature that he observes that "the manner of the priestly service" was derived from Corinth. Unfortunately we know nothing of the Corinthian ritual referred to. The Corinthian Aphrodite-worship was Oriental in type, and any feature in it which reappears at Cyprus is almost certainly Phœnician. That Cyprus borrowed from Corinth is far less likely than that both borrowed from the East, and the authority of Lydus is not enough to outweigh this probability. The allusion to Corinth, however, is of value as teaching us that the peculiar rite was not merely local; and further, the allusion to "priestly service" shows that the sacrifice in question—as indeed is implied in the word συνέθυον—was not a private offering, but a public rite performed at a great temple. But this does not explain the words κωδίῳ ἐσκεπασμένον. It is plain that the meaning cannot be "a sheep with a woolly fleece," as Engel renders, nor does it seem possible to understand with the Duc de Luynes (*Num. et Insc. Cypr.* p. 6), "un bélier couvert de toute sa toison." If the words could bear this meaning, the rendering would be plausible enough, for we have seen that in the Syrian form of the festival the victims were given to the flames alive. But if Lydus had meant that the victim was consumed by fire, skin and all, he would have given κωδίῳ the article, and would have used a more precise word than συνέθυον. And can κώδιον be used of the sheep-skin on the sheep, or ἐσκεπασμένον of the natural coat? The plain sense of the words is that the sheep was wrapped in a sheep-skin when it was presented for sacrifice, not that its skin was left upon it, or wrapped round the sacrificial flesh before it was laid on the altar.

If the skin had been that of a different kind of animal, we might have explained the rite by the same principle of make-believe which we find in the Roman offering of the *cervaria ovis*, the sheep that was made to pass for a stag; for the ordinary meaning of skin-wearing in early religion is to simulate identification with the animal whose skin is worn. But to wrap a sheep in a sheep-skin is like gilding gold. I propose therefore to change a single letter, and read ἐσκεπασμένοι, a change which produces a sense good in itself and strongly recommended by the context and by analogy.

The significance of the κώδιον or sheep-skin in ancient ritual has been illustrated by Lobeck in his *Aglaophamus*, and by Preller in his commentary on Polemo. It always appears in connection with atoning and mystic rites, and in the majority of Greek examples the practice appears to have been that the person to be purged of guilt set his feet, or his left foot, upon the skin of a sacrificed ram. But this was not the only way of using the κώδιον. In Thessaly there was, according to Dicæarchus, a ceremony, observed at the greatest heat of summer, in which the worshippers ascended Mount Pelion to the temple of Zeus Acræus, clad in new sheep-skins (*Fr. Hist. Gr.* ii. 262). When Pythagoras was purified by the priests of Morgus in Crete, he was made to lie beside water (the sea by day, the river by night), wrapped in the fleece of a black lamb, and descended to the tomb of Zeus clad in black wool (Porph., *Vita Pyth.* § 17). Again, the first sacrifice of every worshipper at Hierapolis was a sheep. Having partaken of the flesh, the sacrificer laid the skin on the ground, and knelt on it, taking up the feet and head over his own head. In this posture he besought the deity to accept his offering. Here it is evident that the ceremony expresses the identification of the sacrificer with the victim. He has taken its flesh into his body, and he covers himself with its skin. It is, as it were, the idea of substitution turned outside in. The direct symbolism of vicarious sacrifice, where an animal's life is accepted in place of the life of a human being, is to treat the victim as if it were a man. At Tenedos, for example, the bull-calf sacrificed to Bacchus wears the cothurnus, and the mother cow is treated like a woman in child-bed. But in our case the symbolism is inverted; instead of making believe that the victim is a man, the ritual makes believe that the man is the victim, and so brings the atoning force of the sacrifice into immediate application to him.

It is evident that if this kind of symbolism be applied, not to purification of an individual, but to a general and public atoning service, the priests, as the representatives of the community on whose behalf the rite is performed, are the persons to whom the skin of the victim must be applied. And if there are many priests and only one victim, it will be convenient not to use the actual skin of the sacrifice, which only one can wear at a time, but to clothe all the ministers in skins of the same kind. This, according to my conjecture, is what was done in Cyprus. And here I would ask whether the context, which alludes to the manner of the priestly service, does not show that some reference to the priests has been already made or implied. Such a reference the proposed emendation supplies.

Upon this view of the passage it is necessarily involved that the rite described was expiatory. And that it was so seems to appear from several arguments. The sacrifice of the following day consisted in wild boars, and was explained in connection with the Adonis myth, so that its Semitic origin is not doubtful. Even in Greece the pig is the great purificatory sacrifice; but in Semitic religion the offering of this animal is not a mere ordinary *piaculum*, but a mystic rite of the most exceptional kind (*supra*, p. 290). Now, if the sacrifice of the second day of the feast was mystic, and therefore piacular in the highest degree, we may be sure that the first day's sacrifice was no ordinary sacrificial meal of a joyous character. For a man must first be purified, and then sit down gladly at the table of the gods, and not conversely. Again, the Syrian and Roman rites, which we have found reason to regard as forms of the same observance, were plainly piacular or purificatory. In Rome we have the women bathing, which is a form of lustration, and wearing myrtle, which had purifying virtues, for it was with myrtle twigs that the Romans and Sabines in the time of Romulus purged themselves at the temple of Venus Cloacina (Preller, *Röm. Myth.* 3rd ed., i. 439). And in the Syrian rite, where animals are burnt alive to the goddess, the atoning nature of the sacrifice is unmistakable, and the idea of a mere sacrificial feast is entirely excluded.

A further argument for the atoning character of the rite may be derived from the choice of the victim, for next to the swine the ram was perhaps the commonest sin-offering in antiquity (cf.

Hesychius, *s.v.* 'Ἀφροδισία ἄγρα); so much so, that Stephani, in the *Compte-rendu*, 1869, p. 130 *sqq.*, explains the frequent occurrence of rams' heads and the like in ancient ornament as derived from the association of the animal with the power of averting calamity. Such ornaments are in fact ἀποτρόπαια. It is always dangerous to apply general arguments of this kind to the interpretation of a particular ritual; for the same victim may be an atoning sacrifice in one rite and an ordinary sacrifice in another, and it by no means follows that because, for example, a piacular bull was offered to Zeus, the same piaculum would be appropriate to the Eastern Aphrodite. But in the case of the sheep used as a sin-offering, we have evidence that there was no limitation to a single deity; for when Epimenides was brought to Athens to check the plague, he suffered black and white sheep to stray at will from the Areopagus, and ordered each to be sacrificed, where it lay down, to the nameless deity of the spot (Diog. Laert. i. 10). This form of atonement came from Crete, which was one of the stepping-stones by which Oriental influence reached Greece, so that the example is the more appropriate to our present argument. And that, in point of fact, sheep or rams were offered as piacular sacrifices at the altars of the Eastern Aphrodite, seems to follow from the Hierapolitan ritual already mentioned. The same thing is implied for Carthage in the *Pœnulus* of Plautus, where the sacrifice of six male lambs is directed to propitiate the angry goddess.

These considerations will, I hope, be found sufficient to justify my general view of the Cyprian rite, and to support the proposed correction of the text. The sacrifice was piacular, and the κώδιον was therefore appropriate to the ritual; but on the received text the use of it is entirely unintelligible, whereas the correction ἐσκεπασμένοι restores a sense which gives to this feature the same character as it possesses in analogous ceremonies. But the most interesting aspect of the ceremony is only brought out when we connect it with a fact which I have hitherto kept in the background, because its significance depends on a theory of piacular and mystic sacrifice which is not yet generally accepted. A sheep, or a sheep's head, is a religious symbol of constant occurrence on Cyprian coins; and some of these coins show us a figure, which experts declare to be that of Aphrodite, clinging to the neck and fleece of a running ram. This device has been compared with others, which appear to be Eastern though not Cyprian, in which Aphrodite rides on a ram (see De Luynes, *Num. Cypr.* Pl. v. 3, vi. 5, and the references in Stephani, *Compte-rendu* for 1869, p. 87). The inference is that in Cyprus the sheep was the sacred animal of Aphrodite-Astarte. In this connection it is important to note that the sheep is of frequent occurrence on Semitic votive cippi of the class dedicated to Tanith (a form of Astarte) and Baal-Ḥammān. Examples will be found in *CIS.* Pt. I. Nos. 398, 419, and in a cippus from Sulci, figured in Perrot and Chipiez, iii. 253. The figures on this class of cippi are of various kinds, and sometimes convey allusions to sacrifices (*CIS.* p. 282 *sq.*), but it appears to have been essential to introduce a figure or symbol of the deity. And when animals are figured, they appear to be such symbols. Thus we find fish, which are known to have been sacred to Astarte, and forbidden food to her worshippers; a bull or cow couching, the symbol of the Sidonian Astarte; the elephant, which was not a sacrifice; the horse, which appears so often on the coins of Carthage, and is certainly a divine symbol, as it is sometimes winged. On these analogies I conclude that among the Carthaginians, as in Cyprus, the sheep was sacred to and symbolic of Astarte. To speak quite exactly, one ought to say to a particular type of Astarte; for as this goddess, in the progress of syncretism so characteristic of Semitic religion, absorbed a great number of local types, she had a corresponding multiplicity of sacred animals, each of which was prominent at particular sanctuaries or in particular rites. Thus the dove-Aphrodite is specially associated with Ascalon, and the Cow-goddess with Sidon, where she was identified with Europa, the bride of the bull-Zeus (*Dea Syria,* iv.), and, according to Philo Byblius, placed the head of a bull upon her own. The sheep-Astarte is another type, but it also seems to have its original home in Canaan, for in Deut. vii. 13 the produce of the flock is called "the Ashtaroth of the sheep." A phrase like this, which has descended from religion into ordinary life, and is preserved among the monotheistic Hebrews, is very old evidence for the association of Astarte with the sheep; and it is impossible to explain it except by frankly admitting that Astarte, in one of her types, had originally the form of a sheep, and was a sheep herself, just as in other types she was a dove or a fish.

To this it may be objected that the ram or sheep is not the symbol of Tanith, but of the associated male deity Baal-Ḥammān, who in a terra-cotta of the Barre collection (Perrot et Chipiez, iii.

73) is represented with ram's horns, and laying his hand on the head of a sheep. But the inscription (*CIS.* No. 419), cited above, is dedicated to Tanith, not to Tanith and Baal-Ḥammān conjointly, from which it appears that the accompanying symbol was appropriate to the goddess as well as to her male partner.

It is reasonable that the same animal symbol should belong to the male and female members of a syzygy; and in the case of a goddess who was often represented as androgynous, it is not even necessary to suppose that her symbol would be the ewe and her partner's the ram. But in fact the sheep-symbols on the Tanith cippi, which are commonly called rams, are hornless, and so presumably stand for ewes. On the other hand, all wild sheep and many domestic breeds are horned in both sexes, so that there is no difficulty about a horned Sheep-goddess. The triangle surmounted by a circle, with horns bent outwards, which is commonly found on Tanith cippi, is probably a symbol of the god or the goddess indifferently. And here the horns, being concave outwards, can neither be bull's horns nor the horns of the crescent moon, but must be the horns of sheep.

The Cypriote coins of Aphrodite, in which she clings in a swimming attitude to a running ram, recall the legend of Helle and the golden ram, but they also are obviously parallel to the type of Europa and the bull. On this analogy we ought to remember that the male god specially associated with the ram is Hermes, and that the Cyprian goddess was worshipped in an androgynous form, to which Theophrastus gives the name of Hermaphroditus. I have already cited this androgynous character to explain why the Paphian (and apparently the Punic) Aphrodite preferred male victims; it now supplies an additional reason for supposing that it was the androgynous or bearded Astarte that was specially connected with the ram. On one of the cippi already cited, in which Tanith is figured under the symbol of a sheep (*CIS.* 419), the inscription is not, as usually, "to the Lady Tanith," but "to my Lord Tanith." If this is not a sculptor's error it points in the same direction. And it seems not unlikely that the standing title, תנת פן בעל, which has given rise to so much discussion, means nothing more than Tanith with Baal's face—the bearded goddess.

If, now, the Cyprian goddess was a Sheep-deity, our rite presents us with a piacular sacrifice in which priests, disguised as sheep, offer to the Sheep-goddess an animal of her own kind. The ceremony, therefore, is exactly parallel to the Roman Lupercalia, a purificatory sacrifice to Faunus under the name of Lupercus. The image of Lupercus at the Lupercal was naked, and was clad in a goat-skin (Justin, xliii. 1. 7). Here, at the great lustration of 15th February, the Luperci, who have the same name as their god, sacrifice goats and run about the city naked, daubed with mud and girt with goat-skins, applying to the women who desire to participate in the benefits of the rite strokes of thongs which were cut from the skins of the victims, and were called *februa.* Both sacrifices are complete types of that most ancient form of sacramental and piacular mystery in which the worshippers attest their kinship with the animal-god, and offer in sacrifice an animal of the same kind, which, except on these mystical occasions, it would be impious to bring upon the altar.

ADDITIONAL NOTE H (p. 315)

FURTHER REMARKS ON THE BLOOD COVENANT

An evidence for the survival among the Arabs of the form of covenant described by Herodotus, in which blood is drawn from the parties themselves, seems to lie in the expression *miḥāsh,* "scarified," for "confederates" (Nābigha, xxiv. 1, ed. Ahlw. = xvii. 1, ed. Derenb.). Goldziher, in an interesting review of my *Kinship* (*Literaturbl. f. or. Phil.* 1886, p. 25), thinks that the term properly means "the burnt ones," which is the traditional interpretation, and suggests that we have in it an example of a covenant by fire, such as Jauharī (see Wellh. p. 124) and Nowairī (Rasm., *Add.* p. 75, l. 11 *sqq.*) speak of under the head of *nār al-hūla.* It does not, however, seem that in the latter case the fire touched the parties; what we are told is that every tribe had a sacred fire, and that, when two men (obviously two tribesmen) had a dispute, they were made to swear beside the fire, while the priests cast salt on it. An oath by ashes and salt is mentioned by Al-A'shā in a line cited by Wellhausen from *Agh.* xx. 139, and as the ashes of the cooking pot (*ramād al-cidr*) are a metonym for hospitality, there is perhaps nothing more in the oath by fire and salt than an appeal to the bond of common food that unites tribesmen. This does not indeed fully account for the fact that the fire is called "the fire of terror," and that the poetical references to it show the oath to have really been a terrible one, *i.e.* dangerous to the man that perjured himself; but it is to be remembered that, according to Arabian belief, a man who broke an oath of purgation was likely to die by divine judgment (Bokhārī, iv. 219 *sq.*, viii. 40 *sq.*). I think, therefore, that in the present state of the evidence we must not attempt to connect the *miḥāsh* with the *nār al-hūla.* If the former term really means "burnt ones," we must rather suppose that the reference is to the practice of branding with the tribal mark or *wasm* (which is also called *nār*, Rasm., *Add.* p. 76); for we learn from *Agh.* vii. 110, l. 26, that the *wasm* was sometimes applied to men as well as to cattle. But ماحش primarily means "to scarify," and as it is plain from the article in the *Lisān* that the traditional explanation of the word was uncertain, I take it that the best and most natural view is to interpret *miḥāsh* as "scarified ones."

In process of time the Arabs came to use various substitutes for the blood of covenant, *e.g.* *robb*, *i.e.* inspissated fruit juice (or perhaps the lees of clarified butter), perfumes, and even holy water from a sacred spring (*Kinship*, p. 261; Wellh. p. 121). In all these cases we can still see that there was something about the substitute which made it an equivalent for blood. As regards "living water," this is obvious from what has been said in Lecture V. p. 173 *sqq.* on the holiness of sacred springs. Again, perfumes were habitually used in the form of unguents; and unguents—primarily sacred suet—are equivalent to blood, as has appeared in Lecture X. p. 383 *sqq.* If *robb* in this connection means lees of butter, the use of it in covenant making is explained by the sacredness of unguents; but if, as the traditions imply, it is fruit juice, we must remember that, in other cases also, vegetable juices are looked upon as a kind of blood (*supra*, pp. 133, 230). Compare what Lydus, *De mensibus*, iv. 29, says of the use of bean juice for blood in a Roman ceremony, with the explanation that the bean (κύαμος) κύει αἷμα: the whole passage is notable, and helps to explain the existence of a bean-clan, the *gens Fabia*, at Rome; cf. also the Attic hero Κυαμίτης.

The Hebrew phrase כרת ברית, "to make (*literally*, to cut) a covenant," is generally derived from the peculiar form of sacrifice mentioned in Gen. xv., Jer. xxxiv. 18, where the victim is cut in twain and the parties pass between the pieces; and this rite again is explained as a symbolic form of imprecation, as if those who swore to one another prayed that, if they proved unfaithful, they might be similarly cut in pieces. But this does not explain the characteristic feature in the ceremony—the passing between the pieces; and, on the other hand, we see from Ex. xxiv. 8, "this is the blood of the covenant which Jehovah hath cut with you," that the dividing of the sacrifice and the application of the blood to both parties go together. The sacrifice presumably was divided into two parts (as in Ex. *l.c.* the blood is divided into two parts), when both parties joined in eating it; and when it ceased to be eaten, the parties stood between the pieces, as a symbol that they were taken within the mystical life of the victim. This interpretation is confirmed by the usage of Western nations, who practised the same rite with dogs and other extraordinary victims, as an atoning or purificatory ceremony; see the examples collected by Bochart, *Hierozoicon*, lib. ii. capp. 33, 56. There are many examples of a sacrifice being carried, or its blood sprinkled, round the place or persons to which its efficacy is to extend.

ADDITIONAL NOTE I (p. 333)

THE TABOOS INCIDENT TO PILGRIMAGES AND VOWS

The subject of the taboos, or sacred restrictions, imposed on a pilgrim or other votary, is important enough to deserve a detailed examination. These restrictions are sometimes optional, so that they have to be expressed when the vow is taken; at other times they are of the nature of fixed and customary rules, to which every one who takes a vow is subject. To the latter class belong, *e.g.* the restrictions imposed upon every Arab pilgrim—he must not cut or dress his hair, he must abstain from sexual intercourse, and from bloodshed and so forth; to the former class belong the special engagements to which the Hebrews give the name of *ĕsār* or *issār* (obligatio), *e.g.* Ps. cxxxii. 3 *sq.*, "I will not enter my house or sleep on my bed until," etc.; Acts xxiii. 14, "We will not eat until we have killed Paul." It is to be observed that restrictions of the optional class are evidently more modern than the other, and only come in when the fixity of ancient custom begins to break down; in old Arabia it was the rule that one who was engaged on a blood-feud must abstain from women, wine and unguents, but in the time of the prophet we find these abstinences made matter of special engagements, *e.g.* Wācidī, ed. Kremer, 182. 6 = Ibn Hishām, 543. 8; *Agh.* vi. 99. 24, 30. Where the engagement is optional, it naturally assumes the character of an incentive to prompt discharge of the vow; the votary stimulates his own zeal by imposing on himself abstinence from certain of the comforts of life till his task is discharged; see Marzūcī as quoted by Reiske, Abulfeda, vol. i. p. 18 of the *Adnotationes*, where the phrase *mā taktarithu 'l-nafsu bihi* may be compared with the אסר לענות נפש of Num. xxx. 14. But the stated abstinences which go as a matter of course with certain vows cannot be explained on this principle, and when they are examined in detail it becomes manifest that they are simply taboos incident to a state of consecration, the same taboos, in fact, which are imposed, without a vow, on everyone who is engaged in worship or priestly service in the sanctuary, or even everyone who is present in the holy place. Thus the Hebrew Nazarite was required to abstain from wine, and from uncleanness due to contact with the dead, and the same rules applied to priests, either generally or when they were on service (Lev. x. 9, xxi. 1 *sqq.*). Again, the taboo on sexual intercourse which lay on the Arabian pilgrim applies, among the Semites generally, to everyone who is engaged in an act of worship or present in a holy place (see above, p. 454); and the prohibition of bloodshed, and therefore also of hunting and killing game, is only an extension of the general rule that forbids bloodshed on holy ground. Further, when the same taboos that attach to a pilgrim apply also to braves on the war-path, and especially to men who are under a vow of blood-revenge (*Diw. Hodh.* cvi. 14), it is to be remembered that with the Semites, and indeed with all primitive peoples, war is a sacred function, and the warrior a consecrated person (cf. pp. 402, 455). The Arabic root *ḥalla* (Heb. חלל) applied to the discharge (*lit.* the untying) of a vow, is the same which is regularly used of emergence from a state of taboo (the *iḥrām*, the *'idda* of widowhood, etc.) into ordinary life.

Wellhausen observes that the Arabic *nadhara* and the Hebrew נזר both mean primarily "to consecrate." In an ordinary vow a man consecrates some material thing, in the vow of pilgrimage or war he consecrates himself for a particular purpose. The Arabs have but one root to express both forms of vow, but in Hebrew and Syriac the root is differentiated into two: נדר, ܢܕܪ, "to vow," but נזיר, ܢܙܝܪ, "a consecrated person." The Syriac *nĕzīr*, notwithstanding its medial *z*, is not a mere loan-word from the Old Testament, but is applied, for example, to maidens consecrated to the service of Belthis (Is. Ant. i. 212, l. 130).

In the case of pilgrimage, it seems that the votary consecrates himself by devoting his hair, which is part of himself, as an offering at the sanctuary. Whether the consecration of the warrior was originally effected in the same way, and the discharge of the vow accomplished by means of a hair-offering, can only be matter of conjecture, but is at least not inconceivable. If it was so, the deity to whom the hair was dedicated must have been the kindred god of the clan, who alone, in primitive religion, could be conceived as interested in the avenging of the tribal blood; and we may suppose that the hair-offering of the warriors took place in connection with the "sacrifice of the home-comers," to be spoken of in Note M, *infra*. It must, however, be observed that all over the world the head and hair of persons under taboo are peculiarly sacred and inviolable, and that the primitive notions about the hair as a special seat of life, which have been spoken of at p. 324, are quite sufficient to account for this, without reference to the hair-offering, which is only one out of many applications of these ideas. It is easy, for example, to understand why, if an important part of the life resides in the hair, a man whose whole life is consecrated—*e.g.* a Maori chief, or the Flamen Dialis, or in the Semitic field such a person as Samuel or Samson—should either be forbidden to cut his hair at all, or should be compelled, when he does so, to use special precautions against the profanation of the holy growth. From Ezek. xliv. 20 we may conclude that some Semitic priests let their hair grow unpolled, like Samuel, and that others kept it close shaved, like the priests of Egypt; both usages may be explained on a single principle, for the risk of profaning the hair could be met by not allowing it to grow at all, as well as by not allowing it to be touched. Among the Hebrews, princes as well as priests were consecrated persons, and *nazīr* sometimes means a prince, while *nezer*, "consecration," means "a diadem." As a diadem is in its origin nothing more than a fillet to confine hair that is worn long, I apprehend that in old times the hair of Hebrew princes, like that of a Maori chief, was taboo, and that Absalom's long locks (2 Sam. xiv. 26) were the mark of his political pretensions, and not of his vanity. When the hair of a Maori chief was cut, it was collected and buried in a sacred place or hung on a tree; and it is noteworthy that Absalom's hair was cut annually at the end of the year—*i.e.* in the sacred season of pilgrimage, and that it was collected and weighed, which suggests a religious rite similar to that mentioned by Herod. ii. 65.

While the general principle is clear, that the restrictions laid on persons under a vow were originally taboos, incident to a state of consecration, it is not to be supposed that we can always explain these taboos in detail; for, in the absence of direct evidence, it is often almost impossible for modern men to divine the workings of the primitive mind.

Something, however, may be said about two or three rules which seem, at first sight, to lend colour to the notion that the restrictions are properly privations, designed to prevent a man from delaying to fulfil his vow. The Syrian pilgrim, during his whole journey, was forbidden to sleep on a bed. With this rule Wellhausen compares the custom of certain Arabs, who, during the *iḥrām*, did not enter their houses by the door, but broke in from behind,—a practice which is evidently an evasive modification of an older rule that forbade the house to be entered at all. The link required to connect the Syrian and Arabian rules is supplied by Ps. cxxxii. 3, and with the latter may also be compared the refusal of Uriah to go down to his house during a campaign (2 Sam. xi. 11), and perhaps also the Hebrew usage of living in booths at the Feast of Tabernacles, to which there are many parallels in ancient religion. From the point of view of taboo, this rule is susceptible of two interpretations: it may either be a precaution against uncleanness, or be meant to prevent the house and bed from becoming taboo, and unfit for profane use, by contact with the consecrated person. In favour of the second view may be cited the custom of Tahiti, where the kings habitually abstained from entering an ordinary house, lest it should become taboo, and be lost to its owner. However this may be, the Syrian practice can hardly be separated from the case of priests like the Selli at Dodona, who were ἀνιπτόποδες χαμαιεῦναι, nor the rule against entering a house from the similar restriction imposed on the religious order of the Rechabites (Jer. xxxv. 9 *sq.*). The

Rechabites, like the Nazarites and Arabian votaries, abstained also from wine, and the same abstinence was practised by Egyptian priests (Porph., *De Abst.* iv. 6) and by the Pythagoreans, whose whole life was surrounded by a network of taboos. These parallels leave no doubt that the rule of abstinence is not an arbitrary privation, but a taboo incident to the state of consecration. From Judg. xiii. 4 it would seem that fermented drinks fall into the same class with unclean meats; compare the prohibition of ferments in sacrifice. Again, the Arabian rule against washing or anointing the head is not ascetic, but is simply a consequence from the inviolability of the head, which must not be touched in a way that might detach hairs. The later Arabs did not fully understand these rules, as appears from the variations of the statements by different authorities about one and the same vow; cf., for example, the references given at the beginning of this note for the vow of Abū Sofyān. Finally, the peculiar dress prescribed to the Arabian pilgrim is no doubt a privation to the modern Moslem, but the dress is really nothing else than the old national garb of Arabia, which became sacred under the influence of religious conservatism, combined with the principle already explained (*supra*, p. 451), that a man does not perform a sacred function in his everyday clothes, for fear of making them taboo.

ADDITIONAL NOTE K (pp. 379, 384)

THE ALTAR AT JERUSALEM

THAT there was always an altar of some kind before the temple at Jerusalem might be taken for granted, even without the express mention of it in 2 Kings xi. 11, xii. 9 [10], (1 Kings viii. 22, 54); but this passage throws no light on the nature of the altar. Let us consider separately (*a*) the altar of burnt-offering, (*b*) the brazen altar.

(*a*) According to 1 Kings x. 25, Solomon *built* an altar of burnt-offering, and offered on it three times a year. A built altar is an altar of stone, such as Ahaz's altar and the altar of the second temple were. There is no other trace of the existence of such an altar before the time of Ahaz, and the verse, which is omitted by the Septuagint, belongs to a series of fragmentary notices, which form no part of the original narrative of Solomon's reign, and are of various dates and of uncertain authority. Apart from this passage, we first read of a built altar in 2 Kings xvi., viz. that which Ahaz erected on the model of the altar (*i.e.* the chief altar) at Damascus. Ahaz's innovation evidently proved permanent, for the altar of the second temple was also a platform of stone. According to the Massoretic text of 2 Kings xvi. 14, as it is usually translated, a brazen altar was removed to make way for Ahaz's altar, but this sense is got by straining a corrupt text; ויקרב cannot govern the preceding accusative, and to get sense we must either omit ואת המזבח at the beginning of the verse or read על for את. The former course, which has the authority of the LXX., seems preferable; but in either case it follows that we must point וַיַּקְרֵב, and that the whole verse is an elaborate description of the new ritual introduced by the king. The passage in fact now runs thus (ver. 12): "The king went up upon the new altar (ver. 13) and burned his holocaust and his cereal oblation, and poured out his libation; and he dashed the blood of the peace-offerings that were for himself against the altar (ver. 14) of brass that was before Jehovah, and drew nigh from before the *naos*, between the *naos* and the (new) altar (cf. Ezek. viii. 16; Joel ii. 17) and applied it (*i.e.* some of the blood) to the northern flank of the altar." The brazen altar, therefore, stood quite close to the *naos*, and the new altar stood somewhat further off, presumably in the middle of the court, which since Solomon's time had been consecrated as the place of burnt-offering. Further, it appears that the brazen altar was essentially an altar for the sprinkling of blood; for the king dashes the blood of his *shelāmīm* against it before applying the blood to the new altar. But, according to ver. 15, he ordains that in future the blood of sacrifices shall be applied to the new or great altar, while the brazen altar is reserved for one particular kind of offering by the king himself (לי לבקר, E.V. "for me to inquire by"). The nature of this offering is not clear from the words used in ver. 15, but from ver. 14 it appears that it consisted of *shelāmīm* offered by the king in person. In short, the old altar is not degraded but reserved for special use; henceforth none but the king himself is to pour sacrificial blood upon it.

(*b*) It appears, then, that the brazen altar was an ancient and sacred thing, which had existed long before Ahaz, and continued after his time. Yet there is no separate mention of a brazen altar either in the description of Solomon's temple furniture (1 Kings vii.) or in the list of brazen utensils carried off by the Chaldæans. The explanation suggested by Wellhausen (*Prolegomena*, 3rd ed., p. 45), that the making of the brazen altar has been omitted from 1 Kings vii. by some redactor, who did not see the need of a new brazen altar in addition to that which the priestly author of the Pentateuch ascribes to Moses, does not fully meet the case, and I can see no way out of the difficulty except to suppose that the brazen altar of 2 Kings xvi. is identical with one of the two pillars Jachin and Boaz. In the old time there was no difference between an altar and a sacred stone or pillar, and the brazen pillars are simply the ancient sacred stones—which often occur in pairs—translated into metal. Quite similarly in Strabo (iii. 5. 5), the brazen pillars of Hercules at Gades, which were twelve feet high, are the place at which sailors do sacrifice. Of course an altar of this type belongs properly to the old fireless type of sacrifice; but so long as the holocaust was a rare offering, it was not necessary to have a huge permanent hearth altar; it was enough to erect from time to time a pyre of wood in the middle of the court. It is true that 2 Kings xvi. speaks only of one brazen altar used for the sprinkling of the sacrificial blood, but it is intelligible that usage may have limited this function to one of the two pillars.

I am inclined therefore to think that the innovation of Ahaz lay in the erection of a permanent altar hearth, and in the introduction of the rule that in ordinary cases this new altar should serve for the blood ritual as well as for the fire ritual. One can thus understand the fulness with which the ritual of the new altar is described, for the rule of Ahaz was that which from his time forward was the law of the sanctuary of Jerusalem. I feel, however, that there still remains a difficulty as regards the burning of the fat of the *shelāmīm*, which was practised in Israel even before the royal period (1 Sam. ii. 16). In great feasts it would appear that the fat of ordinary offerings was burned, along with the holocaust, on the pavement of the court (1 Kings viii. 64), but what was done with it on other occasions it is not so easy to say. It is very noteworthy, however, that the details of the capitals of the brazen pillars are those of huge candlesticks or cressets. They had bowls (1 Kings vii. 41) like those of the golden candlestick (Zech. iv. 3), and gratings like those of an altar hearth. They seem therefore to have been built on the model of those altar candlesticks which we find represented on Phœnician monuments; see *CIS.* Pt. I. pl. 29, and Perrot and Chipiez, *Hist. de l'Art*, vol. iii. figs. 81 *sqq.* The similarity to a candlestick, which strikes us in the description of the Hebrew pillars, is also notable in the twin detached pillars which are represented on coins as standing before the temple at Paphos. See the annexed figure. Similar cressets, with worshippers before them in the act of adoration, are figured on Assyrian engraved stones; see, for example, Menant, *Glyptique Orient.* vol. ii. fig. 46. In most of the Assyrian examples it is not easy to draw the line between the candelabrum and the sacred tree crowned with a star or crescent moon. The Hebrew pillar altars had also associations with the sacred tree, as appears from their adornment of pomegranates, but so had the golden candlestick, in which the motive of the ornament was taken from the almond tree (Ex. xxxvii. 17 *sqq.*).

It seems difficult to believe that the enormous pillars of Solomon's temple, which, if the measures are not exaggerated, were twenty-seven feet high, were actually used as fire altars; but if they were, the presumption is that the cressets were fed with the suet of the sacrifices. And perhaps this is after all a less violent supposition than that the details of a Phœnician altar candelabrum were reproduced in them in a meaningless way. At any rate there can be no doubt that one type of fire altar among the Phœnicians and Assyrians was a cresset rather than a hearth, and as this type comes much nearer to the old cippus than the broad platform fitted to receive a holocaust, I fancy that it must be regarded as the oldest type of fire altar. In other words, the permanent fire altar began by adding to the sacred stone an arrangement for consuming the fat of ordinary sacrifices, at a time when holocausts were still burned on a pyre. If the word "Ariel," "hearth of El," originally meant such a pillar altar, we get rid of a serious exegetical difficulty in 2 Sam. xxiii. 20; for on this view it will appear that Benaiah's exploit was to overthrow the twin fire pillars of the national sanctuary of Moab—an act which in these days probably needed more courage than to kill two "lion-like men," as the English Version has it. On the stele of Mesha (l. 12), an *Ariel* appears as something that can be moved from its place, which accords with the view now suggested. Compare the twin pillars of the Tyrian Baal, one of which shone by night (Herod. ii. 44). It will be observed that this line of argument lends some plausibility to Grotius's suggestion that the *ḥammānīm* of Isa. xvii. 8, xxvii. 9, etc., are πυρεῖα.

Finally, it may be noted that Amos ix. 1 becomes far more intelligible if the altar at Bethel was a pillar crowned by a sort of capital bearing a bowl like those at Jerusalem. For then it will be the altar itself that is overthrown, as the context and the parallelism of chap. iii. 14 seem to require: "smite the capital till the bowls ring again, and dash them in pieces on the heads of the worshippers."

ADDITIONAL NOTE L (p. 387)

HIGH PLACES

In the text of the lectures I have tried to work out the history of the fire altar, and show how the place of slaughter and the pyre ultimately met in the altar hearth. In the present note I will give some reasons for thinking that the gradual change of view, which made the burning and not the slaughter the chief thing in sacrifice, also left its mark in another way, by influencing the choice of places for worship.

It has been observed in Lecture V. (p. 172) that the sanctuaries of the Northern Semites commonly lay outside and above the town. This does not seem to have been the case in Arabia, where, on the contrary, most sanctuaries seem to have lain in moist hollows, beside wells and trees. And even in the Northern Semitic lands we have found traces of sanctuaries beside fountains, beneath the towns, which were older than the high places on the hills. At Jerusalem the sanctity of Gihon and En-rogel is older than that of the waterless plateau of Zion above the town.

Now, in the discussion of the natural marks of holy places, we saw how well-watered spots, thickets and the like, might naturally come to be taken as sanctuaries, and we also found it to be intelligible that mountain ranges should be holy tracts; but we have not found any natural reason for fixing a sanctuary on a bare and barren eminence. It is often supposed that altars were built on such spots because they were open to the heaven, and nearer than other points of earth to the heavenly gods; but this explanation takes a great deal for granted that we have no right to assume. On the other hand, if the explanation of the origin of burnt-offering given above is correct, it is obvious that the barren and unfrequented hill-top above a town would be one of the most natural places to choose for burning the holocaust. In process of time a particular point on the hill would become the established place of burning, and, as soon as the burnt flesh began to be regarded as a food-offering presented to the deity, the place of burning would be itself a sanctuary. Ultimately it would become the chief sanctuary of the town, and be fitted up with all the ancient apparatus of sacred posts and sacrificial pillars.

That the high places, or hill sanctuaries, of the Semites were primarily places of burnt-sacrifice cannot be proved by direct evidence, but may, I think, be made probable, quite apart from the argument that has just been sketched. In Arabia we read of only one sanctuary that had "a place of burning," and this is the hill of Cozah at Mozdalifa. Among the Hebrews the sacrifice of Isaac takes place on a mountain (Gen. xxii. 2), and so does the burnt-sacrifice of Gideon. The annual mourning on the mountains at Mizpeh in Gilead must have been connected with a sacrifice on the mountains, which, like that of Laodicea, was thought to represent an ancient human sacrifice (Judg. xi. 40). In Isa. xv. 2 the Moabites in their distress go up to the high places to mourn, and presumably to offer atoning holocausts. It is to offer burnt-sacrifice that Solomon visits the high place at Gibeon (1 Kings iii. 4), and in general, קטר, "to burn sacrificial flesh" (not as E.V., "to burn incense"), is the usual word applied to the service of the high places. A distinction between a high place (*bāma*) and an altar (*mizbeăḥ*) is acknowledged in the Old Testament down to the close of the kingdom (2 Kings xxiii. 15; Isa. xxxvi. 7); but ultimately *bāma* is the name applied to any idolatrous shrine or altar.

ADDITIONAL NOTE M (p. 403)

SACRIFICE BY VICTORIOUS WARRIORS

According to Abū 'Obaida, the Arabs, after a successful foray, sacrificed one beast from the spoil, and feasted upon it before the division of the booty (*Ḥam.* p. 458; Reiske, *An. Musl.* i. 26 *sqq.* of the notes; cf. *Lisān*, x. 240). This victim is called *nacīʽa*, or more fully *nacīʽat al-coddām*, "the *nacīʽa* of the home-comers." The verb نقع is used generally of sacrificing for a guest, but its primary sense is to split or rend, so that the name of *nacīʽa* seems to denote some peculiar way of killing the victim. Now it appears from the narrative of Nilus that the victims of the Saracens were derived from the choicest part of the booty, from which they selected for sacrifice, by preference a handsome boy, or, if no boys had been captured, a white and immaculate camel. The camel exactly corresponds to the *nacīʽa* of the Arabs, and the name probably means a victim torn to pieces in the way described by Nilus It seems probable, therefore, that the sacrifice made for warriors on their return from a foray was not an ordinary feast, but an antique rite of communion, in which the victim was a sacred animal, or might even be an actual man.

That the warriors on their return should unite in a solemn act of service is natural enough; the thing falls under the same category with the custom of shaving one's head at the sanctuary on returning from a journey, and is, in its oldest meaning, simply a retying of the sacred links of common life, which may have grown weak through absence from the tribal seat. But of course a sacrifice of this kind would in later times appear to be piacular or lustral, and accordingly, in the Levitical law, an elaborate purification is prescribed for warriors returning from battle, before they are allowed to re-enter their homes (Num. xxxi. 19 *sqq.*). In ancient Arabia, on the other hand, where warriors were under the same taboos as a man engaged on pilgrimage, the *nacīʽa* was no doubt the means of untying the taboo, and so returning to ordinary life.

These remarks enable us to put the sacrifice of captives, or of certain chosen captives, in a somewhat clearer light. This sacrifice is not an act of blood-revenge, for revenge is taken in hot blood on the field of battle. The captive is simply, as Nilus puts it, the choicest part of the prey, chosen for a religious purpose; and the custom of preferring a human victim to a camel is probably of secondary growth, like other customs of human sacrifice. It seems, however, to be very ancient, for Saul undoubtedly spares Agag in order that he may be sacrificed, and Samuel actually accomplishes this offering by slaying him "before the Lord" in Gilgal. And in this, as in other cases of human sacrifice, the choice of an alien instead of a tribesman is not of the essence of the rite, for Jephthah looses his vow on his return from smiting the Ammonites by the sacrifice of his own daughter.

According to the Arabian lexicographers, the term *nacī'a* may be applied to sacrifices made on various occasions other than return from war, *e.g.* to a coronation feast, or that which a man makes for his intimates on his marriage; while ultimately the word appears to assume a very general sense, and to be applied to any slaughter to entertain a guest. For the occasions on which the Arabs were wont to kill a victim, which are very much the same as those on which slaughter of the sacred cattle is permitted by African peoples (*supra*, p. 298), note the verse cited in *Lisān*, vi. 226, x. 240 (and with a variation, *Tāj*, v. 519, l. 2), where the desirable meats include the *khors*, the *'idhār*, and the *nacī'a*. The first, which is the name applied to the broth given to women in child-bed, denotes also the feast made at a birth; the *'idhār* is the feast at a circumcision. In *Journ. Phil.* xiv. 124, I have connected the *khors* with the Hebrew חרשים, "charms." Charmed food is of course primarily holy food.

INDEX OF PASSAGES OF SCRIPTURE

GENERAL INDEX

CPSIA information can be obtained at www.ICGtesting.com
Printed in the USA
BVOW11s0314240714

360320BV00008B/218/P